The Theodore Roosevelt Association
Film Collection

A Catalog

The Theodore Roosevelt Association Film Collection

A Catalog

Prepared by
Wendy White-Hensen and Veronica M. Gillespie

With the Assistance of Harriet Harrison

Motion Picture, Broadcasting, and Recorded Sound Division

LIBRARY OF CONGRESS   WASHINGTON   1986

Library of Congress Cataloging-in-Publication Data

Library of Congress. Motion Picture, Broadcasting, and
   Recorded Sound Division.
   The Theodore Roosevelt Association film collection.

   Bibliography: p.
   Includes indexes.
   Supt. of Docs. no.: LC 40.2:R67
   1. Roosevelt, Theodore, 1858-1919—Film catalogs.
2. United States—History—1901-1909—Film catalogs.
3. Library of Congress. Motion Picture, Broadcasting,
and Recorded Sound Division—Catalogs. I. White-Hensen,
Wendy, 1948–   . II. Gillespie, Veronica M. III. Harrison,
Harriet. IV. Theodore Roosevelt Association. V. Title.
E757.L76 1985   016.97391'092'4   84-600384
ISBN 0-8444-0492-6

For sale by the Superintendent of Documents, U.S. Government Printing Office
Washington, D.C. 20402

Contents

Foreword

The Theodore Roosevelt Association, originally called the Roosevelt Memorial Association, was founded in 1919 and chartered by an Act of Congress on May 31, 1920. The purpose of the organization is, quoting the Congressional charter, "to perpetuate the memory of Theodore Roosevelt for the benefit of the people of the United States of America and the world." In realizing this objective, the Association has been involved through the years in many projects and programs, including the reconstruction of Theodore Roosevelt's birthplace in New York City, the publication of books, the preservation of the president's Long Island home, Sagamore Hill, and the creation of the Theodore Roosevelt Collection of motion pictures at the Library of Congress.

The motion picture collection had its genesis in the Bureau of Roosevelt Research and Information established by the Association in 1920 to collect books, photographs, papers, letters, cartoons, "moving picture films," and bibliographical materials relating to the life and times of Theodore Roosevelt. In 1923 the Roosevelt Memorial Association, in conjunction with the Women's Roosevelt Memorial Association (the two groups later merged to form the present Theodore Roosevelt Association), opened what is now the Theodore Roosevelt Birthplace National Historic Site, 28 East 20th Street, New York City. There, in the brownstone town house, the organizations maintained a house museum with period rooms, exhibits on the life of Theodore Roosevelt, and a research library and archives—a facility comparable in concept and purpose to the various later presidential libraries. By 1924 the Association's film collection, which included movies of Theodore Roosevelt's contemporaries and times as well as of the former president, was so extensive that a Roosevelt Motion Picture Library was established as a separate department from the Roosevelt Research Library. In time the archival and research collections outgrew the space and the resources of the Theodore Roosevelt Birthplace. Thus, in 1943, the Association's books, papers, letters, photographs, cartoons, and bibliographical materials were donated to the Harvard University Library to become the present Harvard Theodore Roosevelt Collection; and, in the 1960s, shortly after the Theodore Roosevelt Association gave the Theodore Roosevelt Birthplace to the National Park Service, the motion picture collection was sent to the Library of Congress, where it became a component of the National Film Collection.

The film collection assembled by the Theodore Roosevelt Association has been in existence since the 1920s, but never before has it been as accessible to the public as it will be now with the publication of this catalog by the Library of Congress, supported by a generous grant from the National Endowment of the Humanities. Because of the wide variety of subjects included in the collection—political campaigns, conservation, naval history, the Panama Canal, Theodore Roosevelt's opponents as well as supporters, world leaders, social and public events, World War I, Roosevelt's trips to Africa, Europe, and South America, and many other topics—the catalog and the collection will be of great use not only to researchers interested in Theodore Roosevelt, but also to those concerned with many other areas of world and American history during Theodore Roosevelt's era.

This catalog of the Theodore Roosevelt Collection of motion pictures at the Library of Congress is in a real sense a companion to the Library's three-volume *Index to the Theodore Roosevelt Papers*, published in 1969, which lists the letters, papers, speeches, and other materials in the Library's Theodore Roosevelt Papers collection; and also to the five-volume *Theodore Roosevelt Collection: Dictionary Catalogue and Shelf List,* published by the Harvard University Press in 1970, which is the printed guide to the Harvard Theodore Roosevelt Collection. The availability of these two sets of directories and of this motion picture catalog is of inestimable value to scholars everywhere. The Theodore Roosevelt Association, now as always vitally interested in preserving the record of Theodore Roosevelt's life and career, commends the National Endowment for the Humanities and the Library of Congress for publishing this catalog of the Theodore Roosevelt Collection of motion pictures.

JOHN ALLEN GABLE
Executive Director
Theodore Roosevelt Association
Oyster Bay, New York

Acknowledgments

Special appreciation for their assistance in preparing this catalog goes to Mary Bader, Jurij Dobczansky, Susan Kline, and John Pontius—former staff members of the Library's Motion Picture, Broadcasting, and Recorded Sound Division.

Pat Parker, David Spaans, and Kathy Mierke of the Library's Automated Systems Office were absolutely essential to the "TR Project." Without their expertise and patience we could never have completed the catalog. We would also like to acknowledge the help of the staff of the Library's Newspaper and Current Periodical Reading Room. They provided at all times cheerful advice in locating obscure and difficult-to-handle material. Ford Peatross of the Library's Prints and Photographs Division was invaluable in identifying buildings that appeared in the films, often providing the clue that led to appropriate documentation.

But a truce to politics! We want to present Colonel Roosevelt to the reader . . . as a picture man: that is, one in sympathy with the best aspects of the picture.[1]

TR On Film

by Veronica M. Gillespie

It has been said that during the silent newsreel period no president was more photogenic than Theodore Roosevelt. He was unusually cooperative with motion picture photographers, often pausing in the midst of official ceremonies to face the camera, bow, wave, smile, gesture, or otherwise accommodate the cameraman.[2] Because of TR's love affair with the camera, and other fortunate circumstances, the Theodore Roosevelt Association Film Collection in the Library of Congress now constitutes a major visual record of the first decades of the twentieth century. The collection contains rare early motion picture footage, some of which is believed to be unique.

The actual compilation of the collection was undertaken by the Theodore Roosevelt Association (TRA), originally established as the Roosevelt Memorial Association (RMA) in January 1919. The RMA, in conjunction with the Women's Roosevelt Memorial Association, founded the Bureau of Roosevelt Research and Information and, by resolution, appointed Hermann Hagedorn as director on November 8, 1920. The bureau was delegated, among other tasks, to collect all available papers, books, pamphlets, articles, photographs, and motion pictures pertaining to the life and times of the president. As a direct result, in 1924 the Roosevelt Motion Picture Library, where the films were first assembled and preserved, was established at Roosevelt House, the president's birthplace in New York City. Caroline Gentry, experienced in the motion picture industry and art, was appointed director of films at the library. For approximately thirty years the RMA successfully gathered a large quantity of motion picture negative and positive stock from old film vaults, newsreel files, movie companies, individuals, and various other sources throughout the United States, Europe, South America, and Africa.

Films were acquired through various transactions. Many were outright cash purchases; some were donations by individuals, such as Lyman Howe, Charles Urban, William Fox, and John Demarest, as well as by pioneer film companies, such as Biograph, Paramount, Kinograms, and Bray Studios. Still others were obtained by loans, gifts, copy negatives, and trade-ins. Collaboration with the various leading motion picture producers was essential to procuring the Roosevelt films. A Film Research Committee was appointed consisting of Will H. Hays, chairman of the Republican National Committee and president of the Motion Picture Producers and Distributors of America; Elmer Pearson of Pathé Frères; J. Stuart Blackton of Vitagraph; E. W. Hammons of Educational Films; George M. Baynes of Kinograms; and Edwin C. Hill of Fox News. A few of the larger producers made notable contributions; Mr. Blackton, for example, gave the first important impetus by donating all of the Roosevelt negatives located in the Vitagraph vaults. Brokers and dealers in old, junked, and obsolete films, along with independent cameramen, or footage men as they were called in the newsreel world, were also invited to contribute all available film stock on Roosevelt subjects. Eventually, the collection totaled well over 140,000 feet of negative, duplicate negative, and positive stock of the scenes, events, and individuals attendant to the illustrious career of Theodore Roosevelt.

In addition to directing the compilation of materials in the collection, Miss Gentry organized the production of the Roosevelt films, which were available on 16mm noninflammable stock for use by various institutions in exhibitions or for household projection.[3] With a keen sense of historical purpose, Miss Gentry assembled these documentaries by combining old newsreels and other types of films with interior titles and still shots of cartoons, photographs, and sites dealing with the principal phases of Roosevelt's life. Since the RMA productions, originally assembled in the 1920s and 1930s, were periodically reedited and retitled, they are not easily identified. For this reason, an accurate count of them is very difficult to determine; it has, however, been estimated that there were at least fifteen completed ones.

In 1962 Roosevelt House became the Theodore Roosevelt Birthplace National Historic Site, administered by the National Park Service. The Roo-

THE ROOSEVELT FILMS

on 16 mm. Stock
for Household Projection

THE ROOSEVELT FILMS are available on 16 mm. non-inflammable stock for household projection, and orders for single productions, or for the series, may now be placed with the Roosevelt Film Library.

The productions immediately available are:

> T. R. Himself
> Roosevelt, Friend of the Birds
> The Roosevelt Dam
> Roosevelt, the Great Scout

The following will be ready at a later date:

> The Panama Canal
> The River of Doubt
> Roosevelt at Home
> Roosevelt's Return through Europe
> T. R. Comes Back
> Roosevelt in the Great War
> The Roosevelt Policies
> Roosevelt, Big Game Hunter

Further information may be had by applying to Miss Caroline Gentry, Director of Films, Roosevelt House, 28 East 20th Street.

Advertisements like this one promoting the use of the RMA assembled film productions appeared in the *Roosevelt House Bulletin* in 1929.

sevelt Motion Picture Library was then transferred to the Library of Congress, which the TRA believed was the best institution for the storage, preservation, and scholarly utilization of such valuable visual documents.[4]

The Theodore Roosevelt Collection is but a small component of the National Film Collection in the Library of Congress. It had its origins in 1894 with the copyright registration of the early motion pictures of Thomas A. Edison and is now considered one of the most significant collections in existence. The Roosevelt Collection consists of 381 titles of nitrate-base films, which have now been preserved on safety-base stock since nitrate stock is highly flammable and given to autocatalytic disintegration under certain atmospheric conditions. The majority of the films in the collection are black and white (though some are tinted), silent (there is one sound film), 16 or 35 mm in size, and one reel in length (some have two reels). Each title usually has at least one copy of the reference print, the duplicate negative, the archival positive or master positive, and the nitrate original.

In 1975 the National Endowment for the Humanities awarded the Library of Congress a grant to prepare full cataloging and computer-generated access to the entire Theodore Roosevelt Collection. The staff of the Library of Congress National Endowment for the Humanities Cataloging Project prepared individual cataloging records with detailed filmographic and subject analyses for each film. In attempting to provide complete and accurate identification of the motion pictures, the project staff encountered numerous difficulties. With the exception of the RMA productions, the films were, for the most part, untitled newsreel segments and newsfilms. Filmographic data are both incomplete and speculative. There are no reliable written records for most of the films other than the accounts published in the RMA annual reports.

The two most significant descriptors in film identification are the proper title of the film and the name of the company responsible for its production and/or release. Since almost every important event was photographed simultaneously by newsreel cameramen from several different production companies, identification was severely limited if, as frequently happened with unedited footage, a company's name or logo did not appear on the film along with the main title. If the date of an event in a newsreel segment could be verified, then the film could be identified completely or at least tentatively through a laborious research procedure.

However, when complete film productions were involved, they had to be validated through an even more exhaustive search using a variety of film research tools.[5]

After the film had been identified, the project staff utilized cataloging policies adapted from the *Anglo-American Cataloging Rules* for filmographic description and the *Library of Congress Subject Headings* for subject access. Each cataloging entry contains, when possible, the following data: title, production and/or releasing company, date of production, archival physical description, series title, general cataloger's notes, summary of contents, subject headings, added entries, language code, geographic area code, and shelflisting information. These cataloging records were then coded and translated into the MARC (*MA*chine-*R*eadable *C*ataloging) format for films to generate computer end products in the form of catalogs, indexes, publications, and cards for use in manual systems. These retrieval tools will facilitate more efficient use of the collection while eliminating unnecessary handling and viewing of films. All data compiled by the project staff are available to researchers in the Motion Picture, Broadcasting, and Recorded Sound Division of the Library.

The Films

Roosevelt became a major picture personality during the early twentieth century because he was newsworthy as well as photogenic and because newsfilms were novelties and very popular during their formative years. He was the first U.S. president whose life was extensively recorded and preserved in the motion picture format. The collection reveals that although Roosevelt obtained fame before the motion picture form was perfected, he was one of the most frequently photographed subjects among public men. The majority of films in the collection are views of Roosevelt and other national figures participating in political ceremonies, delivering campaign speeches, and attending social activities. These items made excellent newsfilm topics primarily because of the high interest factor involved and the relative ease with which the filming could be preplanned and executed.[6] The film collection reflects the myriad interests and accomplishments of Roosevelt as a statesman, scholar, naturalist, explorer, traveler, advocate of the strenuous life, conservationist, historian, hunter, Rough Rider, orator, family man, vice-president, president, and Progressive party leader.

Motion picture cameraman photographed both of Roosevelt's inaugural ceremonies. *TR's Inauguration, 1905 [1]* and *[2]* include clear views of Roosevelt taking the oath of office and delivering his inaugural address.

Although Roosevelt was photographed many times during his administrations, there are relatively few films that actually portray him as the twenty-sixth president. *TR in San Francisco, 1903* is one of the more unusual items from a sociological point of view. He is parading through San Francisco along Van Ness Avenue on May 12, 1903, during a western presidential tour. There are long shots of military escorts, Roosevelt's horse-drawn carriage, and preceding the carriage, the Ninth U.S. Cavalry Regiment, which according to newspaper accounts, was one of the first black companies to have had so prominent a position in a public procession.[7] *TR's Inaugural Ceremony, 1905,* and *TR's Inauguration, 1905* [1 and 2] are political newsfilms of eminent historical status.[8] There are shots from various camera positions of Roosevelt on the front steps of the Capitol on March 4, 1905, being sworn in by Chief Justice Melville W. Fuller, delivering his inaugural address, and leaving with the rest of his presidential party. *TR's Arrival in Panama, November, 1906* [1 and 4], also of major historical importance, record the first time an American president visited a foreign country while in office.[9] Roosevelt considered the Panama Canal construction one of his most valuable contributions to foreign affairs. He is shown on November 15, 1906, visiting Panama City, where he is officially received by Manuel Amador Guerrero, first president of the republic of Panama. There is a long shot of President Amador Guerrero delivering the welcome address as other prominent officials look on.

Selig Polyscope Company issued this poster to promote the film *Hunting Big Game in Africa*, which was released and accepted in theatrical circles as a genuine moving picture of Roosevelt killing lions in Africa. Later it was reputed to be the most "brazen hoax" of the period involving the fake production of an actual news event. The Library of Congress has the only authentic footage of Roosevelt's African expedition, photographed by Cherry Kearton.

Coverage of Roosevelt's activities during the last decade of his life is rather extensive. His expedition to Africa (1909–10) gave rise to the most notable films depicting him as an "apostle of the strenuous life."[10] *TR in Africa* [1909, 1 and 4] contain scenes of Roosevelt and his party on a safari in East Africa (most likely in the vicinity of Mt. Kenya, in what was then British East Africa and is now Kenya), views of what is probably part of the Kikuyu and Masai cultural dances being performed for Roosevelt in the village of Nyeri in August 1909, and a medium-close shot of Roosevelt planting a tree in Mombasa. *African Animals* shows hippopotamuses sunning on rocks and swimming in what is probably the Tana River in British East Africa, and, in a different location, rhinoceroses grazing in a grove of trees. There are medium-close shots of lions roaring and moving through the underbrush, as well as long shots of various animals including elephants, warthogs, zebras, giraffes, monkeys, African buffalo, and lions. Roosevelt's love of hunting and exploring is evident in these films on his African hunting trip, or as he preferred to call it, his "scientific expedition" sponsored by the Smithsonian Institution.

King Edward's Funeral, 1910 [1 and 2] and *TR's Return from Africa, 1910* [1 and 2] are remarkable examples of an official political ceremony in which Roosevelt participated with other prominent foreign dignitaries. He is shown representing the United States during the ceremonial funeral procession of King Edward VII of Great Britain in London on May 20, 1910. Also in the procession were Kaiser Wilhelm II of Germany, King Ferdinand of Bulgaria, King George I of Greece, King Manuel II of Portugal, King George V of Great Britain, King Haakon VII of Norway, King Alfonso XIII of Spain, and King Frederick VIII of Denmark.

Colonel Roosevelt Is Invited to Fly in Arch Hoxsey's Plane at St. Louis, Mo., 1910 contains footage of the first airplane flight by a president. While participating in the Missouri State Republican campaign on October 11, 1910, he was invited to fly in a Wright biplane with Arch Hoxsey as pilot. Included in the film are views of Roosevelt arriving at the Kinloch aviation field accompanied by Herbert S. Hadley, governor of Missouri (1909–13), a medium-close shot of TR entering the passenger seat, and long shots of the plane flying and of Roosevelt descending and joining his waiting party. He later commented to a *New York Times* reporter, "You know I didn't intend to do it, but when I saw the thing there, I could not resist it."[11] Hoxsey died in a plane crash a year later.

One of the most distinguished groups of films concerns Roosevelt's campaign for the presidency under the banner of the Progressive party, formed when Roosevelt bolted the Republican party. Among the notable titles are *TR at Fargo, N.D., during Progressive Campaign, 1912* [1 and 2].[12] As part of a western campaign tour, the former president appears speaking to crowds and rallying support for the third party in Fargo on September 6, 1912. There are several views from varying distances of him speaking to crowds from the rear of a train, as well as a fairly close silhouette of TR, conversing with three men, one of whom appears to be George E. Roosevelt, his cousin and campaign secretary in the 1912 election.

Hopi Indians Dance for TR at [Walpi, Ariz.] 1913 is

Theodore Roosevelt displaying his vigorous campaigning style before the newsreel cameras.

illustrative of Roosevelt's intense interest in people and culture.[13] There are sequences of TR traveling through the Southwest with his sons Archie and Quentin and a cousin, Nicholas Roosevelt, on August 20, 1913, as well as a medium-close shot of Roosevelt observing a snake dance on the Hopi Indian Reservation.

Roosevelt the conservationist and protector of wildlife is depicted in *TR [in Louisiana], 1915* [1–4].[14] Herbert K. Job of the National Audubon Society photographed the former president and others along the beaches of the bird sanctuary on June 8–12, 1915, Roosevelt joined an Audubon expedition devoted to filming the society's protective work with water birds and appears on an unidentified island off the Louisiana coast with J. H. Coquille, a New Orleans photographer, William Sprinkle, game warden, and M. L. Alexander, head of the Louisiana Conservation Commission.

One of the events receiving massive coverage by the newsreel cameramen was, of course, the memorial services for Roosevelt. Universal Film Manufac-

turing Company released *TR's Funeral at Oyster Bay, 1919* as a segment of its January Universal Current Events series. There are views of Christ Episcopal Church, the funeral procession on January 8, 1919, and Youngs Memorial Cemetery in Oyster Bay, New York. Other notable segments of the film include: a medium-close shot of specially delegated New York City mounted police guards passing along the road in front of the church and followed by the hearse; a long shot at the church entrance of the flag-draped casket being placed in the hearse, with a line of funeral procession autos parked behind; a close shot from a different angle of the casket being borne through the church entrance to the hearse, with a flag bearer following behind; a close-up of Rev. George E. Talmadge, rector of Christ Episcopal Church and officiant at the ceremony; and a long shot in the cemetery of the casket being shouldered and carried up a steep pathway to the grave site, followed by Archie Roosevelt and other family members. In attendance at the funeral were Gen. Peyton C. March, Army Chief of Staff,

Vice-President Thomas R. Marshall, who was the official representative of the U.S. government at the funeral, Rear Adm. Cameron M. Winslow, and William Howard Taft.

The Roosevelt Collection reflects the ambitious newsreel coverage that this particular period enjoyed. Large volumes of footage were devoted to Roosevelt's intimate friends, political associates, intellectual peers, and family members, including Henry Fairfield Osborn, paleontologist, first curator of the Department of Vertebrate Paleontology at the American Museum of Natural History in New York City, and recipient of the Roosevelt Medal for Distinguished Service in 1923 for contributions to natural history; Will H. Hays, chairman of the Republican National Committee (1918–21) and postmaster general in Harding's cabinet (1921–22); Gifford Pinchot, governor of Pennsylvania (1923–27, 1931–35), participating in the first gubernatorial bill-signing filmed in the Pennsylvania State Capitol on May 10, 1923; William Boyce Thompson, first president of the RMA, appearing with his wife, Gertrude Hickman Thompson; Oscar S. Straus, secretary of commerce and labor in TR's cabinet (1906–9); Owen D. Young, coauthor with Charles Dawes of the Dawes Plan for German Reparations; Owen Wister, author of *The Virginian* and close literary friend of Roosevelt's, appearing outdoors on a country estate; and Herbert Putnam, eighth Librarian of Congress (1899–1939), Librarian Emeritus (1939–55), and recipient of the Roosevelt Medal for Distinguished Service in 1929 for the administration of public office, appearing both inside and outside the Library of Congress.

Several films are composed of very short, one-shot images of various senators in or around the Capitol, White House, or other federal government buildings in Washington, D.C. There are views of Gilbert M. Hitchcock, Democratic senator from Nebraska (1911–23); Porter J. McCumber, Republican senator from North Dakota (1899–1923); Boies Penrose, Republican senator from Pennsylvania (1897–1921); Hiram Warren Johnson, Republican senator from California (1917–45); Atlee Pomerene, Democratic senator from Ohio (1911–23); Thomas Edward Watson, Democratic senator from Georgia (1921–22); and Reed Smoot, Republican senator from Utah (1903–33).

The Roosevelt Collection provides a wealth of primary source material for those scholars investigating the historical, political, and social roles of women during the first decades of the twentieth century. Some significant sequences include a close shot of Margaret Hill McCarter of Kansas, author, vice-president of the Republican National Women's Committee and in 1920 the first woman to address the National Republican Convention; a medium close shot of French actress Sarah Bernhardt speaking in Prospect Park, Brooklyn, New York, on July 4, 1917, on behalf of French-American cooperation in the war effort; scenes of women suffragists visiting Roosevelt at Sagamore Hill, Oyster Bay, New York, on September 8, 1917, and participating in the opening of the second New York state suffrage campaign, with views of Vira B. Whitehouse, state chairwoman of the New York State Woman's Suffrage Party, Helen Rogers Reid, and Harriet B. Laidlaw. Some other well-known women presented in the films are Elizabeth Wood, Cornelia B. Pinchot, Florence K. Harding, Edith Wilson, Edith Roosevelt, Corinne R. Robinson, Grace G. Coolidge, Elizabeth A. Bryce, Mary S. Alger, Sallie W. Bolling, and Helen H. Taft.

Foreign personages also figure prominently in the films. There are various shots from many different camera positions of Viscount James Bryce, ambassador to the United States, with his wife, Elizabeth A. Bryce; King George V and Queen Mary of Great Britain; King Edward VIII of Great Britain; Ferdinand Foch, French marshal; Armando duca della Vittoria Diaz, Italian marshal; and Robert G. Nivelle, former commander in chief of the French army. There are also views of King Albert I and Queen Elisabeth of the Belgians; Raymond Poincaré, president of France, and Madame Henriette Poincaré; King Leopold III of the Belgians; and Charles, count of Flanders, all attending the dedication ceremony laying to rest the body of the French unknown soldier in Laeken, Belgium, on July 17, 1927.

This collection may also serve as a useful pictorial history of architectural developments in American buildings and cities during the early twentieth century. There are numerous exterior views and panning shots of the various structural features of architecturally influential historic buildings such as the White House, the Capitol, the Library of Congress, and the Old State House in Boston. The American cities photographed provide an extensive geographical index to the time period; included are scenes of San Francisco, New York, Boston, Chicago, Pittsburgh, Los Angeles, Washington, D.C., Ann Arbor, Albuquerque, Detroit, Saint Paul, and San Diego, as well as lesser-known cities such as Thomson, Georgia; Springfield, Illinois; Roswell, Georgia; Rockford, Illinois; Oyster Bay, New York;

Northampton, Massachusetts; Mineola, New York; Medora, North Dakota; Fargo, North Dakota; Deadwood, South Dakota; Battle Creek, Michigan; and Billings, Montana.

The collection is of indispensable value as primary source material to the historian, film scholar, educator, sociologist, political scientist, and indeed to anyone concerned with interpreting the human experience. These newsfilms reconstruct the past, ascertain the facts about people, places, and events, and authenticate customs, dress, manners, and artifacts of everyday living by supplying irrefutable historical evidence. Of far more than a transitory interest, the films emphatically reiterate that Theodore Roosevelt is "something more than a picture personality: he is A PICTURE MAN."[15]

NOTES

1. "Theodore Roosevelt: The Picture Man," *Moving Picture World* 7 (October 22, 1910): 920.

2. Raymond Fielding, *The American Newsreel, 1911–1967* (Norman: University of Oklahoma Press, 1972), pp. 50, 90.

3. Eight of the original films are still distributed by the TRA in 16mm and video cassette tape. They may be viewed upon request to Sagamore Hill, Oyster Bay, New York.

4. "The Theodore Roosevelt Association and the T.R.A. Motion Picture Collection," *Theodore Roosevelt Association Journal* 2 (Winter–Spring 1976): 14–15.

5. For example, *Moving Picture World;* Raymond Fielding, *The American Newsreel;* Kemp R. Niver, *Motion Pictures from the Library of Congress Paper Print Collection, 1894–1912* (Berkeley: University of California Press, 1967); Terry Ramsaye, *A Million and One Nights: A History of the Motion Picture* (New York: Simon and Schuster, 1926); Howard L. Walls, *Motion Pictures, 1894–1912, Identified from the Records of the U.S. Copyright Office* (Washington: Library of Congress, 1953); and *Catalog of Copyright Entries* (Washington: Library of Congress, 1951–). The single most knowledgeable source on the history of the Roosevelt films is John A. Gable, historian, Roosevelt scholar, and executive director of the TRA, who has been invaluable in identifying people, places, events, and dates contained in the footage.

6. Fielding, *The American Newsreel,* p. 54.

7. *San Francisco Chronicle,* May 12–13, 1903.

8. Niver, *Motion Pictures from the Library of Congress,* p. 259.

9. *Washington Post,* November 16, 1906.

10. For additional information on this period of Roosevelt's life, see Cherry Kearton, *Adventures with Animals and Men* (London: Longmans, Green, 1935), pp. 65–74; Cherry Kearton, *Wild Life across the World* (London: Hodder and Stoughton, 1914), pp. 100–101; and Frederick W. Unger, *Roosevelt's African Trip* (Philadelphia: J. C. Winston Co., 1909).

11. *New York Times,* October 12, 1910.

12. *Fargo Forum and Daily Republican* (Fargo, N.D.), September 6, 1912.

13. Theodore Roosevelt, *A Book-Lover's Holidays in the Open* (New York: Scribner's Sons, 1926), pp. 225–45.

14. *Times-Picayune* (New Orleans), June 7, 8, 10, and 12, 1915.

15. "Theodore Roosevelt: The Picture Man," *Moving Picture World,* p. 920.

A version of this article appeared in the January 1977 issue of the *Quarterly Journal of the Library of Congress.*

How to Use the Catalog

The films in this catalog are arranged alphabetically by title. Data are provided for each entry in the following order: title, production statement, copyright statement, physical description, series statement, shelf location, general note, reference sources note, genre note, summary, personal credits, review citation, subject headings, other index entries (added entries), and an internal computer control number. Each data element or type of information may not be appropriate or available for every title in the catalog.

Title
Entry is by the title assigned by the Roosevelt Memorial Association unless a different title appears on the film itself, or the cataloger has verified the original release title. Because of the nature of the collection, there are few films for which original release titles could be established. Titles supplied by the cataloger appear in brackets, and portions of titles are bracketed when accurate information has been substituted for inaccurate or misleading information. Films with identical titles and similar, but not identical footage and/or sequences have been given bracketed numbers to distinguish them. In many instances the differences are slight and may only be in the order of sequences, rather than in content. The decision was made to descriptively identify footage and to leave any qualitative judgments to the viewer-researcher.

Examples:
Crowd listening to TR speak during Progressive campaign, 1912.
[Flag services for TR at Oyster Bay, October 1919]
General [Diaz] of Italy visits TR's grave [1921]
TR in Africa [1909, 1]
TR himself [2]

Production Statement
A majority of the titles in the Theodore Roosevelt Association Collection comprise newsreel or factual footage and do not include any information identifying the original producer, production company, director, etc. The words "Producer unknown" appear in the production statement for these titles. When the production company can be identified, it appears here; in many instances the film has been identified as a portion of a newsreel or as a Roosevelt Memorial Association production. The words "Various producers" appear in the production statement when more than one company name appears on the film. Explanatory notes follow in the cataloging record. If it was impossible to establish a production or release date, the month, if known, and year of the event or occasion recorded on the film is used. Brackets and question marks are used for questionable dates, and explanatory notes appear later in the entry.

Examples:
Producer unknown, Oct 1910.
Producer unknown [1917?]
Roosevelt Memorial Association, Oct 1923.
Hearst-Pathe Pub. Corp., Jul 1919.
International Film Service Co., Oct 1919.
Various producers [192–?]

Copyright Statement
Because most of the films in the collection are fragments or sequences from unidentified productions, no copyright information could be established. In these instances the copyright statement reads, "© No reg." When the title was registered, the copyright statement includes the following information: the copyright symbol (©), the copyright registration number, the name of the claimant, and the date of registration.

Examples:
© No reg.
© H27382, American Mutoscope & Biograph Co., 22 Jan 1903
© MP5938, Roosevelt Memorial Association, 1Feb28

Physical Description
The physical description of the film notes the number of reels in the Library's collection and, for titles that have been identified as complete works, the number of original copy reels are also included. Most of the titles in the catalog are composed of segments of news or factual footage and are listed as 1r, rather than 1r of 1, since there are no criteria for completeness. Information about footage, sound status, color, gauge (width), presentation format,

Sample Entry

Title	Women suffragettes visit TR at Sagamore [1917]
Production Statement	Hearst-Pathe News, Sep 1917.
Copyright Statement	© No reg.
Physical Description	1r, 4 ft. si. b&w. 16mm. ref print. 1r, 4 ft. si. b&w. 16mm. dupe neg. 1r, 11 ft. si. b&w. 35mm. pos ntr.
Series Statement	(Hearst-Pathe News [newsreel])
Shelf Location	SHELF LOC'N: FAB741 (print); FRA5787 (neg)
General Note	RMA lists date in title as 1918.
Reference Sources Note	Ref sources: Harper, Ida H., ed. History of woman suffrage. v. 6, 1969; Bain, George Grantham. [News photos of woman suffrage in the United States, mostly New York City, 1905–1917.] lot 11052. P&P; League of Women Voters in the United States. . . . [W]omen active in the women's suffrage movement and as members of the National League of Women Voters. lot 5544. P&P; The Brooklyn Daily Eagle. 9/9/17:1, 4.
Genre Note	Newsfilm.
Summary	SUMMARY: Film is the opening of the second New York State suffrage campaign on Sept. 8, 1917 at Sagamore Hill. The first campaign, beginning in 1913, was unsuccessful; the woman suffrage amendment was rejected by the voters in 1915. On Nov. 6, 1917, the suffrage amendment to the New York State Constitution was approved by the voters. The suffragists invited to Sagamore were headed by Mrs. Norman deR. Whitehouse, State Chairman of the New York State Woman Suffrage Party. Sequence on TR talking to three women: the woman in the dark hat and coat is Mrs. Ogden Mills Reid; the woman dressed in furs next to TR is Mrs. Whitehouse; and the tall woman in the light hat and jacket is Mrs. James Lees Laidlaw.
Subject Headings (with arabic numbers)	1. Oyster Bay, N.Y. Sagamore Hill. 2. Suffrage. 3. Suffrage—New York (State) 4. Women—Suffrage—New York (State) 5. Women's rights—New York (State) 6. Oyster Bay, N.Y. 7. Roosevelt, Theodore, Pres. U.S., 1858–1919. 8. Whitehouse, Vira B. 9. Reid, Helen Rogers. 10. Laidlaw, Harriet B.
Added Entries (with roman numerals)	I. Hearst-Pathe News. II. Pathe, source. III. Theodore Roosevelt Association Collection.
Computer Control Number	[mp 76–37]

and if more than one, the number of copies (cy) is also included. The base is safety (triacetate) unless otherwise noted.

Examples:
1r, 5 ft. si. b&w. 16mm. ref print.
2r of 2, 1949 ft. si. b&w. 35mm. dupe neg (cy 1)
1r, 58 ft. si. b&w. 16mm. archival pos (2 cy)
1r, 11 ft. si. b&w. 35mm. pos ntr.

Series Statement
Most of the titles in the catalog do not have series statements. For those titles that have been identified as part of a series, the series title is listed in parentheses below the physical description. The word [Series] (in brackets) has been added to series titles when it may not be clear that the title is a series title rather than another type of title. The word [newsreel] has been used as a qualifier when a distinction must be made between the name of a producer and the title of a series. The distinction between the use of "Series" and "newsreel" is a fine one made to conform to cataloging principles and can be ignored by users of the catalog. Series entries in the general index refer researchers to those titles in the catalog which are part of the series.

Examples:
(The Roosevelt series of history and biography, no. 1)
(Kinograms [Series])
(Hearst-Pathe News [newsreel])

Shelf Location
Shelf location numbers follow immediately after the series statement, if there is one. If there is no series statement, the shelf location appears below the physical description. The shelf location numbers are recorded in the same order as the lines of physical description, so that the first set of numbers corresponds to the first line of physical description, the second set to the second line, and so on.

Examples:
See sample entry.

General Notes
General notes about the film concerning its title, production, physical condition, series statement, and so on are provided. Detailed information for data that appear in brackets and with question marks is given in the general notes.

Examples:
RMA lists date in title as 1917.
Flash interior titles note: Kinograms and Paramount Weekly Gazette.
Dates in title unverified.
Film sequence does not follow order of actual events; interior titles and appropriate footage are out of order.
Nitrate deterioration on ref print ca. ft. 316-354.

Reference Source(s) Note
Here are listed reference sources which were particularly helpful to the cataloger. Sources used for more general information are not listed here—see the Bibliography which follows the indexes to this catalog. Citations listed in the reference sources note may refer to serials, manuscript collections, and photographs, as well as to monographs. With the exception of photographic collections at the Houghton Library at Harvard University and at the National Archives, all sources cited are located in the collections of the Library of Congress.

Examples:
See sample entry.

Genre Note
A genre note briefly categorizes the film. Most of the films in the catalog are categorized as "Newsfilm" or as "Factual." The term "Newsfilm" was used for footage of public occasions and events such as speeches, parades, dedications, etc., which could have been released theatrically as a newsreel. This footage was probably shot with the intention of being included in a newsreel. Actuality footage that was shot by individuals or for noncommercial organizations such as the Army Signal Corps, the Roosevelt Memorial Association, the Audubon Society, etc., has been described simply as "Factual." Errors may have been made inadvertently in attempting to distinguish between the two. If applicable, more specific subject and technical descriptors are also included.

Examples:
Newsfilm.
Factual; views, nature film.
Factual; compilation.
Factual; still film.

Summary
The summary describes what the researcher will actually see when he or she views the film. The

approach is a journalistic one; the who, what, and where are succinctly described. For long compilation films, the sequences are numbered and described separately. Each film has been carefully researched and viewed many times. When there is doubt as to the identity of individuals, physical locations, or dates, it is noted in the summary.

Example:
See sample entry.

Personal Credits
Personal name credits are noted immediately after the summary. Because of the nature of the collection, there was limited personal credit information available. The exceptions are a few photography, director, editor, and source (of acquisition) credits. The personal credit the researcher will encounter most frequently is that of source of acquisition of the title. (See **Additional Entries** for corporate sources.) Because documentation available to catalogers could provide only minimal credit information, several personal credits appear as surnames only.

Examples:
Fox, William, source.
Kandel, source.
Gentry, Caroline, editor.
Kearton, Cherry, photographer.

Subject Headings
Library of Congress subject headings used at the time the collection was cataloged have been assigned to each entry. When possible, both general and specific terms have been provided. Subject headings are preceded by arabic numerals.

Examples:
1. Exhibitions.
2. European War, 1914–1918—Public opinion.
3. Oyster Bay, N.Y. Sagamore Hill.
4. Presidents—United States—Election—1912.
5. Women's rights—New York (State)
6. Fargo, N.D.
7. Edward VIII, King of Great Britain, 1894–1972.
8. Roosevelt, Theodore, Pres. U.S., 1858–1919—Addresses, essays, lectures.
9. Indiana (Ship)
10. Panama-Pacific International Exposition, 1915.

Additional Entries (Added Entries)
Additional entries (added entries) are given for individuals or corporate groups responsible in some way for the production or release, or both, of the film. The corporate source, if there is one, receives an added entry. Alternative titles and collection names, other than the Theodore Roosevelt Association Collection, are given entries. Added entries are preceded by roman numerals.

Examples:
I. Stineman, Ralph P.
II. Kinogram Publishing Corporation.
III. Universal Film Manufacturing Company.
IV. Community Motion Picture Service, inc., source.
V. Roosevelt Memorial Association, source.
VI. American Museum of Natural History, New York, source.
VII. Scenes of TR's trip to South America, 1913 [Title]
VIII. Series: Kinograms [Series]
IX. Paper Print Collection.

Computer Control Number
The internal computer control number is the last element of each catalog entry. It may be ignored by the researcher.

Example:
MP 76–261

Abbreviations
The following abbreviations are used in the Roosevelt Collection catalog:

arch pos, archival pos	archival positive (The "archival" positive in the Library of Congress archive is the positive held there that is closest to the original material.)
b&w	black and white
©	copyright symbol
ca	circa
cy	copy, copies
dupe neg	duplicate negative
dupe neg ntr	duplicate negative nitrate
fgmp	fine grain master positive
ft	foot, feet
Kleine	Kleine (George) Collection
LC	Library of Congress
masterpos	fine grain master positive
MPN	*Motion Picture News*
MPW	*Moving Picture World*
neg	negative
neg ntr	negative nitrate
ntr	nitrate base film

NYT	*New York Times*
P&P	Prints and Photographs Division, Library of Congress
Paper	Paper Print Collection
paper	paper print
pos ntr	positive nitrate
print	reference print (viewing copy)
r	reel(s)
ref print	reference print (viewing copy)
ref source(s)	reference source(s)
reg	registration for copyright
RMA	Roosevelt Memorial Association. The association was established in January 1919; it was formally incorporated by Act of Congress, May 31, 1920. In 1953 the present name [Theodore Roosevelt Association] was adopted; it merged with the Women's Theodore Roosevelt Memorial Association in 1955.
si	silent
shelf loc'n	shelf location
TR	Theodore Roosevelt, Pres. U.S., 1858–1919
TR Jr	Theodore Roosevelt, 1887–1944
WRMA	Women's Roosevelt Memorial Association (see also RMA)
WWI	World War I

The Chronological and General Indexes

The chronological and general indexes provide multiple access points to the collection.

In the chronological index, titles are arranged alphabetically under the first date that appears in the production statement. After the title, the following information appears in brackets: terms which describe the production date, such as "Single date," "Questionable date" (where the time span within which the film was possibly or probably produced is given), "Rereleased date" (where date of original release is followed by the rereleased date), or "Multiple dates" (where film includes footage from different years); and the year or years of production or release. The researcher should check the production statement and relevant notes in the film's catalog entry to obtain more precise information concerning the film's production date. (See also the "Production Statement" paragraph in this section.)

Examples:

1901

President McKinley reviewing the troops at the

Pan-American Exposition.
[Single date: 1901]

1910

William Gibbs McAdoo.
[Questionable date: 1910–1919]

1912

A visit to Theodore Roosevelt at his home at Sagamore Hill, Oyster Bay, L.I., 1912.
[Rereleased date: 1912, 1920]

1913

[Scenes of TR on board ship, 1916; Scenes of TR's trip to South America, 1913]
[Multiple dates: 1913, 1916]

1916

Scenes of TR speaking at Sagamore [1916–1918]
[Multiple dates: 1916–1918]

The general index contains integrated entries for alternative titles, series titles, personal credits, subjects (topical, geographic, personal, and corporate), and collection and corporate names. The relevant title entry in the catalog and the corresponding production date or dates appear after the index entry. The word *See* appears below headings *not* used and directs the researcher to the headings that are used. The words *See also* appear at the end of entries and direct the researcher to other headings which may also be useful. A few notes (scope notes) are included which more precisely define the usage of subject headings and direct the researcher to other appropriate headings. The researcher may find the structured cross-references in *Library of Congress Subject Headings* (1975) useful guides in searching for subjects in the general index.

Examples:

Roosevelt [Title]

TR at Fargo, N.D., during Progressive campaign, 1912 [1] 1912

Universal Animated Weekly

TR reviews and addresses troops [Fort Sheridan, Ill.]; TR riding in auto, Chicago, 1917. 1917

Kearton, Cherry, photographer

African animals. 1909

Teddy bears

Still pictures of TR at [Cambridge] 1910. 1910

Little Missouri Badlands, N.D.

Through Roosevelt country with Roosevelt's friends. 1919

Lodge, Henry Cabot

TR's return from Africa, 1910 [1] 1925

Germany, Kriegsmarine
International naval review, Hampton Roads, Virginia, 1907. 1907
National Audubon Society
TR [in Louisiana], 1915 [1] 1915
Paper Print Collection
Launch, U.S. battleship "Kentucky." 1898
Fox Film Corporation
General Goethals. 1923
Expositions
See Exhibitions
Liberty loan acts
See United States. Laws, statutes, etc. Liberty loan acts
Suffrage
See also Women—Suffrage
Exhibitions
See also Flower shows; particular exhibitions, e.g. Pan-American Exposition, 1901; and subdivision Exhibitions under names of cities

A term such as *source* appearing after a person's name distinguishes him or her from a personal subject entry. The word [Title] (in brackets) follows the alternative title entries—title entries not used—to distinguish them from other entries. Other qualifying terms, such as (Ship) and (State), have been added to entries to avoid confusion.

Examples:
Foch, Ferdinand
Marshal Foch visits Roosevelt House, 1921. 1921
Ford, Henry, source
TR in auto [1912] 1912
Theodore Roosevelt, friend of the birds [Title]
Roosevelt, friend of the birds [1] 1924
Queen Maud (Ship)
TR in Denmark, 1910. 1910
Progressive Party (Founded 1912)
TR speaking from train platform, 1912. 1912
Spirit of St. Louis (Airplane)
Colonel Lindbergh, Admiral Byrd, and Clarence Chamberlin at flying field just before Lindbergh's flight, 1927. 1927
Mato Grosso, Brazil (State)
The River of Doubt [3] 1928

The entries in the general index, as well as in the catalog itself, are arranged according to the rules that have been approved for all computer-generated bibliographic products of the Library of Congress. Entries are arranged word by word; words consist of one or more letters or numerals set off by spaces or marks of significant punctuation, such as a hyphen. Letters are arranged according to the order of the English alphabet. Modified letters (e.g., é, ô, ö) are treated in the same way as their plain equivalents (e.g., e, o). Numbers expressed in digits precede letters and are arranged in order of increasing numerical value. Signs and symbols (such as "[" or "?") are ignored in filing and the succeeding letters or numerals are used as the basis of arrangement. Initial articles are ignored in both the catalog and the general index.

Examples:
25th Infantry
Admiral Dewey on the deck of flagship, 1899 [1]
Admiral Dewey on the deck of flagship, 1899 [2]
Arizona
Arizona (Ter.), Governor, 1909-1912 (Sloan)
Close-up of TR speaking [1917]
[Flag services for TR at Oyster Bay, October 1919]
Helm, William P.
Helsingor, Denmark
Reviewing Annapolis middies
The Roosevelt Dam [1]
The Roosevelt Dam [2]
Roosevelt Scenes [1917-1918]
Theodore Roosevelt in the great war [3]
Through Roosevelt country with Roosevelt's friends
TR addresses Cardinal Gibbons at Baltimore, Md., 1918
TR [at Panama-Pacific Exposition, 1915]
[TR getting into parked car]
TR greeting crowds of people, 1917-1918

Subject headings that are not subdivided precede those that are. Subject divisions are arranged alphabetically.

Examples:
Roosevelt, Theodore, Pres. U.S., 1858-1919
Roosevelt, Theodore, Pres. U.S., 1858-1919—Addresses, essays, lectures
Roosevelt, Theodore, Pres. U.S., 1858-1919—Anecdotes
Roosevelt, Theodore, Pres. U.S., 1858-1919—Birthplace
Roosevelt, Theodore, Pres. U.S., 1858-1919—Family
Roosevelt, Theodore, Pres. U.S., 1858-1919—Homes
Roosevelt, Theodore, Pres. U.S., 1858-1919—Personality
Roosevelt, Theodore, Pres. U.S., 1858-1919—Quotations

The Theodore Roosevelt Association
Film Collection

A Catalog

"But what about the films of fact? . . . Collectors ignore them. Very few archives preserve them. But so violently does our way of life alter that films once considered dull, dismissed as 'educational,' can be transformed by the passage of time into priceless relics that recapture our past in an astonishingly vivid manner."

Kevin Brownlow
The War, the West and the Wilderness

The Theodore Roosevelt Association Film Collection

15th Infantry leaving Governors Island for China (Boxer Uprising) 1900.

Producer unknown [1900?]

© No reg.

    lr, 19 ft. si. b&w. 16mm. ref print.

    lr, 19 ft. si. b&w. 16mm. dupe neg.

    lr, 19 ft. si. b&w. 16mm. archival pos.

  SHELF LOC'N: FAB1459 (print); FRA6195 (neg); FRA6119 (arch pos)

Location and date in title unverified.

Possibly a Biograph production produced ca. 1897–1902.

Research indicates soldiers may be members of the 13th rather than the 15th Infantry.

Ref sources: Smith, Edmund B. *Governors Island*. 1923: 73; Azoy, Anastasio C. M. *Three Centuries under Three Flags*. 1951: 74–75.

Factual: war film.

SUMMARY: This film is probably an enactment of Army troops falling into formation and marching double-time. An officer is directing the drill as a bugler summons the men; the men shoulder their rifles and quickly move off-camera while the officer remains. Location is the courtyard of a large building or complex of buildings whose architecture appears to be Spanish. The uniforms worn by the men indicate that the film was made ca. the Spanish-American War.

1. Infantry drill and tactics. 2. Governors Island, N.Y. 3. United States. Army. Infantry—Drill and tactics. I. Biograph Company. II. Biograph Company, source. III. Theodore Roosevelt Association Collection. [mp 76–244]

25th Infantry.

American Mutoscope Co., 1898.

© H17963, American Mutoscope & Biograph Co., 21 May 1902

    lr of l, 20 ft. si. b&w. 16mm. ref print (cy 1)

    lr of l, 51 ft. si. b&w. 35mm. ref print (cy 2)

    lr of l, 20 ft. si. b&w. 16mm. dupe neg.

    lr of l, 20 ft. si. b&w. 16mm. archival pos.

    lr of l, 25 ft. si. b&w. 16mm. ref print.

    lr of l, 25 ft. si. b&w. 16mm. dupe neg.

    lr of l, 52 ft. si. b&w. 35mm. paper (2 cy)

  SHELF LOC'N: FAB1214 (print, cy 1-RMA); FEA7323 (print, cy 2-RMA); FRA6178 (neg-RMA); FRA6109 (arch pos-RMA); FLA3813 (print-Paper); FRA2856 (neg-Paper); LC799 (paper, 2 cy-Paper)

RMA title: *25th Infantry Returning from Mt. Ariat, 1898.*

Possible production dates: June-Aug., 1898.

Ref sources: Johnson, Edward A. *History of Negro Soldiers in the Spanish-American War*. 1899: 20–32; Nankivell, John H. *History of the Twenty-fifth Regiment, United States Infantry, 1869–1926*. 1927: 70–84; Werstein, Irving. *1898: The Spanish-American War*. 1966: 79, 93.

Newsfilm: war film.

SUMMARY: Preceded by officers on horseback, the Twenty-fifth Infantry of the U.S. Army marches along a road, probably in Cuba. The winter uniforms worn by the soldiers are an example of the lack of planning and adequate equipment for U.S. forces sent to Cuba during the Spanish-American War of 1898. The Twenty-fifth Infantry, a black regiment, distinguished itself during the war by the heroic charge it made on the village of El Caney. During TR's second administration, it was the Twenty-fifth Infantry which was involved in the Brownsville riot of 1906.

1. Afro-American soldiers. 2. Cuba. 3. United States—History—War of 1898. 4. United States—History—War of 1898—Afro-American troops. 5. United States. Army. 25th Infantry. I. Biograph Company. II. Biograph Company, source. III. Theodore Roosevelt Association Collection. IV. Paper Print Collection. [mp 76–250]

Admiral Dewey on flagship, 1899.

Thomas A. Edison, inc., Sep 1899.

© No reg.

    lr, 24 ft. si. b&w. 16mm. ref print (3 cy)

    lr, 24 ft. si. b&w. 16mm. archival pos.

  SHELF LOC'N: FAB1129 & 1130 & 1138 (print, 3 cy); FRA6071 (arch pos)

According to the 1905 Edison Manufacturing Co. catalog, Edison's was the only "photographic apparatus" on board the Olympia on the occasion of Dewey's arrival in New York City, Sept. 27–30, 1899.

Film is out of sequence; film is dark.

Admiral Dewey receives TR, governor of New York, aboard Dewey's flagship, the *Olympia*, September 27, 1889, when New York honored the hero of Manila Bay.

Ref sources: King, Moses. *The Dewey Reception and Committee of New York City*. 1899; The *Evening Star*, Washington, D.C. 9/28/99: 1; 9/29/99: 1; Washington *Post*. 9/29/99: 2; The Brooklyn *Daily Eagle*. 9/27/99: 1; 9/28/99: 1; P&P portrait file.

Newsfilm.

SUMMARY: Prior to the water and land parades on Sept. 29 and 30, 1899, part of New York City's enthusiastic welcome to Adm. George Dewey, the admiral remains on board his flagship, the Olympia, anchored at Tompkinsville, Staten Island. Admiral Dewey, the heavy man with a white mustache, and three of his officers await the arrival of visitors; a group of dignitaries, including several naval officers, board; the first person to step on deck may be Rear Adm. William T. Sampson, commander of the North Atlantic Squadron; Dewey greets visitors. These visitors may be members of the Washington or New York City reception committee. Because the film is out of sequence, other individuals also appear on deck; camera angle and distance make positive identification of visitors impossible.

PERSONAL CREDITS: Elmendorf, Dwight L., source.

1. New York Bay. 2. Tompkinsville, N.Y. 3. Dewey, George. 4. Sampson, William Thomas. 5. Olympia (Cruiser) 6. United States. Navy—Officers. 7. United States. Navy—History—War of 1898. I. Edison (Thomas A.) inc. II. Theodore Roosevelt Association Collection. [mp 76–230]

Admiral Dewey on the deck of flagship, 1899 [1]

Thomas A. Edison, inc., Sep 1899.

© No reg.

 lr, 84 ft. si. b&w. 35mm. ref print.

 lr, 33 ft. si. b&w. 16mm. archival pos.

SHELF LOC'N: FEA7633 (print); FRA6072 (arch pos)

According to the 1905 Edison Manufacturing Co. catalog, Edison's was the only "photographic apparatus" on board the Olympia on the occasion of Dewey's arrival in New York City, Sept. 27–30, 1899.

Film may be out of sequence.

Ref sources: King, Moses. *The Dewey Reception and Committee of New York City*. 1899; The *Evening Star*, Washington, D.C. 9/28/99: 1; 9/29/99: 1; Washington *Post*. 9/29/99: 2; The Brooklyn *Daily Eagle*. 9/27/99: 1; 9/28/99: 1; P&P portrait file.

Newsfilm.

SUMMARY: Adm. George Dewey returns triumphantly to New York City, Sept. 27, 1899, from his victory in Manila Bay during the Spanish-American War of 1898. Immediately after his arrival in the New York Bay, many prominent people make formal visits to the Olympia, Dewey's flagship, anchored at Tompkinsville, Staten Island. Naval officers and guests appear on the Olympia's deck; in the second sequence the admiral and several of his officers walk around the deck; Dewey walks toward the camera and doffs his hat, clear shots of Admiral Dewey; prominent visitors, who may be representatives from the Washington or New York reception committees, board from a boat pulled next to the Olympia; the first individual may be Rear Adm. William T. Sampson, commander of the North Atlantic Squadron; Dewey greets visitors.

PERSONAL CREDITS: Elmendorf, Dwight L., source.

1. Ships. 2. New York Bay. 3. Tompkinsville, N.Y. 4. Dewey, George. 5. Sampson, William Thomas. 6. Olympia (Cruiser) 7. United States. Navy—Officers. 8. United States. Navy—History—War of 1898. I. Edison (Thomas A.) inc. II. Theodore Roosevelt Association Collection. [mp 76–234]

Admiral Dewey on the deck of flagship, 1899 [2]

Thomas A. Edison, inc., Sep 1899.

© No reg.

 lr, 16 ft. si. b&w. 16mm. ref print.

 lr, 16 ft. si. b&w. 16mm. dupe neg.

SHELF LOC'N: FAB1131 (print); FRA6073 (neg)

According to the 1905 Edison Manufacturing Co. catalog, Edison's was the only "photographic apparatus" on board the Olympia on the occasion of Dewey's arrival in New York City, Sept. 27–30, 1899.

Film is out of frame ca. ft. 6; image is blurred ca. ft. 8–10.

Ref sources: King, Moses. *The Dewey Reception and Committee of New York City.* 1899; The *Evening Star,* Washington, D.C. 9/28/99: 1; 9/29/99: 1; Washington *Post.* 9/29/99: 2; The Brooklyn *Daily Eagle.* 9/27/99: 1; 9/28/99: 1; P&P portrait file.

Newsfilm.

SUMMARY: When Adm. George Dewey enters New York Bay on Sept. 27, 1899, he receives many visitors who wish to formally welcome him to New York and to complete arrangements for his reception in New York and in Washington, D.C. Admiral Dewey and three of his officers walk on the deck of the Olympia, Dewey's flagship, which is anchored at Tompkinsville, Staten Island; a group of prominent visitors comes on board and the admiral greets them; the first visitor is probably Rear Adm. William T. Sampson, commander of the North Atlantic Squadron.

PERSONAL CREDITS: Elmendorf, Dwight L., source.

1. Ships. 2. New York Bay. 3. Tompkinsville, N.Y. 4. Dewey, George. 5. Sampson, William Thomas. 6. Olympia (Cruiser) 7. United States. Navy—Officers. 8. United States. Navy—History—War of 1898. I. Edison (Thomas A.) inc. II. Theodore Roosevelt Association Collection. [mp 76–235]

Admiral Dewey parade, 1899 [1]
Producer unknown, Sep 1899.

© No reg.

lr, 70 ft. si. b&w. 16mm. ref print.
lr, 70 ft. si. b&w. 16mm. dupe neg (cy 1)
lr, 174 ft. si. b&w. 35mm. dupe neg (cy 2)
lr, 70 ft. si. b&w. 16mm. archival pos.

SHELF LOC'N: FAB1458 (print); FRA6193 (neg, cy 1); FPA7455 (neg, cy 2); FRA 6070 (arch pos)

Ref sources: King, Moses. *The Dewey Reception and Committee of New York City.* 1899; Detroit Photographic Co., 1899. *The Dewey Land Parade.* lot 6325. P&P.

Newsfilm.

SUMMARY: New York gives Adm. George Dewey, hero of Manila Bay, a lavish welcome Sept. 27–30, 1899, and one of the highlights of that welcome is the land parade of Sept. 30. Cheering crowds waving flags line the street as a battalion of sailors from the cruiser Olympia, Dewey's flagship, march by. Included in the battalion are a color guard carrying the American flag and what is probably the battalion flag, men pulling a piece of artillery, and medical personnel. A long line of carriages follows the marching sailors. In the first carriage, drawn by four horses, ride Admiral Dewey and Robert A. Van Wyck, mayor of New York City (1898–1902). Additional carriages containing dignitaries and naval officers follow. At ca. 53 ft. a carriage appears in which a hatless naval officer, who is probably Rear Adm. William T. Sampson, commander of the North Atlantic Squadron, rides; the man wearing a top hat on the far side of the carriage is probably Thomas F. Woods, president of the Board of Aldermen of New York City.

PERSONAL CREDITS: Elmendorf, Dwight L., source.

1. Processions. 2. Carriages and carts. 3. New York (City) 4. New York (City)—Officials and employees. 5. Dewey, George. 6. Van Wyck, Robert A. 7. Sampson, William Thomas. 8. Woods, Thomas Francis. 9. United States. Navy. Asiatic Fleet. 10. United States. Navy—Officers. 11. United States. Navy—History—War of 1898. I. Theodore Roosevelt Association Collection. [mp 76–232]

Admiral Dewey parade, 1899 [2]
Producer unknown, Sep 1899.

© No reg.

lr, 33 ft. si. b&w. 16mm. ref print (2 cy)
lr, 33 ft. si. b&w. 16mm. archival pos (2 cy)

SHELF LOC'N: FAB1139 & 1209 (print, 2 cy); FRA6093 & 6094 (arch pos, 2 cy)

Ref sources: King, Moses. *The Dewey Reception and Committee of New York City.* 1899; Detroit Photographic Co., 1899. *The Dewey Land Parade.* lot 6325. P&P.

Newsfilm.

SUMMARY: Crowds line a street to watch the land parade on Sept. 30, 1899, the last in a series of special events and ceremonies organized by the City of New York to honor Adm. George Dewey. The film consists of views of numerous carriages carrying naval officers and dignitaries. At ca. 17–18 ft. the hatless naval officer in a carriage is probably Rear Adm. William T. Sampson, commander of the North Atlantic Squadron; with him is probably Thomas F. Woods, president of the Board of Aldermen of New York City.

PERSONAL CREDITS: Elmendorf, Dwight L., source.

1. Processions. 2. Carriages and carts. 3. New York (City) 4. New York (City)—Officials and employees. 5. Sampson, William Thomas. 6. Woods,

TR, then governor of New York, preferred to ride on a horse rather than in an automobile during the parade honoring Adm. George Dewey, September 30, 1899, as seen in this stereograph.

Thomas Francis. 7. United States. Navy—Officers. 8. United States. Navy—History—War of 1898. I. Theodore Roosevelt Association Collection. [mp 76–233]

African animals.

Producer unknown [1909?]

© No reg.

lr, 22 ft. si. b&w. 16mm. ref print.
lr, 22 ft. si. b&w. 16mm. dupe neg (cy 1)
lr, 56 ft. si. b&w. 35mm. dupe neg (cy 2)
lr, 56 ft. si. b&w. 35mm. masterpos.
lr, 56 ft. si. b&w. 35mm. pos ntr.

SHELF LOC'N: FAB1070 (print); FRA6044 (neg, cy 1); FPB7355 (neg, cy 2); FPB 7356 (fgmp)

Sources indicate that the photographer is Cherry Kearton.

Ref sources: Kearton, Cherry. *Photographing Wild Life across the World.* [1923]: 105–121; Kearton, Cherry. *Adventures with Animals and Men.* 1935: 65–66; Unger, Frederick W. *Roosevelt's African Trip.* 1909: [2]; *The Moving Picture World.* v. 6, no. 13, 1910: 528–529.

Factual; nature film.

SUMMARY: In what is probably the Tana River in British East Africa (Kenya), hippopotami sun on a rock and swim. In a different location a rhinoceros grazes in a grove of trees.

PERSONAL CREDITS: Kearton, Cherry, photographer.

1. Hippopotamus. 2. Rhinoceros. 3. Tana River. 4. Kenya. I. Community Motion Picture Service, inc., source. II. Theodore Roosevelt Association Collection. [mp 76–241]

African natives.

Producer unknown, Aug 1909.

© No reg.

lr, 23 ft. si. b&w. 16mm. ref print (cy 1)
lr, 58 ft. si. b&w. 35mm. ref print (cy 2)
lr, 23 ft. si. b&w. 16mm. archival pos.
lr, 58 ft. si. b&w. 35mm. neg ntr.

SHELF LOC'N: FAB1114 (print, cy 1); FEA7626 (print, cy 2); FRA6057 (arch pos)

Sources indicate that the photographer is Cherry Kearton.

Ref sources: Roosevelt, Kermit. *A Sentimental Safari.* 1963: [17]; Kearton, Cherry. *Adventures with Animals and Men.* 1935:68–71; *Scribner's Magazine.* v. 47, no. 6, 1910:643–644, 650–652; Kearton, Cherry. *Photographing Wild Life across the World.* [1923]: 105–106; Roosevelt Memorial Association. *Annual Report.* 1926: 18; Library of Congress. African Section.

Factual; sociological.

SUMMARY: Views of what is probably part of the Kikuyu and Masai tribal dances performed for

TR in the village of Nyeri, Kenya, in Aug. 1909. A line of natives with spears and shields dance on an open hill and move toward the camera; the camera pans a crowd of Kikuyu and/or Masai men in tribal dress, with men who may be members of TR's safari party visible briefly in the crowd; close shot of a small boy who is probably Kikuyu, in traditional dress, surrounded by elders, performing a ritual dance.

PERSONAL CREDITS: Kearton, Cherry, photographer.

1. Big game hunting—Africa. 2. Kikuyu tribe. 3. Kikuyu tribe—Dances. 4. Masai. 5. Masai—Dances. 6. Nyeri, Kenya. 7. Roosevelt, Theodore, Pres. U.S., 1858–1919—Journey to Africa, 1909–1910. I. Community Motion Picture Service, inc., source. II. Theodore Roosevelt Association Collection. [mp 76–247]

Aigrette.
Producer unknown [192–?]
© No reg.
    lr, 3 ft. si. b&w. 16mm. ref print.
    lr, 3 ft. si. b&w. 16mm. dupe neg (cy 1)
    lr, 7 ft. si. b&w. 35mm. dupe neg (cy 2)
    lr, 7 ft. si. b&w. 35mm. pos ntr.
SHELF LOC'N: FAB1038 (print); FRA6010 (neg, cy 1); FPB7347 (neg, cy 2)
Factual.
SUMMARY: Close-up shot of a hand holding a spray of feathers, probably from the egret. May be related to TR's conservation efforts for the protection of birds.

1. Feathers. 2. Wildlife conservation. 3. Birds, Protection of. I. Apollo Pictures, source. II. Theodore Roosevelt Association Collection. [mp 76–309]

Airmen honor TR's memory by dropping American Legion wreath on his grave [1919]
Fox Film Corp., Oct 1919.
© No reg.
    lr, 40 ft. si. b&w. 16mm. ref print.
    lr, 40 ft. si. b&w. 16mm. dupe neg.
    lr, 40 ft. si. b&w. 16mm. archival pos.
(Fox news [Series])
SHELF LOC'N: FAB1063 (print); FRA6036 (neg); FRA6037 (arch pos)
RMA lists the date in the title as 1923.
Ref sources: New York *Tribune.* 10/21/19: 6; The New York *Herald.* 10/21/19: 2.
Newsfilm; views.
SUMMARY: On Oct. 20, 1919, as part of opening day ceremonies to honor TR and raise funds for the restoration of Roosevelt House in New York City, military aviators flew from Hazelhurst Field, Mineola, N.Y., to Oyster Bay to drop wreaths on TR's gravesite in Youngs Memorial Cemetery. The film has scenes of two pilots sitting in a biplane with an emblem showing the name of Mitchel Field, the picture of a dog, and the numbers 41866; the rear pilot is given two wreaths, one with a ribbon inscribed American Legion and the other Spanish American War Veterans; sequences of the biplane taking off, with aerial views of what is probably Oyster Bay and the surrounding area; scenes of a wreath being dropped, a group of men retrieving it, then carrying it to TR's gravesite; final views of two men in uniform placing separate wreaths on TR's grave with the tombstone visible.

PERSONAL CREDITS: Fox, William, source.

1. Airplanes. 2. Air pilots. 3. Air bases—New York (State) 4. Youngs Memorial Cemetery. 5. Oyster Bay, N.Y. 6. Oyster Bay, N.Y.—Description—Aerial. 7. Roosevelt, Theodore, Pres. U.S., 1858–1919—Funeral and memorial services. 8. Roosevelt, Theodore, Pres. U.S., 1858–1919— Tomb. 9. United States. Army Air Forces. 10. American Legion. 11. United Spanish War Veterans. I. Fox Film Corporation. II. Theodore Roosevelt Association Collection. [mp 76–204]

Allied armies in China, 1917–1918.
Producer unknown [1918?]
© No reg.
    lr, 69 ft. si. b&w. 16mm. ref print.
    lr, 69 ft. si. b&w. 16mm. archival pos.
    lr, 157 ft. si. b&w. 35mm. dupe neg ntr.
SHELF LOC'N: FAB969 (print); FRA5938 (arch pos)
The dates in the title are unverified.
The RMA list indicates that the photographer is Paul Rainey.
Ref print jumps throughout; interior title printed out of frame.
Ref source: La Fargue, Thomas E. *China and the World War.* 1973.
Newsfilm.
SUMMARY: The opening scene shows men, who may be Bolshevik prisoners, standing behind barbed wire as soldiers march past in Ekaterinburg (Sverdlovsk), Russia. The second sequence is composed of views of dignitaries reviewing detachments from the allied armies in Peking, China; the camera pans the soldiers from various nations as they stand in formation; a group of dignitaries, one identified by interior title as the president of China, reviews

them; the flag of each participating nation is visible in the film.

PERSONAL CREDITS: Rainey, Paul James, photographer.

1. Armies. 2. Prisoners of war—Sverdlovsk, Russia. 3. Prisons—Russia—Sverdlovsk. 4. Communist parties. 5. Soldiers. 6. Flags. 7. Sverdlovsk, Russia. 8. Peking. I. Church of All Nations, New York (City), source. II. Theodore Roosevelt Association Collection. [mp 76–333]

American Legion lays cornerstone of Roosevelt Bridge at Château-Thierry.
International News, Aug 1921.
© No reg.
lr, 12 ft. si. b&w. 16mm. ref print.
lr, 12 ft. si. b&w. 16mm. dupe neg.
lr, 29 ft. si. b&w. 35mm. pos ntr.
(International News [newsreel])
SHELF LOC'N: FAB954 (print); FRA5918 (neg)
Interior title notes foreign snapshots.
Ref source: P&P portrait file.
Newsfilm; views.
SUMMARY: On Aug. 23, 1921, as part of its French tour, the American Legion delegation attended the ceremony of laying the cornerstone for the Roosevelt Bridge, which was built to replace the bridge the Germans destroyed in 1918 over the Marne River in Château-Thierry, France. The bridge was named after TR and his son Quentin, who was killed in action in France. The camera pans the town, the many French and American dignitaries and soldiers attending the event, and the Marne River; the final sequence is composed of long shots of the formal dedication ceremony; identified on the extreme left of the group are Franklin D'Olier, former national commander, and Maj. John G. Emery, current national commander of the American Legion.

1. Corner stones, Laying of. 2. Dedication services. 3. Veterans. 4. Soldiers. 5. Château-Thierry, France. 6. Château-Thierry, France—Bridges—Roosevelt Bridge. 7. Marne River. 8. D'Olier, Franklin. 9. Emery, John G. 10. American Legion. 11. France. Armée. 12. United States. Army. I. International Newsreel Corporation. II. International Newsreel Corporation, source. III. Theodore Roosevelt Association Collection. [mp 76–310]

American Legion places wreath on TR's grave [1919]; Scenes of Oyster Bay from the air.
Producer unknown, Oct 1919.
© No reg.

lr, 59 ft. si. b&w. 16mm. ref print.
lr, 59 ft. si. b&w. 16mm. dupe neg.
lr, 148 ft. si. b&w. 35mm. pos ntr.
SHELF LOC'N: FAB1064 (print); FRA6038 (neg)
RMA lists the date in the title as 1921.
The film is out of sequence, with some scenes appearing twice.
Ref sources: New York *Tribune*. 10/21/19: 6; The New York *Herald*. 10/21/19: 2.
Newsfilm; views.
SUMMARY: On Oct. 20, 1919, as part of opening day ceremonies to honor TR and raise funds for the restoration of Roosevelt House in New York City, military aviators flew from Hazelhurst Field, Mineola, N.Y. to Oyster Bay to drop wreaths on TR's gravesite in Youngs Memorial Cemetery. The first sequence consists of views of two pilots sitting in a biplane with an emblem showing the name of Mitchel Field, the picture of a dog, and the numbers 41866; the rear pilot is given two wreaths, one with a ribbon inscribed American Legion and the other Spanish American War Veterans; views of the biplane taking off with aerial shots of what is probably Oyster Bay and the surrounding area. The last sequence shows at least three biplanes flying, with a close shot of one plane flying towards the camera.

PERSONAL CREDITS: Urban, Charles, source.

1. Airplanes. 2. Air pilots. 3. Air bases—New York (State) 4. Oyster Bay, N.Y. 5. Oyster Bay, N.Y.—Description—Aerial. 6. Roosevelt, Theodore, Pres. U.S., 1858–1919—Funeral and memorial services. 7. United States. Army Air Forces. 8. American Legion. 9. United Spanish War Veterans. I. Theodore Roosevelt Association Collection. II. Scenes of Oyster Bay from the air [Title] [mp 76–205]

Americanism wins, Coolidge elected.
Kinogram Pub. Corp. [1919?]
© No reg.
lr, 14 ft. si. b&w. 16mm. ref print (cy 1)
lr, 17 ft. si. b&w. 16mm. ref print (cy 2)
lr, 14 ft. si. b&w. 16mm. dupe neg.
lr, 29 ft. si. b&w. 16mm. archival pos (cy 1)
lr, 17 ft. si. b&w. 16mm. archival pos (cy 2)
lr, 23 ft. si. b&w. 16mm. archival pos (cy 3)
lr, 36 ft. si. b&w. 35mm. pos ntr.
(Kinograms [Series])
SHELF LOC'N: FAB840 (print, cy 1); FAB841 (print, cy 2); FRA5842 (neg); FRA5843 (arch pos, cy 1); FRA-

5844 (arch pos, cy 2); FRA5845 (arch pos, cy 3)

RMA titles: *Calvin Coolidge as Governor of Massachusetts, 1919; Mr. and Mrs. Calvin Coolidge and Their Sons.*

Copies vary in length due to number and length of titles.

Ref sources: P&P portrait file; McCoy, Donald R. *Calvin Coolidge.* 1967; The *Post-Intelligencer*, Seattle. 9/14/19: 6.

Newsfilm.

SUMMARY: Views of Calvin Coolidge in the months surrounding his reelection as Massachusetts governor, autumn 1919. Close shot of Coolidge, his wife Grace, and their sons John and Calvin, Jr., on the porch of their home at 21 Massasoit St., Northampton, Mass.; Coolidge casts his vote in the gubernatorial election on Nov.3, 1919, possibly in Northampton, in the presence of election officials; Coolidge receives from a man identified by interior title as Major Beckmann the American Legion medal, while Legion members on steps cheer; quotation from the Seattle *Post-Intelligencer* praising Coolidge for his law-and-order approach in the Boston police strike; close shot of Coolidge outdoors.

PERSONAL CREDITS: Stripe, F. C., source. Carver, H. P., source.

1. Elections—Massachusetts. 2. Voting. 3. Northampton, Mass. 4. Coolidge, Calvin, Pres. U.S., 1872–1933. 5. Coolidge, Calvin, Pres. U.S., 1872–1933. 6. Coolidge, Calvin, Pres. U.S., 1872–1933—Homes. 7. Coolidge, Grace Goodhue. 8. Coolidge, John. 9. Coolidge, Calvin, 1908–1924. 10. Massachusetts. Governor, 1919–1921 (Coolidge) 11. American Legion. 12. Seattle post-intelligencer. I. Kinogram Publishing Corporation. II. Kinogram Publishing Corporation, source. III. Theodore Roosevelt Association Collection. [mp 76–92]

Aviators drop American Legion wreath on TR's grave [1919]

Producer unknown, Oct 1919.

© No reg.

lr, 36 ft. si. b&w. 16mm. ref print.

lr, 36 ft. si. b&w. 16mm. archival pos.

lr, 90 ft. si. b&w. 35mm. neg ntr.

SHELF LOC'N: FAB1065 (print); FRA6039 (arch pos)

RMA lists the date in the title as 1920.

Ref sources: New York *Tribune.* 10/21/19: 6; The New York *Herald.* 10/21/19: 2.

Newsfilm; views.

SUMMARY: On Oct.20, 1919, as part of opening day ceremonies to honor TR's memory and raise funds for the restoration of Roosevelt House in New York City, military aviators flew from Hazelhurst Field, Mineola, N.Y. to Oyster Bay to drop wreaths on TR's gravesite in Youngs Memorial Cemetery. The film has scenes of two pilots sitting in a biplane with an emblem showing the name of Mitchel Field, the picture of a dog, and the numbers 41866; the rear pilot is given two wreaths, one with a ribbon inscribed American Legion and the other Spanish American War Veterans; final scenes of the biplane taking off, with aerial views of what is probably Oyster Bay and the surrounding area.

PERSONAL CREDITS: Urban, Charles, source.

1. Airplanes. 2. Air pilots. 3. Air bases—New York (State) 4. Oyster Bay, N.Y. 5. Oyster Bay, N.Y.—Description—Aerial. 6. Roosevelt, Theodore, Pres. U.S., 1858–1919—Funeral and memorial services. 7. United States. Army Air Forces. 8. American Legion. 9. United Spanish War Veterans. I. Theodore Roosevelt Association Collection. [mp 76–203]

Brooklyn children attend services, children sew stars on Roosevelt Flag [1919]

Producer unknown, Oct 1919.

© No reg.

lr, 37 ft. si. b&w. 16mm. ref print.

lr, 37 ft. si. b&w. 16mm. dupe neg.

lr, 37 ft. si. b&w. 16mm. archival pos.

lr, 93 ft. si. b&w. 35mm. neg ntr.

SHELF LOC'N: FAB987 (print); FRA8654 (neg); FRA5963 (arch pos)

RMA lists the date in the title as 1920.

Film is out of sequence, with some scenes appearing twice.

Ref sources: *Daily News.* New York. 10/25/19: 8; 10/27/19: [10–11]: Roosevelt Memorial Association. *Annual Report.* 1919–1921: 14; P&P portrait file.

Newsfilm.

SUMMARY: In honor of TR's birthday the week of Oct.20–27, 1919, was declared Roosevelt Week by the Roosevelt Memorial Association. As one of the events, an official Roosevelt memorial flag, which has been carried across New York State, is ceremoniously received at the Williamsburg Bridge Plaza in Brooklyn on Oct. 24. Opening scene of a man who may be James A. McCabe, superintendent of public schools, leading the crowd of school children and Boy Scouts in singing; close-up of the flag as boy runners display it; Samuel Abbott, originator of the memorial flag idea, speaks from a platform to a cheering crowd. The final scene is of five girls sewing the forty-eighth and final star on the flag at what is probably Cove School in Oyster Bay, N.Y., with a group of children and Boy Scouts visible in the background.

PERSONAL CREDITS: Urban, Charles, source.

1. Memorial rites and ceremonies. 2. Flags. 3. High school students—Political activity. 4. Brooklyn, N.Y. 5. Oyster Bay, N.Y. 6. Roosevelt, Theodore, Pres. U.S., 1858–1919—Funeral and memorial services. 7. McCabe, James A. 8. Abbott, Samuel. 9. Roosevelt Memorial Association. 10. Boy Scouts of America. 11. Cove School. I. Theodore Roosevelt Association Collection. [mp 76–161]

The Building of the Panama Canal upon the occasion of a memorial exhibition held in honor of General George Washington Goethals.

Roosevelt Memorial Association [1928?]
© No reg.
   lr, 57 ft. si. b&w. 35mm. ref print.
   lr, 57 ft. si. b&w. 35mm. dupe neg.
   lr, 57 ft. si. b&w. 35mm. masterpos.
   lr, 57 ft. si. b&w. 35mm. neg ntr.
  SHELF LOC'N: FEA7838 (print); FPB9923 (neg); FPB9924 (fgmp)
RMA title: *Titles and Scenes used in Goethals Memorial reel, 1928.*
Ref sources: Avery, Ralph E. *America's Triumph at Panama.* 1913: 70; P&P portrait file.
Factual; still film.
SUMMARY: This film consists of a still photograph of Gen. George Washington Goethals, credited as the builder of the Panama Canal, on the immediate right, and of Dr. William Crawford Gorgas, chief sanitation officer of the Panama Canal, on the left. Two unidentified men pose in the background. There are no views on the film of the memorial exhibition event.

1. Panama Canal. 2. Goethals, George W. 3. Gorgas, William C. I. Roosevelt Memorial Association. II. Roosevelt Memorial Association, source. III. Theodore Roosevelt Association Collection. [mp 76–34]

Bulloch home, Roswell, Georgia, 1923.

Roosevelt Memorial Association [1923?]
© No reg.
   lr, 193 ft. si. b&w. 35mm. ref print (2 cy)
   lr, 193 ft. si. b&w. 35mm. dupe neg (2 cy)
   lr, 193 ft. si. b&w. 35mm. masterpos.
   lr, 193 ft. si. b&w. 35mm. neg ntr.

  SHELF LOC'N: FEA6746 & 6747 (print, 2 cy); FPB7582 & 7583 (neg, 2 cy); FPB 7584 (fgmp)
Date in title unverified.
Ref sources: Martin, Clarece. *A Glimpse of the Past.* 1973; Writers' Program. Georgia. Atlanta. 1942: 115, 234, 236; Roosevelt Memorial Association. *Annual Report.* 1925: 15.
Factual views.
SUMMARY: Views of the childhood home of TR's mother, Martha (Mittie) Bulloch Roosevelt, in Roswell, Ga., and of the last remaining bridesmaid in Martha's wedding, Mrs. Evelyn King Baker. Long shot of Bulloch Hall, a stately Greek Revival home, designed, as were many other classic homes in the Roswell area, by Willis Ball; medium-close shot of unidentified men sitting and standing on the front porch; closer view of the columned porch; views of the side of the house, with a grape arbor visible, the barn and outbuildings, the skyline, and a well; view from inside the house of men approaching the doorway; medium-close shot of Mrs. Baker, wearing a long dark dress, seated in a chair outdoors.

1. Roswell, Ga. Bulloch Hall. 2. Greek revival (Architecture)—Georgia. 3. Roswell, Ga. 4. Roosevelt, Martha Bulloch. 5. Baker, Evelyn King. 6. Ball, Willis. I. Roosevelt Memorial Association. II. Roosevelt Memorial Association, source. III. Theodore Roosevelt Association Collection. [mp 76–210]

Calvin Coolidge as Governor of Massachusetts.

Producer unknown, Sep 1919.
© No reg.
   lr, 20 ft. si. b&w. 16mm. ref print.
   lr, 20 ft. si. b&w. 16mm. dupe neg (cy 1)
   lr, 49 ft. si. b&w. 35mm. dupe neg (cy 2)
   lr, 49 ft. si. b&w. 35mm. pos ntr.
  SHELF LOC'N: FAB888 (print); FRA5877 (neg, cy 1); FPB7192 (neg, cy 2)
Ref sources: Moran, Philip R., comp. *Calvin Coolidge, 1872–1933.* 1970; Russell, Francis. *A City in Terror.* 1975.
Newsfilm.
SUMMARY: In the State House in Boston Gov. Calvin Coolidge works on documents related to the Boston police strike, Sept. 1919. Front and back views of Coolidge seated at his desk writing; close shot of Coolidge outdoors; close shot of the governor's statement in which he declares his no-compromise position with regard to police violations of law; close shot of the phrase from his Sept. 14 telegram to Samuel L. Gompers, president of the

American Federation of Labor, which states that "There is no right to strike against the public safety by any body, anywhere, anytime." Coolidge's signature appears on the telegram message.

1. Boston, Mass. Old State House. 2. Boston, Mass. 3. Boston, Mass.—Police strike, 1919. 4. Coolidge, Calvin, Pres. U.S., 1872–1933. 5. Massachusetts. Governor, 1919–1921 (Coolidge). I. Apollo Pictures, source. II. Theodore Roosevelt Association Collection. [mp 76–110]

Calvin Coolidge as Governor of Massachusetts, 1919.
Producer unknown [1919?]
© No reg.
   lr, 26 ft. si. b&w. 16mm. ref print.
   lr, 26 ft. si. b&w. 16mm. dupe neg.
   lr, 26 ft. si. b&w. 16mm. archival pos.
   lr, 65 ft. si. b&w. 35mm. pos ntr.
SHELF LOC'N: FAB836 (print); FRA5838 (neg); FRA5837 (arch pos)
Date in title unverified.
Since Gaumont was producing newsfilm in 1919 and the RMA source is Gaumont, the film may be a Gaumont production.
Ref sources: P&P stereo file; *The Moving Picture World.* v. 40, no. 8, 1919: 1248; Federal Writers' Project. Massachusetts. *Massachusetts: A Guide to its Places and People.* 1937.
Newsfilm.
SUMMARY: Calvin Coolidge poses for the camera on what appears to be the upper portico of the State House, Boston, Mass. Medium-close view, front and profile, of Coolidge smoking a cigar, with columns and the window of a building visible in the immediate background.

1. Boston, Mass. Old State House. 2. Boston, Mass. 3. Coolidge, Calvin, Pres. U.S., 1872–1933. 4. Massachusetts. Governor, 1919–1921 (Coolidge) I. Gaumont (Firm), source. II. Theodore Roosevelt Association Collection. [mp 76–89]

Calvin Coolidge sworn in for second term as Governor of Massachusetts.
Kinogram Pub. Corp., Jan 1920.
© No reg.
   lr, 9 ft. si. b&w. 16mm. ref print (cy 1)
   lr, 6 ft. si. b&w. 16mm. ref print (cy 2–2 cy)
   lr, 6 ft. si. b&w. 16mm. archival pos.
(Kinograms [Series])
SHELF LOC'N: FAB891 (print, cy 1); FAB1230 & 1451 (print, cy 2–2 cy); FRA6186 (arch pos)

Ref print (cy 1) differs from ref print (cy 2) due to longer printing of interior title.
Ref sources: The Boston *Herald.* 1/9/20: 7–8; Boston *Post.* 1/9/20: 16; The Boston *Daily Globe.* 1/8/20: 1; *Who's Who in Sate Politics, 1914.* 1914: 38, 312; Hitchings, Sinclair H. & Farlow, Catherine H. *A New Guide to the Massachusetts State House.* 1964: 48–51; *Our State Capitol Illustrated.* 1894: [43], [93]; P&P portrait file.
Newsfilm.
SUMMARY: At the State House in Boston, Calvin Coolidge is sworn in for his second term as governor of Massachusetts, Jan. 8, 1920. The ceremony actually took place in the Chamber of the House of Representatives, but the film is shot in the Council Chamber. Coolidge is sworn in by a man who is probably Edwin T. McKnight, president of the State Senate. Governor Coolidge, members of his staff, and the Executive Council pose for the camera. Standing in the front are Governor Coolidge and Lt. Gov. Channing H. Cox; seated, left to right, are: Councillors James G. Harris, George B. Wason, Matthew J. Whittall, and Harry H. Williams. In the back row, left to right, are: Secretary to the Governor Henry F. Long (visible between Coolidge and Cox), Assistant Secretary Harry S. Fairfield, Councillor Lewis R. Sullivan, Executive Secretary Charles S. Southworth, Councillor Horace A. Carter, Councillor Henry L. Bowles, and Edward Horrigan, the governor's bodyguard.
PERSONAL CREDITS: Stripe, F. C., source. Carver, H. P., source.

1. Boston, Mass. Old State House. 2. Boston, Mass. 3. Massachusetts—Lieutenant-governors. 4. Massachusetts—Officials and employees. 5. Massachusetts—Politics and government. 6. Coolidge, Calvin, Pres. U.S., 1872–1933. 7. McKnight, Edwin Toil. 8. Cox, Channing H. 9. Harris, James G. 10. Wason, George B. 11. Whittall, Matthew J. 12. Williams, Harry H. 13. Long, Henry F. 14. Fairfield, Harry S. 15. Sullivan, Lewis R. 16. Southworth, Charles S. 17. Carter, Horace A. 18. Bowles, Henry. 19. Horrigan, Edward. 20. Massachusetts. Governor, 1919–1921 (Coolidge) 21. Massachusetts. Council. I. Kinogram Publishing Corporation. II. Theodore Roosevelt Association Collection. [mp 76–264]

Cartoon of Mr. Paul Rainey's African trip [1911]
Producer unknown [1911?]
© No reg.
   lr, 233 ft. si. b&w. 16mm. ref print (cy 1)
   lr, 194 ft. si. b&w. 16mm. ref print (cy 2–2cy)
   lr, 192 ft. si. b&w. 16mm. dupe neg.

lr, 192 ft. si. b&w. 16mm. archival pos.

lr, 485 ft. si. b&w. 35mm. neg ntr.

SHELF LOC'N: FAB963 (print, cy 1); FAB1204 & 1205 (print, cy 2–2 cy); FRA 5930 (neg); FRA5931 (arch pos)

RMA lists the date in the title as 1910.

Research indicates Rainey's first African trip was in Feb. 1911.

Copies vary in length due to longer printing of interior titles.

Ref prints (cy 2) are out of sequence.

Short; cartoon.

SUMMARY: An animated cartoon beginning with a character apparently representing Paul J. Rainey, explorer and hunter, being washed overboard; he swims to a barrel, climbs in, grabs hold of the tail of a whale, which tows him toward shore where he lands; a bird resembling an ostrich lays an egg; Rainey sits on the egg, which hatches; he rides the bird while being chased by a lion and is saved by a native; the bird chases the lion and throws him out to sea where he is swallowed by a whale; a native takes Rainey to a wedding feast at which Rainey is the intended groom; Rainey runs away, jumps into a barrel and floats out to sea while natives gather on shore.

1. Caricatures and cartoons. 2. Editorial cartoons. 3. Animals. 4. Africa. 5. Rainey, Paul James. I. Church of All Nations, New York (City), source. II. Theodore Roosevelt Association Collection. [mp 76–51]

Cartoon of TR's reception by crowned heads of Europe.

Producer unknown [1910?]

© No reg.

lr, 3 ft. si. b&w. 16mm. ref print.

lr, 3 ft. si. b&w. 16mm. dupe neg.

lr, 8 ft. si. b&w. 35mm. pos old safety.

SHELF LOC'N: FAB946 (print); FRA5904 (neg)

Short; political; cartoon.

SUMMARY: An animated cartoon of TR's reception in Europe during his Apr.-June 1910 tour. Sequences of crowned heads of Europe sitting in an open automobile, labeled Europe, located on a pier. TR, carrying a big stick, is in the bow of a ship that approaches the pier as the crowned heads wave. Caricatured are: TR; Victor Emanuel III of Italy; Manuel II of Portugal; Franz Joseph I of Austria; Alfonso XIII of Spain; Nicholas II of Russia; Edward VII of Great Britain; Clément Fallières of France; and Wilhelm II of Germany.

1. Caricatures and cartoons. 2. Editorial cartoons.

3. Politics and art. 4. Roosevelt, Theodore, Pres. U.S., 1858–1919—Journey to Europe, 1910. 5. Roosevelt, Theodore, Pres. U.S., 1858–1919—Cartoons, satire, etc. 6. Vittorio Emanuele III, King of Italy, 1869–1947. 7. Manuel II, King of Portugal, 1889–1932. 8. Franz Joseph I, Emperor of Austria, 1830–1916. 9. Alfonso XIII, King of Spain, 1868–1941. 10. Nicholas II, Emperor of Russia, 1868–1918. 11. Edward VII, King of Great Britain, 1841–1910. 12. Fallières, Clément Armand, Pres. France, 1841–1931. 13. Wilhelm II, German Emperor, 1859–1941. I. Roosevelt Memorial Association, source. II. Theodore Roosevelt Association Collection. [mp 76–182]

Cartoon: TR's arrival in Africa.

Producer unknown [1909?]

© No reg.

lr, 11 ft. si. b&w. 16mm. ref print (cy 1)

lr, 33 ft. si. b&w. 35mm. ref print (cy 2)

lr, 33 ft. si. b&w. 35mm. ref print (cy 3)

lr, 11 ft. si. b&w. 16mm. dupe neg (cy 1)

lr, 33 ft. si. b&w. 35mm. dupe neg (cy 2)

lr, 33 ft. si. b&w. 35mm. masterpos.

lr, 11 ft. si. b&w. 16mm. archival pos.

lr, 33 ft. si. b&w. 35mm. pos ntr.

lr, 28 ft. si. b&w. 35mm. neg ntr.

SHELF LOC'N: FAB884 (print, cy 1); FEA6732 (print, cy 2); FEA9652 (print, cy 3); FRA8205 (neg, cy 1); FPB 7189 (neg, cy 2); FPC0474 (fgmp); FRA5871 (arch pos)

Ref print (cy 1) and arch pos lack interior title.

Appears to be based on Homer Davenport's cartoon, "The Frightened animals; hist! see who's coming," originally published in the *Evening Mail*, New York, March 23, 1909.

Ref sources: Shaw, Albert. *A Cartoon History of Roosevelt's Career.* 1910: 194; Lorant, Stefan. *The Life and Times of Theodore Roosevelt.* 1959: 515.

Short; cartoon.

SUMMARY: Animated caricature of the animals' attitude towards TR's arrival in Africa. Views of a huge tree filled with frightened animals, as a monkey on the ground peers over a cliff; he begins jumping up and down, pointing, and climbing the tree as TR appears over the rim of the cliff with a gun in his hand.

PERSONAL CREDITS: Geiss, A., source.

1. Caricatures and cartoons. 2. Editorial cartoons. 3. Animals. 4. Big game hunting—Africa. 5. Africa. 6. Roosevelt, Theodore, Pres. U.S., 1858–1919—Journey to Africa, 1909–1910. 7. Roosevelt, Theo-

dore, Pres. U.S., 1858–1919—Cartoons, satire, etc. I. Theodore Roosevelt Association Collection. [mp 76–108]

Charles E. Hughes speaking during campaign, Duquesne, Pa., 1916.
Universal Film Manufacturing Co., Sep 1916.
 © No reg.
  lr, 13 ft. si. b&w. 16mm. ref print.
  lr, 13 ft. si. b&w. 16mm. dupe neg.
  lr, 17 ft. si. b&w. 16mm. archival pos.
 (Universal animated weekly, v. 4, issue no. 40)
 SHELF LOC'N: FAB671 (print); FRA5710 (neg);
     FRA5709 (arch pos)
Originally part of a Universal animated weekly newsreel segment including footage of the Wilson campaign entitled "Two Candidates Busy."
 Ref source: The Pittsburgh *Post.* 9/28/16: 1.
Newsfilm.
SUMMARY: Presidential candidate Charles Evans Hughes campaigns in the Pittsburgh vicinity on Sept. 27, 1916. Hughes was on a strenuous tour in an attempt to knit together various Republican factions. In the Pittsburgh area he was joined by Republican notables, some of whom had been at odds with him: Sen. Boies Penrose, Philander Knox, and William Flinn. Hughes spoke in opposition to the eight-hour day and was silent on female suffrage. In the film Hughes is attended by an official who appears, according to newspaper accounts and photos, to be William H. Coleman, Republican county chairman. There are three different sequences: Hughes shaking hands with an official, both apparently on a flag-draped platform, with young girls in the background; Hughes addressing a crowd of men in front of a stone building; and Hughes speaking to a group of workers in the street, with a background view of row houses. Women and children are visible on house porches. An interior title lists the location as Duquesne, Pa.
 CITATION: MPW30.1: 445.
 1. Presidents—United States—Election—1916. 2. Steel workers. 3. Pittsburgh. 4. Duquesne, Pa. 5. Hughes, Charles Evans. 6. Coleman, William H. I. Universal Film Manufacturing Company. II. Community Motion Picture Service, inc., source. III. Theodore Roosevelt Association Collection. [mp 76–24]

Charles Evans Hughes served as governor of New York (1907–1910), was an associate justice of the Supreme Court, and unsuccessfully ran for president in 1916. Hughes later served as secretary of state under Coolidge and Harding, held many significant national and international positions, and was appointed chief justice of the Supreme Court in 1930.

Chauncey Depew, Senator Perkins, and Governor Whitman of New York, at GOP Convention, 1916, Chicago, Ill.
Pathe News, Jun 1916.
 © No reg.
  lr, 41 ft. si. b&w. 16mm. ref print.
  lr, 21 ft. si. b&w. 16mm. dupe neg.
  lr, 21 ft. si. b&w. 16mm. archival pos.
  lr, 52 ft. si. b&w. 35mm. pos ntr.
 (Pathe News [newsreel])
 SHELF LOC'N: FAB976 (print); FRA5945 (neg);
     FRA5946 (arch pos)
Segment of Pathe News no. 46 released June 7, 1916.
 Ref sources: P&P portrait file; Republican Party. National Convention, 16th Chicago, 1916. *Official Report of the Proceedings of the Sixteenth Republican National Convention.* 1916.
 Newsfilm; political.
SUMMARY: Scenes from the Sixteenth Republican National Convention held in Chicago, June 7–10, 1916. Long shot of delegates outside the Congress Hotel. Medium shots, from left to right, of Mrs. Olive H. Whitman; Gov. Charles S. Whitman

of New York (1915–1918); Francis Hendricks, former New York state senator (1886–1891); George W. Perkins, a leader in the Progressive movement (1912–1916); Chauncey M. Depew, former New York state senator (1899–1911); and a medium shot of the Coliseum where the convention was in session.

CITATION: MPW28.2: 2300; MPW29.1: 20.

1. Political conventions. 2. Political parties. 3. Chicago. Coliseum. 4. Chicago. Congress Hotel. 5. Presidents—United States—Election—1916. 6. United States—Politics and government—1913–1921. 7. Chicago. 8. Depew, Chauncey M. 9. Perkins, George W. 10. Whitman, Charles S. 11. Whitman, Olive H. 12. Hendricks, Francis. 13. Republican Party. 14. Republican Party. National Convention. 16th, Chicago, 1916. I. Pathe. II. Pathe, source. III. Theodore Roosevelt Association Collection. [mp 76–207]

Children sewing stars on flag, placing flag on TR's grave [1919]
International Film Service Co., Oct 1919.
© No reg.
  lr, 28 ft. si. b&w. 16mm. ref print.
  lr, 28 ft. si. b&w. 16mm. dupe neg.
  lr, 70 ft. si. b&w. 35mm. pos ntr.
(International [Series])
SHELF LOC'N: FAB1013 (print); FRA5988 (neg)
RMA lists date in title as 1920.
Ref sources: *Daily News*, New York. 10/25/19: 8; The New York *Times Mid-week Pictorial*, v. 10, no. 10, 1919: [9]; New York *American*. 10/25/19: 11.
Newsfilm.
SUMMARY: On Oct. 27, 1919, the Roosevelt memorial flag, which has been carried across New York State in TR's honor, is brought to rest at his grave in Youngs Memorial Cemetery, Oyster Bay, N.Y. Shots from different angles of the memorial flag as it is borne by young men up the steep pathway to the gravesite; five girls sew the forty-eighth and final star on the flag at what is probably Cove School in Oyster Bay with a group of children and Boy Scouts visible in the background; view of children and adults on the cemetery grounds. Final scene of Samuel Abbott, originator of the memorial flag idea, placing the flag on TR's gravesite.

1. Memorial rites and ceremonies. 2. Flags. 3. High school students—Political activity. 4. Youngs Memorial Cemetery. 5. Oyster Bay, N.Y. 6. Roosevelt, Theodore, Pres. U.S., 1858–1919—Funeral and memorial services. 7. Abbott, Samuel. 8. Cove School. 9. Boy Scouts of America. I. International Film Service Company. II. International Newsreel Corporation, source. III. Theodore Roosevelt Association Collection. [mp 76–167]

Children visit TR's grave, 1920.
Fox Film Corp. [1920?]
© No reg.
  lr, 12 ft. si. b&w. 16mm. ref print.
  lr, 12 ft. si. b&w. 16mm. dupe neg.
  lr, 12 ft. si. b&w. 16mm. archival pos.
(Fox news [Series])
SHELF LOC'N: FAB960 (print); FRA5926 (neg); FRA5927 (arch pos)
The date in the title is unverified.
Ref sources: *The Moving Picture World*. v. 42, no. 2, 1919: 236; Fielding, Raymond. *The American Newsreel, 1911–1967*. 1972: 106.
Newsfilm.
SUMMARY: Two young girls and a boy pay homage to TR at his grave in Youngs Memorial Cemetery, Oyster Bay, N.Y. Girls throw flower bouquets through the fence surrounding the grave; the boy leaves a flag; children kneel with bowed heads, then arise and walk away. An interior title notes that the children were TR's neighbors.

PERSONAL CREDITS: Fox, William, source.

1. Tombs. 2. Memorial rites and ceremonies. 3. Youngs Memorial Cemetery. 4. Oyster Bay, N.Y. 5. Roosevelt, Theodore, Pres. U.S., 1858–1919—Tomb. I. Fox Film Corporation. II. Theodore Roosevelt Association Collection. [mp 76–142]

Close-up of TR speaking [1917]
Producer unknown, Sep 1917.
© No reg.
  lr, 5 ft. si. b&w. 16mm. ref print.
  lr, 5 ft. si. b&w. 16mm. dupe neg.
  lr, 5 ft. si. b&w. 16mm. archival pos.
SHELF LOC'N: FAB1073 (print); FRA6047 (neg); FRA6048 (arch pos)
RMA lists dates in title as 1917–1918.
Ref sources: St. Paul *Pioneer Press*. 9/29/17: 1; Chrislock, Carl H. *The Progressive Era in Minnesota, 1899–1918*. 1971.
Newsfilm.
SUMMARY: TR speaks in support of military preparedness at a large pro-war gathering assembled in his honor at St. Paul, Minn. on Sept. 28, 1917. Close side shot of TR speaking from a platform to crowds; a parade passes along the street in the background while he speaks. Joseph A. A.

Burnquist, governor of Minnesota (1915–1921), stands on the platform behind him.

1. Preparedness. 2. European War, 1914–1918—Public opinion. 3. Processions. 4. St. Paul, Minn. 5. Roosevelt, Theodore, Pres. U.S., 1858–1919—Addresses, essays, lectures. 6. Burnquist, Joseph A. A. 7. Minnesota. Governor, 1915–1921 (Burnquist) I. Roosevelt Memorial Association, source. II. Theodore Roosevelt Association Collection. [mp 76–208]

Close-up of TR's grave, 1920.
Producer unknown [1920?]
© No reg.
lr, 4 ft. si. b&w. 16mm. ref print.
lr, 4 ft. si. b&w. 16mm. dupe neg.
lr, 10 ft. si. b&w. 35mm. pos old safety.
SHELF LOC'N: FAB959 (print); FRA5925 (neg)
The date in the title is unverified.
Newsfilm.
SUMMARY: Close shot of TR's gravestone, Youngs Memorial Cemetery, Oyster Bay, N.Y. Birth and death dates of TR and birth date of his wife, Edith, are visible.
PERSONAL CREDITS: Urban, Charles, source.
1. Tombs. 2. Youngs Memorial Cemetery. 3. Oyster Bay, N.Y. 4. Roosevelt, Theodore, Pres. U.S., 1858–1919—Tomb. I. Theodore Roosevelt Association Collection. [mp 76–119]

Close-up scenes of TR speaking during World War I, 1917–18.
Producer unknown [1917?]
© No reg.
lr, 23 ft. si. b&w. 16mm. ref print.
lr, 23 ft. si. b&w. 16mm. archival pos.
SHELF LOC'N: FAB1022 (print); FRA5998 (arch pos)
Dates in the title are unverified.
Factual; views.
SUMMARY: Two unidentified sequences of TR addressing groups on what appear to be two different occasions.
1. European War, 1914–1918—Public opinion. 2. Roosevelt, Theodore, Pres. U.S., 1858–1919—Addresses, essays, lectures. I. Roosevelt Memorial Association, source. II. Theodore Roosevelt Association Collection. [mp 76–270]

Col. William Boyce Thompson.
Producer unknown [192–?]
© No reg.
lr, 6 ft. si. b&w. 16mm. ref print.

lr, 6 ft. si. b&w. 16mm. archival pos (2 cy)
SHELF LOC'N: FAB706 (print); FRA5761 & 5762 (arch pos, 2 cy)
Ref sources: Hagedorn, Hermann. *The Magnate.* 1935; Roosevelt Memorial Association. *Annual Report.* 1925: 15.
Factual; views.
SUMMARY: William Boyce Thompson, a wealthy financier, founder of the Boyce Thompson Institute for Plant Research at Yonkers, and first president of the Roosevelt Memorial Association, actively began supporting TR for the 1920 Republican presidential nomination just before TR's death in Jan. 1919. He appears here with friends, posing in front of an unidentified monument and walking through a city park; the woman standing beside him may be his wife, Gertrude Hickman Thompson.
PERSONAL CREDITS: Stripe, F. C., source. Carver, H. P., source.
1. Thompson, William Boyce. 2. Roosevelt Memorial Association. I. Theodore Roosevelt Association Collection [mp 76–44]

Colonel Lindbergh, Admiral Byrd, and Clarence Chamberlin at flying field just before Lindbergh's flight, 1927.
Producer unknown, May 1927.
© No reg.
lr, 5 ft. si. b&w. 16mm. ref print.
lr, 5 ft. si. b&w. 16mm. dupe neg.
lr, 5 ft. si. b&w. 16mm. archival pos.
lr, 12 ft. si. b&w. 35mm. pos ntr.
SHELF LOC'N: FAB832 (print); FRA5820 (neg); FRA5831 (arch pos)
Research indicates that the film was probably taken at Curtiss Field, L.I. on May 13, 1927, rather than at Roosevelt Field, L.I., before Lindbergh's takeoff, May 21, 1927.
Ref sources: Lindbergh, Charles A. *The Spirit of St. Louis.* 1953; Ellis, Frank H. and Ellis, Elsie M. *Atlantic Air Conquest.* 1963; Byrd, Richard E. *Skyward.* 1928; P&P portrait file.
Newsfilm.
SUMMARY: Charles Lindbergh talks with Commdr. (later Adm.) Richard E. Byrd and Clarence Chamberlin. Commander Byrd crashed on a test flight in Apr. and did not cross the Atlantic until late June. Chamberlin, missing a chance at the Orteig prize, flew to within a few miles of Berlin in early June and set a new world's record for the longest nonstop flight. The three men appear in front of a plane which is probably the Spirit of

St. Louis. Lindbergh is wearing a light-colored jacket; Byrd appears in the middle of the group holding his hat and wearing a cast on his arm because of his accident in Apr.; Chamberlin is wearing a bow tie and holding a folded newspaper.

1. Transatlantic flights. 2. Long Island, N.Y. 3. Lindbergh, Charles A. 4. Byrd, Richard Evelyn. 5. Chamberlin, Clarence D. 6. Spirit of St. Louis (Airplane) I. Pathe, source. II. Theodore Roosevelt Association Collection. [mp 76–67]

Colonel Roosevelt is invited to fly in Arch Hoxsey's plane at St. Louis, Mo., 1910.

Producer unknown, Oct 1910.

© No reg.

lr, 267 ft. si. b&w. 35mm. ref print.
lr, 267 ft. si. b&w. 35mm. dupe neg.
lr, 267 ft. si. b&w. 35mm. masterpos (2 cy)
lr, 235 ft. si. b&w. 35mm. pos ntr.
lr, 241 ft. si. b&w. 35mm. dupe neg ntr.

SHELF LOC'N: FEA6729 (print); FPB7136 (neg); FPC7389 & 7390 (fgmp, 2 cy)

Charles Lindbergh receives best wishes from Clarence Chamberlin and Richard Byrd before Lindbergh's transatlantic flight May 21, 1927. Byrd, standing between Lindbergh and Chamberlin, wears a cast because of a flying accident in April 1927. The *Spirit of St. Louis*, Lindbergh's plane, is visible behind the three men.

Ref sources: St. Louis *Globe-Democrat*. 10/12/10: 1–2; St. Louis *Republic*. 10/12/10: 1,3; P&P portrait file.

Newsfilm.

SUMMARY: While participating in the Missouri State Republican Party's campaign on Oct.11,1910, TR is invited to fly in a biplane with Arch Hoxsey, as pilot. Accompanied by Herbert S. Hadley, governor of Missouri (1909–1913) and two men who appear to be Henry W. Kiel, mayor of St. Louis, and Sheriff Louis Nolte, TR arrives in a motorcade at Kinloch aviation field; a man, who appears to be Hoxsey, inspects the plane: medium shot of TR as he enters the passenger seat of the biplane; long shot of the plane flying; TR alights from the plane, joins the waiting crowd, enters an automobile, and drives away in a motorcade.

PERSONAL CREDITS: Jackson, Thomas, source.

1. Airplanes. 2. Air pilots. 3. Aeronautics—Exhibitions. 4. Kinloch, Mo. Lambert Field. 5. Kinloch, Mo. 6. Roosevelt, Theodore, Pres. U.S., 1858–1919. 7. Hoxsey, Arch. 8. Hadley, Herbert S. 9. Kiel, Henry W. 10. Nolte, Louis. 11. Missouri. Governor, 1909–1913 (Hadley) I. Theodore Roosevelt Association Collection. [mp 76–114]

Commander Dyott sailing from [Hoboken, N.J.] for South America, 1926.

Pathe News, Jul 1926.

© No reg.

lr, 38 ft. si. b&w. 16mm. ref print.
lr, 38 ft. si. b&w. 16mm. dupe neg.
lr, 96 ft. si. b&w. 35mm. pos ntr.

(Pathe News [newsreel])

SHELF LOC'N: FAB1072 (print); FRA6046 (neg)

RMA lists the location in the title as New York City.

Interior title contains the logo: Pathe News 62.

Ref sources: *Daily News*, New York, 7/25/26:28; Roosevelt Memorial Association. *Annual Report*. 1926: 19.

Newsfilm.

SUMMARY: On July 24, 1926, under the auspices of the Roosevelt Memorial Association, Commdr. George M. Dyott, a British explorer, and his party undertook an expedition to retrace and film TR's journey down the River of Doubt in western Brazil. Opening scene of Dyott on board the Lambert & Holt liner, S.S. Vandyck, anchored in what appears to be Hoboken, N.J., prior to departure; medium-close panning views of the party of

A pioneering president, Roosevelt was the first to ride in an automobile (1901) and the first to fly in an airplane (1910). During an aviation meet at Kinloch Field in St. Louis, Missouri, President Roosevelt was a passenger in the biplane piloted by Arch Hoxsey.

explorers, from right to left: Eugene Bussey, Dyott, Robert Young, and Arthur L. Perkins; Dyott bids bon voyage to some unidentified friends and tugs maneuver the ship away from the dock; final views of passengers aboard ship and people on the pier waving.

1. Scientific expeditions. 2. Explorers. 3. Ships. 4. Hoboken, N.J. 5. Dyott, George M. 6. Bussey, Eugene. 7. Young, Robert. 8. Perkins, Arthur L. 9. Roosevelt Memorial Association. 10. Vandyck (Ship) I. Pathe. II. Pathe, source. III. Theodore Roosevelt Association Collection. [mp 76–271]

Count von Bernstorff of Germany.
Producer unknown [191–?]
© No reg.
   lr, 5 ft. si. b&w. 16mm. ref print.
   lr, 5 ft. si. b&w. 16mm. archival pos.
   lr, 14 ft. si. b&w. 35mm. neg ntr.
SHELF LOC'N: FAB958 (print); FRA5924 (arch pos)
Ref source: P&P portrait file.
Factual; views.
SUMMARY: Medium-close shot of Count Johann von Bernstorff, German ambassador to the U.S. (1908–1917), sitting and talking with an unidentified man in a car.
PERSONAL CREDITS: Futter, Walter A., source.

1. Bernstorff, Johann Heinrich Andreas Her-mann Albrecht, Graf Von. I. Theodore Roosevelt Association Collection. [mp 76–217]

Crowd exterior of Buckingham Palace.
Producer unknown [1910?]
© No reg.
   lr, 17 ft. si. b&w. 16mm. ref print.
   lr, 17 ft. si. b&w. 16mm. dupe neg (cy 1)
   lr, 42 ft. si. b&w. 35mm. dupe neg (cy 2)
   lr, 42 ft. si. b&w. 35mm. pos ntr.
SHELF LOC'N: FAB837 (print); FRA5839 (neg, cy 1); FPB7957 (neg, cy 2)
Edge code date on nitrate is 1928; research indicates that the film may have been taken during the week of King Edward's funeral (May 20, 1910).
Factual.
SUMMARY: Film includes panoramic views of Buckingham Palace, the Queen Victoria Memorial, and crowds lining the Mall. A military band marches toward the palace gates. A group of automobiles and a single carriage proceed down the Mall toward the palace.

1. Crowds. 2. London. Queen Victoria Memorial. 3. London. Buckingham Palace. 4. Bands (Music) 5. London. 6. London—Palaces. 7. London—Streets— The Mall. 8. London—Monuments. I. Kinogram Publishing Corporation, source. II. Theodore Roosevelt Association Collection. [mp 76–74]

Crowd listening to TR, Cardinal Gibbons and priests in foreground, 1917.

Producer unknown [1917?]

© No reg.

   lr, 3 ft. si. b&w. 16mm. ref print.

   lr, 3 ft. si. b&w. 16mm. dupe neg.

   lr, 3 ft. si. b&w. 16mm. archival pos.

SHELF LOC'N: FAB689 (print); FRA5723 (neg); FRA5724 (arch pos)

The date in the title is unverified.

Ref source: P&P portrait file.

Newsfilm; views.

SUMMARY: Medium-close shot of a crowd, including Cardinal James Gibbons of Baltimore in the center of the film, sitting in chairs outdoors as they supposedly listen to TR delivering a speech. There are no views of TR on the film.

1. Priests. 2. Gibbons, James. I. General Vision Company, source. II. Theodore Roosevelt Association Collection. [mp 76–11]

Crowd listening to TR speak during Progressive campaign, 1912.

Producer unknown, Sep 1912.

© No reg.

   lr, 5 ft. si. b&w. 16mm. ref print.

   lr, 5 ft. si. b&w. 16mm. dupe neg.

   lr, 14 ft. si. b&w. 16mm. archival pos.

   lr, 13 ft. si. b&w. 35mm. pos ntr.

SHELF LOC'N: FAB1019 (print); FRA5995 (neg); FRA5996 (arch pos)

Archival pos longer than dupe neg and ref print due to longer printing of interior title.

Newsfilm.

SUMMARY: Campaigning for the presidency under the banner of the newly established Progressive party in the area of Fargo, N.D., on Sept. 6, 1912, TR is cheered as his train pulls away from a crowd. The film was shot from the rear of a moving train; neither TR nor any of his party is visible in the picture.

1. Presidents—United States—Election—1912. 2. Fargo, N.D. 3. Roosevelt, Theodore, Pres. U.S., 1858–1919. 4. Progressive Party (Founded 1912) I. Warner Brothers, source. II. Theodore Roosevelt Association Collection. [mp 76–193]

Czar Nicholas of Russia.

Producer unknown [191–?]

© No reg.

   lr, 11 ft. si. b&w. 16mm. ref print.

   lr, 11 ft. si. b&w. 16mm. dupe neg.

   lr, 11 ft. si. b&w. 16mm. archival pos.

SHELF LOC'N: FAB1135 (print); FRA6077 (neg); FRA5797 (arch pos)

Ref print is very dark.

Ref source: P&P portrait file.

Newsfilm; views.

SUMMARY: Long shots of Czar Nicholas II and Czarina Alexandra leaving what may be a church located in Russia and passing between two lines of men who appear to be the Cossack Escort of the Imperial Guard; Alexandra walks toward a carriage and the Czar mounts a horse and rides away.

PERSONAL CREDITS: Futter, Walter A., source.

1. Russia. 2. Russia—History—Nicholas II, 1894–1917. 3. Nicholas II, Emperor of Russia, 1868–1918. 4. Alexandra, consort of Nicholas II, Emperor of Russia, 1872–1918. 5. Russia. Armiîa. I. Theodore Roosevelt Association Collection. [mp 76–70]

Daniel C. Beard and Ernest T. Seton.

Producer unknown [190–?]

© No reg.

   lr, 1 ft. si. b&w. 16mm. ref print.

   lr, 1 ft. si. b&w. 16mm. dupe neg.

   lr, 4 ft. si. b&w. 35mm. pos ntr.

SHELF LOC'N: FAB983 (print); FRA5957 (neg)

Newsfilm.

SUMMARY: Close shot of the two principal founders of the Boy Scouts of America standing outdoors in front of a tent: Daniel C. Beard, wildlife illustrator, magazine editor, and a national scout commissioner until his death; and Ernest T. Seton, naturalist, artist, and author of the first Boy Scout manual.

1. Beard, Daniel C. 2. Seton, Ernest T. 3. Boy Scouts of America. I. Community Motion Picture Service, inc., source. II. Theodore Roosevelt Association Collection. [mp 76–162]

Daniel C. Beard, TR Jr., and Boy Scouts visit TR's grave, 1920.

Producer unknown, Nov 1920.

© No reg.

   lr, 176 ft. si. b&w. 35mm. ref print.

   lr, 176 ft. si. b&w. 35mm. dupe neg.

   lr, 176 ft. si. b&w. 35mm. masterpos.

   lr, 176 ft. si. b&w. 35mm. pos ntr.

SHELF LOC'N: FEA7309 (print); FPB7737 (neg); FPC7391 (fgmp)

Ref sources: *Daily News*, New York. 11/27/20: 11; The New York *Herald*. 11/27/20: 16; *Boys' Life*. v.

11, no. 1, 1921: 25; The New York *Times Mid-week Pictorial*. v. 12, no. 15, 1920: [1]

Newsfilm.

SUMMARY: On Nov. 26, 1920, fifteen hundred Boy Scouts held the first annual pilgrimage to TR's grave in Oyster Bay, New York. National Scout Commissioner Daniel C. Beard leads a parade of scouts, including a band, through Oyster Bay; TR, Jr., and others walk up the hill in Youngs Memorial Cemetery; Beard leads the scout processional into the cemetery; Beard, TR, Jr., and scouts pose in the cemetery; close shot of Beard, TR, Jr., and scouts at TR's grave; close shot of the gravestone with scouts behind an iron fence; scouts walk up in a line to the grave, pause, some throw flowers on the grave, and then leave.

1. Processions. 2. Youngs Memorial Cemetery. 3. Oyster Bay, N.Y. 4. Beard, Daniel C. 5. Roosevelt, Theodore, 1887–1944. 6. Roosevelt, Theodore, Pres. U.S., 1858–1919—Tomb. 7. Roosevelt, Theodore, Pres. U.S., 1858–1919—Funeral and memorial services. 8. Boy Scouts of America. I. International Newsreel Corporation, source. II. Theodore Roosevelt Association Collection. [mp 76–227]

Dedication of Cuban memorial, 1924 [1]

Roosevelt Memorial Association, Dec 1924.

© No reg.

lr, 956 ft. si. b&w. 35mm. ref print.
lr, 956 ft. si. b&w. 35mm. dupe neg.
lr, 956 ft. si. b&w. 35mm. masterpos.
lr, 960 ft. si. b&w. 35mm. neg ntr.

SHELF LOC'N: FEA9948 (print); FPC0774 (neg); FPB9662 (fgmp)

Film is dark ca. ft. 116–135.

Ref sources: Roosevelt Memorial Association. *Annual Report*. 1924: 19; 1925: 18, 28–29; The Havana *Post*. 12/15/24: 1–2; 12/21/24: 15; Freidel, Frank B. *The Splendid Little War*. 1958; Detroit Publishing Co. [Havana, Cuba. 1898–1914] lot 9319. P&P; Detroit Publishing Co. [Cuba. 1898–1914] lot 9320. P&P; P&P portrait file.

Factual.

SUMMARY: A monument to TR, jointly sponsored by the RMA, the Rough Riders Association, and the Rotary Club of Santiago, Cuba, is dedicated on Dec. 14, 1924, in Santiago. Mrs. Edith Roosevelt sailed to Havana and traveled to Santiago by train for the dedication ceremony. She was accompanied by representatives of the RMA and the Rough Riders Association, who visited the site of the Battle of San Juan Hill and the surrounding area. Views of Havana, including the Morro Castle, taken from a ship. Mrs. Roosevelt with Alfredo Zayas, president of Cuba (1921–1925), arrives at a building, probably in Santiago; mounted Cuban soldiers accompany an automobile procession through a Santiago street. Shots of what are probably Daiquiri, where the Rough Riders landed, and Siboney; footage of soldiers landing during the Spanish-American War is included; views of hills outside Santiago. Men, who may be former Rough Riders Lafayette Young, Frank Knox, Colton Reed, and Eugene W. Waterbury, visit monuments and battlegrounds; the man in the dark suit on the far right at the ocean monument may be Frank Knox. Views of what may be the sugar factory and farmhouse on El Pozo Hill, where the Rough Riders camped before the Battle of San Juan Hill. Four men climb Kettle Hill and a group of men and women poses by a large kettle. Various views of the village of El Caney, where a fierce battle was fought on the same day as the Battle of San Juan Hill. The men also visit the large ceiba tree where the peace treaty was signed. Prior to the dedication ceremony, a huge Cuban flag is raised by Cuban veterans. President Zayas and Mrs. Roosevelt listen to an address read by Priscilliano Espinosa of the Santiago Rotary Club. Henry J. Allen, former governor of Kansas (1919–1923), who also served as a newspaper correspondent during the Spanish-American War, speaks. The American ambassador to Cuba, Enoch H. Crowder, stands beside President Zayas. Final views of the monument, which consists of a bronze bust by James Earle Fraser set against a granite background designed by Henry Bacon; carved in Spanish on the granite are TR's words, "Only those are fit to live who do not fear to die."

1. Monuments—Cuba. 2. Battles—Cuba. 3. San Juan Hill, Battle of, 1898. 4. Havana Morro Castle. 5. El Caney, Battle of, 1898. 6. Santiago de Cuba. 7. Havana. 8. Havana—Harbor. 9. Santiago de Cuba—Monuments. 10. Santiago de Cuba—Parks. 11. Daiquiri, Cuba. 12. Siboney, Cuba. 13. El Caney, Cuba. 14. United States—History—War of 1898—Campaigns and battles. 15. Roosevelt, Theodore, Pres. U.S., 1858–1919—Monuments, etc. 16. Roosevelt, Edith. 17. Zayas y Alfonso, Alfredo, Pres. Cuba, 1861–1934. 18. Knox, Franklin. 19. Espinosa, Priscilliano. 20. Allen, Henry J. 21. Crowder, Enoch H. 22. Fraser, James Earle. 23. Bacon, Henry, 1866–1924. 24. Roosevelt Memorial Association. 25. Rough Riders Association. 26. United States. Army. 1st Cavalry (Volunteer) 27. Club Rotario de Santiago de Cuba. 28. Cuba. Presidente, 1921–1925

(Zayas y Alfonso) 29. Cuba. Ejército. I. Roosevelt Memorial Association. II. Roosevelt Memorial Association, source. III. Theodore Roosevelt Association Collection. [mp 76–364]

Dedication of Cuban memorial, 1924 [2]
Roosevelt Memorial Association, Dec 1924.
© No reg.
    lr, 866 ft. si. b&w. 35mm. ref print.
    lr, 866 ft. si. b&w. 35mm. dupe neg.
    lr, 863 ft. si. b&w. 35mm. pos ntr.
  SHELF LOC'N: FEA9457 (print); FPC0147 (neg)
Title on film: *Part two.*
Ref sources: The Havana *Post.* 12/21/24: 15; Freidel, Frank B. *The Splendid Little War.* 1958: 144–160; P&P portrait file.
Factual.
SUMMARY: Views of significant landmarks of the Battle of San Juan Hill including: Kettle Hill and the large kettle which the Rough Riders used for shelter; the sugar factory, probably on El Pozo Hill, where the Rough Riders camped before the battle; the village of El Caney; San Juan Hill; the tree where the armistice was signed; and other memorials commemorating the Spanish-American War. Mrs. Edith Roosevelt and Alfredo Zayas, president of Cuba (1921–1925), participate in memorial services that include the raising of a huge flag by Cuban and American veterans and the dedication of a bronze bust of TR set against a granite background. The monument, jointly sponsored by the RMA, the Rough Riders Association, and the Rotary Club of Santiago, Cuba, is dedicated on Dec. 14, 1924, in Santiago. Priscilliano Espinosa of the Santiago Rotary Club reads an address in front of the monument. Henry J. Allen, former governor of Kansas (1919–1923), who also served as a newspaper correspondent during the Spanish-American War, speaks as President Zayas and Enoch H. Crowder, American ambassador to Cuba, listen. Mrs. Roosevelt unveils the bust. Representing President Coolidge, retired Gen. James G. Harbord makes the principal dedication speech. President Zayas animatedly addresses the crowd. Additional shots of the bust, designed by James Earle Fraser, and the granite work by Henry Bacon upon which is inscribed, in Spanish, TR's words, "Only those are fit to live who do not fear to die." The final interior titles represent TR's thoughts about the requirements for self-government.
1. Monuments—Cuba. 2. Battles—Cuba. 3. San Juan Hill, Battle of, 1898. 4. El Caney, Battle of, 1898. 5. El Caney, Cuba. 6. United States—History—

War of 1898—Campaigns and battles. 7. Santiago de Cuba. 8. Santiago de Cuba—Parks. 9. Santiago de Cuba—Monuments. 10. Roosevelt, Edith. 11. Zayas y Alfonso, Alfredo, Pres. Cuba, 1861–1934. 12. Roosevelt, Theodore, Pres. U.S., 1858–1919—Monuments, etc. 13. Espinosa, Priscilliano. 14. Allen, Henry J. 15. Crowder, Enoch H. 16. Harbord, James G. 17. Fraser, James Earle. 18. Bacon, Henry, 1866–1924. 19. United States. Army. 1st Cavalry (Volunteer) 20. Cuba. Presidente, 1921–1925 (Zayas y Alfonso) 21. Cuba. Ejército. 22. Roosevelt Memorial Association. 23. Rough Riders Association. 24. Club Rotario de Santiago de Cuba. I. Roosevelt Memorial Association. II. Roosevelt Memorial Association, source. III. Theodore Roosevelt Association Collection. [mp 76–379]

Dedication of Roosevelt House, 1923.
Roosevelt Memorial Association, Oct 1923.
© No reg.
    lr, 49 ft. si. b&w. 16mm. ref print (cy 1)
    lr, 122 ft. si. b&w. 35mm. ref print (cy 2)
    lr, 122 ft. si. b&w. 35mm. dupe neg.
    lr, 122 ft. si. b&w. 35mm. masterpos.
    lr, 49 ft. si. b&w. 16mm. archival pos.
    lr, 124 ft. si. b&w. 35mm. neg ntr.
  SHELF LOC'N: FAB754 (print, cy 1); FEA 6750 (print, cy 2); FPB7588 (neg); FPB7589 (fgmp); FRA5809 (arch pos)
Ref sources: Roosevelt Memorial Association. *Annual Report.* 1925: 15; *Roosevelt House Bulletin.* v. 2, no. 2, 1923: 1–4; P&P portrait file.
Factual.
SUMMARY: Exterior views of TR's birthplace, Roosevelt House, on its dedication day. Bought and restored by the Women's Roosevelt Memorial Association, the brownstone is offically opened to visitors on Oct. 27, 1923. Views of street crowds; the Gloria Trumpeters, four young women in Grecian costume who herald the event with trumpet music from the balcony of Roosevelt House; William T. Manning, bishop of the Episcopal Diocese of New York, who is to deliver an opening prayer; Governor and Mrs. Gifford Pinchot of Pennsylvania; Acting Mayor of New York City Murray Hulbert; and other unidentified guests arriving.
1. New York (City). Roosevelt House. 2. Dedication services. 3. New York (City) 4. Roosevelt, Theodore, Pres. U.S., 1858–1919—Birthplace. 5. Roosevelt, Theodore, Pres. U.S., 1858–1919—Homes. 6. Manning, William T. 7. Pinchot, Gifford. 8. Pinchot, Cornelia Bryce. 9. Hulbert, Murray. 10. Wo-

men's Theodore Roosevelt Memorial Association. 11. Gloria Trumpeters. 12. Pennsylvania. Governor, 1923–1927 (Pinchot) I. Roosevelt Memorial Association. II. Roosevelt Memorial Association, source. III. Theodore Roosevelt Association Collection. [mp 76–62]

Dedication of Roosevelt House, Oct. 27, 1923.
Roosevelt Memorial Association, Oct 1923.
© No reg.
   lr, 42 ft. si. b&w. 16mm. ref print.
   lr, 42 ft. si. b&w. 16mm. dupe neg.
   lr, 106 ft. si. b&w. 35mm. pos ntr.
SHELF LOC'N: FAB753 (print); FRA5808 (neg)
Ref sources: Roosevelt Memorial Association. *Annual Report.* 1925: 15; *Roosevelt House Bulletin.* v. 2, no. 2, 1923: 1–4; P&P portrait file.
Factual.
SUMMARY: Exterior views of TR's birthplace, Roosevelt House, on its dedication day. Attending its ceremonial opening are the Gloria Trumpeters, four young women in Grecian costume who play from the balcony of Roosevelt House to crowds below; distinguished guests, including William T. Manning, bishop of the Episcopal Diocese of New York, who is to deliver an opening prayer; Governor and Mrs. Gifford Pinchot of Pennsylvania; Acting Mayor of New York City Murray Hulbert; and other unidentified guests. The event celebrates the Women's Roosevelt Memorial Association's restoration of the birthplace as a museum and library devoted to TR's ideals.
1. New York (City). Roosevelt House. 2. Dedication services. 3. New York (City) 4. Roosevelt, Theodore, Pres. U.S., 1858–1919—Birthplace. 5. Roosevelt, Theodore, Pres. U.S., 1858–1919—Homes. 6. Manning, William T. 7. Pinchot, Gifford. 8. Pinchot, Cornelia Bryce. 9. Hulbert, Murray. 10. Women's Theodore Roosevelt Memorial Association. 11. Gloria Trumpeters. 12. Pennsylvania. Governor, 1923–1927 (Pinchot) I. Roosevelt Memorial Association. II. Roosevelt Memorial Association, source. III. Theodore Roosevelt Association Collection. [mp 76–63]

Dedication of Roosevelt Mountain at Deadwood, S.D., 1919.
Kinogram Pub. Corp., July 1919.
© No reg.
   lr, 115 ft. si. b&w. 16mm. ref print.
   lr, 115 ft. si. b&w. 16mm. archival pos.
   lr, 288 ft. si. b&w. 35mm. neg ntr.
(Kinograms [Series])

SHELF LOC'N: FAB992 (print); FRA5972 (arch pos)
The RMA list indicates that the footage may be composed of outtakes.
The film is out of sequence, with some scenes appearing twice.
Ref sources: Federal Writers' Project. South Dakota. *A South Dakota Guide.* 1938: 107, 109–110; P&P portrait file; Society of Black Hills Pioneers. *Constitution and By-laws Together with a Roll of Members.* 1891; Fite, Gilbert C. *Peter Norbeck.* 1948; The *Daily Argus-Leader*, Sioux Falls, S.D. 7/4/19: 3.
Newsfilm.
SUMMARY: On July 4, 1919, a mountain peak in the Black Hills is renamed and dedicated to Theodore Roosevelt. Located near Deadwood, S.D., in the region where TR hunted and ranched in the 1880s, Mount Roosevelt is dedicated by the Society of Black Hills Pioneers, of which TR had been an honorary member. Panoramic views of the Black Hills taken from Mount Roosevelt; a crowd gathers for the dedication service, with Leonard Wood, a close friend of TR and the principal speaker at the ceremony, and Capt. Seth Bullock, TR's neighbor in his ranching days, speaking informally with crowd members; views of the speakers' platform, with the following men speaking at various points in the service: South Dakota Governor Peter Norbeck, master of ceremonies; Leonard Wood; and former South Dakota Representative to Congress Eben W. Martin (1901–1907, 1908–1915); also identified on the platform are Captain Bullock, at whose suggestion the mountain is being renamed, and Roosevelt Memorial Association member Hermann Hagedorn. Long shots of Roosevelt Monument, a circular tower with a parapet; on the parapet three men raise an American flag. View of Leonard Wood walking along a narrow ledge of the monument to reach the speakers' platform, erected in front of the monument; close shot of a bronze plaque attached to the monument, on which is written: In Memory of Theodore Roosevelt, The American.
PERSONAL CREDITS: Urban, Charles, source.
1. Dedication services. 2. Memorial service. 3. Legislators—South Dakota. 4. Roosevelt Monument, S.D. 5. Mount Roosevelt, S.D. 6. Black Hills, S.D. 7. Deadwood, S.D. 8. Roosevelt, Theodore, Pres. U.S., 1858–1919—Monuments, etc. 9. Roosevelt, Theodore, Pres. U.S., 1858–1919—Funeral and memorial services. 10. Wood, Leonard. 11. Bullock, Seth. 12. Norbeck, Peter. 13. Martin, Eben W. 14. Hagedorn, Hermann. 15. Society of Black Hills Pioneers. 16. South Dakota. Governor, 1917–

1921 (Norbeck) 17. Roosevelt Memorial Association. I. Kinogram Publishing Corporation. II. Theodore Roosevelt Association Collection. [mp 76–184]

Disappearing gun at testing grounds, Sandy Hook, 1898.
Producer unknown [1898?]
© No reg.
    lr, 26 ft. si. b&w. 35mm. ref print (2 cy)
    lr, 10 ft. si. b&w. 16mm. archival pos.
  SHELF LOC'N: FEA7638 & 7639 (print, 2 cy);
            FRA6061 (arch pos)
The date and location in the title are unverified.
Ref sources: United States. Ordnance Dept. *Report of the Chief of Ordnance.* 1899: 41, 409; Manucy, Albert C. *Artillery through the Ages.* 1949: 21, 87.
  Factual; technological.
  SUMMARY: In 1898 the use of disappearing carriages on guns was tested by the Ordnance Dept. at the Sandy Hook Proving Ground in Sandy Hook, N.J. A gun is fired at a wooden scaffold-type target on a beach; the carriage of the gun collapses after firing and the smoke clears.
  PERSONAL CREDITS: Elmendorf, Dwight L., source.
  1. Artillery. 2. Gun-carriages, Disappearing. 3. Ordnance. 4. Ordnance testing. 5. Proving grounds. 6. Sandy Hook, N.J. 7. United States. Sandy Hook Proving Ground, N.J. 8. United States. Ordnance Dept. I. Theodore Roosevelt Association Collection. [mp 76–213]

Dr. Gorgas who had charge of sanitation during building of the Panama Canal.
Producer unknown [191–?]
© No reg.
    lr, 8 ft. si. b&w. 16mm. ref print.
    lr, 8 ft. si. b&w. 16mm. archival pos (cy 1)
    lr, 7 ft. si. b&w. 16mm. archival pos (cy 2)
  SHELF LOC'N: FAB990 (print); FRA5968 (arch
          pos, cy 1); FRA5969 (arch pos,
          cy 2)
Archival pos (cy 1) is longer than arch pos (cy 2) due to longer printing of final scene.
  Ref source: P&P portrait file.
  Factual; views.
  SUMMARY: Medium shots of Dr. William Crawford Gorgas, chief sanitation officer of the Panama Canal (1904–1913) and surgeon general of the U.S. Army (1914–1918), sitting outdoors in a rocking chair and conversing with an unidentified man; close-up of Gorgas.
  PERSONAL CREDITS: Lewis, Samuel, source.

1. Gorgas, William C. I. Theodore Roosevelt Association Collection. [mp 76–135]

Dr. William Gorgas.
Producer unknown [190–?]
© No reg.
    lr, 18 ft. si. b&w. 16mm. ref print.
    lr, 18 ft. si. b&w. 16mm. dupe neg.
    lr, 45 ft. si. b&w. 35mm. pos ntr.
  SHELF LOC'N: FAB985 (print); FRA5959 (neg)
  Ref sources: Abbot, Willis J. *Panama and the Canal.* 1914; Heald, Jean S. *Picturesque Panama.* 1928; Gorgas, Marie D. and Hendrick, Burton J. *William Crawford Gorgas.* 1924; Barrett, John. *Panama Canal.* 1913: 19; P&P portrait file.
  Factual; views.
  SUMMARY: The film has ca. 2 ft. of views of Dr. William Crawford Gorgas, chief sanitation officer of the Panama Canal (1904–1913) and a member of the Isthmian Canal Commission, standing in front of a building; the location of this sequence is undetermined. The remainder of the film shows Dr.

William Crawford Gorgas, appointed chief sanitary officer of the Panama Canal in 1904, was responsible for eradicating yellow fever and malaria in the Canal Zone.

Gorgas and an unidentified man riding on a Panama Canal Company train. The two men are silhouetted against the passing scenery of the Canal Zone as Dr. Gorgas shows the other man points of interest. The train passes a body of water which is probably a part of the canal, countryside, and buildings, probably on Front Street, Colón, including a YMCA club; the final scene shows people walking across the tracks after the train passes.

1. Railroads—Canal Zone. 2. Physicians. 3. Canal Zone. 4. Panama Canal. 5. Canal Zone—Views. 6. Colón, Panama. 7. Colón, Panama—Streets—Front Street. 8. Gorgas, William C. 9. Panama Canal Company. 10. Young Men's Christian Associations. I. Apollo Pictures, source. II. Theodore Roosevelt Association Collection. [mp 76–276]

Elihu Root and Mayor Mitchel of New York, Mr. Root and American delegates return from Russia [1917]
Producer unknown, Aug 1917.
© No reg.
  lr, 6 ft. si. b&w. 16mm. ref print.
  lr, 6 ft. si. b&w. 16mm. dupe neg.
  lr, 16 ft. si. b&w. 35mm. pos ntr.
SHELF LOC'N: FAB975 (print); FRA5944 (neg)
RMA lists the dates in the title as 1917–1918.
Ref sources: New York *Tribune*. 8/11/17: 1,3; The New York *Times*. 8/26/17: pt. 5: [4]; P&P portrait file.
Newsfilm.
SUMMARY: On Aug. 15, 1917, the Special Diplomatic Mission to Russia was offically welcomed in New York City with a series of ceremonies. Medium and close panning shots of men posing for the camera on the steps of New York City Hall; identified in the first row, left to right, are: George T. Wilson, member of the welcoming committee; Gen. Hugh L. Scott, member of the special mission; Oscar S. Straus, member of the welcoming committee; Elihu Root, ambassador extraordinary of the special mission; John P. Mitchel, mayor of New York City; Rear Adm. James H. Glennon, member of the special mission; William A. Prendergast, member of the welcoming committee; and elsewhere among the group possibly James Duncan, Basil Miles, and Samuel R. Bertron, all members of the special mission.

1. Diplomats. 2. Government missions, American. 3. European War, 1914–1918. 4. New York (City). City Hall. 5. New York (City) 6. Russia—Foreign relations—United States. 7. United States—Foreign relations—Russia. 8. Root, Elihu. 9. Mitchel, John P. 10. Wilson, George T. 11. Scott, Hugh L. 12. Straus, Oscar S. 13. Glennon, James H. 14. Prendergast, William A. 15. Duncan, James. 16. Miles, Basil. 17. Bertron, Samuel Reading, 1865–1938. 18. United States. Special Diplomatic Mission to Russia. I. Pathe, source. II. Theodore Roosevelt Association Collection. [mp 76–189]

Emperor Francis Joseph of Austria greeted by his people.
Producer unknown [Apr 1910?]
© No reg.
  lr, 27 ft. si. b&w. 16mm. ref print.
  lr, 68 ft. si. b&w. 35mm. masterpos.
  lr, 27 ft. si. b&w. 16mm. archival pos.
  lr, 68 ft. si. b&w. 35mm. neg ntr.
SHELF LOC'N: FAB868 (print); FPB8230 (fgmp); FRA5896 (arch pos)
The location in the title is unverified.
Ref source: P&P portrait file.
Newsfilm; views.
SUMMARY: Views of Francis Joseph I, emperor of Austria-Hungary, and an entourage of military officers and civilians walking down a wide avenue; the street is lined with people greeting the emperor. Interior title notes the location as Vienna, Austria, and notes that TR is being entertained by the emperor at the palace. TR visited the emperor in Apr. 1910; there are no views of TR on the film.
PERSONAL CREDITS: Elmendorf, Dwight L., source.

1. Emperors. 2. Processions. 3. Vienna. 4. Franz Joseph I, Emperor of Austria, 1830–1916. I. Theodore Roosevelt Association Collection. [mp 76–311]

Exterior scenes of Sagamore Hill.
Producer unknown [1918?]
© No reg.
  lr, 41 ft. si. b&w. 35mm. ref print.
  lr, 41 ft. si. b&w. 35mm. dupe neg.
  lr, 41 ft. si. b&w. 35mm. pos ntr.
SHELF LOC'N:FEA7629 (print); FPB8065 (neg)
Edge code date on nitrate is 1918.
Ref. source: Hagedorn, Hermann. *A Guide to Sagamore Hill.* 1953.
Factual; views.
SUMMARY: Views of Sagamore Hill from the driveway and from other angles; long shots of the house including the portecochère and the piazza, the section of the porch from which the railing was removed and where TR made so many speeches. The film appears to have been shot in winter.

1. Oyster Bay, N.Y. Sagamore Hill. 2. Oyster Bay,

N.Y. 3. Roosevelt, Theodore, Pres. U.S., 1858–1919—Homes. I. International Newsreel Corporation, source. II. Theodore Roosevelt Association Collection. [mp 76–259]

Extermination of mosquitoes by spraying swamps.
Bray Studios [191–?]
© No reg.
    lr, 88 ft. si. b&w. 35mm. ref print.
    lr, 88 ft. si. b&w. 35mm. dupe neg.
SHELF LOC'N: FEA6739 (print); FPB7186
        (neg)
Ref source: Avery, Ralph E. *America's Triumph at Panama.* 1913: 80–88.
Factual; scientific.
SUMMARY: The film demonstrates the applied methods of disease control and prevention by exterminating mosquitoes in the Panama Canal. There are views of a man spraying a small stream with kerosene to prevent mosquitoes from breeding, a close-up through a glass at water level of surfaced mosquito larvae, and a close-up of a model of a mosquito as screening is superimposed over the model.
1. Mosquitoes. 2. Mosquito control. 3. Mosquitoes— Larvae. 4. Panama Canal. I. Bray Studios, inc. II. Bray Studios, inc., source. III. Theodore Roosevelt Association Collection. [mp 76–77]

Flag at half-mast, Oyster Bay, Jan. 1919.
Producer unknown [Jan 1919?]
© No reg.
    lr, 2 ft. si. b&w. 16mm. ref print.
    lr, 2 ft. si. b&w. 16mm. dupe neg.
    lr, 6 ft. si. b&w. 35mm. pos ntr.
SHELF LOC'N: FAB980 (print); FRA5952 (neg)
Newsfilm.
SUMMARY: A view of what appears to be downtown Oyster Bay, N.Y., with what may be the municipal building and a stone gazebo visible beside a flag, which is flying at half-mast; the ground is snow-covered. The occasion may be the mourning period following TR's death on Jan. 6, 1919.
1. Flags. 2. Oyster Bay, N.Y. 3. Roosevelt, Theodore, Pres. U.S., 1858–1919—Funeral and memorial services. I. Pathe, source. II. Theodore Roosevelt Association Collection. [mp 76–153]

[Flag services for TR at Oyster Bay, October 1919]
Kinogram Pub. Corp., Oct. 1919.
© No Reg.
    lr, 28 ft. si. b&w. 16mm. ref print.
    lr, 28 ft. si. b&w. 16mm. archival pos.

    lr, 71 ft. si. b&w. 35mm. neg ntr.
(Kinograms [Series])
SHELF LOC'N: FAB988 (print); FRA5965 (arch
        pos)
RMA title: *Children Visit TR's Grave, 1920.*
The date of the first sequence, children at the grave, is unverified.
Ref sources: The *Daily News,* New York. 10/25/19: 8; The New York *Times Mid-week Pictorial.* v. 10, no. 10, 1919: [6]; P&P portrait file.
Newsfilm.
SUMMARY: On Oct. 27, 1919, the Roosevelt memorial flag, which has been carried across New York State in TR's honor, is brought to rest at his grave in Youngs Memorial Cemetery, Oyster Bay, N.Y. View of two young girls and a boy placing a flower bouquet and a flag through the fence surrounding TR's grave (the event may not be part of the flag ceremonies). Shots from different angles of the memorial flag as it is borne by young men up the steep pathway to the gravesite; five girls sew the forty-eighth and final star on the flag at what is probably Cove School in Oyster Bay, with a group of children and Boy Scouts visible in the background; view of children and adults on the cemetery grounds. The final scene shows Samuel Abbott, originator of the memorial flag idea, placing the flag on TR's gravesite.
PERSONAL CREDITS: Urban, Charles, source.
1. Memorial rites and ceremonies. 2. Flags. 3. High school students—Political activity. 4. Youngs Memorial Cemetery. 5. Oyster Bay, N.Y. 6. Roosevelt, Theodore, Pres. U.S., 1858–1919—Funeral and memorial services. 7. Abbott, Samuel. 8. Cove School. 9. Boy Scouts of America. I. Kinogram Publishing Corporation. II. Theodore Roosevelt Association Collection. [mp 76–143]

The Forbidden City, Pekin.
American Mutoscope & Biograph Co., 1903.
© H34805, American Mutoscope & Biograph Co., 19 Aug 1903
    lr, of 1, 10 ft. si. b&w. 16mm. ref print.
    lr, of 1, 10 ft. si. b&w. 16mm. dupe neg.
    lr, of 1, 10 ft. si. b&w. 16mm. archival pos.
    lr, of 1, 15 ft. si. b&w. 16mm. ref print.
    lr, of 1, 15 ft. si. b&w. 16mm. dupe neg.
    lr, of 1, 25 ft. si. b&w. 35mm. paper (2 cy)
SHELF LOC'N: FAB1457 (print-RMA); FRA6194
        (neg-RMA); FRA5847 (arch pos-
        RMA); FLA4142 (print-Paper);
        FRA1312 (neg-Paper); LC1128
        (paper, 2 cy-Paper)

RMA title: *City of Pekin, China, 1903.*

Paper Print copies are longer due to print differences.

Ref sources: MacFarquhar, Roderick. *The Forbidden City.* 1972: [73]; Dorn, Frank. *The Forbidden City.* 1970.

Newsfilm; views.

SUMMARY: Views of the Forbidden City (Imperial Palace), Peking, China: the camera, probably located top the Meridian Gate (Wu Men) pans from the east, past the Gate of Great Harmony (T'ai Ho Men) with the Hall of Supreme Harmony (T'ai Ho Tien) behind it, past the White Pagoda (Pai Ta) in Pei-Hai Park, and then past the West Flowery Gate.

1. Peking. Imperial Palace. 2. Peking. Gate of Great Harmony. 3. Peking. Hall of Supreme Harmony. 4. Peking. White Pagoda. 5. Peking. West Flowery Gate. 6. Peking. 7. Peking—Description—Views. I. Biograph Company. II. Biograph Company, source. III. Theodore Roosevelt Association Collection. IV. Paper Print Collection. [mp 76–90]

Friends and admirers visit TR's grave, 1920.
Producer unknown [1920?]

© No reg.

lr, 43 ft. si. b&w. 16mm. ref print (cy 1)

lr, 41 ft. si. b&w. 16mm. ref print (cy 2)

lr, 41 ft. si. b&w. 16mm. dupe neg.

lr, 43 ft. si. b&w. 16mm. archival pos.

lr, 102 ft. si. b&w. 35mm. pos ntr.

lr, 108 ft. si. b&w. 35mm. dupe neg ntr.

SHELF LOC'N: FAB690 (print, cy 1); FAB942 (print, cy 2); FRA5900 (neg); FRA5725 (arch pos)

Ref print (cy 1) and arch pos appear under RMA title: *TR's grave, Oyster Bay, N.Y.*

The date in the title is unverified.

Ref source: *Roosevelt House Bulletin.* v. 4, no. 1, 1932: 5–6

Factual; views.

SUMMARY: Close-up of TR's gravesite, enclosed by an iron gate, in Youngs Memorial Cemetery, Oyster Bay, N.Y.; a group of men and women walk around the gravesite. The woman on the immediate right appears to be Sara L. Straus, widow of Oscar S. Straus, secretary of commerce and labor in TR's cabinet. This may be a sequence from the annual pilgrimage to TR's grave sponsored by the Roosevelt Memorial Association. Close view of the site and tomb, with various flags and funeral tributes. The last scene is of a man, who may be Theodore Roosevelt, Jr., walking up the path to the gravesite and posing at the gate.

PERSONAL CREDITS: Urban, Charles, source.

1. Tombs. 2. Youngs Memorial Cemetery. 3. Memorial rites and ceremonies. 4. Oyster Bay, N.Y. 5. Roosevelt, Theodore, Pres. U.S., 1858–1919—Tomb. 6. Roosevelt, Theodore, Pres. U.S., 1858–1919—Funeral and memorial services. 7. Straus, Sara L. 8. Roosevelt, Theodore, 1887–1944. 9. Roosevelt Memorial Association. I. Theodore Roosevelt Association Collection. [mp 76–10]

Gen. Pershing speaking to Scouts in New York.
International Film Service, Sep 1919.

© No reg.

lr, 61 ft. si. b&w. 16mm. ref print.

lr, 54 ft. si. b&w. 16mm. dupe neg.

lr, 54 ft. si. b&w. 16mm. archival pos.

(International [Series] v. 1, no. 37)

SHELF LOC'N: FAB1056 (print); FRA6027 (neg); FRA6028 (arch pos)

Last segment of dupe neg and arch pos is unrelated footage on the Scout Parade at Cartagena, Colombia, 1920.

Ref sources: Pershing, John J. Papers, 1882–1949. Box 4–5, 393. Library of Congress, Manuscript Division; Beard, Daniel C. *Hardly a Man is Now Alive.* 1939.

Newsfilm.

SUMMARY: Gen. John J. Pershing, Commander in Chief of the American Expeditionary Force, received a hero's welcome in New York when he returned from Europe in Sept. 1919. On the afternoon of Sept. 9, the general addressed a group of 50,000 school children assembled at Sheep Meadow in Central Park for a reception in his honor. Escorted by Boy Scouts, General Pershing stands in a flag-bedecked car and waves to the crowd as he enters the park; he salutes the flag and kisses it as the crowd of children cheers and waves flags; a man who is probably Rodman Wanamaker, chairman of the Mayor's Committee on Reception to Distinguished Guests, is visible as General Pershing leans forward to kiss the flag. The film includes views of Pershing addressing a crowd, planting a tree with Wanamaker again standing behind him, and posing for photographers. Daniel C. Beard, national scout commissioner, with a white goatee and wearing a broad-brimmed hat, marches with Boy Scouts before Pershing's car and stands in the group as Pershing plants a tree.

PERSONAL CREDITS: Beard, Daniel C., source.

1. Children. 2. New York (City) 3. New York

(City)—Parks—Central Park. 4. Pershing, John J. 5. Wanamaker, Rodman. 6. Beard, Daniel C. 7. Boy Scouts of America. 8. United States. Army—Officers. I. International Film Service Company. II. Theodore Roosevelt Association Collection. [mp 76-224]

General [Diaz] of Italy visits TR's grave [1921]
International Newsreel Corp., Oct 1921.
  © No reg.
    lr, 6 ft. si. b&w. 16mm. ref print.
    lr, 6 ft. si. b&w. 16mm. dupe neg.
    lr, 15 ft. si. b&w. 35mm. pos ntr.
  (International news [Series])
  SHELF LOC'N: FAB947 (print); FRA5905 (neg)
  RMA title: *General Nivelle of Italy Visits TR's Grave, 1920.*
  Ref source: P&P portrait file.
  Newsfilm.
  SUMMARY: The Italian army officer and hero of the Piave, Gen. Armando Diaz, made an unofficial visit to the U.S. in Oct. 1921, as the guest of the American Legion. He also attended the conference on armaments limitation. Accompanied by his three aides, Gen. Kennedy De Luca, Major Coccone, and Prince Ruspoli, and by a guard of honor which included a man who may be Lt. Sidney Gumpertz, Sgt. Ernest Janson, and Sgt. Fred Dickman, all World War I veterans and holders of the Congressional Medal of Honor; General Diaz drove to Oyster Bay on Oct. 20, 1921, to pay homage to the memory of TR. The film consists of two sequences: General Diaz, an aide, and an American army officer place a wreath of asters and chrysanthemums on the grave in Youngs Memorial Cemetery; General Diaz salutes, turns and walks away. General De Luca stands behind General Diaz. There are few clear shots of Diaz's face in the film.
  1. Memorial rites and ceremonies. 2. Youngs Memorial Cemetery. 3. Oyster Bay, N.Y. 4. Diaz, Armando, duca della Vittoria. 5. De Luca, Kennedy. 6. Roosevelt, Theodore, Pres. U.S., 1858-1919—Tomb. 7. Italy, Esercito—Officers. I. International Newsreel Corporation. II. International Newsreel Corporation, source. III. Theodore Roosevelt Association Collection. [mp 76-165]

General Goethals.
Fox Film Corp., Apr 1923.
  © No reg.
    lr, 12 ft. si. b&w. 16mm. ref print (cy 1)
    lr, 32 ft. si. b&w. 35mm. ref print (cy 2)
    lr, 20 ft. si. b&w. 35mm. ref print (cy 3)

    lr, 12 ft. si. b&w. 16mm. dupe neg. (cy 1)
    lr, 32 ft. si. b&w. 35mm. dupe neg. (cy 2)
    lr, 20 ft. si. b&w. 35mm. dupe neg. (cy 3)
    lr, 32 ft. si. b&w. 35mm. masterpos.
    lr, 31 ft. si. b&w. 35mm. pos ntr. (cy 1)
    lr, 20 ft. si. b&w. 35mm. pos ntr. (cy 2)
    lr, 33 ft. si. b&w. 35mm. dupe neg ntr.
  (Fox news [Series])
  SHELF LOC'N: FAB974 (print, cy 1); FEA6728 (print, cy 2); FEA7627 (print, cy 3); FRA5943 (neg, cy 1); FPB 7135 (neg, cy 2); FPB8063 (neg, cy 3); FPB7134 (fgmp)
  Copies vary in length due to printing of scenes and interior title.
  Segment of Fox news, v. 4, no. 54, released Apr. 1923.
  Ref sources: *Motion Picture News.* v. 27, no. 16, 1923: 1965; P&P portrait file.
  Newsfilm; views.
  SUMMARY: Gen. George Washington Goethals, builder of the Panama Canal and New York State fuel administrator, resigned his state position on Apr. 1, 1923. The film contains two scenes of Goethals: a long shot of him standing on the stairs of a building in New York City, and a close-up of him talking.
  PERSONAL CREDITS: Fox, William, source.
  CITATION: MPN27. 16: 1965.
  1. New York (City) 2. Goethals, George W. I. Fox Film Corporation. II. Theodore Roosevelt Association Collection. [mp 76-196]

General Nivelle visits TR's grave [1921]
Pathe News, Jan 1921.
  © No reg.
    lr, 7 ft. si. b&w. 16mm. ref print.
    lr, 7 ft. si. b&w. 16mm. dupe neg.
    lr, 19 ft. si. b&w. 35mm. pos ntr.
  (Pathe News [newsreel])
  SHELF LOC'N: FAB870 (print); FRA5898 (neg)
  RMA lists the date in the title as 1920; the interior title states, "General Nivelle, hero of Verdun, pays tribute at the tomb of Roosevelt on the second anniversary of his death."
  Ref sources: Azan, Paul J. L. *Souvenirs de Casablanca.* 1911: frontispiece; Spears, Edward L. *Prelude to Victory.* 1939: frontispiece; P&P portrait file.
  Newsfilm.
  SUMMARY: Gen. Robert George Nivelle, hero of Verdun and former Commander in Chief of the French Army, represented his country at the National Mayflower Tercentenary celebration held in

American cities throughout Nov. 1920. He toured the U.S. and on Jan. 2, 1921, he laid a wreath on TR's grave in Youngs Memorial Cemetery. In the film General Nivelle, his aide Col. Paul J. Azan, an American officer who may be Col. Mervyn C. Buckey, and other unidentified people walk up the hill to the gravesite. General Nivelle places a wreath upon the grave and the camera moves in for a close-up view of the tomb and the wreath.

1. Memorial rites and ceremonies. 2. Youngs Memorial Cemetery. 3. Oyster Bay, N.Y. 4. Nivelle, Robert G. 5. Roosevelt, Theodore, Pres. U.S., 1858–1919—Tomb. 6. Azan, Paul J. 7. Buckey, Mervyn C. I. Pathe. II. Pathe, source. III. Theodore Roosevelt Association Collection. [mp 76–177]

General Pershing at Camp Grant.

Producer unknown, Jan 1920.

© No reg.

lr, 25 ft. si. b&w. 16mm. ref print (2 cy)

lr, 25 ft. si. b&w. 16mm. archival pos (2 cy)

SHELF LOC'N: FAB1015 & 1123 (print, 2 cy); FRA5990 & 5991 (arch pos, 2 cy)

The film sequence does not follow the order of actual events.

Ref sources: Pershing, John J. Papers, 1882–1949. Box 4–5. Library of Congress, Manuscript Division; P&P portrait file.

Newsfilm.

SUMMARY: As part of an inspection tour of military camps in the midwest, Gen. John Joseph Pershing visits Camp Grant in Rockford, Ill., on Jan. 5, 1920. Opening scene of Pershing standing with Gen. George J. Bell, Jr., commander of the Sixth Division's Provisional Regiment stationed at Camp Grant; a train with members of Bell's staff unloading is in the background; long shot of Pershing, with an unidentified man to his left, and Robert Rew, mayor of Rockford, posing outside the Hotel Nelson after attending a luncheon in Pershing's honor: the mayor is carrying a saddle and bridle which were presented to Pershing by the citizens of Rockford; views of the Sixth Division in formation; long shot of Pershing, Bell, and possibly Regiment Col. Mathias Crowley walking toward the camera through lines of soldiers; views of tractors pulling cannon along the snow-covered streets; the last scene is of Pershing and a man who may be Crowley standing in a flag-draped reviewing stand as Pershing delivers a speech.

PERSONAL CREDITS: Stripe, F. C., source. Carver, H. P., source.

1. Military training camps—Illinois. 2. Rockford, Ill. Hotel Nelson. 3. Military ceremonies, honors, and salutes. 4. Processions. 5. Rockford, Ill. 6. Pershing, John J. 7. Bell, George J. 8. Rew, Robert. 9. Crowley, Mathias. 10. Camp Grant. 11. United States. Army. 6th Division. I. Theodore Roosevelt Association Collection. [mp 76–299]

General Wood and Calvin Coolidge in Chicago, 1920.

Producer unknown, Jun 1920.

© No reg.

lr, 164 ft. si. b&w. 16mm. ref print.

lr, 164 ft. si. b&w. 16mm. dupe neg.

lr, 164 ft. si. b&w. 16mm. masterpos.

lr, 411 ft. si. b&w. 35mm. pos ntr.

SHELF LOC'N: FAB694 (print); FRA5729 (neg); FRA8650 (fgmp)

Ref sources: Republican Party. National Convention, 17th, Chicago, 1920. *Official Report of the Proceedings of the Seventeenth Republican National Convention.* 1920; P&P presidential file; P&P portrait file.

Newsfilm; political.

SUMMARY: Various scenes from the proceedings of the Seventeenth Republican National Convention held in Chicago, June 8–12, 1920. Long shot of crowd gathering as women march around carrying banners; views of photographers taking pictures, five women dressed in costume, and of a crowd, probably delegates, alternates and visitors at the Chicago Coliseum. The camera pans the exterior of the flag-draped Coliseum. Back view of Margaret Hill McCarter of Kansas, the first woman to address a Republican National Convention, on the speaking platform with Henry Cabot Lodge, convention chairman. Close shot of Gen. Leonard Wood, presidential nominee, with three unidentified men. Scattered sequences of Gov. Calvin Coolidge of Massachusetts, selected as the vice-presidential candidate by the convention: medium-close views of Coolidge sitting at his desk in Boston, standing outside delivering his acceptance speech to a large crowd at the official notification ceremonies in Northampton, Mass., on July 22, and standing with two unidentified women. Sequences of Sen. Warren G. Harding of Ohio, selected as the presidential candidate by the convention: close-up of Harding in an undetermined location with an unidentified man and of him with his wife, Florence Kling Harding, at their home in Marion, Ohio. Medium shot of Harding and Coolidge with Will H. Hays, Republican National Committee chairman, conversing outside the old Senate Office Building in Washington, with the Capitol visible in the background, on June 30. Closing scene of the three men seated at a desk in what appears to be Harding's office in the Senate building.

1. Political parties. 2. Political conventions. 3. Chicago. Coliseum. 4. Presidents—United States—Nomination. 5. Washington, D.C. Capitol. Senate Office Building. 6. Presidents—United States—Election—1920. 7. United States—Politics and government—1919–1933. 8. Chicago. 9. Northampton, Mass. 10. Marion, Ohio. 11. Washington, D.C. 12. Wood, Leonard. 13. Coolidge, Calvin, Pres. U.S., 1872–1933. 14. McCarter, Margaret Hill. 15. Lodge, Henry Cabot. 16. Harding, Warren Gamaliel, Pres. U.S., 1865–1923. 17. Harding, Florence Kling. 18. Hays, Will H. 19. Republican Party. 20. Republican Party. National Convention, 17th, Chicago, 1920. 21. Republican Party. National Committee, 1920–1924. 22. Massachusetts. Governor, 1919–1921 (Coolidge) I. Community Motion Picture Service, Inc., source. II. Theodore Roosevelt Association Collection [mp 76–32]

Gifford Pinchot, 1923.

Producer unknown, May 1923.

© No reg.

lr, 44 ft. si. b&w. 16mm. ref print.

lr, 44 ft. si. b&w. 16mm. dupe neg.

lr, 44 ft. si. b&w. 16mm. archival pos.

lr, 111 ft. si. b&w. 35mm. neg ntr.

SHELF LOC'N: FAB699 (print); FRA5748 (neg); FRA5747 (arch pos)

Ref sources: The *Philadelphia Inquirer*. 5/11/23: 1; The *Patriot*, Harrisburg, Pa. 5/11/23: 11; P&P portrait file; Klein, Philip S. and Hoogenboom, Ari. *A History of Pennsylvania*. 1973.

Newsfilm.

SUMMARY: On May 10, 1923, Gov. Gifford Pinchot of Pennsylvania (1923–1927, 1931–1935) signed into law an old age pension bill which authorized payment of allowances to indigents more than seventy years old, guaranteeing a minimum daily income of one dollar. The first time a gubernatorial bill-signing was filmed in the Pennsylvania State Capitol, the event drew reporters, public officials, and members of the Fraternal Order of Eagles, an organization which strongly supported the measure. Present for the occasion were State Sen. William S. Vare, a significant force behind the bill; U.S. Rep. John M. Morin, from Pittsburgh; and Miss Helen Grimes, representing Rep. Joseph C. Steedle, sponsor of the measure in the House. The

Gifford Pinchot, a close personal friend of TR's, was an early proponent of conservation and served as the chief of the Bureau of Forestry during TR's administration. At the 1908 White House Conservation Conference, TR paid special tribute to Pichot as the man "to whom we owe so much of the progress we have already made in handling this matter of the co-ordination and conservation of national resources" (Joseph L. Gardner, *Departing Glory*). Pinchot later served as governor of Pennsylvania (1923–27 and 1931–35).

film includes shots of Governor Pinchot seated in his private office, attended by a young man who may be his personal secretary, P. Stephen Stahlnecker; Pinchot looks over documents and imprints one with the official seal; Pinchot in an executive chair signs the old age pension bill, surrounded by standing reporters, officials, and a woman who may be Miss Grimes; Vare and Morin are seated on either side of Pinchot, who rises, gives his pen to Vare in appreciation for his support, and begins to speak; Pinchot shakes hands with men who appear to be verterans of the Grand Army of the Republic and members of the Fraternal Order of Eagles; view from over the shoulder of a man who may be Pinchot of the governor's desk, on which the calendar for May 1923, is visible; the motto on the calendar is a quote from Pinchot's friend and political associate, Theodore Roosevelt, concerning the need for pioneer virtues in post-pioneer days.

PERSONAL CREDITS: Roycroft, source.

1. Old age pensions—Pennsylvania. 2. Bills, legislative—Pennsylvania. 3. Moving-picture journalism. 4. Harrisburg, Pa. 5. Pennsylvania—Governors. 6. Pinchot, Gifford. 7. Vare, William S. 8. Morin, John M. 9. Grimes, Helen. 10. Stahlnecker, P. Stephen. 11. Pennsylvania. Governor, 1923–1927 (Pinchot) 12. Fraternal Order of Eagles. I. Theodore Roosevelt Association Collection [mp 76–4]

Governor Goodrich of Indiana.
Producer unknown [1918?]

© No reg.

lr, 154 ft. si. b&w. 35mm. ref print.
lr, 154 ft. si. b&w. 35mm dupe neg.
lr, 154 ft. si. b&w. 35mm. neg ntr.

SHELF LOC'N: FEA8931 (print); FPB9881 (neg)

Ref sources: The Indianapolis News. 8/29/18: 1; The Indianapolis Star. 8/29/18: 1–2; 8/30/18: 1, 5; Boruff, Blanche F. Women of Indiana. 1941: 162.

Factual; views.

SUMMARY: Various views of James Putnam Goodrich, governor of Indiana (1917–1921) walking with the support of a cane in each scene. Goodrich received a fractured left hip when he was involved in an auto accident, Aug. 19, 1918. He was hospitalized for about two months in St. Vincent's Hospital, Indianapolis, and confined to walking with a cane for about six months thereafter. Opening scene of Goodrich leaving a building that may be St. Vincent's Hospital, accompanied by two people who appear to be his wife, Cora Frist Goodrich, and his son in uniform, Pierre Frist Goodrich, a captain in the U.S. Army; long shot of Goodrich sitting in a chair, book in hand, conversing with his wife and son; close-up of Goodrich talking, with the building filling the immediate background; medium view of Goodrich talking with three unidentified men on the hospital grounds; scene of him walking towards the camera, with his son and an unidentified couple; the final view shows Goodrich walking down a long flight of stairs towards the camera.

PERSONAL CREDITS: Lewis, Samuel, source.

1. Indianapolis. 2. Goodrich, James P. 3. Goodrich, Cora Frist. 4. Goodrich, Pierre F. 5. Indiana. Governor, 1917–1921 (Goodrich) 6. St. Vincent's Hospital, Indianapolis. I. Theodore Roosevelt Association Collection [mp 76–284]

Governor's Foot Guards, Conn.
American Mutoscope & Biograph Co., Sep 1899.

© H17969, American Mutoscope & Biograph Co., 21May1902

lr, of 1, 12 ft. si. b&w. 16mm. ref print.
lr, of 1, 12 ft. si. b&w. 16mm. dupe neg.
lr, of 1, 12 ft. si. b&w. 16mm. archival pos.
lr, of 1, 21 ft. si. b&w. 16mm. ref print.
lr, of 1, 21 ft. si. b&w. 16mm. dupe neg.
lr, of 1, 29 ft. si. b&w. 35mm. paper (2 cy)

SHELF LOC'N: FAB1460 (print-RMA); FRA 6196 (neg-RMA); FRA6108 (arch pos-RMA); FLA4025 (print-Paper); FRA1217 (neg-Paper); LC1011 (paper, 2 cy-Paper)

RMA title: Old Guard Parade, New York.

Ref sources: New York Tribune. 10/1/99: pt. 1: 1–2; Connecticutt. Governor's Foot Guard. Second Company, New Haven. Second Company Governor's Foot Guards. [1925]: 34; Fowles, Lloyd W. An Honor to the State. 1971: 114; King, Moses. The Dewey Reception and Committee of New York City. 1899: 141.

Newsfilm.

SUMMARY: many military and patriotic organizations participate in the land parade of Sept. 30, 1899, held in honor of Adm. George Dewey by the City of New York. The First and Second Companies of the Governor's Foot Guards of Connecticut are one of the most picturesque groups marching; they are wearing uniforms of the Continental Army.

1. Processions. 2. Uniforms, Military. 3. New York (City). 4. United States—History—War of 1898. 5. Connecticut. Governor's Foot Guards. First Company, Hartford. 6. Connecticut, Governor's Foot Guards. Second Company, New Haven. I. Biograph Company. II. Biograph Company, source. III. Theodore Roosevelt Association Collection. IV. Paper Print Collection. [mp 76–255]

Governors of New England meet in Governor Coolidge's office in Boston to discuss fuel.
Kinogram Pub. Corp., Dec 1919.

© No reg.

lr, 17 ft. si. b&w. 16mm. ref print (cy 1)
lr, 12 ft. si. b&w. 16mm. ref print (cy 2)
lr, 12 ft. si. b&w. 16mm. archival pos (2 cy)
(Kinograms [Series])

SHELF LOC'N: FAB871 (print, cy 1); FAB1027 (print, cy 2); FRA5856 & 5857 (arch pos, 2 cy)

Ref print (cy 1) is longer than ref print (cy 2) due to longer printing of interior titles; final ca. 5 ft. of ref print (cy 1) is very dark.

Ref sources: P&P portrait file; The Boston Daily Globe. 10/11/19: 1.

Newsfilm.

SUMMARY: On Dec. 10, 1919, Gov. Calvin Coolidge hosts five New England governors in a conference on transportation and fuel conditions. At the State House in Boston the governors pledge support of coal regulation and continuing financial aid for New England's railroads after their return to private control in peacetime. Attending the conference are governors Coolidge, Mass.; Percival W. Clement, Vt.; Robert Livingston Beeckman, R.I.; John H. Bartlett, N.H.; Carl E. Milliken, Me.; and Marcus H. Holcomb, Conn. Views of the governors on the upper portico of the State House and posed in Governor Coolidge's office.

PERSONAL CREDITS: Stripe, F. C., source. Carver, H. P., source.

1. Railroads—New England—Finance. 2. Coal trade—New England. 3. Boston, Mass. Old State House. 4. New England. 5. Boston, Mass. 6. Coolidge, Calvin, Pres. U.S., 1872–1933. 7. Clement, Percival W. 8. Beeckman, Robert Livingston. 9. Bartlett, John H. 10. Milliken, Carl E. 11. Holcomb, Marcus H. 12. Massachusetts. Governor, 1919–1921 (Coolidge) 13. Vermont. Governor, 1919–1921 (Clement) 14. Rhode Island. Governor, 1915–1921 (Beeckman) 15. New Hampshire. Governor, 1919–1921 (Bartlett) 16. Maine. Governor, 1917–1920 (Milliken) 17. Connecticut. Governor, 1915–1921 (Holcomb) I. Kinogram Publishing Corporation. II. Theodore Roosevelt Association Collection [mp 76–102]

Herbert Putnam.
Producer unknown [192–?]
© No reg.
  lr, 58 ft. si. b&w. 16mm. ref print.
  lr, 58 ft. si. b&w. 16mm. archival pos (2 cy)
  SHELF LOC'N: FAB830 (print); FRA5816 & 5817 (arch pos, 2 cy)
Ref source: Library of Congress. *Herbert Putnam, 1861*–1955. 1956.
Factual.
SUMMARY: Herbert Putnam, eighth Librarian of Congress (1899–1939) and Librarian Emeritus (1939–1955), appears inside and outside the Library building, probably between 1925 and 1935. Seated at a desk, Putnam looks at an illuminated volume; in two similar scenes he walks down the front steps of the Library building and pauses, with the Capitol visible in the background; close shot of Putnam at the same location.

1. Washington, D.C. Capitol. 2. Washington, D.C. 3. United States—Public buildings. 4. Putnam, Herbert. 5. United States. Library of Congress. I.

Kinogram Publishing Corporation, source. II. Theodore Roosevelt Association Collection [mp 76–68]

Hopi Indians dance for TR at [Walpi, Ariz.] 1913.
Producer unknown, Aug 1913.
© No reg.
  lr, 103 ft. si. b&w. 16mm. ref print.
  lr, 103 ft. si. b&w. 16mm. dupe neg.
  lr, 103 ft. si. b&w. 16mm. archival pos.
  SHELF LOC'N: FAB1134 (print); FRA6075 (neg); FRA5714 (arch pos)
RMA lists the location in the title as Albuquerque, N.M.
Newsfilm; sociological.
SUMMARY: On Aug. 20, 1913, TR, numerous visitors, and Hopi Indians observe the performance of the ritual Hopi snake dance at Walpi, Ariz., on the Hopi reservation. TR was on a journey through the Southwest with his sons Archie and Quentin, and a young cousin, Nicholas Roosevelt. Crowds, seated and standing, are scattered over adobe dwellings watching the ceremony. The snake dance takes place around a rough column of rock, with Hopis, in native dress and carrying snakes in their hands and mouths, circling the rock. Close shot of TR, seated and apparently awaiting the beginning of the ritual. Brief shot of the Arizona landscape.

1. Hopi Indians—Social life and customs. 2. Snake-dance. 3. Hopi Indian Reservation, Ariz. 4. Walpi, Ariz. 5. Roosevelt, Theodore, Pres. U.S., 1858–1919. I. United States. Bureau of Reclamation, source. II. Theodore Roosevelt Association Collection [mp 76–109]

International naval review, Hampton Roads, Virginia, 1907.
Producer unknown, Apr 1907.
© No reg.
  lr, 38 ft. si. b&w. 16mm. ref print (cy 1)
  lr, 96 ft. si. b&w. 35mm. ref print (cy 2)
  lr, 95 ft. si. b&w. 35mm. dupe neg.
  lr, 38 ft. si. b&w. 16mm. archival pos.
  lr, 95 ft. si. b&w. 35mm. pos ntr.
  lr, 96 ft. si. b&w. 35mm. neg ntr.
  SHELF LOC'N: FAB1222 (print, cy 1); FEA7630 (print, cy 2); FPB8066 (neg); FRA6118 (arch pos)
Ref sources: United States. Jamestown Ter-Centennial Commission. *Final Report of the Jamestown Ter-Centennial Commission.* 1909: 58–59; *Collier's.* v. 39, no. 7, 1907: 16–19; The New York

Herald. 4/27/07: 3–4; *Jane's Fighting Ships.* 1906–7: 61, 63, 90–122, 241, 247; *Heraldry & Regalia of War.* 1973: 90–92, 96; Bain, George Grantham. [News photos of U.S. Navy Atlantic Fleet in New York harbor, ca. 1910–1915.] lot 11276. P&P; Bain, George Grantham. [News photos of return of U.S. Navy Atlantic Fleet from cruise around the world.] lot 11282. P&P.

Newsfilm.

SUMMARY: Ships of foreign countries and the U.S. Atlantic Fleet participate in the international naval review which marks the opening of the Jamestown Exposition Apr. 26, 1907. TR, with his family and guests, had traveled from Washington aboard the presidential yacht Mayflower. As TR passed the rows of anchored ships flying pennants, bunting, and flags, each greeted him with a twenty-one gun salute. Panoramic shots of ships in the Hampton Roads. It is difficult to identify individual ships; however, those painted with dark colors are probably foreign vessels, with the exception of the German ships, which were given new coats of white paint in honor of the occasion. The first ship in the film is one of the British armored cruisers; at ca. ft. 13, the American ship is probably the presidential yacht Mayflower; a ship which is probably the German imperial flagship Roon is visible at ca. ft. 20. In the last sequence, there are views of the monitor Canonicus; a Civil War relic, she was refurbished and served as an exhibit during the exposition.

PERSONAL CREDITS: Kleine, George, source.

1. Warships—Visits to foreign ports. 2. Naval ceremonies, honors, and salutes. 3. Battleships. 4. Cruisers (Warships). 5. Turret ships. 6. Yachts and yachting. 7. Hampton Roads. 8. United States. Navy. Atlantic Fleet. 9. United States. President, 1901–1909 (Roosevelt). 10. Mayflower (Yacht). 11. Germany. Kriegsmarine. 12. Great Britain. Navy. 13. Roon (Cruiser). 14. Canonicus (Ship). 15. Jamestown Exposition, 1907. I. Theodore Roosevelt Association Collection. [mp 76–258]

Jamestown Exposition, 1907.
American Mutoscope & Biograph Co., 1907.
    lr, 272 ft. si. b&w. 16mm. ref print.
    lr, 272 ft. si. b&w. 16mm. dupe neg.
    SHELF LOC'N: FAB842 (print); FRA5846 (neg)
A compilation film containing two segments: [1] Opening day, Jamestown Exposition, April 26, 1907. H94003, American Mutoscope & Biograph Co., 18 May 1907; [2] Georgia Day at the Jamestown Exposition, June 10, 1907. Copyright notice appears on the film, but there is no copyright

TR participated in an international naval review on opening day, April 26, 1907, of the Jamestown Exposition. Battleships flying flags appear in the background, and the steam launch that transported the Roosevelt party ashore from the presidential yacht appears in the foreground.

registration. LC has *Opening Day, Jamestown Exposition, April 26, 1907*, in the Paper Print Collection.

The RMA list notes that several scenes were removed and used in the RMA production *President Roosevelt*.

The film is very light due to nitrate deterioration; out of sequence; main and interior titles appear to be negative emulsion.

Ref sources: Jamestown Exposition, Norfolk, Va., April 1907. Stereographs of the Exposition commemorating the 300th anniversary of the first permanent English settlement in America. lot 2832. P&P; Jamestown Exposition, Norfolk, Va., April 1907. Stereographs of military parades at the Exposition. lot 2836. P&P; Niver, Kemp R. *Motion Pictures from the Library of Congress Paper Print Collection, 1894–1912.* 1967: 254–255; Jamestown Official Photograph Corporation. *Scenes at the Jamestown Exposition.* 1907.

Newsfilm; compilation.

SUMMARY: Scenes of Theodore Roosevelt at the Jamestown Exposition, Apr. and June 1907, Norfolk, Va. Participating in Jamestown's tercentennial celebration on Apr. 26, its opening day, and later on Georgia Day, June 10, TR appears with family members disembarking from a launch at Discovery Landing, the official docking area of the Exposition. From an awning-covered platform he speaks to a large crowd on the Lee Parade

Ground; Frederick Dent Grant, son of the former president, is visible beside him on the stand. At the Lee Parade Ground he reviews West Point cadets and other military units. View of naval and military officials of thirty-seven participating nations passing before the camera. The appearance of flag bunting in the Lee Parade Ground scenes is the only clue to the date of individual scenes; footage in which wrapped bunting appears was probably shot on June 10, loose bunting scenes on Apr. 26.

CITATION: MPW1: 158.

1. Military ceremonies, honors, and salutes. 2. Marching. 3. Georgia Day. 4. Norfolk, Va. Discovery Landing. 5. Norfolk, Va.—Plazas—Lee Parade Ground. 6. Jamestown, Va. 7. Jamestown, Va.—Exhibitions. 8. Norfolk, Va. 9. Roosevelt, Theodore, Pres. U.S., 1858–1919—Addresses, essays, lectures. 10. Grant, Frederick Dent. 11. United States. President, 1901–1909 (Roosevelt) 12. Jamestown Exposition, 1907. I. Biograph Company. II. Biograph Company, source. III. Theodore Roosevelt Association Collection. IV. Opening day, Jamestown Exposition, April 26, 1907 [Title] V. Georgia Day at the Jamestown Exposition, June 10, 1907 [Title] [mp 76–116]

Japanese and Russian peace delegates [leaving New York City], 1905.

Producer unknown, Aug 1905

© No reg.

lr, 201 ft. si. b&w. 35mm. ref print.
lr, 201 ft. si. b&w. 35mm. masterpos.
lr, 202 ft. si. b&w. 35mm. pos ntr.
lr, 201 ft. si. b&w. 35mm. neg ntr.

SHELF LOC'N: FEA7828 (print); FPB7746 (fgmp)

RMA titles: *Japanese and Russian Peace Delegates Arriving at Portsmouth, N.H., 1905; Russian and Japanese Peace Delegates arrive at Portsmouth, N.H., 1905.*

The film is dark and slightly out of frame.

Ref sources: The Boston *Daily Globe.* 8/5/05: 1–6; The Brooklyn *Daily Eagle.* 8/6/05: 1, 7; P&P stereo file.

Newsfilm.

SUMMARY: On Aug. 5, 1905, the Japanese and Russian delegations to the Portsmouth Peace Conference left New York City to board ships which would take them first to Oyster Bay to talk with TR and then to the conference in Portsmouth, N.H. Views at the wharf of the New York Yacht Club of the Japanese delegation boarding two U.S. Navy steam launches; part of the Russian delegation walks down a ramp to the wharf; the first three men are

unidentified; the last two men are the chief Russian envoys, Sergius Witte and Baron Roman Rosen; the delegation is greeted by third Assistant Secretary of State Herbert H. D. Peirce and others; the Russians board a steam launch; final view of a man walking down the ramp and then boarding another launch.

PERSONAL CREDITS: Kleine, George, source.

1. Diplomats. 2. Russo-Japanese War, 1904–1905. 3. Diplomatic negotiations in international disputes. 4. Ships. 5. New York (City) 6. Witte, Sergeĭ IUl'evich, graf, 1849–1915. 7. Rosen, Roman Romanovich, baron, 1847–1921. 8. Peirce, Herbert H. D. 9. New York Yacht Club. 10. United States. Navy. 11. Russia. Armiia. 12. Portsmouth, Treaty of, 1905. I. Theodore Roosevelt Association Collection. [mp 76–340]

Jules Jusserand, 1924.

Producer unknown [1924?]

© No reg.

lr, 21 ft. si. b&w. 16mm. ref print.
lr, 21 ft. si. b&w. 16mm. archival pos.
lr, 53 ft. si. b&w. 35mm. dupe neg ntr.

SHELF LOC'N: FAB679 (print); FRA5721 (arch pos)

The date in the title is unverified.

Ref source: P&P portrait file.

Factual; views.

SUMMARY: Jules Jusserand, diplomat, scholar,

On April 26, 1907, TR delivers the opening address at the Jamestown Exposition in Norfolk, Virginia.

Jules Jusserand, diplomat, scholar, and French ambassador to the U.S. (1903–25). He was a member of TR's "Tennis Cabinet," a group of companions who played tennis, rode, and participated in rough cross-country walks with President Roosevelt.

and French ambassador to the U.S. (1903–1925), poses outside a building with an unidentified man and woman; close-up of Jusserand.

1. Jusserand, Jules. I. Kinogram Publishing Corporation, source. II. Theodore Roosevelt Association Collection. [mp 76–15]

Kaiser Wilhelm.
Producer unknown [191–?]
© No reg.
    lr, 30 ft. si. b&w. 16mm. ref print (2 cy)
    lr, 30 ft. si. b&w. 16mm. dupe neg.
    lr, 30 ft. si. b&w. 16mm. archival pos.
    SHELF LOC'N: FAB971 & 1207 (print, 2 cy); FRA6099 (neg); FRA5940 (arch pos)
Ref source: P&P portrait file.
Factual; views.
SUMMARY: Various scenes of Wilhelm II, emperor of Germany, in different locations: clear view of the kaiser walking towards the camera, with German officers on his left, and a postal delivery service building in the immediate background; view of Wilhelm and an unidentified man entering a carriage; the kaiser with a group of men on horseback; the kaiser greeting a line of dignitaries; and a final long shot of Wilhelm posing for the camera with a large group.
PERSONAL CREDITS: Kandel, source.
1. Germany. 2. Wilhelm II, German Emperor, 1859–1941. 3. Germany. Heer—Officers. 4. Germany. Kriegsmarine—Officers. I. Theodore Roosevelt Association Collection. [mp 76–341]

Kaiser Wilhelm and his admiralty staff attend launching at Kiel.
Producer unknown [191–?]
© No reg.
    lr, 18 ft. si. b&w. 16mm. ref print.
    lr, 18 ft. si. b&w. 16mm. dupe neg.
    lr, 46 ft. si. b&w. 35mm. masterpos.
    lr, 18 ft. si. b&w. 16mm. archival pos.
    lr, 46 ft. si. b&w. 35mm. neg ntr.
    SHELF LOC'N: FAB941 (print); FRA8656 (neg); FPB8229 (fgmp); FRA 5899 (arch pos)
The location in the title is unverified.
Ref sources: P&P portrait file; Wile, Frederic W. *Men around the Kaiser.* 1913: 2.
Factual.
SUMMARY: Kaiser Wilhelm, on the left, Admiral von Tirpitz, Admiral von Koester and an unidentified woman, naval officers, army officers, and other officials walk past a stationary camera and the hull of a ship. The interior title is a TR quotation concerning his efforts towards arms limitations.
PERSONAL CREDITS: Howe, Lyman, source.
1. Kiel. 2. Wilhelm II, German Emperor, 1859–1941. 3. Koester, Hans Ludwig Raimund Von. 4. Tirpitz, Alfred Peter Friedrich Von. 5. Germany. Heer—Officers. 6. Germany. Kriegsmarine—Officers. I. Theodore Roosevelt Association Collection. [mp 76–132]

King Albert of Belgium visits TR's grave, 1919.
Producer unknown, Oct 1919.
© No reg.
    lr, 13 ft. si. b&w. 16mm. ref print.
    lr, 13 ft. si. b&w. 16mm. dupe neg.
    lr, 32 ft. si. b&w. 35mm. pos ntr.
    SHELF LOC'N: FAB874 (print); FRA5860 (neg)
Ref sources: Shumway, Harry I. *Albert, the Soldier-King.* 1934; P&P portrait file.
Newsfilm.

SUMMARY: The king and queen of Belgium and Crown Prince Leopold visited the United States in Oct. 1919, at the invitation of President Wilson. An admirer of TR, King Albert, with the prince, drove to Youngs Memorial Cemetery in Oyster Bay to lay a wreath on TR's grave. The film shows King Albert, Theodore Roosevelt, Jr., and a man in a dark hat who is probably Joseph M. Nye, chief of special agents, Dept. of State, walking with a group of men down the path from the gravesite. Prince Leopold, wearing a Belgian Army uniform and an overseas cap, is walking behind the king. There are medium-close shots of the king and Theodore Roosevelt, Jr., and an unidentified man getting into an open car.

1. Memorial rites and ceremonies. 2. Youngs Memorial Cemetery. 3. Oyster Bay, N.Y. 4. Albert I, King of the Belgians, 1875–1934. 5. Roosevelt, Theodore, Pres. U.S., 1858–1919—Tomb. 6. Leopold III, King of the Belgians, 1901– 7. Roosevelt, Theodore, 1887–1944. 8. Nye, Joseph M. I. International Newsreel Corporation, source. II. Theodore Roosevelt Association Collection. [mp 76–95]

King Albert of Belgium visited the United States in October 1919. The king, an admirer of TR, made the journey to Oyster Bay to lay a wreath on TR's grave.

King Albert of Belgium visits TR's grave, October, 1919.

Fox Film Corp., Oct 1919.

© No reg.

lr, 21 ft. si. b&w. 16mm. ref. print.
lr, 19 ft. si. b&w. 16mm. dupe neg.
lr, 19 ft. si. b&w. 16mm. archival pos.

(Fox news [Series])

SHELF LOC'N: FAB996 (print); FRA5979 (neg); FRA5980 (arch pos)

Image is blurred on ref print.

Ref source: P&P portrait file.

Newsfilm.

SUMMARY: King Albert visits TR's grave in Youngs Memorial Cemetery, Oyster Bay, and is accompanied by his son Prince Leopold, Theodore Roosevelt, Jr., and several dignitaries. Identified in the film are Brand Whitlock, ambassador to Belgium, walking in the rear of the group, and a man who may be Joseph M. Nye walking beside King Albert. An interior title states that King Albert requested that no pictures be taken at the gravesite; the film contains only shots of the king's party walking from the grave and of Theodore Roosevelt, Jr., King Albert, and an unidentified man sitting in an open car ready to depart.

PERSONAL CREDITS: Fox, William, source.

1. Memorial rites and ceremonies. 2. Youngs Memorial Cemetery. 3. Oyster Bay, N.Y. 4. Albert I, King of the Belgians, 1875–1934. 5. Roosevelt, Theodore, Pres. U.S., 1858–1919—Tomb. 6. Leopold III, King of Belgians, 1901– 7. Roosevelt, Theodore, 1887–1944. 8. Whitlock, Brand. 9. Nye, Joseph M. I. Fox Film Corporation. II. Theodore Roosevelt Association Collection. [mp 76–156]

The King and Queen of Belgium and Premier Poincaré of France [1]

Kinogram Pub. Corp., Jul 1927.

© No reg.

lr, 17 ft. si. b&w. 16mm. ref print.
lr, 17 ft. si. b&w. 16mm. dupe neg (cy 1)
lr, 43 ft. si. b&w. 35mm. dupe neg (cy 2)
lr, 43 ft. si. b&w. 35mm. pos ntr.

(Kinograms [Series])

SHELF LOC'N: FAB898 (print); FRA5893 (neg, cy 1); FPB7952 (neg, cy 2)

Ref sources: The *Illustrated War News*, pt. 58, 1917: 35; P&P portrait file; The *Times*, London. 7/18/27: 13; *La Libre Belgique*, Brussels. 7/19/27: 1; *L'Independance Belge*, Brussels. 7/17/27; suppl.: 6–7; New York *Herald Tribune*, Paris. 7/18/27: 1.

Newsfilm.

SUMMARY: On July 17, 1927, a solemn ceremony was held at the cemetery at Laeken, Belgium, to dedicate a monument to an unknown French soldier who fell on Belgian soil during World War I. King Albert of Belgium and Raymond Poincaré, president of France, were the principal speakers. Views of the crowd awaiting the arrival of the royal party are included; the monument is visible in the center of the picture; it is a replica of one at the entrance to the Père Lachaise cemetery in Paris, erected in memory of Belgian soldiers who fell in France. On the right is a platform built in front of the church of Notre-Dame, where the speeches are to be given. King Albert, Queen Elisabeth, and M. Poincaré, followed by the Count of Flanders (Prince Charles), walking behind Poincaré, and the Duke of Brabant (Prince Leopold), walking behind the king, pass through the crowd. The last sequence consists of views of the royal party seated on the platform in front of the church, probably prior to the ceremony. Madame Poincaré, wearing a light-colored hat, is seated next to King Albert.

1. Memorial rites and ceremonies—Belgium. 2. Cemeteries—Belgium—Laeken. 3. War memorials— Belgium. 4. Soldiers' monuments—Belgium. 5. Sepulchral monuments—Belgium. 6. Tombs—Belgium. 7. Laeken, Belgium. 8. Albert I, King of the Belgians, 1875–1934. 9. Elisabeth, consort of Albert I, King of the Belgians, 1876–1965. 10. Poincaré, Raymond, Pres. France, 1860–1934. 11. Charles, Count of Flanders, 1903– 12. Leopold·III, King of the Belgians, 1901– 13. Poincaré, Henriette. 14. Église Notre-Dame, Laeken, Belgium. I. Kinogram Publishing Corporation. II. Kinogram Publishing Corporation, source. III. Theodore Roosevelt Association Collection. [mp 76–133]

The King and Queen of Belgium and Premier Poincaré of France [2]
Producer unknown, Jul 1927.

© No reg.

lr, 35 ft. si. b&w. 35mm. ref print.
lr, 35 ft. si. b&w. 35mm. dupe neg.
lr, 35 ft. si. b&w. 35mm. masterpos.
lr, 35 ft. si. b&w. 35mm. neg ntr.

SHELF LOC'N: FEA9936 (print); FPC0766 (neg); FPB7953 (fgmp)

Ref sources: The *Illustrated War News*. pt. 58, 1917: 35; P&P portrait file; The *Times,* London. 7/18/27: 13; *La Libre Belgique*, Brussels. 7/19/27: 1; *L'Independance Belge*, Brussels. 7/17/27: suppl.: 6–7;

New York *Herald Tribune*, Paris, 7/18/27: 1.
Newsfilm.

SUMMARY: On July 17, 1927, a solemn ceremony was held at the cemetery at Laeken, Belgium to dedicate a monument to an unknown French soldier who fell on Belgian soil during World War I. King Albert of Belgium and Raymond Poincaré, president of France, were the principal speakers. The crowd waits for the arrival of the royal party; the monument is visible in the center of the picture; it is a replica of one at the entrance to the Père Lachaise cemetery in Paris, erected in memory of Belgian soldiers who fell in France. On the right is a platform built in front of the church of Notre-Dame, where the speeches are to be given. King Albert, Queen Elisabeth, and M. Poincaré, followed by the Count of Flanders (Prince Charles), walking behind Poincaré, and the Duke of Brabant (Prince Leopold), walking behind the king, pass through the crowd.

1. Memorial rites and ceremonies—Belgium. 2. War memorials—Belgium. 3. Cemeteries—Belgium— Laeken. 4. Soldiers' monuments—Belgium. 5. Sepulchral monuments—Belgium. 6. Tombs—Belgium. 7. Laeken, Belgium. 8. Albert I, King of the Belgians, 1875–1934. 9. Elisabeth, consort of Albert I, King of the Belgians, 1876–1965. 10. Poincaré, Raymond, Pres. France, 1860–1934. 11. Charles Count of Flanders, 1903– 12. Leopold III, King of the Belgians, 1901– 13. Église Notre-Dame, Laeken, Belgium. I. Kinogram Publishing Corporation, source. II. Theodore Roosevelt Association Collection. [mp] 76–134]

King and Queen of Spain attend a military review.
Producer unknown [192–?]

© No reg.

lr, 11 ft. si. b&w. 16mm. ref print.
lr, 29 ft. si. b&w. 35mm. masterpos.
lr, 11 ft. si. b&w. 16mm. archival pos.
lr, 29 ft. si. b&w. 35mm. neg ntr.

SHELF LOC'N: FAB895 (print); FPB8231 (fgmp); FRA5890 (arch pos)

Events probably occurred between 1913 and 1929, since construction began in 1913 for the Ibero-American Exposition, which was postponed during WWI and finally opened on May 7, 1929.

Ref sources: Fernández Almagro, Melchor. *Historia del Reinado de Don Alfonso XIII*. 1933; P&P portrait file.

Newsfilm.

SUMMARY: Views of King Alfonso XIII of

Spain on horseback reviewing military units in what is probably the Plaza de España at the future Ibero-American Exposition site in Seville, Spain, since the building in the background, the main building at the exposition, is far from completion. In the final sequence the king, Queen Victoria Eugenia, and various officers stand on the reviewing stand while one officer reads from a prepared text.

PERSONAL CREDITS: Foster, source.

1. Military ceremonies, honors, and salutes. 2. Seville. 3. Alfonso XIII, King of Spain, 1886–1941. 4. Victoria Eugenia, consort of Alfonso XIII, King of Spain, 1887–1969. I. Theodore Roosevelt Association Collection. [mp 76–315]

King Edward's funeral, 1910 [1]

Producer unknown, May 1910. Later released by Kineto Company of America [1920?]
  © No reg.
    lr, 196 ft. si. b&w. 16mm. ref print.
    lr, 196 ft. si. b&w. 16mm. dupe neg.
    lr, 491 ft. si. b&w. 35mm. pos ntr.
(Urban popular classics [Series])
SHELF LOC'N: FAB675 (print); FRA5717 (neg)
The imprint "Urban popular classics" appears on the interior title. The reissue date is based on information in *The Moving Picture World*; date of original release is unverified.

Ref source: *The Moving Picture World*. v. 47, no. 8, 1920: 1088.

Newsfilm.

SUMMARY: The ceremonial funeral of King Edward VII (1901–1910) proceeds through the streets of London on May 20, 1910. TR, while on a European tour, was requested by President Taft to represent the United States; he attended in ordinary evening dress, while all other dignitaries were more elaborately attired. An interior title notes the presence of King George V, Kaiser Wilhelm II, the kings of Spain, Portugal, and Denmark, Archduke Ferdinand, and Theodore Roosevelt. There is no positive identification of TR in the procession. The film includes views of diverse military units in formal uniform; two views of the moving casket; and views of heads of state.

PERSONAL CREDITS: Stripe, F. C., source. Carver, H. P., source.

1. Funeral service. 2. Heads of state. 3. London. 4. Edward VII, King of Great Britain, 1841–1910. 5. Edward VII, King of Great Britain, 1841–1910—Funeral and memorial services. I. Kineto Company of America. II. Theodore Roosevelt Association Collection. [mp 76–26]

King Edward's funeral, 1910 [2]

Producer unknown, May 1910.
  © No reg.
    lr, 180 ft. si. b&w. 16mm. ref print.
    lr, 180 ft. si. b&w. 16mm. dupe neg.
    lr, 436 ft. si. b&w. 35mm. pos ntr.
SHELF LOC'N: FAB673 (print); FRA5713 (neg)
Film goes in and out of frame.

Newsfilm.

SUMMARY: The ceremonial funeral procession of King Edward VII (1901–1910) passing through the streets of London on May 20, 1910. Views of the moving casket, heads of state walking behind the casket, the royal carriage, and various marching military units. Attending the ceremony were Kaiser Wilhelm II, Stéphen Pichon, the kings of Spain, Portugal, and Denmark, Archduke Franz Ferdinand, and Theodore Roosevelt, representing the United States. TR is visible at ca. ft. 16–21, 126–129, 168–170.

PERSONAL CREDITS: Howe, Lyman, source.

1. Funeral service. 2. Heads of state. 3. London. 4. Edward VII, King of Great Britain, 1841–1910. 5. Edward VII, King of Great Britain, 1841–1910—Funeral and memorial services. 6. Roosevelt, Theodore, Pres. U.S., 1858–1919. I. Theodore Roosevelt Association Collection. [mp 76–25]

King George and Queen Mary of England [1]

Kinogram Pub. Corp. [1928?]
  © No reg.
    lr, 9 ft. si. b&w. 16mm. ref print.
    lr, 9 ft. si. b&w. 16mm. dupe neg (cy 1)
    lr, 30 ft. si. b&w. 35mm. dupe neg (cy 2)
    lr, 23 ft. si. b&w. 35mm. pos ntr.
(Kinograms [Series])
SHELF LOC'N: FAB843 (print); FRA5848 (neg, cy 1); FPB7954 (neg, cy 2)
Edge code date on nitrate is 1928.

Newsfilm.

SUMMARY: King George, wearing a top hat, and Queen Mary, carrying a parasol, are attending some ceremonial affair. The film consists of three sequences: 1) the king and queen are walking through a crowd, accompanied by a woman in a dark hat and a man with a medal around his neck, and a little girl presents a bouquet to Queen Mary; 2) a crowd of children is cheering the king and queen; pennants and tents are in the background; 3) King George and Queen Mary are seated in the midst of a group of people, probably posing for photographers.

1. Children. 2. Crowds. 3. George V, King of

Great Britain, 1865–1936. 4. Mary, consort of George V, King of Great Britain, 1867–1953. I. Kinogram Publishing Corporation. II. Kinogram Publishing Corporation, source. III. Theodore Roosevelt Association Collection. [mp 76–81]

King George and Queen Mary of England [2]
Producer unknown [1928?]
© No reg.
  lr, 28 ft. si. b&w. 35mm. ref print.
  lr, 28 ft. si. b&w. 35mm. dupe neg.
  lr, 28 ft. si. b&w. 35mm. masterpos.
  lr, 28 ft. si. b&w. 35mm. neg ntr.
  SHELF LOC'N: FEA9937 (print); FPC0765 (neg); FPB8064 (fgmp)
May be a Kinograms production; edge code date on nitrate is 1928.
Newsfilm.
SUMMARY: King George and Queen Mary are sitting amidst a group of people probably posing for photographers. The king, barely visible on the left, and queen walk through a crowd and are accompanied by a woman in a dark hat and a man wearing a medal around his neck; a little girl presents a bouquet to Queen Mary. The royal couple are attending some ceremonial affair; the location is undetermined.
1. George V, King of Great Britain, 1865–1936. 2. Mary, consort of George V, King of Great Britain, 1867–1953. I. Kinogram Publishing Corporation. II. Kinogram Publishing Corporation, source. III. Theodore Roosevelt Association Collection. [mp 76–80]

King Gustav of Sweden greeted by his people.
Producer unknown [192–?]
© No reg.
  lr, 9 ft. si. b&w. 16mm. ref print.
  lr, 23 ft. si. b&w. 35mm. masterpos.
  lr, 9 ft. si. b&w. 16mm. arhcival pos.
  lr, 23 ft. si. b&w. 35mm. dupe neg ntr.
  SHELF LOC'N: FAB896 (print); FPB8069 (fgmp); FRA5891 (arch pos)
Ref source: P&P portrait file.
Factual.
SUMMARY: Long shots of King Gustav V and Queen Victoria of Sweden talking with a group of people, mainly children, in an unverified location in Sweden.
PERSONAL CREDITS: Howe, Lyman, source.
1. Sweden—Kings and rulers. 2. Sweden—Queens. 3. Gustaf V, King of Sweden, 1858–1950. 4. Victoria, consort of Gustavus V, King of Sweden, 1862–1930. I. Theodore Roosevelt Association Collection. [mp 76–159]

The King of Italy entertains King Edward of England on his yacht.
Producer unknown [1907?]
© No reg.
  lr, 60 ft. si. b&w. 16mm. ref print.
  lr, 60 ft. si. b&w. 16mm. dupe neg (cy 1)
  lr, 149 ft. si. b&w. 35mm. dupe neg (cy 2)
  lr, 148 ft. si. b&w. 35mm. pos ntr.
  SHELF LOC'N: FAB962 (print); FRA5929 (neg, cy 1); FPB7352 (neg, cy 2)
Film is out of frame ca. first 5 ft.
Ref sources: The Times, London. 4/19/07: 5; Brook-Shepherd, Gordon. Uncle of Europe. 1976; Gildea, James. King Edward VII. 1914: 330; Gernsheim, Helmut and Gernsheim, Alison. Edward VII and Queen Alexandra. 1962; P&P portrait file.
Factual.
SUMMARY: Research indicates that the film is of King Edward's 1907 Mediterranean cruise, during which the royal party was entertained aboard King Victor Emanuel's yacht, the Trinacria, in Gaeta, Italy. Queen Alexandra, King Edward, King Victor Emanuel, and probably Princess Victoria are seated and are posing for the photographer; Italian and British naval officers and other dignitaries stand behind them. There are less formal views of the royal group chatting with each other and with other members of the party: King Edward lights a cigarette; Princess Victoria hands an object to naval officers standing next to her; King Edward talks with a man in civilian clothes who is probably Sir Edwin Egerton, British ambassador to Italy, while an Italian officer takes their picture. Standing near a railing, King Edward and probably King Victor Emanuel talk with Signor Tommaso Tittoni, Italian minister for foreign affairs.
PERSONAL CREDITS: Howe, Lyman, source.
1. Kings and rulers. 2. Voyages and travels. 3. Ocean travel. 4. Yachts and yachting—Italy. 5. Gaeta, Italy. 6. Vittorio Emanuele III, King of Italy, 1869–1947. 7. Edward VII, King of Great Britain, 1841–1910. 8. Alexandra, consort of Edward VII, King of Great Britain, 1844–1925. 9. Victoria, Princess of Great Britain, 1868–1935. 10. Egerton, Edwin H., Sir. 11. Tittoni, Tommaso. 12. Trinacria (Ship) I. Theodore Roosevelt Association Collection. [mp 76–160]

Last known home of Czar Nicholas.
Producer unknown [1918?]
© No reg.

lr, 47 ft. si. b&w. 16mm. ref print.

lr, 47 ft. si. b&w. 16mm. archival pos.

SHELF LOC'N: FAB744 (print); FRA5796 (arch pos)

The RMA list indicates that the photographer is Paul Rainey.

The last 22 frames of the film are printed upside down.

Ref sources: Martin, John S., ed. *A Picture History of Russia.* 1945: 211; P&P portrait file.

Newsfilm.

SUMMARY: The camera pans the home of a merchant named Ipatiev, where Nicholas II, last Russian emperor, and the royal family were executed in Ekaterinburg (Sverdlovsk), July 1918. The second sequence is composed of views of men, identified by interior title as Bolshevik prisoners, standing behind barbed wire as guards patrol.

PERSONAL CREDITS: Rainey, Paul James, photographer.

1. Prisons—Russia—Sverdlovsk. 2. Prisoners of war—Sverdlovsk, Russia. 3. Communist parties. 4. Russia—History—Politics and government—1917. 5. Russia—History—Revolution, 1917-1921. 6. Sverdlovsk, Russia. 7. Nicholas II, Emperor of Russia, 1868-1918. 8. Ipatiev. I. Church of All Nations, New York (City), source. II. Theodore Roosevelt Association Collection. [mp 76-69]

Launch, U.S. battleship "Kentucky."

American Mutoscope Co., Mar 1898.

© H32833, American Mutoscope & Biograph Co., 18June1903

lr, of 1, 50 ft. si. b&w. 35mm. ref print.

lr, of 1, 20 ft. si. b&w. 16mm. dupe neg.

lr, of 1, 20 ft. si. b&w. 16mm. archival pos.

lr, of 1, 28 ft. si. b&w. 16mm. ref print.

lr, of 1, 28 ft. si. b&w. 16mm. dupe neg.

lr, of 1, 51 ft. si. b&w. 35mm. paper (2 cy)

SHELF LOC'N: FEA7632 (print-RMA); FRA6180 (neg-RMA); FRA6114 (arch pos-RMA); FLA3550 (print-Paper); FRA0826 (neg-Paper); LC536 (paper, 2 cy-Paper)

RMA title: *Launching U.S. Battleship Kentucky, Newport News, Va.*

Ref source: *Jane's Fighting Ships.* 1903: 197.

Newsfilm.

SUMMARY: View from the James River of the launching of the battleship Kentucky at Newport News, Va. Built by the Newport News Shipbuilding and Dry Dock Company, the Kentucky is laun-

ched shortly after the U.S. battleship Kearsarge on Mar. 24, 1898. Long shot of the ship on launching skids, sliding into the river, and moving past the stationary camera.

1. Ships—launching. 2. Battleships. 3. James River. 4. Newport News, Va. 5. Kentucky (Ship) 6. Newport News Shipbuilding and Dry Dock Company. I. Biograph Company. II. Biograph Company, source. III. Theodore Roosevelt Association Collection. IV. Paper Print Collection. [mp 76-253]

Laying cornerstone of Roosevelt School, New Rochelle, N.Y. [1920]

Kinogram Pub. Corp., Jan 1920.

© No reg.

lr, 10 ft. si. b&w. 16mm. ref print.

lr, 10 ft. si. b&w. 16mm. dupe neg.

lr, 26 ft. si. b&w. 35mm. pos old safety.

(Kinograms [Series])

SHELF LOC'N: FAB1133 (print); FRA6074 (neg)

RMA lists the date in the title as 1921.

Newsfilm.

SUMMARY: Lt. Col. Theodore Roosevelt, Jr., is participating in the laying of the cornerstone of the Roosevelt School in New Rochelle, N.Y., Jan. 3, 1920. Dedicated to his father's memory, the public school is located in the Wykagyl area of New Rochelle. Lieutenant Colonel Roosevelt wears a mourning band as he stands on a flag-draped scaffold. The film includes medium-close shots of Lieutenant Colonel Roosevelt.

PERSONAL CREDITS: Urban, Charles, source.

1. Corner stones, Laying of. 2. Dedication services. 3. Memorial service. 4. Schools. 5. New Rochelle, N.Y. 6. Wykagyl, N.Y. 7. Roosevelt, Theodore, Pres. U.S., 1858-1919—Funeral and memorial services. 8. Roosevelt, Theodore, 1887-1944. 9. Roosevelt School. I. Kinogram Publishing Corporation. II. Theodore Roosevelt Association Collection. [mp 76-27]

Leonard Wood at Battle Creek, Michigan.

Producer unknown, Mar 1920.

© No reg.

lr, 213 ft. si. b&w. 16mm. ref print.

lr, 213 ft. si. b&w. 16mm. dupe neg.

SHELF LOC'N: FAB943 (print); FRA5901 (neg)

Film sequence does not follow the order of actual events.

Nitrate deterioration, the film is occasionally very light.

Ref sources: P&P portrait file; The Detroit *Free Press.* 3/2/20: 5; 3/3/20: 1–2.

Newsfilm.

SUMMARY: Leonard Wood campaigns in southern Michigan for the Republican presidential nomination, Mar. 1920. Greeted by residents of Battle Creek, Ann Arbor, and Detroit, Wood speaks in each community on the need for universal military training, Americanization of immigrants, and cooperative working relationships between labor and capital. Views of Wood on Mar. 3 in Battle Creek as he is greeted by local officials; his wife, Mrs. Louisa Wood, poses outdoors for the photographer; Wood enters and leaves the Masonic Temple, where he and his wife are greeted by local farmers. Prominent citizens identified by interior titles in the Battle Creek segment include: Charles W. Ryan, mayor and physician; Paul A. Martin, editor of the *Enquirer and Evening News* and commander of the American Legion in Battle Creek; William H. Shippy, president of the Exchange Club; Frederick M. Alger, chairman of the Leonard Wood League of Michigan and active in the American Legion. Men who appear to be Chauncey B. Baker, head of the Motor Transport Divison of the Army (1918–1921), and Edwin Denby, who was to become secretary of the navy in 1921, accompany Wood in several scenes. On Mar. 1, Wood is met by an Ann Arbor reception committee as he steps from a train; Wood poses in the archway of an unidentified building with the committee, which includes Prof. William H. Hobbs, director of the geological laboratory at the University of Michigan, Mayor Ernst E. Wurster, and William H. Faust, chairman of the reception committee. On the University of Michigan campus, Wood shakes hands with students in front of the school's new clubhouse, the Michigan Union. In Detroit on Mar. 2, Wood poses with prominent citizens, speaks at a banquet, and visits with workers at the Dodge Brothers auto manufacturing plant. Officials identified by interior titles include: Edwin Denby; Walter C. Piper, prominent realtor; and Frederick M. Alger. A panning shot of a banquet table at the Hotel Statler includes views of Mrs. Harriet N. Atterbury, incorrectly identified on the film as Mrs. H. M. Atterbury; Mrs. Frederick M. Alger; Mrs. Leonard Wood; Henry M. Leland, past president of General Motors and current president of the Lincoln Motor Company; Leonard Wood; Frank Hecker, Detroit financier and businessman; and Chauncey B. Baker. Interior title identification of a Sen. Alton F. Roberts is questionable, since no state or United States senator or representative by that name held office in 1920.

1. Presidents—United States—Election—1920. 2. Battle Creek, Mich. Masonic Temple. 3. Detroit. Hotel Statler. 4. Battle Creek, Mich. 5. Ann Arbor, Mich. 6. Detroit. 7. Wood, Leonard. 8. Wood, Louisa Smith. 9. Ryan, Charles W. 10. Martin, Paul A. 11. Shippy, William H. 12. Alger, Frederick M. 13. Baker, Chauncey B. 14. Denby, Edwin. 15. Hobbs, William H. 16. Wurster, Ernst E. 17. Faust, William H. 18. Piper, Walter C. 19. Atterbury, Harriet N. 20. Alger, Mary Swift. 21. Leland, Henry M. 22. Hecker, Frank J. 23. Roberts, Alton F. 24. Republican Party. Michigan. 25. Leonard Wood League of Michigan. 26. Michigan. University. Michigan Union. 27. Dodge Brothers, inc. I. Roosevelt Memorial Association, source. II. Theodore Roosevelt Association Collection. [mp 76–127]

Leonard Wood lays cornerstone of Roosevelt House, 1921.

Pathe News, Jan 1921.

© No reg.

lr, 8 ft. si. b&w. 16mm. ref print.
lr, 8 ft. si. b&w. 16mm. dupe neg.
lr, 20 ft. si. b&w. 35mm. pos ntr.

(Pathe News [newsreel])

SHELF LOC'N: FAB759 (print); FRA5814 (neg)

Ref sources: *Roosevelt House Bulletin.* v. 3, no. 1, 1927: 2; *The Roosevelt Quarterly.* v. 10, no. 4, 1933.

Newsfilm.

SUMMARY: On Jan. 6, 1921, the restoration of TR's birthplace by the Women's Roosevelt Memorial Association is officially begun with the laying of the Roosevelt House cornerstone. Views of crowds pressing around a platform; Maj. Gen. Leonard Wood, TR's longtime friend and political associate, preparing to set the stone in place; Corinne Robinson, TR's sister and a frequent participant in Roosevelt House activities, speaking to the assembled crowd. The woman seated on the platform is Mrs. John Henry Hammond, president of the WRMA.

1. Corner stones, Laying of. 2. New York (City). Roosevelt House. 3. New York (City) 4. Wood, Leonard. 5. Roosevelt, Theodore, Pres. U.S., 1858–1919—Birthplace. 6. Roosevelt, Theodore, Pres. U.S., 1858–1919—Homes. 7. Robinson, Corinne Roosevelt. 8. Hammond, Emily Vanderbilt Sloane. 9. Women's Theodore Roosevelt Memorial Association. I. Pathe. II. Roosevelt Memorial Association, source. III. Theodore Roosevelt Association Collection. [mp 76–64]

Lieutenant-Colonel Theodore Roosevelt arrives in New York after the World War.
Producer unknown, Mar 1919.
© No reg.
  lr, 4 ft. si. b&w. 16mm. ref print.
  lr, 4 ft. si. b&w. 16mm. dupe neg.
  lr, 11 ft. si. b&w. 35mm. pos ntr.
SHELF LOC'N: FAB875 (print); FRA5861 (neg)
Interior title contains logo: H-N.
Ref sources: New York *Tribune.* 3/7/19: 2; P&P portrait file.
Newsfilm.
SUMMARY: Theodore Roosevelt, Jr., suffering from a machine gun wound in the leg, returned as a casualty from France to New York City aboard the Mauretania on Mar. 6, 1919. Medium-close shot of TR, Jr., dressed in uniform, aboard what may be the liner Mauretania, docked at the Cunard pier, North River, New York City.
1. European War, 1914-1918. 2. New York (City) 3. Roosevelt, Theodore, 1887-1944. 4. Mauretania (Ship) I. International Newsreel Corporation, source. II. Theodore Roosevelt Association Collection. [mp 76-99]

Lord and Lady Bryce.
Producer unknown [191-?]
© No reg.
  lr, 9 ft. si. b&w. 16mm. ref print.
  lr, 9 ft. si. b&w. 16mm. dupe neg (cy 1)
  lr, 22 ft. si. b&w. 35mm. dupe neg (cy 2)
  lr, 22 ft. si. b&w. 35mm. pos ntr.
SHELF LOC'N: FAB743 (print); FRA5795 (neg, cy 1); FPB7955 (neg, cy 2)
Ref source: P&P portrait file.
Newsfilm.
SUMMARY: Viscount James Bryce, prominent British statesman, scholar, and ambassador to the United States (1907-1913), appears with his wife, Elizabeth A. Bryce, entering a building. They pose in front of the building, which is guarded by men who appear to be British policemen. Brief shot of a car at the curb.
1. Statesmen—Great Britain. 2. Great Britain—Peerage. 3. Bryce, James. 4. Bryce, Elizabeth A. I. United States. Army. Signal Corps, source. II. Theodore Roosevelt Association Collection. [mp 76-49]

Major General Wm. C. Gorgas.
Producer unknown [191-?]
© No reg.
  lr, 4 ft. si. b&w. 16mm. ref print (2 cy)
  lr, 4 ft. si. b&w. 16mm. archival pos (2 cy)
SHELF LOC'N: FAB989 & 1202 (print, 2 cy);
            FRA5966 & 5967 (arch pos, 2 cy)
Factual; views.
SUMMARY: Dr. William Crawford Gorgas, chief sanitation officer of the Panama Canal (1904-1913) and surgeon general of the U.S. Army (1914-1918), with an unidentified man on the observation platform of a train. Gorgas poses for the camera.
PERSONAL CREDITS: Stripe, F. C., source. Carver, H. P., source.
1. Railroads—Passenger cars. 2. Gorgas, William C. I. Theodore Roosevelt Association Collection. [mp 76-219]

[Man speaking at Faneuil Hall, Boston]
Producer unknown [191-?]
© No reg.
  lr, 5 ft. si. b&w. 16mm. ref print (3 cy)
  lr, 5 ft. si. b&w. 16mm. archival pos.
SHELF LOC'N: FAB1020 & 1021 & 1035 (print, 3 cy); FRA5997 (arch pos)
RMA title: *League of Nations in Session.*
Ref sources: Hamlin, Talbot F. *The American Spirit in Architecture.* 1926: 62; P&P geographic file (brochures); P&P stereo file; *Practical Politics.* v. 18, no. 19, 1916: 8022.
Factual.
SUMMARY: A man addresses an audience in a building which is probably Faneuil Hall in Boston. An American flag is draped across the lectern and men are taking notes at tables below the speaker's platform. The man may be TR, but distance and camera angle make positive identification impossible.
PERSONAL CREDITS: Stripe, F. C., source. Carver, H. P., source.
1. Boston, Mass. Faneuil Hall. 2. Orators. 3. Boston, Mass. I. Theodore Roosevelt Association Collection. [mp 76-185]

Marshal Foch visits Roosevelt House, 1921.
Pathe News, Nov 1921.
© No reg.
  lr, 5 ft. si. b&w. 16mm. ref print.
  lr, 5 ft. si. b&w. 16mm. dupe neg.
  lr, 13 ft. si. b&w. 35mm. pos ntr.
(Pathe News [newsreel])
SHELF LOC'N: FAB838 (print); FRA5840 (neg)
Ref source: P&P portrait file.
Newsfilm.
SUMMARY: At midday on Nov. 19, 1921,

French Marshal Ferdinand Foch, commander of the allied armies in World War I, visits Roosevelt House and is greeted by prominent members of the Women's Roosevelt Memorial Association. After a large public reception along Fifth Avenue, Foch is ceremonially received on the street in front of the house, visible in the background and in a state of partial restoration. Views of a crowd outside the building, including military personnel, civilians, and photographers; Marshal Foch and women who may be Mrs. John Henry Hammond, president of the WRMA, and Mrs. Henry A. Wise Wood, chairman of the organization's education committee, pose for the camera in front of the house, with a large painting of TR suspended in the background; Frederic R. Coudert, prominent New York lawyer and resident of Oyster Bay, is identified in the group.

1. New York (City). Roosevelt House. 2. New York (City) 3. Foch, Ferdinand. 4. Roosevelt, Theodore, Pres. U.S., 1858–1919—Homes. 5. Roosevelt, Theodore, Pres. U.S., 1858–1919—Birthplace. 6. Hammond, Emily Vanderbilt Sloane. 7. Wood, Elizabeth Ogden Brower. 8. Coudert, Frederic R. 9.

Marshal Ferdinand Foch, commander of the Allied Armies during World War I, appears on the steps of the New York City Hall with the mayor of New York City, John F. Hylan, on Foch's left, and with the governor of New York, Nathan I. Miller, on Foch's right on October 28, 1921. Foch later visited Roosevelt House, TR's birthplace.

Women's Theodore Roosevelt Memorial Association. I. Pathe. II. Roosevelt Memorial Association, source. III. Theodore Roosevelt Association Collection. [mp 76–79]

Mayor Mitchel of New York.
Producer unknown [1917?]
  © No reg.
    lr, 5 ft. si. b&w. 16mm. ref print.
    lr, 5 ft. si. b&w. 16mm. archival pos.
    lr, 13 ft. si. b&w. 35mm. neg ntr.
  SHELF LOC'N: FAB883 (print); FRA5870 (arch pos)
  Ref print is out of frame.
  Ref source: P&P portrait file.
  Newsfilm.
  SUMMARY: Views of John P. Mitchel, mayor of New York City (1914–1917), with visiting dignitaries. Close shot of Mitchel and Japanese visitors in formal attire; the occasion may be part of the ceremonies welcoming the Imperial Japanese Commission to New York City, Sept. 1917. In a separate sequence Mitchel walks with unidentified foreign military officers past the camera.
  PERSONAL CREDITS: Futter, Walter A., source.
  1. New York (City) 2. Mitchel, John P. I. Theodore Roosevelt Association Collection. [mp 76–107]

McKinley's funeral, 1901.
Producer unknown, Sep 1901.
  © No reg.
    lr, 28 ft. si. b&w. 35mm. ref print.
    lr, 28 ft. si. b&w. 35mm. dupe neg.
    lr, 28 ft. si. b&w. 35mm. masterpos.
  SHELF LOC'N: FEA9941 (print); FPC0769 (neg); FPB7964 (fgmp)
  Film is dark and slightly out of frame.
  Ref sources: [Davis, Oscar K. and Mumford, John K.] *The Life of William McKinley.* 1901: 117–118, 126–127; P&P stereo file.
  Newsfilm.
  SUMMARY: On Sept. 15, 1901, the body of William McKinley was taken to City Hall in Buffalo, N.Y., where it lay in state until that evening; views of mourners entering and leaving the Buffalo City Hall as a crowd gathers outside.
  PERSONAL CREDITS: Kleine, George, source.
  1. Funeral service. 2. Buffalo. City and County Hall. 3. Buffalo. 4. McKinley, William, Pres. U.S., 1843–1901—Funeral and memorial services. 5. United States. President, 1897–1901 (McKinley) I. Theodore Roosevelt Association Collection. [mp 76–319]

McKinley's funeral, Washington, D.C. 1901.
Producer unknown, Sep 1901.
© No reg.
  lr, 30 ft. si. b&w. 35mm. ref print.
  lr, 30 ft. si. b&w. 35mm. dupe neg.
  lr, 30 ft. si. b&w. 35mm. masterpos.
  SHELF LOC'N: FEA9940 (print); FPC0768 (neg); FPB7966 (fgmp)
Film is dark and slightly out of frame.
  Ref sources: The Canton Repository. *Pictorial Life of William McKinley*. 1943: 26; [Davis, Oscar K. and Mumford, John K.] *The Life of William McKinley*. 1901: [115], 127–128; P&P stereo file.
  Newsfilm.
  SUMMARY: Scenes of the state funeral held for President William McKinley at the Capitol in Washington, D.C., on Sept. 17, 1901; from above, the camera pans the crowds gathered at the East Front of the Capitol, waiting to view the body.
  PERSONAL CREDITS: Kleine, George, source.
  1. Funeral service. 2. Washington, D.C. Capitol. 3. Washington, D.C. 4. McKinley, William, Pres. U.S., 1843–1901—Funeral and memorial services. 5. United States. President, 1897–1901 (McKinley) I. Theodore Roosevelt Association Collection. [mp 76–318]

Memorial services for TR at Van Cortlandt Park, New York, Oct. 1919.
Producer unknown, Oct 1919.
© No reg.
  lr, 46 ft. si. b&w. 16mm. ref print (2 cy)
  lr, 46 ft. si. b&w. 16mm. dupe neg.
  lr, 46 ft. si. b&w. 16mm. archival pos (3 cy)
  lr, 116 ft. si. b&w. 35mm. pos ntr.
  lr, 115 ft. si. b&w. 35mm. neg ntr.
  SHELF LOC'N: FAB712 & 1228 (print, 2 cy); FRA5770 (neg); FRA5771 & 5772 & 6171 (arch pos, 3 cy)
Archival pos (cy 1) and dupe neg appear under RMA title: *Flag Service at Van Cortlandt Park, Oct. 1919.*
  Newsfilm.
  SUMMARY: Scenes of Roosevelt Memorial Association ceremonies on Oct. 20–21, 1919, at Van Cortlandt Park and Roosevelt High School, New York City. In honor of Roosevelt's death a memorial flag, carried across New York State, is officially received, first at Van Cortlandt Park in the Bronx on Oct. 20, and the following day at Roosevelt High School. Shots at the park include Samuel Abbott, originator of the memorial flag idea, and an unidentified official displaying the backpack in which the flag has been carried, then displaying the flag in front of gathered scouts; the scout troop saluting as the flag is raised, with what appears to be Van Cortlandt House in the background. At Roosevelt High School young women march on the school walkway toward the camera; in the following sequence five of the women are shown sewing on the flag's forty-third star; at the school entrance a young runner gives the backpack containing the flag to officials.
  PERSONAL CREDITS: Urban, Charles, source.
  1. Flags. 2. High school students—Political activity. 3. New York (City). Van Cortlandt House. 4. New York (City) 5. New York (City)—Parks—Van Cortlandt Park. 6. Roosevelt, Theodore, Pres. U.S., 1858–1919—Funeral and memorial services. 7. Abbott, Samuel. 8. Roosevelt Memorial Association. 9. Roosevelt High School, New York (City) 10. Boy Scouts of America. I. Theodore Roosevelt Association Collection. [mp 76–31]

Memorial services for TR on the steps of the New York Public Library, 1919 [1]
Kinogram Pub. Corp., Oct 1919.
© No reg.
  lr, 28 ft. si. b&w. 16mm. ref print.
  lr, 28 ft. si. b&w. 16mm. archival pos.
  lr, 71 ft. si. b&w. 35mm. neg ntr.
(Kinograms [Series])
  SHELF LOC'N: FAB713 (print); FRA5773 (arch pos)
The film sequence does not follow the order of actual events.
  Ref sources: *Daily News,* New York. 10/25/19:8; 10/27/19: [10–11]; New York *American.* 10/25/19: 11; P&P portrait file.
  Newsfilm.
  SUMMARY: In honor of TR's birthday the week of Oct. 20–27, 1919, was declared Roosevelt Week by the Roosevelt Memorial Association. As one of the events, an official Roosevelt memorial flag, which has been carried across New York State, is ceremoniously received at the Williamsburg Bridge Plaza in Brooklyn on Oct. 24, and the following day, Oct. 25, at the New York Public Library. Opening scene of a crowd gathered on Fifth Ave. in front of the public library, with views of the Roosevelt Guard of Honor composed of Boy Scouts, members of the Naval Reserve, and veterans of the Civil War, Spanish-American War, and World War I. Long shots of notables standing on the library's steps. Possible identifications from right to left are: Henry Cabot Lodge, honorary vice-president of RMA; the man

next to Lodge is probably Henry J. Allen, governor of Kansas; William Boyce Thompson, president of RMA, is holding the flag with the help of a man who appears to be Henry D. Lindsley, chairman of the event; William Loeb, Jr., vice-president of RMA, is visible in back of Thompson; next to Loeb is probably William Gibbs McAdoo; and the man to the far left with his hands to his side may be Elihu Root, an RMA trustee. Scene of the flag being carried by Boy Scouts across the platform and presented to Thompson. Five school girls sew the forty-seventh star on the flag. The last sequence is of the ceremony in the Williamsburg Bridge Plaza; the camera pans down a statue of George Washington to a group of school children holding American flags; a man who may be James A. McCabe, superintendent of public schools, leads the crowd in singing as Samuel Abbott, originator of the memorial flag idea, looks on in the foreground; the camera pans the crowd.

PERSONAL CREDITS: Urban, Charles, source. 1. Memorial rites and ceremonies. 2. Flags. 3. High school students—Political activity. 4. Veterans. 5. New York (City) 6. Brooklyn, N.Y. 7. Roosevelt, Theodore, Pres. U.S., 1858–1919—Funeral and memorial services. 8. Lodge, Henry Cabot. 9. Allen, Henry J. 10. Thompson, William Boyce. 11. Lindsley, Henry D. 12. Loeb, William, 1866–1937. 13. McAdoo, William Gibbs. 14. Root, Elihu. 15. McCabe, James A. 16. Abbott, Samuel. 17. New York (City). Public Library. 18. Roosevelt Memorial Association. 19. Boy Scouts of America. 20. United States. Naval Reserve. 21. Kansas. Governor, 1919–1923 (Henry J. Allen) I. Kinogram Publishing Corporation. II. Theodore Roosevelt Association Collection. [mp 76–19]

Memorial services for TR on the steps of the New York Public Library, 1919 [2]
Producer unknown, Oct 1919.
© No reg.
    lr, 14 ft. si. b&w. 16mm. ref print.
    lr, 14 ft. si. b&w. 16mm. archival pos.
    lr, 34 ft. si. b&w. 35mm. neg ntr.
SHELF LOC'N: FAB714 (print); FRA5774 (arch pos)
Ref sources: *Daily News*, New York. 10/25/19:8; 10/27/19: [10–11]; New York *American.* 10/25/19: 11; P&P portrait file.
Newsfilm.
SUMMARY: In honor of TR's birthday the week of Oct. 20–27, 1919, was declared Roosevelt Week by the Roosevelt Memorial Association. As one of the events, an official Roosevelt memorial flag, which has been carried across New York State, is ceremoniously received at the New York Public Library on Oct. 25. Long shots of notables standing on the library's steps. Possible identifications from right to left are Henry Cabot Lodge, honorary vice-president of RMA; the man next to Lodge is probably Henry J. Allen, governor of Kansas; William Boyce Thompson, president of RMA, is holding the flag with the help of a man who appears to be Henry D. Lindsley, chairman of the event; William Loeb, Jr., vice-president of RMA, is visible in back of Thompson; next to Loeb is probably William Gibbs McAdoo; and the man to the far left with his hands to his side may be Elihu Root, an RMA trustee. Sequence of Boy Scouts and members of the Naval Reserve preparing to raise the flag up a flagpole as an unidentified man leads the crowd in singing.

PERSONAL CREDITS: Urban, Charles, source. 1. Memorial rites and ceremonies. 2. Flags. 3. New York (City) 4. Roosevelt, Theodore, Pres. U.S., 1858–1919—Funeral and memorial services. 5. Lodge, Henry Cabot. 6. Allen, Henry J. 7. Thompson, William Boyce. 8. Lindsley, Henry D. 9. Loeb, William, 1866–1937. 10. McAdoo, William Gibbs. 11. Root, Elihu. 12. New York (City). Public Library. 13. Roosevelt Memorial Association. 14. Kansas. Governor, 1919–1923 (Henry J. Allen) 15. Boy Scouts of America. 16. United States. Naval Reserve. I. Theodore Roosevelt Association Collection. [mp 76–20]

Memorializing Roosevelt.
Roosevelt Memorial Association [1925?]
© No reg.
    lr, 422 ft. si. b&w. 35mm. ref print.
    lr, 422 ft. si. b&w. 35mm. dupe neg.
    lr, 422 ft. si. b&w. 35mm. masterpos.
SHELF LOC'N: FEA9949 (print); FPB9663 (neg); FPB9664 (fgmp)
Ref sources: Roosevelt Memorial Association. *Annual Report.* 1921: 9; 1924: 12–14; 1925: 18, 22; 1926: 20; P&P portrait file.
Factual; still photography.
SUMMARY: Still photos and interior titles describe the Roosevelt Memorial Association and the Women's Theodore Roosevelt Memorial Association activities, "To perpetuate the ideals of Theodore Roosevelt by spreading the knowledge of his character and career." Projects such as the cataloging of TR's correspondence at the Library of Congress by a woman who may be Elizabeth K. Fitzpatrick are described. Still of a woman who is probably Ethel M. Armes and Joe Murray as Murray participates in

Miss Armes's series of Roosevelt anecdotes, "Roosevelt's Trail." TR's friends are interviewed; stills of TR's cowboy friends on the banks of the Little Missouri River; photo of a man who may be Daniel C. Beard, Gifford Pinchot, and a third unidentified man. Albert Bushnell Hart and an assistant work on a collection of TR quotations, "The Theodore Roosevelt Cyclopedia, " at Harvard University.

1. New York (City). Roosevelt House. 2. Cowboys. 3. New York (City) 4. Washington, D.C. 5. Little Missouri River. 6. Boston, Mass. 7. Roosevelt, Theodore, Pres. U.S., 1858–1919—Anecdotes. 8. Roosevelt, Theodore, Pres. U.S., 1858–1919—Personality. 9. Fitzpatrick, Elizabeth K. 10. Armes, Ethel M. 11. Murray, Joe. 12. Beard, Daniel C. 13. Pinchot, Gifford. 14. Hart, Albert Bushnell, Theodore Roosevelt cyclopedia. 15. Roosevelt, Theodore, Pres. U.S., 1858–1919—Quotations. 16. Roosevelt Memorial Association. 17. Women's Theodore Roosevelt Memorial Association. 18. United States. Library of Congress. 19. Harvard University. Library. I. Roosevelt Memorial Association. II. Roosevelt Memorial Association, source. III. Theodore Roosevelt Association Collection. [mp 76–365]

Moving exhibits into Roosevelt House, 1923.
Producer unknown, Oct 1923.

© No reg.

lr, 93 ft. si. b&w. 16mm. ref print (cy 1-2 cy)
lr, 231 ft. si. b&w. 35mm. ref print (cy 2)
lr, 93 ft. si. b&w. 16mm. dupe neg (cy 1)
lr, 231 ft. si. b&w. 35mm. dupe neg (cy 2)
lr, 231 ft. si. b&w. 35mm. masterpos.
lr, 93 ft. si. b&w. 16mm. archival pos.
lr, 232 ft. si. b&w. 35mm. pos ntr.
lr, 232 ft. si. b&w. 35mm. neg ntr.
SHELF LOC'N: FAB751 & 752 (print, cy 1-2 cy); FEA6753 (print, cy 2); FRA5807 (neg, cy 1); FPB7594 (neg, cy 2); FPB7595 (fgmp); FRA5806 (arch pos)

Ref print (cy 1-cy 2) and dupe neg (cy 1) appear under RMA title: *Roosevelt Relics Arrive at Roosevelt House, 1924.*

Ref print (cy 1-cy 2) has ca. 1 ft. of slug at ca. ft. 80.

Ref source: *The Roosevelt Quarterly.* v. 2, no. 2, 1924; v. 3, no. 1, 1925.

Factual.

SUMMARY: In preparation for the ceremonial dedication of Roosevelt House, TR's birthplace at 28 E. Twentieth St., New York City, a moving van filled with TR memorabilia is unloaded in Oct.

1923. Parking in front of the brownstone, restored by the Women's Roosevelt Memorial Association and to be dedicated on TR's birthday, Oct. 27, the movers display for the camera the following items: framed etchings, photographs, etc., of TR; a worn chair used by him in the White House and presented to the Roosevelt Memorial Association by President Harding; TR's baby crib; items form TR's western adventures, such as a lariat, a saddle, a pistol, a sword, a gun, and antlers. Exterior view of the stairs and entrance to Roosevelt House, with a floor repairer working in the doorway; one shot from inside the house of movers entering with their loads.

1. New York (City). Roosevelt House. 2. New York (City) 3. Roosevelt, Theodore, Pres. U.S., 1858–1919—Birthplace. 4. Roosevelt, Theodore, Pres. U.S., 1858–1919—Homes. 5. Women's Theodore Roosevelt Memorial Association. I. Roosevelt Memorial Association, source. II. Theodore Roosevelt Association Collection. [mp 76–59]

Mr. Garfield presenting medals to 1929 medalists.
Producer unknown, Oct 1929.

© No reg.

lr, 41 ft. sd. b&w. 16mm. ref print.
lr, 41 ft. sd. b&w. 16mm. dupe neg (cy 1)
lr, 41 ft. si. b&w. 16mm. dupe neg (cy 2)
lr, 102 ft. sd. b&w. 35mm. pos ntr.
SHELF LOC'N: FAB1079 (print); FRA6051 (neg, cy 1); FRA6052 (neg, cy 2)

Ref sources: P&P portrait file; Roosevelt Memorial Association. *Annual Report.* 1930: 11; *Roosevelt House Bulletin.* v. 3, no. 7, 1929: 3.

Newsfilm; views.

SUMMARY: On Oct. 27, 1929, during a banquet at Roosevelt House in New York City, James R. Garfield, president of RMA, presents the Roosevelt Medals for Distinguished Service to: Dr. Herbert Putnam, Librarian of Congress, for the administration of public office; Owen D. Young, statesman, in the field of international affairs; and Owen Wister, author, in the field of American literature. Medium shot of the ceremony, with Garfield standing to the immediate right, followed by Putnam, Young, and Wister. A large photo of TR is visible in the center of the film.

PERSONAL CREDITS: Fox, William, source.

1. Medalists. 2. New York (City). Roosevelt House. 3. Roosevelt Medal for Distinguished Service. 4. New York (City) 5. Garfield, James R. 6. Roosevelt, Theodore, Pres. U.S., 1858–1919—Medals. 7. Putnam, Herbert. 8. Young, Owen D. 9. Wister, Owen. 10. Roosevelt Memorial Association.

I. Theodore Roosevelt Association Collection. [mp 76–201]

Mr. Hagedorn and Mr. Akeley at Roosevelt House, 1925 [1]

Producer unknown [1925?]

© No reg.

lr, 211 ft. si. b&w. 35mm. ref print.

lr, 211 ft. si. b&w. 35mm. dupe neg.

lr, 211 ft. si. b&w. 35mm. masterpos.

lr, 211 ft. si. b&w. 35mm. neg ntr.

SHELF LOC'N: FEA7316 (print); FPB7748 (neg); FPB8232 (fgmp)

Possible production dates: 1923–1926; Roosevelt House opened 10/27/23; Akeley died 11/17/26.

The RMA list indicates that the photographer is E. Maase.

Film sequence is repeated.

Ref. source: P&P portrait file.

Factual; views.

SUMMARY: Various views from many different camera angles of Hermann Hagedorn, RMA director and secretary, and Carl E. Akeley, RMA trustee, in Roosevelt House: Hagedorn, standing on the stage in the auditorium and speaking, introduces Akeley, who stands and speaks; medium and close shots of Hagedorn speaking; two takes of Akeley sitting at a desk, unfolding a letter, putting on glasses, reading the letter and marking it with a pen; the stage in the auditorium is empty except for three chairs and a table with a book and papers on it; Hagedorn and Akeley enter, Akeley sits, Hagedorn speaks and introduces Akeley, who speaks as Hagedorn sits down; the final view is a medium shot of Akeley speaking.

PERSONAL CREDITS: Maase, E., photographer.

1. New York (City). Roosevelt House. 2. New York (City) 3. Hagedorn, Hermann. 4. Akeley, Carl E. 5. Roosevelt Memorial Association. I. Roosevelt Memorial Association, source. II. Theodore Roosevelt Association Collection. [mp 76–312]

Mr. Hagedorn and Mr. Akeley at Roosevelt House, 1925 [2]

Producer unknown [1925?]

© No reg.

lr, 137 ft. si. b&w. 35mm. ref print.

lr, 137 ft. si. b&w. 35mm. dupe neg.

lr, 137 ft. si. b&w. 35mm. masterpos.

lr, 137 ft. si. b&w. 35mm. neg ntr.

SHELF LOC'N: FEA7317 (print); FPB7749 (neg); FPB8228 (fgmp)

Possible production dates: 1923–1926; Roosevelt House opened 10/27/23; Akeley died 11/17/26.

The RMA list indicates that the photographer is E. Maase.

Film sequence is repeated.

Ref source: P&P portrait file.

Factual; views.

SUMMARY: Various views from many different camera angles of Hermann Hagedorn, RMA director and secretary, and Carl E. Akeley, RMA trustee, in Roosevelt House: Akeley is shown standing and speaking on the stage in the auditorium; view of Akeley speaking, Hagedorn sitting behind Akeley, and a bust of TR; a close-up of Akeley speaking fades out to a motion picture screen; side view of Akeley speaking; the final view is a close shot of Hagedorn at a desk, browsing through a notebook.

PERSONAL CREDITS: Maase, E., photographer.

1. New York (City). Roosevelt House. 2. New York (City) 3. Hagedorn, Hermann. 4. Akeley, Carl E. 5. Roosevelt Memorial Association. I. Roosevelt Memorial Association, source. II. Theodore Roosevelt Association Collection. [mp 76–313]

Mr. Hagedorn and Mr. Akeley at Roosevelt House, 1925 [3]

Producer unknown [1925?]

© No reg.

lr, 355 ft. si. b&w. 35mm. ref print (2 cy)

lr, 355 ft. si. b&w. 35mm. dupe neg (2 cy)

lr, 357 ft. si. b&w. 35mm. pos ntr.

SHELF LOC'N: FEA7318 & 7319 (print, 2 cy); FPB7750 & 7751 (neg. 2 cy)

Possible production dates: 1923–1926; Roosevelt House opened 10/27/23; Akeley died 11/17/26.

The RMA list indicates that the photographer is E. Maase.

Film sequence is repeated.

Ref source: P&P portrait file.

Factual; views.

SUMMARY: Various views from many different camera angles of Hermann Hagedorn, RMA director and secretary, and Carl E. Akeley, RMA trustee, in Roosevelt House. The stage in the auditorium is empty except for three chairs and a table with a book and papers on it; Hagedorn and Akeley enter, Akeley sits, Hagedorn speaks and introduces Akeley, who speaks as Hagedorn sits; view of Akeley, Hagedorn sitting behind him, and a bust of TR; a close-up of Akeley speaking fades out to a motion picture screen; Hagedorn is shown sitting at a desk browsing through a notebook and looking into space as if thinking; view of Hagedorn standing and talking in the auditorium; two takes of Akeley sitting at a desk, unfolding a letter, putting on glasses, reading the letter and marking it with a pen.

PERSONEL CREDITS: Maase, E., photographer.

1. New York (City). Roosevelt House. 2. New York (City) 3. Hagedorn, Hermann. 4. Akeley, Carl E. 5. Roosevelt Memorial Association. I. Roosevelt Memorial Association, source. II. Theodore Roosevelt Association Collection. [mp 76–314]

Mr. Hagedorn and Mrs. Wood at Roosevelt House [1924, Long version]

Roosevelt memorial Association [1924?]

© No reg.

lr, 70 ft. si. b&w 16mm. ref print.
lr, 70 ft. si. b&w 16mm. dupe neg.
lr, 70 ft. si. b&w 16mm. archival pos.
lr, 175 ft. si. b&w. 35mm. neg ntr.

SHELF LOC'N: FAB708 (print); FRA8647 (neg); FRA5764 (arch pos)

RMA lists the date in the title as 1925; edge code date on nitrate is 1924.

Sequence of scenes varies from that of short version with the same title.

The RMA list indicates that the photographer is E. Maase.

Ref. source: *The Roosevelt Quarterly.* v. 2, no. 1, 1924: 1.

Factual.

SUMMARY: Scenes of Hermann Hagedorn, director and secretary of the Roosevelt Memorial Association, and Mrs. Henry A. Wise Wood, vice-president of the Women's Roosevelt Memorial Association and chairman of its Education Committee. In separate sequences first Hagedorn, then Wood appear seated at a desk in the library of Roosevelt House, birthplace of Theodore Roosevelt and headquarters of the Women's Roosevelt Memorial Association. In the final sequence Hagedorn and Wood, seated at the desk, talk together.

PERSONAL CREDITS: Maase, E., photographer.

1. New York (City). Roosevelt House. 2. New York (City) 3. Hagedorn, Hermann. 4. Wood, Elizabeth Ogden Brower. 5. Roosevelt Memorial Association. 6. Women's Theodore Roosevelt Memorial Association. I. Roosevelt Memorial Association. II. Roosevelt Memorial Association, source. III. Theodore Roosevelt Association Collection. [mp 76–35]

Mr. Hagedorn and Mrs. Wood at Roosevelt House [1924, Short version]
Roosevelt Memorial Association [1924?]

© No reg.

lr, 52 ft. si. b&w. 16mm. ref print.
lr, 52 ft. si. b&w. 16mm. dupe neg.
lr, 133 ft. si. b&w. 35mm. pos ntr.

SHELF LOC'N: FAB707 (print); FRA5763 (neg)

RMA lists the date in the title as 1925; edge code date on nitrate is 1924.

Sequence of scenes varies from that of the long version with the same title.

The RMA list indicates that the photgrapher is E. Maase.

Ref source: *The Roosevelt Quarterly.* v. 2, no. 1, 1924: 1.

Factual.

SUMMARY: Scenes of Hermann Hagedorn, director and secretary of the Roosevelt Memorial Association, and Mrs. Henry A. Wise Wood, vice-president of the Women's Roosevelt Memorial Association and chairman of its Education Committee. In separate sequences first Hagedorn, then Wood appear seated at a desk in the library of Roosevelt House, birthplace of Theodore Roosevelt and headquarters of the Women's Roosevelt Memorial Association. In the final sequence Hagedorn and Wood, seated at the desk, talk together.

PERSONAL CREDITS: Maase, E., photographer.

1. New York (City). Roosevelt House. 2. New York (City) 3. Hagedorn, Hermann. 4. Wood, Elizabeth Ogden Brower. 5. Roosevelt Memorial Association. 6. Women's Theodore Roosevelt Memorial Association. I. Roosevelt Memorial Association. II. Roosevelt Memorial Association, source. III. Theodore Roosevelt Association Collection. [mp 76–36]

Mrs. Roosevelt, Sr., and Mrs. J. H. Hammond photographed on the roof of Roosevelt House, 1927; Mrs. Roosevelt arrives at Roosevelt House.

Producer unknown, Apr 1927.

© No reg.

lr, 53 ft. si. b&w. 35mm. ref print (cy 1)
lr, 51 ft. si. b&w. 35mm. ref print (cy 2)
lr, 53 ft. si. b&w. 35mm. dupe neg (cy 1)
lr, 51 ft. si. b&w. 35mm. dupe neg (cy 2)
lr, 53 ft. si. b&w. 35mm. masterpos.
lr, 51 ft. si. b&w. 35mm. pos ntr.
lr, 53 ft. si. b&w. 35mm. neg ntr.

SHELF LOC'N: FEA7303 (print, cy 1); FEA7315 (print, cy 2); FPB7599 (neg, cy

1); FPB7747 (neg, cy 2); FPB 7600 (fgmp)

Ref sources: The New York *Herald Tribune.* 4/4/27: 15; 4/5/27: 18, 25; New York (City). Roosevelt House. Photographic file.

Factual.

SUMMARY: Mrs. Edith Roosevelt is helped out of a car by a chauffeur. She is probably arriving at Roosevelt House, TR's birthplace in New York City, for a tea held in her honor Apr. 4, 1927, by the Women's Roosevelt Memorial Association. The second sequence consists of medium shots of Mrs. Roosevelt talking to Mrs. John Henry Hammond, president of the WRMA, as both women stand in front of a brick wall.

1. New York (City). Roosevelt House. 2. New York (City) 3. Roosevelt, Edith. 4. Hammond, Emily Vanderbilt Sloane. 5. Women's Theodore Roosevelt Memorial Association. I. Pathe, source. II. Theodore Roosevelt Association Collection. III. Mrs. Roosevelt arrives at Roosevelt House, 1927 [Title] [mp 76–237]

Mrs. Theodore Roosevelt Jr. attends Women in War Work Congress in Paris [1918]

Mutual Film Corp., Aug 1918.

© No reg.

lr, 40 ft. si. b&w. 35mm. ref print.

lr, 40 ft. si. b&w. 35mm. dupe neg.

lr, 40 ft. si. b&w. 35mm. pos ntr.

(Screen telegram [Series])

SHELF LOC'N: FEA7304 (print); FPB7601 (neg)

RMA lists the dates in the tital as 1917–1918.

Mutual Film Corp. produced and released Screen telegram from Mar.–Nov., 1918.

Ref sources: Roosevelt, Eleanor Butler Alexander, *Day before Yesterday.* 1959: 76–118; P&P portrait file; United States. National Archives and Records Service. Audiovisual Archives Division; United States. War Dept. General Staff. *Catalogue of Official A.E.F. Photographs Taken by the Signal Corps.* 1919: 226.

Newsfilm.

SUMMARY: During World War I, Mrs. Theodore Roosevelt, Jr., worked for the YMCA in France running canteens, clubs, and leave centers for soldiers and teaching French. She also designed the uniforms worn by the women workers in the YMCA. Views of Mrs. Roosevelt entertaining women YMCA workers in the garden of the home of her aunt, Mrs. Alice Green Hoffman, in Paris. There are medium-close shots of Mrs. Roosevelt,

In 1917 Eleanor Alexander Roosevelt, wife of Theodore Roosevelt, Jr., went to Paris to work for the YMCA against the wishes of both her husband and her father-in-law. She appears in this 1918 family snapshot in the uniform she designed for the women YMCA workers.

the woman not wearing a hat, as she stands among a group of women.

CITATION: MPW38.2: 988.

1. European War. 1914–1918—War work—Y.M.C.A. 2. European War, 1914–1918—Women's work. 3. Paris. 4. Roosevelt, Eleanor Butler Alexander. 5. Young Men's Christian Associations. I.

Mutual Film Corporation. II. International News-reel Corporation, source. III. Theodore Roosevelt Association Collection. [mp 76–226]

Original U.S. documents.
Producer unknown, Jan 1920.
© No reg.
  lr, 45 ft. si. b&w. 16mm. ref print.
  lr, 45 ft. si. b&w. 16mm. dupe neg.
  lr, 112 ft. si. b&w. 35mm. pos ntr.
SHELF LOC'N: FAB758 (print); FRA5813 (neg)
Ref sources: P&P portrait file; The New York *Times Mid-week Pictorial,* v. 10, no. 22, 1920: [20]
Newsfilm.
SUMMARY: The Declaration of Independence and United States Constitution are displayed for students in the State Dept. on Jan. 15, 1920, prior to their transfer by President Harding to the Library of Congress as a safety measure in 1921. Aided by two men, Secretary of State Robert Lansing (1915–1920) pulls a document from a cabinet. Views of young women filing past documents under glass. Close shots of the Declaration; Articles V, VI, and VII of the Constitution; signatures of George Washington and other delegates to the Constitutional Convention from Connecticut, Massachusetts, New York, and New Hampshire.
1. United States—Public buildings. 2. Washington, D.C. 3. Lansing, Robert. 4. United States. Dept of State. 5. United States. Declaration of Independence. 6. United States. Constitution. 7. United States. Constitution—Signers. I. Community Motion Picture Service, inc., source. II. Theodore Roosevelt Association Collection. [mp 76–58]

Oscar Straus.
Producer unknown [191–?]
© No reg.
  lr, 6 ft. si. b&w. 16mm. ref print (cy 1)
  lr, 14 ft. si. b&w. 35mm. ref print (cy 2)
  lr, 6 ft. si. b&w. 16mm. dupe neg (cy 1)
  lr, 14 ft. si. b&w. 35mm. dupe neg (cy 2)
  lr, 15 ft. si. b&w. 35mm. pos. ntr.
SHELF LOC'N: FAB839 (print, cy 1); FEA6749 (print, cy 2); FRA5841 (neg, cy 1); FPB7587 (neg, cy 2)
Ref source: P&P portrait file.
Factual; views.
SUMMARY: Close shot of Oscar S. Straus, author, United States ambassador, member of the Permanent Court of Arbitration at The Hague for six thee-year terms beginning in 1902, and secretary of commerce and labor in TR's cabinet (1906–1909).

Oscar S. Straus served as a member of the Permanent Court of Arbitration at the Hague, as secretary of commerce and labor in TR's cabinet (1906–9), and as U.S. ambassador to Turkey.

Seated at a desk, Straus answers a telephone and talks.
PERSONAL CREDITS: Straus, Roger, source.
1. Straus, Oscar S. I. Theodore Roosevelt Association Collection. [mp 76–243]

Owen D. Young [1]
Kinogram Pub. Corp., 1927
© No reg.
  lr, 11 ft. si. b&w. 16mm. ref print.
  lr, 11 ft. si. b&w. 16mm. archival pos (2 cy)
(Kinograms [Series])
SHELF LOC'N: FAB876 (print); FRA5862 & 5863 (arch pos, 2 cy)
Ref sources: P&P portrait file; Tarbell, Ida M. *Owen D. Young.* 1932.
Newsfilm.
SUMMARY: Scenes of Owen D. Young, chairman of the board of General Electric and coauthor with Charles G. Dawes of the Dawes Plan for German reparations, in various locations. At Harvard University on June 4, 1927, Young speaks at

the dedication of buildings comprising the Graduate School of Business Administration. View of Young speaking from a podium, with the donor of the buildings, George F. Baker, identified in the group seated behind him; panning shot of the audience. At a separate location Young and other men are seated around a conference table with crowds pressed around them. Close shot of Young outdoors, in hat and coat, at an unidentified location.

1. Dedication services. 2. Cambridge, Mass. 3. Boston, Mass. 4. Young, Owen D. 5. Baker, George F. 6. Harvard University. 7. Harvard University. Graduate School of Business Administration. I. Kinogram Publishing Corporation. II. Roosevelt Memorial Association, source. III. Theodore Roosevelt Association Collection. [mp 76–97]

Owen D. Young [2]
Kinogram Pub. Corp., 1927.
© No reg.
  lr, 30 ft. si. b&w. 16mm. ref print.
  lr, 30 ft. si. b&w. 16mm. dupe neg.

Owen Wister, author of *The Virginian*, was a Harvard classmate and close friend of TR's.

  lr, 74 ft. si. b&w. 35mm. pos ntr.
(Kinograms [Series])
  SHELF LOC'N: FAB877 (print); FRA5864 (neg)
  Ref sources: P&P portrait file; Tarbell, Ida M. *Owen D. Young*. 1932.
  Newsfilm.
  SUMMARY: Scenes of Owen D. Young, chairman of the board of General Electric and coauthor with Charles G. Dawes of the Dawes Plan for German reparations, in various locations. Young speaks at the dedication of buildings comprising the Graduate School of Business Administration, Harvard University, on June 4, 1927. Panning shots of campus buildings; Young speaks from a podium, with the donor of the new buildings, George F. Baker, identified in the group seated behind him; panning shots of the audience seated during the ceremony and standing informally. At a separate location Young and other men are seated around a conference table surrounded by a crowd. Close shot of Young outdoors at an unidentified location.

1. Dedication services. 2. Cambridge, Mass. 3. Boston, Mass. 4. Young, Owen D. 5. Baker, George F. 6. Harvard University. 7. Harvard University. Graduate School of Business Administration. I. Kinogram Publishing Corporation. II. Kinogram Publishing Corporation, source. III. Theodore Roosevelt Association Collection. [mp 76–96]

Owen Wister.
Producer unknown [192–?]
© No reg.
  lr, 45 ft. si. b&w. 16mm. ref print.
  lr, 45 ft. si. b&w. 16mm. archival pos (cy 1)
  lr, 41 ft. si. b&w. 16mm. archival pos (cy 2)
  SHELF LOC'N: FAB831 (print); FRA5818 (arch pos, cy 1); FRA5819 (arch pos, cy 2)
  Archival pos (cy 2) is shorter than arch pos (cy 1) due to briefer scenes, with no apparent content lost.
  Ref sources: Wister, Owen. *Owen Wister Out West*. 1958; Vorpahl, Ben M. *My Dear Wister*. 1972.
  Factual; views.
  SUMMARY: Owen Wister, author of *The Virginian* and other western novels and a close friend of Theodore Roosevelt, appears outdoors on a country estate and seated at a desk, location(s) unknown. Wister walks toward the camera through trees on a large, sloping lawn; comes out the front door of an ivy-covered, two-storied home onto a terrace, and sits on a stone bench; picks a flower outside the doorway and puts it into his lapel; view of Wister

indoors, writing at a desk. The location may be Butler Place, a family estate in the vicinity of Philadelphia, Pa.

1. Wister, Owen. I. Kinogram Publishing Corporation, source. II. Theodore Roosevelt Association Collection. [mp 76–78]

Oyster Bay from the air [1919]
Producer unknown, Oct 1919.
   © No reg.
      lr, 25 ft. si. b&w. 16mm. ref print.
      lr, 25 ft. si. b&w. 16mm. archival pos.
   SHELF LOC'N: FAB1066 (print); FRA6040 (arch pos)
RMA lists the date in the title as 1920.
Ref sources: New York *Tribune*. 10/21/19: 6; The New York *Herald*. 10/21/19: 2.
Newsfilm; views.
SUMMARY: On Oct. 20, 1919, as part of opening day ceremonies to honor TR and raise funds for the restoration of Roosevelt House in New York City, military aviators flew from Hazelhurst Field, Mineola, N.Y., to Oyster Bay to drop wreaths on TR's gravesite in Youngs Memorial Cemetery. The film has aerial views of at least three biplanes flying, with a camera in one of the planes, over what is probably Oyster Bay and the surrounding area; medium-close shot of one plane flying toward the camera.
PERSONAL CREDITS: Urban, Charles, source.
1. Airplanes. 2. Air pilots. 3. Oyster Bay, N.Y. 4. Oyster Bay, N.Y.—Description—Aerial. 5. Roosevelt, Theodore, Pres. U.S., 1858–1919—Funeral and memorial services. 6. United States. Army Air Forces. I. Theodore Roosevelt Association Collection. [mp 76–206]

Pack mules with ammunition on the Santiago trail, Cuba.
Thomas A. Edison, 1898.
   © 46693, Thomas A. Edison, 5 Aug 1898
      lr of 1, 24 ft. si. b&w. 16mm. ref print (cy 1)
      lr of 1, 59 ft. si. b&w. 35mm. ref print (cy 2–2 cy)
      lr of 1, 24 ft. si. b&w. 16mm. dupe neg.
      lr of 1, 24 ft. si. b&w. 16mm. archival pos.
      lr of 1, 60 ft. si. b&w. 35mm. neg ntr.
      lr of 1, 25 ft. si. b&w. 16mm. ref print.
      lr of 1, 25 ft. si. b&w. 16mm. dupe neg.
      lr of 1, 48 ft. si. b&w. 35mm. paper (2 cy)
   SHELF LOC'N: FAB1215 (print, cy 1-RMA); FEA7324 & 7618 (print, cy 2–2 cy-RMA); FRA 6177 (neg-RMA); FRA6110 (arch pos-RMA); FLA3337 (print-Paper); FRA 0648 (neg-Paper); LC323 (paper, 2 cy-Paper)
RMA title: *Pack Mules on Trail, 1898.*
The location in the title is unverified.
RMA copies include an additional sequence at the beginning of the film.
Ref sources: *Photographic History of the Spanish-American War.* 1898: 224–225, 238; Westein, Irving. *1898: the Spanish-American War.* 1966: 41.
Factual; war film.
SUMMARY: About 12,000 mules were taken to Cuba and used primarily for transporting immediate reserves of small-arms ammunition during the Spanish-American War. A group of mules loaded with boxes of ammunition is being driven along a trail, probably near Santiago, Cuba. Some of the men may be civilian mule skinners hired by the Army to handle the pack mules.
PERSONAL CREDITS: Kleine, George, source.
1. Ammunition—Transportation. 2. Mules. 3. Military supplies. 4. Muleteers. 5. Pack transportation. 6. Transportation, Military. 7. Trails—Cuba. 8. Cuba. 9. United States—History—War of 1898—Supplies. I. Edison (Thomas A.) inc. II. Theodore Roosevelt Association Collection. III. Paper Print Collection. [mp 76–252]

The Panama Canal.
Roosevelt Film Library [1927?]
   © No reg.
      2r of 2, 1660 ft. si. b&w. 35mm. ref print.
      2r of 2, 1660 ft. si. b&w. 35mm. dupe neg.
      2r of 2, 1660 ft. si. b&w. 35mm. pos ntr.
   SHELF LOC'N: FEA7831, 7836 (print); FPB 9908–9909 (neg)
The main title appears on reel two.
Ref sources: Roosevelt Memorial Association. *Annual Report.* 1927: 17–18; Avery, Ralph E. *America's Triumph at Panama.* 1913; Roosevelt Memorial Association. *The Panama Canal* (script)
Factual; industrial, compilation.
SUMMARY: Compilation film revealing the story of the Panama Canal's construction, which TR considered one of his most valuable contributions to foreign affairs. The most prominent views are those demonstrating the need for building the canal, and those of the early attempts, the actual construction, and finally the canal in operation. Sequences of stills, mostly maps, showing the need for a shorter way from ocean to ocean; views of the early attempts by Ferdinand de Lesseps; the USS

Oregon, which had to sail around South America from the Pacific to fight in the Spanish-American War; scenes of President William McKinley and TR in 1901; a brief shot of TR. Lyman J. Gage, Philander C. Knox, Ethan Allen Hitchcock, William R. Day, Elihu Root, Charles E. Smith, and James Wilson at McKinley's funeral in Canton, Ohio, 1901; medium-close shot of Dr. William C. Gorgas, who had charge of sanitation during the building of the Panama Canal; workers clearing the canal of yellow fever; TR's visit to Panama in 1906 and his meeting with President Manuel Amador Guerrero; scenes of Secretary of War William Howard Taft's visit to the canal in Nov. 1904; medium-close shot of Col. George W. Goethals, chief engineer and first governor; sequences of machinery, huge cranes, gigantic steam shovels and men working on the actual construction of the canal; various shots of Gamboa Dike, Miraflores Locks, and Gaillard (Culebra) Cut; launch of two barges in a lock, boats, and battleships using the canal; the final sequence shows President Calvin Coolidge speaking.

PERSONAL CREDITS: Gentry, Caroline, editor.

1. Canals, Interoceanic. 2. Battleships. 3. Yellow fever—Panama Canal—Prevention. 4. Construction equipment. 5. Construction workers. 6. Locks (Hydraulic engineering) 7. Panama Canal. 8. Canal Zone. 9. Gorgas, William C. 10. Taft, William Howard, Pres. U.S., 1857–1930. 11. Goethals, George W. 12. Oregon (Ship) 13. United States. President, 1897–1901 (McKinley) 14. United States. President, 1901–1909 (Roosevelt) 15. Panama. Presidente, 1904–1908 (Amador Guerrero) 16. United States. President, 1923–1929 (Coolidge) I. Roosevelt Memorial Association. Film Library. II. Roosevelt Memorial Association, source. III. Theodore Roosevelt Association Collection. [mp 76–320]

Panama Canal Scenes.
Producer unknown [191–?]
  © No reg.
    lr, 182 ft. si. b&w. 16mm. ref print.
    lr, 182 ft. si. b&w. 16mm. dupe neg.
    lr, 456 ft. si. b&w. 35mm. pos ntr.
  SHELF LOC'N: FAB1116 (print); FRA6059 (neg)
The earliest possible production date is 1914, since the Panama Canal was not officially in operation until 1914.
  Ref sources: Avery, Ralph E. *America's Triumph at Panama.* 1913; Roosevelt Memorial Association. *The Panama Canal* (script)
  Factual; industrial, views.

SUMMARY: Various views of the Panama Canal during its construction, which TR considered one of his most valuable contributions to foreign affairs. The most prominent views are of the construction machinery, such as dredges, steam shovels, cranes, concrete mixers, and hydraulic pumps, in operation; construction workers dynamiting for excavation purposes; drill operations; final views are of the construction of the locks and the testing of the lock gates upon completion.

1. Canals, Interoceanic. 2. Construction equipment. 3. Construction workers. 4. Dynamite. 5. Locks (Hydraulic engineering) 6. Panama Canal. 7. Canal Zone. I. Paramount, source. II. Theodore Roosevelt Association Collection. [mp 76–321]

Panama Canal; scenes of the finished Canal.
Producer unknown [1919?]
  © No reg.
    lr, 358 ft. si. b&w. 16mm. ref print.
    lr, 358 ft. si. b&w. 16mm. archival pos.
    lr, 895 ft. si. b&w. 35mm. neg ntr.
  SHELF LOC'N: FAB1115 (print); FRA6058 (arch pos)
Edge code date on nitrate is 1919.
Flash titles are very dark.
  Ref sources: Abbot, Willis J. *Panama and the Canal.* 1913; Avery, Ralph E. *America's Triumph at Panama.* 1913.
  Factual views.

SUMMARY: Scenes of the Panama Canal, generally in the natural order of passage, from a ship moving from the Atlantic to the Pacific. The ship passes by the Panamanian city of Colón on the Atlantic end, through the channel to Gatun Locks and into Gatun Lake; views of the Gatun spillway and the Chagres River. From here she passes from Gaillard (Culebra) Cut into the Pedro Miguel Locks and into Miraflores Locks and into the final portion of the canal, and passing the Canal Zone towns of Ancon, Balboa, and Balboa Heights. Final views are of the Ancon (Gorgas) Hospital and the U.S. Administration Building at Balboa.

PERSONAL CREDITS: Lewis, Samuel, source.

1. Canals, Interoceanic. 2. Ships. 3. Locks (Hydraulic engineering) 4. Spillways. 5. Panama Canal. 6. Panama Canal—Navigation. 7. Colón, Panama. 8. Gatun Lake. 9. Chagres River. 10. Miraflores Lake. 11. Ancon, Canal Zone. 12. Balboa, Canal Zone. 13. Balboa Heights, Canal Zone. 14. Balboa, Canal Zone—Buildings. 15. United States—Public buildings—Balboa, Canal Zone. I. Theodore Roosevelt Association Collection. [mp 76–322]

Presentation of Roosevelt Medals, May 1925, Washington, D.C.

Roosevelt Memorial Association, May 1925.

© No reg.

    lr, 153 ft. si. b&w. 35mm. ref print (2 cy)

    lr, 153 ft. si. b&w. 35mm. dupe neg (2 cy)

    lr, 153 ft. si. b&w. 35mm. masterpos.

    lr, 151 ft. si. b&w. 35mm. pos ntr.

    lr, 154 ft. si. b&w. 35mm. neg ntr.

SHELF LOC'N: FEA6725 & 6726 (print, 2 cy);
               FPB 7130 & 7131 (neg, 2 cy);
               FPB7129 (fgmp)

Film is slightly out of frame.

Ref sources: Roosevelt Memorial Association. *Annual Report.* 1925: 15, 20, 35; P&P portrait file.

Factual; views.

SUMMARY: On May 15, 1925, the Roosevelt Medal for Distinguished Service was presented to Gifford Pinchot, Martha Berry, and George Grinnell by President Calvin Coolidge in the White House. The film consists of close shots of nine men, all members of the RMA's Board of Trustees. In order of appearance they are: 1) Alexander Lambert; 2) Albert Shaw; 3) James R. Garfield; 4) Gifford Pinchot; 5) Raymond Robins; 6) Mark Sullivan; 7) Carl E. Akeley; 8) an unidentified man; and 9) Edwin A. Van Valkenburg.

1. Roosevelt Medal for Distinguished Service. 2. Washington, D.C. 3. Roosevelt, Theodore, Pres. U.S., 1858–1919—Medals. 4. Pinchot, Gifford. 5. Lambert, Alexander. 6. Shaw, Albert. 7. Garfield, James R. 8. Robins, Raymond. 9. Sullivan, Mark. 10. Akeley, Carl E. 11. Van Valkenburg, Edwin A. 12. Roosevelt Memorial Association. Board of Trustees. I. Roosevelt Memorial Association. II. Kinogram Publishing Corporation, source. III. Theodore Roosevelt Association Collection. [mp 76–117]

President Coolidge speaking at Black Hills, S.D., 1927.

Producer unknown, Aug 1927.

© No reg.

    lr, 8 ft. si. b&w. 16mm. ref print (3 cy)

    lr, 8 ft. si. b&w. 16mm. dupe neg.

    lr, 8 ft. si. b&w. 16mm. archival pos.

SHELF LOC'N: FAB872 & 1028 & 1128 (print,
               3 cy); FRA8659 (neg); FRA5858
               (arch pos)

Ref sources: Peattie, Roderick, ed. *The Black Hills.* 1952: 226–228; The *Daily Argus-Leader*, Sioux Falls, S.D. 8/10/27: 1; Fite, Gilbert C. *Mount Rushmore.* 1952.

Newsfilm.

SUMMARY: On Aug. 10, 1927, President Calvin Coolidge speaks at the dedication of Mount Rushmore, Keystone, S.D. Designed by Gutzon Borglum, the sculpture of the faces of Presidents Washington, Jefferson, Lincoln, and Roosevelt is ceremonially begun. Coolidge's speech, which is the first he has made since announcing his intention not to run for a second presidential term, concerns the particular merits of the four presidents whose faces will be cut into the mountainside. Views of the crowd looking toward the mountain; the eastern face of Mount Rushmore before carving; and President Coolidge speaking from notes, with sculptor Borglum and Sen. William H. McMaster of South Dakota identified in the crowd of dignitaries seated behind him.

1. Dedication services. 2. Granite sculpture—South Dakota. 3. Mount Rushmore National Memorial. 4. Black Hills, S.D. 5. Keystone, S.D. 6. Coolidge, Calvin, Pres. U.S., 1872–1933—Addresses, essays, lectures. 7. Borglum, Gutzon. 8. McMaster, William H. 9. United States. President, 1923–1929 (Coolidge) I. International Newsreel Corporation, source. II. Theodore Roosevelt Association Collection. [mp 76–100]

President Harding and Calvin Coolidge [1]

Producer unknown, Jul 1920.

© No reg.

    lr, 248 ft. si. b&w. 16mm. ref print.

    lr, 248 ft. si. b&w. 16mm. dupe neg.

    lr, 627 ft. si. b&w. 35mm. pos ntr.

SHELF LOC'N: FAB716 (print); FRA5778 (neg)

Ref sources: Republican Party. National Convention, 17th, Chicago, 1920. *Official Report of the Proceedings of the Seventeenth Republican National Convention.* 1920: 254–282; P&P presidential file; P&P portrait file.

Newsfilm; political.

SUMMARY: Various scenes of the official notification ceremonies held on July 22, 1920, for Warren G. Harding, selected as the presidential candidate by the Seventeenth Republican National Convention, and Calvin Coolidge, selected as the vice-presidential nominee. Opening views of Harding, followed by scenes of him and his wife, Florence Kling Harding, in Marion, Ohio; Harding, Coolidge, and Will H. Hays, Republican National Committee chairman, getting out of an auto with other members of the Republican party; several scenes from varying distances of Harding and his wife greeting large crowds, Harding delivering a

Henry Cabot Lodge, TR's friend and closest political confidant, appears in many films in the collection. Lodge served as senator from Massachusetts for thirty-one years.

Election—1920. 5. United States—Politics and government—1919–1933. 6. Marion, Ohio. 7. Northampton, Mass. 8. Plymouth, Vt. 9. Harding, Warren Gamaliel, Pres. U.S., 1865–1923. 10. Coolidge, Calvin, Pres. U.S., 1872–1933. 11. Harding, Florence Kling. 12. Hays, Will H. 13. Harding, George T. 14. Lodge, Henry Cabot. 15. Morrow, Edwin P. 16. Republican Party. 17. Republican Party. National Convention, 17th, Chicago, 1920. 18. Republican Party. Notification Committee, 1920. 19. Kentucky. Governor, 1919–1923 (Morrow) 20. Massachusetts. Governor, 1919–1921 (Coolidge) I. Community Motion Picture Service, inc., source. II. Theodore Roosevelt Association Collection. [mp 76–342]

President Harding and Calvin Coolidge [2]
Producer unknown, Jul 1920.
© No reg.
  1r, 252 ft. si. b&w. 16mm. ref print.
  1r, 252 ft. si. b&w. 16mm. dupe neg.
  1r, 625 ft. si. b&w. 35mm. pos ntr.
SHELF LOC'N: FAB717 (print); FRA5779 (neg)
Ref sources: Republican Party. National Convention, 17th, Chicago, 1920. *Official Report of the Proceedings of the Seventeenth Republican National Convention.* 1920: 254–282; Barck, Oscar T. [and] Blake, Nelson M. *Since 1900.* 1947: 324–326; P&P portrait file.

Newsfilm; political.

SUMMARY: Various scenes of the official notification ceremonies held on July 22, 1920, for Warren G. Harding, selected as the presidential candidate by the Seventeenth Republican National Convention, and Calvin Coolidge, selected as the vice-presidential nominee. Opening views of Harding, followed by views of him, Coolidge, and Will H. Hays, Republican National Committee chairman, getting out of an auto with other members of the Republican party; several scenes from varying distances of Harding and his wife, Florence Kling Harding, greeting large crowds, Harding delivering a speech from his porch, and standing in a formal receiving line shaking hands; close shot of a man, identified by interior title as Harding's father, George T. Harding; views of Hays opening the official ceremony, with Henry Cabot Lodge and other members of the Notification Committee visible on the speakers' platform. Sequences of Coolidge's notification ceremony held in Northampton, Mass.; views of Coolidge delivering his acceptance speech; views of Edwin P. Morrow, governor of Kentucky, incorrectly identified by interior title as

speech from his porch, and standing in a formal receiving line shaking hands; close shot of man, identified by interior title as Harding's father, George T. Harding; views of Hays opening the official ceremony, with Henry Cabot Lodge and other members of the Notification Committee visible on the speakers' platform. Sequences of Coolidge's notification ceremony held in Northampton, Mass.; views of Coolidge delivering his acceptance speech; views of Edwin P. Morrow, governor of Kentucky, incorrectly identified by interior title as Edward, delivering the formal notification speech; medium shot of Coolidge and Lodge, surrounded by a crowd; several sequences of Coolidge seated at his desk in Boston and performing duties in the rural setting of his home in Plymouth, Vt. Final scene of Harding, Coolidge, and Hays conversing outside the old Senate Office Building in Washington on June 30, with the Capitol visible in the background.

1. Political parties. 2. Presidents—United States—Nomination. 3. Washington, D.C. Capitol. Senate Office Building. 4. Presidents—United States—

Edward, delivering the formal notification speech; medium shot of Coolidge and Lodge, surrounded by a crowd, and of Coolidge seated at his desk in Boston. Following are unrelated segments on Washington, D.C., Yellowstone National Park, and the Muscle Shoals, Ala., area; panoramic views showing the heart of Washington, including the Capitol, many government buildings, monuments, and the surrounding area; many different views from varying distances of Yellowstone National Park, including mountains, lakes, waterfalls, and cataracts (this segment may be a Park Service advertisement); final sequence on the Muscle Shoals area, which was the site of a major utilities power struggle during the 20s; views of the Wilson Dam, Tennessee River, and tanks for production of atmospheric nitrogen, explosives, and fertilizers.

1. Political parties. 2. Presidents—United States—Nomination. 3. Presidents—United States—Election—1920. 4. Wilson Dam. 5. United States—Politics and government—1919–1933. 6. Marion, Ohio. 7. Northampton, Mass. 8. Washington, D.C. 9. Washington, D.C.—Description—Aerial. 10. Yellowstone National Park. 11. Muscle Shoals, Ala. 12. Harding, Warren Gamaliel, Pres. U.S., 1865–1923. 13. Coolidge, Calvin, Pres. U.S., 1872–1933. 14. Hays, Will H. 15. Harding, Florence Kling. 16. Harding, George T. 17. Lodge, Henry Cabot. 18. Morrow, Edwin P. 19. Republican Party. 20. Republican Party. National Convention, 17th, Chicago, 1920. 21. Republican Party. Notification Committee, 1920. 22. Kentucky, Governor, 1919–1923 (Morrow) 23. Massachusetts. Governor, 1919–1921 (Coolidge) I. Community Motion Picture Service, inc., source. II. Theodore Roosevelt Association Collection. [mp 76–343]

President Harding presenting chair used by TR at the White House to the directors of RMA, October 1921.

Producer unknown, Oct 1921.

© No reg.

lr, 28 ft. si. b&w. 16mm. ref print.
lr, 28 ft. si. b&w. 16mm. dupe neg.
lr, 28 ft. si. b&w. 16mm. archival pos.

SHELF LOC'N: FAB833 (print); FRA5832 (neg); FRA5833 (arch pos)

Ref source: P&P portrait file.

Newsfilm.

SUMMARY: On Oct. 5, 1921, President Harding officially presents TR's White House chair to prominent RMA members on the White House lawn. Harding, with his back to the camera, shakes hands with assembled men and then poses for the camera, seated in the chair; close shot of the worn chair. RMA members identified on the film include: William Boyce Thompson, head of the delegation and president of the association; Charles Evans Hughes, secretary of state and honorary president of the association; Henry C. Wallace, secretary of agriculture; Will H. Hays, postmaster general; Henry Cabot Lodge, Republican senator from Massachusetts; Frank B. Kellogg, Republican senator from Minnesota; Oscar S. Straus, secretary of commerce and labor in TR's Cabinet; Frederick C. Hicks, Republican congressman from New York; Dr. Alexander Lambert, TR's personal physician; Albert Shaw, editor of the *Review of Reviews*; Edwin A. Van Valkenburg, editor of the Philadelphia *North American*; Mark Sullivan, syndicated columnist and former editor of *Collier's*; Henry J. Whigham, publisher of *Metropolitan Magazine*; and Hermann Hagedorn, secretary of the RMA.

PERSONAL CREDITS: Fox, William, source.

1. Washington, D.C. White House. 2. Washington, D.C. 3. Harding, Warren Gamaliel, Pres. U.S.,1865–1923. 4. Roosevelt, Theodore, Pres. U.S., 1858–1919. 5. Thompson, William Boyce. 6. Hughes, Charles Evans. 7. Wallace, Henry C. 8. Hays, Will H. 9. Lodge, Henry Cabot. 10. Kellogg, Frank B. 11. Straus, Oscar S. 12. Hicks, Frederick C. 13. Lambert, Alexander. 14. Shaw, Albert. 15. Van Valkenburg, Edwin A. 16. Sullivan, Mark. 17. Whigham, Henry J. 18. Hagedorn, Hermann. 19. United States. President, 1921–1923 (Harding) 20. Roosevelt Memorial Association. I. Theodore Roosevelt Association Collection. [mp 76–75]

President McKinley inauguration, 1901.

Producer unknown, Mar 1901.

© No reg.

lr, 162 ft. si. b&w. 35mm. ref print.
lr, 162 ft. si. b&w. 35mm. dupe neg.
lr, 162 ft. si. b&w. 35mm. pos ntr.

SHELF LOC'N: FEA8962 (print); FPB9925 (neg)

Ref sources: Washington, D.C. Inaugural Committee, 1901. *Official Souvenir Program, Inaugural Ceremonies, March 4, 1901*.[1901]; P&P presidential file; P&P stereo file; Eskew, Garnett L. *Willard's of Washington*. 1954.

Newsfilm.

SUMMARY: The first ca. 49 ft., views of President William McKinley speaking, may be unrelated footage. Views of crowds on Pennsylvania Ave., NW, in front of the old Willard Hotel during the Mar. 4, 1901, inaugural festivities. A mounted military unit rides through what is probably the court of honor, the area on Pennsylvania Ave., NW, from Fifteenth to Seventeenth Sts.; the president and his party reviewed the inaugural parade from a stand in this area. McKinley doffs his hat to the crowd as his carriage passes the Willard Hotel. Sen. Marcus A. Hanna of Ohio (1897–1904) sits beside McKinley in the carriage. Several members of the president's special escort, Troop A of the Ohio National Guard, are visible, along with aides and guards. The man riding alone in the second carriage may be TR. The last sequence, McKinley in a carriage in the court of honor, is repeated.

1. Inauguration Day. 2. Presidents—United States—Inauguration. 3. Processions. 4. Washington, D.C. 5. Washington, D.C.—Streets—Pennsylvania Avenue, N.W. 6. McKinley, William, Pres. U.S., 1843–1901—Inauguration, 1901. 7. McKinley, William, Pres. U.S., 1843–1901—Addresses, essays, lectures. 8. Hanna, Marcus A. 9. Roosevelt, Theodore, Pres. U.S., 1858–1919. 10. United States. President, 1897–1901 (McKinley) 11. Willard Hotel, Washington, D.C. 12. Ohio. National Guard. Troop A. I. Paramount, source. II. Theodore Roosevelt Association Collection. [mp 76–380]

President McKinley reviewing the troops at the Pan-American Exposition.

Thomas A. Edison, Sep 1901.

© H8588, Thomas A. Edison, 11Sep1901

lr of 1, 34 ft. si. b&w. 16mm. ref print.
lr of 1, 34 ft. si. b&w. 16mm. dupe neg (cy 1)
lr of 1, 86 ft. si. b&w. 35mm. dupe neg (cy 2)
lr of 1, 86 ft. si. b&w. 35mm. pos ntr.
lr of 1, 35 ft. si. b&w. 16mm. ref print.
lr of 1, 40 ft. si. b&w. 16mm. dupe neg.
lr of 1, 86 ft. si. b&w. 35mm. paper (cy 1)
lr of 1, 85 ft. si. b&w. 35mm. paper (cy 2)

SHELF LOC'N: FAB1224 (print-RMA); FRA 5799 (neg, cy 1-RMA); FPB8071 (neg, cy 2-RMA); FLA4824 (print-Paper); FRA1833 (neg-Paper); LC1810 (paper, cy 1-Paper); LC1810 (paper, cy 2-Paper)

RMA title: *President McKinley Reviewing Troops at Pan-American Exposition, Buffalo, 1901.*

RMA copies have 3 ft. of unrelated footage at the beginning of the film.

Paper Print copies vary in length due to printing differences.

Ref sources: Buffalo *Morning Express.* 9/8/01: pt. 1: 2; Buffalo *Courier.* 9/5/01: 1; Washington *Post.* 9/6/01: 1; *All About the Pan-American City and Vicinity.* 1901; Barry, Richard H. *An Historic Memento of the Nation's Loss; The True Story of the Assassination of President McKinley at Buffalo.* 1901: 11; Johnston, Frances B. [Pan-American Exposition, Buffalo, N.Y., 1901.] lot 2967. P&P; Arnold, C. D. [Pan-American Exposition, Buffalo, N.Y., 1901.] lot 4654. P&P.

Newsfilm.

SUMMARY: On Sept. 5, 1901, President's Day at the Pan-American Exposition in Buffalo, N.Y., President William McKinley reviews troops at the stadium on the exposition grounds. Troops reviewed include members of the U.S. Marine Corps, the Seventy-third Coast Artillery, and the Sixty-fifth and Seventy-fourth Regiments of the New York State National Guard. As troops march in front of the reviewing stand, President McKinley, members of the diplomatic corps, and specially invited guests are visible in the background. The man slightly behind and to McKinley's right is probably George B. Cortelyou, who served as McKinley's secretary, as well as TR's, and as the first secretary of commerce and labor (1903–04); the tall man next to Cortelyou is probably John G. Milburn, president of the exposition; present, but not identified in the group, is James Wilson, secretary of agriculture (1897–1913). Views of the crowd in the stadium are also included.

1. Exhibitions. 2. Military ceremonies, honors, and salutes. 3. Stadia. 4. Buffalo. Stadium. 5. Buffalo. 6. McKinley, William, Pres. U.S., 1843–1901. 7. Cortelyou, George B. 8. Milburn, John G. 9. United States. President, 1897–1901 (McKinley) 10. United States. Marine Corps. 11. United States. Coast Artillery. 12. New York Infantry. 65th Regiment. 13. New York Infantry. 74th Regiment. 14. Pan-American Exposition, 1901. I. Edison (Thomas A.) inc. II. Paramount, source. III. Theodore Roosevelt Association Collection. IV. Paper Print Collection. [mp 76–266]

President McKinley speaking, 1901.

Producer unknown [1901?]

© No reg.

lr, 8 ft. si. b&w. 16mm. ref print.
lr, 8 ft. si. b&w. 16mm. dupe neg.
lr, 8 ft. si. b&w. 16mm. archival pos.
lr, 20 ft. si. b&w. 35mm. pos ntr.

SHELF LOC'N: FAB1208 (print); FRA6100 (neg); FRA6101 (arch pos)

The date in the title is unverified.

Newsfilm.

SUMMARY: President William McKinley speaks to a group of people. A platform draped with bunting is in the background; McKinley is standing near what may be a fence on the side of a street in an undetermined location.

PERSONAL CREDITS: Chessman, A., source.

1. McKinley, William, Pres. U.S., 1843–1901—Addresses, essays, lectures. 2. United States. President, 1897–1901 (McKinley) I. Theodore Roosevelt Association Collection. [mp 76–238]

President McKinley speaking at Buffalo, 1901.
Producer unknown, Sep 1901.

© No reg.

lr, 39 ft. si. b&w. 35mm. ref print.
lr, 39 ft. si. b&w. 35mm. dupe neg.
lr, 39 ft. si. b&w. 35mm. masterpos.

SHELF LOC'N: FEA9935 (print); FPC0767 (neg); FPB8070 (fgmp)

May be an Edison production.

Ref sources: Buffalo Morning Express. 9/5/01: 8; New York Tribune. 9/6/01: 1; All about the Pan-American City and Vicinity. 1901: 11; Niver, Kemp R. Motion Pictures from the Library of Congress Paper Print Collection, 1984–1912. 1967: 258; P&P portrait file; P&P presidential file.

Newsfilm.

SUMMARY: President McKinley delivers a speech before a large crowd on Sept. 5, 1901, President's Day at the Pan-American Exposition in Buffalo, N.Y. His speech is delivered from an elaborately decorated grandstand erected on the Esplanade, part of the central plaza area of the exposition grounds; in front of the stand the heads of reporters are visible. McKinley helps his wife, Ida Saxton McKinley, to her seat and seats himself; John G. Milburn, president of the exposition, introduces McKinley; the president rises and acknowledges the crowd's greeting. The bearded man next to Milburn is probably James Wilson, secretary of agriculture (1897–1913); next to Wilson is George B. Cortelyou, who served as McKinley's secretary, as well as TR's, and as the first secretary of commerce and labor (1903–04), postmaster general (1905–07), and secretary of the treasury (1907–09).

PERSONAL CREDITS: Kleine, George, source.

1. Exhibitions. 2. Buffalo. 3. McKinley, William, Pres. U.S., 1843–1901—Addresses, essays, lectures. 4. McKinley, Ida Saxton. 5. Milburn, John G. 6. Wilson, James, 1835–1920. 7. Cortelyou, George B. 8. United States. President, 1897–1901 (McKinley) 9. Pan-American Exposition, 1901. I.

Edison (Thomas A.) inc. II. Theodore Roosevelt Association Collection. [mp 76–280]

President McKinley's funeral, 1901 [1]
Producer unknown, Sep 1901.

© No reg.

lr, 278 ft. si. b&w. 16mm. ref print.
lr, 278 ft. si. b&w. 16mm. dupe neg.
lr, 278 ft. si. b&w. 16mm. archival pos.
lr, 694 ft. si. b&w. 35mm. dupe neg ntr.

SHELF LOC'N: FAB756 (print); FRA8649 (neg); FRA5811 (arch pos)

May be an American Mutoscope and Biograph Company production.

Film sequence does not follow the order of actual events.

Film is dark and slightly out of frame.

Ref sources: [Davis, Oscar K. and Mumford, John K.] The Life of William McKinley. 1901: 111–128; The Canton Repository. Pictorial Life of William McKinley. 1943: 26–28; The New York Herald. 9/17/01: 4–5; P&P presidential file; P&P stereo file.

Newsfilm.

SUMMARY: Three sequences of the funeral ceremonies held for President William McKinley; 1) McKinley's body lay in state in the Rotunda of the Capitol, Washington, D.C., on Sept. 17, 1901; views of officers on horseback, the Artillery Band (wearing dark headdresses), a squadron of cavalry, a battalion of artillery and coast artillery, the Marine Band (wearing white helmets), a battalion of Marines, civilians carrying umbrellas (may be the diplomatic corps), other civilians, the guard of honor, pallbearers, and the horsedrawn hearse all turning the corner off what may be Pennsylvania Avenue on their way to the Capitol; the camera pans the hearse, as a procession of carriages turns the corner; 2) McKinley's body first lay in state for public viewing in Buffalo, N.Y., on Sept. 15–16; views of carriages, the horsedrawn hearse, and marchers stopping in front of the Buffalo City Hall; medium-close shots of the casket being unloaded from the hearse and carried up the stairs of City Hall; crowds of mourners lining up to view the body as a group of soldiers enters City Hall; the camera pans the crowd gathered outside as mourners enter and leave City Hall. An unrelated sequence of Washington ceremonies follows; the camera pans from different angles the crowds gathered at the east front of the Capitol; 3) McKinley's body was conveyed to its final resting place at Canton, Ohio, on Sept. 18–19; views of mounted military units, marching civilians, carriages, and the horsedrawn hearse turning and entering what is probably Westlawn Cemetery where McKinley is buried; military units marching down a street as gathered crowds watch; final pans of mourners, crowds, and soldiers outside the McKinley home in Canton.

1. Funeral service. 2. Washington, D.C. Capitol. 3. Processions. 4. Military music. 5. Buffalo. City and County Hall. 6. Westlawn Cemetery. 7. Washington, D.C. 8. Buffalo. 9. Canton, Ohio. 10. McKinley, William, Pres. U.S., 1843–1901—Funeral and memorial services. 11. McKinley, William, Pres. U.S., 1843–1901—Homes. 12. United States. President, 1897–1901 (McKinley) 13. United States. Army. 14. United States. Marine Corps. 15. United States. Navy. I. Biograph Company. II. Biograph Company, source. III. Theodore Roosevelt Association Collection. [mp 76–323]

President McKinley's funeral, 1901 [2]
Producer unknown, Sep 1901.

© No reg.

lr, 68 ft. si. b&w. 16mm. ref print.

lr, 68 ft. si. b&w. 16mm. dupe neg (cy 1)

lr, 169 ft. si. b&w. 35mm. dupe neg (cy 2)

lr, 169 ft. si. b&w. 35mm. pos ntr.

SHELF LOC'N: FAB1213 (print); FRA6107 (neg, cy 1); FPB8080 (neg, cy 2)

Film is dark and slightly out of frame.

Ref sources: [Davis, Oscar K. and Mumford, John K.] *The Life of William McKinley.* 1901: 127; The Canton Repository. *Pictorial Life of William McKinley.* 1943: 26; The New York *Herald.* 9/17/01: 4–5; P&P stereo file.

Newsfilm.

SUMMARY: Scenes of the state funeral held for President William McKinley in Washington, D.C., on Sept. 17, 1901; views of officers on horseback, the Artillery Band (wearing dark headdresses), a squadron of cavalry, a battalion of artillery and coast artillery, and the Marine Band (wearing white helmets) turning the corner off what may be Pennsylvania Avenue on their way to the Capitol; from ground level, the camera pans the mourners waiting in line to view the body.

1. Funeral service. 2. Processions. 3. Military music. 4. Washington, D.C. Capitol. 5. Washington, D.C. 6. McKinley, William, Pres. U.S., 1843–1901 —Funeral and memorial services. 7. United States. President, 1897–1901 (McKinley) 8. United States. Army. 9. United States. Marine Corps. 10. United States. Navy. I. Paramount, source. II. Theodore Roosevelt Association Collection. [mp 76–324]

President McKinley's funeral, Canton, Ohio, 1901 [1]
Producer unknown, Sep 1901.

© No reg.

lr, 177 ft. si. b&w. 35mm. ref print.

lr, 177 ft. si. b&w. 35mm. dupe neg.

lr, 177 ft. si. b&w. 35mm. masterpos.

SHELF LOC'N: FEA9942 (print); FPC0770 (neg); FPB7961 (fgmp)

Film sequence is repeated.

Film is dark and slightly out of frame with nitrate deterioration.

Ref sources: The Canton Repository. *Pictorial Life of William McKinley.* 1943: 21; P&P portrait file.

Newsfilm.

SUMMARY: On Sept. 18–19, 1901, the body of assassinated President William McKinley is returned to his hometown of Canton, Ohio, for the final funeral ceremonies and burial. Views of the casket being loaded into the hearse at what is probably the Canton train station; two men, probably TR and his brother-in-law, Comdr. William S. Cowles, entering a carriage; the camera pans the crowd, carriages, soldiers, and procession.

PERSONAL CREDITS: Kleine, George, source.

1. Funeral service. 2. Processions. 3. Canton, Ohio. 4. McKinley, William, Pres. U.S., 1843–1901—Funeral and memorial services. 5. Roosevelt, Theodore, Pres. U.S., 1858–1919. 6. Cowles, William Sheffield, 1846–1923. 7. United States. President, 1897–1901 (McKinley) 8. United States. President, 1901–1909 (Roosevelt) I. Theodore Roosevelt Association Collection. [mp 76–325]

President McKinley's funeral, Canton, Ohio, 1901 [2]
Producer unknown, Sep 1901.

© No reg.

lr, 131 ft. si. b&w. 35mm. ref print.

lr, 131 ft. si. b&w. 35mm. dupe neg.

lr, 131 ft. si. b&w. 35mm. masterpos.

SHELF LOC'N: FEA9944 (print); FPC0772 (neg); FPB8241 (fgmp)

The first scene of the film is printed upside down.

The film is very dark and slightly out of frame with nitrate deterioration.

Ref sources: The Canton Repository. *Pictorial Life of William McKinley.* 1943: 21–31; [Davis, Oscar K. and Mumford, John K.] *The Life of William McKinley.* 1901: 122–128; P&P portrait file.

Newsfilm.

SUMMARY: On Sept. 18–19, 1901, the body of assassinated President William McKinley is returned to his hometown of Canton, Ohio, for the final funeral ceremonies and burial. Opening scene of a group of people meeting the train which conveyed McKinley's body to Canton; long panning shots of a large group waiting in line to view the body at McKinley's home; view of the casket being loaded into a horsedrawn hearse, briefly visible in the background are TR, Secretary of the Treasury Lyman J. Gage, Attorney General Philander C. Knox, and Secretary of the Interior Ethan A. Hitchcock; the final scene is of the hearse leaving for Westlawn Cemetery, with crowds visible on the sides.

PERSONAL CREDITS: Kleine, George, source.

1. Funeral service. 2. Processions. 3. Canton, Ohio. 4. McKinley, William, Pres. U.S., 1843–1901—Funeral and memorial services. 5. McKinley, William, Pres. U.S., 1843–1901—Homes. 6. Roosevelt, Theodore, Pres. U.S., 1858–1919. 7. Gage, Lyman J. 8. Knox, Philander Chase. 9. Hitchcock, Ethan Allen, 1835–1909. 10. United States. President, 1897–1901 (McKinley) 11. United States. President, 1901–1909 (Roosevelt) I. Theodore Roosevelt Association Collection. [mp 76–326]

President McKinley's funeral in Buffalo, Washington, and Canton, Ohio, 1901.

Producer unknown, Sep 1901.

© No reg.

lr, 376 ft. si. b&w. 16mm. ref print.

lr, 376 ft. si. b&w. 16mm. dupe neg.

lr, 376 ft. si. b&w. 16mm. archival pos.

SHELF LOC'N: FAB1453 (print); FRA6189 (neg); FRA6106 (arch pos)

Film sequence does not follow the order of actual events.

Film is dark and slightly out of frame.

Ref sources: The Canton Repository. *Pictorial Life of William McKinley.* 1943: 26–28; [Davis, Oscar K. and Mumford, John K.] *The Life of William McKinley.* 1901: 125; P&P portrait file; P&P presidential file; P&P stereo file.

Newsfilm.

SUMMARY: Three sequences of the funeral ceremonies held for President William McKinley: 1) In Canton, Ohio, on Sept. 19, 1901, views of the official Washington party and others preceding the casket out of the First Methodist Episcopal Church: identified are President TR, Secretary of the Treasury Lyman J. Gage (1897–1902), Secretary of War Elihu Root (1899–1904), Attorney General Philander C. Knox (1901–1904), Postmaster General Charles E. Smith (1891–1902), Secretary of the Interior Ethan Allen Hitchcock (1898–1913), Secre-

tary of Agriculture James Wilson (1897–1913), and McKinley's private secretary George B. Cortelyou (1900–1901); men line the stairs as the casket is placed into the horsedrawn hearse; view from the rear as the hearse and procession move down the street; mounted military units, marching civilians, carriages, and the hearse turning and entering what is probably Westlawn Cemetery, where McKinley is buried; military units march down a street; 2) in Washington, D.C., on Sept. 17, views of a squadron of sailors, civilians carrying umbrellas (may be the diplomatic corps), other civilians, the guard of honor, pallbearers, and the horsedrawn hearse all turning a corner off what may be Pennsylvania Avenue on their way to the Capitol; the camera follows the marchers from the rear; a procession of carriages also turning the corner; from ground level, the camera pans the mourners in line and others at the Capitol; officers on horseback, the Artillery Band (wearing dark headdresses), a squadron of cavalry, a battalion of artillery, other military units, the Marine Band (wearing white helmets), and a battalion of marines, all turning a corner off Pennsylvania Avenue on their way to the Capitol; 3) in Buffalo, N.Y., on Sept. 15–16, views of the procession led by mounted police and consisting of a band and various military marching units, carriages, and marching civilians moving down a street; carriages, the horsedrawn hearse, and marchers stopping in front of the Buffalo City Hall; the casket being unloaded from the hearse and carried up the stairs of City Hall; crowds of mourners line up to view the casket as a group of soldiers enters City Hall; as mounted police march by, the camera pans the crowd and carriages gathered outside what is probably the Milburn house where McKinley died; final pans of carriages laden with flowers, closed carriages, marching policemen and the hearse moving through a downtown street.

PERSONAL CREDITS: Kleine, George, source.

1. Funeral service. 2. Processions. 3. Westlawn Cemetery. 4. Washington, D.C. Capitol. 5. Buffalo. City and County Hall. 6. Buffalo. 7. Washington, D.C. 8. Canton, Ohio. 9. McKinley, William, Pres. U.S., 1843–1901—Funeral and memorial services. 10. Roosevelt, Theordore, Pres. U.S., 1858–1919. 11. Gage, Lyman J. 12. Root, Elihu. 13. Knox, Philander Chase. 14. Smith, Charles Emory, 1842–1908. 15. Hitchcock, Ethan Allen, 1835–1909. 16. Wilson, James, 1835–1920. 17. Cortelyou, George B. 18. United States. President, 1897–1901 (McKinley) 19. First Methodist Episcopal Church, Canton, Ohio. 20. United States. President, 1901–1909

(Roosevelt) 21. United States. Army. 22. United States. Navy. 23. United States. Marine Corps. I. Theodore Roosevelt Association Collection. [mp 76-65]

President McKinley's inauguration, 1901 [1]

Producer unknown, Mar 1901.

© No reg.

    lr, 115 ft. si. b&w. 35mm. ref print.

    lr, 115 ft. si. b&w. 35mm. dupe neg.

    lr, 115 ft. si. b&w. 35mm. masterpos.

    SHELF LOC'N: FEA9943 (print); FPC0771 (neg); FPB8059 (fgmp)

Film is very dark and slightly out of frame with nitrate deterioration.

Ref sources: P&P stereo file; P&P presidential file; New York *Tribune*. 3/5/01:1–2; Washington *Post*. 3/5/01: 1–5.

Newsfilm.

SUMMARY: Scenes of William McKinley's second inaugural parade held in Washington, D.C., on Mar. 4, 1901. Moving down Fifteenth St., NW, and turning onto Pennsylvania Ave. are McKinley's escorts to the Capitol: cavalry units; marching units; the president's immediate escort, Troop A of the Ohio National Guard (on black horses and wearing high fur shakos); followed by the carriage with Mc-Kinley. The final view is of West Point cadets marching.

PERSONAL CREDITS: Kleine, George, source.

1. Inauguration Day. 2. Presidents—United States—Inauguration. 3. Processions. 4. Washington, D.C. 5. Washington, D.C.—Streets—Fifteenth Street, N.W. 6. Washington, D.C.—Streets—Pennsylvania Avenue, N.W. 7. McKinley, William, Pres. U.S., 1843–1901—Inauguration, 1901. 8. United States. President, 1897–1901 (McKinley) 9. Ohio. National Guard. Troop A. 10. United States. Military Academy, West Point. I. Theodore Roosevelt Association Collection. [mp 76-327]

President McKinley's inauguration, 1901 [2]

Producer unknown, Mar 1901.

© No reg.

    lr, 105 ft. si. b&w. 35mm. ref print.

    lr, 105 ft. si. b&w. 35mm. dupe neg.

    lr, 105 ft. si. b&w. 35mm. masterpos.

    lr, 105 ft. si. b&w. 35mm. pos ntr.

    SHELF LOC'N: FEA7832 (print); FPB8237 (neg); FPB8239 (fgmp)

Film is very dark and slightly out of frame with nitrate deterioration.

Ref sources: Washington *Post*. 3/5/01: 1–5; New York *Tribune*. 3/5/01: 1–2; P&P presidential file; P&P stereo file.

Newsfilm.

SUMMARY: Scenes of William McKinley's second inaugural parade held in Washington, D.C., on Mar. 4, 1901. Views from varying distances of McKinley's escorts to the Capitol on Pennsylvania Ave.: mounted cavalry units; marching bands; the president's immediate escort, Troop A of the Ohio National Guard (on black horses and wearing high fur shakos); followed by the final scene of McKinley in his carriage, accompanied by Sen. Marcus A. Hanna of Ohio.

1. Inauguration Day. 2. Presidents—United States—Inauguration. 3. Processions. 4. Washington, D.C. 5. Washington, D.C.—Streets—Pennsylvania Avenue, N.W. 6. McKinley, William, Pres. U.S., 1843–1901—Inauguration, 1901. 7. Hanna, Marcus A. 8. United States. President, 1897–1901 (McKinley) 9. United States. Army. 10. Ohio. National Guard. Troop A. I. Paramount, source. II. Theodore Roosevelt Association Collection. [mp 76-328]

President McKinley's memorial dedicated by William Howard Taft at Niles, Ohio.

Universal Film Manufacturing Co., Oct 1917.

© No reg.

    lr, 40 ft. si. b&w. 16mm. ref print.

    lr, 25 ft. si. b&w. 16mm. dupe neg.

    lr, 24 ft. si. b&w. 16mm. archival pos.

(Universal animated weekly, v. 5, issue no. 93)

    SHELF LOC'N: FAB672 (print); FRA5711 (neg); FRA5712 (arch pos)

Ref print lacks some interior titles; arch pos and dupe neg have flash titles and lack one interior title.

Ref sources: *Ohio State Journal*, Columbus 10/6/17: 1–2; National McKinley Birthplace Memorial Association. *The National McKinley Birthplace Memorial*. 1918; P&P portrait file.

Newsfilm.

SUMMARY: Scenes from the dedication ceremony of the National McKinley Birthplace Memorial in Niles, Ohio, on Oct. 5, 1917. Opening views of the gathered crowd; views of the processional, including the McKinley Club of Canton, moving down a street lined with spectators; former President William Howard Taft delivering the dedication speech to the crowd; views of McKinley's sister, Helen McKinley, and a man who may be Joseph G. Butler, Jr., president of the National McKinley Birthplace Memorial Associatoin, unveiling the large marble statue of McKinley located in the Court of Honor; close shots of the statue. The final sequence is of Joe Fisher, identified by interior title as the only surviving boyhood friend of McKinley.

CITATION: MPW34.4: 577; MPW34.5: 713.

1. Memorials. 2. Processions. 3. Niles, Ohio. National McKinley Birthplace Memorial. 4. Niles, Ohio. 5. McKinley, William, Pres. U.S., 1843–1901—Monuments, etc. 6. Taft, William Howard, Pres. U.S., 1857–1930—Addresses, essays, lectures. 7. McKinley, Helen. 8. Butler, Joseph G. 9. Fisher, Joe. 10. National McKinley Birthplace Memorial Association. 11. McKinley Club. I. Universal Film Manufacturing Company. II. Community Motion Picture Service, inc., source. III. Theodore Roosevelt Association Collection. [mp 76–14]

President Roosevelt, 1901–1909.
Roosevelt Memorial Association [1930?]
© No reg.

    lr of 1, 1008 ft. si. b&w. 35mm. ref print.
    lr of 1, 1008 ft. si. b&w. 35mm. dupe neg.
    lr of 1, 1008 ft. si. b&w. 35mm. masterpos.
    lr of 1, 1008 ft. si. b&w. 35mm. pos ntr.

SHELF LOC'N: FEA9939 (print); FPC0763 (neg); FPB9922 (fgmp)

Ref sources: Roosevelt Memorial Association. *President Roosevelt* (script); Roosevelt Memorial Association. *Annual Report.* 1930: 9.

TR at his desk at Sagamore Hill in the summer of 1905, probably during the Portsmouth Peace Conference.

Factual; compilation.

SUMMARY: Through the use of cartoons, stills, and quotations, this film traces the notable aspirations and achievements of TR's administration. Areas represented are: forest reserve extensions; conservation of natural resources; preservation of water power sites; legislation against trusts and overcapitalization; establishment of the Dept. of Commerce and Labor; the Canal Zone; Cuba restored to Cubans; settlement of the Alaskan boundary dispute; conviction of public land grafters; and negotiations of twenty-four treaties. Sequence of TR preparing legislation to secure natural resources. Stills and cartoons of TR's fight for the square deal and against monopolies; scenes of TR in San Francisco on May 12, 1903; views of TR speaking on the coal strike settlement in Wilkes-Barre, Pa., on Aug. 10, 1905; long shot of TR with a group of priests and in an auto with Cardinal James Gibbons. Scene of TR speaking on corporate trust-busting. Sequences demonstrating TR's conservation policies: TR speaking from the rear platform of a train, with Indians in the foreground; panning shots of Roosevelt Dam on the Salt River in Arizona. Sequences on TR's foreign affairs policies: views of TR with a group of foreign dignitaries and of TR sending the battle fleet around the world in 1907. Sequences on the new Republic of Panama, including several shots of the building and completion of the Panama Canal. Cartoons representing TR's life in the White House. The final sequences show TR's inaugural ceremonies held Mar. 4, 1905: views of TR's carriage arriving; panning shots of crowd at the Capitol, the oath-taking ceremony, and the acceptance speech; parting view of TR entering the carriage with Henry Cabot Lodge.

PERSONAL CREDITS: Gentry, Caroline, director. Manning, Mae, editor.

1. Presidents—United States—Term of office. 2. Caricatures and cartoons. 3. Conservation of natural resources. 4. Trust companies. 5. Roosevelt Dam. 6. Presidents—United States—Election—1905. 7. United States—Politics and government—1901–1909. 8. United States—Social conditions—1865–1918. 9. Panama Canal. 10. San Francisco. 11. Wilkes-Barre, Pa. 12. Salt River, Ariz. 13. Roosevelt, Theodore, Pres. U.S., 1858–1919. 14. Gibbons, James. 15. Roosevelt, Theodore, Pres. U.S., 1858–1919—Inauguration, 1905. 16. Lodge, Henry Cabot. I. Roosevelt Memorial Association. II. Roosevelt Memorial Association, source. III. Theodore Roosevelt Association Collection. [mp 76–52]

President Wilson arrives in New York to lead fourth Liberty Loan parade [1918]
Hearst-Pathe News, Sep 1918.

© No reg.

lr, 52 ft. si. b&w. 16mm. ref print.
lr, 52 ft. si. b&w. 16mm. dupe neg.
lr, 129 ft. si. b&w. 35mm. pos ntr.

(Hearst-Pathe News [newsreel])

SHELF LOC'N: FAB740 (print); FRA5786 (neg)
RMA lists the date in the titles as 1917.

Ref sources: P&P portrait file; P&P presidential file; The New York *Times Mid-week Pictorial.* v. 8, no. 6, 1918: [2]; Washington *Post.* 9/29/18: 3.
Newsfilm.

SUMMARY: Views of the fourth Liberty Loan ceremonies in New York City and Washington, Sept. 1918. Inaugurating a national drive for the sale of liberty bonds, President Wilson, his wife Edith, and his mother-in-law, Mrs. W. H. Bolling, arrive in New York on Sept. 27, 1918. At Pennsylvania Railroad Station they are greeted by crowds and joined by the president's two daughters, Margaret Wilson and Eleanor McAdoo, as they enter a touring car en route to the Waldorf-Astoria. Views of flag-lined Fifth Avenue on the following day, with flags of the twenty-two Allied nations and banners supporting liberty bonds filling the avenue. Emile Cartier, Belgian minister to the United States, speaks at the dedication of the Altar of Liberty, an open-air structure in Madison Square designed by Thomas Hastings in support of the Liberty Loan effort; marching soldiers and a band. On the south portico of the U.S. Treasury Building in Washington, D.C., Geraldine Farrar, a member of the Metropolitan Opera Company, ceremonially sells a bond to Secretary of the Treasury William Gibbs McAdoo as Leo S. Rowe, assistant secretary of the treasury, watches.

1. European War, 1914–1918—Finance—New York (City) 2. European War, 1914–1918—Finance—Washington, D.C. 3. European War, 1914–1918—United States. 4. Flags. 5. Marching. 6. New York (City). Liberty's Altar. 7. New York (City) 8. Washington, D.C. 9. New York (City)—Streets—Fifth Avenue. 10. New York (City)—Plazas—Madison Square. 11. Wilson, Woodrow, Pres. U.S., 1856–1924. 12. Wilson, Edith. 13. Bolling, Sallie White. 14. Wilson, Margaret Woodrow. 15. McAdoo, Eleanor. 16. Cartier, Emile. 17. Hastings, Thomas. 18. Farrar, Geraldine. 19. McAdoo, William Gibbs. 20. Rowe, Leo S. 21. United States. President, 1913–1921 (Wilson) 22. United States. Laws, statues, etc. Liberty loan acts. 23. New York (City). Pennsylvania Station. 24. United States. Treasury Dept.—Buildings. I. Hearst-Pathe News. II. Pathe, source. III. Theodore Roosevelt Association Collection. [mp 76–40]

The Prince of Wales visits TR's grave.
International Film Service Co., Nov 1919.

© No reg.

lr, 8 ft. si. b&w. 16mm. ref print.
lr, 8 ft. si. b&w. 16mm. dupe neg.
lr, 20 ft. si. b&w. 35mm. pos ntr.

(International [Series])

SHELF LOC'N: FAB847 (print); FRA5852 (neg)

Ref sources: Newton, Wilfrid Douglas. *Westward with the Prince of Wales.* 1920; Trevelyan, George M. *Grey of Fallodon.* 1937; Kinross, John P. D. B. *The Windsor Years.* 1967; New York (City). Mayor's Committee on Celebration of Twenty-fifth Anniversary of the Greater City of New York. *Official Book of the Silver Jubilee of Greater New York.* 1923; P&P portrait file.
Newsfilm.

Edward, the Prince of Wales (briefly Edward VIII, king of England and later Duke of Windsor), visited the United States in November 1919 and made a semiprivate journey to Theodore Roosevelt's grave on November 21.

SUMMARY: In the summer of 1919, Edward, the Prince of Wales, later King Edward VIII, embarked on a tour of the Dominions. After touring Canada for several months, the prince decided to spend several days in the United States. His visit was the first visit of a Prince of Wales to the United States since that of his grandfather, Edward VII, fifty years earlier. On his last day in New York, Nov. 21, 1919, the prince made a semiprivate journey to Oyster Bay. The film shows the prince placing a laurel wreath on TR's grave in Youngs Memorial Cemetery; the prince, Theodore Roosevelt, Jr., wearing a mourning band, a man who is probably Joseph M. Nye, chief of special agents, Dept. of State, and a group of men return down the path from the gravesite. Behind the prince, the man wearing dark glasses is probably Viscount Grey, British ambassador to the United States. A man wearing an ascot and walking in the rear of the group may be Rodman Wanamaker, chairman of the Mayor's Committee on Reception to Distinguished Guests. The prince tips his hat to people gathered alongside the path.

1. Memorial rites and ceremonies. 2. Youngs Memorial Cemetery. 3. Oyster Bay, N.Y. 4. Edward VIII, King of Great Britain, 1894–1972. 5. Roosevelt, Theodore, Pres. U.S., 1858–1919—Tomb. 6. Roosevelt, Theodore, 1887–1944. 7. Nye, Joseph M. 8. Grey, Edward Grey, 1st Viscount, 1862–1933. 9. Wanamaker, Rodman. I. International Film Service Company. II. International Newsreel Corporation, source. III. Theodore Roosevelt Association Collection. [mp 76–82]

The prize winning design by John Russell Pope for the proposed memorial to Theodore Roosevelt for the city of Washington.

Motion Picture Library [1926?]

© No reg.

   lr, 334 ft. si. b&w. 35mm. ref print.

   lr, 344 ft. si. b&w. 35mm. dupe neg.

   lr, 344 ft. si. b&w. 35mm. pos ntr.

SHELF LOC'N: FEA7839 (print); FPB9879 (neg)

Model of memorial was built in 1926.

Ref sources: Roosevelt Memorial Association. *Annual Report.* 1925: 6–10; 1926: 6–7; Roosevelt Memorial Association. *Plan and Design for the Roosevelt Memorial in the City of Washington, John Russell Pope Architect.* 1925.

Factual; model film.

SUMMARY: The first goal of the Roosevelt Memorial Association was to erect a monument in memory of TR in Washington, D.C. The original site was the general area between the Washington Monument and the Potomac River, bounded by Fifteenth and Seventeenth streets. The RMA invited architects, sculptors, and landscape designers to compete for the commission to design the memorial with the above site in mind. The design of John Russell Pope, architect from New York, won the award by unanimous vote on Oct. 6, 1925. A model of the design in plaster, based on a scale of one-sixteenth of an inch to a foot, was prepared in 1926 by John Donnelly & Company for study by Congress in resolving the controversy over the location of the memorial. Opening scenes of the model, with long shots of the memorial and its grounds; many different camera angles, including panoramic views, of the memorial: its central feature is a huge shaft of water rising 200 ft. from the center of an island of white granite set in a circular basin, flanked by curving colonnades; many views of the architecture and sculpture, which are classical in style; in two segments ca. ft. 271–305, TR addresses a group of suffragists from the porch at Sagamore Hill, 1917. Final panning views of the colonnades surrounding the memorial.

PERSONAL CREDITS: Gentry, Caroline, director.

1. Memorials. 2. Washington, D.C. Theodore Roosevelt Memorial. 3. Models (Clay, plaster, etc.) 4. Architectural models. 5. Monuments. 6. Granite sculpture. 7. Oyster Bay, N.Y. Sagamore Hill. 8. Women—Suffrage—New York (State) 9. Washington, D.C. 10. Oyster Bay, N.Y. 11. Pope, John Russell. 12. Roosevelt, Theodore, Pres. U.S., 1858–1919—Addresses, essays, lectures. 13. Roosevelt, Theodore, Pres. U.S., 1858–1919—Monuments, etc. 14. John Donnelly & Company. I. Roosevelt Memorial Association. Film Library. II. Roosevelt Memorial Association. III. Roosevelt Memorial Association, source. IV. Theodore Roosevelt Association Collection. [mp 76–285]

Professor Henry Fairfield Osborn, RMA medalist, 1923.

Producer unknown [1934?]

© No reg.

   lr, 19 ft. si. b&w. 16mm. ref print.

   lr, 19 ft. si. b&w. 16mm. dupe neg.

   lr, 49 ft. si. b&w. 35mm. pos ntr.

SHELF LOC'N: FAB899 (print); FRA5894 (neg)

Ref sources: American Museum of Natural History, New York. *Annual Report.* 1935: 1–2; New York (State). Board of Trustees of the Roosevelt

Memorial. *The New York State Theodore Roosevelt Memorial.* [1936]

Newsfilm.

SUMMARY: Long and close shots of Henry Fairfield Osborn, paleontologist, first curator of the Dept. of Vertebrate Paleontology at the American Museum of Natural History, New York City, and president of the museum (1908–1933). Osborn, who received the Roosevelt Medal for Distinguished Service in 1923 for his contributions to natural history, and an unidentified man talk in front of the New York State Roosevelt Memorial, a building erected in memory of TR and his interests as a naturalist. The building is part of the American Museum of Natural History. Carvings in bas-relief of native American and African animals, which decorate the exterior columns of the memorial, are visible behind the two conversing men.

1. Roosevelt Medal for Distinguished Service. 2. Medalists. 3. Paleontologists. 4. New York State Theodore Roosevelt Memorial, New York. 5. Bas-relief. 6. Animal sculpture—New York (City) 7. New York (City) 8. Osborn, Henry Fairfield. 9. Roosevelt, Theodore, Pres. U.S., 1858–1919—Medals. 10. American Museum of Natural History, New York. I. American Museum of Natural History, New York, source. II. Theodore Roosevelt Association Collection. [mp 76–195]

Queen Wilhelmina of Holland, the Prince Consort [and] the Princess.

Various producers [192–?]

© No reg.

lr, 26 ft. si. b&w. 16mm. ref print.
lr, 26 ft. si. b&w. 16mm. dupe neg (cy 1)
lr, 74 ft. si. b&w. 35mm. dupe neg (cy 2)
lr, 65 ft. si. b&w. 35mm. pos ntr.

SHELF LOC'N: FAB893 (print); FRA5888 (neg, cy 1); FPB8067 (neg, cy 2)

RMA title: *Queen Wilhelmina of Holland, the Prince Consort, the Princess and the Queen Mother.*

Flash interior titles note: Kinograms and Paramount Weekly Gazette.

Ref sources: Power, Lionel J. B. *The Royal Ladies of the Netherlands.* [1939]; P&P portrait file.

Newsfilm; view.

SUMMARY: Opening scene of the royal family arriving at an unidentified event; views of Wilhelmina, queen of the Netherlands, seated in the carriage to the left, Princess Juliana seated to the right, and Prince Consort Henry seated opposite them; they descend from the carriage, greet some men, and then enter a building; close-up of Prince Henry,

who, the interior titles notes, officially opens the 1928 Olympic Games; pan of game ceremony and attending crowd; scene of men on horseback; final view of a large crowd walking past a large building.

1. Olympic games. 2. Netherlands. 3. Wilhelmina, Queen of the Netherlands, 1880–1962. 4. Henry, consort of Wilhelmina, Queen of the Netherlands, 1876–1934. 5. Juliana, Queen of the Netherlands, 1909– I. Kinogram Publishing Corporation. II. Paramount. III. Kinogram Publishing Corporation, source. IV. Theodore Roosevelt Association Collection. V. Series: Kinograms [Series] VI. Series: Paramount weekly gazette [Series] [mp 76–344]

[Quentin Roosevelt]; Clemenceau and Foch, 1917–1919.

Producer unknown [1918?]

© No reg.

lr, 24 ft. si. b&w. 16mm. ref print (cy 1)
lr, 60 ft. si. b&w. 35mm. ref print (cy 2–2 cy)
lr, 24 ft. si. b&w. 16mm. dupe neg (cy 1)
lr, 60 ft. si. b&w. 35mm. dupe neg (cy 2–2 cy)
lr, 60 ft. si. b&w. 35mm. masterpos.
lr, 61 ft. si. b&w. 35mm. pos ntr.
lr, 60 ft. si. b&w. 35mm. neg ntr.

SHELF LOC'N: FAB844 (print, cy 1); FEA6752 & 6731 (print, cy 2–2 cy); FRA 5849 (neg, cy 1); FPB7188 & 7593 (neg, cy 2–2 cy); FPB7592 (fgmp)

RMA title: *Quentin and Archie Roosevelt's Regiments; Clemenceau and Foch, 1917–1919.*

The dates in the title are unverified.

Ref sources: Pershing, John J. [Views and activities of military import, 1902–1921.] lot 7729, v. 3. P&P; P&P portrait file.

Newsfilm; war film.

SUMMARY: The film appears to have been photographed in France during WWI. Medium-close shot of Quentin Roosevelt with a small building in the background; brief shot of French and American officers, including Lt. Edward V. Rickenbacker at the immediate right, talking; view of a troop train moving through a European town as people line the tracks waving to the soldiers. The final sequence is composed of medium-close panning shots, from left to right, of: John J. Pershing, commander in chief of American forces; André Tardieu, French diplomat; Premier Georges Clemenceau of France; Marshal Ferdinand Foch, commander in chief of French forces; an unidentified French officer; Gen. Maxime Weygand, staff officer to Foch; and Maj. Gen. James W. McAndrews, general chief of staff of American forces, posing as they leave a building.

1. European War, 1914–1918. 2. Roosevelt, Quentin. 3. Clemenceau, Georges. 4. Foch, Ferdinand. 5. Pershing, John J. 6. Rickenbacker, Edward V. 7. Tardieu, André. 8. Weygand, Maxime. 9. McAndrews, James W. 10. United States. Army—Officers. 11. France. Armée. I. United States. Army. Signal Corps, source. II. Theodore Roosevelt Association Collection. III. Clemenceau and Foch, 1917–1919 [Title] [mp 76–83]

Quentin Roosevelt's grave, 1918.

Producer unknown [1919?]

© No reg.

lr, 2 ft. si. b&w. 16mm. ref print.

lr, 2 ft. si. b&w. 16mm. dupe neg.

lr, 2 ft. si. b&w. 16mm. archival pos.

SHELF LOC'N: FAB1137 (print); FRA6079 (neg); FRA6080 (arch pos)

Possible production dates: July 14, 1918–Sep. 4, 1919.

Ref sources: The New York *Times Mid-week Pictorial.* v. 10, no. 1, 9/4/19: [22]; Mackey, Frank J. and Jernegan, Marcus Wilson. *Forward—March!* 1935: 176.

Newsfilm.

SUMMARY: Quentin Roosevelt, TR's youngest son, was shot down behind enemy lines on July 14, 1918, and buried by the Germans near Chambéry, France. A group of American and what are probably French soliders stand by his grave.

1. Tombs. 2. European War, 1914–1918. 3. Chambéry, France. 4. Roosevelt, Quentin. 5. United States. Army. 6. France. Armée. I. General Vision Company, source. II. Theodore Roosevelt Association Collection. [mp 76–381]

Quentin Roosevelt's grave in France.

Producer unknown [1919?]

© No reg.

lr, 12 ft. si. b&w. 16mm. ref print (cy 1)

lr, 29 ft. si. b&w. 35mm. ref print (cy 2)

lr, 12 ft. si. b&w. 16mm. archival pos.

lr, 29 ft. si. b&w. 35mm. neg ntr.

SHELF LOC'N: FAB1136 (print, cy 1); FEA7302 (print, cy 2); FRA6078 (arch pos)

Possible production dates: July 14, 1918–Sep. 4, 1919.

Ref sources: The New York *Times Mid-week Pictorial.* v. 10, no. 1, 9/4/19: [22]; Mackey, Frank J. and

Jernegan, Marcus Wilson. *Forward—March!* 1935: 176.

SUMMARY: Quentin Roosevelt, TR's youngest son, was shot down behind enemy lines on July 14, 1918, and buried by the Germans near Chambéry, France. A group of American and what are probably French soldiers carry a wooden cross headboard and a fence which they place around Quentin's grave; close shot of the headboard with an inscription in French; an American and a French officer pose with a floral grave decoration at the grave.

PERSONAL CREDITS: Lee, A., source.

1. Tombs. 2. European War, 1914–1918. 3. Chambéry, France. 4. Roosevelt, Quentin. 5. United States. Army. 6. France. Armée. I. Theodore Roosevelt Association Collection. [mp 76–382]

Return of Spanish-American troops, 1898.

Producer unknown [1898?]

© No reg.

lr, 16 ft. si. b&w. 16mm. ref print (cy 1)

lr, 40 ft. si. b&w. 35mm. ref print (cy 2)

lr, 16 ft. si. b&w. 16mm. dupe neg.

lr, 16 ft. si. b&w. 16mm. archival pos.

lr, 40 ft. si. b&w. 35mm. neg ntr.

SHELF LOC'N: FAB1221 (print, cy 1); FEA7631 (print, cy 2); FRA6175 (neg); FRA6117 (arch pos)

Date in title unverified.

Ref sources: Smith, Cleveland H. & Taylor, Gertrude R. *United States Service Symbols.* 1942: 16–19; Rankin, Robert H. *Uniforms of the Sea Services.* 1962: 85, 161, 163.

Newsfilm.

SUMMARY: Views of a parade on a broad street in an undetermined location. The following groups appear: a single line of mounted policemen; a marching band, whose members may be sailors or marines; marching sailors or marines carrying rifles; soldiers marching in formation; following the soldiers, a dignitary riding in a closed carriage; lines of marching policemen. The soldiers and sailors may be returning from the Spanish-American War. People line the street and others wave from windows. A sign on a building in the background says Enrico's. The heavy clothing worn by parade participants indicates that the season is fall or winter.

1. Processions. 2. Police—United States. 3. Marching bands. 4. United States—Armed Forces. 5. United States—History—War of 1898. 6. United States. Navy. 7. United States. Marine Corps. 8. United States. Army. I. Paramount, source. II.

Theodore Roosevelt Association Collection. [mp 76-265]

Reviewing Annapolis middies.
Film by Stineman, Jul 1915.
© No reg.
    lr, 43 ft. si. b&w. 16mm. ref print.
    lr, 39 ft. si. b&w. 16mm. dupe neg.
    lr, 39 ft. si. b&w. 16mm. archival pos (3 cy)
    lr, 131 ft. si. b&w. 35mm. neg ntr.
    SHELF LOC'N: FAB670 (print); FRA5707 (neg); FRA5708 & 5917 & 6200 (arch pos, 3 cy)

Archival pos (cy 2 & 3) appear under RAM title: *TR Attends San Diego Exposition, 1915.*

Interior title contains logo: Film by Stineman, San Diego, Calif.

Ref sources: San Francisco *Chronicle.* 7/29/15: 9; San Francisco *Examiner.* 7/29/15: 1; P&P portrait file; Wittemann, Herman L. [Panama-California Exposition, San Diego, Calif., 1915.] lot 6930. P&P.

Newsfilm; views.

SUMMARY: As part of the festivities at the Panama-California Exposition, TR reviews the Annapolis Naval Academy's midshipmen on July 28, 1915. Long shot of the reviewing officials on the steps of the United States Government Building: TR is fourth in line, with Edward F. Dunne, governor of Illinois (1913-1917), standing at his right, and Rear Adm. William F. Fullam, superintendent of the academy, standing at his left. Various views from many different camera angles of the midshipmen as they march and parade around the Plaza de Panama; long shot of the cadets in formation before the dignitaries.

PERSONAL CREDITS: Ganahal, L., source.
1. Midshipmen. 2. Processions. 3. Marching. 4. Military ceremonies, honors, and salutes. 5. Exhibitions. 6. San Diego, Calif.—Plazas—Plaza de Panama. 7. San Diego, Calif. 8. San Diego, Calif.—Exhibitions. 9. Roosevelt, Theodore, Pres. U.S., 1858-1919. 10. Dunne, Edward F. 11. Fullam, William F. 12. United States. Naval Academy, Annapolis. 13. Illinois. Governor, 1913-1917 (Edward F. Dunne) 14. Panama-California Exposition, 1915-1916. I. Stineman, Ralph P. II. Theodore Roosevelt Association Collection. [mp 76-57]

The River of Doubt [1]
Roosevelt Film Library [1928?]
© No reg.
    2r of 2, 799 ft. si. b&w. 16mm. ref print.
    2r of 2, 799 ft. si. b&w. 16mm. dupe neg.
    2r of 2, 2010 ft. si. b&w.35mm. masterpos.
    2r of 2, 801 ft. si. b&w. 16mm. archival pos.
    2r of 2, 2005 ft. si. b&w. 35mm. neg ntr.
    SHELF LOC'N: FAB1463-1464 (print); FRA 8657-8658 (neg); FPB9891-9892 (fgmp); FRA6204-6205 (arch pos)

Film sequence does not follow the order of actual events; interior titles and appropriate footage are out of order.

Ref sources: Roosevelt Memorial Association. *Annual Report.* 1927: 19; 1928: 16; Roosevelt Memorial Association. *The River of Doubt* (script); Cherrie, George K. *Dark Trails.* 1930: 247-322; Miller, Leo E. *In the Wilds of South America.* 1918: 194-265; Eichner, Erich. *A Cidade Maravilhosa, Rio de Janeiro, e seus arredores.* [194-?]: 71; *Scribner's Magazine.* v. 55, no. 4, 1914: 407-435; v. 55, no. 5, 1914: 538-558; v. 55, no. 6, 1914: 667-689; v. 56, no. 1, 1914: 1-32; v. 56, no. 2, 1914: 163-192; v. 56, no. 3, 1914: 290-314; v. 56, no. 4, 1914: 416-443; v. 56, no. 5, 1914: 587-613; *The Outlook.* v. 105, no. 13, 1913: 694-698; v. 105, no. 16, 1913: 837-841; v. 106, no. 4, 1914: 183-188; P&P stereo file; Rio de Janeiro, Brazil. 1916. lot 3165. P&P.

Factual; adventure, compilation, nature film.

SUMMARY: In the fall of 1913, TR combined speaking engagements in Argentina, Brazil, and Chile with a collecting trip in the Amazon Valley. It is decided that Col. Candido Mariano da Silva Rondon and his assistants and members of the Roosevelt party will attempt the descent of the Rio da Dúvida, the River of Doubt. In 1926, George M. Dyott, an English explorer, was asked by the Roosevelt Memorial Association to retrace TR's voyage down the River of Doubt and to film his trip in order to supplement the footage from the 1914 expedition. This film is a combination of footage from both journeys and includes footage from the Brazilian government and other sources as well as still photos. Members of the Roosevelt party pose on board the ship Vandyck. Left to right are: Anthony Fiala, photographer for a portion of the trip; George K. Cherrie, an ornithologist; Fr. John A. Zahm, a friend of TR; Kermit Roosevelt; TR; Frank Harper, TR's secretary; and Leo E. Miller, a mammalogist. At what is probably the harbor area of Rio de Janeiro, TR appears, preceded by reporters; TR waves from a carriage; TR is seated in a trolley car with Edwin V. Morgan, American ambassador to Brazil (the man closest to the camera); long shot of the Monroe Palace (Palácio Monroe). At the Guanabara Palace (Palácio Guanabara) in

Rio de Janeiro, Lauro S. Müller, Brazilian minister of foreign affairs, walks with TR down the steps and poses behind TR and Edith Roosevelt; other Brazilian and American officials pose on the steps. TR and Edith alight from a small steamer and are met by a uniformed official. There are shots of TR and his party aboard a small launch: TR is visible wearing a light shirt (this sequence may be on the Sepotuba River). Views of the riverbank, probably shot from the Nyoac, Colonel Rondon's river steamer; men disembark as the Nyoac lands. Views of the group leaving the Nyoac to participate in a reception at the Fazenda São João (a ranch) on the Cuiabá River. Views of TR preparing to go hunting and returning with his party, possibly at the ranch, Las Palmeiras, on the Taquary (Taquari) River; Colonel Rondon is next to TR and both are on horseback. TR, Kermit, and Colonel Rondon pose with a jaguar skin. Various views of Kermit, Miller, Colonel Rondon, and Cherrie on board the Nyoac, on a pier, and in what may be a smaller boat. TR steps into a canoe; additional views of the group, probably on the Nyoac, and of TR shooting crocodiles from the boat. Scenes of wildlife such as piranhas (caribes), "the walking stick," grasshoppers, crocodiles, ibis, storks, orioles, ants, bees, monkeys, and plant life such as palms and orchids are included. At Tapirapoan the Roosevelt-Rondon group began the overland portion of their trip to the headwaters of the River of Doubt; there are scenes of oxen and pack mules. The group spent several days at Utiarity (Utiariti), where TR especially admired the nearby waterfalls. There is a still photo of TR, Colonel Rondon, and others with a group of Nhambiquara (Nambicuara) Indians near the Juruena River. Scenes depict the exacting journey down the River of Doubt: long shots of the river and men propelling canoes through rapids; men chopping trees for rollers on which canoes are hauled, transporting supplies and canoes, making paddles, cooking and eating at campsites. A still photo shows TR writing while wearing a protective headnet and gauntlets. The man examining a broken branch may be Commander Dyott; the Dyott party met Indians on their trip down the river and there is footage of several who were called Arara Indians by Dyott. The Roosevelt-Rondon group reached the end of the unknown portion of the river Apr. 15, 1914, when they sighted homes of rubber workers. TR, suffering from illness and injuries, returned from Manaos (Manaus) to New York. Several maps showing the location of the River of Doubt are included throughout the film. The Bra-

zilian government renamed the river Rio Roosevelt (also known as Rio Téodoro).

PERSONAL CREDITS: Gentry, Caroline, editor. Fiala, Anthony, photographer.

1. Rio de Janeiro. Palácio Monroe. 2. Rio de Janeiro. Palácio Guanabara. 3. Nambicuara Indians. 4. Arara Indians. 5. Brazil—Description and travel. 6. Amazon Valley. 7. Rio de Janeiro. 8. Sepotuba River. 9. Cuiabá River. 10. Utiariti, Brazil. 11. Roosevelt River. 12. Roosevelt, Theodore, Pres. U.S., 1858–1919. 13. Roosevelt, Theodore, Pres. U.S., 1858–1919—Journey to South America, 1913–1914. 14. Rondon, Candido Mariano da Silva. 15. Dyott, George M. 16. Fiala, Anthony. 17. Cherrie, George K. 18. Zahm, John A. 19. Roosevelt, Kermit. 20. Harper, Frank. 21. Miller, Leo E. 22. Morgan, Edwin V. 23. Müller, Lauro S. 24. Roosevelt, Edith. 25. Roosevelt Memorial Association. 26. Vandyck (Ship) 27. Nyoac (Steamboat) 28. Roosevelt-Rondon Scientific Expedition. I. Roosevelt Memorial Association. Film Library. II. Roosevelt Memorial Association. III. Roosevelt Memorial Association, source. IV. Theodore Roosevelt Association Collection. [mp 76–366]

The River of Doubt [2]
Roosevelt Film Library [1928?]
© No reg.

   2r of 2, 1949 ft. si. b&w. 35mm. ref print (cy 1)
   2r of 2, 1932 ft. si. b&w. 35mm. ref print (cy 2)
   2r of 2, 1994 ft. si. b&w. 35mm. ref print (cy 3)
   2r of 2, 1949 ft. si. b&w. 35mm. dupe neg (cy 1)
   2r of 2, 1932 ft. si. b&w. 35mm. dupe neg (cy 2)
   2r of 2, 1995 ft. si. b&w. 35mm. dupe neg (cy 3)
   2r of 2, 1951 ft. si. b&w. 35mm. pos ntr (cy 1)
   2r of 2, 1932 ft. si. b&w. 35mm. pos ntr (cy 2)
   2r of 2, 1996 ft. si. b&w. 35mm. pos ntr (cy 3)

SHELF LOC'N: FEA8937–8938 (print, cy 1);
            FEA8941–8942 (print, cy 2);
            FEA8943–8944 (print, cy 3);
            FPB9889–9890 (neg, cy 1);
            FPB9895–9896 (neg, cy 2);
            FPB9897–9898 (neg, cy 3)

Factual; adventure, compilation, nature film.

SUMMARY: This film is a Roosevelt Memorial Association compilation of footage from TR's 1913–1914 trip to South America during which he combined a series of lectures with an expedition in the Amazon Valley of Brazil to collect zoological specimens. The Roosevelt group was combined with a group of Brazilian scientists under the leadership of Col. Candido Mariano da Silva Rondon to explore the course of the uncharted Rio da Dúvida, the River of Doubt. In 1926 George M. Dyott, an English explorer, was asked by the Roosevelt Memorial Association to retrace TR's voyage down the River of Doubt and to film his trip in order to supplement the footage from the 1914 trip. There are shots of Roosevelt's party on board the Vandyck: left to right are Anthony Fiala; George K. Cherrie, an ornithologist; Fr. John A. Zahm, a friend of TR; TR; Kermit Roosevelt; Frank Harper, TR's secretary; and Leo E. Miller, a mammalogist. TR and his wife, Edith Roosevelt, alight from a small steamer and are met by a uniformed official; the location may be Rio de Janeiro. At what is probably the Rio de Janeiro harbor area, there are shots of TR walking, preceded by reporters; TR, with three unidentified men, waves from a carriage; TR is seated in a trolley car, the man next to him (closest to the camera) may be Edwin V. Morgan, American ambassador to Brazil; long shot of the Monroe Palace. On the steps of the Guanabara Palace, Lauro S. Müller, Brazilian foreign minister, TR, and others pose. Shots of TR and party aboard a small launch, probably on the Sepotuba River. Views of the riverbank, probably from the Nyoac, Colonel Rondon's river steamer, which carried the Roosevelt-Rondon expedition up the Paraguay River; men disembark as the Nyoac lands. Views of the group leaving the Nyoac to participate in a reception at the Fazenda São João on the Cuyabá (Cuiabá) River. Shots of TR preparing to go hunting and returning with his party, possibly at the ranch, Las Palmeiras, on the Taquary (Taquari) River; TR, Kermit, and Colonel Rondon pose with a jaguar skin. Views of Kermit, Miller, Colonel Rondon, and Cherrie on the Nyoac; TR shoots crocodiles from the boat. Views of wildlife and plant life are included. Scenes depict the exacting journey down the river. There is a still photo of TR, Colonel Rondon, and others with a group of Nhambiquara (Nambicuara) Indians near the Juruena River. Although the Roosevelt party did not see any Indians on the River of Doubt, their presence in the bordering jungle was evident; the man examining a broken branch may be Commander Dyott; the Dyott party did meet Indians and there is footage of several who were called Arara Indians by Dyott. The Roosevelt-Rondon group reached the end of the unknown portion of the river Apr. 15, 1914. TR, suffering from illness and injuries incurred during his long journey, returned from Manaos (Manaus) to New York; the group of men on the riverboat traveling on the Madeira River are probably members of Fiala's group rather than TR's

(Fiala left Roosevelt-Rondon party at Utiarity to descend the Papagaio, the Juruena, and the Tapajós Rivers).

PERSONAL CREDITS: Gentry, Caroline, editor. Fiala, Anthony, photographer.

1. Rio de Janeiro. Palácio Monroe. 2. Rio de Janeiro. Palácio Guanabara. 3. Nambicuara Indians. 4. Indians of South America—Brazil. 5. Arara Indians. 6. Amazon Valley. 7. Brazil—Description and travel. 8. Rio de Janeiro. 9. Sepotuba River. 10. Cuiabá River. 11. Madeira River. 12. Roosevelt River. 13. Roosevelt, Theodore, Pres. U.S., 1858–1919. 14. Roosevelt, Theodore, Pres. U.S., 1858–1919—Journey to South America, 1913–1914. 15. Rondon, Candido Mariano da Silva. 16. Dyott, George M. 17. Fiala, Anthony. 18. Cherrie, George K. 19. Zahm, John A. 20. Roosevelt, Kermit. 21. Harper, Frank. 22. Miller, Leo E. 23. Roosevelt, Edith. 24. Morgan, Edwin V. 25. Müller, Lauro S. 26. Roosevelt Memorial Association. 27. Vandyck (Ship) 28. Nyoac (Steamer) 29. Roosevelt-Rondon Scientific Expedition. I. Roosevelt Memorial Association. Film Library. II. Roosevelt Memorial Association. III. Roosevelt Memorial Association, source. IV. Theodore Roosevelt Association Collection. [mp 76–367]

The River of Doubt [3]
Roosevelt Film Library [1928?]
© No reg.
lr, 794 ft. si. b&w. 35mm. ref print (cy 1)
lr, 798 ft. si. b&w. 35mm. ref print (cy 2)
lr, 806 ft. si. b&w. 35mm. ref print (cy 3)
lr, 794 ft. si. b&w. 35mm. dupe neg (cy 1)
lr, 798 ft. si. b&w. 35mm. dupe neg (cy 2)
lr, 806 ft. si. b&w. 35mm. dupe neg (cy 3)
lr, 798 ft. si. b&w. 35mm. masterpos.
lr, 795 ft. si. b&w. 35mm. pos ntr (cy 1)
lr, 806 ft. si. b&w. 35mm. pos ntr (cy 2)
lr, 798 ft. si. b&w. 35mm. neg ntr.
SHELF LOC'N: FEA8945 (print, cy 1); FEA8933 (print, cy 2); FEA8946 (print, cy 3); FPB9899 (neg, cy 1); FPB 9883 (neg, cy 2); FPB9900 (neg, cy 3); FPB9884 (fgmp)
Factual; adventure, compilation.
SUMMARY: A shorter compilation film combining footage from TR's 1913–1914 trip to South America with footage from George M. Dyott's 1927 trip retracing TR's voyage down the uncharted River of Doubt in Brazil. Several maps show the location of the River of Doubt, renamed Roosevelt River by the Brazilian government in honor of TR.

Several members of TR's group pose aboard the Vandyck, the ship on which TR sailed from New York. Left to right are: Anthony Fiala, former arctic explorer and photographer for a portion of the journey; George K. Cherrie, ornithologist; Fr. John A. Zahm, a friend of TR; Kermit Roosevelt; Frank Harper, TR's secretary; and Leo E. Miller, mammalogist. Several scenes of TR's arrival in Rio de Janeiro are included: a group of reporters precedes TR as he walks, probably in the harbor area of Rio de Janeiro; TR is in a carriage with unidentified Brazilian officials; on the steps of the Guanabara Palace TR poses with American and Brazilian officials, including Edwin V. Morgan, American ambassador, and Lauro S. Müller, Brazilian minister of foreign affairs. The first person off the Nyoac, the river steamer which carried the Roosevelt-Rondon expedition up the Paraguay River, is TR; Father Zahm is also identifiable as the group leaves the boat, probably on their way to a ceremony at the Fazenda São João on the Cuyabá (Cuiabá) River in the state of Matto Grosso (Mato Grosso). There are shots of TR and a man who may be Col. Candido Mariano da Silva Rondon, explorer and leader of the Brazilian members of the expedition, returning from a hunting trip. Various views of wildlife are included; TR shoots crocodiles from the Nyoac. Pack mules and oxen were used to transport supplies on the overland portion of the trip to the headwaters of the River of Doubt. Orchids and palm trees with birds nesting in them depict the flora and fauna of the area. The party spent several days at Utiarity (Utiariti); TR especially admired the spectacular waterfalls nearby. Footage from both expeditions (Roosevelt and Dyott) recounts the exacting journey down the river. Views of Indians called the Arara Indians by Dyott. In a still photo, the Brazilian paddlers are grouped around the marker bearing the river's new name, Rio Roosevelt, and there is also footage of a member of Dyott's party examining the original marker. The last scenes of TR on a ship were probably taken on board the Vandyck before the expedition, rather than after, since Father Zahm, who left the group at Utiarity, also appears.

1. Rio de Janeiro. Palácio Guanabara. 2. Indians of South America—Brazil. 3. Arara Indians. 4. Brazil—Description and travel. 5. Roosevelt River. 6. Rio de Janeiro. 7. Cuiabá River. 8. Mato Grosso, Brazil (State) 9. Utiariti, Brazil. 10. Amazon Valley. 11.Roosevelt, Theodore, Pres. U.S., 1858–1919. 12. Roosevelt, Theodore, Pres. U.S., 1858–1919—Journey to South America, 1913–1914. 13. Dyott, George M. 14. Fiala, Anthony. 15. Cherrie, George K. 16. Zahm, John A. 17. Roosevelt, Kermit. 18. Harper, Frank. 19. Miller, Leo E. 20. Morgan, Edwin V. 21. Müller, Lauro S. 22. Rondon, Candido Mariano da Silva. 23. Roosevelt Memorial Association. 24. Vandyck (Ship) 25. Nyoac (Steamboat) 26. Roosevelt-Rondon Scientific Expedition. I. Roosevelt Memorial Association. Film Library. II. Roosevelt Memorial Association. III. Roosevelt Memorial Association, source. IV. Theodore Roosevelt Association Collection. [mp 76–368]

The River of Doubt [4]
Roosevelt Film Library [1928?]
  © No reg.
    lr, 501 ft. si. b&w. 35mm. ref print.
    lr, 501 ft. si. b&w. 35mm. dupe neg.
    lr, 501 ft. si. b&w. 35mm. masterpos.
    lr, 501 ft. si. b&w. 35mm. neg ntr.
  SHELF LOC'N: FEA8935 (print); FPB9886
                (neg); FPB9887 (fgmp)
Sequences do not follow the order of events; interior titles and appropriate footage are out of order; based on the RMA script, *The River of Doubt*, the film appears to be outtakes from *The River of Doubt* [3]

Ref print is dark; there are flash titles.
Factual; compilation.
SUMMARY: This film appears to be randomly spliced footage of TR's 1913–1914 trip to South America and George M. Dyott's 1927 journey down the Roosevelt River (the River of Doubt). There are several sequences of TR's activities in Rio de Janeiro: TR sitting in a trolley car beside a man who may be Edwin V. Morgan, American ambassador to Brazil; brief views of the Monroe Palace; formal activities as TR arrives at an unidentified building; Lauro S. Müller, Brazilian minister of foreign affairs, and TR walking down the steps of the Guanabara Palace; TR, Edith Roosevelt, and others alighting from a small launch and being greeted by a uniformed official; additional views of TR and Mrs. Roosevelt on the steps of Guanabara Palace, Müller standing behind them with other Brazilian and American diplomatic personnel. The Roosevelt-Rondon group traveled aboard the Nyoac, Col. Candido Mariano da Silva Rondon's river steamer, to São Luis de Cáceres (Cáceres), where men and supplies had to be transferred to a smaller launch to travel up the Sepotuba River to Tapirapoan, where the overland portion of the trip to the headwaters of the River of Doubt began. There are several views of the group aboard the

small launch, probably on the Sepotuba River; various views of the group during the river journey; Kermit Roosevelt and Fr. John A. Zahm, a member of the Roosevelt group, are frequently visible. Views, probably taken from the Nyoac, of the Fazenda São João on the Cuyabá (Cuiabá) River and the welcoming reception given by officials of the state of Matto Grosso (Mato Grosso). TR made several hunting and collecting trips before reaching the River of Doubt: TR, with a man who is probably Colonel Rondon, steps into a canoe; TR poses for the photographer and then mounts a horse; additional sequences of hunting parties on horseback, with Colonel Rondon and Kermit, as well as TR, appearing in most; the three men pose with a jaguar skin. Views of the flora and fauna of the area. TR and party appear in a still photo with several Nhambiquara (Nanbicuara) Indians. Shots of rapids in the River of Doubt and of the Brazilian paddlers represent the voyage through the river's unknown portion.

PERSONAL CREDITS: Gentry, Caroline, editor. 1. Rio de Janeiro. Palácio Monroe. 2. Rio de Janeiro. Palácio Guanabara. 3. Indians of South America—Brazil. 4. Nambicuara Indians. 5. Roosevelt River. 6. Rio de Janeiro. 7. Brazil—Description and travel. 8. Sepotuba River. 9. Cuiabá River. 10. Mato Grosso, Brazil (State) 11. Amazon Valley. 12. Roosevelt, Theodore, Pres. U.S., 1858–1919. 13. Roosevelt, Theodore, Pres. U.S., 1858–1919— Journey to South America, 1913–1914. 14. Dyott, George M. 15. Morgan, Edwin V. 16. Müller, Lauro S. 17. Roosevelt, Edith. 18. Rondon, Candido Mariano da Silva. 19. Roosevelt, Kermit. 20. Zahm, John A. 21. Roosevelt-Rondon Scientific Expedition. 22. Nyoac (Steamboat) I. Roosevelt Memorial Association. Film Library. II. Roosevelt Memorial Association. III. Roosevelt Memorial Association, source. IV. Theodore Roosevelt Association Collection. [mp 76–369]

The River of Doubt [5]
Roosevelt Film Library [1928?]
© No reg.
   lr, 1030 ft. si. b&w. 35mm. ref print.
   lr, 1030 ft. si. b&w. 35mm. dupe neg.
   lr, 1030 ft. si. b&w. 35mm. pos ntr.
   SHELF LOC'N: FEA8936 (print); FPB9888 (neg)
   Film sequence does not follow the order of actual events.
   Factual; compilation.
   SUMMARY: This compilation film appears to be a randomly spliced account of TR's travels in Brazil prior to beginning the descent of the River of Doubt. There are several scenes of the Roosevelt-Rondon party on board the Nyoac, Col. Candido Mariano da Silva Rondon's river steamer, which transported the group up the Paraguay River, and on a small launch which carried the men and their supplies up the Sepotuba River to Tapirapoan, where pack mules and oxen were used to transport supplies on the overland portion of the journey to the headwaters of the River of Doubt. TR shoots at crocodiles from the Nyoac; several views of the small launch, probably on the Sepotuba River; TR appears on the launch wearing a white shirt as he stands and leans against the rail; several members of the party watch the river for piranhas; Kermit Roosevelt turns toward the camera; a man who is probably Fr. John A. Zahm disembarks from a boat that is moored along a riverbank; Kermit, Leo E. Miller, a mammalogist, George K. Cherrie, an ornithologist, and an unidentified man watch the water from the side of a boat or pier; additional views of TR talking informally with Father Zahm, Miller, and Kermit on the Nyoac; shots of the Fazenda São João on the Cuyabá (Cuiabá) River, probably taken from the Nyoac; TR, Father Zahm, and others leave the Nyoac to attend a reception at the ranch given by officials and prominent citizens of the State of Matto Grosso (Mato Grosso). TR and others leave for hunting trips in canoes and on horseback; Kermit and Colonel Rondon accompany TR and pose with a jaguar shot by TR. Views of palm trees, birds (storks and scarlet ibis), insects ("the walking stick" and a grasshopper), and piranhas are examples of plant life and wildlife observed by TR. In Rio de Janeiro TR receives a formal welcome; TR and Edith Roosevelt pose with American and Brazilian diplomatic personnel on the steps of the presidential residence, the Guanabara Palace; Lauro S. Müller, Brazilian minister of foreign affairs, is visible behind the Roosevelts; Edwin V. Morgan, American ambassador to Brazil, and Father Zahm appear on the right portion of the picture, in the following sequence Morgan stands on the right side of TR, and Müller is on TR's left; a man who is probably Anthony Fiala, former arctic explorer and official photographer of the Roosevelt group, and Father Zahm stand behind TR. Maps and panning shots of Guanabara Bay, the harbor of Rio de Janeiro, are included. In the harbor area, TR, preceded by reporters and photographers, tips his hat to the welcoming crowd; in a carriage with three unidentified men, TR waves and speaks; a man who may be Morgan sits next to TR in a trolley car;

long shots of Monroe Palace; soldiers await the arrival of TR at the entrance of a large building; TR and officials arrive in a carriage; Müller and TR walk down the steps of the Guanabara Palace; TR and Mrs. Roosevelt are greeted by a uniformed official as they alight from a small launch. There are medium-close views of Colonel Rondon sitting at his desk. The final sequence is of Fiala, Cherrie, Father Zahm, TR, Kermit, Frank Harper, TR's secretary, and Miller posing on the deck of the Vandyck some time after Kermit joined the group at Bahia, Brazil.

PERSONAL CREDITS: Gentry, Caroline, editor. Fiala, Anthony, photographer.

1. Rio de Janeiro. Palácio Guanabara. 2. Rio de Janeiro. Palácio Monroe. 3. Brazil—Description and travel. 4. Sepotuba River. 5. Cuiabá River. 6. Mato Grosso, Brazil (State) 7. Rio de Janeiro. 8. Amazon Valley. 9. Roosevelt, Theodore, Pres. U.S., 1858–1919. 10. Roosevelt, Theodore, Pres. U.S., 1858–1919—Journey to South America, 1913–1914. 11. Rondon, Candido Mariano da Silva. 12. Roosevelt, Kermit. 13. Zahm, John A. 14. Miller, Leo E. 15. Cherrie, George K. 16. Roosevelt, Edith. 17. Müller, Lauro S. 18. Morgan, Edwin V. 19. Fiala, Anthony. 20. Harper, Frank. 21. Roosevelt-Rondon Scientific Expedition. 22. Nyoac (Steamboat) 23. Vandyck (Ship) I. Roosevelt Memorial Association. Film Library. II. Roosevelt Memorial Association. III. Roosevelt Memorial Association, source. IV. Theodore Roosevelt Association Collection. [mp 76–370]

The River of Doubt [6]
Roosevelt Film Library [1928?]
   © No reg.
      lr, 462 ft. si. b&w. 35mm. ref print.
      lr, 462 ft. si. b&w. 35mm. dupe neg.
      lr, 462 ft. si. b&w. 35mm. masterpos ntr.
   SHELF LOC'N: FEA8934 (print); FPB9885 (neg)
   Ref source: Roosevelt Memorial Association. *The River of Doubt* (script)
   Factual; compilation.
   SUMMARY: A short compilation film of TR's voyage down the River of Doubt in early 1914. Some of the footage was taken by Anthony Fiala, who, though he was the official photographer for the Roosevelt group, did not accompany them down the River of Doubt; Fiala descended the Papagaio, the Juruena, and the Tapajós Rivers. In 1927 George M. Dyott, an English explorer, under the auspices of the Roosevelt Memorial Association, led a party down the River of Doubt, or the Roosevelt

River as it was renamed by the Brazilian government. Footage from his trip, footage from other sources, and still photos were combined with Fiala's film to create a pictorial record of TR's expedition. Included are views of ants, which are a constant torment during the voyage; a still photo shows TR writing while wearing a headnet and gauntlets for protection. There are also close-up shots of a small monkey which visits Dyott's camp. The presence of Indians in the bordering jungle during the river trip was evident to TR's group, but they did not encounter any, unlike the Dyott party: a man, who may be Commander Dyott, examines a broken branch; views of several Indians who are called Arara Indians by Dyott. Several sequences show various activities of the Brazilian paddlers: men cooking and eating at a campsite, pulling a canoe ashore, standing around the marker bearing the river's new name, Rio Roosevelt. A member of Dyott's group examines the marker post thirteen years later. Still photos of TR standing in front of a tent; the still of TR seated in a canoe was probably taken immediately before the descent of the River of Doubt. The end of the voyage is marked by the sighting of homes of rubber workers on the riverbank; scenes of men unloading rubber or supplies from boats. The River of Doubt flows into the Madeira River. The men on the boat, on what is identified as the Madeira River, are probably members of Fiala's group rather than TR's; long shots of a river which may be either the Madeira or the Amazon; a map shows the location of the newly charted river. Final views of TR walking on the deck of a ship were probably taken at the beginning of the voyage aboard the Vandyck, rather than at the end when TR was ill.

PERSONAL CREDITS: Fiala, Anthony, photographer.

1. Ants—Brazil. 2. Insects—Brazil. 3. Monkeys. 4. Indians of South America—Brazil. 5. Arara Indians. 6. Roosevelt River. 7. Brazil—Description and travel. 8. Madeira River. 9. Amazon Valley. 10. Roosevelt, Theodore, Pres. U.S., 1858–1919. 11. Roosevelt, Theodore, Pres. U.S., 1858–1919—Journey to South America, 1913–1914. 12. Dyott, George M. 13. Roosevelt-Rondon Scientific Expedition. 14. Roosevelt Memorial Association. 15. Vandyck (Ship) I. Roosevelt Memorial Association, source. II. Theodore Roosevelt Association Collection. [mp 76–371]

The River of Doubt [7]
Roosevelt Film Library [1928?]

© No reg.

2r of 2, 2027 ft. si. b&w. 35mm. ref print.

2r of 2, 2121 ft. si. b&w. 35mm. dupe neg.

2r of 2, 2028 ft. si. b&w. 35mm. pos ntr.

SHELF LOC'N: FEA8939–8940 (print); FPB 9893–9893–894 (neg)

Dupe neg is longer than ref print due to 93 ft. of unrelated footage at the beginning of r2.

Factual; adventure, compilation, nature film.

SUMMARY: This film is a Roosevelt Memorial Association compilation of footage from TR's 1913–1914 trip to South America during which he combined a series of lectures with an expedition in the Amazon Valley of Brazil to collect zoological specimens. There are shots of Roosevelt's party on board the Vandyck: left to right are Anthony Fiala, former arctic explorer and official photographer for a portion of the trip; George K. Cherrie, an ornithologist; Fr. John A. Zahm, a friend of TR and an experienced traveler in South America; TR; Kermit Roosevelt; Frank Harper, TR's secretary; and Leo E. Miller, mammalogist; the location is probably Bahia or Rio de Janeiro. Pans of Guanabara Bay, the harbor of Rio de Janeiro. TR and Edith Roosevelt alight from a small steamer and are met by a uniformed official; the location may be Rio de Janeiro. At what is probably the Rio de Janeiro harbor area, there are shots of TR walking, preceded by reporters; TR, with three unidentified men, waves from a carriage; TR is seated in a trolley car, the man next to him (closest to the camera) may be Edwin V. Morgan, American ambassador to Brazil; long shot of the Monroe Palace. At the Guanabara Palace in Rio de Janeiro, the man preceding TR down the steps and then posing behind TR and his wife is Lauro S. Müller, Brazilian minister of foreign affairs; Brazilian and American diplomatic personnel and others pose on the steps. Shots of TR and his party aboard a launch, probably on the Sepotuba River. There are views of the riverbank, probably taken from the Nyoac, Col. Candido Mariano da Silva Rondon's river steamer, which carried the Roosevelt-Rondon expedition up the Paraguay River; men disembark from the Nyoac. Views of the group leaving the Nyoac to participate in a reception at the Fazenda São João on the Cuyabá (Cuiabá) River. TR prepares to go hunting and returns with his party, possibly at the ranch, Las Palmeiras, on the Taquary (Taquari) River; Colonel Rondon is next to TR and both are on horseback. TR, Kermit, and Colonel Rondon pose with a jaguar skin. Views of Kermit, Miller, Colonel Rondon, Cherrie, and other members of the group engaged in various activities on the river. TR steps into a canoe preparing for a hunt; additional views of the group, probably on the Nyoac; TR shoots crocodiles from the boat. Views of wildlife and plant life are included. There is a still photo of TR, Colonel Rondon, and others with a group of Nhambiquara (Nambicuara) Indians near the Juruena River. Scenes depict the exacting journey down the river. Although the Roosevelt party didn't see any Indians on the River of Doubt, their presence in the bordering jungle was evident: the man examining a broken branch may be Commander Dyott; the Dyott party did meet Indians and there is footage of several who were called Arara Indians by Dyott. The Roosevelt-Rondon group reached the end of the unknown portion of the river Apr. 15, 1914, when they sighted the homes of rubber workers. TR, suffering from illness and injuries incurred during his long journey, returned from Manaos (Manaus) to New York. Several maps showing the location of the River of Doubt as correctly charted by the Roosevelt-Rondon Expedition are included throughout the film.

PERSONAL CREDITS: Gentry, Caroline, editor. Fiala, Anthony, photographer.

1. Rio de Janeiro. Palácio Monroe. 2. Rio de Janeiro. Palácio Guanabara. 3. Indians of South America—Brazil. 4. Nambicuara Indians. 5. Arara Indians. 6. Amazon Valley. 7. Brazil—Description and travel. 8. Rio de Janeiro. 9. Sepotuba River. 10. Cuiabá River. 11. Roosevelt River. 12. Roosevelt, Theodore, Pres. U.S., 1858–1919. 13. Roosevelt, Theodore, Pres. U.S., 1858–1919—Journey to South America, 1913–1914. 14. Fiala, Anthony. 15. Cherrie, George K. 16. Zahm, John A. 17. Roosevelt, Kermit. 18. Harper, Frank. 19. Miller, Leo E. 20. Roosevelt, Edith. 21. Morgan, Edwin V. 22. Müller, Lauro S. 23. Rondon, Candido Mariano da Silva. 24. Dyott, George M. 25. Roosevelt Memorial Association. 26. Vandyck (Ship) 27. Nyoac (Steamboat) 28. Roosevelt-Rondon Scientific Expedition. I. Roosevelt Memorial Association. Film Library. II. Roosevelt Memorial Association. III. Roosevelt Memorial Association, source. IV. Theodore Roosevelt Association Collection. [mp 76–372]

RMA ceremonies at [Hearst Greek Theatre, University of California, Berkeley, Calif.]

Producer unknown [1919?]

© No reg.

1r, 41 ft. si. b&w. 16mm. ref print.

1r, 41 ft. si. b&w. 16mm. dupe neg.

1r, 103 ft. si. b&w. 35mm. pos old safety.

SHELF LOC'N: FAB720 (print); FRA5782 (neg)

RMA lists the location and the date in the title as Oakland, Calif., 1920.

Research indicates that the film may be a Kinogram production.

Ref source: Abell, Carl. *The Campus, University of California.* 1919.

Newsfilm.

SUMMARY: Military personnel and civilians attend a Roosevelt memorial ceremony on the campus of the University of California at Berkeley. The service is held in the Hearst Greek Theatre, given to the university by journalist William Randolph Hearst. The film includes shots of uniformed men filing into the open-air theater, an unidentified man speaking from the stage, and men carrying an American flag as the assemblage disperses.

PERSONAL CREDITS: Urban, Charles, source.

1. Armed Forces. 2. Berkeley, Calif. 3. Roosevelt, Theodore, Pres. U.S., 1858–1919—Funeral and memorial services. 4. Roosevelt Memorial Association. 5. University of California, Berkeley. 6. Hearst Greek Theatre. I. Theodore Roosevelt Association Collection. [mp 76–46]

RMA flag ceremonies, children sew stars on flag, 1919.

Kinogram Pub. Corp., Oct 1919.

© No reg.

lr, 52 ft. si. b&w. 16mm. ref print.

lr, 52 ft. si. b&w. 16mm. dupe neg.

lr, 55 ft. si. b&w. 16mm. archival pos.

lr, 131 ft. si. b&w. 35mm. pos ntr.

(Kinograms [Series])

SHELF LOC'N: FAB711 (print); FRA5768 (neg); FRA5769 (arch pos)

Film sequence does not follow the order of actual events.

Ref sources: *Daily News,* New York. 10/25/19: 8; 10/27/19: [10–11]; Roosevelt Memorial Association. *Annual Report.* 1919–1921; 14; P&P portrait file.

Newsfilm.

SUMMARY: In honor of TR's birthday the week of Oct. 20–27, 1919, was declared Roosevelt Week by the Roosevelt Memorial Association. As one of the events, an official Roosevelt memorial flag, which has been carried across New York State, is ceremoniously received at the Williamsburg Bridge Plaza in Brooklyn on Oct. 24. Opening scene of five school girls sewing the forty-seventh star on the flag; the camera pans down a statue of George Washington to a group of school children holding flags and participating in the ceremony; a man who

may be James A. McCabe, superintendent of public schools, leads the crowd in singing; close-up of the flag as boy runners stand on a table to display it to the crowd; Samuel Abbott, originator of the memorial flag idea, speaks from a platform to the cheering crowd. The final scene is of five girls sewing the forty-eighth and final star on the flag at what is probably Cove School in Oyster Bay, N.Y., with a group of children and Boy Scouts visible in the background.

PERSONAL CREDITS: Urban, Charles, source.

1. Memorial rites and ceremonies. 2. Flags. 3. High school students—Political activity. 4. Brooklyn, N.Y. 5. Oyster Bay, N.Y. 6. Roosevelt, Theodore, Pres. U.S., 1858–1919—Funeral and memorial services. 7. McCabe, James A. 8. Abbott, Samuel. 9. Roosevelt Memorial Association. 10. Cove School. 11. Boy Scouts of America. I. Kinogram Publishing Corporation. II. Theodore Roosevelt Association Collection. [mp 76–42]

RMA flag service on the steps of New York Public Library, 1919.

Kinogram Pub. Corp., Oct 1919.

© No reg.

lr, 42 ft. si. b&w. 16mm. ref print.

lr, 42 ft. si. b&w. 16mm. dupe neg.

lr, 42 ft. si. b&w. 16mm. archival pos.

lr, 104 ft. si. b&w. 35mm. pos ntr.

(Kinograms [Series])

SHELF LOC'N: FAB994 (print); FRA5976 (neg); FRA5977 (arch pos)

Film sequence does not follow the order of actual events; the second sequence, children at the grave, is unverified.

Ref sources: *Daily News,* New York. 10/25/19: 8; The New York *Times Mid-week Pictorial.* v. 10, no. 10,1919: [9]; New York *American.* 10/25/19: 11; P&P portrait file.

Newsfilm.

SUMMARY: On Oct. 27, 1919, the Roosevelt memorial flag, which has been carried across New York State in TR's honor, is brought to rest at his grave in Youngs Memorial Cemetery, Oyster Bay, N.Y. Views of Samuel Abbott, originator of the memorial flag idea, placing the flag on TR's grave. Sequence of two young girls and a boy placing a flower bouquet and a flag through the fence surrounding TR's grave; this event may not be part of the flag ceremonies. Final scenes of a flag ceremony sponsored by the Roosevelt Memorial Association on the steps of the New York Public Library, Oct. 25; long shots of notables standing on a platform. Possible identifications from right to left are: Henry Cabot Lodge, honorary vice-president of RMA; the man next to Lodge is probably Henry J. Allen, governor of Kansas; William Boyce Thompson, president of RMA, is holding the flag with the help of a man who appears to be Henry D. Lindsley, chairman of the event; William Loeb, Jr., vice-president of RMA, is visible in back of Thompson; next to Loeb is probably William Gibbs McAdoo; and the man to the far left with his hands to his side may be Elihu Root, an RMA trustee. Sequence of Boy Scouts and members of the Naval Reserve hoisting the flag up a flagpole as an unidentified man leads the crowd in singing.

PERSONAL CREDITS: Urban, Charles, source.

1. Memorial rites and ceremonies. 2. Flags. 3. Youngs Memorial Cemetery. 4. New York (City) 5. Oyster Bay, N.Y. 6. Roosevelt, Theodore, Pres. U.S., 1858–1919—Funeral and memorial services. 7. Abbott, Samuel. 8. Lodge, Henry Cabot. 9. Allen, Henry J. 10. Thompson, William Boyce. 11. Lindsley, Henry D. 12. Loeb, William, 1866–1937. 13. McAdoo, William Gibbs. 14. Root, Elihu. 15. Roosevelt Memorial Association. 16. New York (City). Public Library. 17. Kansas. Governor, 1919–1923 (Henry J. Allen) 18. Boy Scouts of America. 19. United States. Naval Reserve. I. Kinogram Publishing Corporation. II. Theodore Roosevelt Association Collection. [mp 76–141]

RMA pilgrimage to TR's grave, 1930.

Producer unknown [1930?]

© No reg.

lr, 135 ft. si. b&w. 35mm. ref print.

lr, 135 ft. si. b&w. 35mm. dupe neg.

lr, 135 ft. si. b&w. 35mm. masterpos.

SHELF LOC'N: FEA6741 (print); FPB7350 (neg); FPB7349 (fgmp)

The date in the title is unverified.

Ref sources: *Roosevelt House Bulletin.* v. 4, no. 1, 1932: 5–6; P&P portrait file.

Factual; views.

SUMMARY: Scenes from an annual pilgrimage sponsored by RMA whereby a group of personal friends visit TR's gravesite in Youngs Memorial Cemetery in Oyster Bay, N.Y., and then call on Edith Roosevelt at Sagamore Hill. Long shots of a group of men, one carrying a large wreath, and women walking up the hill to TR's gravesite; medium-close view of a man, who may be William Loeb, Jr., reading from an open book as a group listens; identified in the crowd, from left to right in the first line are: Hermann Hagedorn, executive

secretary of RMA; Alexander Lambert, TR's personal physician; and Albert Bushnell Hart, historian and trustee of RMA. The final sequence is composed of views of Sagamore Hill, as a car pulls up and members of the pilgrimage party leave the auto to enter the house.

1. Memorial rites and ceremonies. 2. Youngs Memorial Cemetery. 3. Oyster Bay, N.Y. Sagamore Hill. 4. Oyster Bay, N.Y. 5. Roosevelt, Theodore, Pres. U.S., 1858–1919—Funeral and memorial services. 6. Loeb, William, 1866–1937. 7. Hagedorn, Hermann. 8. Lambert, Alexander. 9. Hart, Albert Bushnell. 10. Roosevelt Memorial Association. I. Kinogram Publishing Corporation, source. II. Theodore Roosevelt Association Collection. [mp 76–172]

RMA services at [Hearst Greek Theatre, University of California, Berkeley, Calif.]; Laying cornerstone of Roosevelt School at New Rochelle, N.Y. [1920]

Producer unknown, Jan 1920.

© No reg.

lr, 50 ft. si. b&w. 16mm. ref print.

lr, 50 ft. si. b&w. 16mm. archival pos.

lr, 124 ft. si. b&w. 35mm. neg ntr.

SHELF LOC'N: FAB719 (print); FRA5783 (arch pos)

Research indicates the production date of the first segment may be 1919; RMA lists the date in the title of the second segment as 1919–1920.

RMA lists the location in the title of the first segment as the Oakland, Calif. Stadium.

Laying Cornerstone of Roosevelt School at New Rochelle, N.Y. [1920] is clearly identified as a Kinogram production; *RMA Services . . .* may also be a Kinogram production.

Ref source: Abell, Carl. *The Campus, University of California.* 1919.

Newsfilm.

SUMMARY: The first segment consists of views of military personnel and civilians attending a Roosevelt memorial ceremony on the campus of the University of California at Berkeley. The service is held in the Hearst Greek Theatre, given to the university by journalist William Randolph Hearst. The film includes shots of uniformed men filing into the open-air theater, an unidentified man speaking from the stage, and men carrying an American flag as the assemblage disperses. In the second segment, Lt. Col. Theodore Roosevelt, Jr., is participating in the laying of the cornerstone of the Roosevelt School in New Rochelle, N.Y., Jan. 3,

1920. Dedicated to his father's memory, the public school is located in the Wykagyl area of New Rochelle. Lieutenant Colonel Roosevelt wears a mourning band as he stands on a flag-draped scaffold. The segment includes medium-close shots of Lieutenant Colonel Roosevelt.

PERSONAL CREDITS: Urban, Charles, source.

1. Memorial service. 2. Armed Forces. 3. Corner stones, Laying of. 4. Schools. 5. Dedication services. 6. Berkeley, Calif. 7. New Rochelle, N.Y. 8. Wykagyl, N.Y. 9. Roosevelt, Theodore, Pres. U.S., 1858–1919—Funeral and memorial services. 10. Roosevelt, Theodore, 1887–1944. 11. University of California, Berkeley. 12. Hearst Greek Theatre. 13. Roosevelt School. I. Kinogram Publishing Corporation. II. Theodore Roosevelt Association Collection. III. Laying cornerstone of Roosevelt School at New Rochelle, N.Y. [1920] [Title] IV. Series: Kinograms [Series] [mp 76–249]

RMA trustees at Roosevelt House, 1923 [1]

Roosevelt Memorial Association [1923?]

© No reg.

    lr, 70 ft. si. b&w. 16mm. ref print.

    lr, 70 ft. si. b&w. 16mm. archival pos.

    lr, 167 ft. si. b&w. 35mm. neg ntr.

SHELF LOC'N: FAB982 (print); FRA5955 (arch pos)

The date in the title is unverified.

The RMA list indicates that the surname of the photographer is Ruby.

Ref sources: Roosevelt Memorial Association. *Annual Report.* 1923: 13–14; P&P portrait file.

Factual; views.

SUMMARY: Several close shots of five men, identified as RMA trustees, posing behind a desk filled with books and papers in what appears to be the library in Roosevelt House: 1) Hermann Hagedorn; 2) Alexander Lambert; 3) William Loeb, Jr.; 4) and 5) are unidentified.

PERSONAL CREDITS: Ruby, photographer.

1. New York (City). Roosevelt House. 2. New York (City) 3. Hagedorn, Hermann. 4. Lambert, Alexander. 5. Loeb, William, 1866–1937. 6. Roosevelt Memorial Association. 7. Roosevelt Memorial Association. Board of Trustees. I. Roosevelt Memorial Association. II. Roosevelt Memorial Association, source. III. Theodore Roosevelt Association Collection. [mp 76–123]

RMA trustees at Roosevelt House, 1923 [2]

Roosevelt Memorial Association [1923?]

    © No reg.

    lr, 57 ft. si. b&w. 16mm. ref print.

    lr, 57 ft. si. b&w. 16mm. archival pos.

    lr, 142 ft. si. b&w. 35mm. neg ntr.

SHELF LOC'N: FAB981 (print); FRA5956 (arch pos)

The date in the title is unverified.

The RMA list indicates that the surname of the photographer is Ruby.

Ref sources: Roosevelt Memorial Association. *Annual Report.* 1923: 13–14; P&P portrait file.

Factual; views.

SUMMARY: Several close shots of five men, identified as RMA trustees, posing behind a desk filled with books and papers in what appears to be the library in Roosevelt House: 1) an unidentified man; 2) Will H. Hays; 3) John H. Finley; 4) Elihu Root; and 5) Edwin A. Van Valkenburg.

PERSONAL CREDITS: Ruby, photographer.

1. New York (City). Roosevelt House. 2. New York (City) 3. Hays, Will H. 4. Finley, John H. 5. Root, Elihu. 6. Van Valkenburg, Edwin A. 7. Roosevelt Memorial Association. 8. Roosevelt Memorial Association. Board of Trustees. I. Roosevelt Memorial Association. II. Roosevelt Memorial Association, source. III. Theodore Roosevelt Association Collection. [mp 76–122]

Robert Bacon and Army officers.

Producer unknown, May 1918.

    © No reg.

    lr, 15 ft. si. b&w. 16mm. ref print.

    lr, 15 ft. si. b&w. 16mm. dupe neg (cy 1)

    lr, 38 ft. si. b&w. 35mm. dupe neg (cy 2)

    lr, 37 ft. si. b&w. 35mm. pos ntr.

SHELF LOC'N: FAB973 (print); FRA5942 (neg, cy 1); FPB7951 (neg, cy 2)

May be a Signal Corps production.

Film is out of frame ca. first 6 ft. on ref print and dupe neg (cy 1).

Ref sources: Scott, James B. *Robert Bacon.* 1975; Pershing, John J. *My Experiences in the World War.* v. 1, 1931: 164; United States. National Archives and Records Service. Audiovisual Archives Division; P&P portrait file; United States. War Dept. General Staff. *Catalogue of Official A.E.F. Photographs Taken by the Signal Corps.* 1919: 179.

Factual; views.

SUMMARY: Col. Robert Bacon, former secretary of state and ex-ambassador to France, served as chief of the American Military Mission to British General Headquarters and as Field Marshal Sir Douglas Haig's personal liaison officer with American units in the British area. Colonel Bacon, Brig.

Gen. Cyril M. Wagstaff, chief of the British Mission, and Brig. Gen. William W. Harts, chief of the American Mission (after Colonel Bacon) and commanding general of American troops with the British Expeditionary Forces, walk out of a building in Montreuil, France, the location of British headquarters; the three men talk and pose for the camera. A woman and several children walk past the group. Colonel Bacon is the man on the left, the British officer in the center is Brigadier General Wagstaff, and the other American officer is Brigadier General Harts. Brief shots of buildings and the street are included.

1. European War, 1914–1918. 2. Montreuil-sur-Mer, France. 3. Bacon, Robert, 1860–1919. 4. Wagstaff, Cyril M. 5. Harts, William W. 6. United States. Army—Officers. 7. Great Britain. Army—Officers. I. United States. Army. Signal Corps. II. United States. Army. Signal Corps, source. III. Theodore Roosevelt Association Collection. [mp 76–166]

Roosevelt at home: Sagamore Hill, Oyster Bay, L.I. [1]

Roosevelt Film Library, 1930.
© No reg.
   lr of 1,356 ft. si. b&w. 16mm. ref print.
   lr of 1,356 ft. si. b&w. 16mm. dupe neg.
   lr of 1,913 ft. si. b&w. 35mm. masterpos.
   lr of 1,356 ft. si. b&w. 16mm. archival pos.

lr of 1,923 ft. si. b&w. 35mm. pos ntr.
lr of 1,890 ft. si. b&w. 35mm. neg ntr.
SHELF LOC'N: FAB1469 (print); FRA8655 (neg); FPB4605 (fgmp); FRA6198 (arch pos)
Nitrate deterioration on ref print ca. ft. 316–354.
Ref sources: Roosevelt Memorial Association. *Annual Report.* 1930: 9; Roosevelt Memorial Association. *Roosevelt at Home* (script)
Factual; biographical.

SUMMARY: This Roosevelt Memorial Association production employs interior titles, quotations from TR, still photos, and factual footage to depict TR's enduring love of his home and family. Both interior and exterior views of Sagamore Hill, including shots of trophies, gifts, and mementos in the house; still photos of Mrs. Roosevelt, the Roosevelt children, and relatives; TR walking with friends and addressing a large group from the porch at Sagamore; William P. Helm, an Associated Press correspondent for New York City and Washington (1910–1918) speaks with TR; TR poses with his horse, Sidar, and his dogs, chops a tree down, and rows along the shore of Oyster Bay; the final sequences represent TR's sons' service in the armed forces during World War I, and TR's ideas about patriotism as he participates in the 1916 Fourth of July celebration in Oyster Bay.

1. Oyster Bay, N.Y. Sagamore Hill. 2. Sidar (Horse) 3. Pets. 4. Horses. 5. Dogs. 6 Trees. 7.

The Roosevelt family on a picnic in 1916. Left to right are: Archie Roosevelt, Quentin Roosevelt, Ethel Roosevelt Derby, a woman who may be Eleanor Alexander Roosevelt (wife of Theodore Roosevelt, Jr.), TR, and Edith Roosevelt.

Fourth of July celebrations. 8. Processions. 9. Oyster Bay, N.Y. 10. Roosevelt, Theodore, Pres. U.S., 1858–1919. 11. Roosevelt, Theodore, Pres. U.S., 1858–1919—Homes. 12. Roosevelt family. 13. Roosevelt, Theodore, Pres. U.S., 1858–1919—Family. 14. Roosevelt, Theodore, Pres. U.S., 1858–1919—Personality. 15. Helm, William P. 16. Associated Press. I. Roosevelt Memorial Association. II. Roosevelt Memorial Association. Film Library. III. Pathe. IV. Roosevelt Memorial Association, source. V. Theodore Roosevelt Association Collection. [mp 76–272]

Roosevelt at home: Sagamore Hill, Oyster Bay, L.I. [2]
Roosevelt Film Library, 1930.
© No reg.
lr, 914 ft. si. b&w. 35mm. ref print.
lr, 914 ft. si. b&w. 35mm. dupe neg.
lr, 914 ft. si. b&w. 35mm. pos ntr.
SHELF LOC'N: FEA8338 (print); FPB9876 (neg)
Ref sources: Roosevelt Memorial Association. *Annual Report*. 1930: 9; Roosevelt Memorial Association. *Roosevelt at Home* (script)
Factual; biographical.
SUMMARY: Quotations and still photos are interspersed with factual footage of TR's home and family in Oyster Bay, N.Y. Exterior views of Sagamore Hill and surrounding land and interior views of the entrance hall, the North Room (Trophy Room), and the library; photos of Mrs. Roosevelt, the Roosevelt children, and relatives; TR walking with friends and addressing a large group from the porch at Sagamore; children are greeted by TR at a building which may be the Cove School in Oyster Bay, which the Roosevelt children attended; William P. Helm, an Associated Press correspondent for New York City and Washington (1910–1918) speaks with TR; TR rides and poses with his horse, Sidar, and his dogs, chops down a tree, and rows along the shore of Oyster Bay; the final sequences represent TR's sons' service in the armed forces during World War I, and TR's ideas about patriotism as he participates in the 1916 Fourth of July celebration in Oyster Bay.
PERSONAL CREDITS: Gentry, Caroline, director.
1. Oyster Bay, N.Y. Sagamore Hill. 2. Sidar (Horse) 3. Pets. 4. Horses. 5. Dogs. 6. Trees. 7. Fourth of July celebrations. 8. Processions. 9. Oyster Bay, N.Y. 10. Roosevelt, Theodore, Pres. U.S., 1858–1919. 11. Roosevelt, Theodore, Pres. U.S., 1858–1919—Homes. 12. Roosevelt family. 13.

Roosevelt, Theodore, Pres. U.S., 1858–1919—Family. 14. Roosevelt, Theodore, Pres. U.S., 1858–1919—Personality. 15. Helm, William P. 16. Cove School. 17. Associated Press. I. Roosevelt Memorial Association. II. Roosevelt Memorial Association. Film Library. III. Pathe. IV. Roosevelt Memorial Association, source. V. Theodore Roosevelt Association Collection. [mp 76–273]

Roosevelt cartoons.
Producer unknown [191–?]
© No reg.
lr, 45 ft. si. b&w. 35mm. ref print.
lr, 45 ft. si. b&w. 35mm. dupe neg.
lr, 45 ft. si. b&w. 35mm. neg ntr.
SHELF LOC'N: FEA8932 (print); FPB9882 (neg)
Ref sources: Gros, Raymond, ed. *T.R. in Cartoon*. 1910; Shaw, Albert. *A Cartoon History of Roosevelt's Career*. 1910: 19.
Short; political; still film.
SUMMARY: Five political cartoons of TR depicting different phases of his career: 1) TR as trust-buster and reformer in the White House; 2) TR as Rough Rider; 3) TR as man of the hour, after the charge up San Juan Hill and the Russo-Japanese peace negotiations; 4) TR as Uncle Sam; and 5) TR's policies on public indifference and special privileges.
1. Caricatures and cartoons. 2. Editorial cartoons. 3. Politics and art. 4. Roosevelt, Theodore, Pres. U.S., 1858–1919—Cartoons, satire, etc. 5. Roosevelt, Theodore, Pres. U.S., 1858–1919—Personality. I. Prizma Pictures, source. II. Theodore Roosevelt Association Collection. [mp 76–286]

The Roosevelt Dam [1]
Roosevelt Memorial Association Film Library [1928?]
© No reg.
lr, 949 ft. si. b&w. 35mm. ref print (cy 1)
lr, 950 ft. si. b&w. 35mm. ref print (cy 2)
lr, 949 ft. si. b&w. 35mm. dupe neg (cy 1)
lr, 950 ft. si. b&w. 35mm. dupe neg (cy 2)
lr, 950 ft. si. b&w. 35mm. pos ntr.
SHELF LOC'N: FEA8949 (print, cy 1); FEA8950 (print, cy 2); FPB9906 (neg, cy 1); FPB9907 (neg, cy 2)
Ref print (cy 1) and dupe neg (cy 1) have additional RMA material at the beginning and end of the film.
Ref sources: Roosevelt Memorial Association. *The Roosevelt Dam* (script); Roosevelt Memorial Association. *Annual Report*. 1928: 16; Harbaugh, William

H. *The Life and Times of Theodore Roosevelt.* 1963: 304–319; Sloan, Richard E., ed. *History of Arizona.* v. 2, 1930: 316–322; *Arizona Republican,* Phoenix. 3/18/11: 1–2; 3/19/11: sec. 1: 1; 3/19/11: sec. 2: 4–6; P&P portrait file; *Portrait and Biographical Record of Arizona.* 1901: [334]

Factual; compilation, views.

SUMMARY: This film depicts TR's commitment to the reclamation of desert land and his belief that natural resources exist for the public benefit. Included are close-up views of Frederick H. Newell, first director of the U.S. Reclamation Service, and Gifford Pinchot, first chief forester and leader of the conservation movement in the U.S.; both influenced TR's thinking and action on conservation. TR fought successfully for the passage of the Reclamation Act of 1902, which authorized the creation of the reclamation service. In 1906 work on the Roosevelt Dam on the Salt River in Arizona began; it was completed in 1911. The film consists of views of a desert area, including many varieties of cactus; construction of the dam; the completed dam, hydroelectric plant, reservoir, and irrigation system. Scenes of fields and orchards, sheep and cattle grazing, men clearing, plowing, and harvesting fields with various types of farm equipment, and scenes of crops of wheat, alfalfa, and melons all represent the benefits brought to the Salt River Valley area by the availability of water. At the formal dedication of the dam on Mar. 18, 1911, TR presses an electric switch opening sluice gates; TR speaks and shakes hands with Indian workers. Behind him on the platform are, left to right: a woman who may be Edith Roosevelt; a bald man who is probably Louis C. Hill, supervising engineer of the project; an unidentified man; Benjamin A. Fowler, president of the National Irrigation Congress; another unidentified man; Richard E. Sloan, territorial governor of Arizona; and a man who is probably John P. Orme, President of the Salt River Valley Water Users' Association.

PERSONAL CREDITS: Gentry, Caroline, editor.

1. Roosevelt Dam. 2. Reclamation of land—Arizona. 3. Cactus. 4. Dams—Arizona—Design and construction. 5. Water-power electric plants—Arizona. 6. Reservoirs—Arizona. 7. Irrigation—Arizona. 8. Farm equipment. 9. Irrigation farming—Arizona. 10. Dedication services. 11. Indians of North America—Arizona—Employment. 12. United States—Public Lands. 13. Salt River, Ariz. 14. Arizona. 15. Salt River Valley, Ariz. 16. Roosevelt, Theodore, Pres. U.S., 1858–1919. 17. Newell, Frederick H. 18. Pinchot, Gifford. 19. Roosevelt, Theodore, Pres. U.S., 1858–1919—Addresses, essays, lectures. 20. Roosevelt, Edith. 21. Hill, Louis C. 22. Fowler, Benjamin A. 23. Sloan, Richard E. 24. Orme, John P. 25. United States. Bureau of Reclamation. 26. Arizona (Ter.). Governor, 1909–1912 (Sloan) I. Roosevelt Memorial Association. Film Library. II. Roosevelt Memorial Association, source. III. Theodore Roosevelt Association Collection [mp 76–354]

The Roosevelt Dam [2]

Roosevelt Memorial Association Film Library [1928?]

© No reg.

  lr, 986 ft. si. b&w. 35mm. ref print.
  lr, 986 ft. si. b&w. 35mm. dupe neg.
  lr, 959 ft. si. b&w. 35mm. masterpos.
  lr, 961 ft. si. b&w. 35mm. neg ntr.

SHELF LOC'N: FEA9947 (print); FPB9904 (neg); FPB9905 (fgmp)

Dupe neg is longer than the masterpos due to printing of interior title and sequence.

Some interior titles and appropriate footage are not in order.

Ref sources: Roosevelt Memorial Association. *The Roosevelt Dam* (script); Roosevelt Memorial Association. *Annual Report.* 1928: 16.

Factual; compilation, views.

SUMMARY: TR's involvement in the reclamation of desert land from the beginning of his presidential administration to the formal dedication of Roosevelt Dam on the Salt River in Arizona, on Mar. 18 1911, is represented in this film. Included are close-up views of Frederick H. Newell, first director of the U.S. Reclamation Service, and Gifford Pinchot, first chief forester and leader of the conservation movement in the U.S. Views of the desert include varieties of cactus, a man and woman farming land using irrigation, and fields and orchards. At the formal dedication of the dam on Mar. 18, TR presses an electric switch opening sluice gates. TR speaks at the dedication ceremonies and shakes hands with Indian workers. Behind him on the platform are, left to right: a woman who may be Edith Roosevelt; a bald man who is probably Louis C. Hill, supervising engineer of the project; an unidentified man; Benjamin A. Fowler, president of the National Irrigation Congress; another unidentified man; Richard E. Sloan, territorial governor of Arizona; and a man who is probably John P. Orme, president of the Salt River Valley Water Users' Association. There are long shots and pans of the construction of the dam, and of the completed dam, hydroelectric plant, reservoir, and irrigation system. Scenes of sheep and cattle grazing; men clearing, plowing, and harvesting fields with various types of farm equipment; crops of wheat, alfalfa, and melons all represent the benefits brought to the Salt River Valley by the availability of water.

PERSONAL CREDITS: Gentry, Caroline, editor. 1. Roosevelt Dam. 2. Reclamation of land—Arizona. 3. Dams—Arizona. 4. Cactus. 5. Irrigation farming—Arizona. 6. Dedication services. 7. Indians of North America—Arizona—Employment. 8. Dams—Arizona—Design and construction. 9. Water-power electric plants—Arizona. 10. Reservoirs—Arizona. 11. Farm equipment. 12. United States—Public lands. 13. Salt River, Ariz. 14. Arizona. 15. Salt River Valley, Ariz. 16. Roosevelt, Theodore, Pres. U.S., 1858–1919. 17. Newell, Frederick H. 18. Pinchot, Gifford. 19. Roosevelt, Theodore, Pres. U.S., 1858–1919—Addresses, essays, lectures. 20. Roosevelt, Edith. 21. Hill, Louis C. 22. Fowler, Benjamin A. 23. Sloan, Richard E. 24. Orme, John P. 25. United States. Bureau of Reclamation. 26. Arizona (Ter.). Governor, 1909–1912 (Sloan) I. Roosevelt Memorial Association. Film Library. II. Roosevelt Memorial Association, source. III. Theodore Roosevelt Association Collection. [mp 76–355]

Roosevelt, friend of the birds [1]

Roosevelt Memorial Association Film Library [1924?]

© MP5938, Roosevelt Memorial Association, 1Feb28

lr of 1, 980 ft. si. b&w. 35mm. ref print.
lr of 1, 980 ft. si. b&w. 35mm. dupe neg.
lr of 1, 648 ft. si. b&w. 35mm. pos ntr.

SHELF LOC'N: FEA6700 (print); FPB7074 (neg)

The copyright catalog lists the title as *Theodore Roosevelt, Friend of the Birds,* and the author as Caroline Gentry.

Interior titles suggest that the TR sequences were filmed at Pelican Island in the Indian River, a bird sanctuary off the eastern coast of Florida, which TR had established by unnumbered Executive Order in March 1903 (not 1904 as the RMA title states). Pelican Island marked the beginning of the national wildlife refuge system. Research indicates that the film's locations are the Breton Island Reservation and Audubon bird sanctuaries off the coast of Louisiana; areas visited by TR included the Chandeleur Islands, Grand Isle, Breton Island, Bird

Island, Last Island, Battledore Island, and Barataria Bay. Breton Island Reservation was established by Executive Order 369–A on Nov. 11, 1905. The exact locations of the sequences are undetermined.

The film is composed of footage taken in 1915 by Herbert K. Job on a National Audubon Society expedition with TR and undated dramatic footage of the plight of the snowy egret.

Ref sources: The *Times-Picayune,* New Orleans. 6/7/15: 2; 6/8/15: 16; 6/10/15: 10; 6/12/15: 1; 6/13/15: (real estate sec.): 7; Harvard University. Library. Theodore Roosevelt Collection; Roosevelt Memorial Association. *Roosevelt, Friend of the Birds* (script); Roosevelt Memorial Association. *Annual Report.* 1924: 10; *Scribner's Magazine.* v. 59, no. 3, 1916: 261–280; *Audubon Magazine.* v. 17, no. 5, 1915: 410–412; *Louisiana History.* v. 12, no. 1, 1971: 5–19; Gabrielson, Ira N. *Wildlife Refuges.* 1943: 10–11, 70–71; Historical Records Survey. New York (City). *Presidential Executive Orders.* v. 1, 1944: 38; *Harper's Magazine.* v. 119, 1909: 290–299; United States. Congress. Senate. Committee on Interior and Insular Affairs. *Designating Pelican Island Wilderness Area.* 1969.

Factual; nature film.

SUMMARY: A narrative of TR's role in bird preservation which includes factual footage taken on his visit under the auspices of the National Audubon Society to bird sanctuary islands off the coast of Louisiana, June 1915. Mating habits and domestic life of snowy egrets and their plunder by hunters are dramatized. Scenes of an egret's nest and the hunting, killing, and plucking of birds serve as the prologue to the depiction of TR as a bird preservationist. Views of TR and John M. Parker, leader of the Louisiana Progressive party, aboard the Audubon Society's boat, the Royal Tern; views of TR standing in marshes, with what is perhaps the Louisiana Conservation Commission yacht in the background. Herbert K. Job, photographer for the expedition and noted ornithologist, appears on the beach with his camera; TR examines eggs and talks with other members of the expedition: a man who is probably J. Hippolyte Coquille, a local photographer; M. L. Alexander, president of the Louisiana Conservation Commission, in light pants; John Parker, with his back to the camera; and game warden William Sprinkle. Additional scenes of TR exploring an island and observing birds along the beach and views of a variety of shore birds including royal terns, black skimmers, laughing gulls, brown pelicans, blue herons, and egrets complete the film.

PERSONAL CREDITS: Gentry, Caroline, director. Job, Herbert K., photographer.

1. Birds, Protection of. 2. Wildlife refuges—Louisiana. 3. Herons. 4. Water-birds. 5. Terns. 6. Black skimmer. 7. Laughing gull. 8. Brown pelican. 9. Breton Island Reservation, La. 10. Louisiana. 11. Gulf of Mexico. 12. Roosevelt, Theodore, Pres. U.S., 1858–1919—Journey to Louisiana, 1915. 13. Parker, John Milliken. 14. Job, Herbert K. 15. Coquille, J. Hippolyte. 16. Alexander, M. L. 17. Sprinkle, William. 18. National Audubon Society. 19. Royal Tern (launch) 20. Louisiana. Dept. of Conservation. I. Roosevelt Memorial Association. Film Library. II. Roosevelt Memorial Association, source. III. Theodore Roosevelt Association Collection. IV. Theodore Roosevelt, friend of the birds [Title] [mp 76–356]

Roosevelt, friend of the birds [2]

Roosevelt Memorial Association Film Library [1924?]

© No reg.

lr, 1003 ft. si. b&w. 35mm. ref print (cy 1)
lr, 989 ft. si. b&w. 35mm. ref print (cy 2)
lr, 984 ft. si. b&w. 35mm. ref print (cy 3)
lr, 1003 ft. si. b&w. 35mm. dupe neg (cy 1)
lr, 989 ft. si. b&w. 35mm. dupe neg (cy 2)
lr, 984 ft. si. b&w. 35mm. dupe neg (cy 3)
lr, 1003 ft. si. b&w. 35mm. pos ntr (cy 1)
lr, 989 ft. si. b&w. 35mm. pos ntr (cy 2)
lr, 983 ft. si. b&w. 35mm. pos ntr (cy 3)

SHELF LOC'N: FEA8958 (print, cy 1); FEA8959 (print, cy 2); FEA8960 (print, cy 3); FPB9916(neg, cy 1); FPB9917 (neg, cy 2); FPB9918 (neg, cy 3)

"Produced by Caroline Gentry, Director of Films" appears on ref print (cy 3) and dupe neg (cy 3).

Interior titles suggest that the TR sequences were filmed at Pelican Island in the Indian River, a bird sanctuary off the eastern coast of Florida which TR had established by unnumbered Executive Order in March 1903 (not 1904 as the RMA title states). Pelican Island marked the beginning of the national wildlife refuge system. Research indicates that the film's locations are the Breton Island Reservation and Audubon bird sanctuaries off the coast of Louisiana; areas visited by TR included the Chandeleur Islands, Grand Isle, Breton Island, Bird Island, Last Island, Battledore Island, and Barataria Bay. Breton Island Reservation was established by Executive Order

369–A on Nov. 11, 1905. The exact locations of the sequences are undetermined.

The film is composed of footage taken in 1915 by Herbert K. Job on a National Audubon Society expedition with TR and undated dramatic footage of the plight of the snowy egret.

Some interior titles differ slightly from *Roosevelt, Friend of the Birds [1]*

Ref sources: Roosevelt Memorial Association. *Roosevelt, Friend of the Birds* (script); Roosevelt Memorial Association. *Annual Report.* 1924: 10.

Factual; nature film.

SUMMARY: A narrative of TR's role in bird preservation which includes factual footage taken on his visit under the auspices of the National Audubon Society to bird sanctuary islands off the coast of Louisiana, June 1915. Mating habits and domestic life of snowy egrets and their plunder by hunters are dramatized. Scenes of an egret's nest and the hunting, killing, and plucking of birds serve as the prologue to the depiction of TR as a bird preservationist. Views of TR and John M. Parker, leader of the Louisiana Progressive party aboard the Audubon Society's boat, the Royal Tern; views of TR standing in marshes, with what is perhaps the Louisiana Conservation Commission yacht in the background. Herbert K. Job, photographer for the expedition and noted ornithologist, appears on the beach with his camera; TR examines eggs and talks with other members of the expedition: a man who is probably J. Hippolyte Coquille, a local photographer; M. L. Alexander, president of the Louisiana Conservation Commission, in light pants; John Parker, with his back to the camera; and game warden William Sprinkle. Additional scenes of TR exploring an island and observing birds along the beach and views of a variety of shore birds including royal terns, black skimmers, laughing gulls, brown pelicans, blue herons, and egrets complete the film.

PERSONAL CREDITS: Gentry, Caroline, director. Job, Herbert K., photographer.

1. Birds, Protection of. 2. Wildlife refuges—Louisiana. 3. Herons. 4. Water-birds. 5. Terns. 6. Black skimmer. 7. Laughing gull. 8. Brown pelican. 9. Breton Island Reservation, La. 10. Louisiana. 11. Gulf of Mexico. 12. Roosevelt, Theodore, Pres. U. S., 1858–1919—Journey to Louisiana, 1915. 13. Parker, John Milliken. 14. Job, Herbert K. 15. Coquille, J. Hippolyte. 16. Alexander, M. L. 17. Sprinkle, William. 18. National Audubon Society. 19. Royal Tern (Launch) 20. Louisiana. Dept. of Conservation. I. Roosevelt Memorial Association.

Film Library. II. Roosevelt Memorial Association, source. III. Theodore Roosevelt Association Collection. IV. Theodore Roosevelt, friend of the birds [Title] [mp 76–357]

Roosevelt, friend of the birds [3]

Roosevelt Memorial Association Film Library [1924?]

© No reg.

lr, 379 ft. si. b&w. 16mm. ref print.
lr, 379 ft. si. b&w. 16mm. dupe neg.
lr, 380 ft. si. b&w. 16mm. archival pos.
SHELF LOC'N: FAB1018(print); FRA5801 (neg); FRA5994 (arch pos)

Film lacks main credits and is out of sequence.

Interior titles suggest that the TR sequences were filmed at Pelican Island in the Indian River, a bird sanctuary off the eastern coast of Florida which TR had established by unnumbered Executive Order in March 1903 (not 1904 as the RMA title states). Pelican Island marked the beginning of the national wildlife refuge system. Research indicates that the film's locations are the Breton Island Reservation and Audubon bird sanctuaries off the coast of Louisiana; areas visited by TR included the Chandeleur Islands, Grand Isle, Breton Island, Bird Island, Last Island, Battledore Island, and Barataria Bay. Breton Island Reservation was established by Executive Order 369–A on Nov. 11, 1905. The exact locations of the sequences are undetermined.

The film is composed of footage taken in 1915 by Herbert K. Job on a National Audubon Society expedition with TR and undated dramatic footage of the plight of the snowy egret.

Ref sources: Roosevelt Memorial Association. *Roosevelt, Friend of the Birds* (script); Roosevelt Memorial Association. *Annual Report.* 1924: 10.

Factual; nature film.

SUMMARY: Scenes from TR's June 1915 visit to the Breton Island Reservation and Audubon bird sanctuary islands portray TR as a bird lover and preservationist. Views of TR and John M. Parker, leader of the Louisiana Progressive party, aboard the Audubon Society's boat, the Royal Tern; views of TR standing in marshes, with what is perhaps the Louisiana Conservation Commission yacht in the background. Herbert K. Job, photographer for the expedition and noted ornithologist, appears on the beach with his camera; TR examines eggs and talks with other members of the expedition: a man who is probably J. Hippolyte Coquille, a local photographer; M. L. Alexander, in light pants and shirt, president of the Louisiana Conservation

Commission; John Parker, with his back to the camera; and game warden William Sprinkle. TR explores an island and observes birds on the beach. Mating habits and domestic life of snowy egrets and their plunder by hunters are dramatized with scenes of an egret's nest and the hunting, killing, and plucking of the birds. There are also views of a variety of shore birds including royal terns, black skimmers, laughing gulls, brown pelicans, blue herons, and egrets.

PERSONAL CREDITS: Job, Herbert K., photographer.

1. Wildlife refuges—Louisiana. 2. Birds, Protection of. 3. Water-birds. 4. Herons. 5. Terns. 6. Black skimmer. 7. Laughing gull. 8. Brown pelican. 9. Breton Island Reservation, La. 10. Louisiana. 11. Gulf of Mexico. 12. Roosevelt, Theodore, Pres. U.S., 1858–1919—Journey to Louisiana, 1915. 13. Parker, John Milliken. 14. Job, Herbert K. 15. Coquille, J. Hippolyte. 16. Alexander, M. L. 17. Sprinkle, William. 18. National Audubon Society. 19. Royal Tern (Launch) 20. Louisiana. Dept. of Conservation. I. Roosevelt Memorial Association. Film Library. II. Eastman Kodak Company, source. III. Theodore Roosevelt Association Collection. [mp 76–358]

Roosevelt, friend of the birds [4]; The Roosevelt Dam [3]

Roosevelt Memorial Association Film Library [1928?]

© No reg.

lr, 835 ft. si. b&w. 35mm. ref print.
lr, 835 ft. si. b&w. 35mm. dupe neg.
lr, 833 ft. si. b&w. 35mm. pos ntr.
SHELF LOC'N: FEA7830 (print); FPB9920 (neg)

RMA title: *The Roosevelt Dam and Roosevelt, Friend of the Birds.*

Ref sources: Roosevelt Memorial Association. *Roosevelt, Friend of the Birds* (script); Roosevelt Memorial Association. *The Roosevelt Dam* (script)

Factual; views, nature film.

SUMMARY: This film is composed of short versions of two RMA productions: the first portion of Roosevelt, friend of the birds [4] describes the plunder of snowy egrets for their plumes; the second portion includes views of TR's June 1915 expedition to bird sanctuary islands off the coast of Louisiana; the location is not Pelican Island, Fla., as an interior title notes, but is probably Audubon bird sanctuaries or the Breton Island Reservation. TR and John M. Parker, leader of the Louisiana Progressive party, wave from the Audubon Society's boat, the Royal Tern. Herbert K. Job, an ornithologist from the National Audubon Society who also served as photographer for the expedition, appears on the beach with his camera; examining bird eggs are J. Hippolyte Coquille, a local photographer; TR; M. L. Alexander, president of the Louisiana Conservation Commission; and William Sprinkle, game warden. View of TR exploring the island and observing birds. Included are shots of herons, royal terns, black skimmers, laughing gulls, and brown pelicans. The Roosevelt Dam, built on the Salt River in Ariz., was dedicated on Mar. 18, 1911; it was a result of TR's continued interest and support of reclamation of desert land. The Roosevelt Dam [3] consists of various shots of the completed dam, the hydroelectric plant, the highway on top of the dam, irrigation machinery, and the reservoir formed by the dam. Scenes of fields, sheep, cattle, horses pulling a plow, and the harvesting of alfalfa and melons depict the dramatic impact the irrigation system had on the Salt River Valley.

PERSONAL CREDITS: Gentry, Caroline.

1. Birds, Protection of. 2. Roosevelt Dam. 3. Herons. 4. Wildlife refuges—Louisiana. 5. Waterbirds. 6. Terns. 7. Black skimmer. 8. Laughing gull. 9. Brown pelican. 10. Dams—Arizona. 11. Reclamation of land—Arizona. 12. Irrigation farming—Arizona. 13. Louisiana. 14. Gulf of Mexico. 15. Breton Island Reservation, La. 16. Salt River, Ariz. 17. Arizona. 18. Salt River Valley, Ariz. 19. Roosevelt, Theodore, Pres. U.S., 1858–1919—Journey to Louisiana, 1915. 20. Parker, John Milliken. 21. Job, Herbert K. 22. Coquille, J. Hippolyte. 23. Alexander, M. L. 24. Sprinkle, William. 25. National Audubon Society. 26. Royal Tern (Launch) I. Roosevelt Memorial Association. Film Library. II. Eastman Kodak Company, source. III. Theodore Roosevelt Association Collection. IV. Roosevelt Dam [3], The [Title] [mp 76–359]

Roosevelt scenes [1917–1918]
Hearst-Pathe News, 1917–1918.
© No reg.
   lr, 83 ft. si. b&w. 16mm. ref print.
   lr, 83 ft. si. b&w. 16mm. dupe neg.
   lr, 101 ft. si. b&w. 16mm. archival pos.
(Hearst-Pathe News [newsreel])
SHELF LOC'N: FAB1057 (print); FRA6029 (neg); FRA6030 (arch pos)
RMA lists the date in the title as 1917.
Newsfilm; compilation.
SUMMARY: Views of TR at various public functions in support of the war effort: 1) TR stands with Brig. Gen. Michael J. Lenihan, fellow officer in the Spanish-American War, and speaks to the camera during an informal visit to Camp Mills, near Garden City, N.Y., on Sept. 2, 1917; 2) on the lawn of Sagamore Hill on Aug. 22, 1917, TR and members of the Belgian mission pose for the camera; identified in the group are Capt. Thomas C. Cook, an American army officer; Hector Carlier, a secretary of the mission; Maj. Leon Osterrieth, Belgian army officer; George T. Wilson and Frederic Coudert, prominent New Yorkers; Baron Ludovic Moncheur, former ambassador to the United States and head of the mission; Gen. Mathieu Leclercq, commander of the Belgian Cavalry; Jean D. Mertens, a secretary of the mission; T. P. O'Connor, Irish political leader and writer; and Count Louis d'Ursel, Belgian army officer and diplomat; 3) at Forest Hills, N.Y., on July 4, 1917, TR reviews and marches with the Forest Hills Rifle Club; 4) on Sept. 28, 1917, TR speaks at a large pro-war parade in St. Paul, Minn., with Minnesota Governor Joseph A. A. Burnquist (1915–1921) standing behind him on the platform; 5) supporting the Liberty Loan effort in Billings, Mont., TR parades through a downtown Billings street, preceded by cowboys on horseback; 6) at Camp Grant, Rockford, Ill., TR and Thomas H. Barry, commander of the camp, address troops on Sept. 26, 1917; 7) TR speaks to crowds at the launching of the U.S.S. Newburgh in Newburgh, N.Y., Sept. 2, 1918; 8) from the porch at Sagamore TR addresses volunteer workers for the third Liberty Loan on Apr. 2, 1918; 9) TR is in Springfield, Ill. on Aug. 26, 1918, to endorse a rapid ending of the war; 10) the final sequence may be of TR arriving at the Naval Service Club in Boston on May 2, 1918, in an open car with a man who is probably the president of the club, F. Nathaniel Perkins.

1. European War, 1914–1918. 2. Oyster Bay, N.Y. Sagamore Hill. 3. Government missions, Belgian. 4. Garden City, N.Y. 5. Oyster Bay, N.Y. 6. Forest Hills, N.Y. 7. St. Paul, Minn. 8. Billings, Mont. 9. Rockford, Ill. 10. Newburgh, N.Y. 11. Springfield, Ill. 12. Boston, Mass. 13. Lenihan, Michael J. 14. Roosevelt, Theodore, Pres. U.S., 1858–1919—Addresses, essays, lectures. 15. Roosevelt, Theodore, Pres. U.S., 1858–1919—Military leadership. 16. Cook, Thomas C. 17. Carlier, Hector. 18. Osterrieth, Leon. 19. Wilson, George T. 20. Coudert, Frederic R. 21. Moncheur, Ludovic, Baron. 22. Leclercq, Mathieu. 23. Mertens, Jean D. 24. O'Connor, Thomas Power. 25. Ursel, Louis, comte d' 26. Burnquist, Joseph A. A. 27. Barry,

Thomas H. 28. Perkins, F. Nathaniel. 29. Camp Mills. 30. Forest Hills Rifle Club. 31. United States. Laws, statutes, etc. Liberty loan acts. 32. Camp Grant. 33. Newburgh (Ship) 34. New York (City). Liberty Loan Committee. 35. Naval Service Club, Boston, Mass. I. Hearst-Pathe News. II. Pathe, source. III. Theodore Roosevelt Association Collection. [mp 76–200]

Roosevelt scenes from RMA productions.

Producer unknown, 1912–1924.
© No reg.
  lr, 155 ft. si. b&w. 16mm. ref print.
  lr, 156 ft. si. b&w. 16mm. archival pos.
  lr, 390 ft. si. b&w. 35mm. neg ntr.
SHELF LOC'N: FAB1780 (print); FRA7738 (arch pos)
Ref sources: The New York *Times*. 9/15/18: pt. 5: [1]; 12/28/24: pt. 5: [1]; Roosevelt Memorial Association. *Annual Report*. 1925: 28; P&P portrait file.
Newsfilm; compilation.

SUMMARY: This compilation film includes many short sequences representing TR's varied activities and interests. He waves from the steps of City Hall in New York City, Sept. 6, 1918, after delivering an address during the Lafayette-Marne Day exercises; TR poses with members of his 1913–1914 expedition to South America and with American and Brazilian officials in Rio de Janeiro. Views of what is probably TR's 1912 Progressive campaign; a large rally at Sagamore Hill on May 27, 1916; a Memorial Day address in 1917 at Mineola, N.Y. At Oriole Baseball Park in Baltimore, TR greets Cardinal James Gibbons and speaks on behalf of the fourth Liberty Loan campaign. Men march up Sagamore Hill for the May 27, 1916, demonstration; from the porch TR addresses suffragists on Sept. 8, 1917. TR reviews the Forest Hills Rifle Club and speaks at the Forest Hills Gardens railroad station July 4, 1917. With Mayor John P. Mitchel of New York City, Charles Evans Hughes, and other notables, TR reviews a parade of drafted men Sept. 4, 1917. At Camp Grant, near Rockford, Ill., TR addresses soldiers. After his funeral on Jan. 8, 1919, pallbearers carry TR's casket from Christ Episcopal Church in Oyster Bay; views of former President William H. Taft and others at Youngs Memorial Cemetery. A monument to TR is dedicated Dec. 14, 1924, in Santiago, Cuba. Participating in the ceremony are, left to right: the president of Cuba (1921–1925), Alfredo Zayas; Mrs. Edith Roosevelt; and Enoch H. Crowder, American ambassador to Cuba. King Albert of Belgium, accompanied by Theodore Roosevelt, Jr., lays a wreath on TR's grave in Oct. 1919. Final views of a soldier standing watch over TR's grave.
PERSONAL CREDITS: Horst, source.

1. Presidents—United States—Election—1912. 2. Presidents—United States—Nomination. 3. Oyster Bay, N.Y. Sagamore Hill. 4. Women—Suffrage—New York (State) 5. New York (City) 6. Rio de Janeiro. 7. Oyster Bay, N.Y. 8. Mineola, N.Y. 9. Baltimore. 10. Forest Hills, N.Y. 11. Santiago de Cuba—Monuments. 12. Roosevelt, Theodore, Pres. U.S., 1858–1919. 13. Roosevelt, Theodore, Pres. U.S., 1858–1919—Addresses, essays, lectures. 14. Gibbons, James. 15. Mitchel, John P. 16. Hughes, Charles Evans. 17. Roosevelt, Theodore, Pres. U.S., 1858–1919—Funeral and memorial services. 18. Taft, William Howard, Pres. U.S., 1857–1930. 19. Roosevelt, Theodore, Pres. U.S., 1858–1919—Monuments, etc. 20. Zayas y Alfonso, Alfredo, Pres. Cuba, 1861–1934. 21. Roosevelt, Edith. 22. Crowder, Enoch H. 23. Albert I, King of the Belgians, 1875–1934. 24. Roosevelt, Theodore, 1887–1944. 25. Roosevelt, Theodore, Pres. U.S., 1858–1919—Tomb. 26. New York (City). City Hall. 27. Roosevelt-Rondon Scientific Expedition. 28. United States. Laws, statutes, etc. Liberty loan acts. 29. Forest Hills Rifle Club. 30. Camp Grant. 31. Cuba. Presidente, 1921–1925 (Zayas y Alfonso) I. Theodore Roosevelt Association Collection. [mp 76–373]

Rough Riders greet TR during Liberty Loan drive out west [1918]

Producer unknown, Oct 1918.
© No reg.
  lr, 3 ft. si. b&w. 16mm. ref print.
  lr, 3 ft. si. b&w. 16mm. dupe neg.
  lr, 8 ft. si. b&w. 35mm. pos ntr.
SHELF LOC'N: FAB1053 (print); FRA6021 (neg)
RMA lists the dates in the title as 1917–1918.
Ref sources: The Anaconda *Standard*. 10/6/18: 10; The Helena *Independent*. 10/6/18: 1, 3.
Newsfilm.

SUMMARY: TR appears in Billings, Montana, on Oct. 5, 1918, to speak on behalf of the Liberty Loan drive. The film has long shots of a touring car with six men inside, one of whom may be TR; the car is followed by a group of men on horseback who may be the Rough Riders. The street is lined with Billings citizens as car and riders pass.

1. Processions. 2. Horsemen. 3. Billings, Mont. 4. Roosevelt, Theodore, Pres. U.S., 1858–1919. 5.

United States. Army. 1st Cavalry (Volunteer) 6. United States. Laws, statutes, etc. Liberty loan acts. I. Pathe, source. II. Theodore Roosevelt Association Collection. [mp 76–277]

Runners carrying flag to TR's grave [1919]
Kinogram Pub. Corp., Oct 1919.
   © No reg.
      lr, 16 ft. si. b&w. 16mm. ref print (2 cy)
      lr, 16 ft. si. b&w. 16mm. dupe neg.
      lr, 16 ft. si. b&w. 16mm. masterpos.
      lr, 39 ft. si. b&w. 35mm. pos ntr.
   (Kinograms [Series])
   SHELF LOC'N: FAB1210 & 1219 (print, 2 cy); FRA6103 (neg); FRA8652 (fgmp)
   RMA lists the date in the title as 1920.
   Ref sources: *Daily News*, New York. 10/27/19: 3; 10/28/19: 1–2; New York *Tribune*. 10/28/19: 4; P&P portrait file.
   Newsfilm.
   SUMMARY: On Oct. 27, 1919, the Roosevelt memorial flag, which has been carried across New York State in TR's honor, is brought to rest at his grave in Youngs Memorial Cemetery, Oyster Bay, N.Y. There are shots from different angles of the memorial flag as it is borne by young men up the steep pathway to the gravesite; five girls sew the forty-eighth and final star on the flag at what is probably Cove School in Oyster Bay, with a group of children and Boy Scouts visible in the background. The final view is of children and adults on the cemetery grounds.
   PERSONAL CREDITS: Urban, Charles, source.
   1. Memorial rites and ceremonies. 2. Flags. 3. High school students—Political activity. 4. Youngs Memorial Cemetery. 5. Oyster Bay, N.Y. 6. Roosevelt, Theodore, Pres. U.S., 1858–1919—Funeral and memorial services. 7. Cove School. 8. Boy Scouts of America. I. Kinogram Publishing Corporation. II. Theodore Roosevelt Association Collection. [mp 76–239]

Sarah Bernhardt addresses crowd in Prospect Park, Brooklyn, 1917.
Producer unknown, Jul 1917.
   © No reg.
      lr, 4 ft. si. b&w. 16mm. ref print.
      lr, 4 ft. si. b&w. 16mm. dupe neg.
      lr, 10 ft. si. b&w. 35mm. pos ntr.
   SHELF LOC'N: FAB984 (print); FRA5958 (neg)
   Ref sources: P&P portrait file; Castelot, André. *Ensorcelante Sarah Bernhardt*. 1973: [15]

French actress Sarah Bernhardt participating in the celebration supporting French-American cooperation in the war effort on July 4, 1917.

Newsfilm.
   SUMMARY: On July 4, 1917, French actress Sarah Bernhardt speaks in Prospect Park, Brooklyn, N.Y., on behalf of French-American cooperation in the war effort. Addressing more than 50,000 people gathered around a decorated music platform, Mme. Bernhardt stands and speaks from an open touring car parked in front of the platform. Medium-close shot of Mme. Bernhardt speaking and gesturing, with a man who may be her personal physician, Dr. Felix Marot, and a woman who is probably her secretary and translator, Miss Elizabeth Ormsby, seated in the car.
   1. Fourth of July orations. 2. European War, 1914–1918—Public opinion. 3. Brooklyn, N.Y.—Parks—Prospect Park. 4. Brooklyn, N.Y. 5. Bernhardt, Sarah. 6. Marot, Felix. 7. Ormsby, Elizabeth. I. Roosevelt Memorial Association, source. II. Theodore Roosevelt Association Collection. [mp 76–157]

Scene of Clemenceau, Tardieu, Foch, Poincaré and Pershing, 1917–1918.
Producer unknown [1918?]
   © No reg.
      lr, 11 ft. si. b&w. 16mm. ref print.
      lr, 11 ft. si. b&w. 16mm. dupe neg.
      lr, 27 ft. si. b&w. 35mm. pos ntr.
   SHELF LOC'N: FAB873 (print); FRA5859 (neg)
   Dates in the title are unverified.
   Ref sources: Pershing, John J. [Views and activities of military import, 1902–1921.] lot 7729, v. 3. P&P; P&P portrait file.
   Newsfilm; war film.
   SUMMARY: Views of Philippe Pétain, commander in chief of French forces, French Premier Georges Clemenceau, and French President Raymond Poincaré reviewing a contingent of French soldiers. Gen. Cyriaque Gillain, Belgian chief of staff; Gen. John J. Pershing, commander of the

American Expeditionary Forces; Marshal Ferdinand Foch, commander of the allied armies; Field Marshal Sir Douglas Haig, commander in chief of British forces; Gen. Alberico Albrucci, commander of the Italian armies; French Marshal Joseph J. Joffre; French Gen. Maxime Weygand, chief of staff to Foch; and other unidentified officers. André Tardieu is not identified on film.

1. Processions. 2. European War, 1914–1918. 3. Clemenceau, Georges. 4. Foch, Ferdinand. 5. Poincaré, Raymond, Pres. France, 1860–1934. 6. Pershing, John J. 7. Pétain, Henri Philippe. 8. Gillain, Cyriaque C. 9. Haig, Douglas Haig. 10. Albrucci, Alberico. 11. Joffre, Joseph J. 12. Weygand, Maxime. 13. France. Président, 1913–1920 (Poincaré) 14. France. Armée. 15. France. Armée—Officers. 1. Pathe, source. II. Theodore Roosevelt Association Collection. [mp 76–334]

Scenes of African animals [1911]
Producer unknown [1911?]
© No reg.
  lr, 380 ft. si. b&w. 16mm. ref print.
  lr, 380 ft. si. b&w. 16mm. dupe neg.
  lr, 951 ft. si. b&w. 35mm. pos ntr.
SHELF LOC'N: FAB1121 (print); FRA6064 (neg)

RMA lists the date in the title as 1910; since Rainey's earliest African expedition was made in 1911, that is the earliest possible date of production.

RMA lists the photographer as Paul Rainey; since sources indicate that the official photographer on Rainey's early expeditions was John C. Hemment, he may be the actual photographer of the film.

Ref sources: *The Moving Picture World.* v. 8, no. 6, 1911:290; v. 12, no. 3, 1912: 214–215; Ramsaye, Terry. *A Million and One Nights.* 1964: 600.

Factual; nature film.

SUMMARY: Long shots in Africa of various animals, including, among others: elephants, zebras, giraffes, monkeys, African buffalo, a rhinoceros, a lion and possibly warthogs. There are brief scenes of a dog chasing a lion, and several men on horseback riding toward the camera, preceded by a pack of dogs.

PERSONAL CREDITS: Rainey, Paul James. Hemment, John C., photographer. Rainey, Paul James, source.

1. Big game animals—Africa. 2. African elephant. 3. Swine—Africa. 4. Zebras. 5. Giraffes. 6. Monkeys. 7. Buffaloes. 8. Rhinoceros. 9. Lions. 10. Hunting dogs. 11. Africa. I. Theodore Roosevelt Association Collection. [mp 76–242]

Scenes of Dr. Frank Chapman.
Producer unknown [192–?]
© No reg.
  lr, 31 ft. si. b&w. 16mm. ref print.
  lr, 31 ft. si. b&w. 16mm. archival pos.
  lr, 76 ft. si. b&w. 35mm. neg ntr.
SHELF LOC'N: FAB965 (print); FRA5934 (arch pos)

Ref sources; *New York, Greetings from the Great Metropolis Beautiful.* [19—?]; [7]; P&P portrait file.

Factual; views.

SUMMARY: Various views of Dr. Frank M. Chapman, ornithologist, curator of ornithology at the American Museum of Natural History in New York City (1908–1942) and recipient of the Roosevelt Distinguished Service Medal (1928). Medium shot of Chapman sitting at a desk in an undetermined location; view of him walking toward the camera, down what may be the staircase of the museum; and a long shot of a man who may be Chapman walking across the street with the museum visible in the background.

1. Roosevelt Medal for Distinguished Service. 2. Medalists. 3. Ornithologists. 4. New York (City) 5. Chapman, Frank Michler. 6. Roosevelt, Theodore, Pres. U.S., 1858–1919—Medals. 7. American Museum of Natural History, New York. I. Roosevelt Memorial Association, source. II. Theodore Roosevelt Association Collection. [mp 76–138]

Scenes of flowers and birds in Washington, D.C.
Producer unknown [192–?]
© No reg.
  lr, 277 ft. si. b&w. 35mm. ref print.
  lr, 277 ft. si. b&w. 35mm. dupe neg.
  lr, 277 ft. si. b&w. 35mm. pos ntr.
SHELF LOC'N: FEA7829 (print); FPB8233 (neg)

Ref sources: Rickett, Harold W. *Wild Flowers of the United States.* v. 1, pt. 1, 2, 1966; Library of Congress. Science and Technology Division. Reference Section.

Factual; views, nature film.

SUMMARY: Various views from many different camera angles of wild flowers and flora on the White House lawn. Medium and close shots of bluets; long shot of apple trees in bloom; medium shot of wild violets; two close-up shots of apple blossoms; medium shot and close shot of anemones at the base of a tree; close shot of bellworts in leaves; two long shots of dogwood beside a stream; medium shot of spring beauties; and a medium shot of dogwood with a stream flowing behind them. A long shot of the south portico of the White

House and the south lawn; two pans of flora on what is probably the south lawn of the White House; and a long shot of the northeast corner of the grounds with the North Portico of the White House in the background. There are no views of birds on the film.

PERSONAL CREDITS: Reiker, M., source.

1. Wild flowers. 2. Washington, D.C. White House. 3. Bluets. 4. Fruit trees. 5. Violets. 6. Anemones. 7. Bellworts. 8. Flowering trees. 9. Dogwood. 10. Washington, D.C. I. Theodore Roosevelt Association Collection. [mp 76–278]

[Scenes of flowers in Washington, D.C.]

Producer unknown [192–?]

© No reg.

  lr, 583 ft. si. b&w. 35mm. ref print.

  lr, 583 ft. si. b&w. 35mm. dupe neg.

  lr, 583 ft. si. b&w. 35mm. masterpos.

SHELF LOC'N: FEA9938 (print); FPC0764 (neg); FPB9921 (fgmp)

Ref sources: Rickett, Harold W. *Wild Flowers of the United States.* v. 1, 1966; Library of Congress. Science and Technology Division. Reference Section.

Factual; views, nature film.

SUMMARY: Various views from many different camera angles of flowers and flora on the White House lawn and around what appears to be the Washington, D.C. area: long shot of the White House with a group of people walking around; several scenes of flora; shots of cherry blossoms, violets, apple blossoms, anemones at the base of trees, bellworts in leaves, dogwood along a running stream, and spring beauties; pans of the south and north porticos of the White House and lawn, followed by additional scenes of flora.

1. Wild flowers. 2. Washington, D.C. White House. 3. Flowering trees. 4. Flowering cherries. 5. Violets. 6. Anemones. 7. Bellworts. 8. Dogwood. 9. Washington, D.C. I. Roosevelt Memorial Association, source. II. Theodore Roosevelt Association Collection. [mp 76–53]

Scenes of Hastings Hart, 1930 medalist.

Producer unknown [1930?]

© No reg.

  lr, 48 ft. si. b&w. 16mm. ref print.

  lr, 48 ft. si. b&w. 16mm. archival pos.

  lr, 121 ft. si. b&w. 35mm. neg ntr.

SHELF LOC'N: FAB972 (print); FRA5941 (arch pos)

Ref source: *Roosevelt House Bulletin.* v. 3, no. 10, 1930: 2.

Factual; views.

SUMMARY: Scenes of Hastings Hornell Hart, penologist, consultant in delinquency and penology for the Russell Sage Foundation, and recipient of the 1930 Roosevelt Medal for Distinguished Service for the promotion of social justice; opening scene of Hart greeting two guard officers at what appears to be a prison building in New York State; long shot of Hart posing with a group of inmates and guards; and a medium view of Hart talking with an unidentified inmate in a jail cell.

1. Prisons—New York (State) 2. Prisoners. 3. Roosevelt Medal for Distinguished Service. 4. Medalists. 5. New York (State) 6. Hart, Hastings Hornell. I. Kinogram Publishing Corporation, source. II. Theodore Roosevelt Association Collection. [mp 76–137]

Scenes of John Burroughs.

Producer unknown [191–?]

© No reg.

  lr, 34 ft. si. b&w. 35mm. ref print.

  lr, 34 ft. si. b&w. 35mm. dupe neg.

  lr, 34 ft. si. b&w. 35mm. neg ntr.

SHELF LOC'N: FEA8930 (print); FPB9880 (neg)

Ref source: P&P portrait file.

Factual; views.

SUMMARY: Two sequences of John Burroughs, naturalist, eminent author, and hunting companion of TR; close-up of Burroughs talking and a long shot of him sitting in a chair reading a book; the immediate background is filled with trees and vegetation, location unknown; the final sequence is of a bird moving around on a window ledge.

PERSONAL CREDITS: Foster, source.

1. Naturalists. 2. Burroughs, John. I. Theodore Roosevelt Association Collection. [mp 76–287]

Scenes of lions.

Producer unknown [191–?]

© No reg.

  lr, 12 ft. si. b&w. 16mm. ref print.

  lr, 12 ft. si. b&w. 16mm. dupe neg.

  lr, 30 ft. si. b&w. 35mm. pos ntr.

SHELF LOC'N: FAB1071 (print); FRA6045 (neg)

Several frames of dramatic footage have apparently been spliced on in ft. 6.

Factual; nature film.

SUMMARY: Medium-close shots of lions roaring and moving through underbrush.

1. Lions. I. Famous Players-Lasky Corporation, source. II. Theodore Roosevelt Association Collection. [mp 76–240]

Scenes of Oyster Bay.
Roosevelt Memorial Association, 1924.
© No reg.
    lr, 320 ft. si. b&w. 16mm. ref print.
    lr, 320 ft. si. b&w. 16mm. archival pos.
    SHELF LOC'N: FAB695 (print); FRA5730 (arch pos)
The RMA list indicates that the surname of the photographer is Ruby.
Ref source: Roosevelt Memorial Association. *Annual Report.* 1924: 3–4, 8–11.
Factual; views.
SUMMARY: Various scenes of Oyster Bay, N.Y., and the surrounding area, commissioned by the RMA as part of its efforts to establish a memorial park in honor of Theodore Roosevelt. The most prominent views are of the midtown intersection of East Main St. and South St., and the area around Oyster Bay railroad station, which borders on the park site. Various shots of the intersection, in some of which campaign banners of the 1924 election are visible: pictures of Coolidge, Dawes, and Theodore Roosevelt, Jr. who unsuccessfully ran for New York governor against Al Smith in 1924, appear on the banners. Panning shots of a frame home by railroad tracks, a steam engine with a crew posed in front, and the railroad station. Shots of a garbage dump and homes beside the bay, the harbor area, a row of frame houses fronting on the garbage dump, and a passenger train. These areas were to be included in the park.
PERSONAL CREDITS: Ruby, photographer.
1. Architecture, American—Oyster Bay, N.Y. 2. Locomotives. 3. Landscape. 4. Oyster Bay, N.Y. 5. Oyster Bay, N.Y.—Harbor. 6. Oyster Bay, N.Y.—Description—Views. 7. Oyster Bay, N.Y.—Parks—Theodore Roosevelt Memorial Park. I. Roosevelt Memorial Association. II. Roosevelt Memorial Association, source. III. Theodore Roosevelt Association Collection. [mp 76–8]

Scenes of Roosevelt Dam.
Producer unknown [1911?]
© No reg.
    lr, 23 ft. si. b&w. 16mm. ref print.
    lr, 23 ft. si. b&w. 16mm. dupe neg.
    lr, 58 ft. si. b&w. 35mm. pos ntr.
    SHELF LOC'N: FAB1206(print); FRA5932 (neg)
Ref sources: *Arizona: Its People and Resources.*

1972: 121–124; *Along the Apache Trail of Arizona.* [191–?]
Factual; views.
SUMMARY: Panoramic views of the Roosevelt Dam on the Salt River in Arizona: shots include a rocky hill above the dam, water rushing through portions of the dam, and a car being driven on the road across the dam. Since a flag waves from the back of the car, the film may have been shot at the dedication ceremonies, Mar. 18, 1911, at which TR delivered the principal address. The Roosevelt Dam, a major irrigation project in the Salt River Valley near Phoenix, is largely a result of TR's land reclamation efforts when he was president.
1. Roosevelt Dam. 2. Dams—Arizona. 3. Reclamation of land—Arizona. 4. Salt River, Ariz. 5. Salt River Valley, Ariz. I. Pathe, source. II. Theodore Roosevelt Association Collection. [mp 76–231]

Scenes of Sagamore Hill.
Roosevelt Memorial Association [1923?]
© No reg.
    lr of 1, 354 ft. si. b&w. 16mm. ref print.
    lr of 1, 354 ft. si. b&w. 16mm. archival pos.
    lr of 1, 894 ft. si. b&w. 35mm. neg ntr.
    SHELF LOC'N: FAB742 (print); FRA5794 (arch pos)
Edge code date on nitrate is 1923; producer verified by RMA list and annual report.
The RMA list indicates that the surname of the photographer is Ruby.
Ref source: Roosevelt Memorial Association. *Annual Report.* 1925: 15.
Factual; views.
SUMMARY: Clear exterior views of Sagamore Hill and surrounding land in summertime. Shots of the house, including the veranda and side porch, from a variety of angles and distances; antlers attached to the roof peak; a cannon beside the house; rolling grounds and the bay as seen from the veranda; a rough wooden gazebo covered with vines; a pet cemetery; benches along a footpath; the entrance rock and road leading to Sagamore; meadows, cows, and horses; and what appears to be a neighboring home.
PERSONAL CREDITS: Ruby, photographer.
1. Oyster Bay, N.Y. Sagamore Hill. 2. Architecture, American—Oyster Bay, N.Y. 3. Oyster Bay, N.Y. 4. Roosevelt, Theodore, Pres. U. S., 1858–1919—Homes. I. Roosevelt Memorial Association. II. Roosevelt Memorial Association, source. III. Theodore Roosevelt Association Collection. [mp 76–38]

[Scenes of the British royal family]
Producer unknown, Aug 1918.
© No reg.
lr, 15 ft. si. b&w. 16mm. ref print.
lr, 15 ft. si. b&w. 16mm. dupe neg (cy 1)
lr, 39 ft. si. b&w. 35mm. dupe neg (cy 2)
lr, 39 ft. si. b&w. 35mm. pos ntr.
   SHELF LOC'N: FAB880 (print); FRA5867 (neg, cy 1); FPB7950 (neg, cy 2)
   RMA title: *King George and Queen Mary of England.*
   Ref sources: The *Times,* London. 8/5/18: 4; The *Daily Telegraph,* London. 8/5/18: 5; The *Morning Post,* London. 8/5/18: 3; P&P portrait file; Bullock, Albert E., ed. *Westminister Abbey and St. Margaret's Church.* v. 1, 1920: 7.
   Factual.
SUMMARY: Queen Mary, King George in the uniform of an Admiral of the Fleet, members of the royal family, a clergyman, and other unidentified people are walking in procession into St. Margaret's Church, Westminster. The occasion is probably "Remembrance Day," Aug. 4, 1918, the fourth anniversary of the beginning of World War I. The royal family, joined by the two houses of Parliament and representatives of the overseas dominions and of the U.S., attend a special service of remembrance and rededication. Queen Alexandra and the Duke of Connaught follow Queen Mary and King George; Princess Mary, wearing a white collar, and Princess Victoria follow. In the second sequence, the royal party leaves the church followed by members of Parliament. The final sequence consists of brief shots of colonial troops with a British officer.
   1. Memorial rites and ceremonies. 2. European War, 1914–1918—Religious aspects. 3. London. 4. Mary, consort of George V, King of Great Britain, 1867–1953. 5. George V, King of Great Britain, 1865–1936. 6. Alexandra, consort of Edward VII, King of Great Britain, 1844–1925. 7. Connaught, Arthur William Patrick Albert, Duke of, 1850–1942. 8. Mary, Princess of Great Britain, 1897–1965. 9. Victoria, Princess of Great Britain, 1868–1935. 10. Westminster, Eng. St. Margaret's Church. 11. Great Britain. Parliament. 12. Great Britain. Army—Colonial forces. I. United States. Army. Signal Corps, source. II. Theodore Roosevelt Association Collection. [mp 76–94]

Scenes of the Capitol, Washington, D.C.
Producer unknown [192–?]
© No reg.
   lr, 21 ft. si. b&w. 16mm. ref print.

lr, 21 ft. si. b&w. 16mm. dupe neg.
lr, 21 ft. si. b&w. 16mm. archival pos (2 cy)
   SHELF LOC'N: FAB890 (print); FRA8660 (neg); FRA5879 & 6185 (arch pos, 2 cy)
Factual; views.
SUMMARY: Various exterior views of the United States Capitol building, its dome, and the bronze Statue of Freedom atop the dome.
   1. Washington, D.C. Capitol. 2. Washington, D.C. 3. Washington, D.C.—Statues. 4. United States—Public buildings. I. Roosevelt Memorial Association, source. II. Theodore Roosevelt Association Collection. [mp 76–112]

Scenes of the River of Doubt photographed by G.M. Dyott, 1926–1927 [1]
Producer unknown [1927?]
© No reg.
   lr, 305 ft. si. b&w. 16mm. ref print.
   lr, 304 ft. si. b&w. 16mm. dupe neg.
   lr, 762 ft. si. b&w. 35mm. pos ntr.
   SHELF LOC'N: FAB1465 (print); FRA6206 (neg)
   Ref source: Roosevelt Memorial Association. *Annual Report.* 1927: 19.
   Factual; compilation.
SUMMARY: In 1926, with the support of the New York Zoological Society and the RMA, Comdr. George M. Dyott, a noted explorer, organized a party to retrace TR's 1914 journey down the River of Doubt, now the Roosevelt River. The primary objectives of Dyott's trip were to settle the geographic controversy over the validity of the Roosevelt-Rondon Expedition's charting of the River of Doubt and to record the voyage pictorially, since much of the footage from the original journey had been lost. Dyott used TR's book, *Through the Brazilian Wilderness,* as a guide on the journey; the film is a compilation of Dyott's observations and experiences. There are sequences of: various insects, including stingless bees which tormented travelers in the Amazon Valley, a caterpillar, ants, a grasshopper, and a beetle; unusual webs and a hat damaged by ants; birds such as orioles, ibis, and storks; a small monkey; a lizard; several piranhas; mules; and palm trees and orchids. The River of Doubt is photographed at several different points: the dangerous rapids contrast with the wide, calm parts of the river. Scenes of waterfalls, probably those at Utiarity, which TR so admired. A member of Dyott's party inspects the post which held the first sign for the Rio Roosevelt. Two men appear in the panning shots of Rio de Janeiro and its harbor,

Guanabara Bay. There are also close-up views of Col. Candido Mariano da Silva Rondon, whom Dyott visited in Rio de Janeiro. Shots of several Indians whom Dyott called Arara Indians because of the sound they made. Various scenes of Dyott's men: sitting around a campfire; pulling a dugout canoe over log rollers; laying the log rollers; a man riding a mule in open country and observing a large anthill. A sequence shows supplies or what may be raw rubber on a riverbank; final views show men in a larger boat, probably near the mouth of the River of Doubt where it empties into the Madeira River, the portion that is settled by rubber workers.

PERSONAL CREDITS: Dyott, George M., source.

1. Discoveries (in geography) 2. Stingless bees. 3. Caterpillars. 4. Ants—Brazil. 5. Locusts—Brazil. 6. Beetles—Brazil. 7. Spider webs. 8. Orioles. 9. Ibis. 10. Storks. 11. Monkeys. 12. Lizards—Brazil. 13. Caribe. 14. Mules. 15. Palms—Brazil. 16. Orchids—Brazil. 17. Waterfalls—Brazil. 18. Indians of South America—Brazil. 19. Arara Indians. 20. Canoes and canoeing—Brazil. 21. Roosevelt River. 22. Brazil. 23. Brazil—Description and travel. 24. Amazon Valley. 25. Utiariti, Brazil. 26. Rio de Janeiro—Harbor. 27. Guanabara Bay. 28. Madeira River. 29. Dyott, George M. 30. Rondon, Candido Mariano da Silva. 31. New York Zoological Society. 32. Roosevelt Memorial Association. 33. Roosevelt-Rondon Scientific Expedition. I. Theodore Roosevelt Association Collection. [mp 76–54]

Scenes of the River of Doubt photographed by G.M. Dyott, 1926–1927 [2]

Producer unknown [1927?]
© No reg.
    lr, 244 ft. si. b&w. 16mm. ref print.
    lr, 248 ft. si. b&w. 16mm. dupe neg.
    lr, 620 ft. si. b&w. 35mm. pos ntr.
    SHELF LOC'N: FAB1466 (print); FRA6207 (neg)
Ref source: Roosevelt Memorial Association. *Annual Report.* 1927: 19.
Factual; compilation.
SUMMARY: This compilation film of Comdr. George M. Dyott's 1927 descent of the River of Doubt (now the Roosevelt River) consists of scenes of wildlife noted by TR in his book, *Through the Brazilian Wilderness,* and observed by Commander Dyott; Arara Indians encountered by Dyott; several sequences of Dyott and his men; and miscellaneous scenes such as views of Rio de Janeiro and

Guanabara Bay at the beginning of the film and shots of a town or village the Dyott party visited. Wildlife sequences include: piranhas, a lizard, birds (possibly orioles) nesting in a palm tree, bees in a honeycomb, a caterpillar, ants, other insects, a turtle, a tall palm tree, and a monkey. Included are geographic features such as waterfalls, probably those at Utiariy, the River of Doubt, and probably the rock on which TR and Colonel Rondon stood to observe the Navaité Rapids on the River of Doubt. Dyott and his men appear in several scenes: two men appear to tap a tree; three men traveling on horseback; men with equipment, probably preparing to load boats. Two men pose by a set of rapids; there are medium-close shots of Dyott wearing protective headgear. Accompanying Dyott, but not identified, were Eugene Bussey, Ramon da Paz, and Robert Young.

PERSONAL CREDITS: Dyott, George M., source.

1. Discoveries (in geography) 2. Indians of South America—Brazil. 3. Arara Indians. 4. Caribe. 5. Lizards—Brazil. 6. Orioles. 7. Palms—Brazil. 8. Bees— Brazil. 9. Caterpillars. 10. Ants—Brazil. 11. Turtles—Brazil. 12. Monkeys. 13. Waterfalls—Brazil. 14. Horses. 15. Roosevelt River. 16. Brazil. 17. Brazil—Description and travel. 18. Rio de Janeiro. 19. Rio de Janeiro—Harbor. 20. Guanabara Bay. 21. Utiariti, Brazil. 22. Amazon Valley. 23. Dyott, George M. I. Theodore Roosevelt Association Collection. [mp 76–55]

Scenes of the White House.

Producer unknown [192–?]
© No reg.
    lr, 19 ft. si. b&w. 16mm. ref print.
    lr, 19 ft. si. b&w. 16mm. archival pos (2 cy)
    SHELF LOC'N: FAB892 (print); FRA5880 & 5887 (arch pos, 2 cy)
Factual; views.
SUMMARY: Exterior views of the White House, flag flying atop, as the camera pans down the south portico.

1. Washington, D.C. White House. 2. Flags—United States. 3. United States—Public buildings. 4. Washington, D.C. I. Roosevelt Memorial Association, source. II. Theodore Roosevelt Association Collection. [mp 76–105]

[Scenes of TR, 1913–1915]

Producer unknown [1913–1915]
© No reg.
    lr, 78 ft. si. b&w. 35mm. ref print (3 cy)

lr, 78 ft. si. b&w. 35mm. dupe neg (2 cy)
lr, 78 ft. si. b&w. 35mm. masterpos.
lr, 80 ft. si. b&w. 35mm. pos ntr.
lr, 79 ft. si. b&w. 35mm. neg ntr.
SHELF LOC'N: FEA7623 & 7624 & 7625 (print, 3 cy); FPB8060 & 8061 (neg, 2 cy); FPB8062 (fgmp)

RMA title: *TR and Party in South America, TR Walking toward Camera, TR Greeting Navy Officers, TR Seated in Auto, TR with Group of People, Children Drilling for TR.*

Ref sources: New York *Tribune.* 6/7/13: 18; The New York *Herald.* 6/7/13: 7; Cherrie, George K. *Dark Trails.* 1930; Roosevelt Memorial Association. *The River of Doubt* (script)

Newsfilm; compilation.

SUMMARY: Three individual sequences of TR in South America, San Francisco, and New York City: 1) TR, with Edwin V. Morgan, American ambassador to Brazil, on his right, and Dr. Lauro S. Müller, Brazilian minister of foreign affairs, on his left (closest to the camera), poses on the steps of the Guanabara Palace in Rio de Janeiro; a man who may be Anthony Fiala and Fr. John A. Zahm, both members of TR's party on his 1913–1914 trip to South America, stand behind him; other Brazilians and Americans are also included; a crowd surrounds TR as he tips his hat and walks in the harbor area of Rio de Janeiro; Dr. Müller walks beside TR with ships visible in the background; 2) attending "Roosevelt Day" at the Panama-Pacific International Exposition July 21, 1915, TR talks animatedly outside what is probably one of the exposition buildings; army and navy officers are in the background; the man behind TR, wearing a top hat, is Hiram W. Johnson, governor of California (1911–1917), Progressive party candidate for the vice presidency in 1912, and later senator from California (1917–1945); views of TR sitting in an open car beside the same building, tipping his hat; 3) TR attends the program of applied athletics and field day games presented by boys of the New York Public Schools Athletic League in Central Park, on June 6, 1913; medium-close views, from left to right, of Gustavus T. Kirby, president of the Amateur Athletic Union and chairman of the Demonstration Committee, Public Schools Athletic League; TR; Gen. George W. Wingate, president of the league; Vincent Astor, member, Demonstration Committee; and Solomon R. Guggenheim, treasurer of the league; the final scene is a long shot of boys in formation doing gymnastics and then running off the field.

1. Rio de Janeiro. Palácio Guanabara. 2. Ships. 3. Exhibitions. 4. Athletics. 5. Gymnastics. 6. Rio de Janeiro. 7. Rio de Janeiro—Harbor. 8. San Francisco. 9. San Francisco—Exhibitions. 10. New York (City) 11. New York (City)—Parks—Central Park. 12. Roosevelt, Theodore, Pres. U.S., 1858–1919. 13. Roosevelt, Theodore, Pres. U.S., 1858–1919—Journey to South America, 1913–1914. 14. Morgan, Edwin V. 15. Müller, Lauro S. 16. Fiala, Anthony. 17. Zahm, John A. 18. Johnson, Hiram W. 19. Kirby, Gustavus T. 20. Wingate, George W. 21. Astor, William Vincent. 22. Guggenheim, Solomon R. 23. United States. Army—Officers. 24. United States. Navy— Officers. 25. California. Governor, 1911–1917 (Johnson) 26. Public Schools Athletic League, New York. 27. Panama-Pacific International Exposition, 1915. 28. Panama-Pacific International Exposition, 1915 —Buildings. I. Gaumont (Firm), source. II. Theodore Roosevelt Association Collection. [mp 76–293]

Scenes of TR and his sons Quentin and Archie, 1917–1918 [1]

Various producers, 1917–1918.
© No reg.
lr, 26 ft. si. b&w. 16mm. ref print.
lr, 26 ft. si. b&w. 16mm. dupe neg.
lr, 35 ft. si. b&w. 16mm. archival pos.
lr, 76 ft. si. b&w. 35mm. neg ntr.
SHELF LOC'N: FAB678 (print); FRA5719 (neg); FRA5720 (arch pos)

The first segment is identified by interior title as *Universal Animated Weekly,* issue no. 78, v. 5, produced by Universal Film Manufacturing Co. and released June 27, 1917; the last segment is from a Danish newsreel with the title, *Ex-praesident Theodore Roosevelt og hans berømte Smil* [Ex-president Theodore Roosevelt and his famous smile]

Ref source: P&P portrait file.

Newsfilm; compilation.

SUMMARY: Unrelated segments of Quentin, Archie, and TR at various times and locations: medium-close view of Quentin wearing a WWI uniform and standing by a wooden shed in Mineola, New York, May 1917; long shot of Archie in uniform, with a cane, standing by a building, possibly in 1918; Archie in uniform astride a horse, possibly in 1917; medium shot of TR speaking from the porch at Sagamore Hill; close shot of TR sitting at the Fifth Annual International Flower Show in the Grand Central Palace, New York City, on Mar. 20, 1917; long shot of crowds and TR in a motorcade, probably during 1917, location unknown; and

TR with an unidentified man standing and talking on the outside steps of a house, identified by interior title as in Washington, D.C.

CITATION: MPW33.1: 843.

1. European War, 1914–1918. 2. Oyster Bay, N.Y. Sagamore Hill. 3. Flower shows. 4. New York (City). Grand Central Palace. 5. Processions. 6. Mineola, N.Y. 7. Oyster Bay, N.Y. 8. New York (City) 9. Washington, D.C. 10. Roosevelt, Theodore, Pres. U.S., 1858–1919. 11. Roosevelt, Quentin. 12. Roosevelt, Archibald B. 13. Roosevelt, Theodore, Pres. U.S., 1858–1919—Addresses, essays, lectures. 14. International Flower Show, 5th, New York City, 1917. I. Universal Film Manufacturing Company. II. United States. Army. Signal Corps. Army Pictorial Service, source. III. Theodore Roosevelt Association Collection. [mp 76–303]

Scenes of TR and his sons Quentin and Archie, 1917–1918 [2]

Various producers, 1917–1918.

© No reg.

lr, 76 ft. si. b&w. 35mm. ref print.
lr, 76 ft. si. b&w. 35mm. dupe neg.
lr, 76 ft. si. b&w. 35mm. masterpos.
lr, 76 ft. si. b&w. 35mm. neg ntr.

SHELF LOC'N: FEA6694(print); FPB7073(neg); FPB7072 (fgmp)

Last segment is from a Danish newsreel entitled *Ex-praesident Theodore Roosevelt og hans berømte Smil* [Ex-president Theodore Roosevelt and his famous smile]

Ref source: P&P portrait file.

Newsfilm; compilation.

SUMMARY: Unrelated segments of Quentin, Archie, and TR at various times and locations. Medium-close view of Quentin wearing a WWI uniform standing by a wooden shed in Mineola, New York, May 1917; long shot of Archie in uniform astride a horse possibly in 1917; Archie in uniform, with a cane, standing by a building possibly in 1918; medium shot of TR speaking from the porch at Sagamore Hill; close shot of TR sitting at the Fifth Annual International Flower Show in the Grand Central Palace, New York City, on Mar. 20, 1917; long shot of crowds and TR in a motorcade, probably during 1917, location unknown; TR speaking from a flag-decked platform, possibly in 1917; and TR with an unidentified man standing and talking on the outside steps of a house, identified by interior title as in Washington, D.C.

1. European War, 1914–1918. 2. Oyster Bay, N.Y. Sagamore Hill. 3. Flower shows. 4. New York

(City). Grand Central Palace. 5. Processions. 6. Mineola, N.Y. 7. Oyster Bay, N.Y. 8. New York (City) 9. Washington, D.C. 10. Roosevelt, Theodore, Pres. U.S., 1858–1919. 11. Roosevelt, Quentin. 12. Roosevelt, Archibald B. 13. Roosevelt, Theodore, Pres. U.S., 1858–1919—Addresses, essays, lectures. 14. International Flower Show, 5th, New York City, 1917. I. Roosevelt Memorial Association, source. II. Theodore Roosevelt Association Collection. [mp 76–304]

Scenes of TR at Sagamore Hill, 1912.

Pathé Frères, Oct 1912.

© No reg.

lr, 148 ft. si. b&w. 35mm. ref print.
lr, 148 ft. si. b&w. 35mm. dupe neg.
lr, 148 ft. si. b&w. 35mm. pos ntr.

SHELF LOC'N: FEA6730 (print); FPB7187 (neg)

Ref source: Roosevelt Memorial Association. *Annual Report.* 1925: 18.

Newsfilm.

SUMMARY: The first film footage taken of TR at Sagamore Hill, summer of 1912. TR on his horse Sidar shakes hands with William P. Helm, Associated Press correspondent for New York City and Washington (1910–1918) and detailed by AP to Wilson and TR during the 1912 campaign. TR rides his horse away from Sagamore, returns to Sagamore, dismounts and feeds the horse from his hand, plays with his three dogs, and then reviews his mail assisted by his son Archie. The final scene shows TR, with ax in hand, walking down the driveway.

CITATION: MPW13: 1304.

1. Oyster Bay, N.Y. Sagamore Hill. 2. Sidar (Horse) 3. Oyster Bay, N.Y. 4. Roosevelt, Theodore, Pres. U.S., 1858–1919. 5. Roosevelt, Theodore, Pres. U.S., 1858–1919—Homes. 6. Helm, William P. 7. Roosevelt, Archibald B. 8. Associated Press. I. Pathe. II. Roosevelt Memorial Association, source. III. Theodore Roosevelt Association Collection. [mp 76–76]

[Scenes of TR on board ship, 1916; Scenes of TR's trip to South America, 1913]

Producer unknown, 1913–1916.

© No reg.

lr, 12 ft. si. b&w. 16mm. ref print (2 cy)
lr, 12 ft. si. b&w. 16mm. archival pos.

SHELF LOC'N: FAB676 & 677 (print, 2 cy); FRA5718 (arch pos)

RMA title: *TR and Party on Ship before Sailing for South America, October 4, 1913; TR and Party on Steps of Palace in South America.*

Ref sources: Cherrie, George K. *Dark Trails*. 1930; Roosevelt Memorial Association. *The River of Doubt* (script); *Scribner's Magazine*. v. 55, no. 4, 1914: 411; *The Outlook*. v. 105, no. 13, 1913: 694[a]

Newsfilm; compilation.

SUMMARY: This film consists of three sequences: 1) TR posing on the deck of the ship Guiana in New York Harbor prior to sailing to the West Indies on Feb. 11, 1916; 2) TR journeys to South America to combine a lecture tour with a scientific expedition to the Amazon Valley of Brazil in Oct. 1913. TR and members of his party standing on the deck of the Vandyck some time after picking up Kermit Roosevelt at Bahia, Brazil on Oct. 17. Left to right are: Anthony Fiala, former arctic explorer; George K. Cherrie, ornithologist; Fr. John A. Zahm, scientist; TR; Kermit Roosevelt; Frank Harper, TR's secretary; and at the edge of the picture, Leo E. Miller, mammalogist; 3) side view of TR with American and Brazilian officials on the steps of the Guanabara Palace in Rio de Janeiro: to TR's right is Edwin V. Morgan, American ambassador to Brazil; a man who may be Anthony Fiala and Fathern Zahm stand behind TR; on TR's left is Dr. Lauro S. Müller, Brazilian minister of foreign affairs, the person who encouraged TR's exploration of the River of Doubt.

1. Voyages and travels. 2. Scientific expeditions. 3. Rio de Janeiro. Palácio Guanabara. 4. New York Harbor. 5. South America. 6. Rio de Janeiro. 7. Roosevelt River. 8. Roosevelt, Theodore, Pres. U. S., 1858–1919—Journey to South America, 1913–1914. 9. Roosevelt, Kermit. 10. Roosevelt, Theodore, Pres. U.S., 1858–1919. 11. Fiala, Anthony. 12. Cherrie, George K. 13. Zahm, John A. 14. Harper, Frank. 15. Miller, Leo E. 16. Morgan, Edwin V. 17. Müller, Lauro S. 18. Guiana (Ship) 19. Vandyck (Ship) I. Weiss Brothers, source. II. Theodore Roosevelt Association Collection. III. Scenes of TR's trip to South America, 1913 [Title] [mp 76–22]

Scenes of TR on board ship before sailing for West Indies, 1916.

Producer unknown, Feb 1916.

© No reg.

lr, 11 ft. si. b&w. 16mm. ref print.
lr, 11 ft. si. b&w. 16mm. dupe neg.
lr, 29 ft. si. b&w. 35mm. pos ntr.

SHELF LOC'N: FAB1061 (print); FRA6033 (neg)

Ref source: King, Moses. *King's Views of New York*. [1915]: 6.

Newsfilm.

SUMMARY: Beginning a tour of the West Indies with his wife on Feb. 11, 1916, TR appears on deck of the ship Guiana in New York Harbor. Medium-close shot of TR posing for the camera, with smiling young men and an older man on the deck behind him; TR gives instructions to an off-camera person or persons, then turns away; medium-close shot of the steamship Guiana as it pulls away from the dock; long shot of the Guiana passing under Manhattan Bridge.

1. Steamboats. 2. Bridges, Suspension. 3. New York (City)—Bridges—Manhattan Bridge. 4. New York Bay. 5. New York (City) 6. New York (City)—Harbor. 7. Roosevelt, Theodore, Pres. U.S., 1858–1919—Journey to the West Indies, 1916. 8. Guiana (Ship) I. International Newsreel Corporation, source. II. Theodore Roosevelt Association Collection. [mp 76–211]

[Scenes of TR, Panama Canal construction, and William McKinley]

Producer unknown, 1901–[1918?]

© No reg.

lr, 69 ft. si. b&w. 35mm. ref print.
lr, 69 ft. si. b&w. 35mm. dupe neg.
lr, 69 ft. si. b&w. 35mm. masterpos.

SHELF LOC'N: FEA9950(print); FPC0775 (neg); FPA8395 (fgmp)

RMA title: *The Panama Canal*.

Factual.

SUMMARY: Three unrelated sequences: 1) medium-close shots of TR speaking animatedly to a crowd outdoors, probably during WWI (1917–1918); 2) panning shots of construction of the Panama Canal; men move materials along a railroad track; 3) President McKinley speaks at the Pan-American Exposition in Buffalo, N.Y., on Sept. 5, 1901; the bearded man to McKinley's left is probably James Wilson, secretary of agriculture (1897–1913); next to Wilson is George B. Cortelyou, who served as McKinley's secretary as well as TR's, and as the first secretary of commerce and labor (1903–04), postmaster general (1905–07), and secretary of the treasury (1907–09).

1. Canals, Interoceanic. 2. Exhibitions. 3. Panama Canal. 4. Buffalo. 5. Roosevelt, Theodore, Pres. U.S., 1858–1919—Addresses, essays, lectures. 6. McKinley, William, Pres. U.S., 1843–1901—Addresses, essays, lectures. 7. Wilson, James, 1835–1920. 8. Cortelyou, George B. 9. United States. President, 1897–1901 (McKinley) 10. Pan-American Exposition, 1901. I. Roosevelt Memorial

Association, source. II. Theodore Roosevelt Association Collection. [mp 76–374]

Scenes of TR speaking at Sagamore [1916–1918]

Producer unknown, 1916–1918.

© No reg.

   lr, 143 ft. si. b&w. 16mm. ref print.
   lr, 358 ft. si. b&w. 35mm. masterpos.
   lr, 143 ft. si. b&w. 16mm. archival pos.
   lr, 358 ft. si. b&w. 35mm. neg ntr.
   SHELF LOC'N: FAB1058 (print); FPB7742 (fgmp); FRA6031 (arch pos)

RMA title: *Scenes of TR Speaking at Sagamore, 1916.*

Ref sources: New York *Tribune.* 5/28/16: pt. 1: 1–2; 6/4/16: pt. 5: 1; Harvard University. Library. Theodore Roosevelt Collection; The New York *Times.* 9/16/17: pt. 5: [1]

Newsfilm; compilation.

SUMMARY: On different occasions TR addresses and speaks informally with crowds from the porch and lawn of Sagamore Hill. Panning shots of a large crowd assembled on May 27, 1916, to demonstrate their support for TR as a 1916 presidential candidate; TR speaks on "Americanism" and shakes hands; the men with him on the porch are probably members of the Roosevelt Non-Partisan League, organizers of the event; additional footage at ca. ft. 83–89 and 122–126. Sequences at ca. ft. 36–41, 53–83, 90–91, 96–108, and 133–143 are of the Apr. 2, 1918, visit of volunteer workers for the third Liberty Loan from the New York District; close-up and medium-close views of TR addressing the group; in front of the porch men and women file past TR to shake hands with him as an aide announces names; additional shots of TR speaking. The opening of the second New York State suffrage campaign, Sept. 8, 1917, at Sagamore Hill, is represented by sequences at ca. ft. 41–53, 92–96, and 110–122. Views of TR speaking to suffragists; at ca. ft. 94 TR speaks to leaders of the suffrage campaign: Mrs. Norman de R. Whitehouse, state chairman of the New York State Woman Suffrage Party, stands next to TR; the woman in the dark hat and coat is Mrs. Ogden Mills Reid; and the tall woman in the light hat and jacket is Mrs. James Lees Laidlaw. There is a short segment at ca. ft. 108–109 of TR speaking from the end of a long rectangular platform surrounded by a large crowd at Albuquerque, N.M., Oct. 23, 1916. A sequence of TR reading a paper or letter and laughing with three men, ca. ft. 127–133, is unidentified.

1. Oyster Bay, N.Y. Sagamore Hill. 2. Presidents— United States—Nomination. 3. Presidents— United States—Election—1916. 4. Suffrage—New York (State) 5. Women—Suffrage—New York (State) 6. Women's rights—New York (State) 7. Oyster Bay, N.Y. 8. Albuquerque, N.M. 9. Roosevelt, Theodore, Pres. U.S., 1858—1919—Addresses, essays, lectures. 10. Roosevelt, Theodore, Pres. U.S., 1858–1919. 11. Whitehouse, Vira B. 12. Reid, Helen Rogers. 13. Laidlaw, Harriet B. 14. Roosevelt Non-Partisan League. 15. New York (City). Liberty Loan Committee. 16. United States. Laws, statutes, etc. Liberty loan acts. I. Roosevelt Memorial Association, source. II. Theodore Roosevelt Association Collection. [mp 76–175]

Scenes showing Blue Line Tour route to Roosevelt House in 1925.

Roosevelt Memorial Association [1925?]

© No reg.

   lr, 107 ft. si. b&w. 16mm. ref print (cy 1)
   lr, 339 ft. si. b&w. 35mm. ref print (cy 2)
   lr, 267 ft. si. b&w. 35mm. ref print (cy 3)
   lr, 136 ft. si. b&w. 16mm. dupe neg (cy 1)
   lr, 339 ft. si. b&w. 35mm. dupe neg (cy 2)
   lr, 267 ft. si. b&w. 35mm. dupe neg (cy 3)
   lr, 267 ft. si. b&w. 35mm. master pos.
   lr, 107 ft. si. b&w. 16mm. archival pos (cy 1)
   lr, 136 ft. si. b&w. 16mm. archival pos (cy 2)
   lr, 339 ft. si. b&w. 35mm. pos ntr.
   lr, 267 ft. si. b&w. 35mm. neg ntr.
   SHELF LOC'N: FAB715 (print, cy 1); FEA6734 (print, cy 2); FEA7834 (print, cy 3); FRA5775 (neg, cy 1); FPB7199 (neg, cy 2); FPB8234 (neg, cy 3); FPB8235 (fgmp); FRA5776 (arch pos, cy 1); FRA 5777 (arch pos, cy 2)

RMA list indicates these scenes were used as a trailer on *Memorializing Roosevelt,* but were not included in the assembled negative.

The date in the title is unverified.

Copies vary in length due to longer printing of the map sequence.

Factual.

SUMMARY: The opening scene shows a group entering a tour bus in front of the Hotel McAlpin, Thirty-fourth and Broadway, New York City; the bus begins moving down Broadway. Sequence of a map with lines tracing the route from the Hotel McAlpin, Penn Station at Thirty-second Street and Seventh Avenue, Grand Central Station at Forty-second Street and Park Avenue to Roosevelt House at 28 East Twentieth Street. The bus stops in front of the Roosevelt House; its passengers enter the house, then reboard the bus as the camera pans down from the flag to the house's entrance.

1. Sightseeing business. 2. New York (City). Roosevelt House. 3. New York (City). Hotel McAlpin. 4. New York (City) 5. Blue Line Sightseeing Tours, inc. I. Roosevelt Memorial Association. II. Roosevelt Memorial Association, source. III. Theodore Roosevelt Association Collection. [mp 76–33]

Scout parade, Cartagena, Colombia, 1920.
Caribe Syndicate L.t.d. Films, Aug 1920.
© No reg.
   lr, 76 ft. si. b&w. 16mm. ref print.
   lr, 76 ft. si. b&w. 16mm. dupe neg.
   lr, 77 ft. si. b&w. 16mm. archival pos.
SHELF LOC'N: FAB1023 (print); FRA5999 (neg); FRA6000 (arch pos)
   Ref source: Cartagena, Colombia. Cámara de Comercio. *Souvenir History of Cartagena de Indias.* 1925: 13.
   Factual.
SUMMARY: According to an interior title, this film is of a San Roque's Day procession, on Aug. 22, 1920, in Cartagena, Colombia. The camera, which is probably positioned on the city wall, pans the Market Harbour area, beginning on the left at what is probably a railroad station. The procession is led by a crucifer followed by choir boys, ranks of Boy Scouts and soldiers, and people carrying banners; it is difficult to distinguish the Boy Scouts or soldiers. Children dressed in white line the street and a float appears near the end of the procession.
PERSONAL CREDITS: Beard, Daniel C., source.
   1. Processions, Ecclesiastical—Cartagena, Colombia. 2. Saints—Cartegena, Colombia—Commemoration. 3. Boy Scouts. 4. Cartagena, Colombia. 5. Cartagena, Colombia—Plazas. 6. Cartagena, Colombia—Walls. 7. Cartagena, Colombia—Description—Views. 8. Rochus, Saint, 1295 (ca.)–1327. I. Caribe Syndicate L.t.d. Films. II. Theodore Roosevelt Association Collection. [mp 76–220]

Scouts on their way to TR's grave, Daniel C. Beard and TR Jr. attend services, 1920.
Producer unknown, Nov 1920.
© No reg.
   lr, 4 ft. si. b&w. 16mm. ref print.
   lr, 4 ft. si. b&w. 16mm. dupe neg.
   lr, 4 ft. si. b&w. 16mm. archival pos.
   lr, 9 ft. si. b&w. 35mm. pos ntr.
SHELF LOC'N: FAB885 (print); FRA5872 (neg); FRA5873 (arch pos)

Ref sources: P&P portrait file; The New York *Times Mid-week Pictorial.* v. 12, no. 15, 1920: [1]
   Newsfilm.
SUMMARY: On Nov. 26, 1920, a group of fifteen hundred Boy Scouts from various troops in New York City attend memorial ceremonies at TR's grave in Youngs Memorial Cemetery, Oyster Bay, N.Y., honoring TR, who had been honorary president and chief scout citizen of the organization; the scouts are led by Daniel C. Beard, founder and national commissioner of the Boy Scouts of America, and TR, Jr. Long shots of the group walking along a road toward the cemetery, with residents of Oyster Bay watching from the roadside; scouts file through the cemetery, with hats over their hearts; close shot of Beard and TR, Jr., as scouts look over their shoulders toward the camera.
   1. Memorial service. 2. Youngs Memorial Cemetery. 3. Oyster Bay, N.Y. 4. Roosevelt, Theodore, Pres. U.S., 1858–1919—Funeral and memorial services. 5. Roosevelt, Theodore, Pres. U.S., 1858–1919—Tomb. 6. Beard, Daniel C. 7. Roosevelt, Theodore, 1887–1944. 8. Boy Scouts of America. I. General Vision Company, source. II. Theodore Roosevelt Association Collection. [mp 76–104]

Senator Hiram Johnson.
Selznick Pictures Corp. [1922?]
© No reg.
   lr, 14 ft. si. b&w. 16mm. ref print (2 cy)
   lr, 14 ft. si. b&w. 16mm. archival pos (cy 1)
   lr, 21 ft. si. b&w. 16mm. archival pos (cy 2)
(Selznick news [Series])
SHELF LOC'N: FAB718 & 1126 (print, 2 cy); FRA5780 (arch pos, cy 1); FRA 5781 (arch pos, cy 2)
   The earliest possible date of production is 1920 since Selznick news was first released on Apr. 4, 1920, and stopped in Mar. 1923.
   Archival pos (cy 2) is longer than arch pos (cy 1) due to longer printing of interior titles.
   Ref source: P&P portrait file.
   Newsfilm; views.
SUMMARY: Two sequences of Hiram Warren Johnson, Republican senator from California (1917–1945); close-up of him seated near a window and a long shot of him standing outdoors.
PERSONAL CREDITS: Stripe, F. C., source. Carver, H. P., source.
   1. Legislators—California. 2. Johnson, Hiram W. I. Selznick Pictures Corporation. II. Theodore Roosevelt Association Collection. [mp 76–28]

Senator Hitchcock.
Producer unknown [191–?]
  © No reg.
    lr, 6 ft. si. b&w. 16mm. ref print.
    lr, 6 ft. si. b&w. 16mm. archival pos (3 cy)
  SHELF LOC'N: FAB702 (print); FRA5752 & 6004 & 5753 (arch pos, 3 cy)
  Ref source: P&P portrait file.
  Factual; views.
  SUMMARY: Sen. Gilbert M. Hitchcock, Democrat from Nebraska (1911–1923), poses for the camera in front of what appears to be the Capitol in Washington.
  PERSONAL CREDITS: Stripe, F. C., source. Carver, H. P., source.
  1. Legislators—Nebraska. 2. Washington, D.C. Capitol. 3. Washington, D.C. 4. United States—Public buildings. 5. Hitchcock, Gilbert M. I. Theodore Roosevelt Association Collection. [mp 76–39]

Senator McCumber of North Dakota.
Producer unknown [1920?]
  © No reg.
    lr, 2 ft. si. b&w. 16mm. ref print.
    lr, 2 ft. si. b&w. 16mm. archival pos (2 cy)
  SHELF LOC'N: FAB704 (print); FRA5757 & 5758 (arch pos, 2 cy)
  Ref source: P&P portrait file.
  Factual; views.
  SUMMARY: Porter J. McCumber, Republican senator from North Dakota (1899–1923), poses for the camera on the terrace of the Capitol building in Washington; the Washington Monument is visible in the background.
  PERSONAL CREDITS: Stripe, F.C., source. Carver, H. P., source.
  1. Legislators—North Dakota. 2. Washington, D.C. Capitol. 3. Washington, D.C. Washington Monument. 4. United States—Public buildings. 5. Washington, D.C. 6. McCumber, Porter J. I. Theodore Roosevelt Association Collection. [mp 76–45]

Senator Penrose.
Producer unknown [191–?]
  © No reg.
    lr, 7 ft. si. b&w. 16mm. ref print (2 cy)
    lr, 7 ft. si. b&w. 16mm. dupe neg.
    lr, 7 ft. si. b&w. 16mm. archival pos (2 cy)
  SHELF LOC'N: FAB703 & 1030 (print, 2 cy); FRA5756 (neg); FRA5754 & 5755 (arch pos, 2 cy)
  Ref source: P&P portrait file.
  Factual; views.
  SUMMARY: On the grounds of what appears to be the Capitol in Washington, D.C., Republican Senator Boies Penrose of Pennsylvania (1897–1921) appears seated in an open car.
  PERSONAL CREDITS: Stripe, F. C., source. Carver, H. P., source.
  1. Legislators—Pennsylvania. 2. Washington, D.C. Capitol. 3. United States—Public buildings. 4. Washington, D.C. 5. Penrose, Boies. I. Theodore Roosevelt Association Collection. [mp 76–29]

Senator Pomerene.
Producer unknown [191–?]
  © No reg.
    lr, 5 ft. si. b&w. 16mm. ref print.
    lr, 5 ft. si. b&w. 16mm. archival pos (2 cy)
  SHELF LOC'N: FAB998 (print); FRA5983 & 5984 (arch pos, 2 cy)
  Ref source: P&P portrait file.
  Factual; views.
  SUMMARY: Medium-close frontal view of Atlee Pomerene, Democratic senator from Ohio (1911–1923), posing outside the United States Capitol, Washington, D.C.
  PERSONAL CREDITS: Stripe, F. C., source. Carver, H. P., source.
  1. Legislators—Ohio. 2. Washington, D.C. Capitol. 3. Washington, D.C. 4. Pomerene, Atlee. I. Theodore Roosevelt Association Collection. [mp 76–148]

Senator Smoot.
Kinogram Pub. Corp. [192–?]
  © No reg.
    lr, 2 ft. si. b&w. 16mm. ref print (2 cy)
    lr, 2 ft. si. b&w. 16mm. dupe neg.
    lr, 2 ft. si. b&w. 16mm. archival pos (cy 1)
    lr, 5 ft. si. b&w. 16mm. archival pos (cy 2)
  (Kinograms [Series])
  SHELF LOC'N: FAB993 & 1125 (print, 2 cy); FRA5973 (neg); FRA5974 (arch pos, cy 1); FRA5975 (arch pos, cy 2)
  Archival pos (cy 2) is longer than arch pos (cy 1) due to longer printing of interior title.
  Ref source: P&P portrait file.
  Factual; views.
  SUMMARY: Close shot of Reed Smoot, Republican senator from Utah (1903–1933), in an undetermined location.
  PERSONAL CREDITS: Stripe, F. C., source. Carver, H. P., source.
  1. Legislators—Utah. 2. Smoot, Reed. I. Kino-

gram Publishing Corporation. II. Theodore Roosevelt Association Collection. [mp 76-146]

Senator Watson.

Selznick Pictures Corp. [1921?]

© No reg.

lr, 35 ft. si. b&w. 16mm. ref print (cy 1)

lr, 26 ft. si. b&w. l6mm. ref print (cy 2)

lr, 26 ft. si. b&w. 16mm. archival pos (2 cy)

(Selznick news [Series])

SHELF LOC'N: FAB955 (print, cy 1); FAB1124 (print, cy 2); FRA5919 & 5920 (arch pos, 2 cy)

The earliest possible date of production is 1920 since Selznick news was first released on Apr. 4, 1920; the latest possible date of production is 1922 since Watson died in Sept. 1922.

Ref print (cy 1) is longer than ref print (cy 2) due to longer printing of interior titles.

Ref sources: The Atlanta *Journal.* 9/26/22: 12; Brewton, William W. *The Life of Thomas E. Watson.* 1926; P&P portrait file.

Factual; views.

SUMMARY: Various views of Thomas Edward Watson at Hickory Hill, his home in Thomson, Georgia. In two scenes he is probably with his two granddaughters, Georgia Lee and Georgia Watson. Watson was a Georgia state legislator (1882-1883); a Populist party representative from Georgia in Congress (1891-1893); the vice presidential candidate of the Populist party (1896); the People's party presidential candidate (1904); and a United States senator from Georgia (1921-1922).

PERSONAL CREDITS: Stripe, F. C., source. Carver, H. P., source.

1. Legislators—Georgia. 2. Thomson, Ga. Hickory Hill. 3. Thomson, Ga. 4. Watson, Thomas E. 5. Lee, Georgia Watson. 6. Watson, Georgia Doremus. I. Selznick Pictures Corporation. II. Theodore Roosevelt Association Collection. [mp 76-228]

Senators Curtis, Cummins, Moses, and [Representative] Mondell.

Kinogram Pub. Corp. [1919?]

© No reg.

lr, 17 ft. si. b&w. 16mm. ref print (2 cy)

lr, 30 ft. si. b&w. 16mm. archival pos (cy 1)

lr, 17 ft. si. b&w. 16mm. archival pos (cy 2)

(Kinograms [Series])

SHELF LOC'N: FAB951 & 1029 (print, 2 cy); FRA5953 (arch pos, cy 1); FRA5913 (arch pos, cy 2)

Since the interior title suggests that Senator Cummins has recently been named president pro tempore of the Senate, and since his service in that capacity began in 1919, the date of production is probably 1919 or 1920.

Archival pos (cy 1) is longer than archival pos (cy 2) due to longer printing of interior titles.

Ref source: P&P portrait file.

Newsfilm.

SUMMARY: Views in unknown location(s) of prominent Republican congressional leaders, including: Charles Curtis, senator from Kansas (1907-1913, 1915-1929) and vice president under Herbert Hoover (1929-1933); Albert B. Cummins, former governor of Iowa (1902-1908), senator from that state (1908-1926), and president pro tempore of the Senate (1919-1925); George H. Moses, former U.S. minister to Greece and Montenegro (1909-1912), senator from New Hampshire (1918-1933), and president pro tempore of the Senate (1925-1933); James W. Wadsworth, Jr., senator from New York (1915-1927); Harry S. New, senator from Indiana (1917-1923) and postmaster general (1923-1929); and Frank W. Mondell, representative from Wyoming (1899-1923) and House whip (1919-1923).

PERSONAL CREDITS: Stripe, F. C., source. Carver, H. P., source.

1. Legislators—Kansas. 2. Legislators—Iowa. 3. Legislators—New Hampshire. 4. Legislators—New York (State) 5. Legislators—Indiana. 6. Legislators— Wyoming. 7. Iowa—Governors. 8. Curtis, Charles. 9. Cummins, Albert B. 10. Moses, George H. 11. Mondell, Frank W. 12. Wadsworth, James W., 1877-1952. 13. New, Harry S. I. Kinogram Publishing Corporation. II. Theodore Roosevelt Association Collection. [mp 76-147]

Shall we prepare?

Paramount Pictures, Feb 1916.

© No reg.

lr, 101 ft. si. b&w. 16mm. ref print (cy 1)

lr, 106 ft. si. b&w. 35mm. ref print (cy 2)

lr, 206 ft. si. b&w. 35mm. ref print (cy 3)

lr, 107 ft. si. b&w. 16mm. dupe neg (cy 1)

lr, 106 ft. si. b&w. 35mm. dupe neg (cy 2)

lr, 206 ft. si. b&w. 35mm. dupe neg (cy 3)

lr, 106 ft. si. b&w. 35mm. masterpos.

lr, 101 ft. si. b&w. 16mm. archival pos.

lr, 106 ft. si. b&w. 35mm. pos ntr.

lr, 106 ft. si. b&w. 35mm. neg ntr.

(Paramount pictographs, no. 2)

SHELF LOC'N: FAB691 (print, cy 1); FEA7636 (print, cy 2); FFA7637 (print, cy 3); FRA5726 (neg, cy 1); FPB 8076 (neg, cy 2); FPB8077 (neg, cy 3); FPB8078 (fgmp); FRA 5727 (arch pos)

RMA title: *TR Speaking at Sagamore; TR in Metropolitan Magazine Office, 1916.*

Copies vary in length due to longer printing of interior titles.

Ref sources: *The Moving Picture World.* v. 27, no. 8, 1916: 1236; *Metropolitan Magazine.* v. 43, no. 5, 1916: 72–73.

Newsfilm; views.

SUMMARY: Two sequences of TR: 1) views of TR walking onto the porch of Sagamore Hill, Oyster Bay, N.Y., facing the camera, and then speaking on military preparedness during WWI; 2) views of TR sitting at his desk in the *Metropolitan Magazine* office in New York City and speaking with a man who may be Carl Hovey, editor of the magazine.

PERSONAL CREDITS: Palmer, Frederick, editor. Reuterdahl, Henry, editor.

CITATION: MPW27.7: 1116; MPW27.8: 1380.

1. Preparedness. 2. Oyster Bay, N.Y. Sagamore Hill. 3. Oyster Bay, N.Y. 4. New York (City) 5. Roosevelt, Theodore, Pres. U.S., 1858–1919—Addresses, essays, lectures. 6. Hovey, Carl. 7. Roosevelt, Theodore, Pres. U.S., 1858–1919—Military leadership. 8. Metropolitan magazine. I. Paramount. II. Bray Studios, inc., source. III. Theodore Roosevelt Association Collection. [mp 76–6]

Ships in the Panama Canal [1]

Producer unknown [191–?]

© No reg.

lr, 6 ft. si. b&w. 16mm. ref print.
lr, 6 ft. si. b&w. 16mm. archival pos.
lr, 15 ft. si. b&w. 35mm. neg ntr.
SHELF LOC'N: FAB1060 (print); FRA6032 (arch pos)

The earliest possible production date is 1914, since the Panama Canal was not officially in operation until 1914.

Ref sources: Avery, Ralph E. *America's Triumph at Panama.* 1913: 349–367; Bakenhus, Reuben E., Knapp, Harry S., and Johnson, Emory R. *The Panama Canal.* 1915: 80.

Factual; views.

SUMMARY: The film consists of two sequences: views of a large ship in the Panama Canal, with mountains in the background; and views of the ship in one of the series of locks. Towing locomotives are visible on the edge of the lock wall.

1. Ships. 2. Canals, Interoceanic. 3. Locks (Hydraulic engineering) 4. Towing. 5. Electric locomotives. 6. Panama Canal. 7. Canal Zone. I. United States. Dept. of Agriculture, source. II. Theodore Roosevelt Association Collection. [mp 76–178]

Ships in the Panama Canal [2]

Producer unknown [191–?]

© No reg.

lr, 68 ft. si. b&w. 16mm. ref print.
lr, 68 ft. si. b&w. 16mm. archival pos.
lr, 170 ft. si. b&w. 35mm. neg ntr.
SHELF LOC'N: FAB1062 (print); FRA6034 (arch pos)

The earliest possible production date is 1914, since the Panama Canal was not officially in operation until 1914.

Ref sources: *Jane's Fighting Ships.* 1916: 132; Avery, Ralph E. *America's Triumph at Panama.* 1913: 184; [Daniels, Josephus.... USS Missouri, USS Ohio, and USS Wisconsin in various parts of the Panama Canal on July 15–16, 1915.] lot 5415. P&P; Detroit Publishing Co. [Panama and the Panama Canal. 1914–15.] lot 9681. P&P.

Factual; views.

SUMMARY: Several ships, including what is probably an American battleship, pass through the Gaillard (Culebra) Cut, a portion of the Panama Canal; mountainous landscape is in the background. The battleship passes slowly by the camera, and members of her crew appear on deck.

PERSONAL CREDITS: Goethals, George W., source.

1. Ships. 2. Battleships. 3. Canals, Interoceanic. 4. Panama Canal. 5. Canal Zone. 6. Gaillard Cut, Canal Zone. I. Theodore Roosevelt Association Collection. [mp 76–179]

Short scenes of TR [1]

Producer unknown, 1916–1918.

© No reg.

lr, 96 ft. si. b&w. 16mm. ref print.
lr, 96 ft. si. b&w. 16mm. dupe neg.
lr, 259 ft. si. b&w. 35mm. masterpos.
lr, 96 ft. si. b&w. 16mm. archival pos.
lr, 240 ft. si. b&w. 35mm. neg ntr.
SHELF LOC'N: FAB1470 (print); FRA9242 (neg); FPB8831 (fgmp); FRA7845 (arch pos)

Ref sources: The Pittsburgh *Dispatch.* 7/27/17: 1–2; The Pittsburgh *Post.* 7/26/17: 1; United States. National Archives and Records Service. Audiovisual Archives Division; *The North American,* Philadelphia. 1/21/16: 14; *Public Ledger,* Philadelphia. 1/22/16: 1, 9; Harvard University. Library. Theodore Roosevelt Collection; The New York *Times.* 10/28/17: pt. 5: 3.

Factual; biographical, compilation, views.

SUMMARY: Views of TR ca. 1916–1918 engaged in a variety of activities: 1) TR walks underneath the porte-cochere at Sagamore Hill and proceeds toward the camera; the date is probably ca. 1918; 2) TR appears on the deck of the ship Guiana in New York Harbor before sailing to the West Indies on Feb. 11, 1916; 3) TR, with prominent New Mexico politicians, is at the Alvarado Hotel in Albuquerque, N.M., on Oct. 23, 1916, campaigning for Republican presidential candidate Charles Evans Hughes; 4) medium-close shots of TR and Leonard Wood on Mar. 29, 1917, at the Fifth Annual International Flower Show at Grand Central Palace in New York City; 5) views of TR waving a flag and urging universal military training from a stand erected on the steps of the Allegheny County Courthouse in Pittsburgh during the Twenty-ninth Annual Convention of the Loyal Order of Moose; 6) TR alights from an automobile accompanied by a group of men, one of whom may be Edwin A. Van Valkenburg, editor of the Philadelphia *North American*; the sequence was probably shot during TR's Jan. 20–21, 1916, visit to Philadelphia; TR shakes Van Valkenburg's hand and enters what may be the home of Dr. J. William White; 7) TR leaves a building with a group of men and then waves his hat at the crowd; the location and date may be that of the following sequence; 8) TR poses in front of the Naval Service Club on Beacon St. in Boston on May 2, 1918, with officers and sailors; 9) TR emerges from a car with another man; both are wearing medals; the location may be Springfield, Ill.; the mourning band TR wears for his son Quentin indicates that the film was shot after July 1918; 10) the sequence may be of TR arriving at the Naval Service Club in Boston on May 2, 1918, in an open car with a man who is probably president of the club, F. Nathaniel Perkins; 11) from a flag-draped stand, TR enthusiastically speaks to troops at Camp Grant, Rockford, Ill., on Sept. 26, 1917; the man briefly visible behind TR is probably Thomas H. Barry, commander of the camp; 12) at Cooper's Training Camp in Stamford, Conn., TR poses with a group of men; 13) final views of TR at Sagamore Hill, probably in 1918.

1. Oyster Bay, N.Y. Sagamore Hill. 2. Albuquerque, N.M. Alvarado Hotel. 3. Presidents—

United States—Election—1916. 4. Legislators—New Mexico. 5. New York (City). Grand Central Palace. 6. Allegheny Co., Pa. County Courthouse. 7. Oyster Bay, N.Y. 8. New York (City)—Harbor. 9. Albuquerque, N.M. 10. New York (City) 11. Pittsburgh. 12. Philadelphia. 13. Boston, Mass. 14. Springfield, Ill. 15. Rockford, Ill. 16. Stamford, Conn. 17. Roosevelt, Theodore, Pres. U.S., 1858–1919. 18. Roosevelt, Theodore, Pres. U.S., 1858–1919—Addresses, essays, lectures. 19. Wood, Leonard. 20. Van Valkenburg, Edwin A. 21. Perkins, F. Nathaniel. 22.Barry, Thomas H. 23. Guiana (Ship) 24. Loyal Order of Moose. 25. Naval Service Club, Boston, Mass. 26. United States. Navy—Service clubs. 27. United States. Navy—Officers. 28. Camp Grant. 29. Cooper's Training Camp. 30. International Flower Show, 5th, New York City, 1917. 31. Convention of the Loyal Order of Moose, 29th, Pittsburgh, 1917. I. Roosevelt Memorial Association, source. II. Theodore Roosevelt Association Collection. [mp 76–268]

Short scenes of TR [2]

Producer unknown [1912–1916]

© No reg.

    lr, 50 ft. si. b&w. 35mm. ref print.

    lr, 50 ft. si. b&w. 35mm. dupe neg.

    lr, 50 ft. si. b&w. 35mm. pos ntr.

SHELF LOC'N: FEA8335 (print); FPB9872 (neg)

Newsfilm; compilation, political.

SUMMARY: Compilation film of TR speaking and campaigning; several sequences are of his 1912 Progressive campaign: 1) in Los Angeles on Sept. 16, 1912, TR waves from his auto after participating in a parade; 2) scenes shot from aboard a train, of crowds waving as the train pulls away from the Fargo, N.D., area on Sept. 6, 1912; 3) from the rear seat of an open touring car, TR, with a group of men, shakes hands with a sailor, and the car backs away from a group of sailors; 4) close-up views of TR speaking; 5) TR speaks from a balcony or porch, probably during his Oct. 23, 1916, visit to Albuquerque, N.M., while campaigning for Republican presidential nominee Charles Evans Hughes; the location may be the Alvarado Hotel in Albuquerque; 6) views from varying distances of TR campaigning from the rear of a train in the Fargo, N.D., area on Sept. 6, 1912; the crowd includes Indian men, women, and children; the man next to TR, wearing a cap, is probably George E. Roosevelt, TR's cousin and campaign secretary.

PERSONAL CREDITS: Chessman, A., source.

1. Progressive Party (Founded 1912) 2. Presi-

dents—United States—Election—1912. 3. Presidents—United States—Election—1916. 4. Seamen. 5. Albuquerque, N.M. Alvarado Hotel. 6. Los Angeles, Calif. 7. Fargo, N.D. 8. Albuquerque, N.M. 9. Roosevelt, Theodore, Pres. U.S., 1858–1919. 10. Roosevelt, Theodore, Pres. U.S., 1858–1919—Addresses, essays, lectures. 11. Roosevelt, George E. I. Theodore Roosevelt Association Collection. [mp 76–269]

Short scenes of TR as used in Paramount reel.
Producer unknown [1916–1918?]

© No reg.

lr, 31 ft. si. b&w. 16mm. ref print.

lr, 31 ft. si. b&w. 16mm. dupe neg.

lr, 31 ft. si. b&w. 16mm. archival pos.

SHELF LOC'N: FAB1452 (print); FRA6188 (neg); FRA6067 (arch pos)

The Paramount reel referred to in the title is unidentified.

Factual; views, compilation.

SUMMARY: TR delivers addresses to various groups in Oyster Bay: standing in a gazebo, TR speaks to citizens of Oyster Bay during the July 4, 1916, festivities; at Sagamore Hill, TR addresses a group, several of whom are in uniform; medium and close-up shots of TR vigorously speaking; TR, holding a piece of paper, speaks while reporters take notes on the porch at Sagamore Hill; the final sequence is probably his Apr. 2, 1918, address to Liberty Loan workers from the New York District.

1. Oyster Bay, N.Y. Sagamore Hill. 2. Fourth of July orations. 3. Reporters and reporting. 4. Oyster Bay, N.Y. 5. Roosevelt, Theodore, Pres. U.S., 1858–1919—Addresses, essays, lectures. 6. United States. Laws, statutes, etc. Liberty loan acts. 7. New York (City). Liberty Loan Committee, I. Paramount, source. II. Theodore Roosevelt Association Collection. [mp 76–267]

Spanish Mountain Artillery, 1898.
Producer unknown [1898?]

© No reg.

lr, 94 ft. si. b&w. 35mm. ref print.

lr, 37 ft. si. b&w. 16mm. archival pos.

SHELF LOC'N: FEA7825 (print); FRA6181 (arch pos)

The date in the title is unverified.

Ref sources: Funcken, Liliane and Funcken, Fred. *The First World War.* pt. 2, 1974: 76; D'Ami, Rinaldo D. *World Uniforms in Colour.* v. 1, 1968: 20–21.

Factual; war film.

SUMMARY: Soldiers, who may be members of the Spanish Mountain Artillery, dressed in light pants, dark tunics, and berets, walk down a path. The terrain is rough and rocky and what may be a fort or castle appears in the background. The men are leading pack animals loaded with guns, carriages and wheels, and ammunition. In the second sequence the soldiers unload the pack mules, mount two guns on carriages and wheels, load, and fire. Mountains are visible in the background; the location may be Cuba.

PERSONAL CREDITS: Elmendorf, Dwight L., source.

1. Soldiers—Cuba. 2. Artillery, Field and mountain. 3. Pack transportation. 4. Transportation, Military. 5. Mules. 6. Horses. 7. Cuba. 8. Spain. Ejército. Artilleria. I. Theodore Roosevelt Association Collection. [mp 76–257]

Speaker of the House F. H. Gillett.
Producer unknown [1919?]

© No reg.

lr, 2 ft. si. b&w. 16mm. ref print (2 cy)

lr, 2 ft. si. b&w. 16mm. archival pos.

SHELF LOC'N: FAB953 & 1132 (print, 2 cy); FRA5916 (arch pos)

Ref prints lack full film image.

Ref source: P&P portrait file.

Factual; views.

SUMMARY: Medium shot of Frederick H. Gillett of Massachusetts, Speaker of the House (1919–1925), standing at the speaker's rostrum in the House of Representatives, United States Capitol, Washington, D.C.

PERSONAL CREDITS: Stripe, F. C., source. Carver, H. P., source.

1. Legislators—Massachusetts. 2. Washington, D.C. Capitol. 3. Washington, D.C. 4. Gillett, Frederick Huntington. 5. United States. Congress. House. I. Theodore Roosevelt Association Collection. [mp 76–139]

Still photographs of TR on motion picture film.
Producer unknown [192–?]

© No reg.

lr, 51 ft. si. b&w. 16mm. ref print.

lr, 51 ft. si. b&w. 16mm. archival pos.

lr, 127 ft. si. b&w. 35mm. neg ntr.

SHELF LOC'N: FAB964 (print); FRA5933 (arch pos)

Ref source: P&P portrait file.

Factual; still film.

SUMMARY: Miscellaneous photographs of TR in the United States and abroad, including several posed shots of TR and his family at Sagamore Hill; TR and King George V; TR in hunting attire; TR posed beside a tent out West; and TR on a platform with Charles Evans Hughes and New York City Mayor John P. Mitchel in front of what appears to be the New York Public Library.

PERSONAL CREDITS: Buchheister, source.

1. Oyster Bay, N.Y. Sagamore Hill. 2. Oyster Bay, N.Y. 3. New York (City) 4. Roosevelt, Theodore, Pres. U.S., 1858–1919. 5. Roosevelt, Theodore, Pres. U.S., 1858–1919—Family. 6. George V, King of Great Britain, 1865–1936. 7. Hughes, Charles Evans. 8. Mitchel, John P. 9. New York (City). Public Library. I. Theodore Roosevelt Association Collection. [mp 76–136]

Still picture of TR and his family.

Producer unknown [1907?]

© No reg.

lr, 12 ft. si. b&w. 35mm. ref print (2 cy)

lr, 12 ft. si. b&w. 35mm. dupe neg (2 cy)

lr, 12 ft. si. b&w. 35mm. masterpos.

lr, 12 ft. si. b&w. 35mm. pos ntr.

lr, 12 ft. si. b&w. 35mm. neg ntr.

SHELF LOC'N: FEA7305 & 7306 (print, 2 cy);
              FPB7732 & 7733 (neg, 2 cy);
              FPB7734 (fgmp)

Ref source: P&P presidential file.

Factual; still film.

SUMMARY: Film footage of a still photograph, copyrighted in 1907, showing TR and Edith Roosevelt with their children, Kermit, Archie, Ethel, Quentin, and TR, Jr., plus a dog, posing outside their home, Sagamore Hill, Oyster Bay, N.Y.

1. Oyster Bay, N.Y. Sagamore Hill. 2. Oyster Bay, N.Y. 3.Roosevelt,Theodore,Pres. U.S., 1858–1919—Family. 4. Roosevelt, Edith. 5. Roosevelt, Kermit. 6. Roosevelt, Archibald B. 7. Derby, Ethel Roosevelt. 8. Roosevelt, Quentin. 9. Roosevelt, Theodore, 1887–1944. 10. United States. President, 1901–1909 (Roosevelt) I. International Film Service Company, source. II. Theodore Roosevelt Association Collection. [mp 76–294]

Still pictures exposed on scene of McKinley's funeral as used in Paramount reel.

Producer unknown, Sep 1901.

© No reg.

lr, 59 ft. si. b&w. 35mm. ref print.

lr, 59 ft. si. b&w. 35mm. dupe neg.

SHELF LOC'N: FEA9945 (print); FPB7965 (neg)

The Paramount reel referred to in the title is unidentified.

The film is dark and slightly out of frame.

Ref sources: The Canton Repository. *Pictorial Life of William McKinley*. 1943: 26; [Davis, Oscar K. and Mumford, John K.] *The Life of William McKinley*. 1901: [115], 127–128; P&P presidential file.

Newsfilm.

SUMMARY: Scenes of the state funeral held for President William McKinley at the Capitol in Washington, D.C., on Sept. 17, 1901; from above, the camera pans the crowds gathered at the East Front of the Capitol waiting to view the body; a still close-up of McKinley is superimposed over the pan; the Capitol scene dissolves, leaving the still of McKinley.

1. Funeral service. 2. Washington, D.C. Capitol. 3. Washington, D.C. 4. McKinley, William, Pres. U.S., 1843–1901. 5. McKinley, William, Pres. U.S., 1843–1901—Funeral and memorial services. 6. United States. President, 1897–1901 (McKinley) I. Paramount, source. II. Theodore Roosevelt Association Collection. [mp 76–329]

Still pictures of TR at [Cambridge] 1910.

Producer unknown, May 1910.

© No reg.

lr, 48 ft. si. b&w. 35mm. ref print.

lr, 48 ft. si. b&w. 35mm. dupe neg.

lr, 48 ft. si. b&w. 35mm. masterpos.

lr, 51 ft. si. b&w. 35mm. neg ntr.

SHELF LOC'N: FEA6727 (print); FPB 7133 (neg);
              FPB7132 (fgmp)

RMA lists the location in the title as Oxford.

Ref sources: Lorant, Stefan. *The Life and Times of Theodore Roosevelt*. 1959: 533; The *Times*, London. 5/27/10: 8; The *Evening Star*, Washington, D.C. 5/26/10: 1.

Factual; still film.

SUMMARY: On May 26, 1910, Cambridge University conferred an honorary doctor of laws degree on TR, who spoke before the Cambridge Union, a debating society. This film consists of two still photographs: TR and an unidentified man walk between lines of cheering students, a small teddy bear is visible on the ground in the lower left-hand corner; vignetted close-up of the small, stuffed teddy bear, with his paws stretched out in greetings.

PERSONAL CREDITS: Geiss, A., source.

1. Students. 2. Teddy bears. 3. Cambridge, Eng. 4. Roosevelt, Theodore, Pres. U.S., 1858–1919. 5. Cambridge, Eng. Univerity. I. Theodore Roosevelt Association Collection. [mp 76–85]

The Story of the Panama Canal [1]
Roosevelt Film Library [1927?]
© No reg.
 2r of 2, 1886 ft. si. b&w. 35mm. ref print.
 2r of 2, 1886 ft. si. b&w. 35mm. dupe neg.
 2r of 2, 1886 ft. si. b&w. 35mm. pos ntr.
SHELF LOC'N: FEA7833, 7835 (print); FPB
    8238, 8240 (neg)
RMA title: *The Panama Canal.*

Ref sources: Roosevelt Memorial Association. *Annual Report.* 1927: 17–18; Avery, Ralph E. *America's Triumph at Panama.* 1913; Roosevelt Memorial Association. *The Panama Canal* (script)

Factual; industrial, compilation.

SUMMARY: Compilation film revealing the story of the construction of the Panama Canal, which TR considered one of his most valuable contributions to foreign affairs. The most prominent views demonstrate the need for building the canal and show the early attempts, the actual construction, and finally the canal in operation. Sequences of stills, mostly maps, showing the need for a shorter way from ocean to ocean; views of the early attempts by Ferdinand de Lesseps; the USS Oregon, which had to sail around South America from the Pacific to fight in the Spanish-American War; scenes of President William McKinley and TR in 1901; a brief shot of TR, Lyman J. Gage, Philander C. Knox, Ethan Allen Hitchcock, William R. Day, Elihu Root, Charles E. Smith, and James Wilson at McKinley's funeral in Canton, Ohio, 1901; a medium-close shot of Dr. William C. Gorgas, who was in charge of sanitation during the building of the Panama Canal; workers clearing the canal of yellow fever; TR's visit to Panama in 1906 and his meeting with President Manuel Amador Guerrero; a view of Col. George W. Goethals, chief engineer and first governor; sequences of machinery, huge cranes, gigantic steam shovels, and men working on the actual construction of the canal; various shots of Gamboa Dike, Miraflores Locks, and Gaillard (Culebra) Cut; scenes showing the launch of two barges in a lock, boats, and battleships using the canal; the final sequence shows President Calvin Coolidge speaking.

PERSONAL CREDITS: Gentry, Caroline, editor. 1. Canals, Interoceanic. 2. Battleships. 3. Yellow fever—Panama Canal—Prevention. 4. Construction equipment. 5. Construction workers. 6. Locks (Hydraulic engineering) 7. Panama Canal. 8. Canal Zone. 9. Gorgas, William C. 10. Goethals, George W. 11. Oregon (Ship) 12. United States. President, 1897–1901 (McKinley) 13. United States. President, 1901–1909 (Roosevelt) 14. Panama. Presidente, 1904–1908 (Amador Guerrero) 15. United States. President, 1923–1929 (Coolidge) I. Roosevelt Memorial Association. Film Library. II. Roosevelt Memorial Association, source. III. Theodore Roosevelt Association Collection. [mp 76–330]

The Story of the Panama Canal [2]
Roosevelt Film Library [1927?]
© No reg.
 2r of 2, 1900 ft. si. b&w. 35mm. ref print.
 2r of 2, 1900 ft. si. b&w. 35mm. dupe neg.
 2r of 2, 1899 ft. si. b&w. 35mm. neg ntr.
SHELF LOC'N: FEA6702–6703 (print); FPB
    7076, 7126 (neg)
RMA title: *The Panama Canal.*

Ref sources: Roosevelt Memorial Association. *Annual Report.* 1927: 17–18; Avery, Ralph E. *America's Triumph at Panama.* 1913; Roosevelt Memorial Association. *The Panama Canal* (script)

Factual; industrial, compilation.

SUMMARY: Compilation film revealing the story of the construction of the Panama Canal, which TR considered one of his most valuable contributions to foreign affairs. The most prominent views demonstrate the need for building the canal and show the early attempts, the actual construction, and finally the canal in operation. Sequences of stills, mostly maps, showing the need for a shorter way from ocean to ocean; views of the early attempts by Ferdinand de Lesseps; the USS Oregon, which had to sail around South America from the Pacific to fight in the Spanish-American War; scenes of President William McKinley and TR in 1901; a brief shot of TR, Lyman J. Gage, Philander C. Knox, Ethan Allen Hitchcock, William R. Day, Elihu Root, Charles E. Smith, and James Wilson at McKinley's funeral in Canton, Ohio, 1901; a medium-close shot of Dr. William C. Gorgas, who was in charge of sanitation during the building of the Panama Canal; workers clearing the canal of yellow fever; TR's visit to Panama in 1906 and his meeting with President Manuel Amador Guerrero; scenes of Secretary of War William Howard Taft's visit to the canal in Nov., 1904; a medium-close shot of Col. George W. Goethals, chief engineer and first governor; sequences of machinery, huge cranes, gigantic steam shovels and men working on the actual construction of the canal; various shots of Gamboa Dike, Miraflores Locks, and Gaillard (Culebra) Cut; scenes showing the launch of two barges in a lock, boats, and battleships using the canal; the final sequence shows President Calvin Coolidge speaking.

PERSONAL CREDITS: Gentry, Caroline, editor.

1. Canals,Interoceanic. 2. Battleships. 3. Yellow fever—Panama Canal—Prevention. 4. Construction equipment. 5. Construction workers. 6. Locks (Hydraulic engineering) 7. Panama Canal. 8. Canal Zone. 9. Gorgas, William C. 10. Taft, William Howard, Pres. U.S., 1857–1930. 11. Goethals, George W. 12. Oregon (Ship) 13. United States. President, 1897–1901 (McKinley) 14. United States. President, 1901–1909 (Roosevelt) 15. Panama. Presidente, 1904–1908 (Amador Guerrero) 16. United States. President, 1923–1929 (Coolidge) I. Roosevelt Memorial Association. Film Library. II. Roosevelt Memorial Association, source. III. Theodore Roosevelt Association Collection. [mp 76–331]

Street scenes in Naples, Italy.
Producer unknown [191–?]
© No reg.
   lr, 14 ft. si. b&w. 16mm. ref print.
   lr, 14 ft. si. b&w. 16mm. dupe neg (cy 1)
   lr, 36 ft. si. b&w. 35mm. dupe neg (cy 2)
   lr, 36 ft. si. b&w. 35mm. pos ntr.
SHELF LOC'N: FAB869 (print); FRA5897 (neg, cy 1); FPB8079 (neg, cy 2)
Ref sources: Lukas, Jan. *Naples*. 1965: 24–25; P&P stereo file.
Factual; views.
SUMMARY: Scenes of soldiers and civilians on the steps and in front of the Royal Palace in Naples; a long shot of the Piazza Plebiscito in Naples; long shots of the Parliament building in Budapest and men leaving automobiles and entering the building; final views of German troops in formation before an unidentified building.
1. Soldiers. 2. Naples. Palazzo reale. 3. Budapest. Országház. 4. Naples. 5. Naples—Plazas—Piazza del Plebiscito. 6. Budapest. I. Kinogram Publishing Corporation, source. II. Theodore Roosevelt Association Collection. [mp 76–188]

Theodore Roosevelt: fighter for social justice.
Roosevelt Memorial Association, 1934.
© No reg.
   lr, 214 ft. si. b&w. 16mm. ref print.
   lr, 214 ft. si. b&w. 16mm. dupe neg (cy 1)
   lr, 536 ft. si. b&w. 35mm. dupe neg (cy 2)
   lr, 536 ft. si. b&w. 35mm. pos ntr.
SHELF LOC'N: FAB1051 (print); FRA6018 (neg, cy 1); FPB7348 (neg, cy 2)
RMA title: *Social Justice*.
Ref source: Roosevelt Memorial Association. *Theodore Roosevelt, Fighter for Social Justice* (script)
Factual.

Dr. TR: "You're a very sick man. I'm the only one that can help you." Lafollette: "Quack! That's all!" Pen and ink drawing by Clifford Berryman, August 6, 1912.

SUMMARY: This compilation film consists of scenes of TR during his 1912 Progressive campaign: in North Dakota TR speaks to crowds from a train and is silhouetted as he stands with his cousin and campaign secretary, George E. Roosevelt, and some unidentified men on the rear platform of his train; TR addresses a crowd in Pueblo, Colo. (the photographer's sign reads Mile High Photo Co., Denver). Interior titles consisting of excerpts from TR's speeches and/or writings are interspersed throughout the film. The RMA list indicates that the film was assembled and shown at the RMA medals dinner, Oct. 27, 1934.
1. Presidents—United States—Election—1912. 2. North Dakota. 3. Pueblo, Colo. 4. Roosevelt, Theodore, Pres. U.S., 1858–1919—Addresses, essays, lectures. 5. Roosevelt, George E. 6. Roosevelt, Theodore, Pres. U.S., 1858–1919—Quotations. 7. Progressive Party (Founded 1912) I. Roosevelt Memorial Association. II. Roosevelt Memorial Association, source. III. Theodore Roosevelt Association Collection. [mp 76–183]

Theodore Roosevelt, great scout [1]
Film Library, Roosevelt Memorial Association [1925?]

© No reg.

2r of 2, 1726 ft. si. b&w. 35mm. ref print.

2r of 2, 1726 ft. si. b&w. 35mm. dupe neg.

2r of 2, 1726 ft. si. b&w. 35mm. pos ntr.

SHELF LOC'N: FEA8953–8954 (print); FPB 9911–9912 (neg)

Ref sources: Roosevelt Memorial Association. *Theodore Roosevelt, Great Scout* (script); Roosevelt Memorial Association. *Annual Report.* 1925: 17; Murray, William D. *The History of the Boy Scouts of America.* 1937; *Roosevelt House Bulletin.* v. 2, no. 5, 1925: 1, 5.

Factual; compilation.

SUMMARY: A film-within-a-film format links TR's enthusiasm and support for the Boy Scouts of America with his love of adventure in the outdoors. From the steps of Roosevelt House in New York City, Robert W. G. Vail, RMA librarian, speaks to scouts who attended the 1924 World Jamboree in Copenhagen; on Vail's left is Colin H. Livingstone, national president of the Boy Scouts; the other man is unidentified. Local Boy Scouts visit the museum in the house as interior titles and still photos describe TR's boyhood; boys enter the auditorium to view a film on TR. A still photo of TR in a cowboy outfit, scenes of western landscape, cowboys riding horses and herding cattle and horses, and TR speaking during his 1912 Progressive campaign represent his visits to the Dakotas as a young man. Footage of TR's 1909 trip to East Africa includes TR and party in a crowd of Kikuyu and/or Masai tribesmen, tribesmen performing a ritual dance carrying shields and spears, a campsite, elephants, lions, TR on a hunting trip, African buffalo, and a giraffe. Before beginning the 1913 River of Doubt expedition in Brazil, TR poses with Kermit Roosevelt, Frank Harper, and Leo E. Miller on the ship Vandyck. Views of Rio de Janeiro and its harbor; the gates of what is probably the Guanabara Palace; TR, Lauro S. Müller, Edwin V. Morgan, Anthony Fiala, and Fr. John A. Zahm on the steps of the Guanabara Palace. The Roosevelt-Rondon group is on a small launch on the Sepotuba River; TR, hatless in a light shirt, leans on the rail. Men paddle on a river and portage canoes through the river's rapids. At Sagamore Hill TR poses with his horse Sidar. Walking with a group of men, TR is at Cooper's Training Camp in Stamford, Conn. TR poses with Boy Scouts at Sagamore Hill; a group of men march up the hill; from the porch TR speaks to a group of suffragists. TR, with Mayor John P. Mitchel, Charles Evans Hughes, and Alton B. Parker, reviews a parade of drafted men on

Sept. 4, 1917, in New York City. At a Fourth of July celebration in 1917 at Forest Hills, TR reviews the Forest Hills Rifle Club, and at the Forest Hills Gardens railroad station he speaks in support of American war involvement. Indicative of the close relationship between TR and the Boy Scouts organization are scenes of scouts attending memorial services for TR at the New York Public Library on Oct. 25, 1919, and participating in the annual pilgrimage to his grave on Oct. 27, TR's birthday; there are close-up shots of national commissioner of the Boy Scouts Daniel C. Beard and Theodore Roosevelt, Jr., at the grave in 1920. Views of TR speaking at Camp Grant in Rockford, Ill., during the war and of scouts in the auditorium conclude the film.

1. Scouts and scouting. 2. New York (City). Roosevelt House. 3. Oyster Bay, N.Y. Sagamore Hill. 4. Africa. 5. Brazil. 6. Vail, Robert W. G. 7. Livingstone, Colin H. 8. Roosevelt, Theodore, Pres. U.S., 1858–1919—Childhood and youth. 9. Roosevelt, Theodore, Pres. U.S., 1858–1919—Addresses, essays, lectures. 10. Roosevelt, Theodore, Pres. U.S., 1858–1919—Journey to Africa, 1909–1910. 11. Roosevelt, Theodore, Pres. U.S., 1858–1919—Journey to South America, 1913–1914. 12. Roosevelt, Theordore, Pres. U.S., 1858–1919—Funeral and memorial services. 13. Beard, Daniel C. 14. Roosevelt, Theodore, 1887–1944. 15. Boy Scouts of America. I. Roosevelt Memorial Association. Film Library. II. Roosevelt Memorial Association, source. III. Theodore Roosevelt Association Collection. [mp 76–337]

Theodore Roosevelt, great scout [2]

Film Library, Roosevelt Memorial Association [1925?]

© No reg.

2r, 1850 ft. si. b&w. 35mm. ref print.

2r, 1850 ft. si. b&w. 35mm. dupe neg.

2r, 1854 ft. si. b&w. 35mm. pos ntr.

SHELF LOC'N: FEA5446, 8951 (print); FPA 8326–8327 (neg)

Ref sources: Roosevelt Memorial Association. *Theodore Roosevelt, Great Scout* (script); Roosevelt Memorial Association. *Annual Report.* 1925: 17; *Roosevelt House Bulletin.* v. 2, no. 5, 1925: 1, 5.

Factual; compilation.

SUMMARY: TR's love of the West is portrayed in scenes of cowboys, western landscape, cattle, horses, and TR speaking during his 1912 Progressive campaign. From the steps of Roosevelt House in New York City, RMA librarian Robert W.G. Vail speaks to scouts who attended the 1924 World Jamboree in Copenhagen; Colin H. Livingstone, national president of the Boy Scouts of America, is on Vail's left; the third man is unidentified. Local Boy Scouts visit Roosevelt House and learn about TR's active life and his support of the BSA from its founding in 1910. TR's 1909–1910 hunting and collecting trip to Africa is recounted with scenes of TR and his party with a group of Kikuyu and/or Masai tribesmen, a ritual dance performed by tribesmen carrying shields and spears, a campsite, elephants, lions, TR on horseback, African buffalo, and a giraffe. On the ship Vandyck, TR poses with Kermit Roosevelt, Frank Harper, and Leo E. Miller prior to his 1913 expedition to explore the River of Doubt in Brazil. Views of Rio de Janeiro and its harbor; the gates of what is probably the Guanabara Palace; TR, Lauro S. Müller, Edwin V. Morgan, Anthony Fiala, and Fr. John A. Zahm on the steps of the Guanabara Palace. The Roosevelt-Rondon group is on a small launch on the Sepotuba River; TR, hatless in a light shirt, leans on the rail. Men paddle on a river and portage canoes through the river's rapids. At his home, Sagamore Hill, in Oyster Bay, N.Y., TR walks with his dogs, rides his horse Sidar, and chops down a tree. Walking with several men, TR is at Cooper's Training Camp in Stamford, Conn. A group of men march up the hill at Sagamore Hill; from the porch TR speaks to a group of suffragists. In 1920, Daniel C. Beard, national commissioner of the Boy Scouts, Theodore Roosevelt, Jr., and scouts participate in the annual pilgrimage to TR's grave on his birthday. Active in promoting the war effort, TR speaks at Camp Grant in Rockford, Ill.; with Mayor John P. Mitchel, Charles Evans Hughes, and Alton B. Parker, TR reviews a parade of drafted men on Sept. 4, 1917, in New York City. At a Fourth of July celebration in 1917 at Forest Hills, TR reviews the Forest Hills Rifle Club, and at the Forest Hills Gardens railroad station, he speaks in support of American war involvement. The film concludes with scenes of memorial services held for TR at the New York Public Library on Oct. 25, 1919, and scouts in the auditorium of Roosevelt House.

1. Scouts and scouting. 2. New York (City). Roosevelt House. 3. Oyster Bay, N.Y. Sagamore Hill. 4. Africa. 5. Brazil. 6. Roosevelt, Theodore, Pres. U.S., 1858–1919—Childhood and youth. 7. Roosevelt, Theodore, Pres. U.S., 1858–1919—Addresses, essays, lectures. 8. Vail, Robert W.G. 9. Livingstone, Colin H. 10. Roosevelt, Theodore, Pres. U.S., 1858–1919—Journey to Africa, 1909–1910. 11. Roosevelt, Theodore, Pres. U.S., 1858–1919—Journey to South America, 1913–1914. 12. Beard, Daniel C. 13. Roosevelt, Theodore, 1887–1944. 14. Roosevelt, Theodore, Pres. U.S., 1858–1919—Funeral and memorial services. 15. Boy Scouts of America. I. Roosevelt Memorial Association. Film Library. II. Eastman Kodak Company, source. III. Theodore Roosevelt Association Collection. [mp 76–338]

Theodore Roosevelt, great scout [3]

Film Library, Roosevelt Memorial Association [1925?]

© No reg.

    lr of 1, 348 ft. si. b&w. 16mm. ref print (cy 1)
    lr of 1, 820 ft. si. b&w. 35mm. ref print (cy 2)
    lr of 1, 820 ft. si. b&w. 35mm. dupe neg.
    lr of 1, 823 ft. si. b&w. 35mm. pos ntr.

SHELF LOC'N: FAB1653 (print, cy 1); FEA8952 (print, cy 2); FPB9910 (neg)

Caroline Gentry is listed as editor on the ref print (cy 2) and the dupe neg.

Ref sources: Roosevelt Memorial Association. *Theodore Roosevelt, the Great Scout* (script); Roosevelt Memorial Association. *Annual Report.* 1925: 17; *Roosevelt House Bulletin.* v. 2, no. 5, 1925: 1, 5.

Factual; compilation.

SUMMARY: This short biographical film highlights TR's close relationship with the Boy Scouts of America. RMA librarian Robert W. G. Vail, Colin H. Livingstone, national president of the BSA, and an unidentified man welcome scouts who have returned from the 1924 World Jamboree in Copenhagen to Roosevelt House in New York City. Local scouts visit the museum in the house and learn about TR's youth and his love of the West. During his 1909–1910 hunting and collecting trip to East Africa, TR and his party visit Kikuyu and/or Masai tribesmen and tribesmen perform a dance; views of lions, African buffalo, and a giraffe. TR poses with Kermit Roosevelt, Frank Harper, and Leo E. Miller on the ship Vandyck before beginning the River of Doubt expedition. On the steps of the Guanabara Palace in Rio de Janeiro, TR appears with Lauro S. Muller, Edwin V. Morgan, Anthony Fiala, and Fr. John A. Zahm. TR, in a light shirt, leans on the rail of a small launch, probably on the Sepotuba River, as his party travels to the headwaters of the River of Doubt. At Sagamore Hill TR walks with dogs and vigorously chops down a tree. Urging active participation in the war effort, TR reviews the Forest Hills Rifle Club and speaks at

Camp Grant in Rockford, Ill. Scouts in the auditorium of Roosevelt House cheer.

PERSONAL CREDITS: Gentry, Caroline, editor.

1. Scouts and scouting. 2. New York (City). Roosevelt House. 3. The West. 4. Oyster Bay, N.Y. Sagamore Hill. 5. Africa. 6. Brazil. 7. Vail, Robert W. G. 8. Livingstone, Colin H. 9. Roosevelt, Theodore, Pres. U.S., 1858–1919—Childhood and youth. 10. Roosevelt, Theodore, Pres. U.S., 1858–1919—Journey to Africa, 1909–1910. 11. Roosevelt, Theodore, Pres. U.S., 1858–1919—Journey to South America, 1913–1914. 12. Roosevelt, Theodore, Pres. U.S., 1858–1919—Addresses, essays, lectures. 13. Boy Scouts of America. 14. Forest Hills Rifle Club. I. Roosevelt Memorial Association. Film Library. II. Eastman Kodak Company, source. III. Theodore Roosevelt Association Collection. [mp 76–339]

Theodore Roosevelt in the great war [1]
Roosevelt Film Library [1930?]

© No reg.

lr, 1042 ft. si. b&w. 35mm. ref print.

lr, 1042 ft. si. b&w. 35mm. dupe neg.

lr, 1041 ft. si. sepia. 35mm. archival pos old safety.

lr, 1029 ft. si. b&w. 35mm. pos ntr.

lr, 1011 ft. si. b&w. 35mm. masterpos ntr.

SHELF LOC'N: FEA9951 (print); FPB4606(neg); FPA6239 (arch pos)

RMA title: *Roosevelt in the Great War.*

Ref sources: Roosevelt Memorial Association. *Annual Report.* 1930: 9; Roosevelt Memorial Association. *Theodore Roosevelt in the Great War* (script); United States. National Archives and Records Service. Audiovisual Archives Division; The New York *Times Mid-week Pictorial.* v. 6, no. 2, 1917: [12–13]; Harvard University. Library. Theodore Roosevelt Collection.

Factual; biographical, historical, war film.

SUMMARY: A film tracing TR's concern before and during the United States' participation in WWI. Quotations and footage depict the beginning of the war in Europe and the entry of the United States; views of President Woodrow Wilson signing the declaration of war. TR visits Gen. Leonard Wood at the Plattsburgh camp; soldiers visit Sagamore Hill. Urging active involvement in the war effort and supporting the Liberty Loan, TR makes many speeches and appearances: on July 4, 1917, he addresses a crowd at Forest Hills Gardens; talking with reporters, TR is at the White House after President Wilson rejects his offer to lead a division

in France; crowds at the Altar of Liberty in Madison Square; TR speaks at the Panama-Pacific International Exposition in San Francisco on July 21, 1915; preceded by cowboys, TR parades through a crowed Billings, Mont., street; on Sept. 26, 1917, TR addresses soldiers at Camp Grant in Rockford, Ill.; reviewing the Sept. 4, 1917, parade of men drafted into the new National Army in New York City are TR, Mayor John P. Mitchel, and Charles Evans Hughes, among other officials and military leaders. Several sequences represent the mobilization of U.S. forces. Shots of TR delivering a Memorial Day address in 1917 at Mineola, N.Y. Views of an infantry unit and Quentin Roosevelt and his Ninety-fifth Aero Squadron represent TR's sons' war involvement. TR speaks at the opening of the fourth Liberty Loan campaign at Oriole Baseball Park, Sept. 28, 1918. At a factory, possibly located in St. Paul, Minn., TR speaks to workers. Views of soldiers and civilians celebrating the surrender of Germany. Views of TR's burial in Youngs Memorial Cemetery in Oyster Bay Jan. 8, 1919, conclude the film.

PERSONAL CREDITS: Gentry, Caroline, director. Manning, Mae, editor.

1. European War, 1914–1918. 2. Preparedness. 3. Oyster Bay, N.Y. Sagamore Hill. 4. European War, 1914–1918—Finance. 5. Washington, D. C. White House. 6. New York (City). Liberty's Altar. 7. Baltimore. Oriole Baseball Park. 8. Plattsburgh, N.Y. 9. Oyster Bay, N.Y. 10. Forest Hills, N.Y. 11. Washington, D.C. 12. New York (City) 13. New York (City)—Plazas—Madison Square. 14. San Francisco. 15. Billings, Mont. 16. Rockford, Ill. 17. Mineola, N.Y. 18. Baltimore. 19. St. Paul, Minn. 20. Roosevelt, Theodore, Pres. U.S., 1858–1919—Quotations. 21. Wilson, Woodrow, Pres. U.S., 1856–1924. 22. Wood, Leonard. 23. Roosevelt, Theodore, Pres. U.S., 1858–1919—Addresses, essays, lectures. 24. Mitchel, John P. 25. Hughes, Charles Evans. 26. Roosevelt, Quentin. 27. Roosevelt, Theodore, Pres. U.S., 1858–1919—Family. 28. Roosevelt, Theodore, Pres. U.S., 1858–1919—Funeral and memorial services. 29. United States. president, 1913–1921 (Wilson) 30. Plattsburgh Barracks. 31. United States. Laws, statutes, etc. Liberty loan acts. 32. Camp Grant. 33. United States. Army. A.E.F., 1917–1920. 34. United States. Army. 95th Aero Squadron. 35. Panama-Pacific International Exposition, 1915. I. Roosevelt Memorial Association. Film Library. II. Roosevelt Memorial Association. III. Roosevelt Memorial Association, source. IV. Theodore Roosevelt Association Collec-

tion. V. Roosevelt in the great war [Title] [mp 76–289]

Theodore Roosevelt in the great war [2]
Roosevelt Film Library [1930?]
© No reg.
 lr, 1038 ft. si. b&w. 35mm. ref print (cy 1)
 lr, 1078 ft. si. b&w. 35mm. ref print (cy 2)
 lr, 1038 ft. si. b&w. 35mm. dupe neg (cy 1)
 lr, 1078 ft. si. b&w. 35mm. dupe neg (cy 2)
 lr, 1038 ft. si. b&w. 35mm. pos ntr (cy 1)
 lr, 1078 ft. si. b&w. 35mm. pos ntr (cy 2)
SHELF LOC'N: FEA8337 (print, cy 1); FEA8955 (print, cy 2); FPB9875 (neg, cy 1); FPA8330 (neg, cy 2)
RMA title: *Roosevelt in the great war.*
Factual; biographical, historical, war film.
SUMMARY: A film tracing TR's concern before and during the United States' participation in WWI. Quotations and footage depict the beginning of the war in Europe and the entry of the United States; views of President Woodrow Wilson signing the declaration of war. TR visits Gen. Leonard Wood at the Plattsburgh camp; soldiers visit Sagamore Hill. Urging active involvement in the war effort and supporting the Liberty Loan, TR makes many speeches and appearances: on July 4, 1917, he addresses a crowd at Forest Hills Gardens; talking with reporters, TR is at the White House after President Wilson rejects his offer to lead a division in France; crowds at the Altar of Liberty in Madison Square; TR speaks at the Panama-Pacific International Exposition in San Francisco on July 21, 1915; preceded by cowboys, TR parades through a crowded Billings, Mont., street; on Sept. 26, 1917, TR addresses soldiers at Camp Grant in Rockford, Ill.; reviewing the Sept. 4, 1917, parade of men drafted into the new National Army in New York City are TR, Mayor John P. Mitchel, and Charles Evans Hughes, among other officials and military leaders. Several sequences represent the mobilization of U.S. forces. Shots of TR delivering a Memorial Day address in 1917 at Mineola, N.Y. Views of an infantry unit and Quentin Roosevelt and his Ninety-fifth Aero Squadron represent TR's sons' war involvement. TR speaks at the opening of the fourth Liberty Loan campaign at Oriole Baseball Park, Sept. 28, 1918. At a factory, possibly located in St. Paul, Minn., TR speaks to workers. Views of soldiers and civilians celebrating the surrender of Germany. Views of TR's burial in Youngs Memorial Cemetery in Oyster Bay Jan. 8, 1919, conclude the film.

PERSONAL CREDITS: Gentry, Caroline, director. Manning, Mae, editor.
1. European War, 1914–1918. 2. Preparedness. 3. Oyster Bay, N.Y. Sagamore Hill. 4. European War, 1914–1918—Finance. 5. Washington, D.C. White House. 6. New York (City). Liberty's Altar. 7. Baltimore. Oriole Baseball Park. 8. Plattsburgh, N.Y. 9. Oyster Bay, N.Y. 10. Forest Hills, N.Y. 11. Washington, D.C. 12. New York (City) 13. New York (City)—Plazas—Madison Square. 14. San Francisco. 15. Billings, Mont. 16. Rockford, Ill. 17. Mineola, N.Y. 18. Baltimore. 19. St. Paul, Minn. 20. Roosevelt, Theodore, Pres. U.S., 1858–1919—Quotations. 21. Wilson, Woodrow, Pres. U.S., 1856–1924. 22. Wood, Leonard. 23. Roosevelt, Theodore, Pres. U. S., 1858–1919—Addresses, essays, lectures. 24. Mitchel, John P. 25. Hughes, Charles Evans. 26. Roosevelt, Quentin. 27. Roosevelt, Theodore, Pres. U.S., 1858–1919—Family. 28. Roosevelt, Theodore, Pres. U.S., 1858–1919—Funeral and memorial services. 29. United States. President, 1913–1921 (Wilson) 30. Plattsburgh Barracks. 31. United States. Laws, statutes, etc. Liberty loan acts. 32. Camp Grant. 33. United States. Army. A.E.F., 1917–1920. 34. United States. Army. 95th Aero Squadron. 35. Panama-Pacific International Exposition, 1915. I. Roosevelt Memorial Association. Film Library. II. Roosevelt Memorial Association. III. Roosevelt Memorial Association, source. IV. Theodore Roosevelt Association Collection. V. Roosevelt in the great war [Title] [mp 76–290]

Theodore Roosevelt in the great war [3]
Roosevelt Film Library [1930?]
© No reg.
 lr, 417 ft. si. b&w. 16mm. ref print.
 lr, 417 ft. si. b&w. 16mm. archival pos.
 lr, 1043 ft. si. b&w. 35mm. neg ntr.
SHELF LOC'N: FAB1468 (print); FRA6199 (arch pos)
RMA title: *Roosevelt in the Great War.*
Factual; biographical, historical, war film.
SUMMARY: TR's beliefs and activities before and during WWI are presented. The first ca. 49 ft. are out of sequence. Quotations and various scenes depict the beginning of the war in Europe and the entry of the United States; views of President Woodrow Wilson signing the declaration of war. TR visits Gen. Leonard Wood at the Plattsburgh camp. Urging active involvement in the war effort and supporting the Liberty Loan, TR makes many speeches and appearances: on July 4, 1917, he addresses a crowd at Forest Hills Gardens; talking

with reporters, TR is at the White House after President Wilson rejects his offer to lead a division in France; crowds at the Altar of Liberty in Madison Square; TR speaks at the Panama-Pacific International Exposition in San Francisco on July 21, 1915; TR parades through a crowded Billings, Mont., street; on Sept. 26, 1917, TR addresses soldiers at Camp Grant in Rockford, Ill.; reviewing the Sept. 4, 1917, parade of men drafted into the new National Army in New York City are TR, Mayor John P. Mitchel, and Charles Evans Hughes, among other officials and military leaders. Several sequences represent the mobilization of U.S. forces. Shots of TR delivering a Memorial Day address in 1917 at Mineola, N.Y. Views of an infantry unit and Quentin Roosevelt and his Ninety-fifth Aero Squadron represent TR's sons' war involvement. TR speaks at the opening of the fourth Liberty Loan campaign at Oriole Baseball Park, Sept. 28, 1918. At a factory, possibly located in St. Paul, Minn., TR speaks to workers. Views of soldiers and civilians celebrating the surrender of Germany. Views of TR's burial in Youngs Memorial Cemetery in Oyster Bay Jan. 8, 1919, conclude the film.

PERSONAL CREDITS: Gentry, Caroline, director. Manning, Mae, editor.

1. European War, 1914–1918. 2. Preparedness. 3. European War, 1914–1918—Finance. 4. Washington, D.C. White House. 5. New York (City). Liberty's Altar. 6. Baltimore. Oriole Baseball Park. 7. Plattsburgh, N.Y. 8. Forest Hills, N.Y. 9. Washington, D.C. 10. New York (City) 11. New York (City)— Plazas—Madison Square. 12. San Francisco. 13. Billings, Mont. 14. Rockford, Ill. 15. Mineola, N.Y. 16. Baltimore. 17. St. Paul, Minn. 18. Oyster Bay, N.Y. 19. Roosevelt, Theodore, Pres. U.S., 1858–1919—Quotations. 20. Wilson, Woodrow, Pres. U.S., 1856–1924. 21. Wood, Leonard. 22. Roosevelt, Theodore, Pres. U.S., 1858–1919—Addresses, essays, lectures. 23. Mitchel, John P. 24. Hughes, Charles Evans. 25. Roosevelt, Quentin. 26. Roosevelt, Theodore, Pres. U.S., 1858–1919—Family. 27. Roosevelt, Theodore, Pres. U.S., 1858–1919—Funeral and memorial services. 28. United States. President, 1913–1921 (Wilson) 29. Plattsburgh Barracks. 30. United States. Laws, statutes, etc. Liberty loan acts. 31. Camp Grant. 32. United States. Army. A.E.F., 1917–1920. 33. United States. Army. 95th Aero Squadron. 34. Panama-Pacific International Exposition, 1915. I. Roosevelt Memorial Association. Film Library. II. Roosevelt Memorial Association. III. Roosevelt Memorial Association, source. IV. Theodore Roosevelt Association Collection. V. Roosevelt in the great war [Title] [mp 76–291]

Theodore Roosevelt leaving the White House.

American Mutoscope Co. [1897?]

© H27382, American Mutoscope & Biograph Co., 22Jan1903

    lr of 1, 6 ft. si. b&w. 16mm. ref print (cy 1)
    lr of 1, 15 ft. si. b&w. 35mm. ref print (cy 2)
    lr of 1, 6 ft. si. b&w. 16mm. dupe neg (2 cy)
    lr of 1, 15 ft. si. b&w. 35mm. masterpos (2 cy)
    lr of 1, 15 ft. si. b&w. 35mm. pos ntr.
    lr of 1, 13 ft. si. b&w. 16mm. ref print.
    lr of 1, 13 ft. si. b&w. 16mm. dupe neg.
    lr of 1, 16 ft. si. b&w. 35mm. paper (2 cy)
SHELF LOC'N: FAB1229 (print, cy 1–RMA); FEA7826 (print, cy 2–RMA); FRA6182 & 6183 (neg, 2 cy–RMA); FPB8058 & 9689 (fgmp, 2 cy-RMA); FLA3351 (print-Paper); FRA0688 (neg-Paper); LC337 (paper, 2 cy-Paper)

RMA title: *TR as Assistant Secretary of the Navy Leaving the White House, 1897.*

Possible production dates: Apr. 1897–May 1898, since TR was assistant secretary of the Navy during this period.

Ref sources: Roosevelt Memorial Association. *Annual Report.* 1925: 16; P&P geographic file; P&P presidential file.

Newsfilm; views.

SUMMARY: TR, in formal dress with a hat, walks down the stairs of the old State, War and Navy Building in Washington, D.C.; he turns and walks toward the stationary camera; the south portico of the White House is visible through trees in the background. According to the Roosevelt Memorial Association, this is the first motion picture of TR.

1. Washington, D.C. White House. 2. Washington, D.C. State, War and Navy Building. 3. Washington, D.C. 4. Washington, D.C.—Public buildings. 5. Roosevelt, Theodore, Pres. U.S., 1858–1919. I. Biograph Company. II. Biograph Company, source. III. Paramount, source. IV. Theodore Roosevelt Association Collection. V. Paper Print Collection. [mp 76–279]

Three children visit TR's grave, 1920.

Producer unknown [1920?]

© No reg.

    lr, 2 ft. si. b&w. 16mm. ref print.
    lr, 2 ft. si. b&w. 16mm. dupe neg.
    lr, 6 ft. si. b&w. 35mm. pos old safety.

SHELF LOC'N: FAB961 (print); FRA5928 (neg)
The date in the title is unverified.
Newsfilm.
SUMMARY: Two young girls and a boy pay homage to TR at his grave in Youngs Memorial Cemetery, Oyster Bay, New York. The boy, holding a flag, watches while the girls throw flower bouquets through the fence surrounding the grave.
PERSONAL CREDITS: Urban, Charles, source. 1. Tombs. 2. Youngs Memorial Cemetery. 3. Memorial rites and ceremonies. 4. Oyster Bay, N.Y. 5. Roosevelt, Theodore, Pres. U.S., 1858–1919—Tomb. I. Theodore Roosevelt Association Collection. [mp 76–152]

Through the Roosevelt country with Roosevelt's friends.

Roosevelt Memorial Association [1919?]
© No reg.
    2r of 2, 691 ft. si. b&w. 16mm. ref print.
    2r of 2, 691 ft. si. b&w. 16mm. dupe neg.
    2r of 2, 1632 ft. si. b&w. 35mm. pos ntr.
SHELF LOC'N: FAB845–846 (print); FRA5850–5851 (neg)
RMA title: *Through the Roosevelt Country.*
Ref sources: Hagedorn, Hermann. *Roosevelt in the Bad Lands.* 1921; *The Moving Picture World.* v. 42, no. [2], 1919: [214]
Factual; western.
SUMMARY: Sequences of TR's ranching life in the Dakotas, hunting grounds in Wyoming and Montana, and views of his friends and neighbors in the Little Missouri Badlands during the 1880s, with quotations from TR and his friends interspersed. The opening scene of TR speaking at Sagamore Hill is followed by various stills of TR. Panning shots and panoramic views of a large geographic area, part of which is identified by interior title as Medora, N.D. Long shot of a building labeled Rough Rider's Hotel, with a group of men gathered outside. Following are sequences of TR's Badlands friends, his cattle ranches, and his hunting grounds, mainly identified by interior titles: Joe Ferris, partner with TR in the Chimney Butte Ranch (Maltese Cross); Old Frenchy; Bill Dantz, TR's law partner; Nitch Kendley, incorrectly identified on the film as Kinley; Sylvane Ferris, partner with TR in both the Chimney Butte and Elkhorn Ranches; a view of three men riding horses across a grassy plateau; an unidentified man and a woman are shown sitting in chairs; A. W. Merrifield, foreman of the Chimney Butte Ranch; sequences of TR's three closest friends, Merrifield and the Ferris

brothers, talking with a group of men, pointing out the site of Chimney Butte Ranch, and sitting on a cliff above the Chimney Butte site; scenes of men roping and branding cattle, with panning shots of the area and the butte formation in the background; Margaret Roberts; Pete Pellessier, incorrectly identified on the film as Pelissier; panning shots of the Elkhorn site and surrounding area; scenes of a roundup, men on horseback flanking range horses into the corral at Elkhorn; a view from the Elkhorn site of the Little Missouri River bordered by cliffs, peaks, a plateau, and grassy meadows; Victor Stickney, a frontier doctor; sequences of two unidentified men on a hunting trip in the Big Horn Mountains, where TR hunted; scene of elks; medium shot of the Eaton brothers, Howard on the right, their dude ranch in Wyoming, and a scene of Howard talking with a group; panning shot of a man who appears to be Merrifield shooting from a boat; scenes of a buffalo herd, possibly in Montana; Dutch Wannigan(John Reuter), who worked for TR; a view of a man riding horseback; panning shots of a river, a grassy plateau, and a forest. The closing scene shows TR speaking at Sagamore Hill.
PERSONAL CREDITS: Hagedorn, Hermann, director. Reid, W. W., photographer.
1. Hunting. 2. Medora, N.D. Rough Rider's Hotel. 3. Chimney Butte Ranch, N.D. 4. Elkhorn Ranch, N.D. 5. Dude ranches. 6. Wyoming. 7. Montana. 8. Little Missouri Badlands, N.D. 9. Medora, N.D. 10. Medora, N.D.—Description—Views. 11. Little Missouri River. 12. Big Horn Mountains. 13. Roosevelt, Theodore, Pres. U.S., 1858–1919. 14. Ferris, Joseph A. 15. Frenchy. 16. Dantz, William T. 17. Kendley, Nitch. 18. Ferris, Sylvane M. 19. Merrifield, Arthur W. 20. Roberts, Margaret. 21. Pellessier, Pete. 22. Stickney, Victor H. 23. Eaton, Howard. 24. Reuter, John. I. Roosevelt Memorial Association. II. Roosevelt Memorial Association, source. III. Theodore Roosevelt Association Collection. [mp 76–91]

TR addresses large crowd for the Liberty Loan in Baltimore, 1918.

Producer unknown, Sep 1918.
© No reg.
    lr, 15 ft. si. b&w. 16mm. ref print.
    lr, 15 ft. si. b&w. 16mm. dupe neg.
    lr, 39 ft. si. b&w. 35mm. pos ntr.
SHELF LOC'N: FAB966 (print); FRA5935 (neg)
Ref sources: Baltimore *American.* 9/28/18: 8; The

Evening Sun, Baltimore. 9/28/18: 1; P&P portrait file.

Newsfilm.

SUMMARY: At the opening of the fourth Liberty Loan rally on Sept. 28, 1918, TR addresses a large crowd in Oriole Baseball Park, Baltimore, Md. Views from above the stadium of the seated crowd; long and close shots of TR, wearing a mourning armband for his son Quentin, delivering his address from a platform; seated among the notables behind him are, left to right: Dr. Thomas J. Preston, Mrs. Thomas J. Preston, who was the wife of former President Grover Cleveland, and Emerson C. Harrington, governor of Maryland.

1. Baltimore. Oriole Baseball Park. 2. Baltimore—Sports facilities. 3. Baltimore. 4. Preston, Thomas J. 5. Preston, Frances Folsom Cleveland. 6. Roosevelt, Theodore, Pres. U.S., 1858–1919—Addresses, essays, lectures. 7. Harrington, Emerson C. 8. United States. Laws, statutes, etc. Liberty loan acts. 9. Maryland. Liberty Loan Committee. 10. Maryland. Governor, 1916–1920 (Harrington) I. International Newsreel Corporation, source. II. Theodore Roosevelt Association Collection. [mp 76–163]

TR and Cardinal Gibbons at Baltimore, Md., 1918.

Producer unknown, Sep 1918.

© No reg.

lr, 9 ft. si. b&w. 16mm. ref print.
lr, 9 ft. si. b&w. 16mm. dupe neg.
lr, 22 ft. si. b&w. 35mm. pos ntr.

SHELF LOC'N: FAB1034 (print); FRA6007 (neg)

Ref sources: Baltimore *American*. 9/28/18: 8; The *Evening Sun*, Baltimore. 9/28/18: 1; P&P portrait file.

Newsfilm.

SUMMARY: On Sept. 28, 1918, TR addresses crowds in Baltimore in support of the fourth Liberty Loan. At Oriole Park, TR and a man who appears to be Phillips L. Goldsborough, chairman of the Liberty Loan Committee for Maryland and former Maryland governor (1912–1916), walk across the field with other officials; TR stops and speaks with Cardinal James Gibbons of Baltimore, whose back is to the camera; beside a flag-decorated table TR, wearing a mourning armband for his son Quentin, speaks from a platform to the packed stadium, with a man who appears to be current Maryland Governor Emerson C. Harrington among the notables seated behind him.

PERSONAL CREDITS: Braunstein, Cy, source.

1. Baltimore. Oriole Baseball Park. 2. Baltimore—Sports facilities. 3. Maryland—Governors. 4. Baltimore. 5. Roosevelt, Theodore, Pres. U.S., 1858–1919—Addresses, essays, lectures. 6. Gibbons, James. 7. Goldsborough, Phillips L. 8. Harrington, Emerson C. 9. United States. Laws, statutes, etc. Liberty loan acts. 10. Maryland. Liberty Loan Committee. 11. Maryland. Governor, 1916–1920 (Harrington) I. Theodore Roosevelt Association Collection. [mp 76–180]

TR and expedition party on the [Sepotuba] River [1914]

Producer unknown [Jan 1914?]

© No reg.

lr, 5 ft. si. b&w. 16mm. ref print (cy 1)
lr, 12 ft. si. b&w. 35mm. ref print (cy 2)
lr, 5 ft. si. b&w. 16mm. archival pos.
lr, 12 ft. si. b&w. 35mm. neg ntr.

SHELF LOC'N: FAB1122 (print, cy 1); FEA6745 (print, cy 2); FRA6065 (arch pos)

RMA title: *TR and Expedition Party on the Amazon River, 1913–1914.*

Research indicates that the photographer is Anthony Fiala, the probable location is the Sepotuba River, and the probable date is Jan. 1914.

Film has nitrate deterioration and scratches.

Ref sources: Roosevelt Memorial Association. *The River of Doubt* (script); *Scribner's Magazine*. v. 56, no. 1, 1914: 9, 23–24.

Factual.

SUMMARY: TR combines a lecture tour with exploration of the River of Doubt (Roosevelt River) in the Amazon Valley during his 1913–1914 trip to South America. In Jan. 1914, the Roosevelt-Rondon Scientific Expedition travels in Brazil on the Paraguay River and the Sepotuba River to Tapirapoan, where the overland portion of their journey to the headwaters of the River of Doubt began. A native trading boat appears to be lashed to the small launch carrying the Roosevelt party; the launch moves slowly toward the camera. The man wearing a white shirt, seated to the right on the boat, is probably TR. The location may be the Sepotuba River. Camera distance and film quality make positive identification of individuals impossible.

PERSONAL CREDITS: Fiala, Anthony, photographer. Fiala, Anthony, source.

1. Scientific expeditions. 2. Launches. 3. Boats and boating. 4. Sepotuba River. 5. Roosevelt River. 6. Amazon Valley. 7. Brazil. 8. Roosevelt, Theodore, Pres. U.S., 1858–1919—Journey to South America, 1913–1914. 9. Roosevelt-Rondon Scientific Expe-

dition. I. Theodore Roosevelt Association Collection. [mp 76–223]

TR and Leonard Wood at the New York flower show, 1917.

Producer unknown, Mar 1917.

© No reg.

    lr, 43 ft. si. b&w. 16mm. ref print.

    lr, 43 ft. si. b&w. 16mm. dupe neg.

    lr, 108 ft. si. b&w. 35mm. pos ntr.

SHELF LOC'N: FAB835 (print); FRA5836 (neg)

Newsfilm.

SUMMARY: Shots of TR and Leonard Wood on Mar. 20, 1917, at the Fifth Annual International Flower Show, Grand Central Palace in New York City. Medium-close view of TR and Wood standing together and talking, facing camera; TR, seated, poses for the photographer, with Wood and an unidentified man standing behind him.

    1. Flower shows. 2. New York (City). Grand Central Palace. 3. New York (City) 4. Roosevelt, Theodore, Pres. U.S., 1858–1919. 5. Wood, Leonard. 6. International Flower Show, 5th, New York City, 1917. I. International Newsreel Corporation, source. II. Theodore Roosevelt Association Collection. [mp 76–72]

TR and Mr. Helm, a newspaper reporter, exterior of Sagamore Hill, 1912.

Pathé Frères, Oct 1912.

© No reg.

    lr, 5 ft. si. b&w. 16mm. ref print (2 cy)

    lr, 5 ft. si. b&w. 16mm. archival pos.

SHELF LOC'N: FAB692 & 693 (print, 2 cy);
                  FRA5728 (arch pos)

Ref source: Roosevelt Memorial Association. *Annual Report.* 1925: 18.

Newsfilm.

SUMMARY: Medium-close shot of TR speaking with William P. Helm, Associated Press correspondent for New York City and Washington (1910–1918), part of the first film footage taken of TR at Sagamore Hill, summer of 1912; long shot of TR riding towards the camera on his favorite horse, Sidar; Sagamore Hill, Oyster Bay, N.Y., is visible in the background.

    CITATION: MPW13: 1304.

    1. Oyster Bay, N.Y. Sagamore Hill. 2. Sidar (Horse) 3. Oyster Bay, N.Y. 4. Roosevelt, Theodore, Pres. U.S., 1858–1919—Homes. 5. Roosevelt, Theodore, Pres. U.S., 1858–1919—Addresses, essays, lectures. 6. Helm, William P. I. Pathe. II.

Pathe, source. III. Theodore Roosevelt Association Collection. [mp 76–9]

TR and Mrs. Roosevelt [at the Panama-California Exposition, 1915]

Producer unknown, Jul 1915.

  © No reg.

    lr, 3 ft. si. b&w. 16mm. ref print.

    lr, 3 ft. si. b&w. 16mm. archival pos.

    lr, 8 ft. si. b&w. 35mm. neg ntr.

SHELF LOC'N: FAB979 (print); FRA5951 (arch
                  pos)

RMA title: *TR and Mrs. Roosevelt about 1915, Location Unknown.*

Ref source: Pourade, Richard F. *Gold in the Sun.* 1965: 197–198.

Newsfilm.

SUMMARY: At the Panama-California Exposition, San Diego, Calif., on July 27, 1915, TR and Edith Roosevelt speak with officials on the steps of what is probably the United States Government Building. Close view of the group smiling and talking.

    1. Exhibitions. 2. San Diego, Calif.—Exhibitions. 3. San Diego, Calif. 4. Roosevelt, Theodore, Pres. U.S., 1858–1919. 5. Roosevelt, Edith. 6. Panama-California Exposition, 1915–1916. I. Roosevelt Memorial Association, source. II. Theodore Roosevelt Association Collection. [mp 76–120]

TR and several men.

Producer unknown [191–?]

  © No reg.

    lr, 7 ft. si. b&w. 16mm. ref print.

    lr, 7 ft. si. b&w. 16mm. dupe neg.

    lr, 16 ft. si. b&w. 35mm. pos ntr.

SHELF LOC'N: FAB1050 (print); FRA6017
                  (neg)

RMA lists the location as unknown.

Ref source: P&P portrait file.

Factual.

SUMMARY: TR and a small group of men, one of whom appears to be Edwin A. Van Valkenburg, editor and publisher of the Philadelphia *North American*, stand on a city street beside an auto and talk, nodding to the camera; TR moves up the steps of a row house, turns and shakes Van Valkenburg's hand, then enters the house with an unidentified man.

    1. Roosevelt, Theodore, Pres. U.S., 1858–1919. 2. Van Valkenburg, Edwin A. I. International Newsreel Corporation, source. II. Theodore Roosevelt Association Collection. [mp 76–169]

TR as Father Curran's guest at Wilkes-Barre, Pa., August 10, 1905.

Producer unknown, Aug 1905.

© No reg.

   lr, 141 ft. si. b&w. 16mm. ref print.

   lr, 141 ft. si. b&w. 16mm. dupe neg.

   lr, 351 ft. si. b&w. 35mm. pos ntr.

SHELF LOC'N: FAB 1026 (print); FRA6003 (neg)

Ref sources: The Philadelphia *Inquirer*. 8/11/05: 1–2; The Pittsburgh *Post*. 8/11/05: 1, 4; P&P portrait file; P&P presidential file.

Newsfilm; views.

SUMMARY: On Aug. 10, 1905, TR appeared as the joint guest of the United Mine Workers of America and the Catholic Total Abstinence Union of America during their annual convention in Wilkes-Barre, Pa. The opening scene shows Cardinal James Gibbons, archbishop of Baltimore, with other unidentified clergymen walking toward the camera through a huge crowd. TR and his party arrive. Identified in the group are: Fr. John J. Curran, temperance leader and labor arbitrator; Fred C. Kirkendall, mayor of Wilkes-Barre; and John Mitchell, president of the UMW. In a long shot of the flag-draped stand, TR is visible delivering a speech with the prepared text in hand; views of TR and party leaving the platform; TR enters an auto, Gibbons follows. Views of a long procession of priests and clergymen with TR following; this may be a sequence from part of the parade held in TR's honor or from an unrelated event. In the final scene, TR and noted clergymen pose on the steps of a house.

PERSONAL CREDITS: Howe, Lyman, source.

1. Trade-unions—Miners. 2. Temperance societies. 3. Priests. 4. Processions. 5. Wilkes-Barre, Pa. 6. Roosevelt, Theodore, Pres. U.S., 1858–1919—Addresses, essays, lectures. 7. Curran, John J. 8. Gibbons, James. 9. Kirkendall, Fred C. 10. Mitchell, John, 1870–1919. 11. United States. President, 1901–1909 (Roosevelt) 12. United Mine Workers of America. 13. Catholic Total Abstinence Union of America. I. Theodore Roosevelt Association Collection. [mp 76–16]

TR at Baltimore [1918]; TR at Sagamore [Hill, 1918]

Producer unknown, 1918.

© No reg.

   lr, 22 ft. si. b&w. 16mm. ref print.

   lr, 22 ft. si. b&w. 16mm. dupe neg (cy 1)

   lr, 56 ft. si. b&w. 35mm. dupe neg (cy 2)

   lr, 57 ft. si. b&w. 35mm. pos ntr.

SHELF LOC'N: FAB950 (print); FRA5912 (neg, cy 1); FPB7346 (neg, cy 2)

RMA title: *TR at Baltimore; TR at Sagamore, 1917.*

Ref sources: Baltimore *American.* 9/28/18: 8; The *Evening Sun*, Baltimore. 9/28/18: 1; P&P portrait file; Harvard University. Library. Theodore Roosevelt Collection.

Newsfilm.

SUMMARY: Sequences of TR speaking on two occasions: on Sept. 28, 1918, he addresses crowds in Baltimore in support of the fourth Liberty Loan; at Sagamore Hill on Apr. 2, 1918, he encourages workers for the third Liberty Loan. At Oriole Park in Baltimore TR, wearing a mourning armband for his son, Quentin, helps open the fourth Liberty Loan campaign. Views of TR and a man who appears to be Phillips L. Goldsborough, chairman of the Liberty Loan Committee for Maryland and former Maryland governor (1912–1916), walking across Oriole field with other officials; TR stops and speaks with Cardinal James Gibbons of Baltimore, whose back is to the camera; beside a flag-decorated table TR speaks to the packed stadium, with a man who appears to be current Maryland

Left to right are: Father John J. Curran, temperance leader and labor arbitrator, Cardinal James Gibbons, archbishop of Baltimore, TR, and John Mitchell, president of the United Mine Workers, at Wilkes-Barre, Pennsylvania, during the annual convention of the United Mine Workers and the Catholic Total Abstinence Union of America, August 10, 1905.

Governor Emerson C. Harrington, Mrs. Thomas J. Preston (who had been the wife of former President Grover Cleveland), and Dr. Thomas J. Preston among the notables on the platform; close-up of TR as he vigorously delivers an address. At Sagamore Hill, with reporters behind him, TR addresses Liberty Loan workers from the New York District on Apr. 2, 1918.

1. Baltimore. Oriole Baseball Park. 2. Oyster Bay, N.Y. Sagamore Hills. 3. Oyster Bay, N.Y. 4. Baltimore—Sports facilities. 5. Baltimore. 6. Maryland—Governors. 7. Roosevelt, Theodore, Pres. U. S., 1858–1919—Addresses, essays, lectures. 8. Goldsborough, Phillips L. 9. Gibbons, James. 10. Harrington, Emerson C. 11. Preston, Frances Folsom Cleveland. 12. Preston, Thomas J. 13. United States. Laws, statutes, etc. Liberty loan acts. 14. Maryland. Liberty Loan Committee. 15. Maryland. Governor, 1916–1920 (Harrington) 16. New York (City). Liberty Loan Committee. I. Eclair Film Company, source. II. Theodore Roosevelt Association Collection. III. TR at Sagamore [Hill, 1918–] [Title] [mp 76–164]

TR at Billings, Montana [1918]
Producer unknown, Oct 1918.

© No reg.

lr, 9 ft. si. b&w. 16mm. ref print.
lr, 9 ft. si. b&w. 16mm. archival pos.
SHELF LOC'N: FAB 1016 (print); FRA5992
(arch pos)

RMA lists the dates in the title as 1917–1918.

Ref sources: The Anaconda *Standard*. 10/6/18: 10; The Helena *Independent*. 10/6/18: 1, 3. Newsfilm.

SUMMARY: In Billings, Mont., on Oct. 5, 1918, to speak on behalf of the Liberty Loan and to denounce the Nonpartisan League of Farmers for its pacifist orientation, TR appears in a touring car greeting Billings citizens. Long shot of TR doffing his hat and shaking hands from a parked car in downtown Billings; after he is seated, the car moves through a crowded, flag-draped street.

1. Billings, Mont. 2. Roosevelt, Theodore, Pres. U.S., 1858–1919—Addresses, essays, lectures. 3. United States. Laws, statutes, etc. Liberty loan acts. I. Roosevelt Memorial Association, source. II. Theodore Roosevelt Association Collection. [mp 76–170]

TR at Camp Mills [1917]
Producer unknown, Sep 1917.

© No reg.

lr, 9 ft. si. b&w. 16mm. ref print.
lr, 9 ft. si. b&w. 16mm. archival pos.
SHELF LOC'N: FAB1080 (print); FRA6053
(arch pos)

RMA lists dates in title as 1917–1918.

Ref sources: New York *American*. 9/3/17: 3; New York *Tribune*. 9/3/17: 10; The New York *Herald*. 9/3/17: 13; 9/9/17: pt. 6: 6; P&P portrait file. Newsfilm.

SUMMARY: On Sept. 2, 1917, during an informal call at Camp Mills near Garden City, N.Y., TR meets officers and old friends who saw action with him in the Santiago Campaign, Spanish-American War. Opening scene of TR, flanked on his immediate left by Col. Charles Hine, regiment commander of the 165th Infantry, and Lt. Col. Latham R. Reed, former commander of the 165th, and on his right by William W. Cocks, former congressman from New York (1905–1911); a large crowd of men and soldiers is following TR; medium-close view of TR talking with a group of men under Hine's tent; the final scene shows TR speaking to an unseen audience, with Brig. Gen. Michael J. Lenihan, another comrade of the Cuban campaign, standing to his left.

1. Military training camps—New York (State) 2. Soldiers. 3. Military ceremonies, honors, and salutes. 4. Garden City, N.Y. 5. United States—History—War of 1898. 6. Roosevelt, Theodore, Pres. U.S., 1858–1919. 7. Hine, Charles. 8. Reed, Latham R. 9. Cocks, William W. 10. Lenihan, Michael J. 11. Camp Mills. 12. United States. Army. 165th Infantry. I. Roosevelt Memorial Association, source. II. Theodore Roosevelt Association Collection. [mp 76–300]

TR at dedication of Roosevelt Dam, 1911.
Producer unknown, Mar 1911.

© No reg.

lr, 19 ft. si. b&w. 16mm. ref print (cy 1)
lr, 12 ft. si. b&w. 16mm. ref print (cy 2)
lr, 17 ft. si. b&w. 16mm. ref print (cy 3)
lr, 19 ft. si. b&w. 16mm. dupe neg.
lr, 19 ft. si. b&w. 16mm. archival pos (2 cy)
SHELF LOC'N: FAB1647 (print, cy 1); FAB1648
(print, cy 2); FAB1649 (print, cy 3); FRA6208 (neg); FRA5923 & 6209 (arch pos, 2 cy)

Ref prints differ due to longer printing of second sequence; ref print (cy 1) out of frame first 6 ft.; arch pos (cy 2) out of frame first 8 ft.

Ref sources: Sloan, Richard E., ed. *History of Ari-*

zona. v. 2, 1930: 316–322; *Arizona Republican,* Phoenix. 3/18/11: 1–2; 3/19/11: l; P&P portrait file.

Newsfilm.

SUMMARY: On Mar. 18, 1911, TR makes the principal address at the dedication of Roosevelt Dam on the Salt River, a major irrigation project in the territory of Arizona which is largely the result of TR's reclamation efforts while president. The dam is significantly to affect the agricultural productivity of the Salt River Valley area of Arizona. Views of TR speaking, with the following officials identified behind him on the speaker's platform: Territorial Governor of Arizona Richard E. Sloan; Louis C. Hill, engineer in charge of dam construction; and Benjamin A. Fowler, president of the National Irrigation Congress. Medium-close shot of the milling crowd.

PERSONAL CREDITS: Howe, Lyman, source.

1. Roosevelt Dam. 2. Dedication services. 3. Dams—Arizona. 4. Reclamation of land—Arizona. 5. Salt River Valley, Ariz. 6. Salt River, Ariz. 7. Roosevelt, Theodore, Pres. U.S., 1858–1919— Addresses, essays, lectures. 8. Sloan, Richard E. 9. Hill, Louis C. 10. Fowler, Benjamin A. 11. Arizona (Ter.). Governor, 1909–1912 (Sloan) I. Theodore Roosevelt Association Collection. [mp 76–125]

TR at Fargo, N.D., during Progressive campaign, 1912 [1]

Producer unknown, Sep 1912.

© No reg.

   lr, 133 ft. si. b&w. 16mm. ref print.

   lr, 133 ft. si. b&w. 16mm. dupe neg.

SHELF LOC'N: FAB848 (print); FRA5853 (neg)

Main title "Roosevelt" appears on the film; it appears to have been spliced on. "General Film Publicity & Sales Co.," which is probably a film distributor, also appears on the film.

Ref sources: P&P portrait file; The Fargo *Forum.* 9/6/12: 1.

Newsfilm.

SUMMARY: As part of a western campaign tour TR speaks to crowds and firms up the Progressive party structure in the area of Fargo, N.D., Sept. 6, 1912. Several views from varying distances of TR greeting and speaking to crowds from the rear of a train; TR addressing a large crowd from a decorated platform, apparently in a stadium; TR speaking from the rear of a train to Indian men, women, and children assembled on open plains; several long shots of crowds; medium-close silhouette of TR conversing with three men, one of whom appears

to be George E. Roosevelt, TR's cousin and campaign secretary in the 1912 election.

PERSONAL CREDITS: Chessman, A., source.

1. Political parties—North Dakota. 2. Presidents— United States—Election—1912. 3. Fargo, N.D. 4. Roosevelt, Theodore, Pres. U. S., 1858–1919— Addresses, essays, lectures. 5. Roosevelt, George E. 6. Progressive Party (Founded 1912) I. General Film Publicity & Sales Company. II. Theodore Roosevelt Association Collection. III. Roosevelt [Title] [mp 76–130]

TR at Fargo, N.D., during Progressive campaign, 1912 [2]

Producer unknown, Sep 1912.

© No reg.

   lr, 38 ft. si. b&w. 16mm. ref print.

   lr, 38 ft. si. b&w. 16mm. archival pos.

   lr, 95 ft. si. b&w. 35mm. neg ntr.

SHELF LOC'N: FAB849 (print); FRA5854 (arch pos)

Ref sources: P&P portrait file; The Fargo *Forum.* 9/6/12: 1.

Newsfilm.

SUMMARY: In the area of Fargo, N.D., TR addresses crowds in his campaign for the presidency under the Progressive party banner, Sept. 6, 1912. Views from varying distances of TR speaking from the rear of a train and from a campaign platform; view from aboard a train of crowds waving as the train pulls away; shot of Indian men, women, and children gathering at the rear of the train; close shot of TR speaking with three men, one of whom may be George E. Roosevelt, TR's cousin and campaign secretary in the 1912 election.

PERSONAL CREDITS: Chessman, A., source.

1. Political parties—North Dakota. 2. Presidents— United States—Election—1912. 3. Fargo, N.D. 4. Roosevelt, Theodore, Pres. U. S., 1858–1919— Addresses, essays, lectures. 5. Roosevelt, George E. 6. Progressive Party (Founded 1912) I. Theodore Roosevelt Association Collection. [mp 76–131]

TR at Forest Hills, New York, 1917 [1]

Producer unknown, Jul 1917.

© No reg.

   lr, 121 ft. si. b&w. 16mm. ref print.

   lr, 121 ft. si. b&w. 16mm. archival pos.

SHELF LOC'N: FAB1048 (print); FRA6014 (arch pos)

Film sequence does not follow the order of actual events.

Ref sources: P&P portrait file; Federal Writers'

Project. New York (City). *New York City Guide*. 1939: 581–582; Goudy, Frederic W. *Why We Have Chosen Forest Hills Gardens for Our Home*. 1915; The Brooklyn *Daily Eagle*. 7/5/17: 4.

Newsfilm.

SUMMARY: At a Forest Hills Fourth of July celebration in 1917, TR speaks in support of vigorous American war involvement and attacks conscientious objectors in an address at the Forest Hills Gardens railroad station; in a nearby field he later reviews the Forest Hills Rifle Club. Views of TR marching with rifle club members, standing at attention as the club marches past, speaking informally with individuals, and talking with an officer who may be Col. J. A. Delafield. Long shot of the speaker's balcony on the outdoor stairway of the railroad station, with TR acknowledging his introduction by Frederick Burgess, bishop of Long Island; close shots of TR speaking from a prepared speech.

1. Fourth of July celebrations. 2. Fourth of July orations. 3. Railroad terminals—New York (City) 4. Marching. 5. Military ceremonies, honors, and salutes. 6. Forest Hills, N.Y. 7. Roosevelt, Theodore, Pres. U.S., 1858–1919—Addresses, essays, lectures. 8. Burgess, Frederick. 9. Forest Hills Rifle Club. I. Roosevelt Memorial Association, source. II. Theodore Roosevelt Association Collection. [mp 76–173]

TR at Forest Hills, New York, 1917 [2]

Producer unknown, Jul 1917.

© No reg.

lr, 152 ft. si. b&w. 16mm. ref print.
lr, 152 ft. si. b&w. 16mm. dupe neg.
lr, 380 ft. si. b&w. 35mm. pos ntr.

SHELF LOC'N: FAB1049 (print); FRA6015 (neg)

Film sequence does not follow the order of actual events.

Ref sources: P&P portrait file; Federal Writers' Project. New York (City). *New York City Guide*. 1939: 581–582; Goudy, Frederic W. *Why We Have Chosen Forest Hills Gardens for Our Home*. 1915; The Brooklyn *Daily Eagle*. 7/5/17: 4.

Newsfilm.

SUMMARY: At Forest Hills, July 4, 1917, TR speaks in support of vigorous American war involvement and attacks conscientious objectors in an address at the Forest Hills Gardens railroad station; he later reviews the Forest Hills Rifle Club in a nearby field. Views of TR marching with rifle club members, speaking informally with individuals, standing at attention as the club marches past, and

talking with an officer who may be Col. J. A. Delafield. Long shot of the speaker's balcony on the outdoor stairway of the Forest Hills Gardens railroad station, with Frederick Burgess, bishop of Long Island, speaking and introducing TR; the crowd cheers TR, who then begins to speak; panning shots of crowds.

PERSONAL CREDITS: Demarest, John, source.

1. Fourth of July celebrations. 2. Fourth of July orations. 3. Railroad terminals—New York (City) 4. Marching. 5. Military ceremonies, honors, and salutes. 6. Forest Hills, N.Y. 7. Roosevelt, Theodore, Pres. U.S., 1858–1919—Addresses, essays, lectures. 8. Burgess, Frederick. 9. Forest Hills Rifle Club. I. Theodore Roosevelt Association Collection. [mp 76–174]

TR at limousine window, 1917.

Producer unknown [1917?]

© No reg.

lr, 5 ft. si. b&w. 16mm. ref print.
lr, 5 ft. si. b&w. 16mm. archival pos (3 cy)
lr, 13 ft. si. b&w. 35mm. dupe neg ntr.

SHELF LOC'N: FAB680(print); FRA5722 & 6201 & 6202 (arch pos, 3 cy)

Date in the title is unverified.

Archival pos (cy 2 and 3) appear under RMA title: *T. R. Greeting Friends from Automobile, 1917.*

Newsfilm; views.

SUMMARY: Close shot of TR sitting in an automobile and shaking hands with people through the window.

PERSONAL CREDITS: Miles, H., source. Lee, A., source.

1. Roosevelt, Theodore, Pres. U.S., 1858–1919. I. Theodore Roosevelt Association Collection. [mp 76–12]

TR [at Panama-Pacific Exposition, 1915]

Producer unknown, Jul 1915.

© No reg.

lr, 6 ft. si. b&w. 16mm. ref print.
lr, 6 ft. si. b&w. 16mm. dupe neg.
lr, 16 ft. si. b&w. 35mm. pos ntr.

SHELF LOC'N: FAB1068 (print); FRA6042 (neg)

RMA title: *TR Visits Naval Club in Boston, 1917.*

Research indicates that the film is probably of TR's July 1915 visit to the Panama-Pacific International Exposition in San Francisco.

Ref sources: San Francisco *Examiner*. 7/21/15: 1–2; 7/22/15: 4; San Francisco *Chronicle*. 7/22/15: 5; *Snap shots of scenes at the Panama-Pacific*

Exposition, San Francisco, 1915. 1915; Harvard University. Library. Theodore Roosevelt Collection; Todd, Frank M. *The Story of the Exposition.* v. 3, 1921: 94–99.

Factual.

SUMMARY: On July 21, 1915, TR attends "Roosevelt Day" at the Panama-Pacific Internatonal Exposition in San Francisco. He gives two addresses, one to enlisted men and officers, and the second to the general public. TR talks animatedly outside what is probably one of the exposition buildings; army and navy officers are in the background. The man wearing a top hat directly behind TR is Hiram Johnson, governor of California (1911–1917) and TR's running mate in the 1912 Progressive campaign. In the last sequence, TR sits in an open car and tips his hat to the camera.

1. Exhibitions. 2. Exhibition buildings. 3. San Francisco. 4. San Francisco—Exhibitions. 5. Roosevelt, Theodore, Pres. U.S., 1858–1919. 6. Johnson, Hiram W. 7. United States. Army—Officers. 8. United States. Navy—Officers. 9. California. Governor, 1911–1917 (Johnson) 10. Panama-Pacific International Exposition, 1915. 11. Panama-Pacific International Exposition, 1915—Buildings. I. Pathe, source. II. Theodore Roosevelt Association Collection. [mp 76–190]

TR at Sagamore, 1917.

Producer unknown [1917?]

© No reg.

lr, 15 ft. si. b&w. 35mm. ref print (cy 1)
lr, 13 ft. si. b&w. 35mm. ref print (cy 2)
lr, 15 ft. si. b&w. 35mm. dupe neg (cy 1)
lr, 13 ft. si. b&w. 35mm. dupe neg (cy 2)
lr, 15 ft. si. b&w. 35mm. masterpos.
lr, 13 ft. si. b&w. 35mm. pos ntr.
lr, 14 ft. si. b&w. 35mm. neg ntr.

SHELF LOC'N: FEA7320 (print, cy 1); FEA7321 (print, cy 2); FPB7947 (neg, cy 1); FPB7948 (neg, cy 2); FPB 7949 (fgmp)

Location and date in the title are unverified.

Copies vary in length due to blank frames between sequences.

Film sequence is repeated.

Factual; views.

SUMMARY: Close shot of TR speaking on what appears to be the grounds of Sagamore Hill, Oyster Bay, N.Y.

1. Oyster Bay, N.Y. Sagamore Hill. 2. Oyster Bay, N.Y. 3. Roosevelt, Theodore, Pres. U.S., 1858–1919—Addresses, essays, lectures. I. Roosevelt

Memorial Association, source. II. Theodore Roosevelt Association Collection. [mp 76–281]

TR at Sagamore Hill [1916]

Producer unknown, 1915–1916.

© No reg.

lr, 51 ft. si. b&w. 16mm. ref print.
lr, 51 ft. si. b&w. 16mm. dupe neg.

SHELF LOC'N: FAB948 (print); FRA5906 (neg)

RMA title: *TR at Sagamore Hill, 1917–1918.*

Unrelated footage of TR speaking at the Panama-Pacific International Exposition ca. ft. 43–48.

Ref sources: The New York *Herald.* 5/28/16: sec. 1: pt. 3: 5; New York *Tribune.* 5/28/16: pt. 1: 1–2; 6/4/16: pt. 5: 1; Harvard University. Library. Theodore Roosevelt Collection.

Newsfilm.

SUMMARY: On May 27, 1916, shortly before the Republican party and Progressive party conventions, the newly formed Roosevelt Non-Partisan League sponsors a demonstration of support for TR at Sagamore Hill. Many prominent men are included in the over 2,000 people who traveled from New York City to Oyster Bay to see TR and hear him speak on "Americanism." Panning shots of the crowd gathered around the porch; TR shakes hands. The man who appears to be addressing TR may be Richard M. Hurd, chairman of the committee which arranged the demonstration. TR addresses the crowd. At ca. ft. 43, there is a brief sequence of TR speaking in the Court of the Universe at the Panama-Pacific International Exposition in San Francisco, on July 21, 1915. Final views of TR speaking at Sagamore Hill.

PERSONAL CREDITS: Fox, William, source.

1. Oyster Bay, N.Y. Sagamore Hill. 2. Presidents—United States—Nomination. 3. Presidents—United States—Election—1916. 4. Exhibitions. 5. Oyster Bay, N.Y. 6. San Francisco. 7. San Francisco—Plazas—Court of the Universe. 8. Roosevelt, Theodore, Pres. U.S., 1858–1919. 9. Roosevelt, Theodore, Pres. U.S., 1858–1919—Addresses, essays, lectures. 10. Hurd, Richard M. 11. Roosevelt Non-Partisan League. 12. Panama-Pacific International Exposition, 1915. I. Theodore Roosevelt Association Collection. [mp 76–128]

TR at Sagamore Hill [1916–1918]

Producer unknown, 1916–1918.

© No reg.

lr, 37 ft. si. b&w. 16mm. ref print.
lr, 37 ft. si. b&w. 16mm. dupe neg.

SHELF LOC'N: FAB949 (print); FRA5907 (neg)

RMA title: *TR at Sagamore Hill, 1917–1918*.
Film image is occasionally blurred.
Newsfilm.

SUMMARY: This film is composed of alternately spliced footage of two separate occasions when TR spoke to groups from the porch at Sagamore Hill. The first sequence, to ca. ft. 2, and other similar footage of TR formally dressed in a dark suit and holding a prepared text are probably of his Apr. 2, 1918, speech to New York District volunteer workers (primarily businessmen) for the third Liberty Loan; medium-close views of TR speaking, with reporters standing behind him, are included. The second sequence, ca. ft. 2–4, and additional similar footage are from the May 27, 1916, rally organized by the Roosevelt Non-Partisan League to demonstrate support for TR for the 1916 presidential nomination. TR, informally dressed in a light-colored riding suit, speaks on "Americanism" to the large crowd assembled on the lawn.

PERSONAL CREDITS: Fox, William, source.

1. Oyster Bay, N.Y. Sagamore Hill. 2. Presidents—United States—Nomination. 3. Presidents—United States—Election—1916. 4. Oyster Bay, N.Y. 5. Roosevelt, Theodore, Pres. U. S., 1858–1919—Addresses, essays, lectures. 6. New York (City). Liberty Loan Committee. 7. United States. Laws, statutes, etc. Liberty loan acts. 8. Roosevelt Non-Partisan League. I. Theodore Roosevelt Association Collection. [mp 76–129]

TR at San Diego Exposition, 1915.

Film by Stineman, Jul 1915.

© No reg.

  lr, 18 ft. si. b&w. 16mm. ref print (cy 1)
  lr, 14 ft. si. b&w. 16mm. ref print (cy 2)
  lr, 18 ft. si. b&w. 16mm. dupe neg.
  lr, 25 ft. si. b&w. 16mm. archival pos.

SHELF LOC'N: FAB669 (print, cy 1); FAB1380 (print, cy 2); FRA5705 (neg); FRA5706 (arch pos)

Ref print (cy 2) appears under the RMA title: *TR Attends San Diego Exposition, 1915.*

The interior title contains the logo: Film by Stineman, San Diego, Calif.

Ref print (cy 2) is shorter than ref print (cy 1) due to the lack of the last sequence; both copies lack one interior title.

Ref sources: Pourade, Richard F. *Gold in the Sun.* 1965: 197–198; The New York *Times.* 8/8/15: pt. 1: [9]

Newsfilm.

SUMMARY: TR attends the Panama-California Exposition on Roosevelt Day, July 27, 1915. Scenes of TR arriving at the United States Government Building in an open touring car with two men in the rear seat; the one wearing a ribbon on his coat appears to be George W. Marston, park commissioner. Gilbert Aubrey Davidson, president of the exposition, and others greet TR and his party. The final scenes show TR and his wife, Edith, speaking with various officials and a child on the steps of the building; there is a close shot of the group talking.

PERSONAL CREDITS: Ganahal, L., source.

1. Exhibitions. 2. San Diego, Calif.—Exhibitions. 3. San Diego, Calif. 4. Roosevelt, Theodore, Pres. U.S., 1858–1919. 5. Marston, George M. 6. Davidson, Gilbert Aubrey. 7. Roosevelt, Edith. 8. Panama-California Exposition, 1915–1916. I. Stineman, Ralph P. II. Theodore Roosevelt Association Collection. [mp 76–56]

TR at Wilkes-Barre, Pa., 1905.

Producer unknown, Aug 1905.

© No reg.

  lr, 87 ft. si. b&w. 16mm. ref print.
  lr, 216 ft. si. b&w. 35mm. masterpos.
  lr, 87 ft. si. b&w. 16mm. archival pos.
  lr, 218 ft. si. b&w. 35mm. dupe neg ntr.

SHELF LOC'N: FAB1025 (print); FPB7345 (fgmp); FRA6002 (arch pos)

Ref sources: The Philadelphia *Inquirer.* 8/11/05: 1–2; The Pittsburgh *Post.* 8/11/05: 1, 4; P&P portrait file; P&P presidential file.

Newsfilm; views.

SUMMARY: On Aug. 10, 1905, TR appeared as the guest of the United Mine Workers of America and the Catholic Total Abstinence Union of America during their annual convention in Wilkes-Barre, Pa. Views of a long procession of priests and clergymen, with TR following; this may be a sequence from part of the parade held in TR's honor or from an unrelated event; the final scene is of TR and noted clergymen posing on the steps of a house.

1. Temperance societies. 2. Priests. 3. Processions. 4. Wilkes-Barre, Pa. 5. Roosevelt, Theodore, Pres. U.S., 1858–1919. 6. United States. President, 1901–1909 (Roosevelt) 7. Catholic Total Abstinence Union of America. I. Paramount, source. II. Theodore Roosevelt Association Collection. [mp 76–305]

TR attends dinner of Cincinnati, Ohio, Business Men's Club, Dec. 14, 1917 [1]

Producer unknown, Dec 1917.

© No reg.

lr, 142 ft. si. b&w. 35mm. ref print.

lr, 142 ft. si. b&w. 35mm. dupe neg.

lr, 142 ft. si. b&w. 35mm. pos ntr.

SHELF LOC'N: FEA8339(print); FPB9877 (neg)

Ref sources: The Cincinnati *Enquirer*. 12/14/17: 9; 12/15/17: 1, 7; P&P portrait file.

Newsfilm.

SUMMARY: TR attends a luncheon, speaks on the war, and commemorates the twenty-fifth anniversary of the Business Men's Club held at Music Hall in Cincinnati, Ohio, on December 14, 1917. The opening scene shows TR, flanked on his left by James M. Cox, governor of Ohio (1917–1920); there is a medium view of TR and Cox shaking hands and talking; the man slightly behind TR on his left appears to be the other guest speaker of the club, Carl E. Milliken, governor of Maine (1917–1920); medium-close shots of TR and Cox standing in an informal receiving line, shaking the hands of the guests as they file past a stationary camera; the last scene shows men of the Cincinnati Home Guard Regiment filing past the camera.

PERSONAL CREDITS: Runey, source.

1. Luncheons. 2. European War, 1914–1918—Public opinion. 3. Cincinnati. Music Hall. 4. Cincinnati. 5. Cincinnati—Clubs. 6. Roosevelt, Theodore, Pres. U.S., 1858–1919. 7. Cox, James M. 8. Milliken, Carl E. 9. Business Men's Club, Cincinnati. 10. Ohio. Governor, 1917–1920 (Cox) 11. Maine. Governor, 1917–1920 (Milliken) 12. Cincinnati. Home Guard. I. Theodore Roosevelt Association Collection. [mp 76–301]

TR attends dinner of Cincinnati, Ohio, Business Men's Club, Dec. 14, 1917 [2]

Producer unknown, Dec 1917.

© No reg.

lr, 68 ft. si. b&w. 35mm. ref print (2 cy)

lr, 68 ft. si. b&w. 35mm. dupe neg (2 cy)

lr, 68 ft. si. b&w. 35mm. masterpos.

lr, 68 ft. si. b&w. 35mm. neg ntr.

SHELF LOC'N: FEA8947 & 8948 (print, 2 cy); FPB9902 & 9903 (neg, 2 cy); FPB9901 (fgmp)

Ref sources: The Cincinnati *Enquirer*. 12/14/17: 9; 12/15/17: 1, 7; P&P portrait file.

Newsfilm.

SUMMARY: TR attends a luncheon, speaks on the war, and commemorates the twenty-fifth anniversary of the Business Men's Club held in Cincinnati, Ohio, on December 14, 1917. The film consists of several medium-close panning views of TR, flanked by James M. Cox, governor of Ohio (1917–1920)

and Carl E. Milliken, governor of Maine (1917–1920) seated at tables eating lunch with the entire reception committee. Each member wore a ribbon with "reception committee" printed on it. According to the newspaper account, the reception committee consists of: Charles A. Hinsch, chairman, George Puchta, Judson Harmon, William C. Proctor, John Galvin, Alfred G. Allen, A. Clifford Shinkle, John L. Shuff, C. H. M. Atkins, B. H. Kroger, L. A. Auit, Lawrence Maxwell, E. W. Edwards, W. B. Melish, Otto Armleder, Nicholas Longworth, A. Julian, J. C. Clore, M. J. Freiburg, Casper Rowe, James P. Orr, Walter F. Ernst, H. H. Suydam, William Geoghegan, and W. S. Rowe. The men in uniform may be members of the Cincinnati Home Guard Regiment.

PERSONAL CREDITS: Runey, source.

1. Luncheons. 2. European War, 1914–1918—Public opinion. 3. Cincinnati. 4. Cincinnati—Clubs. 5. Roosevelt, Theodore, Pres. U.S., 1858–1919. 6. Cox, James M. 7. Milliken, Carl E. 8. Business Men's Club, Cincinnati. 9. Business Men's Club, Cincinnati. Reception Committee. 10. Ohio. Governor, 1917–1920 (Cox) 11. Maine. Governor, 1917–1920 (Milliken) 12. Cincinnati. Home Guard. I. Theodore Roosevelt Association Collection. [mp 76–302]

TR attends his son Archie's wedding at Boston, 1917.

Producer unknown, Apr 1917.

© No reg.

lr, 21 ft. si. b&w. 16mm. ref print (cy 1)

lr, 53 ft. si. b&w. 35mm. ref print (cy 2–2 cy)

lr, 21 ft. si. b&w. 16mm. dupe neg (cy 1)

lr, 53 ft. si. b&w. 35mm. dupe neg (cy 2–3 cy)

lr, 53 ft. si. b&w. 35mm. masterpos.

lr, 53 ft. si. b&w. 35mm. archival pos.

lr, 51 ft. si. b&w. 35mm. pos ntr (cy 1)

lr, 53 ft. si. b&w. 35mm. pos ntr (cy 2)

lr, 56 ft. si. b&w. 35mm. dupe neg ntr.

SHELF LOC'N: FAB894 (print, cy 1); FEA6733 & 7827 (print, cy 2–2 cy); FRA 5964 (neg, cy 1); FPB7195 & 7196 & 7197 (neg, cy 2–3 cy); FPB7194 (fgmp); FPB7198 (arch. pos)

Film sequence does not follow the order of actual events.

Ref source: The Boston *Daily Globe*. 4/14/17: 3.

Newsfilm.

SUMMARY: On Apr. 14, 1917, Archie Roosevelt marries Grace S. Lockwood at the Emmanuel Church in Boston, Mass. Side view of TR entering an automobile with two women, the one following TR may be his wife Edith; TR doffs his hat as he faces the camera; a view of the crowd outside the Emmanuel Church; and a long shot of a woman holding a blanket up, perhaps to shield the bride's entrance into the church. The last two segments appear to be unrelated scenes: a medium-close shot of TR sitting in a car with an unidentified man, and a close-up of TR with a man in uniform; both scenes are outside in undetermined locations.

PERSONAL CREDITS: Kandel, source.

1. Weddings. 2. Boston, Mass. 3. Roosevelt, Theodore, Pres. U.S., 1858–1919. 4. Roosevelt, Theodore, Pres. U.S., 1858–1919—Family. 5. Roosevelt, Archibald B. 6. Lockwood, Grace S. 7. Roosevelt, Edith. 8. Emmanuel Church, Boston, Mass. I. Theodore Roosevelt Association Collection. [mp 76–115]

TR attends McKinley's funeral, 1901.

Producer unknown, Sep 1901.

© No reg.

lr, 11 ft. si. b&w. 16mm. ref print.
lr, 11 ft. si. b&w. 16mm. dupe neg (cy 1)
lr, 26 ft. si. b&w. 35mm. dupe neg (cy 2)
lr, 14 ft. si. b&w. 35mm. masterpos (cy 1)
lr, 13 ft. si. b&w. 35mm. masterpos (cy 2)
lr, 27 ft. si. b&w. 35mm. pos ntr.
SHELF LOC'N: FAB1212 (print); FRA6105 (neg, cy 1); FPB7962 (neg, cy 2); FPB7963 (fgmp, cy 1); FPB 9690 (fgmp, cy 2)

Film is dark and slightly out of frame.

Ref sources: The Canton Repository. *Pictorial Life of William McKinley.* 1943: 28; P&P portrait file. Newsfilm.

SUMMARY: On Sept. 18, 1901, the body of assassinated President William McKinley was returned to his hometown of Canton, Ohio, for the final funeral ceremonies and burial. Long shot at the Canton train station of pallbearers carrying the casket of McKinley past two lines of men representing the official Washington party. Identified, standing next to a building, left to right, are: TR, president; Secretary of the Treasury Lyman J. Gage (1897–1902); Attorney General Philander C. Knox (1901–1904); Secretary of the Interior Ethan Allen Hitchcock (1898–1907); and former Secretary of State William R. Day (Apr.-Sept. 1898); second in the opposite line is Secretary of War Elihu Root (1899–1904). Further possible identifications of men standing behind Root are Postmaster General Charles E. Smith (1891–1902) and Secretary of

Agriculture James Wilson (1897–1913). After the casket passes, the men follow in two lines.

1. Funeral service. 2. Canton, Ohio 3. Roosevelt Theodore, Pres. U.S., 1858–1919. 4. McKinley, William, Pres. U.S., 1843–1901—Funeral and memorial services. 5. Gage, Lyman J. 6. Knox, Philander Chase. 7. Hitchcock, Ethan Allen, 1835–1909. 8. Day, William Rufus, 1849–1923. 9. Root, Elihu. 10. Smith, Charles Emory, 1842–1908. 11. Wilson, James, 1835–1920. 12. United States. President, 1897–1901 (McKinley) 13. United States. President, 1901–1909 (Roosevelt) I. Paramount, source. II. Theodore Roosevelt Association Collection. [mp 76–332]

TR attends McKinley's funeral, Canton, Ohio, 1901.

Producer unknown, Sep 1901.

© No reg.

lr, 26 ft. si. b&w. 35mm. ref print.
lr, 26 ft. si. b&w. 35mm. dupe neg.
lr, 26 ft. si. b&w. 35mm. masterpos.
SHELF LOC'N: FEA9946(print); FPC0773(neg); FPB7976 (fgmp)

Film sequence does not follow the order of actual events.

Film is dark and slightly out of frame.

Ref sources: The Canton Repository. *Pictorial Life of William McKinley.* 1943: 28; P&P portrait file. Newsfilm.

SUMMARY: On Sept. 18, 1901, the body of assassinated President William McKinley was returned to his hometown of Canton, Ohio, for the final funeral ceremonies and burial. Long shot at the Canton train station of TR and cabinet members standing and then walking out of camera range; views of McKinley's casket being carried between two lines of men representing the official Washington party. Identified from left to right are: TR, Secretary of the Treasury Lyman J. Gage (1897–1902); Attorney General Philander C. Knox (1901–1904); Secretary of the Interior Ethan Allen Hitchcock (1898–1907); former Secretary of State William R. Day (Apr.-Sept. 1898); second in the opposite line is Secretary of War Elihu Root (1899–1904); Postmaster General Charles E. Smith (1891–1902) and Secretary of Agriculture James Wilson (1897–1913) may also be in that line.

PERSONAL CREDITS: Kleine, George, source.

1. Funeral service. 2. Canton, Ohio. 3. Roosevelt, Theodore, Pres. U.S., 1858–1919. 4. McKinley, William, Pres. U.S., 1843–1901—Funeral and memorial services. 5. Gage, Lyman J. 6. Knox, Philan-

der Chase. 7. Hitchcock, Ethan Allen, 1835–1909. 8. Day, William Rufus, 1849–1923. 9. Root, Elihu. 10. Smith, Charles Emory, 1842–1908. 11. Wilson, James, 1835–1920. 12. United States. President, 1901–1909 (Roosevelt) 13. United States. President, 1897–1901 (McKinley) I. Theodore Roosevelt Association Collection. [mp 76–335]

TR calls on neighbors at Christmas, 1917.
Producer unknown [Dec 1917?]
© No reg.
   lr, 39 ft. si. b&w. 35mm. ref print.
   lr, 39 ft. si. b&w. 35mm. dupe neg.
   lr, 39 ft. si. b&w. 35mm. pos ntr.
SHELF LOC'N: FEA7307 (print); FPB7735 (neg)
Date and event in the title are unverified.
Factual.
SUMMARY: The opening scene shows a man, a woman, and two children with presents walking up to a house in Oyster Bay, N.Y.; one child enters the house and comes back out, then the woman enters; two older girls stand in the doorway; TR, carrying a present, walks up to the house. In the final scene, TR talks with the group as they all pose while a small girl peeks out of the door.
1. Christmas. 2. Oyster Bay, N.Y. 3. Roosevelt, Theodore, Pres. U.S., 1858–1919. I. International Newsreel Corporation, source. II. Theodore Roosevelt Association Collection. [mp 76–306]

TR, Charles E. Hughes, and Mayor Mitchel of New York, on reviewing stand in front of the New York Public Library [1917]
Producer unknown, Sep 1917.
© No reg.
   lr, 4 ft. si. b&w. 16mm. ref print.
   lr, 4 ft. si. b&w. 16mm. archival pos.
SHELF LOC'N: FAB 1037 (print); FRA6009 (arch pos)
RMA lists the dates in the title as 1917–18.
Ref sources: The New York *Herald.* 9/5/17: 11; The New York *Times Mid-week Pictorial.* v. 6, no. 2, 1917: [12–13]; The New York *Times.* 9/9/17: pt. 5: [3]; P&P portrait file.
Newsfilm.
SUMMARY: On Labor Day, Sept. 4, 1917, a parade is held in honor of the first group of men being sent overseas as part of the new National Army. Long shots of dignitaries watching the parade and paying tribute to the men from a reviewing platform in front of the New York Public Library. Identified on the film from left to right are: Col. Daniel Appleton, Seventh Regiment, New York National Guard; Rear Adm. Nathaniel R. Usher, commandant, New York Navy Yard; Maj. Gen. J. Franklin Bell, commander, Seventy-seventh Division, Camp Upton, National Army; TR; John P. Mitchel, mayor of New York; Charles Evans Hughes, head of the District Exemption Board; Alton B. Parker, jurist and Democratic nominee for the presidency in 1904; Brig. Gen. Charles H. Sherrill, in charge of the United States draft in New York State; Rear Adm. Albert Gleaves, commander, Cruiser and Transport Force, Atlantic Fleet; and Brig. Gen. Eli D. Hoyle, commander, Eastern Dept., Governors Island, N.Y.
1. Labor Day. 2. Military ceremonies, honors, and salutes. 3. New York (City) 4. Roosevelt, Theodore, Pres. U.S., 1858–1919. 5. Hughes, Charles Evans. 6. Mitchel, John P. 7. Appleton, Daniel. 8. Usher, Nathaniel Reilly. 9. Bell, James Franklin, 1856–1919. 10. Parker, Alton B. 11. Sherrill, Charles Hitchcock. 12. Gleaves, Albert. 13. Hoyle, Eli D. 14. United States. Army. 15. New York (City). Public Library. I. Roosevelt Memorial Association, source. II. Theodore Roosevelt Association Collection. [mp 76–187]

TR comes back.
Roosevelt Memorial Association [1925?]
© No reg.
   lr, 613 ft. si. b&w. 35mm. ref print.
   lr, 613 ft. si. b&w. 35mm. dupe neg.
SHELF LOC'N: FEA9040 (print); FPB9688 (neg)
Factual; still film.
SUMMARY: Still photos depict TR's arrival in New York Harbor, his speech at the Battery, and the parade held in his honor June 18, 1910, when he returns from his extensive African and European travels. Ships shown in the harbor include a battleship, probably the dreadnought South Carolina, the reception committee cutter Androscoggin, the liner Kaiserin Auguste Victoria, on which the Roosevelt party sailed from Europe, a smaller cutter, the Manhattan, and other vessels. William Loeb, TR's former secretary, is among the welcoming dignitaries. William J. Gaynor, mayor of New York City, and TR appear on the speaker's stand at the Battery where TR expresses his joy on returning to his native country. Final views of the parade include Rough Riders and other veterans of the Spanish-American War who serve as escort for TR.
PERSONAL CREDITS: Gentry, Caroline.
1. Processions. 2. Ships. 3. New York Bay. 4. New York (City)—Harbor. 5. New York (City)—Parks—Battery. 6. New York (City)—Streets. 7.

Roosevelt, Theodore, Pres. U.S., 1858–1919. 8. Roosevelt, Theodore, Pres. U.S. 1858–1919—Addresses, essays, lectures. 9. Loeb, William, 1866–1937. 10. Gaynor, William J. 11. South Carolina (Ship) 12. Androscoggin (Ship) 13. Kaiserin Auguste Victoria (Ship) 14. Manhattan (Ship) 15. United States. Army. lst Cavalry (Volunteer) I. Roosevelt Memorial Association. II. Roosevelt Memorial Association, source. III. Theodore Roosevelt Association Collection. [mp 76–149]

TR during Progressive campaign, 1912.

Producer unknown [1912?]
© No reg.
   lr, 20 ft. si. b&w. 16mm. ref print.
   lr, 20 ft. si. b&w. 16mm. dupe neg.
   lr, 20 ft. si. b&w. 16mm. archival pos.
SHELF LOC'N: FAB1455 (print); FRA6191 (neg); FRA6035 (arch pos)
The date in the title is unverified.
Newsfilm.
SUMMARY: In a small community TR addresses townspeople from the rear of a train which is crowded with TR supporters and reporters; the train pulls away as the townspeople cheer and wave flags. The tall man holding a newspaper under his arm and standing next to TR may be TR's cousin and campaign secretary in the 1912 presidential campaign, George E. Roosevelt.
PERSONAL CREDITS: Lee, A., source.
1. Presidents—United States—Election—1912. 2. Roosevelt, Theodore, Pres. U. S., 1858–1919—Addresses, essays, lectures. 3. Roosevelt, George E. 4. Progressive Party (Founded 1912) I. Theodore Roosevelt Association Collection. [mp 76–192]

TR, exterior of building, Washington, D.C. 1918.

Hearst-Pathe News, Jan 1918.
© No reg.
   lr, 5 ft. si. b&w. 16mm. ref print.
   lr, 5 ft. si. b&w. 16mm. dupe neg.
   lr, 13 ft. si. b&w. 35mm. pos ntr.
(Hearst-Pathe News [newsreel])
SHELF LOC'N: FAB1014 (print); FRA5989 (neg)
Newsfilm.
SUMMARY: During a visit to Washington, D.C., Jan. 22, 1918, TR helps those urging war reorganization and speedup of war work. TR appears with an unidentified man standing and talking on the steps outside a building.
1. European War, 1914–1918—Public opinion. 2. Washington, D.C. 3. Roosevelt, Theodore, Pres.

U.S., 1858–1919. I. Hearst-Pathe News. II. Pathe, source. III. Theodore Roosevelt Association Collection. [mp 76–282]

[TR getting into parked car]

Producer unknown [191-?]
© No reg.
   lr, 16 ft. si. b&w. 16mm. ref print.
   lr, 16 ft. si. b&w. 16mm. archival pos.
   lr, 40 ft. si. b&w. 35mm. neg ntr.
SHELF LOC'N: FAB1078 (print); FRA6024 (arch pos)
RMA title: *TR Exterior Building Enters Auto, 1917?*
Factual.
SUMMARY: At what may be the beginning of a parade, TR, a sailor, and other men crowd into an open touring car; TR removes a newspaper from the back seat, acknowledges the camera, sits, talks with the men in the car, and shakes hands with the sailor. A brick building or wall fills the immediate background.
PERSONAL CREDITS: Chessman, A., source.
1. Roosevelt, Theodore, Pres. U.S., 1858–1919. I. Theodore Roosevelt Association Collection. [mp 76–194]

TR greeting crowds of people, 1917–18

Producer unknown [1917?]
© No reg.
   lr, 13 ft. si. b&w. 16mm. ref print.
   lr, 13 ft. si. b&w. 16mm. archival pos.
SHELF LOC'N: FAB1033 (print); FRA6006 (arch pos)
Dates in the title are unverified.
Newsfilm.
SUMMARY: Two unidentified sequences of TR: 1) TR standing and waving to a large crowd from the rear of an open touring car; 2) TR walking with a group of men, one of whom is wearing a large Oklahoma pennant; the final view is of TR entering the open touring car.
1. Roosevelt, Theodore, Pres. U.S., 1858–1919—Addresses, essays, lectures. I. Roosevelt Memorial Association, source. II. Theodore Roosevelt Association Collection. [mp 76–316]

TR himself [1]

Roosevelt Memorial Association Film Library [1926?]
© No reg.
   lr, 840 ft. si. b&w. 35mm. ref print.
   lr, 840 ft. si. b&w. 35mm. dupe neg.
   lr, 840 ft. si. b&w. 35mm. pos ntr.

Ref sources: Roosevelt Memorial Association. *T. R. Himself* (script); United States. National Archives and Records Service. Audiovisual Archives Division; P&P portrait file; Harvard University. Library. Theodore Roosevelt Collection.

Factual; biographical, compilation, views.

SUMMARY: By using still photographs and motion picture footage, the film traces TR's life from his youth to his death in 1919. 1) Sequences from his early life, including views of TR, his mother, Martha Bulloch, his father, Theodore, and his birthplace; 2) views of TR delivering his inaugural address at the Capitol, Mar. 4, 1905; 3) delegations to the Russo-Japanese peace conference arriving in Portsmouth, N.H., Aug. 8, 1905; they are greeted by Rear Adm. William W. Mead, commandant of the Portsmouth Navy Yard, and headed by Count Sergius Witte, Baron Roman Rosen, Baron Jutaro Komura, and Baron Kogoro Takahira; 4) TR with King Haakon VII in Christiania (Oslo), Norway, May 4–6, 1910, to give his formal acceptance speech for the 1906 Nobel Peace Prize; 5) pan of the Roosevelt Dam and Roosevelt Reservoir; 6) TR and men posing and talking on the lawn of Sagamore Hill, Oyster Bay, N.Y.; identified between two chairs is George W. Perkins; 7) sequences of TR campaigning in the West, probably before the 1912 election; 8) TR, Lauro S. Müller, and others pose on the steps of Guanabara Palace in Rio de Janeiro in 1913; 9) TR speaks at a Sagamore Hill rally organized by the Roosevelt Non-Partisan League on May 27, 1916; 10) TR greets New York Liberty Loan workers, Apr. 2, 1918; 11) TR at the White House, Apr. 9, 1917; 12) outside a building, probably at the Panama-Pacific Exposition in San Francisco, July 21, 1915, TR speaks to a man; behind TR is Hiram W. Johnson, governor of Calif. (1911–1917); 13) TR speaking for the Liberty Loan and urging active participation in the war effort: at

One of TR's major diplomatic achievements, the 1905 Portsmouth Peace Conference thoroughly captured the public's attention. Newspaper correspondents and artists sent from several countries to record the progress of the conference pose for the camera.

Mineola, N.Y., on Memorial Day in 1917; at Oriole Park, Baltimore, with Cardinal James Gibbons, Dr. and Mrs. Thomas J. Preston, and Maryland Governor Emerson C. Harrington on Sept. 28, 1918; at Camp Grant, Rockford, Ill., on Sept. 26, 1917, with Maj. Gen. Thomas H. Barry; probably in Springfield, Ill., in Aug. 1918; 14) TR at the Lafayette Day celebration at New York City Hall on Sept. 6, 1918; 15) final scenes of TR's funeral on Jan. 8, 1919, at Christ Episcopal Church, Oyster Bay, and Youngs Memorial Cemetery with former President William Howard Taft in attendance and an unidentified soldier at the grave.

1. Inauguration Day. 2. Nobel prizes. 3. Roosevelt Dam. 4. Youngs Memorial Cemetery. 5. Rio de Janeiro. 6. Springfield, Ill. 7. Roosevelt, Theodore, Pres. U.S., 1858–1919—Personality. 8. Roosevelt, Theodore, Pres. U.S., 1858–1919—Family. 9. Mead, William W. 10. Witte, Sergeǐ IUl'evich, graf, 1849–1915. 11. Rosen, Roman Romanovich, baron, 1847–1921. 12. Komura, Jutaro. 13. Takahira, Kogoro. 14. Haakon VII, King of Norway, 1872–1957. 15. Perkins, George W. 16. Müller, Lauro S. 17. Johnson, Hiram W. 18. Barry, Thomas H. 19. Gibbons, James. 20. Preston, Thomas J. 21. Preston, Frances Folsom Cleveland. 22. Harrington, Emerson C. 23. Roosevelt, Theodore, Pres. U.S., 1858–1919—Funeral and memorial services. 24. Progressive Party (Founded 1912) 25. California. Governor, 1911–1917 (Johnson) 26. Maryland. Governor, 1916–1920 (Harrington) 27. Camp Grant. 28. Christ Episcopal Church, Oyster Bay, N.Y. 29. Portsmouth, Treaty of,. 1905. I. Roosevelt Memorial Association. Film Library. II. Roosevelt Memorial Association, source. III. Theodore Roosevelt Association Collection. [mp 76–348]

TR himself [2]
Roosevelt Memorial Association Film Library [1926?]
© No reg.
lr, 848 ft. si. b&w. 35mm. ref print.
lr, 848 ft. si. b&w. 35mm. dupe neg.
lr, 848 ft. si. b&w. 35mm. pos old safety.
SHELF LOC'N: FEA8333 (print); FPB8989 (neg)
Ref sources: Roosevelt Memorial Association. *T. R. Himself* (script); United States. National Archives and Records Service. Audiovisual Archives Division; P&P portrait file; Harvard University. Library. Theodore Roosevelt Collection.
Factual; biographical, compilation, views.
SUMMARY: By using still photographs and motion picture footage, the film traces TR's life from his youth to his death in 1919. 1) Sequences from his early life, including views of TR, his mother, Martha Bulloch, his father, Theodore, and his birthplace; 2) views of TR delivering his inaugural address at the Capitol, Mar. 4, 1905; 3) delegations to the Russo-Japanese peace conference arriving in Portsmouth, N.H., Aug. 8, 1905; they are greeted by Rear Adm. William W. Mead, commandant of the Portsmouth Navy Yard, and headed by Sergius Witte, Baron Roman Rosen, Baron Jutaro Komura, and Baron Kogoro Takahira; 4) TR with King Haakon VII in Christiania (Oslo), Norway, May 4–6, 1910, to give his formal acceptance speech for the 1906 Nobel Peace Prize; 5) TR and men posing and talking on the lawn of Sagamore Hill, Oyster Bay, N.Y.; identified between two chairs is George W. Perkins; 6) sequences of TR campaigning in the West, probably before the 1912 election; 7) TR, Lauro S. Müller, and others pose on the steps of Guanabara Palace in Rio de Janeiro in 1913; 8) TR speaks at a Sagamore Hill rally organized by the Roosevelt Non-Partisan League on May 27, 1916; 9) TR greets New York Liberty Loan workers, Apr. 2, 1918; 10) TR at the White House, Apr. 9, 1917; 11) WWI scenes of TR's sons' efforts: soldiers marching, artillery firing, and airplanes flying; 12) TR speaking for the Liberty Loan and urging active participation in the war effort: in Mineola, N.Y., on Memorial Day in 1917; at Oriole Park, Baltimore, with Cardinal James Gibbons, Dr. and Mrs. Thomas J. Preston, and Maryland Governor Emerson C. Harrington on Sept. 28, 1918; at Camp Grant, Rockford, Ill., on Sept. 26, 1917, with Maj. Gen. Thomas H. Barry; probably in Springfield, Ill., in Aug. 1918; 13) TR at the Lafayette Day celebration at New York City Hall on Sept. 6, 1918; 14) final scenes of TR's funeral on Jan. 8, 1919, at Christ Episcopal Church, Oyster Bay, and Youngs Memorial Cemetery, with former President William Howard Taft in attendance and an unidentified soldier at the grave.

1. Inauguration Day. 2. Nobel prizes. 3. Youngs Memorial Cemetery. 4. Rio de Janeiro. 5. Springfield, Ill. 6. Roosevelt, Theodore, Pres. U.S., 1858–1919—Personality. 7. Roosevelt, Theodore, Pres. U.S., 1858–1919—Family. 8. Mead, William W. 9. Witte, Sergeǐ IUl'evich, graf, 1849–1915. 10. Rosen, Roman Romanovich, baron, 1847–1921. 11. Komura, Jutaro. 12. Takahira, Kogoro. 13. Haakon VII, King of Norway, 1872–1957. 14. Perkins, George W. 15. Müller, Lauro S. 16. Gibbons, James. 17. Preston, Thomas J. 18. Preston, Frances Folsom Cleveland. 19. Harrington, Emerson C. 20.

Barry, Thomas H. 21. Roosevelt, Theodore, Pres. U.S., 1858–1919—Funeral and memorial services. 22. Progressive Party (Founded 1912) 23. Maryland. Governor, 1916–1920 (Harrington) 24. Camp Grant. 25. Christ Episcopal Church, Oyster Bay, N.Y. 26. Portsmouth, Treaty of, 1905. I. Roosevelt Memorial Association. Film Library. II. Roosevelt Memorial Association, source. III. Theodore Roosevelt Association Collection. [mp 76–349]

TR himself [3]
Roosevelt Memorial Association Film Library [1926?]
© No reg.
   lr, 837 ft. si. b&w. 35mm. ref print (2 cy)
   lr, 837 ft. si. b&w. 35mm. dupe neg (2 cy)
   lr, 837 ft. si. b&w. 35mm. masterpos.
   lr, 837 ft. si. b&w. 35mm. pos ntr.
   SHELF LOC'N: FEA8332 & 8956 (print, 2 cy);
                FPB8990 & 9914 (neg, 2 cy);
                FPB9913 (fgmp)
   Ref sources: Roosevelt Memorial Association. *T. R. Himself* (script); United States. National Archives and Records Service. Audiovisual Archives Division; P&P portrait file; Harvard University. Library. Theodore Roosevelt Collection.

Factual; biographical, compilation, views.

SUMMARY: By using still photographs and motion picture footage, the film traces TR's life from his youth to his death in 1919. 1) Sequences from his early life, including views of TR, his mother, Martha Bulloch, his father, Theodore, and his birthplace; 2) views of TR delivering his inaugural address at the Capitol, Mar. 4, 1905; 3) delegations to the Russo-Japanese peace conference arriving in Portsmouth, N.H., Aug. 8, 1905; they are greeted by Rear Adm. William W. Mead, commandant of the Portsmouth Navy Yard, and headed by Count Sergius Witte, Baron Roman Rosen, Baron Jutaro Komura, and Baron Kogoro Takahira; 4) TR with King Haakon VII in Christiania (Oslo), Norway, May 4–6, 1910, to give his formal acceptance speech for the 1906 Nobel Peace Prize; 5) pan of the Roosevelt Dam and Roosevelt Reservoir; 6) TR and men posing and talking on the lawn of Sagamore Hill, Oyster Bay, N.Y.; identified between two chairs is George W. Perkins; 7) sequences of TR campaigning in the West, probably before the 1912 election; 8) TR, Lauro S. Müller, and others pose on the steps of Guanabara Palace in Rio de Janeiro in 1913; 9) TR speaks at a Sagamore Hill rally organized by the Roosevelt Non-Partisan League on May 27, 1916; 10) TR greets New York

Liberty Loan workers Apr. 2, 1918; 11) TR at the White House, Apr. 9, 1917; 12) TR speaking for the Liberty Loan and urging active participation in the war effort: at Mineola, N.Y., on Memorial Day in 1917; at Oriole Park, Baltimore, with Cardinal James Gibbons, Dr. and Mrs. Thomas J. Preston, and Maryland Governor Emerson C. Harrington, on Sept. 28, 1918; at Camp Grant, Rockford, Ill. on Sept. 26, 1917, with Maj. Gen. Thomas H. Barry; probably in Springfield, Ill., in Aug. 1918; 14) TR at the Lafayette Day celebration at New York City Hall on Sept. 6, 1918; 15) final scenes of TR's funeral on Jan. 8, 1919, at Christ Episcopal Church, Oyster Bay, and Youngs Memorial Cemetery, with former President William Howard Taft in attendance and an unidentified soldier at the grave.

1. Inauguration Day. 2. Nobel prizes. 3. Roosevelt Dam. 4. Youngs Memorial Cemetery. 5. Rio de Janeiro. 6. Springfield, Ill. 7. Roosevelt, Theodore, Pres. U.S. 1858–1919—Personality. 8. Roosevelt, Theodore, Pres. U.S., 1858–1919—Family. 9. Mead, William W. 10. Witte, Sergei IUl'evich, graf, 1849–1915. 11. Rosen, Roman Romanovich, baron, 1847–1921. 12. Komura, Jutaro. 13. Takahira, Kogoro. 14. Haakon VII, King of Norway, 1872–1957. 15. Perkins, George W. 16. Müller, Lauro S. 17. Barry, Thomas H. 18. Gibbons, James. 19. Preston, Thomas J. 20. Preston, Frances Folsom Cleveland. 21. Harrington, Emerson C. 22. Roosevelt, Theodore, Pres. U.S., 1858–1919—Funeral and memorial services. 23. Progressive Party (Founded 1912) 24. Maryland. Governor, 1916–1920 (Harrington) 25. Camp Grant. 26. Christ Episcopal Church, Oyster Bay, N.Y. 27. Portsmouth, Treaty of, 1905. I. Roosevelt Memorial Association. Film Library. II. Roosevelt Memorial Association, source. III. Theodore Roosevelt Association Collection. [mp 76–350]

TR himself [4]
Roosevelt Memorial Association Film Library [1926?]
© No reg.
   lr, 904 ft. si. b&w. 35mm. ref print.
   lr, 904 ft. si. b&w. 35mm. dupe neg.
   lr, 904 ft. si. b&w. 35mm. pos ntr.
   SHELF LOC'N: FEA8331 (print); FPB8991 (neg)
   Ref sources: Roosevelt Memorial Association. *T. R. Himself* (script); United States. National Archives and Records Service. Audiovisual Archives Division; P&P portrait file; Harvard University. Library. Theodore Roosevelt Collection.

Factual; biographical, compilation, views.

SUMMARY: By using still photographs and motion picture footage, the film traces TR's life from his youth to his death in 1919. 1) Sequences from his early life, including views of TR, his mother, Martha Bulloch, his father, Theodore, and his birthplace; 2) views of TR delivering his inaugural address at the Capitol, Mar. 4, 1905; 3) delegations to the Russo-Japanese peace conference arriving in Portsmouth, N.H., Aug. 8, 1905; they are greeted by Rear Adm. William W. Mead, commandant of the Portsmouth Navy Yard, and headed by Count Sergius Witte, Baron Roman Rosen, Baron Jutaro Komura, and Baron Kogoro Takahira; 4) TR with King Haakon VII in Christiania (Oslo), Norway, May 4–6, 1910, to give his formal acceptance speech for the 1906 Nobel Peace Prize; 5) pan of the Roosevelt Dam and Roosevelt Reservoir; 6) TR and men posing and talking on the lawn of Sagamore Hill, Oyster Bay, N.Y.; identified between two chairs is George W. Perkins; 7) sequences of TR campaigning in the West, probably before the 1912 election; 8) TR, Lauro S. Müller, and others pose on the steps of Guanabara Palace in Rio de Janeiro in 1913; 9) TR speaks at a Sagamore Hill rally organized by the Roosevelt Non-Partisan League on May 27, 1916; 10) TR greets New York Liberty Loan workers, Apr. 2, 1918; 11) scenes of TR at the White House, Apr. 9, 1917; 12) WWI scenes of TR's sons' efforts; soldiers marching, artillery firing, and airplanes flying; 13) TR speaking for the Liberty Loan and urging active participation in the war effort: at Mineola, N.Y., on Memorial Day in 1917; at Oriole Park, Baltimore, with Cardinal James Gibbons, Dr. and Mrs. Thomas J. Preston, and Maryland Governor Emerson C. Harrington on Sept. 28, 1918; at Camp Grant, Rockford, Ill., on Sept. 26, 1917, with Maj. Gen. Thomas H. Barry; probably in Springfield, Ill., in Aug. 1918; 14) TR at the Lafayette Day celebration at New York City Hall on Sept. 6, 1918; 15) final scenes of TR's funeral on Jan. 8, 1919, at Youngs Memorial Cemetery; TR's son Archie, in uniform, is identified in the line of mourners.

1. Inauguration Day. 2. Nobel prizes. 3. Roosevelt Dam. 4. Youngs Memorial Cemetery. 5. Rio de Janeiro. 6. Springfield, Ill. 7. Roosevelt, Theodore, Pres. U.S., 1858–1919—Personality. 8. Roosevelt, Theodore, Pres. U.S., 1858–1919—Family. 9. Mead, William W. 10. Witte, Sergeĭ IUl'evich, graf, 1849–1915. 11. Rosen, Roman Romanovich, baron, 1847–1921. 12. Komura, Jutaro. 13. Takahira, Kogoro. 14. Haakon VII, King of Norway, 1872–1957. 15. Perkins, George W. 16. Müller, Lauro S. 17. Barry, Thomas H. 18. Gibbons, James. 19. Preston, Thomas J. 20. Preston, Frances Folsom Cleveland. 2l. Harrington, Emerson C. 22. Roosevelt, Theodore, Pres. U.S., 1858–1919—Funeral and memorial services. 23. Roosevelt, Archibald B. 24. Progressive Party (Founded 1912) 25. Maryland. Governor, 1916–1920 (Harrington) 26. Camp Grant. 27. Christ Episcopal Church, Oyster Bay, N.Y. 28. Portsmouth, Treaty of, 1905. I. Roosevelt Memorial Association. Film Library. II. Roosevelt Memorial Association, source. III. Theodore Roosevelt Association Collection. [mp 76–351]

TR himself [5]
Roosevelt Memorial Association Film Library, c 1926.
© MP5815, Roosevelt Memorial Association, 18Mar1926
    lr of 1, 875 ft. si. b&w. 35mm. ref print.
    lr of 1, 875 ft. si. b&w. 35mm. dupe neg.
    lr of 1, 874 ft. si. b&w. 35mm. masterpos.
    lr of 1, 868 ft. si. b&w. 35mm. neg ntr.
(The Roosevelt series of history and biography, no. 1.)
    SHELF LOC'N: FEA8334(print); FPB8988 (neg);
              FPA8366 (fgmp)

Ref sources: Roosevelt Memorial Association. *T. R. Himself* (script) United States. National Archives and Records Service. Audiovisual Archives Division; P&P portrait file; Harvard University. Library Theodore Roosevelt Collection.

Factual; biographical, compilation, views.

SUMMARY: By using still photographs and motion picture footage, the film traces TR's life from his youth to his death in 1919. 1) Sequences from his early life, including views of TR, his mother, Martha Bulloch, his father, Theodore, and his birthplace; 2) TR delivering his inaugural address at the Capitol, Mar. 4, 1905; 3) delegations to the Russo-Japanese peace conference arriving in Portsmouth, N.H., on Aug. 8, 1905; they are greeted by Rear Adm. William W. Mead, commandant of the Portsmouth Navy Yard, and headed by Count Sergius Witte, Baron Roman Rosen, Baron Jutaro Komura, and Baron Kogoro Takahira; 4) TR with King Haakon VII in Christiania (Oslo), Norway, May 4–6, 1910, to give his formal acceptance speech for the 1906 Nobel Peace Prize; 5) pan of the Roosevelt Dam and Roosevelt Reservoir; 6) TR and men posing and talking on the lawn of Sagamore Hill, Oyster Bay, N.Y.; identified between chairs is George W. Perkins; 7) sequences of TR campaigning in the West, probably before the 1912 election; 8) TR, Lauro S. Müller, and others pose on the steps of Guanabara Palace in Rio de Janeiro in 1913; 9) TR speaks at a Sagamore Hill rally organized by the Roosevelt Non-Partisan League on May 27, 1916; 10) TR greets New York Liberty Loan workers Apr. 2, 1918; 11) views of the White House; 12) outside a building, probably at the Panama-Pacific Exposition in San Francisco, July 21, 1915, TR speaks to a man; behind TR is Hiram W. Johnson, governor of Calif. (1911–1917); 13) TR speaking for the Liberty Loan and urging active participation in the war effort: at Mineola, N.Y., on Memorial Day in 1917; at Oriole Park, Baltimore, with Cardinal James Gibbons, Dr. and Mrs. Thomas J. Preston, and Maryland Governor Emerson C. Harrington on Sept. 28, 1918; at Camp Grant, Rockford, Ill., on Sept. 26, 1917, with Maj. Gen. Thomas H. Barry; probably in Springfield, Ill., in Aug. 1918; 14) TR at the Lafayette Day celebration at New York City Hall on Sept. 6, 1918; 15) final scenes of TR's funeral on Jan. 8, 1919, at Christ Episcopal Church, Oyster Bay, and Youngs Memorial Cemetery, with former President William Howard Taft in attendance and an unidentified soldier at the grave.

1. Inauguration Day. 2. Nobel prizes. 3. Roosevelt Dam. 4. Youngs Memorial Cemetery. 5. Rio de Janeiro. 6. Springfield, Ill. 7. Roosevelt, Theodore, Pres. U.S., 1858–1919—Personality. 8. Roosevelt, Theodore, Pres. U.S., 1858–1919—Family. 9. Mead, William W. 10. Witte, Sergeĭ I͡Ul'evich, graf, 1849–1915. 11. Rosen, Roman Romanovich, baron, 1847–1921. 12. Komura, Jutaro. 13. Takahira, Kogoro. 14. Haakon VII, King of Norway, 1872–1957. 15. Perkins, George W. 16. Müller, Lauro S. 17. Johnson, Hiram W. 18. Barry, Thomas H. 19. Gibbons, James. 20. Preston, Thomas J. 21. Preston, Frances Folsom Cleveland. 22. Harrington, Emerson C. 23. Roosevelt, Theodore, Pres. U.S., 1858–1919—Funeral and memorial services. 24. Progressive Party (Founded 1912) 25. California. Governor, 1911–1917 (Johnson) 26. Maryland. Governor, 1916–1920 (Harrington) 27. Camp Grant. 28. Christ Episcopal Church, Oyster Bay, N.Y. 29. Portsmouth, Treaty of, 1905. I. Roosevelt Memorial Association. Film Library. II. Roosevelt Memorial Association, source. III. Theodore Roosevelt Association Collection. [mp 76–352]

TR himself [6]
Roosevelt Memorial Association Film Library [1926?]
© No reg.

lr, 509 ft. si. b&w. 35mm. ref print.
lr, 509 ft. si. b&w. 35mm. dupe neg.
SHELF LOC'N: FEA8957 (print); FPB9915 (neg)
Ref sources: Roosevelt Memorial Association. *T. R. Himself* (script); United States. National Archives and Records Service. Audiovisual Archives Division; P&P portrait file; Harvard University. Library. Theodore Roosevelt Collection.

Factual; biographical, compilation; still film.

SUMMARY: By using still photos, the film traces TR's life from his youth to his death in 1919. 1) Scenes from his early life, including views of TR, his mother, Martha Bulloch, his father, Theodore, and his birthplace; 2) TR delivering his inaugural address at the Capitol, Mar. 4, 1905; 3) delegations to the Russo-Japanese peace conference arriving in Portsmouth, N.H., Aug. 8, 1905; they are greeted by Rear Adm. William W. Mead, commandant of the Portsmouth Navy Yard, and headed by Count Sergius Witte, Baron Roman Rosen, Baron Jutaro Komura, and Baron Kogoro Takahira; 4) TR with King Haakon VII in Christiania (Oslo), Norway, May 4–6, 1910, to give his formal acceptance speech for the 1906 Nobel Peace Prize; 5) TR and a man posing on the lawn of Sagamore Hill, Oyster Bay, N.Y.; 6) TR campaigning in the West, probably before the 1912 election; 7) TR and others pose on the steps of Guanabara Palace in Rio de Janeiro in 1913; 8) TR speaks at a Sagamore Hill rally organized by the Roosevelt Non-Partisan League on May 27, 1916; 9) TR greets New York Liberty Loan workers, Apr. 2, 1918; 10) TR at the White House, Apr. 9, 1917; 11) WWI scenes of TR's sons' efforts: soldiers marching, airplanes, and artillery; 12) TR speaking for the Liberty Loan and urging active participation in the war effort: in Mineola, N.Y., on Memorial Day in 1917; at Oriole Park, Baltimore, with Cardinal James Gibbons, Dr. and Mrs. Thomas J. Preston, and Maryland Governor Emerson C. Harrington on Sept. 28, 1918; at Camp Grant, Rockford, Ill., on Sept. 26, 1917, with Maj. Gen. Thomas H. Barry; probably in Springfield, Ill., in Aug. 1918; 13) TR at the Lafayette Day celebration at New York City Hall on Sept. 6, 1918; 14) final scenes of TR's funeral on Jan. 8, 1919, at Christ Episcopal Church, Oyster Bay, and Youngs Memorial Cemetery, with former President William Howard Taft in attendance and an unidentified soldier at the grave.

1. Inauguration Day. 2. Nobel prizes. 3. Roosevelt Dam. 4. Youngs Memorial Cemetery. 5. Rio de Janeiro. 6. Springfield, Ill. 7. Roosevelt, Theodore, Pres. U.S., 1858–1919—Personality. 8. Roosevelt,

Military procession in Portsmouth, New Hampshire, August 8, 1905, marking the arrival of the Russian and Japanese delegations for the peace conference. Note the hand-cranked motion picture camera in the center foreground.

Theodore, Pres. U.S., 1858–1919—Family. 9. Mead, William W. 10. Witte, Sergeĭ IUl'evich, graf, 1849–1915. 11. Rosen, Roman Romanovich, baron, 1847–1921. 12. Komura, Jutaro. 13. Takahira,

The Japanese delegation arriving in Portsmouth, New Hampshire, August 8, 1905.

Kogoro. 14. Haakon VII, King of Norway, 1872–1957. 15. Barry, Thomas H. 16. Gibbons, James. 17. Preston, Thomas J. 18. Preston, Frances Folsom Cleveland. 19. Harrington, Emerson C. 20. Roosevelt, Theodore, Pres. U.S., 1858–1919—Funeral and memorial services. 21. Progressive Party (Founded 1912) 22. Maryland. Governor, 1916–1920 (Harrington) 23. Camp Grant. 24. Christ Episcopal Church, Oyster Bay, N.Y. 25. Portsmouth, Treaty of, 1905. I. Roosevelt Memorial Association. Film Library. II. Roosevelt Memorial Association. III. Roosevelt Memorial Association, source. IV. Theodore Roosevelt Association Collection.[mp 76–353]

TR in a rowboat on Oyster Bay, Archie assists with boat to shore, 1914.
Hearst-Selig News Pictorial [1914?]
© No reg.

lr, 14 ft. si. b&w. 16mm. ref print.

lr, 14 ft. si. b&w. 16mm. dupe neg.

lr, 35 ft. si. b&w. 35mm. pos ntr.

(Hearst-Selig News Pictorial [newsreel])

SHELF LOC'N: FAB 878 (print); FRA5865 (neg)

Since Hearst-Selig News Pictorial produced films between Feb. 1914 and Dec. 1915, the possible dates of production are 1914–1915.

Ref source: *The Moving Picture World.* v. 19, no. 10, 1914: 1263; v. 26, no. 11, 1915: 1802; v. 26, no. 14, 1915: 2352.

Newsfilm.

SUMMARY: On Oyster Bay TR rows alone away from shore; in the second sequence his son Archie and an unidentified boy beach the boat as TR looks on.

1. Oyster Bay, N.Y.—Harbor. 2. Oyster Bay, N.Y. 3. Roosevelt, Theodore, Pres. U.S., 1858–1919. 4. Roosevelt, Archibald B. I. Hearst-Selig News Pictorial. II. International Newsreel Corporation, source. III. Theodore Roosevelt Association Collection. [mp 76–103]

TR in Africa [1909, 1]

Producer unknown, 1909.

© No reg.

lr, 196 ft. si. b&w. 16mm. ref print.

lr, 196 ft. si. b&w. 16mm. dupe neg (cy 1)

lr, 490 ft. si. b&w. 35mm. dupe neg (cy 2)

lr, 490 ft. si. b&w. 35mm. masterpos.

lr, 491 ft. si. b&w. 35mm. pos ntr.

SHELF LOC'N: FAB1117 (print); FRA6060 (neg, cy 1); FPB7353 (neg, cy 2); FPB7354 (fgmp)

RMA lists the date in the title as 1910.

Sources indicate that the photographer is Cherry Kearton.

Film is out of sequence, with some scenes appearing twice.

Ref sources: *The Moving Picture World.* v. 6, no. 13, 1910: 528–529; v. 6, no. 17, 1910: 682–683; *Scribner's Magazine.* v. 47, no. 6, 1910: 643–644, 650–652; Kearton, Cherry. *Adventures with Animals and Men.* 1935: 65–74; Kearton, Cherry. *Wild Life across the World.* [1914]: 100–102; Unger, Frederick W. *Roosevelt's African Trip.* 1909; Library of Congress. African Section.

Factual; sociological.

SUMMARY: On safari in East Africa, TR and members of his party appear in different locations, all probably in the vicinity of Mt. Kenya, British East Africa (Kenya), in 1909. Medium-close shot of TR and his party in a crowd of Kikuyu and/or Masai tribesmen in traditional dress, carrying shields and spears; tribesmen pose for the camera; members of TR's party watch while he plants a tree in front of a trading post building, possibly located in Mombasa; on horseback TR rides toward the camera over a grassy open hill, followed by an African attendant on foot; carrying shields and spears, unidentified tribesmen individually pose for the camera at close range, with a campsite visible in the background; long shot of TR and his party approaching a stream; at a campsite porters work busily, either setting up or breaking camp, with TR briefly visible after leaving his tent; TR on horseback gallops toward the camera across a grassy open hill; followed by porters, TR on horseback approaches a stream, pauses to let the horse drink, then crosses; several views of what is probably part of the large Kikuyu dance performed in TR's honor at Nyeri in August, with a small number of Masai also participating; view of a large number of what may be Masai women ceremonially forming a circle, through which men with shields pass; tribesmen who may be Kikuyu, holding shields, pose for the camera; medium-close shot of TR and his party in a crowd of Kikuyu and/or Masai tribesmen; TR and other party members examine a gun in the presence of tribesmen; a young boy who is probably Kikuyu dances in traditional dress, surrounded by adult tribesmen.

PERSONAL CREDITS: Kearton, Cherry, photographer. Kearton, Cherry, source.

1. Big game hunting—Africa. 2. Kikuyu tribe. 3. Kikuyu tribe—Dances. 4. Masai. 5. Masai—Dances. 6. Tree planting—Kenya. 7. Africa—Native races. 8. Kenya. 9. Roosevelt, Theodore, Pres. U.S., 1858–1919—Journey to Africa, 1909–1910. I. Theodore Roosevelt Association Collection. [mp 76–260]

TR in Africa [1909, 2]

Producer unknown, 1909.

© No reg.

lr, 298 ft. si. b&w. 16mm. ref print (cy 1)

lr, 746 ft. si. b&w. 35mm. ref print (cy 2)

lr, 298 ft. si. b&w. 16mm. dupe neg (cy 1)

lr, 746 ft. si. b&w. 35mm. dupe neg (cy 2)

lr, 742 ft. si. b&w. 35mm. pos ntr.

SHELF LOC'N: FAB1226 (print, cy 1); FEA7635 (print, cy 2); FRA6172 (neg, cy 1); FPB8075 (neg, cy 2)

RMA lists the date in the title as 1910.

Film appears to be a fragment of the production *Roosevelt in Africa*, released Apr. 18, 1910.

Sources indicate that the photographer is Cherry Kearton.

Ref sources: *Scribner's Magazine*, v. 47, no. 3, 1910; 264; v. 47, no. 6, 1910: 643–644, 650–652; Roosevelt, Kermit. *A Sentimental Safari*. 1963: XXIX; Kearton, Cherry. *Adventures with Animals and Men*. 1935: 68–71; Kearton, Cherry. *Photographing Wild Life across the World*. [1923]: 105–106; Roosevelt Memorial Association. *Annual Report*. 1926: 18; Library of Congress. African Section.

Factual; sociological.

SUMMARY: Scenes of African peoples and of TR's safari party, all probably filmed in British East Africa (Kenya) in 1909. View of TR planting a tree in front of a trading company building, possibly located in the Kenyan seaport of Mombasa; long shot of a busy amusement area in Mombasa, including a shot of a ferris wheel filled with Swahilis; shots, taken from the observation platform on a train engine, of plains along the Uganda Railway, with herdsmen who are probably Masai and railroad workers visible along the tracks; the train pulls into a small community; women who are probably Masai, incorrectly identified by interior title as Zulu, gather water at a spring, accompanied by children; a rainmaker dances in a ritual ceremony, surrounded by Swahilis; members of an unknown tribe draw water from a well, with a large thatched structure in the background; views of Masai men, women, and children in a kraal, with clear shots of mud houses; TR and his party appear in a group of Kikuyu and/or Masai tribesmen; women who are probably Masai, incorrectly identified by interior title as Zulu, form a ceremonial circle on an open plain; TR and members of his party examine a gun in the presence of African tribesmen; unidentified tribesmen pose individually for the camera at close range, with a campsite visible in the background; at a campsite porters work busily, either setting up or breaking camp, with TR briefly visible; view of a Kikuyu and/ or Masai dance, incorrectly identified by interior title as a Zulu dance, in honor of TR's visit; the Roosevelt party crosses a stream, with porters carrying gear and safari members across the water toward the camera.

PERSONAL CREDITS: Kearton, Cherry, photographer.

CITATION: MPW6: 528–529, 682–683.

1. Big game hunting—Africa. 2. Tree planting—Kenya. 3. Masai. 4. Masai—Social life and customs. 5. Masai—Dances. 6. Kikuyu tribe. 7. Kikuyu tribe—Social life and customs. 8. Kikuyu tribe—Dances. 9. Africa—Native races. 10. Kenya. 11. Mombasa, Kenya. 12. Roosevelt, Theodore, Pres. U.S., 1858–1919—Journey to Africa, 1909–1910. I. Community Motion Picture Service, inc., source. II. Theodore Roosevelt Association Collection. III. Roosevelt in Africa [Title] [mp 76–261]

TR in Africa [1909, 3]
Producer unknown, 1909.
© No reg.
   lr, 190 ft. si. b&w. 16mm. ref print.
   lr, 190 ft. si. b&w. 16mm. dupe neg.
   lr, 474 ft. si. b&w. 35mm. pos ntr.
SHELF LOC'N: FAB1227 (print); FRA6173 (neg)
RMA lists the date in the title as 1910.
Film appears to be a fragment of the production *Roosevelt in Africa*, released Apr. 18, 1910.

Sources indicate that the photographer is Cherry Kearton.

Ref sources: Kearton, Cherry. *Photographing Wild Life across the World*. [1923]: 105–121; Kearton, Cherry. *Adventures with Animals and Men*. 1935: 65–66; Library of Congress. African Section.

Factual; nature film.

SUMMARY: Views in Africa of the TR party on safari and scenes of hippopotami, all probably filmed in British East Africa (Kenya) in 1909. On horseback TR approaches a rocky stream followed by a long line of porters; TR permits his horse to drink, then crosses the stream, with porters following. In a different location members of TR's party are carried across a stream by porters. Long shots of several hippopotami swimming and basking on a small island in what is probably the Tana River.

PERSONAL CREDITS: Kearton, Cherry, photographer.

CITATION: MPW6: 528–529, 682–683.

1. Big game hunting—Africa. 2. Hippopotamus. 3. Kenya. 4. Tana River. 5. Roosevelt, Theodore, Pres. U.S., 1858–1919—Journey to Africa, 1909–1910. I. Community Motion Picture Service, inc., source. II. Theodore Roosevelt Association Collection. III. Roosevelt in Africa [Title] [mp 76–262]

TR in Africa [1909, 4]
Producer unknown, 1909.
© No reg.
   lr, 200 ft. si. b&w. 16mm. ref print.
   lr, 200 ft. si. b&w. 16mm. archival pos (2 cy)
   lr, 500 ft. si. b&w. 35mm. neg ntr.
SHELF LOC'N: FAB1113 (print); FRA6054 & 6055 (arch pos, 2 cy)
RMA lists the date in the title as 1910.

Sources indicate that the photographer is Cherry Kearton.

Film is out of sequence, with some scenes appearing twice.

Ref sources: *The Moving Picture World*. v. 6, no. 13, 1910: 528–529; v. 6, no. 17, 1910: 682–683; *Scribner's Magazine*, v. 47, no. 6, 1910: 643–644, 650–652; Kearton, Cherry. *Adventures with Animals and Men*. 1935: 65–74; Kearton, Cherry. *Wild Life across the World*. [1914]: 100–102; Unger, Frederick W. *Roosevelt's African Trip*. 1909; Library of Congress. African Section.

Factual; sociological.

SUMMARY: On safari in East Africa, TR and members of his party appear in different locations, all probably in the vicinity of Mt. Kenya, British East Africa (Kenya), in 1909. View of Kikuyu and/or Masai tribesmen performing a ritual dance, carrying shields and spears; medium-close shot of TR and his party in a crowd of tribesmen, who pose for the camera; members of TR's party watch while he plants a tree in front of a trading post building, possibly located in Mombasa; on horseback TR rides toward the camera over a grassy open hill, followed by an African attendant on foot; carrying shields and spears, unidentified tribesmen individually pose for the camera at close range, with a campsite visible in the background; long shot of TR and his party approaching a stream; at a campsite porters work busily, either setting up or breaking camp, with TR briefly visible in the background; TR on horseback gallops toward the camera across a grassy open hill; followed by porters, TR on horseback approaches a stream, pauses to let his horse drink, then crosses; several views of what is probably part of the large Kikuyu dance performed in TR's honor at Nyeri in August, with a small number of Masai also participating; view of large number of what may be Masai women ceremonially forming a circle, through which men with shields pass; tribesmen who may be Kikuyu, holding shields, pose for the camera; medium-close shot of TR and his party in a crowd of Kikuyu and/or Masai tribesmen; TR and other party members examine a gun in the presence of tribesmen; a young boy who is probably Kikuyu dances in traditional dress, surrounded by adult tribesmen.

PERSONAL CREDITS: Kearton, Cherry, photographer. Kearton, Cherry, source.

1. Big game hunting—Africa. 2. Kikuyu tribe. 3. Kikuyu tribe—Dances. 4. Masai. 5. Masai—Dances. 6. Tree planting—Kenya. 7. Africa—Native races. 8. Kenya. 9. Roosevelt, Theodore, Pres. U.S., 1858–1919—Journey to Africa, 1909–1910. I. Theodore Roosevelt Association Collection. [mp 76–263]

TR in auto [1912]

Producer unknown [1912?]

© No reg.

lr, 9 ft. si. b&w. 16mm. ref print.
lr, 9 ft. si. b&w. 16mm. dupe neg.
lr, 23 ft. si. b&w. 35mm. pos ntr.

SHELF LOC'N: FAB1462 (print); FRA6203 (neg)

RMA lists the date in the title as 1916.

Film sequence is repeated.

Ref source: P&P stereo file.

Newsfilm.

SUMMARY: Research indicates that this may be a sequence of TR in Washington, D.C., during his campaign for the presidency under the Progressive party banner in 1912. Medium-close shot of TR sitting in the back seat of a touring auto; two unidentified men enter and the auto pulls away. A police car with an American flag on the radiator follows.

PERSONAL CREDITS: Ford, Henry, source.

1. Political parties—Washington, D.C. 2. Presidents—United States—Election—1912. 3. Washington, D.C. 4. Roosevelt, Theodore, Pres. U.S., 1858–1919. 5. Progressive Party (Founded 1912) I. Theodore Roosevelt Association Collection. [mp 76–283]

TR in Baltimore during Liberty Loan drive, 1918.

Producer unknown, Sep 1918.

© No reg.

lr, 22 ft. si. b&w. 16mm. ref print.
lr, 22 ft. si. b&w. 16mm. dupe neg.

SHELF LOC'N: FAB952 (print); FRA5915 (neg)

Ref sources: Baltimore *American*. 9/28/18: 8; The *Evening Sun*, Baltimore. 9/28/18: 1; P&P portrait file.

Newsfilm.

SUMMARY: On Sept. 28, 1918, TR is the principal speaker at the opening of the fourth Liberty Loan campaign in Oriole Baseball Park, Baltimore, Md. Wearing a mourning armband for his son, Quentin, TR walks across Oriole field with Liberty Loan officials, including a man who appears to be Phillips L. Goldsborough, chairman of the Loan Committee for Maryland and former governor of the state; TR pauses and speaks with Cardinal James Gibbons; on the speaker's platform TR is cheered by crowds, with Cardinal Gibbons, a man who appears to be Maryland Governor Emerson C. Harrington, Mrs. Thomas J. Preston, who was the wife of former President Grover Cleveland, and her husband Dr. Thomas J. Preston, with the dark mustache, among the notables behind him on the platform; view of TR addressing the crowd; long and close shots of crowds.

PERSONAL CREDITS: Kandel, source.

1. Baltimore. Oriole Baseball Park. 2. Baltimore—Sports facilities. 3. Maryland—Governors. 4. Baltimore. 5. Roosevelt, Theodore, Pres. U.S., 1858–1919—Addresses, essays, lectures. 6. Goldsborough, Phillips L. 7. Gibbons, James. 8. Harrington, Emerson C. 9. Preston, Frances Folsom Cleveland. 10. Preston, Thomas J. 11. United States. Laws, statutes, etc. Liberty loan acts. 12. Maryland. Liberty Loan Committee. 13. Maryland. Governor, 1916–1920 (Harrington) I. Theodore Roosevelt Association Collection. [mp 76–198]

TR in Denmark, 1910.

Producer unknown, May 1910.

© No reg.

lr, 7 ft. si. b&w. 16mm. ref print.

lr, 17 ft. si. b&w. 35mm. masterpos.

lr, 7 ft. si. b&w. 16mm. archival pos.

lr, 17 ft. si. b&w. 35mm. dupe neg ntr.

SHELF LOC'N: FAB944 (print); FPB8081 (fgmp); FRA5902 (arch pos)

Ref sources: P&P portrait file; P&P presidential file; *Politiken*, Copenhagen. 5/3/10: 1,3; 5/4/10:3.

Newsfilm.

SUMMARY: On May 2–3, 1910, TR visited Denmark while on his way to Norway to deliver his formal acceptance speech for the 1906 Nobel Peace prize. Views of TR, a woman who may be Katharine M. Egan, and Dr. Maurice F. Egan, American minister to Denmark, and others boarding the steamer Queen Maud at Helsingør prior to TR's return trip to Copenhagen.

1. Voyages and travels. 2. Helsingør, Denmark. 3. Roosevelt, Theodore, Pres. U.S., 1858–1919—Journey to Norway and Denmark, 1910. 4. Egan, Katharine M. 5. Egan, Maurice F. 6. Queen Maud (Ship) I. Roosevelt Memorial Association, source. II. Theodore Roosevelt Association Collection. [mp 76–199]

TR [in Louisiana], 1915 [1]

Producer unknown, Jun 1915.

© No reg.

lr, 36 ft. si. b&w. 16mm. ref print.

lr, 38 ft. si. b&w. 16mm. archival pos.

SHELF LOC'N: FAB747 (print); FRA5802 (arch pos)

RMA title: *TR on Pelican Island, 1915.*

Research indicates that the location is the Breton Island Reservation or one of the Audubon bird sanctuary islands off the coast of Louisiana; areas visited by TR included the Chandeleur Islands, Grand Isle, Breton Island, Bird Island, Last Island, Battledore Island, and Barataria Bay. Breton Island Reservation was established by Executive Order 369–A on Nov. 11, 1905. The exact location is undetermined.

Ref sources: The *Times-Picayune*, New Orleans. 6/7/15:2; 6/8/15: 16; 6/10/15: 10; 6/12/15: 1; 6/13/15: (real estate sec.): 7; Harvard University. Library. Theodore Roosevelt Collection; *Scribner's Magazine.* v. 59, no. 3, 1916: 261–280; *Audubon Magazine.* v. 17, no. 5, 1915: 410–412.

Factual; nature film.

SUMMARY: Scenes shot by ornithologist Herbert K. Job of TR and others along the beaches of the bird sanctuary islands off the coast of Louisiana, June 8–12, 1915. Joining a National Audubon Society expedition devoted to filming the society's protective work with water-birds, TR appears on an island examining eggs, probably of the royal tern, with J. Hippolyte Coquille, a New Orleans photographer, who is carrying a camera; M. L. Alexander, in light pants and shirt, president of the Louisiana Conservation Commission; and William Sprinkle, game warden. TR and Coquille talk together on the beach and examine an egg; TR and Sprinkle stand at the water's edge and talk, with what is probably the yacht of the Louisiana Conservation Commission in the background.

PERSONAL CREDITS; Job, Herbert K., photographer. Mitchell, Pell, source.

1. Wildlife refuges—Louisiana. 2. Islands—Louisiana. 3. Birds, Protection of. 4. Water-birds. 5. Terns. 6. Breton Island Reservation, La. 7. Louisiana. 8. Gulf of Mexico. 9. Roosevelt, Theodore, Pres. U.S., 1858–1919. 10. Roosevelt, Theodore, Pres. U.S., 1858–1919—Journey to Louisiana, 1915. 11. Coquille, J. Hippolyte. 12. Alexander, M. L. 13. Sprinkle, William. 14. National Audubon Society. 15. Louisiana. Dept. of Conservation. I. Theodore Roosevelt Association Collection. [mp 76–360]

TR [in Louisiana], 1915 [2]

Producer unknown, Jun 1915.

© No reg.

lr, 24 ft. si. b&w. 16mm. ref print.

lr, 24 ft. si. b&w. 16mm. dupe neg.
lr, 60 ft. si. b&w. 35mm. pos ntr.
SHELF LOC'N: FAB748 (print); FRA5803 (neg)
RMA title: *TR on Pelican Island, 1915.*

Research indicates that the location is the Breton Island Reservation or one of the Audubon bird sanctuary islands off the coast of Louisiana; areas visited by TR included the Chandeleur Islands, Grand Isle, Breton Island, Bird Island, Last Island, Battledore Island, and Barataria Bay. Breton Island Reservation was established by Executive Order 369–A on Nov. 11, 1905. The exact location is undetermined.

Ref sources: The *Times-Picayune*, New Orleans. 6/7/15: 2; 6/8/15: 16; 6/10/15: 10; 6/12/15: 1; 6/13/15: (real estate sec.): 7; *Scribner's Magazine*. v. 59, no. 3, 1916: 261–280; *Audubon Magazine*. v. 17, no. 5, 1915: 410–412.

Factual; nature film.

SUMMARY: While on a National Audubon Society expedition to bird sanctuary islands off the coast of Louisiana, TR observes birds on one of the islands. Herbert K. Job, a photographer and noted ornithologist, filmed the expedition to illustrate the Audubon Society's protective work with water-birds. The film includes views of TR walking on shore and standing in island growth and scenes of birds in flight.

PERSONAL CREDITS: Job, Herbert K., photographer. Linnenkohl, source.

1. Wildlife refuges—Louisiana. 2. Islands—Louisiana. 3. Birds, Protection of. 4. Water-birds. 5. Breton Island Reservation, La. 6. Louisiana. 7. Gulf of Mexico. 8. Roosevelt, Theodore, Pres. U.S., 1858–1919. 9. Roosevelt, Theodore, Pres. U.S., 1858–1919—Journey to Louisiana, 1915. 10. National Audubon Society. I. Theodore Roosevelt Association Collection. [mp 76–361]

TR [in Louisiana], 1915 [3]

Producer unknown, Jun 1915.
© No reg.
lr, 25 ft. si. b&w. 16mm. ref print.
lr, 25 ft. si. b&w. 16mm. dupe neg.
lr, 25 ft. si. b&w. 16mm. archival pos.
SHELF LOC'N: FAB1211 (print); FRA6104 (neg); FRA5804 (arch pos)
RMA title: *TR on Pelican Island, 1915.*

Research indicates that the location is the Breton Island Reservation or one of the Audubon bird sanctuary islands off the coast of Louisiana; areas visited by TR included the Chandeleur Islands, Grand Isle, Breton Island, Bird Island, Last Island,

Battledore Island, and Barataria Bay. Breton Island Reservation was established by Executive Order 369–A on Nov. 11, 1905. The exact location is undetermined.

Severe nitrate deterioration from the beginning of the film to ca. ft. 17; the film is barely visible.

Ref sources: The *Times-Picayune*, New Orleans. 6/7/15: 2; 6/8/15: 16; 6/10/15: 10; 6/12/15: 1; 6/13/15: (real estate sec.): 7; *Scribner's Magazine*. v. 59, no. 3, 1916: 261–280; *Audubon Magazine*. v. 17, no. 5, 1915: 410–412.

Factual; nature film.

SUMMARY: TR visits an island bird preserve off the coast of Louisiana in June 1915. Views of TR alone, standing on a beach and in island growth, and looking up at birds wheeling in flight were shot by Herbert K. Job of the National Audubon Society. The society's boat, the Royal Tern, is briefly visible at the beginning of the film.

PERSONAL CREDITS: Job, Herbert K., photographer.

1. Islands—Louisiana. 2. Wildlife refuges—Louisiana. 3. Birds, Protection of. 4. Water-birds. 5. Breton Island Reservation, La. 6. Louisiana. 7. Gulf of Mexico. 8. Roosevelt, Theodore, Pres. U.S., 1858–1919. 9. Roosevelt, Theodore, Pres. U.S., 1858–1919—Journey to Louisiana, 1915. 10. National Audubon Society. 11. Royal Tern (Launch) I. Roosevelt Memorial Association, source. II. Theodore Roosevelt Association Collection. [mp 76–362]

TR [in Louisiana], 1915 [4]

Producer unknown, Jun 1915.
© No reg.
lr, 23 ft. si. b&w. 35mm. ref print.
lr, 23 ft. si. b&w. 35mm. dupe neg.
lr, 23 ft. si. b&w. 35mm. pos ntr.
SHELF LOC'N: FEA8961 (print); FPB9919 (neg)
RMA title: *TR on Pelican Island, 1915.*

Research indicates that the location is the Breton Island Reservation or one of the Audubon bird sanctuary islands off the coast of Louisiana; areas visited by TR included the Chandeleur Islands, Grand Isle, Breton Island, Bird Island, Last Island, Battledore Island, and Barataria Bay. Breton Island Reservation was established by Executive Order 369–A on Nov. 11, 1905. The exact location is undetermined.

Ref sources: The *Times-Picayune*, New Orleans. 6/7/15: 2; 6/8/15: 16; 6/10/15: 10; 6/12/15: 1; 6/13/15: (real estate sec.): 7; *Scribner's Magazine*. v. 59, no. 3,

1916: 261–280; *Audubon Magazine*. v. 17, no. 5, 1915: 410–412.

Factual; nature film.

SUMMARY: Views of TR walking on a beach; holding his hat, TR stands near bushes on an island and follows the flight of birds. The film was photographed by Herbert K. Job of the National Audubon Society on an expedition with TR to bird sanctuary islands off the Louisiana coast in June 1915.

PERSONAL CREDITS: Job, Herbert K., photographer. Mitchell, Pell, source.

1. Islands—Louisiana. 2. Water-birds. 3. Wildlife refuges—Louisiana. 4. Birds, Protection of. 5. Breton Island Reservation, La. 6. Louisiana. 7. Gulf of Mexico. 8. Roosevelt, Theodore, Pres. U.S., 1858–1919. 9. Roosevelt, Theodore, Pres. U.S., 1858–1919—Journey to Louisiana, 1915. 10. National Audubon Society. I. Theodore Roosevelt Association Collection. [mp 76–363]

TR in New Mexico, 1916.

Producer unknown, Oct 1916.

© No reg.

   lr, 27 ft. si. b&w. 16mm. ref print.

   lr, 27 ft. si. b&w. 16mm. dupe neg.

   lr, 68 ft. si. b&w. 35mm. pos ntr.

SHELF LOC'N: FAB1017 (print); FRA5993 (neg)

Ref sources: P&P portrait file; Albuquerque *Journal*. 10/23/16: 8; Coan, Charles F. *A History of New Mexico*. v. 1, 1925: 500; Twitchell, Ralph E. *The Leading Facts of New Mexican History*. v. 2, 1963: 563; Fitzpatrick, George and Caplin, Harvey. *Albuquerque*. 1975; 62–63; [Hening, Horace B.] *Albuquerque, New Mexico*. [1908]

Newsfilm.

SUMMARY: On Oct. 23, 1916, TR campaigns for Republican presidential nominee Charles Evans Hughes and assails the Wilson administration in Albuquerque, N.M. Views of an auto parade, preceded by a young woman on horseback who carries a bouquet of flowers; TR passes by the camera in an open touring car, seated by a man who appears to be Albert B. Fall, one of New Mexico's first U.S. senators (1912–1921) and later to be secretary of the interior under Harding (1921–1923) until exposure of his involvement in the Teapot Dome scandal. Long and close shots of TR, seated on a stone pillar in front of the Alvarado Hotel in downtown Albuquerque, as he amiably talks with men gathered around him; identified in the group are Senator Fall, with a cigar in his hand, and George Curry, the tall man in a light hat, former territorial governor of New Mexico (1907–1911) and U.S. representative (1912–1913). Long shot of TR speaking to a large crowd from a narrow platform erected in front of the Alvarado Hotel; two young women on horseback bring flowers through the crowd to the platform, and TR accepts them.

1. Presidents—United States—Election—1916. 2. Processions. 3. Legislators—New Mexico. 4. Albuquerque, N.M. Alvarado Hotel. 5. New Mexico—Governors. 6. Albuquerque, N.M. 7. Roosevelt, Theodore, Pres. U.S., 1858–1919—Addresses, essays, lectures. 8. Fall, Albert B. 9. Curry, George. I. Pathe, source. II. Theodore Roosevelt Association Collection. [mp 76–168]

TR in Norway, 1910.

Producer unknown, May 1910.

© No reg.

   lr, 25 ft. si. b&w. 16mm. ref print.

   lr, 76 ft. si. b&w. 35mm. masterpos.

   lr, 25 ft. si. b&w. 16mm. archival pos.

   lr, 62 ft. si. b&w. 35mm. neg ntr.

SHELF LOC'N: FAB945(print); FPB8227 (fgmp); FRA5903 (arch pos)

Ref sources: *Aftenposten*, Oslo. 5/4/10: [2]; P&P presidential file; P&P portrait file.

Newsfilm.

SUMMARY: TR visited Christiania (Oslo), Norway on May 4–6, 1910, to deliver his formal address of acceptance for the 1906 Nobel Peace Prize. Edith Roosevelt, Queen Maud, Ethel Roosevelt, and Kermit Roosevelt enter carriages outside the railroad station in Christiania; final views of the carriage processional moving down the street. There are no views of TR in the film.

1. Oslo. 2. Roosevelt, Theodore, Pres. U.S., 1858–1919—Journey to Norway and Denmark, 1910. 3. Roosevelt, Edith. 4. Maud, consort of Haakon VII, King of Norway, 1869–1938. 5. Derby, Ethel Roosevelt. 6. Roosevelt, Kermit. I. Roosevelt Memorial Association, source. II. Theodore Roosevelt Association Collection. [mp 76–202]

TR in Norway and Denmark, 1910 [3]

Producer unknown, May 1910.

© No reg.

   lr, 176 ft. si. b&w. 16mm. ref print.

   lr, 439 ft. si. b&w. 35mm. masterpos.

   lr, 176 ft. si. b&w. 16mm. archival pos.

   lr, 439 ft. si. b&w. 35mm. neg ntr.

SHELF LOC'N: FAB887 (print); FPB7l9l (fgmp); FRA5875 (arch pos)

Film sequence does not follow the order of actual events.

Film is slightly out of frame.

Ref sources: P&P presidential file; P&P portrait file; *Aftenposten*, Oslo. 5/4/10: 1–2; 5/6/10: 1; *Politiken*, Copenhagen. 5/3/10; 1, 3; 5/4/10; 3.

Newsfilm.

SUMMARY: While returning from his African adventure in 1910, TR visited many European countries, including Denmark (May 2–3) and Norway (May 4–6). In Christiania (Oslo), he delivered his formal acceptance speech for the 1906 Nobel Peace Prize. Views of TR and Crown Prince Christian (later King Christian X) entering a carriage in Copenhagen; the carriage carrying TR and Prince Christian arrives at Amalienborg Palace in Copenhagen; TR and others arrive by auto and are greeted at an unidentified location, probably in Denmark; TR leaves the steamer Queen Maud; TR and his entourage arrive as Danish soldiers march by, visit, and bid their hosts goodbye at Kronborg Castle in Denmark; TR entering a carriage in Copenhagen; carriages arriving at the wharf at Helsingør, Denmark; Edith, Queen Maud, Ethel Roosevelt, and Kermit Roosevelt entering carriages outside the railroad station in Christiania; TR and Kermit arrive by carriage outside the National Theater in Christiania, where TR is to deliver his address, and are greeted by King Haakon and others; TR and Prince Christian in a carriage; Kermit, Edith, and Ethel entering a carriage in Copenhagen; at an unidentified location, probably in Denmark, TR, a woman who may be Katharine M. Egan, and Dr. Maurice F. Egan, American minister to Denmark, are greeted by unidentified men; Ethel, probably Edith, and Queen Maud arrive at the National Theater; crowds gather outside King Frederick University, Christiania; carriages outside the railroad station; TR and his entourage bid farewell to their hosts at Kronborg Castle; TR, Mrs. Egan, Dr. Egan, and an unidentified man board the steamer Queen Maud; the ship sails past Kronborg Castle and a Danish naval ship and returns to Copenhagen; TR and King Haakon entering a carriage outside the railroad station; final pan of crowds at Frederiksborg Castle.

1. Voyages and travels. 2. Nobel prizes. 3. Copenhagen. Amalienborg. 4. Helsingør, Denmark. Kronborg slot. 5. Hillerød, Denmark. Frederiksborg slot. 6. Oslo. 7. Copenhagen. 8. Helsingor, Denmark. 9. Roosevelt, Theodore, Pres. U.S., 1858–1919—Journey to Norway and Denmark, 1910. 10. Christian X, King of Denmark, 1870–1947. 11. Egan, Katharine M. 12. Egan, Maurice F. 13. Roosevelt, Edith. 14. Maud, consort of Haakon VII, King of Norway, 1869–1938. 15. Derby, Ethel Roosevelt. 16. Roosevelt, Kermit. 17. Haakon VII, King of Norway, 1872–1957. 18. Queen Maud (Ship) 19. Oslo. Nationaltheatret. I. Nordisk films kompagni, A/s, Copenhagen, source. II. Theodore Roosevelt Association Collection. [mp 76–347]

TR in Norway and Denmark, 1910 [1]
Producer unknown, May 1910.
© No reg.
　lr, 186 ft. si. b&w. 16mm. ref print.
　lr, 186 ft. si. b&w. 16mm. dupe neg (cy 1)
　lr, 465 ft. si. b&w. 35mm. dupe neg (cy 2)
　lr, 465 ft. si. b&w. 35mm. pos ntr.
SHELF LOC'N: FAB886 (print); FRA5874 (neg, cy 1); FPB7190 (neg, cy 2)

Film sequence does not follow the order of actual events.

Film is slightly out of frame.

Ref sources: P&P presidential file; P&P portrait file; *Aftenposten*, Oslo. 5/4/10: 1–2; 5/6/10: 1; *Politiken*, Copenhagen. 5/3/10: 1, 3; 5/4/10: 3.

Newsfilm.

SUMMARY: While returning from his African adventure in 1910, TR visited many European countries, including Denmark (May 2–3) and Norway (May 4–6). Views of TR, King Haakon, Edith Roosevelt, Queen Maud, Ethel Roosevelt, Kermit Roosevelt, and others entering carriages outside the railroad station in Christiania (Oslo); carriages arrive at a wharf at Helsingør, Denmark; TR and Kermit arrive by carriage outside the National Theater in Christiania, where TR is to deliver his acceptance speech for the 1906 Nobel Peace Prize; they are greeted by King Haakon and others; Ethel, probably Edith, and Queen Maud arrive at the theater; crowds gather outside King Frederick University, Christiania; TR, Crown Prince Christian (later King Christian X), Kermit, Edith, and Ethel entering carriages in Copenhagen; the carriage carrying TR and Prince Christian arrives at Amalienborg Palace, Copenhagen; TR, a woman who may be Katharine M. Egan and Dr. Maurice F. Egan, American minister to Denmark (barely visible on the far left), arrive by auto and are greeted by unidentified men; pan of crowds at Frederiksborg Castle in Denmark; TR and his entourage arrive as Danish soldiers march by, visit, and bid their hosts goodbye at Kronborg Castle, Denmark; TR, Mrs. Egan, and Dr. Egan board the steamer Queen Maud; the ship sails past Kronborg Castle and a Danish naval ship and returns to Copenhagen; final views of TR leaving the ship and entering a carriage.

1. Voyages and travels. 2. Nobel prizes. 3. Copenhagen. Amalienborg. 4. Hillerød, Denmark. Frederiksborg slot. 5. Helsingør, Denmark. Kronborg slot. 6. Oslo. 7. Helsingør, Denmark. 8. Copenhagen. 9. Roosevelt,Theodore, Pres. U.S., 1858–1919—Journey to Norway and Denmark, 1910. 10. Haakon VII, King of Norway, 1872–1957. 11. Roosevelt, Edith. 12. Maud, consort of Haakon VII, King of Norway, 1869–1938. 13. Derby, Ethel Roosevelt. 14. Roosevelt, Kermit. 15. Christian X, King of Denmark, 1870–1947. 16. Egan, Katharine M. 17. Egan, Maurice F. 18. Oslo. Nationaltheatret. 19. Queen Maud (Ship) I. Nordisk films kompagni, A/s, Copenhagen, source. II. Theodore Roosevelt Association Collection. [mp 76–345]

TR in Norway and Denmark, 1910 [2]

Producer unknown, May 1910.

© No reg.

   lr, 177 ft. si. b&w. 16mm. ref print.

   lr, 177 ft. si. b&w. 16mm. dupe neg (2 cy)

   lr, 177 ft. si. b&w. 16mm. archival pos.

   lr, 442 ft. si. b&w. 35mm. pos ntr.

SHELF LOC'N: FAB1220 (print); FRA6115 & 6116 (neg, 2 cy); FRA5876 (arch pos)

TR on board the Norwegian ship *Queen Maud* in 1910. TR went to Oslo to receive the Nobel Peace Prize awarded to him in 1906 for his role in the 1905 Portsmouth Peace Treaty which prevented a war between Russia and Japan.

Film sequence does not follow the order of actual events.

Film is slightly out of frame.

Ref sources: P&P presidential file; P&P portrait file; *Aftenposten*, Oslo. 5/4/10: 1–2; 5/6/10: 1; *Politiken*, Copenhagen. 5/3/10: 1, 3; 5/4/10: 3.

Newsfilm.

SUMMARY: While returning from his African adventure in 1910, TR visited many European countries, including Denmark (May 2–3) and Norway (May 4–6). Views of TR, King Haakon, Edith Roosevelt, Queen Maud, Ethel Roosevelt, Kermit Roosevelt, and others entering carriages outside the railroad station in Christiania (Oslo); carriages arrive at a wharf at Helsingør, Denmark; TR and Kermit arrive by carriage outside the National Theater in Christiania, where TR is to deliver his acceptance speech for the 1906 Nobel Peace Prize; they are greeted by King Haakon and others; Ethel, probably Edith, and Queen Maud arrive at the theater; crowds gather outside King Frederick University, Christiania; TR, Crown Prince Christian (later King Christian X), Kermit, Edith, and Ethel entering carriages in Copenhagen; the carriage carrying TR and Prince Christian arrives at Amalienborg Palace, Copenhagen; TR, a woman who may be Katharine M. Egan, wife of Dr. Maurice F. Egan, American minister to Denmark, and others arrive by auto and are greeted by unidentified men; pan of crowds at Frederiksborg Castle in Denmark; TR and his entourage arrive as Danish soldiers march by, visit, and bid their hosts goodbye at Kronborg Castle, Denmark; TR, Mrs. Egan, and Dr. Maurice F. Egan board the steamer Queen Maud; the ship sails past Kronborg Castle and a Danish naval ship and returns to Copenhagen; final views of TR leaving the ship and entering a carriage.

1. Voyages and travels. 2. Nobel prizes. 3. Copenhagen. Amalienborg. 4. Hillerød, Denmark. Frederiksborg slot. 5. Helsingør, Denmark. Kronborg slot. 6. Oslo. 7. Helsingør, Denmark. 8. Copenhagen. 9. Roosevelt, Theodore, Pres. U.S., 1858–1919—Journey to Norway and Denmark, 1910. 10. Haakon VII, King of Norway, 1872–1957. 11. Roosevelt, Edith. 12. Maud, consort of Haakon VII, King of Norway, 1869–1938. 13. Derby, Ethel Roosevelt. 14. Roosevelt, Kermit. 15. Christian X, King of Denmark, 1870–1947. 16. Egan, Katharine M. 17. Egan, Maurice F. 18. Oslo. Nationaltheatret. 19. Queen Maud (Ship) I. Nordisk films kompagni, A/s, Copenhagen, source. II. Theodore Roosevelt Association Collection. [mp 76–346]

TR in San Francisco, 1903.

Producer unknown, May 1903.

© No reg.

    lr, 54 ft. si. b&w. 16mm. ref print.

    lr, 54 ft. si. b&w. 16mm. dupe neg.

    lr, 54 ft. si. b&w. 16mm. archival pos.

  SHELF LOC'N: FAB1454 (print); FRA6190 (neg); FRA6020 (arch pos)

Ref sources: San Francisco *Chronicle.* 5/12/03: 16; 5/13/03: 1–8; San Francisco *Examiner.* 5/12/03: 1–4; San Francisco Chronicle. *The City San Francisco in Pictures.* 1961: 52; Writers' Program. California. *San Francisco.* 1940: 287, 300.

Newsfilm.

SUMMARY: On a western presidential tour in 1903, TR parades through San Francisco along Van Ness Ave., May 12, 1903. Long shots of the parade, including views of military escorts, TR's horsedrawn carriage, and buildings along Van Ness Ave.; view of the Ninth U.S. Cavalry regiment preceding TR's carriage, according to press accounts one of the first black companies to be accorded so prominent a position in a public procession; long shot of TR's carriage, surrounded by walking men, passing crowds at St. Mary's Cathedral at the intersection of Van Ness Ave. and O'Farrell Street; medium-close shot of TR standing in a carriage as it returns along the same street later in the day.

PERSONAL CREDITS: Howe, Lyman, source.

1. Processions. 2. Afro-American soldiers. 3. San Francisco. 4. San Francisco—Streets—Van Ness Avenue. 5. Roosevelt, Theodore, Pres. U.S., 1858–1919. 6. United States. President, 1901–1909 (Roosevelt) 7. United States. Army. 9th Cavalry. 8. United States. Army. Cavalry—History. 9. St. Mary's Cathedral, San Francisco. I. Theodore Roosevelt Association Collection. [mp 76–218]

TR in St. Paul, Minn. [1917]

Producer unknown, Sep 1917.

© No reg.

    lr, 19 ft. si. b&w. 16mm. ref print (cy 1)

    lr, 12 ft. si. b&w. 16mm. ref print (cy 2)

    lr, 12 ft. si. b&w. 16mm. dupe neg.

    lr, 12 ft. si. b&w. 16mm. archival pos (2 cy)

  SHELF LOC'N: FAB651 (print, cy 1); FAB1054 (print, cy 2); FRA5692 (neg); FRA6022 & 6023 (arch pos, 2 cy)

RMA titles: *TR Speaking at St. Paul, Minn., 1918* [and] *TR in St. Paul, Minn., 1918.*

Ref print (cy 1) lacks one interior title but is longer than ref print (cy 2) due to longer printing of other interior titles.

Ref sources: St. Paul *Pioneer Press.* 9/29/17: 1; Chrislock, Carl H. *The Progressive Era in Minnesota, 1899–1918.* 1971: 144.

Newsfilm.

SUMMARY: Roosevelt views a large pro-war parade assembled in his honor in St. Paul, Minn., on Sept. 28, 1917. Long shot of a large American flag as women carry it through the crowd; close shots of officials, including Roosevelt, on a platform observing the parade; Louis W. Hill, parade organizer and civic leader; Joseph A. A. Burnquist, governor of Minnesota (1915–1921); and Vivian R. Irvin, mayor of St. Paul.

PERSONAL CREDITS: Hollis, V. P., source.

1. Processions. 2. European War, 1914–1918—Public opinion. 3. St. Paul, Minn. 4. Roosevelt, Theodore, Pres. U. S., 1858–1919. 5. Hill, Louis W. 6. Burnquist, Joseph A. A. 7. Irvin, Vivian R. 8. Minnesota. Governor, 1915–1921 (Burnquist) I. Theodore Roosevelt Association Collection. [mp 76–1]

TR in Vincennes, France, 1910.

Producer unknown, Apr 1910.

© No reg.

    lr, 12 ft. si. b&w. 16mm. ref print.

    lr, 30 ft. si. b&w. 35mm. masterpos.

    lr, 12 ft. si. b&w. 16mm. archival pos.

    lr, 30 ft. si. b&w. 35mm. neg ntr.

  SHELF LOC'N: FAB967 (print); FPB7193 (fgmp); FRA5936 (arch pos)

Ref sources: Lorant, Stefan. *The Life and Times of Theodore Roosevelt.* 1959; Gardner, Joseph L. *Departing Glory.* 1973; The *Times*, London. 4/28/10: 5; *Le Figaro*, Paris. 4/28/10: 2; P&P portrait file; Enjalric, Marcel. *Château de Vincennes.* [1975?]

Factual.

SUMMARY: TR, fulfilling one of the required duties of a visiting statesman, reviews French troops and observes military maneuvers at Vincennes, France, on Apr. 27, 1910. Gen. Jean B. Dalstein, military governor of Paris, TR, and Robert Bacon, American ambassador to France, are mounted on horses and lead a party of French soldiers through a portion of the courtyard of the Château de Vincennes; the group is probably on its way to the Polygon, the field where the maneuvers take place. The second sequence consists of views of TR and Dalstein on horseback, with Jules Jusserand, French ambassador to the U.S., standing next to them, watching the military maneuvers.

1. Vincennes, Château de. 2. Vincennes, France. Polygon. 3. Military maneuvers. 4. War games. 5. Vincennes, France. 6. Roosevelt, Theodore, Pres. U.S., 1858–1919. 7.Roosevelt, Theodore,Pres. U.S., 1858–1919—Journey to Europe, 1910. 8. Dalstein, Jean B. 9. Bacon, Robert, 1860–1919. 10. Jusserand, Jules. 11. France. Armée—Maneuvers. I. Roosevelt Memorial Association, source. II. Theodore Roosevelt Association Collection. [mp 76–254]

TR in Wilkes-Barre, Pa., 1905.
Producer unknown, Aug 1905.
© No reg.
   lr, 18 ft. si. b&w. 16mm. ref print.
   lr, 18 ft. si. b&w. 16mm. dupe neg (cy 1)
   lr, 45 ft. si. b&w. 35mm. dupe neg (cy 2)
   lr, 45 ft. si. b&w. 35mm. pos ntr.
   SHELF LOC'N: FAB1024(print); FRA6001 (neg, cy 1); FPB7344 (neg, cy 2)
Interior title in Italian refers to the sinking of the Lusitania and Zeppelin flights over London and is unrelated to pictorial footage.
Ref sources: The Philadelphia *Inquirer*. 8/11/05: 1–2; The Pittsburgh *Post*. 8/11/05: 1, 4; P&P portrait file; P&P presidential file.
Newsfilm; views.
SUMMARY: On Aug. 10, 1905, TR appeared as the guest of the United Mine Workers of America and the Catholic Total Abstinence Union of America during their annual convention in Wilkes-Barre, Pa. Views of a long procession of priests ,and clergymen, with TR following; this may be a sequence from part of the parade held in TR's honor or from an unrelated event; the final scene shows TR and noted clergymen posing on the steps of a house.
1. Temperance societies. 2. Processions. 3. Priests. 4. Wilkes-Barre, Pa. 5. Roosevelt, Theodore, Pres. U.S., 1858–1919. 6. United States. President, 1901–1909 (Roosevelt) 7. Catholic Total Abstinence Union of America. I. Apollo Pictures, source. II. Theodore Roosevelt Association Collection. [mp 76–307]

TR Jr. and Will Hays.
Producer unknown [192–?]
© No reg.
   lr, 6 ft. si. b&w. 16mm. ref print.
   lr, 6 ft. si. b&w. 16mm. dupe neg.
   lr, 16 ft. si. b&w. 35mm. pos ntr.
   SHELF LOC'N: FAB850 (print); FRA5855 (neg)
Newsfilm.
SUMMARY: Close shot of Theodore Roosevelt,

Jr., and Will H. Hays, prominent Republican leaders, talking outdoors. A building is visible in the background.
1. Roosevelt, Theodore, 1887–1944. 2. Hays, Will H. I. International Newsreel Corporation, source. II. Theodore Roosevelt Association Collection. [mp 76–84]

TR Jr. with group of sailors and soldiers.
Pathe News [1919?]
© No reg.
   lr, 5 ft. si. b&w. 16mm. ref print.
   lr, 5 ft. si. b&w. 16mm. dupe neg.
   lr, 14 ft. si. b&w. 35mm. pos ntr.
(Pathe News [newsreel])
SHELF LOC'N: FAB957 (print); FRA5922 (neg)
Newsfilm; views.
SUMMARY: Medium-close view of TR, Jr., talking with two sailors and two soldiers. Interior title identifies TR, Jr., as one of the founders of the new Legion, which was incorporated by Congress on Sept. 16, 1919, as the American Legion.
1. Seamen. 2. Soldiers. 3. Roosevelt, Theodore, 1887–1944. 4. American Legion. I. Pathe. II. Pathe, source. III. Theodore Roosevelt Association Collection. [mp 76–144]

TR, Mayor Mitchel and guests at Cooper Sanitarium [1917]
Producer unknown, Oct 1917.
© No reg.
   lr, 2 ft. si. b&w. 16mm. ref print.
   lr, 2 ft. si. b&w. 16mm. dupe neg.
   lr, 6 ft. si. b&w. 35mm. pos ntr.
   SHELF LOC'N: FAB995 (print); FRA5978 (neg)
RMA lists the date in the title as 1916.
Ref sources: New Haven *Journal-Courier*. 10/22/17: 1; The New York *Times*. 10/28/17: pt. 5: [3]; P&P portrait file.
Newsfilm.
SUMMARY: During the period of Oct. 11–21, 1917, TR was resting and losing weight at Cooper's Training Camp, Stamford, Conn. On Oct. 21, TR received a group of visitors. Identified in the first row, left to right, are: William Warren Barbour, later senator from New Jersey; Mayor John P. Mitchel of New York City; TR; Jack Cooper; and a man who may be Mayor John J. Treat of Stamford.
1. Health resorts, watering-places, etc. 2. Stamford, Conn. 3. Roosevelt, Theodore, Pres. U.S., 1858–1919. 4. Mitchel, John P. 5. Barbour, William Warren. 6. Cooper, Jack. 7. Treat, John J. 8. Cooper's Training Camp. I. Pathe, source. II. The-

odore Roosevelt Association Collection. [mp 76–248]

TR, Mayor Mitchel, Governor Charles Whitman of New York, and Myron Herrick, 1917.
Producer unknown, 1917.
 © No reg.
  lr, 3 ft. si. b&w. 16mm. ref print.
  lr, 3 ft. si. b&w. 16mm. archival pos.
  lr, 9 ft. si. b&w. 35mm. neg ntr.
 SHELF LOC'N: FAB889 (print); FRA5878 (arch pos)
Ref print is very light.
Ref sources: The New York *Herald*. 8/31/17: pt. 2: [9], 11–13; New York *Tribune*. 9/9/17: pt. 6: 8; P&P portrait file; Harvard University. Library. Theodore Roosevelt Collection.
Newsfilm.
SUMMARY: Close-up view of New York Governor Charles S. Whitman (1915–1918); Myron T. Herrick, formerly governor of Ohio and United States ambassador to France; and New York City Mayor John P. Mitchel (1914–1917) reviewing a parade of New York National Guardsmen from the balcony of the Union League Club in New York City, Aug. 30, 1917. TR steps forward between Herrick and Mitchel and tips his hat, probably acknowledging applause.
PERSONAL CREDITS: Futter, Walter A., source.
1. New York (City) 2. Roosevelt, Theodore, Pres. U.S., 1858–1919. 3. Mitchel, John P. 4. Whitman, Charles S. 5. Herrick, Myron T. 6. New York (State). Governor, 1915–1918 (Charles S. Whitman) 7. New York (City). Union League Club. I. Theodore Roosevelt Association Collection. [mp 76–106]

TR memorial services at New York Public Library, 1919.
Fox Film Corp., Oct 1919.
 © No reg.
  lr, 33 ft. si. b&w. 16mm. ref print.
  lr, 33 ft. si. b&w. 16mm. dupe neg.
  lr, 36 ft. si. b&w. 16mm. archival pos.
(Fox news [Series])
 SHELF LOC'N: FAB991 (print); FRA5970 (neg); FRA5971 (arch pos)
Ref sources: *Daily News*, New York. 10/25/19: 8; New York *American*. 10/25/19: 11; P&P portrait file.
Newsfilm.
SUMMARY: In honor of TR's birthday the week of Oct. 20–27, 1919, was declared Roosevelt Week by the Roosevelt Memorial Association. As one of the events, an official Roosevelt memorial flag, which has been carried across New York State, is ceremoniously received at the New York Public Library on Oct. 25. Opening scene of a crowd gathered on Fifth Avenue in front of the public library, with a view of the flag on display. Long shots of notables standing on the library's steps. Possible identifications from right to left are: Henry Cabot Lodge, honorary vice-president of RMA; the man next to Lodge is probably Henry J. Allen, governor of Kansas; William Boyce Thompson, president of RMA; William Loeb, Jr., vice-president of RMA, is visible in back of Thompson; next to Loeb is probably William Gibbs McAdoo; and the man to the far left with his hands to his sides may be Elihu Root, an RMA trustee. Sequence of Boy Scouts and members of the Naval Reserve hoisting the flag up a flagpole as an unidentified man leads the crowd in singing. Five school girls sew the forty-seventh star on the flag. Final view of the flag on the pole.
PERSONAL CREDITS: Fox, William, source.
1. Memorial rites and ceremonies. 2. Flags. 3. High school students—Political activity. 4. New York (City) 5. Roosevelt, Theodore, Pres. U.S., 1858–1919—Funeral and memorial services. 6. Lodge, Henry Cabot. 7. Allen, Henry J. 8. Thompson, William Boyce. 9. Loeb, William, 1866–1937. 10. McAdoo, William Gibbs. 11. Root, Elihu. 12. New York (City). Public Library. 13. Roosevelt Memorial Association. 14. Kansas. Governor, 1919–1923 (Henry J. Allen) 15. Boy Scouts of America. 16. United States. Naval Reserve. I. Fox Film Corporation. II. Theodore Roosevelt Association Collection. [mp 76–140]

TR on Fifth Avenue, New York, near St. Patrick's Cathedral after attending Mayor Mitchel's funeral.
Producer unknown, Jul 1918.
 © No reg.
  lr, 7 ft. si. b&w. 16mm. ref print (cy 1)
  lr, 18 ft. si. b&w. 35mm. ref print (cy 2)
  lr, 17 ft. si. b&w. 35mm. ref print (cy 3)
  lr, 7 ft. si. b&w. 16mm. dupe neg (cy 1)
  lr, 18 ft. si. b&w. 35mm. dupe neg (cy 2)
  lr, 17 ft. si. b&w. 35mm. dupe neg (cy 3–2 cy)
  lr, 18 ft. si. b&w. 35mm. masterpos (cy 1)
  lr, 17 ft. si. b&w. 35mm. masterpos (cy 2)
  lr, 17 ft. si. b&w. 35mm. pos ntr.
  lr, 17 ft. si. b&w. 35mm. neg ntr (cy 1)
  lr, 16 ft. si. b&w. 35mm. neg ntr (cy 2)
 SHELF LOC'N: FAB970 (print, cy 1); FEA7322 (print, cy 2); FEA7634 (print, cy 3); FRA5939 (neg, cy 1); FPB 7959 (neg, cy 2); FPB8073 &

8074 (neg, cy 3–2 cy); FPB7960 (fgmp, cy 1); FPB8072 (fgmp, cy 2)

Ref source: P&P portrait file.

Newsfilm.

SUMMARY: As an honorary pallbearer at the funeral of former New York City Mayor John P. Mitchel on July 11, 1918, TR appears with other funeral participants on Fifth Avenue. Surrounded by men in formal dress, TR speaks briefly with an unidentified military officer; standing in the group are men tentatively identified as Nicholas Murray Butler, president of Columbia University, and financier George W. Perkins, both pallbearers with TR at the funeral; close shot of TR speaking with a woman; TR, Butler, and members of the crowd walk past the camera.

1. Funeral service. 2. New York (City)—Streets— Fifth Avenue. 3. New York (City) 4. Roosevelt, Theodore, Pres. U.S., 1858–1919. 5. Mitchel, John P. 6. Butler, Nicholas Murray. 7. Perkins, George W. I. American Motion Picture Company, source. II. Theodore Roosevelt Association Collection. [mp 76–121]

TR on porch at Sagamore Hill, 1917.

Producer unknown [1917?]

© No reg.

lr, 4 ft. si. b&w. 16mm. ref print.
lr, 4 ft. si. b&w. 16mm. dupe neg.
lr, 4 ft. si. b&w. 16mm. archival pos.
lr, 11 ft. si. b&w. 35mm. pos ntr.

SHELF LOC'N: FAB746 (print); FRA5800 (neg); FRA6102 (arch pos)

The date in the title is unverified.

Newsfilm.

SUMMARY: TR, standing on the porch at Sagamore Hill, speaks and gestures with a riding whip. He is dressed in casual clothes: striped vest, coat, and hat.

PERSONAL CREDITS: Kandel, source.

1. Oyster Bay, N.Y. Sagamore Hill. 2. Oyster Bay, N.Y. 3. Roosevelt, Theodore, Pres. U.S., 1858–1919. 4. Roosevelt, Theodore, Pres. U.S., 1858–1919— Homes. I. Theodore Roosevelt Association Collection. [mp 76–50]

TR on reception yacht in New York Bay, 1910.

Producer unknown, Jun 1910.

© No reg.

lr, 27 ft. si. b&w. 16mm. ref print.
lr, 68 ft. si. b&w. 35mm. masterpos.
lr, 27 ft. si. b&w. 16mm. archival pos.

lr, 67 ft. si. b&w. 35mm. neg ntr.

SHELF LOC'N: FAB701 (print); FPB7958 (fgmp); FRA5751 (arch pos)

TR is not positively identified aboard the yacht Androscoggin. The last two segments of footage include shots of policemen and of TR on a platform.

Newsfilm.

SUMMARY: TR received a rousing welcome in New York on June 18, 1910, when he returned from his extensive tour of Africa and western Europe. Flags are raised on the large cutter Androscoggin, which carried the Roosevelt party into the docking area. A smaller cutter, the Manhattan, is shown passing the Androscoggin. The film includes brief shots of policemen waiting by a passageway; the Androscoggin moving into the dock; clear views of TR and William J. Gaynor, mayor of New York, on the speaking platform at the Battery.

1. Ships. 2. New York Bay. 3. New York (City) —Harbor. 4. New York (City)—Parks—Battery. 5. Roosevelt, Theodore, Pres. U.S., 1858–1919. 6. Gaynor, William J. 7. Androscoggin (Ship) 8. Manhattan (Ship) I. Warner Brothers, source. II. Theodore Roosevelt Association Collection. [mp 76–21]

[TR planting a tree in Africa]

Producer unknown, 1909.

© No reg.

lr, 19 ft. si. b&w. 16mm. ref print.
lr, 19 ft. si. b&w. 16mm. dupe neg.
lr, 19 ft. si. b&w. 16mm. archival pos.

SHELF LOC'N: FAB1456 (print); FRA6192 (neg); FRA6056 (arch pos)

Sources indicate that the photographer is Cherry Kearton.

Ref source: Kearton, Cherry. *Wild Life across the World.* [1914]: 100–101.

Factual.

SUMMARY: A view of TR, accompanied by members of his safari party, planting a tree in front of a trading post building; interior title identifies the location as Mombasa, Kenya.

PERSONAL CREDITS: Kearton, Cherry, photographer.

1. Tree planting—Kenya. 2. Mombasa, Kenya. 3. Roosevelt, Theodore, Pres. U.S., 1858–1919— Journey to Africa, 1909–1910. I. Theodore Roosevelt Association Collection. [mp 76–246]

TR receiving Belgian envoys at Sagamore Hill [1917]

Producer unknown, Aug 1917.

© No reg.

lr, 15 ft. si. b&w. 16mm. ref print.

lr, 15 ft. si. b&w. 16mm. archival pos.

SHELF LOC'N: FAB900 (print); FRA5895 (arch
pos)

RMA lists the dates in the title as 1917–1918.

Ref sources: *Empire State Notables, 1914.* 1914: 131; Fyfe, Henry Hamilton. *T. P. O'Connor.* 1934; The New York *Times.* 8/26/17: pt. 5: [4], [6]; New York *Times Mid-week Pictorial. Portfolio of the World War.* 1917: [109]; The *Evening Star*, Washington, D.C. 6/18/17: 2; Londres *L'Independance belge*, London. 7/31/17: 2–3; P&P portrait file.

Newsfilm.

SUMMARY: TR entertains members of the Belgian Mission at Sagamore Hill, Aug. 22, 1917. The mission is headed by Baron Ludovic Moncheur, former ambassador to the United States, and includes Gen. Mathieu Leclercq, commander of the Belgian Cavalry, Maj. Leon Osterrieth, Hector Carlier, Count Louis d'Ursel, and Jean D. Mertens. Those accompanying the Belgian Mission include George T. Wilson, Maj. Gen. Daniel Appleton, Lt. Harry Stratton, Capt. Thomas C. Cook, T. P. O'Connor, Irish political leader and writer, and New York lawyer Frederic Coudert. The camera pans the group standing in front of the porch. Identified are: Count Louis d'Ursel, the Belgian officer standing at the end of the group; T. P. O'Connor, the large man with white hair; a man who is probably Jean D. Mertens; a man who is probably George T. Wilson; General Leclercq; TR; Baron Moncheur; Frederic Coudert, wearing the white vest; Major Osterrieth, the large Belgian officer; Hector Carlier, with a dark beard and wearing a light suit; the large man in an American uniform with a white mustache is possibly Major General Appleton; the smaller American officer standing with his side to the camera and his knee bent is Capt. Thomas C. Cook.

1. Oyster Bay, N.Y. Sagamore Hill. 2. European War, 1914–1918. 3. Government missions, Belgian. 4. Oyster Bay, N.Y. 5. Belgium—Diplomatic and consular service. 6. Belgium—Foreign relations. 7. Roosevelt, Theodore, Pres. U.S., 1858–1919. 8. Moncheur, Ludovic, Baron. 9. Leclercq, Mathieu. 10. Osterrieth, Leon. 11. Carlier, Hector. 12. Ursel, Louis, comte d' 13. Mertens, Jean D. 14. Wilson, George T. 15. Cook, Thomas C. 16. O'Connor, Thomas Power. 17. Coudert, Frederic R. I. Roosevelt Memorial Association, source. II. Theodore Roosevelt Association Collection. [mp 76–118]

TR reviewing and speaking to 13th Regiment at Sagamore Hill, 1917.

Producer unknown [1917?]

© No reg.

lr, 23 ft. si. b&w. 16mm. ref print (cy 1)

lr, 60 ft. si. b&w. 35mm. ref print (cy 2)

lr, 23 ft. si. b&w. 16mm. archival pos.

lr, 57 ft. si. b&w. 35mm. neg ntr.

SHELF LOC'N: FAB1118 (print, cy 1); FEA6744
(print, cy 2); FRA6062 (arch pos)

The date in the title is unverified.

Factual.

SUMMARY: TR speaks to several unidentified people, including a man who looks like TR, on the porch at Sagamore Hill. There are two views of TR addressing soldiers assembled on the lawn of Sagamore Hill: the first segment shows TR's back as he speaks; the second is a long shot of TR, shot from the rear of the group of soldiers.

1. Soldiers. 2. Oyster Bay, N.Y. Sagamore Hill. 3. Oyster Bay, N.Y. 4. Roosevelt, Theodore, Pres. U.S., 1858–1919. 5. Roosevelt, Theodore, Pres. U.S., 1858–1919—Homes. 6. Roosevelt, Theodore, Pres. U.S., 1858–1919—Addresses, essays, lectures. 7. United States. Army. I. Warner Brothers, source. II. Theodore Roosevelt Association Collection. [mp 76–212]

TR reviews and addresses troops [Fort Sheridan, Ill.]; TR riding in auto, Chicago, 1917.

Universal Film Manufacturing Co., Sep 1917.

© No reg.

lr, 28 ft. si. b&w. 16mm. ref print (cy 1)

lr, 106 ft. si. b&w. 35mm. ref print (cy 2)

lr, 61 ft. si. b&w. 35mm. ref print (cy 3)

lr, 25 ft. si. b&w. 16mm. dupe neg (cy 1)

lr, 106 ft. si. b&w. 35mm. dupe neg (cy 2)

lr, 61 ft. si. b&w. 35mm. dupe neg (cy 3)

lr, 106 ft. si. b&w. 35mm. masterpos.

lr, 25 ft. si. b&w. 16mm. archival pos.

lr, 61 ft. si. b&w. 35mm. pos ntr.

lr, 61 ft. si. b&w. 35mm. neg ntr.

SHELF LOC'N: FAB698 (print, cy 1); FEA6742
(print, cy 2); FEA6743 (print, cy
3); FRA5744 (neg, cy 1); FPB
7201 (neg, cy 2); FPB7342 (neg,
cy 3); FPB7343 (fgmp); FRA
5743 (arch pos)

The first segment has *Universal Animated Weekly* v. 5, issue no. 92, released October 4, 1917; the second segment does not have volume numbering.

Copies vary in length due to the number and length of titles.

Ref sources: P&P portrait file; Fort Sheridan Association. *The History and Achievements of the Fort Sheridan Officers' Training Camps.* 1920; Chicago *Daily Tribune.* 9/28/17: 2–3; The Chicago *Daily News.* 9/27/17: 1; 4/28/17: 1–3.

Newsfilm.

SUMMARY: Two segments of TR during a midwestern speaking tour in support of military preparedness. On Sept. 27, 1917, TR visited the officers' training camp at Fort Sheridan, Ill. Views of troops marching past a reviewing stand for inspection by TR and several civilian and military personnel; identified on the platform with TR are Capt. Georges Etienne Bertrand (wearing beret), a visiting Frenchman who instructed the trainees in trench warfare, and Col. James A. Ryan, commanding officer of Fort Sheridan; TR addresses the troops after the review. The second segment shows scenes from a parade staged in TR's honor in Chicago on Apr. 28, 1917. Views of men on horseback who appear to be mounted police, sailors, and cavalry; view of TR standing and waving his hat in an open touring car; in the car with TR are Arthur Meeker and Samuel Insull, Chicago businessmen who are members of the welcoming committee, and some unidentified men.

PERSONAL CREDITS: Foster, source.

CITATION: MPW34.1: 435; MPW34. 1: 526.

1. Marching. 2. Processions. 3. Preparedness. 4. European War, 1914–1918—Public opinion. 5. Military training camps—Illinois. 6. Chicago. 7. Roosevelt, Theodore, Pres. U.S., 1858–1919—Addresses, essays, lectures. 8. Bertrand, Georges Etienne. 9. Ryan, James A. 10. Meeker, Arthur, 1866–1946. 11. Insull, Samuel. 12. Fort Sheridan. 13. United States. Army. 14. United States. Navy. I. Universal Film Manufacturing Company. II. Community Motion Picture Service, inc., source. III. Theodore Roosevelt Association Collection. IV. TR riding in auto, Chicago, 1917 [Title] V. Series: Universal animated weekly. [mp 76–43]

TR reviews French troops at Vincennes, France, 1910.

Producer unknown, Apr 1910.

© No reg.

lr, 88 ft. si. b&w. 16mm. ref print.

lr, 88 ft. si. b&w. 16mm. dupe neg (cy 1)

lr, 221 ft. si. b&w. 35mm. dupe neg (cy 2)

lr, 221 ft. si. b&w. 35mm. pos ntr.

SHELF LOC'N: FAB968 (print); FRA5937 (neg, cy 1); FPB7351 (neg, cy 2)

The film is out of sequence.

Ref sources: Lorant, Stefan. *The Life and Times of Theodore Roosevelt.* 1959; Gardner, Joseph L. *Departing Glory.* 1973; *Le Figaro,* Paris. 4/28/10: 2; *The Times,* London. 4/28/10: 5; *Le Matin,* Paris. 4/28/10: 2; Enaud, François. *Le Château de Vincennes.* 1964: 60, 84; Enjalric, Marcel. *Château de Vincennes.* [1975?]; P&P portrait file.

Factual.

SUMMARY: Robert Bacon, American ambassador to France, TR, Jules Jusserand, French ambassador to the United States, and Gen. Jean B. Dalstein, military governor of Paris, arrive at the Château de Vincennes, a medieval castle and dungeon, parts of which are used by French military schools; the group has been invited to review troops and observe military maneuvers. TR's party arrives in a car and is received by M. Lépine, the prefect of police, General Verand, and Colonel Jacquot. In the courtyard of the dungeon, TR is mounted on a horse while his stirrups are adjusted and leggings are brought to fit over his formal striped trousers. There are several scenes of Bacon, Dalstein, TR,

Robert Bacon. A Harvard classmate of TR's, Bacon served as Assistant Secretary of State (1905–9), Secretary of State (January 27-March 6, 1909), Ambassador to France (1909–12), and as Chief of the American Military Mission to British General Headquarters and Field Marshal Sir Douglas Haig's personal liaison officer during World War I.

and other dignitaries and soldiers riding through an arch, probably La Porte du Bois, on the way to the Polygon, the field where the maneuvers are to take place; and scenes of the group riding past French cavalry units. Views of TR and Dalstein mounted, with Jusserand standing nearby, watching the military maneuvers and sham battle enacted for TR. TR shakes Dalstein's hand as he leaves; Jusserand and TR tip their hats to French officers.

PERSONAL CREDITS: Howe, Lyman, source.

1. Vincennes, Château de. 2. Vincennes, France. Polygon. 3. Military education—France. 4. Military maneuvers. 5. War games. 6. Vincennes, France. 7. Roosevelt, Theodore, Pres. U.S., 1858–1919. 8. Roosevelt, Theodore, Pres. U. S., 1858–1919—Journey to Europe, 1910. 9. Bacon, Robert, 1860–1919. 10. Jusserand, Jules. 11. Dalstein, Jean B. 12. France. Armée—Maneuvers. I. Theodore Roosevelt Association Collection. [mp 76–186]

TR reviews the fleet, 1907.

Producer unknown, Dec 1907.

© No reg.

lr, 40 ft. si. b&w. 35mm. ref print (2 cy)
lr, 16 ft. si. b&w. 16mm. dupe neg (cy 1)
lr, 40 ft. si. b&w. 35mm. dupe neg (cy 2)
lr, 40 ft. si. b&w. 35mm. masterpos.
lr, 40 ft. si. b&w. 35mm. neg ntr.

SHELF LOC'N: FEA8336 & 7837 (print, 2 cy); FRA8662 (neg, cy 1); FPB9873 (neg, cy 2); FPB9874 (fgmp)

Ref sources: The New York *Times*. 12/22/07: pt. 1: [8]; The New York *Herald*. 12/17/07: 4; P&P presidential file; P&P portrait file.

Newsfilm.

SUMMARY: On Dec. 16, 1907, TR, aboard the presidential yacht, Mayflower, travels to Hampton Roads, Va., to see the Great White Fleet off on its voyage around the world. At an informal reception on the Mayflower, TR receives the commander in chief of the fleet, Rear Adm. Robley D. Evans, the three flag officers, their staffs, and captains commanding the sixteen vessels. The man standing next to TR as he greets three naval officers is Evans; the officer on the other side of TR, who walks toward the camera, is probably Rear Adm. Willard H. Brownson, a member of the presidential party. TR greets an unidentified naval officer; his wife, Edith, is visible behind him.

PERSONAL CREDITS: Holmes, Burton, source.

1. Yachts and yachting. 2. Voyages around the world. 3. Hampton Roads. 4. United States—History, Naval—20th century. 5. Roosevelt, Theo-

dore, Pres. U.S., 1858–1919. 6. Evans, Robley D. 7. Brownson, Willard H. 8. Roosevelt, Edith. 9. United States. President, 1901–1909 (Roosevelt) 10. Mayflower (Yacht) 11. United States. Navy—Officers. 12. United States. Navy—History. I. Theodore Roosevelt Association Collection. [mp 76–274]

TR riding in an auto in Chicago, 1917.

Producer unknown [1917?]

© No reg.

lr, 8 ft. si. b&w. 16mm. ref print.
lr, 8 ft. si. b&w. 16mm. dupe neg.
lr, 20 ft. si. b&w. 35mm. pos ntr.

SHELF LOC'N: FAB1052 (print); FRA6019 (neg)

The location and date in the title are unverified.

Newsfilm.

SUMMARY: Views of police on horseback leading a motorcade; TR, standing in an open touring car, waves to a large crowd; several unidentified men are with TR inside the auto. Interior title notes the location as Chicago; this may be a sequence from a parade held in TR's honor during his midwestern speaking tour in support of military preparedness in Apr. 1917.

1. Mounted police—Chicago. 2. Processions. 3. Preparedness. 4. European War, 1914–1918—Public opinion. 5. Chicago. 6. Roosevelt, Theodore, Pres. U.S., 1858–1919. I. Pathe, source. II. Theodore Roosevelt Association Collection. [mp 76–295]

TR riding in auto through crowded streets [1912]

Producer unknown, Sep 1912.

© No reg.

lr, 14 ft. si. b&w. 16mm. ref print.
lr, 14 ft. si. b&w. 16mm. dupe neg.
lr, 14 ft. si. b&w. 16mm. archival pos.
lr, 35 ft. si. b&w. 35mm. neg ntr.

SHELF LOC'N: FAB1120 (print); FRA9241 (neg); FRA6025 (arch pos)

RMA lists the date in the title as 1916.

Ref sources: Los Angeles. Municipal Art Dept. *Mayors of Los Angeles*. 1965: 56–57; Los Angeles *Times*. 9/17/12: pt. 2: 1; San Francisco *Examiner*. 9/17/12:2.

Newsfilm.

SUMMARY: Campaigning in the western states as a third-party presidential candidate under the Progressive banner, TR parades through Los Angeles on Sept. 16, 1912. Clear front shots, taken from a camera moving with the parade, of TR standing in an open touring car and waving his hat to crowds along the sidewalks, with what may be a security car flanking him on the right, mounted police on the left; an open bus carrying officials and members of a band moves past the stationary camera, with a view of parked trolleys in the background; a touring car filled with men and bearing a large moose head passes the camera, followed by TR's car; in the final scene TR's auto pulls to the curb and stops, with crowds filling the sidewalk and streets; the mayor of Los Angeles, George Alexander (1909–1913) is visible in the backseat beside TR.

PERSONAL CREDITS: Chessman, A., source.

1. Processions. 2. Presidents—United States—Election—1912. 3. Trolley buses—Los Angeles, Calif. 4. Los Angeles, Calif. 5. Roosevelt, Theodore, Pres. U.S., 1858–1919. 6. Alexander, George. 7. Progressive Party (Founded 1912) I. Theodore Roosevelt Association Collection. [mp 76–209]

TR scenes purchased from different dealers.
Producer unknown [1912–1927]
© No reg.
    lr, 96 ft. si. b&w. 16mm. ref print.
    lr, 96 ft. si. b&w. 16mm. dupe neg.
    lr, 96 ft. si. b&w. 16mm. archival pos.
SHELF LOC'N: FAB1203 (print); FRA6097 (neg); FRA6098 (arch pos)
The RMA list states that this footage was sent to Famous Players Studio during the filming of *The Rough Riders* and identifying titles were removed. *The Rough Riders* was produced in 1927.

Ref sources: Roosevelt Memorial Association. *Annual Report.* 1927: 20; The *Roosevelt Quarterly.* v. 11, no. 4, 1934; Baltimore *American.* 9/29/18: 6–7, 12; The New York *Times.* 9/16/17: pt. 5: [1]; P&P portrait file; The New York *Herald,* 4/3/18: 16; Harvard University. Library. Theodore Roosevelt Collection.

Newsfilm; compilation.

SUMMARY: A compilation film which consists of views of TR engaging in a variety of activities: 1) TR stands in an open car and tips his hat to a crowd; he walks with a group of men, one of whom wears a pennant bearing the inscription Oklahoma; TR, again in an open automobile; the film was probably taken ca. 1917–1918; 2) TR speaks at the opening of the fourth Liberty Loan campaign in Oriole Park, Baltimore, Md., on Sept. 28, 1918; the people behind him on the platform are Dr. and Mrs. Thomas J. Preston and Emerson C. Harrington, governor of Maryland; 3) TR alights from an automobile accompanied by a group of men, probably during his Jan. 20–21, 1916, visit to Philadelphia; one of the men is Edwin A. Van Valkenburg, edi-

tor of the Philadelphia *North American*; TR shakes Van Valkenburg's hand, then enters a house; 4) on Oyster Bay, TR rows alone away from shore; in the second sequence his son Archie helps TR alight and, with an unidentified boy, secures the boat; 5) TR sits in a chair on the lawn of Sagamore Hill, probably in 1918; 6) on Sept. 8, 1917, TR addresses suffragists at Sagamore Hill; 7) TR speaks vigorously, probably during WWI; 8) wearing a kerchief, TR delivers an address, probably in the West during his 1912 Progressive campaign; 9) TR at his desk at the *Metropolitan Magazine* with a man who is possibly Carl Hovey, the magazine's editor; 10) TR delivers a Memorial Day address at Mineola, N.Y., in 1917; 11) additional footage of TR with suffragists; 12) TR reads a speech to a delegation of volunteer workers for the third Liberty Loan, at Sagamore Hill, Apr. 2, 1918; as an aide gives him names, TR greets members of the group; 13) TR speaks from a decorated stand in Fargo, N.D., during his 1912 Progressive campaign.

1. Baltimore. Oriole Baseball Park. 2. Oyster Bay, N.Y. Sagamore Hill. 3. Suffrage—New York (State) 4. Women—Suffrage—New York (State) 5. Women's rights—New York (State) 6. Presidents—United States—Election—1912. 7. Baltimore. 8. Philadelphia. 9. Oyster Bay, N.Y. 10. Oyster Bay, N.Y.—Harbor. 11. New York (City) 12. Mineola, N.Y. 13. Fargo, N.D. 14. Roosevelt, Theodore, Pres. U.S., 1858–1919. 15. Roosevelt, Theodore, Pres. U.S., 1858–1919—Addresses, essays, lectures. 16. Preston, Thomas J. 17. Preston, Frances Folsom Cleveland. 18. Harrington, Emerson C. 19. Van Valkenburg, Edwin A. 20. Roosevelt, Archibald B. 21. Hovey, Carl. 22. United States. Laws, statutes, etc. Liberty loan acts. 23. Maryland. Liberty Loan Committee. 24. Maryland. Governor, 1916–1920 (Harrington) 25. Progressive Party (Founded 1912) 26. New York (City). Liberty Loan Committee. 27. Metropolitan magazine. I. Roosevelt Memorial Association, source. II. Theodore Roosevelt Association Collection. [mp 76–236]

TR seated at his desk in the Outlook office [1914?]
Producer unknown [1914?]
© No reg.
    lr, 7 ft. si. b&w. 16mm. ref print.
    lr, 7 ft. si. b&w. 16mm. dupe neg.
    lr, 18 ft. si. b&w. 35mm. pos ntr.
SHELF LOC'N: FAB897 (print); FRA5892 (neg)
RMA lists the date in the title as 1917; since TR's affiliation with *The Outlook* ended in 1914, that year is the last probable date of the film.

Newsfilm.

SUMMARY: TR works at his desk in the New York City office of *The Outlook*, a small but influential weekly journal of opinion for which he became a special contributing editor early in 1909.

1. New York (City) 2. Roosevelt, Theodore, Pres. U.S., 1858–1919. 3. Outlook, The. I. International Newsreel Corporation, source. II. Theodore Roosevelt Association Collection. [mp 76–113]

TR speaking at Battery Park, New York, June 1910.

Producer unknown, Jun 1910.

© No reg.

lr, 24 ft. si. b&w. 16mm. ref print.

lr, 24 ft. si. b&w. 16mm. archival pos.

lr, 61 ft. si. b&w. 35mm. neg ntr.

SHELF LOC'N: FAB697 (print); FRA5742 (arch pos)

Ref source: P&P portrait file.

Newsfilm.

SUMMARY: On June 18, 1910, TR was welcomed home to New York City after a fifteen-month tour abroad. City ceremonies included brief speeches delivered by TR and Mayor William J. Gaynor at Battery Park. The film includes side and front views of TR speaking from written notes on the Battery platform, with Mayor Gaynor standing behind him; someone who appears to be a Spanish-American War veteran assisting on the platform; photographers and reporters, as well as top hats of notables, visible around the base of the stand.

1. New York (City) 2. New York (City)—Parks—Battery. 3. Roosevelt, Theodore, Pres. U.S., 1858–1919—Addresses, essays, lectures. 4. Gaynor, William J. 5. United States. Army. 1st Cavalry (Volunteer) I. Warner Brothers, source. II. Theodore Roosevelt Association Collection. [mp 76–23]

TR speaking at Newburgh, N.Y. [1918]

Producer unknown, Sep 1918.

© No reg.

lr, 10 ft. si. b&w. 16mm. ref print.

lr, 10 ft. si. b&w. 16mm. archival pos.

SHELF LOC'N: FAB1036 (print); FRA6008 (arch pos)

RMA lists the dates in the title as 1917–18.

Ref sources: Dunphy, Edward P. *Newburgh in the World War*. 1924: 178–180; The New York *Herald*. 9/3/18: 4; United States. National Archives and Records Service. Audiovisual Archives Division.

Newsfilm.

SUMMARY: On Labor Day, Sept. 2, 1918, TR visits Newburgh, N. Y., where he speaks on the vital need for ships in order to win the war and watches the launching of the S. S. Newburgh. The camera pans as TR speaks to a large crowd from the second-story porch of a building, probably at Newburgh Shipyards, Inc. Long shot of TR and a group of men and women on the platform beside the bow of the S.S. Newburgh; included in the group are Thomas C. Desmond, president of the shipyard, and Maud H. Bush, the woman nearest the bow and sponsor of the ship.

1. Shipyards. 2. Ships—Launching. 3. Labor Day. 4. Newburgh, N.Y. 5. Roosevelt, Theodore, Pres. U.S., 1858–1919—Addresses, essays, lectures. 6. Desmond, Thomas C. 7. Bush, Maud Howard. 8. Newburgh (Ship) 9. Newburgh Shipyards, inc. I. Roosevelt Memorial Association, source. II. Theodore Roosevelt Association Collection. [mp 76–171]

TR speaking at Oyster Bay, July 4, 1916.

Producer unknown, Jul 1916.

© No reg.

lr, 31 ft. si. b&w. 16mm. ref print (cy 1)

lr, 81 ft. si. b&w. 35mm. ref print (cy 2)

lr, 31 ft. si. b&w. 16mm. archival pos.

lr, 77 ft. si. b&w. 35mm. neg ntr.

SHELF LOC'N: FAB881 (print, cy 1); FEA7628 (print, cy 2); FRA5868 (arch pos)

The film is out of sequence.

Newsfilm.

SUMMARY: TR speaks from a decorated gazebo on July 4, 1916, to gathered townspeople in Oyster Bay. Speaking on the possibility of war with Mexico, TR in his unscheduled address stresses the need for national military strength. Close view of TR speaking and acknowledging the cheers of the crowd; long shot of the gazebo filled with people and the crowd below. Frederic R. Coudert, TR's neighbor at Oyster Bay and the scheduled speaker at the celebration, appears, holding his hat, on the platform behind TR. The man beside TR may be Howard C. Smith, identified in newspaper accounts as the master of ceremonies.

1. Fourth of July celebrations. 2. Fourth of July orations. 3. Oyster Bay, N.Y. 4. Roosevelt, Theodore, Pres. U.S., 1858–1919—Addresses, essays, lectures. 5. Coudert, Frederic R. I. Warner Brothers, source. II. Theodore Roosevelt Association Collection. [mp 76–98]

TR speaking at [Pueblo] Colorado, 1912.

Producer unknown, Sep 1912.

THE MIRAGE.

A cartoon from the *New York World*, December 10, 1912, following TR's unsuccessful Progressive campaign.

© No reg.
    lr, 34 ft. si. b&w. 16mm. ref print.
    lr, 34 ft. si. b&w. 16mm. dupe neg.
    lr, 34 ft. si. b&w. 16mm. archival pos.
SHELF LOC'N: FAB674 (print); FRA5715 (neg); FRA5716 (arch pos)

RMA lists the location in the title as Denver, Colorado.

Ref source: *Rocky Mountain News*, Denver. 9/20/12: 1–3.

Newsfilm.

SUMMARY: As part of a western tour, TR addresses a crowd in his campaign for the presidency under the Progressive party banner in what appears to be Pueblo, Colo., on Sept. 19, 1912. Long shots of the crowd, with views of two cameramen on a platform with the sign: Mile High Photo Co., Denver. Views from varying distances of TR, in a decorated gazebo, speaking from a prepared text; three unidentified men are seated inside the gazebo; long shots of the crowd, with some people on horseback and a body of water visible in the background.

PERSONAL CREDITS: Braunstein, Cy, source.

1. Political parties—Colorado. 2. Presidents—United States—Election—1912. 3. Pueblo, Colo. 4. Roosevelt, Theodore, Pres. U.S., 1858–1919—

Addresses, essays, lectures. 5. Progressive Party (Founded 1912) I. Theodore Roosevelt Association Collection. [mp 76–5]

TR speaking at Sagamore Hill [1916–1918] [1]

Producer unknown, 1916–1918.
  © No reg.
    lr, 20 ft. si. b&w. 16mm. ref print (cy 1)
    lr, 59 ft. si. b&w. 16mm. ref print (cy 2)
    lr, 50 ft. si. b&w. 35mm. ref print (cy 3–2 cy)
    lr, 20 ft. si. b&w. 16mm. dupe neg (cy 1)
    lr, 59 ft. si. b&w. 16mm. dupe neg (cy 2)
    lr, 50 ft. si. b&w. 35mm. dupe neg (cy 3–2 cy)
    lr, 50 ft. si. b&w. 35mm. masterpos.
    lr, 50 ft. si. b&w. 16mm. archival pos.
    lr, 50 ft. si. b&w. 35mm. pos ntr (2 cy)
    lr, 148 ft. si. b&w. 35mm. pos ntr.
    lr, 50 ft. si. b&w. 35mm. neg ntr.
SHELF LOC'N: FAB978 (print, cy 1); FAB986 (print, cy 2); FEA7310 & 7311 (print, cy 3–2 cy); FRA5949 (neg, cy 1); FRA5962 (neg, cy 2); FPB7739 & 7740 (neg, cy 3–2 cy); FPB7738 (fgmp); FRA5950 (arch pos)

RMA titles: *TR Speaking at Sagamore Hill*, 1917; *TR Speaking at Sagamore Hill, 1917–1918*.

Films vary in length due to longer printing of interior titles, lack of some titles, and addition of main title.

Ref sources: New York *Tribune*. 5/28/16: pt. 1: 1–2; 6/4/16: pt. 5: 1; Harvard University. Library. Theodore Roosevelt Collection.

Newsfilm; compilation.

SUMMARY: Three sequences of TR addressing groups from the porch at Sagamore Hill. The first sequence shows TR speaking to a group of people on Sept. 8, 1917, at the opening of the second New York State suffrage campaign at Sagamore Hill. The second sequence is probably TR encouraging New York District volunteer workers for the third Liberty Loan on Apr. 2, 1918. Final views of TR addressing the large crowd which came to demonstrate support for him for the 1916 presidential nomination. The May 27, 1916, rally was organized by members of the Roosevelt Non-Partisan League. Interior titles, which appear to be TR quotations, stress the need for loyal American citizens and for judicious American dealings with other nations.

PERSONAL CREDITS: Foster, source.

1. Oyster Bay, N.Y. Sagamore Hill. 2. Suffrage—New York (State) 3. Women—Suffrage—New York

(State) 4. Women's rights—New York (State) 5. Presidents—United States—Nomination. 6. Presidents—United States—Election—1916. 7. Oyster Bay, N.Y. 8. Roosevelt, Theodore, Pres. U.S., 1858–1919—Addresses, essays, lectures. 9. New York (City). Liberty Loan Committee. 10. United States. Laws, statutes, etc. Liberty loan acts. 11. Roosevelt Non-Partisan League. I. Community Motion Picture Service, inc., source. II. Theodore Roosevelt Association Collection. III. Editorial by the late Theodore Roosevelt [Title] [mp 76–150]

TR speaking at Sagamore Hill [1916–1918] [2]
Producer unknown, 1916–1918.

© No reg.

lr, 11 ft. si. b&w. 16mm. ref print.
lr, 11 ft. si. b&w. 16mm. dupe neg.
lr, 27 ft. si. b&w. 35mm. pos ntr.

SHELF LOC'N: FAB1055 (print); FRA6026 (neg)

RMA title: *TR Speaking at Sagamore Hill, 1917.*
Newsfilm; compilation.

SUMMARY: Three sequences of TR addressing groups from the porch at Sagamore Hill. The first sequence shows TR speaking to a group of people on Sept. 8, 1917, at the opening of the second New York State suffrage campaign at Sagamore Hill. The second sequence is probably TR encouraging New York District volunteer workers for the third Liberty Loan on Apr. 2, 1918. Final views of TR addressing the large crowd which came to demonstrate support for him for the 1916 presidential nomination. The May 27, 1916, rally was organized by members of the Roosevelt Non-Partisan League. Interior titles, which appear to be TR quotations, stress the need for loyal American citizens and for judicious American dealings with other nations.

1. Oyster Bay, N.Y. Sagamore Hill. 2. Suffrage—New York (State) 3. Women—Suffrage—New York (State) 4. Women's rights—New York (State) 5. Presidents—United States—Nomination. 6. Presidents—United States—Election—1916. 7. Oyster Bay, N.Y. 8. Roosevelt, Theodore, Pres. U.S., 1858–1919—Addresses, essays, lectures. 9. New York (City). Liberty Loan Committee. 10. United States. Laws, statutes, etc. Liberty loan acts. 11. Roosevelt Non-Partisan League. I. United States. Bureau of Reclamation, source. II. Theodore Roosevelt Association Collection. [mp 76–151]

TR speaking at Sagamore Hill [1916–1918 and scenes of his early career]
Producer unknown [1897?]–1918.

© No reg.

lr, 64 ft. si. b&w. 16mm. ref print.
lr, 64 ft. si. b&w. 16mm. dupe neg.
lr, 64 ft. si. b&w. 16mm. archival pos.

SHELF LOC'N: FAB2277 (print); FRA8316 (neg); FRA7844 (arch pos)

RMA title: *TR Speaking at Sagamore Hill, 1917–1918.*

Factual; biographical, compilation; still film.

SUMMARY: Approximately half of this compilation film shows TR speaking on different occasions from the porch at Sagamore Hill; close and medium shots of TR. At ca. ft. 2, TR speaks to a group of men and boys; at ca. ft. 20, TR addresses Liberty Loan workers from New York City on Apr. 2, 1918; at ca. ft. 28, TR speaks to a large group who came to demonstrate their support for him as a presidential candidate May 27, 1916. The remaining half of the film depicts TR's early career with a still photo of TR standing by a desk; the south portico of the White House is visible in the background as TR walks down the steps of the old State, War, and Navy Building in Washington, D.C. ca. 1897–98, when he was assistant secretary of the navy; a still photo of TR in his Rough Rider uniform; a still photo probably representing his service as assistant secretary of the navy; a photo of TR and President William McKinley sitting outdoors; a portrait of TR; views of TR's 1905 inaugural parade.

PERSONAL CREDITS: Lee, A., source.

1. Oyster Bay, N.Y. Sagamore Hill. 2. Presidents — United States—Election—1916. 3. Presidents—United States—Nomination. 4. Washington, D.C. White House. 5. Washington, D.C. State, War and Navy Building. 6. Inauguration Day. 7. Processions. 8. Oyster Bay, N.Y. 9. Washington, D.C. 10. Washington, D. C.—Public buildings. 11. Roosevelt, Theodore, Pres. U.S., 1858–1919. 12. Roosevelt, Theodore, Pres. U.S., 1858–1919—Addresses, essays, lectures. 13. Roosevelt, Theodore, Pres. U.S., 1858–1919—Military leadership. 14. McKinley, William, Pres. U.S., 1843–1901. 15. Roosevelt, Theodore, Pres. U.S., 1858–1919—Inauguration, 1905. 16. United States. Laws, statutes, etc. Liberty loan acts. 17. New York (City). Liberty Loan Committee. I. Theodore Roosevelt Association Collection. [mp 76–375]

TR speaking at St. Paul, Minn., 1918.
Producer unknown [1918?]

© No reg.

lr, 6 ft. si. b&w. 16mm. ref print.
lr, 6 ft. si. b&w. 16mm. archival pos.

SHELF LOC'N: FAB1069 (print); FRA6043 (arch pos)

The location and date in the title are unverified. Newsfilm; views.

SUMMARY: Close-up of TR holding a prepared text in his hand and speaking to the camera. He wears a mourning armband for his son Quentin, who died in France, July 1918.

PERSONAL CREDITS: Hollis, V. P., source.

1. European War, 1914–1918—Public opinion. 2. St. Paul, Minn. 3. Roosevelt, Theodore, Pres. U.S., 1858–1919—Addresses, essays, lectures. I. Theodore Roosevelt Association Collection. [mp 76–288]

TR speaking at [St. Paul, Minnesota, 1917]
Producer unknown, Sep 1917.

© No reg.

lr, 3 ft. si. b&w. 16mm. ref print.
lr, 3 ft. si. b&w. 16mm. dupe neg.
lr, 7 ft. si. b&w. 35mm. pos ntr.

SHELF LOC'N: FAB882 (print); FRA5869 (neg)

RMA lists the location and date in the title as Albany, New York, 1916. The interior title, which refers to "the late Theodore Roosevelt," indicates that the film may be a reissue; the company and date of reissue are unknown.

Ref sources: St. Paul *Pioneer Press.* 9/29/17: 1; Chrislock, Carl H. *The Progressive Era in Minnesota, 1899–1918.* 1971.

Newsfilm.

SUMMARY: On Sept. 28, 1917, TR speaks in support of military preparedness at a large pro-war gathering assembled in his honor in St. Paul, Minn. Close side shot of TR speaking from a platform to crowds; a parade passes along the street in the background while he speaks. Identified on the platform behind TR is Joseph A. A. Burnquist, governor of Minn. (1915–1921). The interior title, which incorrectly notes the location as Albany, suggest TR's concern for U.S. military superiority on land, sea, and air.

1. Preparedness. 2. European War, 1914–1918—Public opinion. 3. Processions. 4. St. Paul, Minn. 5. Roosevelt, Theodore, Pres. U.S., 1858–1919—Addresses, essays, lectures. 6. Burnquist, Joseph A. A. 7. Minnesota. Governor, 1915–1921 (Burnquist) I. United States. Army Air Forces, source. II. Theodore Roosevelt Association Collection. [mp 76–101]

TR speaking at the Battery, 1910.
Producer unknown, Jun 1910.

© No reg.

lr, 23 ft. si. b&w. 16mm. ref print.
lr, 57 ft. si. b&w. 35mm. masterpos.
lr, 23 ft. si. b&w. 16mm. archival pos.
lr, 57 ft. si. b&w. 35mm. dupe neg ntr.

SHELF LOC'N: FAB696 (print); FPB7956 (fgmp); FRA5741 (arch pos)

Ref source: P&P portrait file.

Newsfilm.

SUMMARY: Upon returning to the United States after an extended tour abroad, TR is welcomed with eleaborate festivities in New York City on June 18, 1910. Views of TR and Cornelius Vanderbilt, chairman of the welcoming committee, walking toward the Battery Park platform, with photographers lining their approach; Mayor William J. Gaynor greeting TR at the base of the Battery platform, with the spectator stand visible in the background; side view of TR and Gaynor on the platform.

1. New York (City) 2. New York (City)—Parks—Battery. 3. Roosevelt, Theodore, Pres. U.S., 1858–1919—Addresses, essays, lectures. 4. Gaynor, William J. 5. Vanderbilt, Cornelius, 1873–1942. I. Roosevelt Memorial Association, source. II. Theodore Roosevelt Association Collection. [mp 76–13]

TR speaking at the dedication of Roosevelt Dam, 1911.
Producer unknown, Mar 1911.

© No reg.

lr, 9 ft. si. b&w. 16mm. ref print.
lr, 9 ft. si. b&w. 16mm. archival pos.
lr, 22 ft. si. b&w. 35mm. neg ntr.

SHELF LOC'N: FAB956 (print); FRA5921 (arch pos)

Ref sources: Sloan, Richard E., ed. *History of Arizona.* v. 2, 1930: 316–322; *Arizona Republican,* Phoenix. 3/18/11: 1–2; 3/19/11: 1; P&P portrait file.

Newsfilm.

SUMMARY: On Mar. 18, 1911, TR speaks at the dedication of the Roosevelt Dam. Providing irrigation for the Salt River Valley area of the territory of Arizona, the dam is largely the result of TR's reclamation efforts while President. On the driveway along the top of the dam, TR, officials, and a crowd look intently over the side of the dam; TR has probably just pushed the electric switch opening the sluice gates on the dam's northern slope. Long shot of TR addressing the crowd, with the following officials identified behind him on the platform: Territorial Governor of Arizona Richard E. Sloan; Louis C. Hill, engineer in charge of dam construction; and Benjamin A. Fowler, president of the National Irrigation Congress.

PERSONAL CREDITS: Howe, Lyman, source.

1. Roosevelt Dam. 2. Dedication services. 3. Dams— Arizona. 4. Reclamation of land—Arizona. 5. Salt River Valley, Ariz. 6. Salt River, Ariz. 7. Roosevelt, Theodore, Pres. U.S., 1858–1919— Addresses, essays, lectures. 8. Sloan, Richard E. 9. Hill, Louis C. 10. Fowler, Benjamin A. 11. Arizona (Ter.). Governor, 1909–1912 (Sloan) I. Theodore Roosevelt Association Collection. [mp 76–124]

TR speaking [at the Panama-Pacific Exposition, 1915]
Producer unknown, Jul 1915.
© No reg.
lr, 7 ft. si. b&w. 16mm. ref print (cy 1)
lr, 12 ft. si. b&w. 16mm. ref print (cy 2)
lr, 12 ft. si. b&w. 16mm. dupe neg.
lr, 7 ft. si. b&w. 16mm. archival pos.
lr, 29 ft. si. b&w. 35mm. pos ntr.
SHELF LOC'N: FAB1032 (print, cy 1); FAB1040 (print, cy 2); FRA6012 (neg); FRA6005 (arch pos)
RMA title: *TR Speaking for YMCA, 1917–18.*
Copies vary in length due to longer printing of a scene.
Ref sources: San Francisco *Examiner.* 7/21/15: 1–2; 7/22/15: 4; San Francisco *Chronicle.* 7/22/15: 5; Harvard University. Library. Theodore Roosevelt Collection.
Newsfilm.
SUMMARY: TR speaks on "Roosevelt Day," July 21, 1915, from the Court of the Universe at the Panama-Pacific International Exposition in San Francisco. Medium-close views from a low camera angle of TR delivering his speech with the prepared text in his hand.

1. Exhibitions. 2. San Francisco—Exhibitions. 3. San Francisco—Plazas—Court of the Universe. 4. San Francisco. 5. Roosevelt, Theodore, Pres. U.S., 1858–1919—Addresses, essays, lectures. 6. Panama-Pacific International Exposition, 1915. I. Roosevelt Memorial Association, source. II. Young Men's Christian Associations, source. III. Theodore Roosevelt Association Collection. [mp 76–296]

TR speaking during War, 1917–1918.
Producer unknown [1917?]
© No reg.
lr, 15 ft. si. b&w. 35mm. ref print.
lr, 15 ft. si. b&w. 35mm. dupe neg.

lr, 16 ft. si. b&w. 35mm. pos ntr.
SHELF LOC'N: FEA7308 (print); FPB7736 (neg)
Dates in the title are unverified.
Factual; views.
SUMMARY: Medium shot of TR speaking from a raised structure, with an American flag in the background, on an unidentified occasion.

1. European War, 1914–1918—Public opinion. 2. Roosevelt, Theodore, Pres. U.S., 1858–1919 —Addresses, essays, lectures. I. International Newsreel Corporation, source. II. Theodore Roosevelt Association Collection. [mp 76–275]

TR speaking from Cathedral steps, Panama.
Producer unknown, Nov 1906.
© No reg.
lr, 44 ft. si. b&w. 16mm. ref print.
lr, 44 ft. si. b&w. 16mm. dupe neg.
lr, 111 ft. si. b&w. 35mm. pos ntr.
SHELF LOC'N: FAB1047 (print); FRA6013 (neg)
Film sequences are partially duplicated.
Ref sources: Washington *Post.* 11/16/06: 1; New York *Tribune.* 11/16/06: 1; United States. President, 1901–1909 (Roosevelt). *Special Message of the President of the United States Concerning the Panama Canal.* 1906.
Newsfilm.
SUMMARY: TR became the first president in office to visit a foreign country while on an inspection tour of the Panama Canal. On Nov. 15, 1906, on a platform on the steps of the Cathedral, Panama City, Manuel Amador Guerrero, first president of Panama, delivers a welcoming address to TR as dignitaries arrive. Two women arrive at the ceremony; the woman on the right may be Edith Roosevelt; TR then speaks.

1. Panama (City) 2. Roosevelt, Theodore, Pres. U.S., 1858–1919—Addresses, essays, lectures. 3. Roosevelt, Theodore, Pres. U.S., 1858–1919— Journey to Panama, 1906. 4. Amador Guerrero, Manuel, Pres. Panama, 1833–1909—Addresses, essays, lectures. 5. Roosevelt, Edith. 6. United States. President, 1901–1909 (Roosevelt) 7. Panama. Presidente, 1904–1908 (Amador Guerrero) 8. Catedral, Panama (City) I. Paramount, source. II. Theodore Roosevelt Association Collection. [mp 76–181]

TR speaking from train platform, 1912.
Producer unknown, Sep 1912.
© No reg.
lr, 10 ft. si. b&w. 16mm. ref print.
lr, 25 ft. si. b&w. 35mm. masterpos.

lr, 10 ft. si. b&w. 16mm. archival pos.

lr, 25 ft. si. b&w. 35mm. neg ntr.

SHELF LOC'N: FAB1059 (print); FPB7586 (fgmp); FRA6016 (arch pos)

Ref sources: P&P portrait file; The Fargo *Forum*. 9/6/12: 1.

Newsfilm.

SUMMARY: In the vicinity of Fargo, N.D., Sept. 6, 1912, TR speaks on behalf of his presidential candidacy under the banner of the newly formed Progressive party. Views of men, women, and children gathered around the rear of the campaign train as TR leans forward over the train railing and speaks; shot of the crowd; medium-close silhouette of TR and three men conversing as the train pulls away: one of the men appears to be George E. Roosevelt, TR's cousin and campaign secretary in the 1912 election.

1. Political parties—North Dakota. 2. Presidents — United States—Election—1912. 3. Fargo, N.D. 4. Roosevelt, Theodore, Pres. U.S., 1858–1919 —Addresses, essays, lectures. 5. Roosevelt, George E. 6. Progressive Party (Founded 1912) I. Roose-

velt Memorial Association, source. II. Theodore Roosevelt Association Collection. [mp 76–197]

TR speaking in Panama, November 1906.

Producer unknown, Nov 1906.

© No reg.

lr, 130 ft. si. b&w. 35mm. ref print.

lr, 130 ft. si. b&w. 35mm. dupe neg.

lr, 131 ft. si. b&w. 35mm. pos ntr.

SHELF LOC'N: FEA7313 (print); FPB7743 (neg)

Ref sources: Washington *Post*. 11/16/06: 1; New York *Tribune*. 11/16/06: 1; United States. President, 1901–1909 (Roosevelt). *Special Message of the President of the United States Concerning the Panama Canal.* 1906.

Newsfilm.

SUMMARY: TR became the first president in office to visit a foreign country while on an inspection tour of the Panama Canal. On Nov. 15, 1906, TR and Manuel Amador Guerrero, first president of Panama, and two unidentified men arrive and stand on a platform on the steps of the Cathedral in Panama City. Medium shot of two women arriv-

Roosevelt broke a 117-year tradition by becoming the first president to visit a foreign country during his term of office. The film *TR Speaking in Panama, November 1906*, contains long shots of Roosevelt responding to the official welcoming address delivered by President Manuel Amador Guerrero of Panama.

ing at the ceremony; the woman on the right may be Edith Roosevelt. Long shot of President Amador Guerrero delivering a welcoming address as dignitaries look on; TR then speaks.

1. Panama (City) 2. Roosevelt, Theodore, Pres. U.S., 1858-1919—Addresses, essays, lectures. 3. Roosevelt, Theodore, Pres. U.S., 1858-1919—Journey to Panama, 1906. 4. Amador Guerrero, Manuel, Pres. Panama, 1833-1909—Addresses, essays, lectures. 5. Roosevelt, Edith. 6. United States. President, 1901-1909 (Roosevelt) 7. Panama. Presidente, 1904-1908 (Amador Guerrero) 8. Catedral, Panama (City) I. Paramount, source. II. Theodore Roosevelt Association Collection. [mp 76-225]

TR speaking in St. Paul, Minnesota, 1918.
Producer unknown [1918?]
© No reg.
   lr, 18 ft. si. b&w. 16mm. ref print.
   lr, 18 ft. si. b&w. 16mm. dupe neg.
   lr, 18 ft. si. b&w. 16mm. archival pos.
SHELF LOC'N: FAB668 (print); FRA5703 (neg); FRA5704 (arch pos)
Location and date in the title are unverified.
Newsfilm; views.
SUMMARY: Views of TR, wearing a mourning armband for his son Quentin, delivering a speech from a covered platform to a large crowd gathered in an open area of what appears to be a factory and surrounding area; close-up of TR, prepared text in hand, speaking to the camera.
PERSONAL CREDITS: Hollis, V. P., source.
1. Factories. 2. European War, 1914-1918—Public opinion. 3. St. Paul, Minn. 4. Roosevelt, Theodore, Pres. U.S., 1858-1919—Addresses, essays, lectures. I. Theodore Roosevelt Association Collection. [mp 76-7]

TR speaking to a group of men from the porch at Sagamore Hill, 1916.
Producer unknown, May 1916.
© No reg.
   lr, 35 ft. si. b&w. 16mm. ref print.
   lr, 35 ft. si. b&w. 16mm. dupe neg.
   lr, 88 ft. si. b&w. 35mm. pos ntr.
SHELF LOC'N: FAB879 (print); FRA5866 (neg)
Ref sources: New York *Tribune*. 5/28/16: pt. 1: 1-2; 6/4/16: pt. 5: 1; Harvard University. Library. Theodore Roosevelt Collection.
Newsfilm.
SUMMARY: On May 27, 1916, groups of men, the Seventh Regiment Band, and several children march on the road from the Oyster Bay railroad

station to Sagamore Hill to demonstrate their support of TR for the 1916 presidential nomination. Views of TR addressing the large crowd assembled on the lawn of Sagamore Hill. The rally was organized by the Roosevelt Non-Partisan League of New York City.

1. Oyster Bay, N.Y. Sagamore Hill. 2. Bands (Music) 3. Presidents—United States—Nomination. 4. Presidents—United States—Election—1916. 5. Oyster Bay, N.Y. 6. Roosevelt, Theodore, Pres. U.S., 1858-1919—Addresses, essays, lectures. 7. New York Infantry. 7th Regiment, 1806-1922 (Militia). Band. 8. Roosevelt Non-Partisan League. I. International Newsreel Corporation, source. II. Theodore Roosevelt Association Collection. [mp 76-93]

TR speaking to a group of suffragettes from the porch at Sagamore Hill [1917]
Producer unknown, Sep 1917.
© No reg.
   lr, 12 ft. si. b&w. 16mm. ref print.
   lr, 12 ft. si. b&w. 16mm. dupe neg.
   lr, 29 ft. si. b&w. 35mm. pos ntr.
SHELF LOC'N: FAB760 (print); FRA5815 (neg)
RMA lists the date in the title as 1916.
Ref sources: Harper, Ida H., ed. *History of Woman Suffrage*. v. 6, 1969; The Brooklyn *Daily Eagle*. 9/9/17: 1, 4; The New York *Times*. 9/16/17: pt. 5: [1]
Newsfilm.
SUMMARY: TR addresses a group of men and women at the opening of the second New York State suffrage campaign on Sept. 8, 1917, at Sagamore Hill. The film includes a side view of TR and a frontal view shot from the rear of the crowd. A woman and a man appear on the porch behind TR; immediately in front of the porch, a man who may be a reporter takes notes.
1. Oyster Bay, N.Y. Sagamore Hill. 2. Suffrage—New York (State) 3. Women's rights—New York (State) 4. Women—Suffrage—New York (State) 5. Women—Legal status, laws, etc. 6. Roosevelt, Theodore, Pres. U.S., 1858-1919—Addresses, essays, lectures. I. International Newsreel Corporation, source. II. Theodore Roosevelt Association Collection. [mp 76-66]

[TR speaks to group at Sagamore Hill, 1]
Producer unknown [1917?]
© No reg.
   lr, 10 ft. si. b&w. 16mm. ref print (3 cy)
   lr, 10 ft. si. b&w. 16mm. archival pos.

SHELF LOC'N: FAB1074 & 1075 & 1140 (print, 3 cy); FRA6049 (arch pos)

RMA title: *TR Speaking at Sagamore Hill to 13th Regiment, May 1917.*

Possible production dates: 1916–1918.

Ref print (cy 1) is out of frame ca. first 6 ft.; ref print (cy 2) is out of frame ca. first 1 ft.; entire ref print (cy 3) is out of frame.

Factual.

SUMMARY: TR speaks to a small group of people, mainly men and boys, from the porch at Sagamore Hill. The season appears to be either spring or fall. The second sequence consists of medium-close shots of TR.

1. Oyster Bay, N.Y. Sagamore Hill. 2. Oyster Bay, N.Y. 3. Roosevelt, Theodore, Pres. U.S., 1858–1919—Addresses, essays, lectures. I. Roosevelt Memorial Association, source. II. Theodore Roosevelt Association Collection. [mp 76–214]

[TR speaks to group at Sagamore Hill, 2]
Producer unknown [1917?]
© No reg.
  lr, 6 ft. si. b&w. 16mm. ref print (2 cy)
  lr, 6 ft. si. b&w. 16mm. dupe neg.
  lr, 18 ft. si. b&w. 35mm. pos ntr.
SHELF LOC'N: FAB1076 & 1077 (print, 2 cy); FRA6050 (neg)

RMA title: *TR Speaking at Sagamore Hill to 13th Regiment, May 1917.*

Possible production dates: 1916–1918.

Factual.

SUMMARY: TR speaks to a small group of people, mainly men and boys, from the porch at Sagamore Hill. The season appears to be either spring or fall.

1. Oyster Bay, N.Y. Sagamore Hill. 2. Oyster Bay, N.Y. 3. Roosevelt, Theodore, Pres. U.S., 1858–1919—Addresses, essays, lectures. I. Roosevelt Memorial Association, source. II. Theodore Roosevelt Association Collection. [mp 76–215]

[TR speaks to group at Sagamore Hill, 3]
Producer unknown [1917?]
© No reg.
  lr, 15 ft. si. b&w. 35mm. ref print (2 cy)
  lr, 15 ft. si. b&w. 35mm. dupe neg (2 cy)
  lr, 15 ft. si. b&w. 35mm. masterpos.
  lr, 16 ft. si. b&w. 35mm. pos ntr.
  lr, 16 ft. si. b&w. 35mm. neg ntr.
SHELF LOC'N: FEA6754 & 7301 (print, 2 cy); FPB7596 & 7597 (neg, 2 cy); FPB7598 (fgmp)

RMA title: *TR Speaking at Sagamore Hill to 13th Regiment, May 1917.*

Possible production dates: 1916–1918.

Flash shot of troops at the end of ref print (cy 1), dupe neg (cy 1), and masterpos may be unrelated footage.

Factual.

SUMMARY: Medium-close shots of TR as he vigorously addresses a group of people from the porch at Sagamore Hill. He then turns and continues to speak with his back to the camera.

1. Oyster Bay, N.Y. Sagamore Hill. 2. Oyster Bay, N.Y. 3. Roosevelt, Theodore, Pres. U.S., 1858–1919—Addresses, essays, lectures. I. Roosevelt Memorial Association, source. II. Theodore Roosevelt Association Collection. [mp 76–216]

TR wearing army coat standing in auto greeting friends at Oyster Bay, 1910.
Producer unknown [1910?]
© No reg.
  lr, 2 ft. si. b&w. 16mm. ref print (cy 1)
  lr, 4 ft. si. b&w. 35mm. ref print (cy 2–2 cy)
  lr, 2 ft. si. b&w. 16mm. dupe neg (cy 1)
  lr, 4 ft. si. b&w. 35mm. dupe neg (cy 2–2 cy)
  lr, 4 ft. si. b&w. 35mm. masterpos.
  lr, 2 ft. si. b&w. 16mm. archival pos.
  lr, 4 ft. si. b&w. 35mm. pos ntr.
  lr, 4 ft. si. b&w. 35mm. dupe neg ntr.
SHELF LOC'N: FAB739 (print, cy 1); FEA6698 & 6699 (print, cy 2–2 cy); FRA-5784 (neg, cy 1); FPB7058 & 7059 (neg, cy 2–2 cy); FPB7057 (fgmp); FRA5785 (arch pos)

Location and date in the title are unverified.

Ref source: P&P presidential file.

Newsfilm; views.

SUMMARY: Medium-close view of TR standing in the rear seat of an auto and addressing a group of people in what may be Oyster Bay, N.Y. A large house fills the immediate background. TR is wearing the army coat he wore during his European trip in 1910.

PERSONAL CREDITS: Farrow, source.

1. Oyster Bay, N.Y. 2. Roosevelt, Theodore, Pres. U.S., 1858–1919—Addresses, essays, lectures. I. Theodore Roosevelt Association Collection. [mp 76–30]

TR with group of men, 1917; TR speaking at dedication of Roosevelt Dam, 1911.
Producer unknown, 1911–[1917?]
© No reg.

lr, 5 ft. si. b&w. 16mm. ref print.

lr, 5 ft. si. b&w. 16mm. dupe neg.

lr, 5 ft. si. b&w. 16mm. archival pos.

SHELF LOC'N: FAB2270 (print); FRA8315 (neg); FRA6360 (arch pos)

The date in the first title is unverified; the location is undetermined.

Ref source: Sloan, Richard E., ed. *History of Arizona.* v. 2, 1930: 316–322.

Factual.

SUMMARY: In the first sequence, TR, attending some kind of rally, poses with a group of men in front of a crowd. In the second sequence, TR speaks at the dedication of Roosevelt Dam on the Salt River in Arizona on Mar. 18, 1911. Seated behind him on the platform are, left to right: a woman who may be Edith Roosevelt; a bald man who is probably Louis C. Hill, supervising engineer of the project; an unidentified man; Benjamin A. Fowler, president of the National Irrigation Congress; another unidentified man; Richard E. Sloan, territorial governor of Arizona; and a man who is probably John P. Orme, president of the Salt River Valley Water Users' Association.

1. Dedication services. 2. Roosevelt Dam. 3. Dams—Arizona. 4. Water-storage—Arizona—Salt River. 5. Arizona. 6. Salt River, Ariz. 7. Salt River Valley, Ariz. 8. Roosevelt, Theodore, Pres. U.S., 1858–1919. 9. Roosevelt, Theodore, Pres. U.S., 1858–1919—Addresses, essays, lectures. 10. Roosevelt, Edith. 11. Hill, Louis C. 12. Fowler, Benjamin A. 13. Sloan, Richard E. 14. Orme, John P. 15. Arizona (Ter.). Governor, 1909–1912 (Sloan) I. Gaumont (Firm), source. II. Theodore Roosevelt Association Collection. III. TR speaking at dedication of Roosevelt Dam, 1911 [Title] [mp 76–308]

TR with naval officers, exterior Navy Club, Boston [1918]

Producer unknown, May 1918.

© No reg.

lr, 3 ft. si. b&w. 16mm. ref print.

lr, 3 ft. si. b&w. 16mm. archival pos.

lr, 8 ft. si. b&w. 35mm. neg ntr.

SHELF LOC'N: FAB1067 (print); FRA6041 (arch pos)

RMA lists the date in the title as 1917.

Ref sources: The Boston *Daily Globe.* 5/3/18: 2; The Boston *Herald.* 5/3/18: 14; *Christian Science Monitor.* 5/3/18: 5, United States. National Archives and Records Service. Audiovisual Archives Division.

Factual.

SUMMARY: In Boston to speak on behalf of the

Liberty Loan, on May 2, 1918, TR also inspects the Naval Service Club on Beacon St. He poses in front of the club with naval officers and enlisted men from the Boston Navy Yard and the Commonwealth Pier.

1. Seamen. 2. Boston, Mass. 3. Roosevelt, Theodore, Pres. U.S., 1858–1919. 4. United States. Navy. 5. United States. Navy—Officers. 6. United States. Navy—Service clubs. 7. Naval Service Club, Boston, Mass. I. Pathe, source. II. Theodore Roosevelt Association Collection. [mp 76–191]

TR with Rough Rider friends.

Producer unknown [191–?]

© No reg.

lr, 30 ft. si. b&w. 35mm. ref print (2 cy)

lr, 30 ft. si. b&w. 35mm. dupe neg (2 cy)

lr, 30 ft. si. b&w. 35mm. masterpos.

lr, 31 ft. si. b&w. 35mm. pos ntr.

lr, 30 ft. si. b&w. 35mm. neg ntr.

SHELF LOC'N: FEA6696 & 6697 (print, 2 cy); FPB7070 & 7061 (neg, 2 cy); FPB7060 (fgmp)

Ref source: P&P portrait file.

Factual; views.

SUMMARY: Scenes of TR in a western setting; the man on TR's immediate left appears to be Albert B. Fall, senator from New Mexico (1913–1921); four unidentified men, two of whom are wearing western hats, may be Rough Riders; a woman is barely visible directly behind TR.

PERSONAL CREDITS: Chessman, A., source.

1. Legislators—New Mexico. 2. Roosevelt, Theodore, Pres. U.S., 1858–1919. 3. Fall, Albert B. 4. United States. Army. 1st Cavalry (Volunteer) I. Theodore Roosevelt Association Collection. [mp 76–41]

Troops making military road in front of Santiago.

Thomas A. Edison, 1898.

© 52059, Thomas A. Edison, 3Sept1898

lr, of 1, 21 ft. si. b&w. 16mm. ref print (cy 1)

lr, of 1, 53 ft. si. b&w. 35mm. ref print (cy 2–2 cy)

lr, of 1, 21 ft. si. b&w. 16mm. dupe neg.

lr, of 1, 21 ft. si. b&w. 16mm. archival pos.

lr, of 1, 53 ft. si. b&w. 35mm. neg ntr.

lr, of 1, 24 ft. si. b&w. 16mm. ref print.

lr, of 1, 24 ft. si. b&w. 16mm. dupe neg.

lr, of 1, 46 ft. si. b&w. 35mm. paper (2 cy)

SHELF LOC'N: FAB1216 (print, cy 1-RMA); FEA7619 & 7620 (print, cy 2–2 cy-RMA); FRA6179 (neg-RMA);

FRA6111 (arch pos-RMA); FLA 4003 (print-Paper); FRA1204 (neg-Paper); LC989 (paper, 2 cy-Paper)

RMA title: *U.S. Troops Making Artillery Road in Santiago, 1898.*

Ref sources: Keller, Allan. *The Spanish-American War.* 1969: 129 [a], 137–140; Freidel, Frank B. *The Splendid Little War.* 1958: 115–117.

Newsfilm; war film.

SUMMARY: Poor roads were a major obstacle in the transporting of men, supplies, and equipment for the attack on Santiago, Cuba, during the last stages of the Spanish-American War of 1898. On portions of the roads there were no bridges, and rainfalls and constant erosion had formed deep gullies; the roads were made usable by corduroying with brush, filling depressions, removing boulders, bridging steams, cutting through woods, and making a new road in part. The soldiers in the film are digging with pickaxes and shovels, probably working on the road that leads to the battlefront near Santiago; in the background, men on horseback are observing.

PERSONAL CREDITS: Kleine, George, source.

1. Roads—Cuba—Maintenance and repair. 2. Transportation, Military. 3. Cuba. 4. United States — History—War of 1898. 5. United States. Army. I. Edison (Thomas A.) inc. II. Theodore Roosevelt Association Collection. III. Paper Print Collection. [mp 76–251]

TR's arrival in Panama, November 1906 [1]
Producer unknown, Nov 1906.

© No reg.

lr, 30 ft. si. b&w. 16mm. ref print.
lr, 30 ft. si. b&w. 16mm. archival pos.
lr, 74 ft. si. b&w. 35mm. dupe neg ntr.

SHELF LOC'N: FAB750 (print); FRA5914 (arch pos)

Ref sources: Washington *Post.* 11/16/06: 1; New York *Tribune.* 11/16/06: 1; United States. President, 1901–1909 (Roosevelt). *Special Message of the President of the United States Concerning the Panama Canal.* 1906.

Newsfilm.

SUMMARY: TR became the first president in office to visit a foreign country while on an inspection tour of the Panama Canal. There are views of the processional on Nov. 15, 1906, in Panama City, including a marching band and escorts on horseback, with spectators gathering; long shot of TR accompanied by Manuel Amador Guerrero, first president of Panama, and two unidentified men standing on a platform on the steps of the Cathedral.

PERSONAL CREDITS: Miles, H., source.

1. Processions. 2. Panama (City) 3. Roosevelt, Theodore, Pres. U. S., 1858–1919—Journey to Panama, 1906. 4. Amador Guerrero, Manuel, Pres. Panama, 1833–1909—Addresses, essays, lectures. 5. United States. President, 1901–1909 (Roosevelt) 6. Panama. Presidente, 1904–1908 (Amador Guerrero) 7. Catedral, Panama (City) I. Theodore Roosevelt Association Collection. [mp 76–86]

TR's arrival in Panama, November 1906 [2]
Producer unknown, Nov 1906.

© No reg.

lr, 87 ft. si. b&w. 35mm. ref print.
lr, 87 ft. si. b&w. 35mm. dupe neg.
lr, 87 ft. si. b&w. 35mm. pos ntr.

SHELF LOC'N: FEA6701 (print); FPB7075 (neg)

Ref sources: Washington *Post.* 11/16/06: 1; New York *Tribune.* 11/16/06: 1; United States. President, 1901–1909 (Roosevelt). *Special Message of the President of the United States Concerning the Panama Canal.* 1906.

Newsfilm.

SUMMARY: TR became the first president in office to visit a foreign country while on an inspection tour of the Panama Canal. There are views of the processional on Nov. 15, 1906, in Panama City, including a marching band and escorts on horseback, with spectators gathering; long shot of TR, accompanied by Manuel Amador Guerrero, first president of Panama, and two unidentified men standing on a platform on the steps of the Cathedral; President Amador Guerrero delivers a welcoming address as dignitaries look on; TR then speaks.

PERSONAL CREDITS: Miles, H., source.

1. Processions. 2. Panama (City) 3. Roosevelt, Theodore, Pres. U.S., 1858–1919—Addresses, essays, lectures. 4. Roosevelt, Theodore, Pres. U.S., 1858–1919—Journey to Panama, 1906. 5. Amador Guerrero, Manuel, Pres. Panama, 1833–1909 —Addresses, essays, lectures. 6. United States. President, 1901–1909 (Roosevelt) 7. Panama. Presidente, 1904–1908 (Amador Guerrero) 8. Catedral, Panama (City) I. Theodore Roosevelt Association Collection. [mp 76–87]

TR's arrival in Panama, November 1906 [3]
Producer unknown, Nov 1906.

© No reg.

lr, 74 ft. si. b&w. 16mm. ref print.
lr, 74 ft. si. b&w. 16mm. dupe neg.
lr, 74 ft. si. b&w. 16mm. archival pos.
lr, 185 ft. si. b&w. 35mm. pos ntr.

SHELF LOC'N: FAB749 (print); FRA8663 (neg); FRA5805 (arch pos)

Ref sources: Washington *Post*. 11/16/06: 1; New York *Tribune*. 11/16/06: 1; United States. President, 1901–1909 (Roosevelt). *Special Message of the President of the United States Concerning the Panama Canal.* 1906.

Newsfilm.

SUMMARY: TR became the first president in office to visit a foreign country while on an inspection tour of the Panama Canal. There are views of the processional on Nov. 15, 1906, in Panama City including a marching band and escorts on horseback, with spectators gathering; long shot of TR, accompanied by Manuel Amador Guerrero, first president of Panama, and two unidentified men standing on a platform on the steps of the Cathedral. Medium shot of two women arriving at the ceremony; the woman on the right may be Edith Roosevelt. Long shot of President Amador Guerrero delivering a welcoming address as dignitaries look on; TR then speaks.

PERSONAL CREDITS: Miles, H., source.

1. Processions. 2. Panama (City) 3. Roosevelt, Theodore, Pres. U.S., 1858–1919—Addresses, essays, lectures. 4. Roosevelt, Theodore, Pres. U.S., 1858–1919—Journey to Panama, 1906. 5. Amador Guerrero, Manuel, Pres. Panama, 1833–1909—Addresses, essays, lectures. 6. Roosevelt, Edith. 7. United States. President, 1901–1909 (Roosevelt) 8. Panama. Presidente, 1904–1908 (Amador Guerrero) 9. Catedral, Panama (City) I. Theodore Roosevelt Association Collection. [mp 76–88]

TR's camp in Africa [1909]

Producer unknown, Aug 1909.

© No reg.

lr, 25 ft. si. b&w. 16mm. ref print (cy 1)
lr, 62 ft. si. b&w. 35mm. ref print (cy 2)
lr, 25 ft. si. b&w. 16mm. archival pos.
lr, 62 ft. si. b&w. 35mm. neg ntr.

SHELF LOC'N: FAB1119 (print, cy 1); FEA6740 (print, cy 2); FRA6063 (arch pos)

RMA lists the date in the title as 1910.

Sources indicate that the photographer is Cherry Kearton.

Ref sources: Kearton, Cherry. *Wild Life across the World.* [1914]: 100–101; *The Moving Picture World.* v. 6, no. 17, 1910: 682–683.

Factual; views.

SUMMARY: Long shots in the area of Mt. Kenya, British East Africa (Kenya) of 1) TR crossing a ford and 2) the Roosevelt campsite, according to the photographer's accounts shot in late Aug. 1909. Views of TR on horseback, followed by porters and members of his party, approaching a rocky stream; TR pauses, permits his horse to drink, then moves to the far bank. A view at the campsite of tents flying the American flag, busy porters, and TR in the background speaking with an unidentified member of his party.

PERSONAL CREDITS: Kearton, Cherry, photographer.

1. Big game hunting—Africa. 2. Kenya. 3. Roosevelt, Theodore, Pres. U.S., 1858–1919—Journey to Africa, 1909–1910. I. Community Motion Picture Service, inc., source. II. Theodore Roosevelt Association Collection. [mp 76–245]

TR's funeral, 1919.

Producer unknown, Jan 1919.

© No reg.

lr, 13 ft. si. b&w. 16mm. ref print.
lr, 13 ft. si. b&w. 16mm. dupe neg.
lr, 13 ft. si. b&w. 16mm. archival pos.

SHELF LOC'N: FAB1000 (print); FRA5986 (neg); FRA5987 (arch pos)

Ref source: P&P portrait file.

Newsfilm.

SUMMARY: Views of Christ Episcopal Church and Youngs Memorial Cemetery, Oyster Bay, N.Y., during TR's funeral, Jan. 8, 1919. Long shots of cars parked in front of the church and crowds on the church lawn; a view of men and women filing up the path to the grave at the cemetery; and a side shot of former President William Howard Taft (1909–1913) and others on the cemetery grounds.

1. Funeral service. 2. Youngs Memorial Cemetery. 3. Oyster Bay, N.Y. 4. Roosevelt, Theodore, Pres. U.S., 1858–1919—Funeral and memorial services. 5. Taft, William Howard, Pres. U.S., 1857–1930. 6. Christ Episcopal Church, Oyster Bay, N.Y. I. General Vision Company, source. II. Theodore Roosevelt Association Collection. [mp 76–158]

TR's funeral at Oyster Bay, 1919.

Universal Film Manufacturing Co., Jan 1919.

© No reg.

lr, 50 ft. si. b&w. 16mm. ref print.
lr, 50 ft. si. b&w. 16mm. dupe neg.
lr, 50 ft. si. b&w. 16mm. masterpos.
lr, 126 ft. si. b&w. 35mm. pos ntr.

(Universal current events [Series])
SHELF LOC'N: FAB999 (print); FRA5982 (neg);
FRA8651 (fgmp)
Ref sources: P&P portrait file; P&P stereo file.
Newsfilm.
SUMMARY: Views of Christ Episcopal Church, the funeral procession, and Youngs Memorial Cemetery during TR's funeral on Jan. 8, 1919, in Oyster Bay, N.Y. Medium-close shot of specially delegated New York City mounted police guards, followed by the hearse, passing on the road in front of the church; long shot at the church entrance of the flag-draped casket being placed in the hearse, with a line of funeral procession autos parked behind, and crowds on the church lawn; closer shot from a different angle of the casket as it is borne through the church entrance to the hearse, with a flag-bearer following behind, and Rev. George E. Talmadge, pastor of Christ Episcopal Church and reader at the simple service, visible in the street beside the hearse; long shot in the cemetery of the casket being shouldered and carried up the steep pathway to the grave site, preceded by Rev. Talmadge and followed by TR's son Archie Roosevelt, in uniform, and other family members; close shot at what appears to be a train station of the following men in attendance at the funeral: Gen. Peyton C. March, Army Chief of Staff; Vice-President Thomas R. Marshall (1913–1921), official representative of the U.S. government at the funeral; and Rear Adm. Cameron M. Winslow; close shots in the crowd at the cemetery of TR's friend, Maj. Gen. Leonard Wood; and Oscar S. Straus, secretary of commerce and labor in TR's cabinet (1906–1909).

1. Funeral service. 2. Youngs Memorial Cemetery. 3. Mounted police—New York (City) 4. Oyster Bay, N.Y. 5. Roosevelt, Theodore, Pres. U.S., 1858–1919—Funeral and memorial services. 6. Roosevelt, Theodore, Pres. U.S., 1858–1919—Family. 7. Talmadge, George E. 8. Roosevelt, Archibald B. 9. March, Peyton C. 10. Marshall, Thomas R. 11. Winslow, Cameron M. 12. Wood, Leonard. 13. Straus, Oscar S. 14. Christ Episcopal Church, Oyster Bay, N.Y. I. Universal Film Manufacturing Company. II. International Newsreel Corporation, source. III. Theodore Roosevelt Association Collection. [mp 76–176]

TR's funeral at Oyster Bay, January 1919 [1]
Producer unknown, Jan 1919.
© No reg.
    lr, 13 ft. si. b&w. 16mm. ref print.

lr, 13 ft. si. b&w. 16mm. dupe neg.
lr, 13 ft. si. b&w. 16mm. archival pos.
SHELF LOC'N: FAB2276 (print); FRA8314
(neg); FRA5981 (arch pos)
Film image is blurred.
Newsfilm.
SUMMARY: Views of TR's funeral on Jan. 8, 1919, at Christ Episcopal Church and Youngs Memorial Cemetery, Oyster Bay, New York. Long shots of crowds on the snow-covered church grounds; cars at the front entrance of the church; men and women filing up the steep cemetery path to TR's grave site; side view of former President William Howard Taft (1909–1913) and unidentified men on the cemetery grounds.
PERSONAL CREDITS: Lee, A., source.

1. Funeral service. 2. Youngs Memorial Cemetery. 3. Oyster Bay, N.Y. 4. Roosevelt, Theodore, Pres. U.S., 1858–1919—Funeral and memorial services. 5. Taft, William Howard, Pres. U.S., 1857–1930. 6. Christ Episcopal Church, Oyster Bay, N.Y. I. Theodore Roosevelt Association Collection. [mp 76–155]

TR's funeral at Oyster Bay, January 1919 [2]
Pathe News, Jan 1919.
© No reg.
    lr, 46 ft. si. b&w. 16mm. ref print.
    lr, 46 ft. si. b&w. 16mm. dupe neg.
    lr, 46 ft. si. b&w. 16mm. masterpos.
    lr, 114 ft. si. b&w. 35mm. pos ntr.

TR's funeral procession in Youngs Memorial Cemetery, overlooking Oyster Bay, January 8, 1919.

153

(Pathe News [newsreel])
SHELF LOC'N: FAB997 (print); FRA5985 (neg);
FRA8653(fgmp)
Ref source: P&P portrait file.
Newsfilm.
SUMMARY: Views of TR's funeral on Jan. 8, 1919, including scenes of the funeral procession, Youngs Memorial Cemetery, and exterior shorts of Christ Episcopal Church, Oyster Bay, N.Y. Specially delegated New York City mounted police lead the funeral procession along a road through snow-covered fields; the procession passes by crowds lining the road; long shot of Christ Episcopal Church, with crowds on the grounds; side view of the casket being borne from the church entrance to a hearse, with a flag-bearer following behind and Rev. George E. Talmadge, pastor of the church and reader at the simple service, visible in the street beside the hearse; the hearse pulls away from the church; men and women walk up the steep pathway to the grave site in Youngs Memorial Cemetery; side view of former President William Howard Taft (1909-1913) and others on the cemetery grounds; long shot of the casket being shouldered and carried up the path, preceded by Rev. Talmadge, and followed by Archie Roosevelt, TR's son, in uniform, and other family members; medium-close shot at what appears to be a train station of Vice-President Thomas R. Marshall (1913–1921), official U. S. government representative at the funeral, and Gen. Peyton C. March, Army Chief of Staff; shot of Taft, assisted by an unidentified man, walking down the hill after the ceremony at the grave site.

1. Funeral service. 2. Youngs Memorial Cemetery. 3. Mounted police—New York (City) 4. Oyster Bay, N. Y. 5. Roosevelt, Theodore, Pres. U. S., 1858–1919—Funeral and memorial services. 6. Roosevelt, Theodore, Pres. U. S., 1858–1919—Family. 7. Talmadge, George E. 8. Taft, William Howard, Pres. U. S., 1857–1930. 9. Roosevelt, Archibald B. 10. Marshall, Thomas R. 11. March, Peyton C. 12. Christ Episcopal Church, Oyster Bay, N. Y. I. Pathe. II. Pathe, source. III. Theodore Roosevelt Association Collection. [mp 76–154]

[TR's inaugural ceremony, 1905]
Producer unknown, Mar 1905.
© No reg.
    lr, 99 ft. si. b&w. 35mm. ref print.
    lr, 99 ft. si. b&w. 35mm. dupe neg.
    lr, 99 ft. si. b&w. 35mm. masterpos (2 cy)
    lr, 98 ft. si. b&w. 35mm. neg ntr.

SHELF LOC'N: FEA7314 (print); FPB7744 (neg); FPB7745 & 8057 (fgmp, 2 cy)
RMA title: *TR's Inaugural Address, 1905.*
Research indicates that the film is of TR taking the oath of office rather than delivering his inaugural address.
Ref sources: Washington, D. C. Inaugural Committee, 1905. *Inauguration of Theodore Roosevelt as President of the United States, March 4, 1905.* [1905]; Washington *Post.* 3/5/05: 1–2; The *Evening Star,* Washington, D. C. 3/4/05: pt. 2: 5; 3/5/05: 1–2; New York *Tribune.* 3/5/05: 3; The New York *Herald.* 3/5/05: 5; P&P stereo file.
Newsfilm.
SUMMARY: On Mar. 4, 1905. TR is inaugurated in Washington, D. C., with much celebration and fanfare. TR rides in an open landau on Fifteenth St., NW, escorted by mounted Rough Riders; Secret Service men and detectives walk on either side of the carriage; TR tips his hat to the crowd. Sitting beside him is Sen. John C. Spooner of Wis., chairman of the Joint Congressional Committee on Inaugural Ceremonies. Opposite, but not clearly visible, are Sen. Henry Cabot Lodge of Mass. and Rep. John Dalzell of Pa., members of the committee. The second sequence consists of long shots of TR taking the oath of office on a platform erected on the East Front of the Capitol; Chief Justice Melville Weston Fuller (1888–1910) administers the presidential oath of office as Chief Clerk of the Supreme Court James H. McKenney holds the Bible. The platform is decorated with plants and garlands and a large banner with the American eagle on it hangs from the center of the railing. West Point cadets and Annapolis midshipmen are assembled below the platform.

PERSONAL CREDITS: Kleine, George, source.
1. Oaths. 2. Inauguration Day. 3. Presidents—United States—Inauguration. 4. Processions. 5. Washington, D. C. Capitol. 6. Midshipmen. 7. Washington, D. C. 8. Washington, D. C.—Streets—Fifteenth Street, N. W. 9. Roosevelt, Theodore, Pres. U. S., 1858–1919—Inauguration, 1905. 10. Spooner, John C. 11. Fuller, Melville Weston. 12. McKenney, James H. 13. United States. President, 1901–1909 (Roosevelt) 14. United States. Army. 1st Cavalry (Volunteer) 15. United States. Congress. Committee on Inaugural Ceremonies. 16. United States. Military Academy, West Point. 17. United States. Naval Academy, Annapolis. I. Theodore Roosevelt Association Collection [mp 76–336]

TR's inauguration, 1905 [1]
Producer unknown, Mar 1905.

As his carriage leaves the U. S. Capitol, TR tips his hat to the crowd. Note his escort of Secret Service men. Following the assassination of President William McKinley, TR became the first president to receive such protection.

© No. reg.

lr, 580 ft. si. b&w. 35mm. ref print.

lr, 580 ft. si. b&w. 35mm. dupe neg (2 cy)

SHELF LOC'N: FEA6695 (print); FPB7200 & 8236 (neg, 2 cy)

The film sequence is repeated and does not follow the order of actual events.

Ref sources: Washington, D. C. Inaugural Committee, 1905. *Inauguration of Theodore Roosevelt as President of the United States, March 4, 1905.* [1905]; Washington *Post.* 3/5/05: 1–2; The New York *Herald.* 3/5/05: 2, 5; New York *Tribune.* 3/5/05: 1–3; P&P presidential file.

Newsfilm.

SUMMARY: Scenes of TR's inauguration on Mar. 4, 1905, in Washington, D.C.: long panning shots of crowds gathered at the Capitol; on a platform erected on the East Front of the Capitol, Chief Justice Melville W. Fuller administers the presidential oath of office to TR as Chief Clerk of the Supreme Court James H. McKenney holds the Bible; TR speaks to the crowd. Views of the West Point band and cadets, the Naval Academy band and midshipmen, men on horseback, and the Citizens Americus Club of Pittsburgh, carrying umbrellas, marching by and turning the corner off Pennsylvania Ave. onto Fifteenth St., NW. Views of the presidential escort—Squadron A of the New York National Guard and mounted Rough Riders—Secret Service and detectives, and TR's carriage

moving on their way to the Capitol. Beside TR in the carriage is Sen. John C. Spooner of Wis., chairman of the Committee of Inaugural Ceremonies; opposite but not visible are Sen. Henry Cabot Lodge of Mass. and Rep. John Dalzell of Pa., both members of the committee. On Pennsylvania Ave., two groups of officers on horseback, a civilian band, and cavalry and marching soldiers parade by.

1. Presidents—United States—Inauguration. 2. Inauguration Day. 3. Oaths. 4. Washington, D. C. Capitol. 5. Midshipmen. 6. Processions. 7. Washington, D. C. 8. Washington, D. C.—Streets—Pennsylvania Avenue, N. W. 9. Washington, D. C.—Streets—Fifteenth Street, N. W. 10. Roosevelt, Theodore, Pres. U. S., 1858–1919—Inauguration, 1905. 11. Fuller, Melville Weston. 12. McKenney, James H. 13. Spooner, John C. 14. United States President, 1901–1909 (Roosevelt) 15. United States. Military Academy, West Point. 16. United States. Naval Academy, Annapolis. 17. Citizens Americus Club, Pittsburgh. 18. New York Cavalry. Squadron A. 19. United States. Army. 1st Cavalry (Volunteer) 20. United States. Army. Cavalry. 21. United States. Secret Service. 22. United States. Congress. Committee on Inaugural Ceremonies. I. Paramount, source. II. Theodore Roosevelt Association Collection. [mp 76–47]

TR's inauguration, 1905 [2]

Producer unknown, Mar 1905.

© No reg.

lr, 287 ft. si. b&w. 35mm ref print.

lr, 287 ft. si. b&w. 35mm. dupe neg.

lr, 187 ft. si. b&w. 35mm. masterpos.

SHELF LOC'N: FEA6693 (print): FPB7071 (neg); FPB8830 (fgmp)

The film sequence is repeated and does not follow the order of actual events.

Ref sources: Washington *Post.* 3/5/05: 1–2; P&P stereo file; P&P presidential file; New York *Tribune.* 3/5/05: 1–3.

Newsfilm.

SUMMARY: Scene of TR's inauguration on Mar. 4, 1905, in Washington, D. C.: a platoon of mounted police, the Fifth Band of the Artillery Corps, officers on horseback probably led by Lt. Gen. Adna R. Chaffee, civilians on horseback, and TR's carriage turn a corner off Pennsylvania Ave.; medium shot of TR and others on a platform erected on the East Front of the Capitol; long shot of Chief Justice Melville W. Fuller administering the oath to TR as Chief Clerk of the Supreme Court James H. McKenney holds the Bible. On Pennsylvania Ave. at the corner of Fifteenth St., NW, the West Point band and cadets, a unit in white-plumed helmets, and soldiers march by; pan of the crowds at the Capitol; medium shot of TR, Sen. Henry Cabot Lodge of Mass., Rep. John Dalzell of Pa., both members of the Committee on Inaugural Ceremonies, and Sen. John C. Spooner of Wis., chairman of the committee, entering a carriage at the East Front of the Capitol; the carriage moves away; medium shot of Vice-President Charles W. Fairbanks, Sen. Augustus O. Bacon of Ga., Sen. John Sharp Williams of Miss., and Rep. Edgar D. Crumpacker of Ind., all three committee members, entering a carriage at the Capitol; West Point cadets march into formation before the inaugural platform on the East Front of the Capitol; TR takes the oath of office from Chief Justice Fuller as McKenney holds the Bible; West Point band and cadets march by; ground-level medium shot of the carriage with TR, Spooner, Lodge, and Dalzell seated in it.

1. Presidents—United States—Inauguration. 2. Inauguration Day. 3. Processions. 4. Mounted police. 5. Washington, D. C. Capitol. 6. Oaths. 7. Washington, D. C. 8. Washington, D. C.—Streets—Pennsylvania Avenue, N. W. 9. Washington, D. C.—Streets—Fifteenth Street, N. W. 10. Roosevelt, Theodore Pres. U. S., 1858–1919—Inauguration, 1905. 11. Fuller, Melville Weston. 12. Roosevelt, Theodore, Pres. U. S., 1858–1919—Addresses, essays, lectures. 13. McKenney, James H. 14. Lodge, Henry Cabot. 15. Dalzell, John. 16. Spooner, John C. 17. Fairbanks, Charles W. 18. Bacon, Augustus O. 19. Williams, John Sharp. 20. Crumpacker, Edgar D. 21. United States. President, 1901–1909 (Roosevelt) 22. United States. Military Academy, West Point. 23. United States. Congress. Committee on Inaugural Ceremonies. I. Paramount, source II. Theodore Roosevelt Association Collection. [mp 76–48]

TR's reception in Albuquerque, N. M., 1916.
Producer unknown, Oct 1916.
© No reg.
lr, 144 ft. si. b&w. 35mm. ref print.
lr, 144 ft. si. b&w. 35mm. dupe neg.
lr, 143 fr. si. b&w. 35mm. pos ntr.
SHELF LOC'N: FEA7312 (print); FPB7741 (neg)
Ref sources: Albuquerque *Journal.* 10/23/16: 8; 10/24/16: 1–2; Coan, Charles F. *A History of New Mexico.* v. 1, 1925: 500; Twitchell, Ralph E. *The Leading Facts of New Mexican History.* v. 2, 1963: 563; Fitzpatrick, George and Caplin, Harvey. *Al-*

buquerque. 1975: 45, 62–63; [Hening, Horace B.] *Albuquerque, New Mexico.* [1908]
Newsfilm.
SUMMARY: TR is cordially received on Oct. 23, 1916, in Albuquerque, N. M., where he speaks on behalf of the Republican presidential candidate, Charles Evans Hughes, and attacks President Wilson's Mexican policies. There are long shots of TR being greeted in the courtyard of the Alvarado Hotel; TR walks with a group of men that includes former Rough Rider George Curry, appointed territorial governor of New Mexico (1907–1911) by TR and a U. S. representative (1912–1913); Curry is the tall man in a dark suit and light hat. TR acknowledges an Indian woman and child sitting by a fountain in the courtyard of the hotel and gives the woman some money. A parade on Central Ave. is held in honor of TR; there are views of a marching band, a mounted escort that includes twelve former Rough Riders, and decorated cars carrying dignitaries; distance and camera angle make positive identification of TR in this sequence impossible. From a narrow platform erected in front of the Alvarado Hotel, TR gives his speech; the seated man behind him is Sen. Albert B. Fall, one of New Mexico's first senators (1912–1921) and later to be secretary of the interior under Harding (1921–1923). The last sequence, showing TR waving from a car, walking with several men through a crowd, and standing in a car, may be unrelated footage.

1. Presidents—United States—Election—1916. 2. Processions. 3. Legislators—New Mexico. 4. Albuquerque, N. M. Alvarado Hotel. 5. New Mexico—Governors. 6. Albuquerque, N. M. 7. Albuquerque, N. M.—Streets—Central Avenue. 8. Roosevelt, Theodore, Pres. U. S., 1858–1919. 9. Roosevelt, Theodore, Pres. U. S. 1858–1919—Addresses, essays, lectures. 10. Curry, George. 11. Fall, Albert B. 12. United States. Army. 1st Cavalry (Volunteer) I. International Newsreel Corporation, source. II. Theodore Roosevelt Association Collection. [mp 76–229]

TR's return from Africa, 1910 [1]
Roosevelt Film Library [1925?]
© No reg.
lr of 1,409 ft. si. b&w. 16mm. ref print.
lr of 1,409 ft. si. b&w. 16mm. dupe neg.
lr of 1,1023 ft. si. b&w. 35mm. pos ntr.
SHELF LOC'N: FAB1791 (print); FRA7794 (neg)
RMA title: *Roosevelt's Return from Africa.*

Ref sources: Roosevelt Memorial Association. *Annual Report*. 1925: 18; Roosevelt Memorial Association. *Theodore Roosevelt's Return from Africa* (script); The Graphic, London. *Funeral of King Edward*. 1910; McNaughton, Arnold. *The Book of Kings*. 1973; The Illustrated London News. *The Funeral Procession of King Edward VII*. 1910.

Factual; compilation.

SUMMARY: This film traces TR's return from his African hunting trip through the countries of the Sudan, France, Denmark, Norway, Germany, Great Britain, and finally his reception in New York City. There are views of: 1) his riverboat on the Nile River in the Sudan; 2) TR's visit in Paris with French Ambassador Jules Jusserand, Gen. Jean B. Dalstein, American Ambassador Robert Bacon, and Mrs. Bacon; TR's trip to Issy-les-Moulineaux; TR reviewing French troops with Jusserand, Bacon, and Dalstein at Vincennes on Apr. 27, 1910; and TR leaving the University of Paris (Sorbonne) on Apr. 23, 1910; 3) TR and Prince Christian in Copenhagen on May 2–3, 1910; 4) TR and King Haakon in Christiania (now Oslo) on May 4–6, 1910; 5) the Brandenburg Gate in Berlin; TR, Kaiser Wilhelm, the kaiserin, and others leaving the University of Berlin on May 12, 1910; 6) the funeral cortege at Windsor on May 20, 1910; identified in the processional, left to right, walking in rows are: Kaiser Wilhelm of Germany, King George V of England, and the Duke of Connaught; the Duke of Cornwall (later King Edward VIII) and Prince Albert (later King George VI); two rows of the king's aides; King Alfonso XIII of Spain, King George I of Greece, and King Haakon VII of Norway; King Manuel II of Portugal, King Frederik VIII of Denmark, and King Ferdinand I of Bulgaria; Archduke Franz Ferdinand of Austria, King Albert I of Belgium, and Prince Yusuf Izzedin of Turkey; the Duke of Aosta, Grand Duke Michael Alexandrovitch of Russia, and Prince Sadanaru Fushimi of Japan; the Crown Prince of Romania (later King Carol II), the Duke of Sparta (later King Constantine I of Greece), and probably Prince Rupprecht of Bavaria; the Crown Prince of Serbia (later Peter I), Duke Albrecht of Wurtemberg, and Prince Henry of the Netherlands; the Grand Duke of Mecklenburg-Strelitz, the Grand Duke of Hesse, and Prince Henry of Prussia; Crown Prince George of Saxony, the Duke of Saxe-Coburg, and Prince Charles (later King Gustav VI) of Sweden; probably the Prince of Waldeck, probably Prince Tsai-tao of China, and Prince Mohammed Ali of Egypt; Prince Christian of Schleswig-Holstein, Prince

Arthur of Connaught, and Prince Albert of Schleswig-Holstein; Prince Alexander of Battenburg; Prince George of Cumberland, and the Duke of Fife; TR is visible at the end of the procession, dressed in evening attire; 7) TR's arrival in New York City; his greeting by Mayor William J. Gaynor, Cornelius Vanderbilt, Henry Cabot Lodge, and William Loeb; his speech at the Battery; and the parade in his honor.

PERSONAL CREDITS: Gentry, Caroline, director. Manning, Mae, editor.

1. Heads of state. 2. Kings and rulers. 3. Berlin. Brandenburger Tor. 4. Copenhagen. 5. Berlin. 6. Oslo. 7. Roosevelt, Theodore, Pres. U.S., 1858–1919—Journey to Europe, 1910. 8. Jusserand, Jules. 9. Dalstein, Jean B. 10. Bacon, Robert, 1860–1919. 11. Christian X, King of Denmark, 1870–1947. 12. Haakon VII, King of Norway, 1872–1957. 13. Wilhelm II, German Emperor, 1859–1941. 14. Edward VII, King of Great Britain, 1841–1910—Funeral and memorial services. 15. George V, King of Great Britain, 1865–1936. 16. Connaught, Arthur William Patrick Albert, Duke of, 1850–1942. 17. Edward VIII, King of Great Britain, 1894–1972. 18. George VI, King of Great Britain, 1895–1952. 19. Alfonso XIII, King of Spain, 1886–1941. 20. George I, King of the Hellenes, 1845–1913. 21. Manuel II, King of Portugal, 1889–1932. 22. Frederik VIII, King of Denmark, 1843–1912. 23. Ferdinand I, Czar of Bulgaria, 1861–1948. 24. Franz Ferdinand, Archduke of Austria, 1863–1914. 25. Albert I, King of the Belgians, 1875–1934. 26. Yusuf Izzedin, 1858–1916. 27. Gaynor, William J. 28. Vanderbilt, Cornelius, 1873–1942. 29. Lodge, Henry Cabot. 30. Loeb, William, 1866–1937. I. Roosevelt Memorial Association. Film Library. II. Roosevelt Memorial Association. III. Roosevelt Memorial Association, source. IV. Theodore Roosevelt Association Collection. V. Roosevelt's return from Africa [Title] [mp 76–376]

TR's return from Africa, 1910 [2]
Roosevelt Film Library [1925?]
© No reg.
2r of 2, 1927 ft. si. b&w. 35mm. ref print.
2r of 2, 1927 ft. si. b&w. 35mm. dupe neg.
2r of 2, 1929 ft. si. b&w. 35mm. pos ntr.
SHELF LOC'N: FEA9051–9052 (print); FPB 4601–4602 (neg)

RMA title: *Roosevelt's Return from Africa.*

Ref sources: Roosevelt Memorial Association. *Annual Report*. 1925: 18; Roosevelt Memorial As-

Kaiser Wilhelm II of Germany about 1915. TR visted the kaiser on his European tour and addressed students at the University of Berlin on May 12, 1910.

sociation. *Theodore Roosevelt's Return from Africa* (script)

Factual; compilation.

SUMMARY: Returning from his African hunting trip, TR visits the Sudan, France, Denmark, Norway, Germany, Great Britain, and attends ceremonies in his honor in New York City. There are views of: 1) his riverboat on the Nile River in the Sudan; 2) TR's visit in Paris with French Ambassador Jules Jusserand, Gen. Jean B. Dalstein, American Ambassador Robert Bacon, and Mrs. Bacon; his trip to Issy-les-Moulineaux; TR reviewing French troops with Jusserand, Bacon, and Dalstein at Vincennes on Apr. 27, 1910; and TR leaving the University of Paris (Sorbonne) on Apr. 23, 1910; 3) TR with Prince Christian and others in Denmark May 2–3, 1910; 4) TR and King Haakon in Christiania (now Oslo) on May 4–6, 1910; 5) views of Berlin including the Brandenburg Gate and the Reichstag; TR, Kaiser Wilhelm, the kaiserin, and others leaving the University of Berlin on May 12, 1910; 6) the funeral cortege at Windsor on May 20, 1910; identified in the processional, left to right, walking in rows are: Kaiser Wilhelm of Germany, King George V of England, and the Duke of Connaught; the Duke of Cornwall (later King Edward VIII) and Prince Albert (later King George VI); two rows of the king's aides; King Alfonso XII of Spain, King George I of Greece, and King Haakon VII of Norway; King Manuel II of Portugal, King Frederik VIII of Denmark, and King Ferdinand I of Bulgaria; Archduke Franz Ferdinand of Austria, King Albert I of Belgium, and Prince Yusuf Izzedin of Turkey; the Duke of Aosta, Grand Duke Michael Alexandrovitch of Russia, and Prince Sadanaru Fushimi of Japan; the Crown Prince of Romania (later King Carol II), the Duke of Sparta (later King Constantine I of Greece), and probably Prince Rupprecht of Bavaria; Crown Prince of Serbia (later Peter I), Duke Albrecht of Wurtemberg, and Prince Henry of the Netherlands; the Grand Duke of Mecklenburg-Strelitz, the Grand Duke of Hesse, and Prince Henry of Prussia; Crown Prince George of Saxony, the Duke of Saxe-Coburg, and Prince Charles (later King Gustav VI) of Sweden; probably the Prince of Waldeck, probably Prince Tsai-tao of China, and Prince Mohammed Ali of Egypt; Prince Christian of Schleswig-Holstein, Prince Arthur of Connaught, and Prince Albert of Schleswig-Holstein; Prince Alexander of Battenburg; Prince George of Cumberland, and the Duke of Fife; TR is visible at the end of the procession; 7) TR's arrival in New York City; his greeting by Mayor William J. Gaynor, Cornelius Vanderbilt, Henry Cabot Lodge, and William Loeb; his speech at the Battery, and the parade in his honor.

PERSONAL CREDITS: Gentry, Caroline, director. Manning, Mae, editor.

1. Heads of state. 2. Kings and rulers. 3. Berlin. Brandenburger Tor. 4. Berlin. Reichstagsgebäude. 5. Denmark. 6. Oslo. 7. Berlin—Streets. 8. Roosevelt, Theodore, Pres. U.S., 1858–1919—Journey to Europe, 1910. 9. Jusserand, Jules. 10. Dalstein, Jean B. 11. Bacon, Robert, 1860–1919. 12. Christian X, King of Denmark, 1870–1947. 13. Haakon VII, King of Norway, 1872–1957. 14. Wilhelm II, German Emperor, 1859–1941. 15. Edward VII, King of Great Britain, 1841–1910—Funeral and memorial services. 16. George V, King of Great Britain, 1865–1936. 17. Connaught, Arthur William Patrick Albert, Duke of, 1850–1942. 18. Edward VIII, King of Great Britain, 1894–1972. 19. George VI, King of Great Britain, 1895–1952. 20.

Alfonso XIII, King of Spain, 1886–1941. 21. George I, King of the Hellenes, 1845–1913. 22. Manuel II, King of Portugal, 1889–1932. 23. Frederik VIII King of Denmark, 1843–1912. 24. Ferdinand I, Czar of Bulgaria, 1861–1948. 25. Franz Ferdinand, Archduke of Austria, 1863–1914. 26. Albert I, King of the Belgians, 1875–1934. 27. Yusuf Izzedin, 1858–1916. 28. Gaynor, William J. 29. Vanderbilt, Cornelius, 1873–1942. 30. Lodge, Henry Cabot. 31. Loeb, William, 1866–1937. 32. Roosevelt, Theodore, Pres. U.S., 1858–1919—Addresses, essays, lectures. I. Roosevelt Memorial Association. Film Library. II. Roosevelt Memorial Association. III. Roosevelt Memorial Association, source. IV. Theodore Roosevelt Association Collection. V. Roosevelt's return from Africa [Title] [mp 76–377]

TR's return to New York, 1910 [1]

Producer unknown, Jun 1910.
© No reg.
    lr, 231 ft. si. b&w. 16mm. ref print.
    lr, 231 ft. si. b&w. 16mm. dupe neg.
    lr, 231 ft. si. b&w. 16mm. archival pos.
SHELF LOC'N: FAB700 (print); FRA5750 (neg); FRA5749 (arch pos)
RMA title: *TR's Return to New York, 1910* (old version); the new version is not identified.
Ref sources: P&P portrait file; P&P presidential file.
Newsfilm.
SUMMARY: On June 18, 1910, TR returned to New York City after a fifteen-month tour abroad, having traveled through Africa and western Europe. An elaborate city celebration drawing a million people marked his homecoming. Aboard the ocean liner Kaiserin Auguste Victoria ex-President and Mrs. Roosevelt were met by a revenue cutter, the Manhattan, carrying the Roosevelt children. TR then went aboard a larger cutter, the Androscoggin, and officially became a guest of the city. After proceeding up the Hudson River along the New Jersey shore to West Fifty-ninth St., the Androscoggin moved back along the Manhattan shore to Battery Park, followed by a water parade of almost one hundred vessels. TR was greeted by Mayor William J. Gaynor at the park, where both briefly spoke to an assembled crowd, with notables seated on a flag-draped stand expanded for the occasion to hold 600 people. Battery ceremonies were followed by a parade up Broadway and Fifth Avenue to the Fifty-ninth St. plaza. In the parade TR, Mayor William J. Gaynor, and chairman of the city's welcoming committee Cornelius Vanderbilt, rode together in an open carriage, preceded by TR's regiment of Rough Riders, the First United States Volunteer Cavalry. Also in the parade were approximately two thousand other veterans of the Spanish-American War. On the film are views of the open harbor, with various vessels assembled for TR's visit, including the Kaiserin Auguste Victoria, the Androscoggin, and the Manhattan; TR alone on the lookout station of what appears to be the Androscoggin as it moves into port; a street scene in which photographers scramble to get a clear view of carriages as notables pass through a street cordoned off with greenery; TR and Vanderbilt move toward the Battery speakers platform, beside which is visible the stand erected for TR's family and dignitaries; TR and Mayor Gaynor, who steps forward to greet TR, ascend the platform; men mill around the base of the platform; side view of TR speaking from written notes, with Gaynor behind him; scenes of crowds and tents in what appears to be Central Park south; the parade moves toward the camera and passes in front of the decorated stands; TR, standing in a carriage, pauses in front of the stands; shots of mounted police, a mounted band, carriages, and a marching band.
PERSONAL CREDITS: Braunstein, Cy, source.
1. Ships. 2. Processions. 3. New York (City) 4. New York (City)—Harbor. 5. New York (City)—Plazas. 6. New York (City)—Streets. 7. New York (City)—Parks—Battery. 8. Roosevelt, Theodore, Pres. U.S., 1858–1919. 9. Roosevelt, Theodore, Pres. U.S., 1858–1919—Addresses, essays, lectures. 10. Gaynor, William J. 11. Vanderbilt, Cornelius, 1873–1942. 12. Kaiserin Auguste Victoria (Ship) 13. Manhattan (Ship) 14. Androscoggin (Ship) 15. United States. Army. 1st Cavalry (Volunteer) I. Theodore Roosevelt Association Collection. [mp 76–2]

TR's return to New York, 1910 [2]

Producer unknown, Jun 1910.
© No reg.
    lr, 317 ft. si. b&w. 16mm. ref print.
    lr, 317 ft. si. b&w. 16mm. dupe neg.
    lr, 317 ft. si. b&w. 16mm. masterpos.
    lr, 317 ft. si. b&w. 16mm. archival pos.
SHELF LOC'N: FAB709 (print); FRA5765 (neg); FRA8648 (fgmp); FRA5766 (arch pos)
RMA title: *TR's Return to New York, 1910* (old version); the new version is not identified.

TR returned to the United States June 18, 1910, after an extensive trip to Africa and Europe. In this stereograph he responds to the enthusiastic welcome given to him by the citizens of New York as William Gaynor, mayor of New York, stands at the rear of the platform, and a reporter takes notes on the right.

Film is out of sequence.

Ref sources: P&P portrait file; P&P presidential file; *Jane's Fighting Ships*. 1914: 170.

Newsfilm.

SUMMARY: TR returned to N. Y. on June 18, 1910, having completed a fifteen-month tour of Africa and western Europe. The Roosevelt party on the liner Kaiserin Auguste Victoria was met by the city revenue cutter Manhattan. From the Manhattan, TR went aboard a larger cutter, the Androscoggin, which carried the official reception committee. After a trip up the Hudson to Fifty-ninth St., the Androscoggin returned to the Battery. There TR and Cornelius Vanderbilt were met by William J. Gaynor, mayor of New York. After the Battery ceremonies, a parade was formed which marched up Broadway and Fifth Ave. to the Fifty-ninth St. plaza, where it dispersed. The film shows several shots of harbor activity: front and side views of the Kaiser; shots of the Androscoggin in the harbor, passing the aquarium, and approaching the flag-draped docking area; pans of naval vessels accompanying the Kaiser, including the dreadnought South Carolina, the steamboat Majestic, flying a pennant which ways "Dee-Lighted," and other miscellaneous vessels; and views of houses overlooking the harbor. Scenes at the Battery show TR

with Cornelius Vanderbilt; TR and dignitaries walking through a passageway, probably on their way to the welcoming ceremonies; Mayor Gaynor and TR on the decorated stand greeting the crowd prior to their speeches. Parade sequences include pans of the New York Produce Exchange Bank at Beaver St. at the beginning of the parade; shots of mounted Rough Riders and other Spanish-American War veterans preceding TR's carriage; TR, with a New York City Police escort, standing in his carriage and waving his top hat; shots of the crowd and flag-draped stands.

1. Ships. 2. Ocean liners. 3. Battleships. 4. Warships. 5. Aquariums, Public. 6. New York Bay. 7. New York (City) 8. New York (City)—Harbor. 9. New York (City)—Parks—Battery. 10. New York (City)—Buildings. 11. New York (City)—Streets. 12. Roosevelt, Theodore, Pres. U.S., 1858–1919. 13. Roosevelt, Theodore, Pres. U.S., 1858–1919—Addresses, essays, lectures. 14. Vanderbilt, Cornelius, 1873–1942. 15. Gaynor, William J. 16. Kaiserin Auguste Victoria (Ship) 17. Manhattan (Ship) 18. Androscoggin (Ship) 19. New York Aquarium. 20. South Carolina (Ship) 21. Majestic (Ship) 22. United States. Army. lst Cavalry (Volunteer) I. Warner Brothers, source. II. Theodore Roosevelt Association Collection. [mp 76–3]

TR's sons' regiments during war, 1917–1918 [1]
Producer unknown [1918?]

© No reg.

lr, 53 ft. si. b&w. 16mm. ref print.

lr, 53 ft. si. b&w. 16mm. dupe neg.

SHELF LOC'N: FAB 1127 (print); FRA6066
(neg)

Dates in the title are unverified.

Ref sources: Roosevelt, Theodore. *Average Americans.* 1919: 23; Buckley, Harold. *Squadron 95.* 1933: 166; [Fullerton, Charles B.] *The Twenty-sixth Infantry in France.* 1919: 100.

Factual; war film.

SUMMARY: Soldiers, accompanied by several mounted men, walk in formation on a road. Because of the soldiers' heavy clothing, it must be winter. This group may be the Twenty-sixth Infantry, Theodore and Archibald Roosevelt's regiment. The following sequence is of biplanes flying in formation; the third sequence is shot at a hangar where men appear to be preparing a plane for flight. The second and third sequences may be of Quentin Roosevelt's squadron, the Ninety-fifth. The last sequence probably represents Kermit Roosevelt's regiment, the Seventh Field Artillery. In this sequence a group of men load and fire a cannon. The location is undetermined; the film, or portions of it, was probably shot in France.

1. Airplanes. 2. Artillery. 3. Soldiers. 4. European War, 1914–1918. 5. European War, 1914–1918—Aerial operations, American. 6. France. 7. Roosevelt, Theodore, 1887–1944. 8. Roosevelt, Archibald B. 9. Roosevelt, Quentin. 10. Roosevelt, Kermit. 11. United States. Army. 26th Infantry. 12. United States. Army. 95th Aero Squadron. 13. United States. Army. 7th Field Artillery. I. United States. Army. Signal Corps, source. II. Theodore Roosevelt Association Collection. [mp 76–222]

TR's sons' regiments during war, 1917–1918 [2]
Producer unknown [1918?]

© No reg.

lr, 55 ft. si. b&w. 35mm. ref print.

lr, 55 ft. si. b&w. 35mm. dupe neg.

lr, 56 ft. si. b&w. 35mm. pos ntr.

SHELF LOC'N: FEA6748 (print); FPB7585 (neg)

The dates in the title are unverified.

Ref sources: Roosevelt, Theodore. *Average Americans.* 1919: 23; [Fullerton, Charles B.] *The Twenty-sixth Infantry in France.* 1919: 100.

Factual; war film.

SUMMARY: Soldiers, accompanied by mounted men, walk in formation on a road; several soldiers wave at the camera. The soldiers' heavy clothing establishes the season as winter. This group may be the Twenty-sixth Infantry, Theodore and Archibald Roosevelt's regiment. The location is undetermined; the film was probably shot in France.

1. Soldiers. 2. European War, 1914–1918. 3. France. 4. Roosevelt, Theodore, 1887–1944. 5. Roosevelt, Archibald B. 6. United States. Army. 26th Infantry. I. United States. Army. Signal Corps, source. II. Theodore Roosevelt Association Collection. [mp 76–221]

U.S. battleship Indiana.
Producer unknown [1898?]

© No reg.

lr, 7 ft. si. b&w. 16mm. ref print.

lr, 7 ft. si. b&w. 16mm. archival pos.

SHELF LOC'N: FAB1225 (print); FRA6120
(arch pos)

May be a Biograph production.

Ref sources: *Jane's Fighting Ships.* 1904: 203; P&P stereo file.

Newsfilm; views.

SUMMARY: Long shot on the starboard side of the battleship U.S.S. Indiana as she steams under way in unidentified waters.

1. Battleships. 2. Indiana (Ship) I. Biograph Company. II. Biograph Company, source. III. Theodore Roosevelt Association Collection. [mp 76–297]

U.S. battleship "Oregon."
American Mutoscope Co. [Aug 1898?]

© H35637, American Mutoscope & Biograph Co.,12Sep1903

lr of 1, 8 ft. si. b&w. 16mm. ref print.

lr of 1, 8 ft. si. b&w. 16mm. dupe neg.

lr of 1, 8 ft. si. b&w. 16mm. archival pos.

lr of 1, 14 ft. si. b&w. 16mm. ref print.

lr of 1, 14 ft. si. b&w. 16mm. dupe neg.

lr of 1, 24 ft. si. b&w. 35mm. paper (2 cy)

SHELF LOC'N: FAB1461 (print-RMA); FRA
6197 (neg-RMA); FRA6184
(arch pos-RMA); FLA3338
(print-Paper); FRA0649 (neg-Paper); LC324 (paper-2 cy-Paper)

Ref sources: *Jane's Fighting Ships.* 1903: 199; P&P stereo file.

Newsfilm; views.

SUMMARY: Views on the starboard side of the battleship U.S.S. Oregon as she passes a camera which is probably on another ship; her crew is at quarters on her deck; other vessels are visible in the foreground. These may be scenes of New York City's welcome to William T. Sampson's fleet after his victory at Santiago Bay, in August 1898.

1. Battleships. 2. New York (City) 3. United States— History—War of 1898. 4. Oregon (Ship) I. Biograph Company. II. Biograph Company, source. III. Theodore Roosevelt Association Collection. IV. Paper Print Collection [mp 76–298]

U.S. troops landing at Daiquiri, Cuba.
Thomas A. Edison, Jun 1898.
© 46690, Thomas A. Edison, 5Aug1898
lr of 1, 21 ft. si. b&w. 16mm. ref print (cy 1)
lr of 1, 49 ft. si. b&w. 35mm. ref print (cy 2)
lr of 1, 48 ft. si. b&w. 35mm. ref print (cy 3)
lr of 1, 19 ft. si. b&w. 16mm. dupe neg.
lr of 1, 19 ft. si. b&w. 16mm. archival pos
lr of 1, 47 ft. si. b&w. 35mm. neg ntr.
lr of 1, 25 ft. si. b&w. 16mm. ref print.
lr of 1, 25 ft. si. b&w. 16mm. dupe neg (cy 1)
lr of 1, 24 ft. si. b&w. 16mm. dupe neg (cy 2)
lr of 1, 49 ft. si. b&w. 35mm. paper (cy 1)
lr of 1, 50 ft. si. b&w. 35mm. paper (cy 2)
SHELF LOC'N: FAB1217 (print, cy 1-RMA); FEA7621 (print, cy 2-RMA); FEA7622 (print, cy 3-RMA); FRA6176 (neg-RMA); FRA 6112 (arch pos-RMA); FLA 3513 (print-Paper); FRA0791 (neg, cy 1-Paper); FRA0792 (neg, cy 2-Paper); LC499 (paper, cy 1-Paper); LC499 (paper, cy 2-Paper)

RMA title: *U.S. Troops Landing at Daiquiri, Cuba, 1898.*

Title on paper print films: *U.S. Troops Landing at Baiquiri, Cuba.*

Ref print (cy 1) is out of frame.

Ref sources: Chidsey, Donald B. *The Spanish-American War.* 1971: 117–120; Freidel, Frank B. *The Splendid Little War.* 1958: 59–97; Keller, Allan. *The Spanish-American War.* 1969: 112–127; Werstein, Irving. *1898: The Spanish-American War.* 1966: 93.

Newsfilm; war film.

SUMMARY: U.S. troops in lifeboats are landing at a wooden pier in Daiquiri, Cuba; the men are part of Gen. William R. Shafter's expeditionary force sent to fight in Cuba during the Spanish-American War in June 1898. The men alight from boats as earlier arrivals walk along the dock toward the camera; the soldiers are equipped with blanket rolls, haversacks, and rifles. One of the transport ships is visible in the background next to a high metal pier. Daiquiri was recommended to General Shafter as a landing site by Gen. Calixto Garcia because of the two piers built by an American mining company and the availability of fresh water. The actual landing proved to be disordered, but was fortunately unopposed by Spanish troops.

PERSONAL CREDITS: Kleine, George, source.

1. Landing operations. 2. Daiquiri, Cuba. 3. United States—History—War of 1898. 4. United States. Army. I. Edison (Thomas A.) inc. II. Theodore Roosevelt Association Collection. III. Paper Print Collection. IV. U.S. troops landing at Daiquiri, Cuba [Title] [mp 76–256]

[Unidentified man]
Producer unknown [191–?]
© No reg.
lr, 9 ft. si. b&w. 16mm. ref print.
lr, 9 ft. si. b&w. 16mm. arch pos (2 cy)
SHELF LOC'N: FAB1781 (print); FRA7846 & 7847 (arch pos, 2 cy)

RMA title: *Senator Poindexter*; research indicates that the identification is incorrect.

Factual; views.

SUMMARY: An unidentified man, possibly a senator, walks down steps and poses for the camera outside the U.S. Capitol, Washington, D.C.

PERSONAL CREDITS: Stripe, F. C., source. Carver, H. P., source.

1. Legislators. 2. Washington, D.C. Capitol. 3. Washington, D.C. I. Theodore Roosevelt Association Collection. [mp 76–378]

A visit to Theodore Roosevelt at his home at Sagamore Hill, Oyster Bay, L.I., 1912.
Pathé Frères, Oct 1912. Roosevelt Memorial Association [1920]
© No reg.
lr, 218 ft. si. b&w. 16mm. ref print.
lr, 218 ft. si. b&w. 16mm. dupe neg (cy 1)
lr, 479 ft. si. b&w. 35mm. dupe neg (cy 2)
lr, 479 ft. si. b&w. 35mm. pos ntr.
SHELF LOC'N: FAB745 (print); FRA5798 (neg, cy 1); FPB7127 (neg, cy 2)

The RMA *Annual Report* notes that the film was originally released by Pathé Frères under the title *A Visit to the Illustrious Colonel*; the MPW review appears under the title *Theodore Roosevelt*. Interior titles were supplied by RMA.

Ref source: Roosevelt Memorial Association. *Annual Report.* 1925: 18.

Newsfilm.

SUMMARY: The first film footage taken of TR at Sagamore Hill, summer of 1912. Views of the house and surrounding grounds; TR reviews his mail, assisted by his son Archie; William P. Helm, who was Associated Press correspondent for New York City and Washington (1910–1918) and detailed by A.P. to Wilson and Roosevelt during the 1912 campaign, speaks informally with TR under some trees; TR rides his "favorite horse" Sidar away from Sagamore and stops to feed the horse from his hand; TR and his dogs set out across a field, with Sagamore visible in the background; TR, in a white shirt and vest, chops down a tree. Shot of a band and a crowd of men on the Sagamore grounds and TR addressing a large group of men from the Sagamore porch; shot of a flying American flag. The last sequences of a band and a crowd were probably not included in the original Pathé production.

CITATION: MPW13: 1304.

1. Oyster Bay, N.Y. Sagamore Hill. 2. Sidar (Horse) 3. Oyster Bay, N.Y. 4. Roosevelt, Theodore, Pres. U.S., 1858–1919—Homes. 5. Roosevelt, Theodore, Pres. U.S., 1858–1919—Addresses, essays, lectures. 6. Roosevelt, Archibald B. 7. Helm, William P. 8. Associated Press. I. Pathe. II. Roosevelt Memorial Association. III. Roosevelt Memorial Association, source. IV. Theodore Roosevelt Association Collection. V. Visit to the illustrious colonel, A [Title] VI. Theodore Roosevelt [Title] [mp 76–126]

Whole nation honors memory of Roosevelt.
Kinogram Pub. Corp., Oct 1919.
  © No reg.
    lr, 31 ft. si. b&w. 16mm. ref print (2 cy)
    lr, 31 ft. si. b&w. 16mm. dupe neg (2 cy)
    lr, 31 ft. si. b&w. 16mm. archival pos (2 cy)
    lr, 78 ft. si. b&w. 35mm. pos ntr.
    lr, 79 ft. si. b&w. 35mm. neg ntr.
(Kinograms [Series])
SHELF LOC'N: FAB710 & 1218 (print, 2 cy);
              FRA5767 & 6113 (neg, 2 cy);
              FRA5960 & 5961 (arch pos, 2 cy)
RMA titles: *Runners Carrying Flag, Girls Sewing Stars on Flag, 1920* [and] *Scouts Carry Roosevelt Flag, Runners Stop for Services at Manor.*
Ref source: The New York *Times Mid-week Pictorial.* v. 10, no. 10, 1919: [9]
Newsfilm.
SUMMARY: In honor of TR's birthday the week of Oct. 20–27, 1919, was declared Roosevelt Week by the Roosevelt Memorial Association. An intensive membership campaign, which sought to raise funds for suitable memorials to TR, was begun on Oct. 20. As one of the first events of the week, an official Roosevelt memorial flag, which has been carried across New York State by Boy Scouts and school boys, is received at Van Cortlandt Park by Park Commissioner Joseph Hennessey of the Bronx. On Oct. 21, the flag was carried to Theodore Roosevelt High School, where a forty-third star was added. The film includes shots in Van Cortlandt Park: a young runner bears the flag to waiting officials and Boy Scouts at Manor House in the park; view of Samuel Abbott, originator of the memorial flag idea; the runner and a Scout display a pack containing the folded flag; the flag is raised while Scouts salute. Scenes at Roosevelt High School ceremonies include the runner arriving and giving the memorial flag to officials at the entrance to the school; five young women sew on the forty-third star; the runner departs from the school with the flag; and a view of marching high school women in robes, each with a single star stitched on the front; marchers are led by the women who sewed the stars.

PERSONAL CREDITS: Urban, Charles, source.

1. Memorial rites and ceremonies. 2. Flags. 3. High school students—Political activity. 4. New York (City). Van Cortlandt House. 5. New York (City) 6. New York (City)—Parks—Van Cortlandt Park. 7. Roosevelt, Theodore, Pres. U.S., 1858–1919—Funeral and memorial services. 8. Abbott, Samuel. 9. Roosevelt Memorial Association. 10. Boy Scouts of America. 11. Roosevelt High School, New York (City) I. Kinogram Publishing Corporation. II. Theodore Roosevelt Association Collection. [mp 76–18]

Will Hays.
Producer unknown [192–?]
  © No reg.
    lr, 22 ft. si. b&w. 16mm. ref print.
    lr, 22 ft. si. b&w. 16mm. dupe neg.
    lr, 22 ft. si. b&w. 16mm. archival pos (2 cy)
SHELF LOC'N: FAB705 (print); FRA8661 (neg);
              FRA5759 & 5760 (arch pos,2 cy)
Ref source: Hays, Will H. *Memoirs.* 1955.
Factual.
SUMMARY: Will H. Hays, chairman of the Republican National Committee between 1918 and 1922, postmaster general in President Harding's cabinet (1921–1922), and head of the Motion Picture Producers and Distributors of America, Inc.

in 1922, appears seated at an office desk, busily working with papers. Immediately behind his desk is a large sculpture of an elephant.

PERSONAL CREDITS: Stripe, F. C., source. Carver, H. P., source.

1. Hays, Will H. I. Theodore Roosevelt Association Collection. [mp 76–17]

William Gibbs McAdoo.

Producer unknown [191–?]

© No reg.

    lr, 4 ft. si. b&w. 16mm. ref print.

    lr, 4 ft. si. b&w. 16mm. dupe neg.

    lr, 4 ft. si. b&w. 16mm. archival pos.

    lr, 10 ft. si. b&w. 35mm. pos ntr.

SHELF LOC'N: FAB977 (print); FRA5947 (neg); FRA5948 (arch pos)

Ref source: P&P portrait file.

Factual; views.

SUMMARY: Medium-close frontal and side views of William Gibbs McAdoo, Secretary of the Treasury (1913–1918), standing and speaking in front of a column.

1. McAdoo, William Gibbs. I. Pathe, source. II. Theodore Roosevelt Association Collection. [mp 76–145]

William H. Taft burns mortgage of Exposition, 1915.

Producer unknown, Sep 1915.

© No reg.

    lr, 23 ft. si. b&w. 35mm. ref print.

    lr, 23 ft. si. b&w. 35mm. dupe neg.

    lr, 10 ft. si. b&w. 35mm. pos ntr.

SHELF LOC'N: FEA8330 (print); FPB9878 (neg)

Film is very dark.

Ref sources: San Francisco *Chronicle*. 9/2/15: 8; 9/3/15: 9; 9/4/15: 4; P&P presidential file.

Newsfilm.

SUMMARY: On Sept. 3, 1915, as part of the ceremonies for the "out of debt night" at the Panama-Pacific International Exposition in San Francisco, William Howard Taft burns the mortgage representing the expo's last debt. The program is held at night in the Court of the Universe on expo grounds and entails the public transfer of the check for the mortgage by Charles C. Moore, president of the expo, and of the mortgage by James J. Fagan, representing the San Francisco Clearing House. Moore presents the mortgage to Taft, who then consigns it to flames in an urn. Opening scene of Moore walking towards the camera onto the platform, followed by Taft, who is carrying the mortgage on top of a long stick; Taft places the document into the burning urn, takes it out, and lays it down; Fagan walks onto the platform; Taft shakes hands with Moore, turns left, and shakes hands with Fagan.

1. Mortgages. 2. Mortgage loans. 3. Exhibitions. 4. San Francisco. 5. San Francisco—Exhibitions. 6. San Francisco—Plazas—Court of the Universe. 7. Taft, William Howard, Pres. U.S., 1857–1930. 8. Moore, Charles C. 9. Fagan, James J. 10. Panama-Pacific International Exposition, 1915. I. Apollo Pictures, source. II. Theodore Roosevelt Association Collection. [mp 76–292]

William H. Taft in Panama [1910?]

Producer unknown [Nov 1910?]

© No reg.

    lr, 64 ft. si. b&w. 16mm. ref print (3 cy)

    lr, 64 ft. si. b&w. 16mm. dupe neg.

    lr, 64 ft. si. b&w. 16mm. archival pos (2 cy)

SHELF LOC'N: FAB1031 & 1650 & 1652 (print, 3 cy); FRA6210 (neg); FRA5889 & 6359 (arch pos, 2 cy)

RMA lists the date in the title as 1907; identification of members of Taft's entourage suggests that the event may be Taft's visit to Panama, Nov. 1910.

Ref sources: Pringle, Henry F. *The Life and Times of William Howard Taft*. 1939; P&P presidential file; P&P portrait file; *Jane's Fighting Ships*. 1915: 174.

Newsfilm.

SUMMARY: On one of many visits to Panama, William Howard Taft inspects canal construction and visits ruins in what may be the Panamanian jungle. Views of a crowd of men and women on a dock, posing for the camera; a tugboat pulls into an unidentified harbor, with Taft and Gen. George W. Goethals, chief engineer of the Panama Canal project, seated on the upper deck; Taft and his entourage in formal dress board what may be the armored cruiser Tennessee, while the crew stands at attention; view of the cruiser's deck; Taft and his entourage disembark from the unidentified vessel, with a crowd gathered on the dock; the Taft party is greeted at a train by General Goethals; the party includes Mrs. Helen Herron Taft, wife of the president, and Federico Alfonso Pezet, minister to the United States from Peru. In the last scene Taft and members of his party visit the site of stone ruins in the jungle.

PERSONAL CREDITS: Futter, Walter A., source.

1. Canals, Interoceanic. 2. Cruisers (Warships) 3. Ships. 4. Architecture, Primitive. 5. Panama. 6. Panama Canal. 7. Taft, William Howard, Pres. U.S.,

1857–1930—Journey to Panama, 1910. 8. Goethals, George W. 9. Taft, Helen Herron. 10. Pezet, Federico Alfonso. 11. United States. President, 1909–1913 (Taft) 12. Tennessee (Ship) I. Theodore Roosevelt Association Collection. [mp 76–111]

William Howard Taft on rear platform of train.
Producer unknown [1908?]
© No reg.
   lr, 5 ft. si. b&w. 16mm. ref print.
   lr, 5 ft. si. b&w. 16mm. dupe neg.
   lr, 5 ft. si. b&w. 16mm. archival pos.
SHELF LOC'N: FAB834 (print); FRA5834 (neg); FRA5835 (arch pos)
Possible production dates: 1908–1910.
Newsfilm.
SUMMARY: Medium-close shot of Taft, hat in hand, speaking from the rear of a train.
1. Taft, William Howard, Pres. U.S., 1857–1930—Addresses, essays, lectures. I. Pathe, source. II. Theodore Roosevelt Association Collection. [mp 76–73]

Woman wearing aigrette in her hat.
Producer unknown [192–?]
© No reg.
   lr, 9 ft. si. b&w. 16mm. ref print.
   lr, 9 ft. si. b&w. 16mm. dupe neg.
   lr, 21 ft. si. b&w. 35mm. pos ntr.
SHELF LOC'N: FAB 1039 (print); FRA6011 (neg)
Factual.
SUMMARY: This appears to be a dramatic sequence from a feature film; medium-close shot of an actress wearing a fur coat and a cloche with a spray of feathers, holding a small dog, and speaking to the camera. The sequence may be related to TR's conservation efforts for the protection of birds.
1. Actresses. 2. Feathers. 3. Wildlife conservation. 4. Birds, Protection of. I. Famous Players—Lasky Corporation, source. II. Theodore Roosevelt Association Collection. [mp 76–317]

Woman's Roosevelt Memorial Association meeting at Roosevelt House, 1923 [1]
Producer unknown, 1923.
© No reg.
   lr, 23 ft. si. b&w. 16mm. ref print (cy 1)
   lr, 57 ft. si. b&w. 35mm. ref print (cy 2)
   lr, 57 ft. si. b&w. 35mm. dupe neg.
   lr, 57 ft. si. b&w. 35mm. masterpos.
   lr, 23 ft. si. b&w. 16mm. archival pos.
   lr, 58 ft. si. b&w. 35mm. neg ntr.

SHELF LOC'N: FAB757 (print, cy 1); FEA6751 (print, cy 2); FPB7590 (neg); FPB7591 (fgmp); FRA5812 (arch pos)
Ref sources: P&P portrait file; *Roosevelt House Bulletin*. v. 4, no. 1, 1932: 5; New York (City). Roosevelt House. Photographic file.
Factual.
SUMMARY: Medium-close shots of a small group of WRMA members standing and sitting around a desk on which a bust of TR is visible. The woman speaking and gesturing with a ledger in her hand is Mrs. John Henry Hammond, president of the organization. The woman wearing a fur collar seated to Mrs. Hammond's right is probably Mrs. William Curtis Demorest; the next woman, wearing a dark hat and dress, is Mrs. A. Barton Hepburn, treasurer of the organization; the woman beside Mrs. Hepburn may be Mrs. Sara L. Straus, wife of American diplomat and secretary of the Department of Commerce and Labor in TR's cabinet Oscar S. Straus. The women shake hands and disperse; the event is probably related to the successful fund-raising campaign for the restoration of Roosevelt House.
1. New York (City). Roosevelt House. 2. New York (City) 3. Roosevelt, Theodore, Pres. U.S., 1858–1919—Birthplace. 4. Hammond, Emily Vanderbilt Sloane. 5. Demorest, Alice G. 6. Hepburn, Emily E. 7. Straus, Sara L. 8. Women's Theodore Roosevelt Memorial Association. I. Roosevelt Memorial Association, source. II. Theodore Roosevelt Association Collection. [mp 76–61]

Woman's Roosevelt Memorial Association meeting at Roosevelt House, 1923 [2]
Producer unknown, 1923.
© No reg.
   lr, 19 ft. si. b&w. 16mm. ref print.
   lr, 19 ft. si. b&w. 16mm. dupe neg.
   lr, 48 ft. si. b&w. 35mm. pos ntr.
SHELF LOC'N: FAB755 (print); FRA5810 (neg)
Ref sources: P&P portrait file; *Roosevelt House Bulletin*. v. 4, no. 1, 1932: 5; New York (City). Roosevelt House. Photographic file.
Factual.
SUMMARY: Medium-close shots of a small group of WRMA members standing and sitting around a desk on which a bust of TR is visible. The woman speaking and gesturing with a ledger in her hand is Mrs. John Henry Hammond, president of the organization. The woman wearing a fur collar seated to Mrs. Hammond's right is probably Mrs.

William Curtis Demorest; the next woman, wearing a dark hat and dress, is Mrs. A. Barton Hepburn, treasurer of the organization; the woman beside Mrs. Hepburn may be Mrs. Sara L. Straus, wife of American diplomat and secretary of the Department of Commerce and Labor in TR's cabinet Oscar S. Straus. The women shake hands and disperse; the event is probably related to the successful fund-raising campaign for the restoration of Roosevelt House.

1. New York (City). Roosevelt House. 2. New York (City) 3. Roosevelt, Theodore, Pres. U.S., 1858–1919—Birthplace. 4. Hammond, Emily Vanderbilt Sloane. 5. Demorest, Alice G. 6. Hepburn, Emily E. 7. Straus, Sara L. 8. Women's Theodore Roosevelt Memorial Association. I. Roosevelt Memorial Association, source. II. Theodore Roosevelt Association Collection. [mp 76–60]

Women suffragettes visit TR at Sagamore [1917]
Hearst-Pathe News, Sep 1917.

© No reg.

lr, 4 ft. si. b&w. 16mm. ref print.

lr, 4 ft. si. b&w. 16mm. dupe neg.

lr, 11 ft. si. b&w. 35mm. pos ntr.

(Hearst-Pathe News [newsreel])

SHELF LOC'N: FAB741 (print); FRA5787 (neg)

RMA lists the date in the title as 1918.

Ref sources: Harper, Ida H., ed. *History of Woman Suffrage.* v. 6, 1969; Bain, George Grantham. [News photos of woman suffrage in the United States, mostly New York City, 1905–1917.] lot 11052. P&P; League of Women Voters in the United States. . . . [W]omen active in the women's suffrage movement and as members of the National League of Women Voters. lot 5544. P&P; the Brooklyn *Daily Eagle.* 9/9/17: 1, 4.

Suffragists on their way to give William J. Gaynor, mayor of New York City, tickets to the Yonkers suffrage event on August 30, 1913.

Newsfilm.

SUMMARY: This film shows the opening of the second New York State suffrage campaign on Sept. 8, 1917, at Sagamore Hill. The first campaign, beginning in 1913, was unsuccessful; the woman suffrage amendment was rejected by the voters in 1915. On Nov. 6, 1917, the suffrage amendment to the New York State Constitution was approved by the voters. The suffragists invited to Sagamore Hill were headed by Mrs. Norman deR. Whitehouse, state chairman of the New York State Woman Suffrage Party. Sequence of TR talking to three women: the woman in the dark hat and coat is Mrs. Ogden Mills Reid; the woman dressed in furs next to TR is Mrs. Whitehouse; and the tall woman in the light hat and jacket is Mrs. James Lees Laidlaw.

1. Oyster Bay, N.Y. Sagamore Hill. 2. Suffrage. 3. Suffrage—New York (State) 4. Women—Suffrage—New York (State) 5. Women's rights—New York (State) 6. Oyster Bay, N.Y. 7. Roosevelt, Theodore, Pres. U.S., 1858–1919. 8. Whitehouse, Vira B. 9. Reid, Helen Rogers. 10. Laidlaw, Harriet B. I. Hearst-Pathe News. II. Pathe, source. III. Theodore Roosevelt Association Collection. [mp 76–37]

Wreck of the "Vizcaya."
American Mutoscope Co., 1898.
© H30726, American Mutoscope & Biograph Co., 24Apr1903
  lr of 1, 10 ft. si. b&w. 16mm. ref print.

lr of 1, 10 ft. si. b&w. 16mm. dupe neg.
lr of 1, 26 ft. si. b&w. 35mm. masterpos.
lr of 1, 16 ft. si. b&w. 16mm. ref print.
lr of 1, 16 ft. si. b&w. 16mm. dupe neg.
lr of 1, 26 ft. si. b&w. 35mm. paper (2 cy)
SHELF LOC'N: FAB1223 (print-RMA); FRA6174 (neg-RMA); FPB8068 (fgmp); FLA3150 (print-Paper); FRA 0483 (neg-Paper); LC136 (paper, 2 cy-Paper)

RMA title: *Wreck of the Viscaya in Santiago, Cuba, 1898.*

Ref sources: Werstein, Irving. *1898: The Spanish-American War.* 1966: 110; Freidel, Frank B. *The Splendid Little War.* 1958: 229.

Newsfilm.

SUMMARY: The Spanish armored cruiser Vizcaya was captured and destroyed by the U.S. Navy on July 4, 1898, while trying to escape a blockade of Santiago Bay in Cuba during the Spanish-American War. The camera, in a boat, moves in a tracking shot along the port side of the damaged Vizcaya, which is resting in shallow water; the shoreline is visible in the background.

1. United States—History—War of 1898. 2. United States—History—War of 1898—Naval operations. 3. Santiago de Cuba. 4. Vizcaya (Ship) 5. United States. Navy. I. Biograph Company. II. Biograph Company, source. III. Theodore Roosevelt Association Collection. IV. Paper Print Collection. [mp 76–71]

Chronological Index

1897

Theodore Roosevelt leaving the White House.
[Single date: 1897]
TR speaking at Sagamore Hill [1916–1918 and
scenes of his early career]
[Multiple dates: 1897–1918]

1898

25th Infantry.
[Single date: 1898]
Disappearing gun at testing grounds, Sandy
Hook, 1898.
[Single date: 1898]
Launch, U.S. battleship "Kentucky."
[Single date: 1898]
Pack mules with ammunition on the Santiago
trail, Cuba.
[Single date: 1898]
Return of Spanish-American troops, 1898.
[Single date: 1898]
Spanish Mountain Artillery, 1898.
[Single date: 1898]
Troops making military road in front of San-
tiago.
[Single date: 1898]
U.S. battleship Indiana.
[Single date: 1898]
U.S. battleship "Oregon."
[Single date: 1898]
U.S. troops landing at Daiquiri, Cuba.
[Single date: 1898]
Wreck of the "Vizcaya."
[Single date: 1898]

1899

Admiral Dewey on flagship, 1899.
[Single date: 1899]
Admiral Dewey on the deck of flagship, 1899 [1]
[Single date: 1899]
Admiral Dewey on the deck of flagship, 1899 [2]
[Single date: 1899]
Admiral Dewey parade, 1899 [1]
[Single date: 1899]
Admiral Dewey parade, 1899 [2]

[Single date: 1899]
Governor's Foot Guards, Conn.
[Single date: 1899]

1900

15th Infantry leaving Governors Island for China
(Boxer Uprising) 1900.
[Single date: 1900]
Daniel C. Beard and Ernest T. Seton.
[Questionable date: 1900–1909]
Dr. William Gorgas.
[Questionable date: 1900–1909]

1901

McKinley's funeral, 1901.
[Single date: 1901]
McKinley's funeral, Washington, D.C., 1901.
[Single date: 1901]
President McKinley inauguration, 1901.
[Single date: 1901]
President McKinley reviewing the troops at the
Pan-American Exposition.
[Single date: 1901]
President McKinley speaking, 1901.
[Single date: 1901]
President McKinley speaking at Buffalo, 1901.
[Single date: 1901]
President McKinley's funeral, 1901 [1]
[Single date: 1901]
President McKinley's funeral, 1901 [2]
[Single date: 1901]
President McKinley's funeral, Canton, Ohio, 1901
[1]
[Single date: 1901]
President McKinley's funeral, Canton, Ohio, 1901
[2]
[Single date: 1901]
President McKinley's funeral in Buffalo, Wash-
ington, and Canton, Ohio, 1901.
[Single date: 1901]
President McKinley's inauguration, 1901 [1]
[Single date: 1901]
President McKinley's inauguration, 1901 [2]
[Single date: 1901]

[Scenes of TR, Panama Canal construction, and William McKinley]
  [Multiple dates: 1901–1918]
Still pictures exposed on scene of McKinley's funeral as used in Paramount reel.
  [Single date: 1901]
TR attends McKinley's funeral, 1901.
  [Single date: 1901]
TR attends McKinley's funeral, Canton, Ohio, 1901.
  [Single date: 1901]

1903

The Forbidden City, Pekin.
  [Single date: 1903]
TR in San Francisco, 1903.
  [Single date: 1903]

1905

Japanese and Russian peace delegates [leaving New York City], 1905.
  [Single date: 1905]
TR as Father Curran's guest at Wilkes-Barre, Pa., August 10, 1905.
  [Single date: 1905]
TR at Wilkes-Barre, Pa., 1905.
  [Single date: 1905]
TR in Wilkes-Barre, Pa., 1905.
  [Single date: 1905]
[TR's inaugural ceremony, 1905]
  [Single date: 1905]
TR's inauguration, 1905 [1]
  [Single date: 1905]
TR's inauguration, 1905 [2]
  [Single date: 1905]

1906

TR speaking from Cathedral steps, Panama.
  [Single date: 1906]
TR speaking in Panama, November 1906.
  [Single date: 1906]
TR's arrival in Panama, November 1906 [1]
  [Single date: 1906]
TR's arrival in Panama, November 1906 [2]
  [Single date: 1906]
TR's arrival in Panama, November 1906 [3]
  [Single date: 1906]

1907

International naval review, Hampton Roads, Virginia, 1907.
  [Single date: 1907]
Jamestown Exposition, 1907.
  [Single date: 1907]
The King of Italy entertains King Edward of England on his yacht.
  [Single date: 1907]
Still picture of TR and his family.
  [Single date: 1907]
TR reviews the fleet, 1907.
  [Single date: 1907]

1908

William Howard Taft on rear platform of train.
  [Single date: 1908]

1909

African animals.
  [Single date: 1909]
African natives.
  [Single date: 1909]
Cartoon: TR's arrival in Africa.
  [Single date: 1909]
TR in Africa [1909, 1]
  [Single date: 1909]
TR in Africa [1909, 2]
  [Single date: 1909]
TR in Africa [1909, 3]
  [Single date: 1909]
TR in Africa [1909, 4]
  [Single date: 1909]
[TR planting a tree in Africa]
  [Single date: 1909]
TR's camp in Africa [1909]
  [Single date: 1909]

1910

Cartoon of TR's reception by crowned heads of Europe.
  [Single date: 1910]
Colonel Roosevelt is invited to fly in Arch Hoxsey's plane at St. Louis, Mo., 1910.
  [Single date: 1910]
Count von Bernstorff of Germany.
  [Questionable date: 1910–1919]

Crowd exterior of Buckingham Palace.
[Single date: 1910]
Czar Nicholas of Russia.
[Questionable date: 1910–1919]
Dr. Gorgas who had charge of sanitation during building of the Panama Canal.
[Questionable date: 1910–1919]
Emperor Francis Joseph of Austria greeted by his people.
[Single date: 1910]
Extermination of mosquitoes by spraying swamps.
[Questionable date: 1910–1919]
Kaiser Wilhelm.
[Questionable date: 1910–1919]
Kaiser Wilhelm and his admiralty staff attend launching at Kiel.
[Questionable date: 1910–1919]
King Edward's funeral, 1910 [1]
[Rereleased date: 1910, 1920]
King Edward's funeral, 1910 [2]
[Single date: 1910]
Lord and Lady Bryce.
[Questionable date: 1910–1919]
Major General Wm. C. Gorgas.
[Questionable date: 1910–1919]
[Man speaking at Faneuil Hall, Boston]
[Questionable date: 1910–1919]
Oscar Straus.
[Questionable date: 1910–1919]
Panama Canal scenes.
[Questionable date: 1910–1919]
Roosevelt cartoons.
[Questionable date: 1910–1919]
Scenes of John Burroughs.
[Questionable date: 1910–1919]
Scenes of lions.
[Questionable date: 1910–1919]
Senator Hitchcock.
[Questionable date: 1910–1919]
Senator Penrose.
[Questionable date: 1910–1919]
Senator Pomerene.
[Questionable date: 1910–1919]
Ships in the Panama Canal [1]
[Questionable date: 1910–1919]
Ships in the Panama Canal [2]
[Questionable date: 1910–1919]
Still pictures of TR at [Cambridge] 1910.
[Single date: 1910]
Street scenes in Naples, Italy.
[Questionable date: 1910–1919]
TR and several men.

[Questionable date: 1910–1919]
[TR getting into parked car]
[Questionable date: 1910–1919]
TR in Denmark, 1910.
[Single date: 1910]
TR in Norway, 1910.
[Single date: 1910]
TR in Norway and Denmark, 1910 [1]
[Single date: 1910]
TR in Norway and Denmark, 1910 [2]
[Single date: 1910]
TR in Norway and Denmark, 1910 [3]
[Single date: 1910]
TR in Vincennes, France, 1910.
[Single date: 1910]
TR on reception yacht in New York Bay, 1910.
[Single date: 1910]
TR reviews French troops at Vincennes, France, 1910.
[Single date: 1910]
TR speaking at Battery Park, New York, June 1910.
[Single date: 1910]
TR speaking at the Battery, 1910.
[Single date: 1910]
TR wearing army coat standing in auto greeting friends at Oyster Bay, 1910.
[Single date: 1910]
TR with Rough Rider friends.
[Questionable date: 1910–1919]
TR's return to New York, 1910 [1]
[Single date: 1910]
TR's return to New York, 1910 [2]
[Single date: 1910]
[Unidentified man]
[Questionable date: 1910–1919]
William Gibbs McAdoo.
[Questionable date: 1910–1919]
William H. Taft in Panama [1910?]
[Single date: 1910]

1911
Cartoon of Mr. Paul Rainey's African trip [1911]
[Single date: 1911]
Scenes of African animals [1911]
[Single date: 1911]
Scenes of Roosevelt Dam.
[Single date: 1911]
TR at dedication of Roosevelt Dam, 1911.
[Single date: 1911]
TR speaking at the dedication of Roosevelt Dam, 1911

[Single date: 1911]
TR with group of men, 1917; TR speaking at dedication of Roosevelt Dam, 1911.
[Multiple dates: 1911, 1917]

1912

Crowd listening to TR speak during Progressive campaign, 1912.
[Single date: 1912]
Roosevelt scenes from RMA productions.
[Multiple dates: 1912–1924]
Scenes of TR at Sagamore Hill, 1912.
[Single date: 1912]
Short scenes of TR [2]
[Multiple dates: 1912–1916]
TR and Mr. Helm, a newspaper reporter, exterior of Sagamore Hill, 1912.
[Single date: 1912]
TR at Fargo, N.D., during Progressive campaign, 1912 [1]
[Single date: 1912]
TR at Fargo, N.D., during Progressive campaign, 1912 [2]
[Single date: 1912]
TR during Progressive campaign, 1912.
[Single date: 1912]
TR in auto [1912]
[Single date: 1912]
TR riding in auto through crowded streets [1912]
[Single date: 1912]
TR scenes purchased from different dealers.
[Multiple dates: 1912–1927]
TR speaking at [Pueblo] Colorado, 1912.
[Single date: 1912]
TR speaking from train platform, 1912.
[Single date: 1912]
A visit to Theodore Roosevelt at his home at Sagamore Hill, Oyster Bay, L.I., 1912.
[Rereleased date: 1912, 1920]

1913

Hopi Indians dance for TR at [Walpi, Ariz.] 1913.
[Single date: 1913]
[Scenes of TR, 1913–1915]
[Multiple dates: 1913, 1915]
[Scenes of TR on board ship, 1916; Scenes of TR's trip to South America, 1913]
[Multiple dates: 1913, 1916]

1914

TR and expedition party on the [Sepotuba] River [1914]
[Single date: 1914]
TR in a rowboat on Oyster Bay, Archie assists with boat to shore, 1914.
[Single date: 1914]
TR seated at his desk in the Outlook office [1914?]
[Single date: 1914]

1915

Reviewing Annapolis middies.
[Single date: 1915]
TR and Mrs. Roosevelt [at the Panama-California Exposition, 1915]
[Single date: 1915]
TR [at Panama-Pacific Exposition, 1915]
[Single date: 1915]
TR at Sagamore Hill [1916]
[Multiple dates: 1915, 1916]
TR at San Diego Exposition, 1915.
[Single date: 1915]
TR [in Louisiana], 1915 [1]
[Single date: 1915]
TR [in Louisiana], 1915 [2]
[Single date: 1915]
TR [in Louisiana], 1915 [3]
[Single date: 1915]
TR [in Louisiana], 1915 [4]
[Single date: 1915]
TR speaking [at the Panama-Pacific Exposition, 1915]
[Single date: 1915]
William H. Taft burns mortgage of Exposition, 1915.
[Single date: 1915]

1916

Charles E. Hughes speaking during campaign, Duquesne, Pa., 1916.
[Single date: 1916]
Chauncey Depew, Senator Perkins, and Governor Whitman of New York, at GOP Convention, 1916, Chicago, Ill.
[Single date: 1916]
Scenes of TR on board ship before sailing for West Indies, 1916.

[Single date: 1916]

Scenes of TR speaking at Sagamore [1916–1918]
  [Multiple dates: 1916–1918]

Shall we prepare?
  [Single date: 1916]

Short scenes of TR [1]
  [Multiple dates: 1916–1918]

Short scenes of TR as used in Paramount reel.
  [Multiple dates: 1916–1918]

TR at Sagamore Hill [1916–1918]
  [Multiple dates: 1916, 1918]

TR in New Mexico, 1916.
  [Single date: 1916]

TR speaking at Oyster Bay, July 4, 1916.
  [Single date: 1916]

TR speaking at Sagamore Hill [1916–1918] [1]
  [Multiple dates: 1916–1918]

TR speaking at Sagamore Hill [1916–1918] [2]
  [Multiple dates: 1916–1918]

TR speaking to a group of men from the porch at Sagamore Hill, 1916.
  [Single date: 1916]

TR's reception in Albuquerque, N.M., 1916.
  [Single date: 1916]

1917

Close-up of TR speaking [1917]
  [Single date: 1917]

Close-up scenes of TR speaking during World War I, 1917–18.
  [Single date: 1917]

Crowd listening to TR, Cardinal Gibbons and priests in foreground, 1917.
  [Single date: 1917]

Elihu Root and Mayor Mitchel of New York, Mr. Root and American delegates return from Russia [1917]
  [Single date: 1917]

Mayor Mitchel of New York.
  [Single date: 1917]

President McKinley's memorial dedicated by William Howard Taft at Niles, Ohio.
  [Single date: 1917]

Roosevelt scenes [1917–1918]
  [Multiple dates: 1917–1918]

Sarah Bernhardt addresses crowd in Prospect Park, Brooklyn, 1917.
  [Single date: 1917]

Scenes of TR and his sons Quentin and Archie, 1917–1918 [1]
  [Multiple dates: 1917–1918]

Scenes of TR and his sons Quentin and Archie, 1917–1918 [2]
  [Multiple dates: 1917–1918]

TR and Leonard Wood at the New York flower show, 1917.
  [Single date: 1917]

TR at Camp Mills [1917]
  [Single date: 1917]

TR at Forest Hills, New York, 1917 [1]
  [Single date: 1917]

TR at Forest Hills, New York, 1917 [2]
  [Single date: 1917]

TR at limousine window, 1917.
  [Single date: 1917]

TR at Sagamore, 1917.
  [Single date: 1917]

TR attends dinner of Cincinnati, Ohio, Business Men's Club, Dec. 14, 1917 [1]
  [Single date: 1917]

TR attends dinner of Cincinnati, Ohio, Business Men's Club, Dec. 14, 1917 [2]
  [Single date: 1917]

TR attends his son Archie's wedding at Boston, 1917.
  [Single date: 1917]

TR calls on neighbors at Christmas, 1917.
  [Single date: 1917]

TR, Charles E. Hughes, and Mayor Mitchel of New York, on reviewing stand in front of the New York Public Library [1917]
  [Single date: 1917]

TR greeting crowds of people, 1917–1918.
  [Single date: 1917]

TR in St. Paul, Minn. [1917]
  [Single date: 1917]

TR, Mayor Mitchel and guests at Cooper Sanitarium [1917]
  [Single date: 1917]

TR, Mayor Mitchel, Governor Charles Whitman of New York, and Myron Herrick, 1917.
  [Single date: 1917]

TR on porch at Sagamore Hill, 1917.
  [Single date: 1917]

TR receiving Belgian envoys at Sagamore Hill [1917]
  [Single date: 1917]

TR reviewing and speaking to 13th Regiment at Sagamore Hill, 1917.
  [Single date: 1917]

TR reviews and addresses troops [Fort Sheridan, Ill.]; TR riding in auto, Chicago, 1917.
  [Single date: 1917]

TR riding in an auto in Chicago, 1917.

[Single date: 1917]
TR speaking at [St. Paul, Minnesota, 1917]
[Single date: 1917]
TR speaking during War, 1917–1918.
[Single date: 1917]
TR speaking to a group of suffragettes from the porch at Sagamore Hill [1917]
[Single date: 1917]
[TR speaks to group at Sagamore Hill, 1]
[Single date: 1917]
[TR speaks to group at Sagamore Hill, 2]
[Single date: 1917]
[TR speaks to group at Sagamore Hill, 3]
[Single date: 1917]
Women suffragettes visit TR at Sagamore [1917]
[Single date: 1917]

1918

Allied armies in China, 1917–1918.
[Single date: 1918]
Exterior scenes of Sagamore Hill.
[Single date: 1918]
Governor Goodrich of Indiana.
[Single date: 1918]
Last known home of Czar Nicholas.
[Single date: 1918]
Mrs. Theodore Roosevelt Jr. attends Women in War Work Congress in Paris [1918]
[Single date: 1918]
President Wilson arrives in New York to lead fourth Liberty Loan parade [1918]
[Single date: 1918]
[Quentin Roosevelt]; Clemenceau and Foch, 1917–1919.
[Single date: 1918]
Robert Bacon and Army officers.
[Single date: 1918]
Rough Riders greet TR during Liberty Loan drive out west [1918]
[Single date: 1918]
Scene of Clemenceau, Tardieu, Foch, Poincaré and Pershing, 1917–1918.
[Single date: 1918]
[Scenes of the British royal family]
[Single date: 1918]
TR addresses large crowd for the Liberty Loan in Baltimore, 1918.
[Single date: 1918]
TR and Cardinal Gibbons at Baltimore, Md., 1918.
[Single date: 1918]

TR at Baltimore [1918]; TR at Sagamore [Hill, 1918]
[Single date: 1918]
TR at Billings, Montana [1918]
[Single date: 1918]
TR, exterior of building, Washington, D.C. 1918.
[Single date: 1918]
TR in Baltimore during Liberty Loan drive, 1918.
[Single date: 1918]
TR on Fifth Avenue, New York, near St. Patrick's Cathedral after attending Mayor Mitchel's funeral.
[Single date: 1918]
TR speaking at Newburgh, N.Y. [1918]
[Single date: 1918]
TR speaking at St. Paul, Minn., 1918.
[Single date: 1918]
TR speaking in St. Paul, Minnesota, 1918.
[Single date: 1918]
TR with naval officers, exterior Navy Club, Boston [1918]
[Single date: 1918]
TR's sons' regiments during war, 1917–1918 [1]
[Single date: 1918]
TR's sons' regiments during war, 1917–1918 [2]
[Single date: 1918]

1919

Airmen honor TR's memory by dropping American Legion wreath on his grave [1919]
[Single date: 1919]
American Legion places wreath on TR's grave [1919]; Scenes of Oyster Bay from the air.
[Single date: 1919]
Americanism wins, Coolidge elected.
[Single date: 1919]
Aviators drop American Legion wreath on TR's grave [1919]
[Single date: 1919]
Brooklyn children attend services, children sew stars on Roosevelt Flag [1919]
[Single date: 1919]
Calvin Coolidge as Governor of Massachusetts.
[Single date: 1919]
Calvin Coolidge as Governor of Massachusetts, 1919.
[Single date: 1919]
Children sewing stars on flag, placing flag on TR's grave [1919]
[Single date: 1919]
Dedication of Roosevelt Mountain at Deadwood, S.D., 1919.

[Single date: 1919]

Flag at half-mast, Oyster Bay, Jan. 1919.
[Single date: 1919]

[Flag services for TR at Oyster Bay, October 1919]
[Single date: 1919]

Gen. Pershing speaking to Scouts in New York.
[Single date: 1919]

Governors of New England meet in Governor Coolidge's office in Boston to discuss fuel.
[Single date: 1919]

King Albert of Belgium visits TR's grave, 1919.
[Single date: 1919]

King Albert of Belgium visits TR's grave, October, 1919.
[Single date: 1919]

Lieutenant-Colonel Theodore Roosevelt arrives in New York after the World War.
[Single date: 1919]

Memorial services for TR at Van Cortlandt Park, New York, Oct. 1919.
[Single date: 1919]

Memorial services for TR on the steps of the New York Public Library, 1919 [1]
[Single date: 1919]

Memorial services for TR on the steps of the New York Public Library, 1919 [2]
[Single date: 1919]

Oyster Bay from the air [1919]
[Single date: 1919]

Panama Canal; scenes of the finished Canal.
[Single date: 1919]

The Prince of Wales visits TR's grave.
[Single date: 1919]

Quentin Roosevelt's grave, 1918.
[Single date: 1919]

Quentin Roosevelt's grave in France.
[Single date: 1919]

RMA ceremonies at [Hearst Greek Theatre, University of California, Berkeley, Calif.]
[Single date: 1919]

RMA flag ceremonies, children sew stars on flag, 1919.
[Single date: 1919]

RMA flag service on the steps of New York Public Library, 1919.
[Single date: 1919]

Runners carrying flag to TR's grave [1919]
[Single date: 1919]

Senators Curtis, Cummins, Moses, and [Representative] Mondell.
[Single date: 1919]

Speaker of the House F. H. Gillett.

[Single date: 1919]

Through the Roosevelt country with Roosevelt's friends.
[Single date: 1919]

TR Jr. with group of sailors and soldiers.
[Single date: 1919]

TR memorial services at New York Public Library, 1919.
[Single date: 1919]

TR's funeral, 1919.
[Single date: 1919]

TR's funeral at Oyster Bay, 1919.
[Single date: 1919]

TR's funeral at Oyster Bay, January 1919 [1]
[Single date: 1919]

TR's funeral at Oyster Bay, January 1919 [2]
[Single date: 1919]

Whole nation honors memory of Roosevelt.
[Single date: 1919]

1920

Aigrette.
[Questionable date: 1920–1929]

Calvin Coolidge sworn in for second term as Governor of Massachusetts.
[Single date: 1920]

Children visit TR's grave, 1920.
[Single date: 1920]

Close-up of TR's grave, 1920.
[Single date: 1920]

Col. William Boyce Thompson.
[Questionable date: 1920–1929]

Daniel C. Beard, TR Jr., and Boy Scouts visit TR's grave, 1920.
[Single date: 1920]

Friends and admirers visit TR's grave, 1920.
[Single date: 1920]

General Pershing at Camp Grant.
[Single date: 1920]

General Wood and Calvin Coolidge in Chicago, 1920.
[Single date: 1920]

Herbert Putnam.
[Questionable date: 1920–1929]

King and Queen of Spain attend a military review.
[Questionable date: 1920–1929]

King Gustav of Sweden greeted by his people.
[Questionable date: 1920–1929]

Laying cornerstone of Roosevelt School, New Rochelle, N.Y. [1920]

[Single date: 1920]
Leonard Wood at Battle Creek, Michigan.
[Single date: 1920]
Original U.S. documents.
[Single date: 1920]
Owen Wister.
[Questionable date: 1920–1929]
President Harding and Calvin Coolidge [1]
[Single date: 1920]
President Harding and Calvin Coolidge [2]
[Single date: 1920]
Queen Wilhelmina of Holland, the Prince Consort [and] the Princess.
[Questionable date: 1920–1929]
RMA services at [Hearst Greek Theatre, University of California, Berkeley, Calif.]; Laying cornerstone of Roosevelt School at New Rochelle, N.Y. [1920]
[Single date: 1920]
Scenes of Dr. Frank Chapman.
[Questionable date: 1920–1929]
Scenes of flowers and birds in Washington, D.C.
[Questionable date: 1920–1929]
[Scenes of flowers in Washington, D.C.]
·[Questionable date: 1920–1929]
Scenes of the Capitol, Washington, D.C.
[Questionable date: 1920–1929]
Scenes of the White House.
[Questionable date: 1920–1929]
Scout parade, Cartagena, Colombia, 1920.
[Single date: 1920]
Scouts on their way to TR's grave, Daniel C. Beard and TR Jr. attend services, 1920.
[Single date: 1920]
Senator McCumber of North Dakota.
[Single date: 1920]
Senator Smoot.
[Questionable date: 1920–1929]
Still photographs of TR on motion picture film.
[Questionable date: 1920–1929]
Three children visit TR's grave, 1920.
[Single date: 1920]
TR Jr. and Will Hays.
[Questionable date: 1920–1929]
Will Hays.
[Questionable date: 1920–1929]
Woman wearing aigrette in her hat.
[Questionable date: 1920–1929]

1921
American Legion lays cornerstone of Roosevelt Bridge at Chateau-Thierry.

[Single date: 1921]
General [Diaz] of Italy visits TR's grave [1921]
[Single date: 1921]
General Nivelle visits TR's grave [1921]
[Single date: 1921]
Leonard Wood lays cornerstone of Roosevelt House, 1921.
[Single date: 1921]
Marshal Foch visits Roosevelt House, 1921.
[Single date: 1921]
President Harding presenting chair used by TR at the White House to the directors of RMA, October 1921.
[Single date: 1921]
Senator Watson.
[Single date: 1921]

1922
Senator Hiram Johnson.
[Single date: 1922]

1923
Bulloch home, Roswell, Georgia, 1923.
[Single date: 1923]
Dedication of Roosevelt House, 1923.
[Single date: 1923]
Dedication of Roosevelt House, Oct. 27, 1923.
[Single date: 1923]
General Goethals.
[Single date: 1923]
Gifford Pinchot, 1923.
[Single date: 1923]
Moving exhibits into Roosevelt House, 1923.
[Single date: 1923]
RMA trustees at Roosevelt House, 1923 [1]
[Single date: 1923]
RMA trustees at Roosevelt House, 1923 [2]
[Single date: 1923]
Scenes of Sagamore Hill.
[Single date: 1923]
Woman's Roosevelt Memorial Association meeting at Roosevelt House, 1923 [1]
[Single date: 1923]
Woman's Roosevelt Memorial Association meeting at Roosevelt House, 1923 [2]
[Single date: 1923]

1924
Dedication of Cuban memorial, 1924 [1]

[Single date: 1924]
Dedication of Cuban memorial, 1924 [2]
  [Single date: 1924]
Jules Jusserand, 1924.
  [Single date: 1924]
Mr. Hagedorn and Mrs. Wood at Roosevelt House [1924, Long version]
  [Single date: 1924]
Mr. Hagedorn and Mrs. Wood at Roosevelt House [1924, Short version]
  [Single date: 1924]
Roosevelt, friend of the birds [1]
  [Single date: 1924]
Roosevelt, friend of the birds [2]
  [Single date: 1924]
Roosevelt, friend of the birds [3]
  [Single date: 1924]
Scenes of Oyster Bay.
  [Single date: 1924]

1925

Memorializing Roosevelt.
  [Single date: 1925]
Mr. Hagedorn and Mr. Akeley at Roosevelt House, 1925 [1]
  [Single date: 1925]
Mr. Hagedorn and Mr. Akeley at Roosevelt House, 1925 [2]
  [Single date: 1925]
Mr. Hagedorn and Mr. Akeley at Roosevelt House, 1925 [3]
  [Single date: 1925]
Presentation of Roosevelt Medals, May 1925, Washington, D.C.
  [Single date: 1925]
Scenes showing Blue Line Tour route to Roosevelt House in 1925.
  [Single date: 1925]
Theodore Roosevelt, great scout [1]
  [Single date: 1925]
Theodore Roosevelt, great scout [2]
  [Single date: 1925]
Theodore Roosevelt, great scout [3]
  [Single date: 1925]
TR comes back.
  [Single date: 1925]
TR's return from Africa, 1910 [1]
  [Single date: 1925]
TR's return from Africa, 1910 [2]
  [Single date: 1925]

1926

Commander Dyott sailing from [Hoboken, N.J.] for South America, 1926.
  [Single date: 1926]
The prize winning design by John Russell Pope for the proposed memorial to Theodore Roosevelt for the city of Washington.
  [Single date: 1926]
TR himself [1]
  [Single date: 1926]
TR himself [2]
  [Single date: 1926]
TR himself [3]
  [Single date: 1926]
TR himself [4]
  [Single date: 1926]
TR himself [5]
  [Single date: 1926]
TR himself [6]
  [Single date: 1926]

1927

Colonel Lindbergh, Admiral Byrd, and Clarence Chamberlin at flying field just before Lindbergh's flight, 1927.
  [Single date: 1927]
The King and Queen of Belgium and Premier Poincaré of France [1]
  [Single date: 1927]
The King and Queen of Belgium and Premier Poincaré of France [2]
  [Single date: 1927]
Mrs. Roosevelt, Sr., and Mrs. J. H. Hammond photographed on the roof of Roosevelt House, 1927; Mrs. Roosevelt arrives at Roosevelt House.
  [Single date: 1927]
Owen D. Young [1]
  [Single date: 1927]
Owen D. Young [2]
  [Single date: 1927]
The Panama Canal.
  [Single date: 1927]
President Coolidge speaking at Black Hills, S.D., 1927.
  [Single date: 1927]
Scenes of the River of Doubt photographed by G. M. Dyott, 1926–1927 [1]
  [Single date: 1927]
Scenes of the River of Doubt photographed by G. M. Dyott, 1926–1927 [2]

[Single date: 1927]
The Story of the Panama Canal [1]
[Single date: 1927]
The Story of the Panama Canal [2]
[Single date: 1927]

1928

The Building of the Panama Canal upon the occasion of a memorial exhibition held in honor of General George Washington Goethals.
[Single date: 1928]
King George and Queen Mary of England [1]
[Single date: 1928]
King George and Queen Mary of England [2]
[Single date: 1928]
The River of Doubt [1]
[Single date: 1928]
The River of Doubt [2]
[Single date: 1928]
The River of Doubt [3]
[Single date: 1928]
The River of Doubt [4]
[Single date: 1928]
The River of Doubt [5]
[Single date: 1928]
The River of Doubt [6]
[Single date: 1928]
The River of Doubt [7]
[Single date: 1928]
The Roosevelt Dam [1]
[Single date: 1928]
The Roosevelt Dam [2]
[Single date: 1928]
Roosevelt, friend of the birds [4]; The Roosevelt Dam [3]
[Single date: 1928]

1929

Mr. Garfield presenting medals to 1929 medalists.
[Single date: 1929]

1930

President Roosevelt, 1901–1909.
[Single date: 1930]
RMA pilgrimage to TR's grave, 1930.
[Single date: 1930]
Roosevelt at home: Sagamore Hill, Oyster Bay, L.I. [1]
[Single date: 1930]
Roosevelt at home: Sagamore Hill, Oyster Bay, L.I. [2]
[Single date: 1930]
Scenes of Hastings Hart, 1930 medalist.
[Single date: 1930]
Theodore Roosevelt in the great war [1]
[Single date: 1930]
Theodore Roosevelt in the great war [2]
[Single date: 1930]
Theodore Roosevelt in the great war [3]
[Single date: 1930]

1934

Professor Henry Fairfield Osborn, RMA medalist, 1923.
[Single date: 1934]
Theodore Roosevelt: fighter for social justice.
[Single date: 1934]

General Index

Abbott, Samuel
Brooklyn children attend services, children sew stars on Roosevelt Flag [1919] 1919
Children sewing stars on flag, placing flag on TR's grave [1919] 1919
[Flag services for TR at Oyster Bay, October 1919] 1919
Memorial services for TR at Van Cortlandt Park, New York, Oct. 1919. 1919
Memorial services for TR on the steps of the New York Public Library, 1919 [1] 1919
RMA flag ceremonies, children sew stars on flag, 1919. 1919
RMA flag service on the steps of New York Public Library, 1919. 1919
Whole nation honors memory of Roosevelt. 1919.

Actresses
Woman wearing aigrette in her hat. 1920

Aeronautics
See Airplanes; Air pilots

Aeronautics—Exhibitions
Colonel Roosevelt is invited to fly in Arch Hoxsey's plane at St. Louis, Mo., 1910. 1910

Africa
Cartoon of Mr. Paul Rainey's African trip [1911] 1911
Cartoon: TR's arrival in Africa. 1909
Scenes of African animals [1911] 1911
Theodore Roosevelt, great scout [1] 1925
Theodore Roosevelt, great scout [2] 1925
Theodore Roosevelt, great scout [3] 1925

Africa—Native races
TR in Africa [1909, 1] 1909
TR in Africa [1909, 2] 1909
TR in Africa [1909, 4] 1909

African elephant
Scenes of African animals [1911] 1911

Afro-American soldiers
25th Infantry, 1898
TR in San Francisco, 1903. 1903

Air bases—New York (State)
Airmen honor TR's memory by dropping American Legion wreath on his grave [1919] 1919
American Legion places wreath on TR's grave [1919]; Scenes of Oyster Bay from the air. 1919
Aviators drop American Legion wreath on TR's grave [1919] 1919.

Air pilots
Airmen honor TR's memory by dropping American Legion wreath on his grave [1919] 1919
American Legion places wreath on TR's grave [1919]; Scenes of Oyster Bay from the air. 1919
Aviators drop American Legion wreath on TR's grave [1919] 1919
Colonel Roosevelt is invited to fly in Arch Hoxsey's plane at St. Louis, Mo., 1910. 1910
Oyster Bay from the air [1919] 1919

Airplanes
Airmen honor TR's memory by dropping American Legion wreath on his grave [1919] 1919
American Legion places wreath on TR's grave [1919]; Scenes of Oyster Bay from the air. 1919
Aviators drop American Legion wreath on TR's grave [1919] 1919
Colonel Roosevelt is invited to fly in Arch Hoxsey's plane at St. Louis, Mo., 1910. 1910
Oyster Bay from the air [1919] 1919
TRs sons' regiments during war, 1917–1918 [1] 1918

Akeley, Carl E.
Mr. Hagedorn and Mr. Akeley at Roosevelt House, 1925 [1] 1925
Mr. Hagedorn and Mr. Akeley at Roosevelt House, 1925 [2] 1925
Mr. Hagedorn and Mr. Akeley at Roosevelt House, 1925 [3] 1925
Presentation of Roosevelt Medals, May 1925, Washington, D. C. 1925

Albert I, King of the Belgians, 1875–1934
King Albert of Belgium visits TR's grave, 1919. 1919
King Albert of Belgium visits TR's grave, October, 1919. 1919
The King and Queen of Belgium and Premier Poincaré of France [1] 1927
The King and Queen of Belgium and Premier Poincaré of France [2] 1927
Roosevelt scenes from RMA productions. 1912
TR's return from Africa, 1910 [1] 1925
TR's return from Africa, 1910 [2] 1925

Albert, Duke of York
See George VI, King of Great Britain, 1895–1952

Albrucci, Alberico
Scene of Clemenceau, Tardieu, Foch, Poincaré and Pershing, 1917–1918. 1918

Albuquerque, N. M.
Scenes of TR speaking at Sagamore [1916-1918] 1916
Short scenes of TR [1] 1916
Short scenes of TR [2] 1912
TR in New Mexico, 1916. 1916
TR's reception in Albuquerque, N. M., 1916. 1916

Albuquerque, N. M.—Streets—Central Avenue
TR's reception in Albuquerque, N. M., 1916. 1916

Albuquerque, N. M. Alvarado Hotel
Short scenes of TR [1] 1916
Short scenes of TR [2] 1912
TR in New Mexico, 1916. 1916
TR's reception in Albuquerque, N. M., 1916. 1916

Alexander, Eleanor Butler
See Roosevelt, Eleanor Butler Alexander

Alexander, George
TR riding in auto through crowded streets [1912] 1912

Alexander, M. L.
Roosevelt, friend of the birds [1] 1924
Roosevelt, friend of the birds [2] 1924
Roosevelt, friend of the birds [3] 1924
Roosevelt, friend of the birds [4]; The Roosevelt Dam [3] 1928
TR [in Louisiana], 1915 [1] 1915

Alexander, Mark L.
See Alexander, M. L.

Alexandra, consort of Edward VII, King of Great Britain, 1844–1925
The King of Italy entertains King Edward of England on his yacht. 1907
[Scenes of the British royal family] 1918

Alexandra, consort of Nicholas II, Emperor of Russia, 1872–1918
Czar Nicholas of Russia. 1910

Alfonso XIII, King of Spain, 1886–1941
Cartoon of TR's reception by crowned heads of Europe. 1910
King and Queen of Spain attend a military review. 1920
TR's return from Africa, 1910 [1] 1925
TR's return from Africa, 1910 [2] 1925

Alger, Frederick M.
Leonard Wood at Battle Creek, Michigan. 1920

Alger, Mary Swift
Leonard Wood at Battle Creek, Michigan. 1920

Allegheny Co., Pa. County Courthouse
Short scenes of TR [1] 1916

Allegheny County Courthouse, Pittsburgh
See Allegheny Co., Pa. County Courthouse

Allen, Henry J.
Dedication of Cuban memorial, 1924 [1] 1924
Dedication of Cuban memorial, 1924 [2] 1924
Memorial services for TR on the steps of the New York Public Library, 1919 [1] 1919
Memorial services for TR on the steps of the New York Public Library, 1919 [2] 1919
RMA flag service on the steps of New York Public Library, 1919. 1919
TR memorial services at New York Public Library, 1919. 1919

Altar of Liberty, New York (City)
See New York (City). Liberty's Altar

Alvarado Hotel, Albuquerque, N. M.
See Albuquerque, N. M. Alvarado Hotel

Amador Guerrero, Manuel, Pres. Panama, 1833–1909
See Panama, Presidente, 1904-1908 (Amador Guerrero)

Amador Guerrero, Manuel, Pres. Panama, 1833–1909—Addresses, essays, lectures
TR speaking from Cathedral steps, Panama. 1906
TR speaking in Panama, November 1906. 1906
TR's arrival in Panama, November 1906 [1] 1906
TR's arrival in Panama, November 1906 [2] 1906
TR's arrival in Panama, November 1906 [3] 1906

Amazon Valley
The River of Doubt [1] 1928
The River of Doubt [2] 1928
The River of Doubt [3] 1928
The River of Doubt [4] 1928
The River of Doubt [5] 1928
The River of Doubt [6] 1928
The River of Doubt [7] 1928
Scenes of the River of Doubt photographed by G. M. Dyott, 1926–1927 [1] 1927
Scenes of the River of Doubt photographed by G. M. Dyott, 1926–1927 [2] 1927
TR and expedition party on the [Sepotuba] River [1914] 1914

American Legion
Airmen honor TR's memory by dropping American Legion wreath on his grave [1919] 1919
American Legion lays cornerstone of Roosevelt Bridge at Château-Thierry. 1921
American Legion places wreath on TR's grave [1919]; Scenes of Oyster Bay from the air, 1919
Americanism wins, Coolidge elected. 1919
Aviators drop American Legion wreath on TR's grave [1919] 1919
TR Jr. with group of sailors and soldiers. 1919

American Motion Picture Company, source
TR on Fifth Avenue, New York, near St. Patrick's Cathedral after attending Mayor Mitchel's funeral. 1918

American Museum of Natural History, New York
Professor Henry Fairfield Osborn, RMA medalist, 1923. 1934
Scenes of Dr. Frank Chapman. 1920

American Museum of Natural History, New York, source
Professor Henry Fairfield Osborn, RMA medalist, 1923. 1934

American Mutoscope and Biograph Company
See Biograph Company

American Mutoscope Company
See Biograph Company

American Spanish War, 1898
See United States—History—War of 1898

Ammunition—Transportation
Pack mules with ammunition on the Santiago trail, Cuba. 1898

Ancon, Canal Zone
Panama Canal; scenes of the finished Canal. 1919

Androscoggin (Ship)
TR comes back. 1925
TR on reception yacht in New York Bay, 1910. 1910
TR's return to New York, 1910 [1] 1910
TR's return to New York, 1910 [2] 1910

Anemones
Scenes of flowers and birds in Washington, D. C. 1920
[Scenes of flowers in Washington, D. C.] 1920

Animal sculpture—New York (City)
Professor Henry Fairfield Osborn, RMA medalist, 1923. 1934

Animals
Cartoon of Mr. Paul Rainey's African trip [1911] 1911
Cartoon: TR's arrival in Africa. 1909

Ann Arbor, Mich.
Leonard Wood at Battle Creek, Michigan. 1920

Annapolis Naval Academy
See United States. Naval Academy, Annapolis

Ants—Brazil
The River of Doubt [6] 1928
Scenes of the River of Doubt photographed by G. M. Dyott, 1926–1927 [1] 1927
Scenes of the River of Doubt photographed by G. M. Dyott, 1926–1927 [2] 1927

Apollo Pictures, source
Aigrette. 1920
Calvin Coolidge as Governor of Massachusetts. 1919
Dr. William Gorgas. 1900
TR in Wilkes-Barre, Pa., 1905. 1905
William H. Taft burns mortgage of Exposition, 1915. 1915

Appleton, Daniel
TR, Charles E. Hughes, and Mayor Mitchel of New York, on reviewing stand in front of the New York Public Library [1917] 1917

Aquariums, Public
TR's return to New York, 1910 [2] 1910

Arara Indians
The River of Doubt [1] 1928
The River of Doubt [2] 1928
The River of Doubt [3] 1928
The River of Doubt [6] 1928
The River of Doubt [7] 1928
Scenes of the River of Doubt photographed by G. M. Dyott, 1926–1927 [1] 1927
Scenes of the River of Doubt photographed by G. M. Dyott, 1926–1927 [2] 1927

Architectural models
The prize winning design by John Russell Pope for the proposed memorial to Theodore Roosevelt for the city of Washington. 1926

Architecture, American—Oyster Bay, N. Y.
Scenes of Oyster Bay. 1924
Scenes of Sagamore Hill. 1923

Architecture, Primitive
William H. Taft in Panama [1910?] 1910

Ariponan River
See Roosevelt River

Arizona
The Roosevelt Dam [1] 1928
The Roosevelt Dam [2] 1928
Roosevelt, friend of the birds [4]; The Roosevelt Dam [3] 1928
TR with group of men, 1917; TR speaking at dedication of **Roosevelt Dam, 1911**. 1911

Arizona (Ter.). Governor, 1909–1912 (Sloan)
The Roosevelt Dam [1] 1928
The Roosevelt Dam [2] 1928
TR at dedication of Roosevelt Dam, 1911. 1911
TR speaking at the dedication of Roosevelt Dam, 1911. 1911
TR with group of men, 1917; TR speaking at dedication of Roosevelt Dam, 1911. 1911

Armed Forces
RMA ceremonies at [Hearst Greek Threatre, University of California, Berkeley, Calif.] 1919.
RMA services at [Hearst Greek Threatre, University of California, Berkeley, Calif.]; Laying cornerstone of Roosevelt School at New Rochelle, N. Y. [1920] 1920
See also Armies; Soldiers; specific branches of the Armed Forces under names of countries, e. g., United States. Army.

Armes, Ethel M.
Memorializing Roosevelt. 1925

Armies
Allied armies in China, 1917–1918. 1918
See also Soldiers; United States. Army; and similar headings.

Armies—Maneuvers
See Military maneuvers

Armies—Supplies
See Military supplies

Army
See United States. Army

Arthur, Duke of Connaught, 1850–1942
See Connaught, Arthur William Patrick Albert, Duke of, 1850–1942.

Artillery
Disappearing gun at testing grounds, Sandy Hook, 1898. 1898
TR's sons' regiments during war, 1917–1918 [1] 1918
See also United States. Army. Artillery; and similar headings.

Artillery, Field and mountain
Spanish Mountain Artillery, 1898. 1898

Ashton, Elizabeth
See Bryce, Elizabeth A.

Asiatic Squadron
See United States. Navy. Asiatic Fleet

Associated Press
Roosevelt at home: Sagamore Hill, Oyster Bay, L.I. [1] 1930
Roosevelt at home: Sagamore Hill, Oyster Bay, L.I. [2] 1930
Scenes of TR at Sagamore Hill, 1912. 1912
A visit to Theodore Roosevelt at his home at Sagamore Hill, Oyster Bay, L.I., 1912. 1912

Astor, Vincent
See Astor, William Vincent

Astor, William Vincent
[Scenes of TR, 1913–1915] 1913

Athletics
[Scenes of TR, 1913–1915] 1913

Atterbury, Harriet N.
Leonard Wood at Battle Creek, Michigan. 1920

Audubon Society
See National Audubon Society

Azan, Paul J.
General Nivelle visits TR's grave [1921] 1921

Bacon, Augustus O.
TR's inauguration, 1905 [2] 1905

Bacon, Henry, 1866-1924
Dedication of Cuban memorial, 1924 [1] 1924
Dedication of Cuban memorial, 1924 [2] 1924

Bacon, Robert, 1860-1919
Robert Bacon and Army officers. 1918
TR in Vincennes, France, 1910. 1910
TR reviews French troops at Vincennes, France, 1910. 1910
TR's return from Africa, 1910 [1] 1925
TR's return from Africa, 1910 [2] 1925

Badlands, N.D.
See Little Missouri Badlands, N.D.

Baiquiri, Cuba
See Daiquiri, Cuba

Baker, Chauncey B.
Leonard Wood at Battle Creek, Michigan. 1920

Baker, Evelyn King
Bulloch home, Roswell, Georgia, 1923. 1923

Baker, George F.
Owen D. Young [1] 1927
Owen D. Young [2] 1927

Balboa, Canal Zone
Panama Canal; scenes of the finished Canal. 1919

Balboa, Canal Zone—Buildings
Panama Canal; scenes of the finished Canal. 1919

Balboa Heights, Canal Zone
Panama Canal; scenes of the finished Canal. 1919

Ball, Willis
Bulloch home, Roswell, Georgia, 1923. 1923

Baltimore
Roosevelt scenes from RMA productions. 1912
Theodore Roosevelt in the great war [1] 1930
Theodore Roosevelt in the great war [2] 1930
Theodore Roosevelt in the great war [3] 1930
TR addresses large crowd for the Liberty Loan in Baltimore, 1918. 1918
TR and Cardinal Gibbons at Baltimore, Md., 1918. 1918
TR at Baltimore [1918]; TR at Sagamore [Hill, 1918] 1918
TR in Baltimore during Liberty Loan drive, 1918. 1918
TR scenes purchased from different dealers. 1912

Baltimore—Sports facilities
TR addresses large crowd for the Liberty Loan in Baltimore, 1918. 1918
TR and Cardinal Gibbons at Baltimore, Md., 1918. 1918
TR at Baltimore [1918]; TR at Sagamore [Hill, 1918] 1918
TR in Baltimore during Liberty Loan drive, 1918. 1918

Baltimore. Oriole Baseball Park
Theodore Roosevelt in the great war [1] 1930
Theodore Roosevelt in the great war [2] 1930
Theodore Roosevelt in the great war [3] 1930
TR addresses large crowd for the Liberty Loan in Baltimore, 1918. 1918
TR and Cardinal Gibbons at Baltimore, Md., 1918. 1918
TR at Baltimore [1918]; TR at Sagamore [Hill, 1918] 1918
TR in Baltimore during Liberty Loan drive, 1918. 1918
TR scenes purchased from different dealers. 1912

Bands (Music)
Crowd exterior of Buckingham Palace. 1910
TR speaking to a group of men from the porch at Sagamore Hill, 1916. 1916

Barbour, W. Warren
See Barbour, William Warren

Barbour, Warren
See Barbour, William Warren

Barbour, William Warren
TR, Mayor Mitchel and guests at Cooper Sanitarium [1917] 1917

Barry, Thomas H.
Roosevelt scenes [1917–1918] 1917
Short scenes of TR [1] 1916
TR himself [1] 1926
TR himself [2] 1926
TR himself [3] 1926
TR himself [4] 1926
TR himself [5] 1926
TR himself [6] 1926

Bartlett, John H.
Governors of New England meet in Governor Coolidge's office in Boston to discuss fuel. 1919

Bas-relief
Professor Henry Fairfield Osborn, RMA medalist, 1923. 1934

Battery Park
See New York (City)—Parks—Battery

Battle Creek, Mich.
Leonard Wood at Battle Creek, Michigan. 1920

Battle Creek, Mich. Masonic Temple
Leonard Wood at Battle Creek, Michigan. 1920

Battles—Cuba
Dedication of Cuban memorial, 1924 [1] 1924
Dedication of Cuban memorial, 1924 [2] 1924

Battleships
International naval review, Hampton Roads, Virginia, 1907. 1907
Launch, U.S. battleship "Kentucky." 1898
The Panama Canal. 1927
Ships in the Panama Canal [2] 1910
The Story of the Panama Canal [1] 1927
The Story of the Panama Canal [2] 1927
TR's return to New York, 1910 [2] 1910
U.S. battleship Indiana. 1898
U.S. battleship "Oregon." 1898

Beard, Daniel C.
Daniel C. Beard and Ernest T. Seton. 1900
Daniel C. Beard, TR Jr., and Boy Scouts visit TR's grave, 1920. 1920
Gen. Pershing speaking to Scouts in New York. 1919
Memorializing Roosevelt. 1925
Scouts on their way to TR's grave, Daniel C. Beard and TR Jr. attend services, 1920. 1920
Theodore Roosevelt, great scout [1] 1925
Theodore Roosevelt, great scout [2] 1925

Beard, Daniel C., source
Gen. Pershing speaking to Scouts in New York. 1919
Scout parade, Cartagena, Columbia, 1920. 1920

Beeckman, Robert Livingston
Governors of New England meet in Governor Coolidge's office in Boston to discuss fuel. 1919

Bees—Brazil
Scenes of the River of Doubt photographed by G. M. Dyott, 1926–1927 [2] 1927

Beetles—Brazil
Scenes of the River of Doubt photographed by G. M. Dyott, 1926–1927 [1] 1927

Belgium—Diplomatic and consular service
TR receiving Belgian envoys at Sagamore Hill [1917] 1917

Belgium—Foreign relations
TR receiving Belgian envoys at Sagamore Hill [1917] 1917

Bell, George J.
General Pershing at Camp Grant. 1920

Bell, J. Franklin
See Bell, James Franklin, 1856–1919

Bell, James Franklin, 1856-1919
TR, Charles E. Hughes, and Mayor Mitchel of New York, on reviewing stand in front of the New York Public Library [1917] 1917

Bellworts
Scenes of flowers and birds in Washington, D.C. 1920
[Scenes of flowers in Washington, D.C.] 1920

Berkeley, Calif.
RMA ceremonies at [Hearst Greek Theatre, University of California, Berkeley, Calif.] 1919
RMA services at [Hearst Greek Theatre, University of California, Berkeley, Calif.]; Laying cornerstone of Roosevelt School at New Rochelle, N.Y. [1920] 1920

Berlin
TR's return from Africa, 1910 [1] 1925

Berlin—Streets
TR's return from Africa, 1910 [2] 1925

Berlin. Bradenburger Tor
TR's return from Africa, 1910 [1] 1925
TR's return from Africa, 1910 [2] 1925

Berlin. Reichstagsgebäude
TR's return from Africa, 1910 [2] 1925

Bernhardt, Sarah
Sarah Bernhardt addresses crowd in Prospect Park, Brooklyn, 1917. 1917

Bernstorff, Johann Heinrich Andreas Hermann Albrecht, Graf Von
Count von Bernstorff of Germany. 1910

Bertrand, Georges Etienne
TR reviews and addresses troops [Fort Sheridan, Ill.]; TR riding in auto, Chicago, 1917. 1917

Bertron, Samuel Reading, 1865–1938
Elihu Root and Mayor Mitchel of New York, Mr. Root and American delegates return from Russia [1917] 1917

Big game animals—Africa
Scenes of African animals [1911] 1911

Big game hunting
See Hunting

Big game hunting—Africa
African natives. 1909
Cartoon: TR's arrival in Africa. 1909
TR in Africa [1909, 1] 1909
TR in Africa [1909, 2] 1909
TR in Africa [1909, 3] 1909
TR in Africa [1909, 4] 1909
TR's camp in Africa [1909] 1909

Big Horn Mountains
Through the Roosevelt country with Roosevelt's friends. 1919

Billings, Mont.
Roosevelt scenes [1917–1918] 1917
Rough Riders greet TR during Liberty Loan drive out west [1918] 1918
Theodore Roosevelt in the great war [1] 1930
Theodore Roosevelt in the great war [2] 1930
Theodore Roosevelt in the great war [3] 1930
TR at Billings, Montana [1918] 1918

Bills, legislative—Pennsylvania
Gifford Pinchot, 1923. 1923

Biograph Company
15th Infantry leaving Governors Island for China (Boxer Uprising) 1900. 1900
25th Infantry. 1898
The Forbidden City, Pekin. 1903
Governor's Foot Guards, Conn. 1899
Jamestown Exposition, 1907. 1907
Launch, U.S. battleship "Kentucky." 1898
President McKinley's funeral, 1901 [1] 1901
Theodore Roosevelt leaving the White House. 1897
U.S. battleship Indiana. 1898
U.S. battleship "Oregon." 1898
Wreck of the "Vizcaya." 1898

Biograph Company, source
15th Infantry leaving Governors Island for China (Boxer Uprising) 1900. 1900
25th Infantry. 1898
The Forbidden City, Pekin. 1903
Governor's Foot Guards, Conn. 1899
Jamestown Exposition, 1907. 1907
Launch, U.S. battleship "Kentucky." 1898
President McKinley's funeral, 1901 [1] 1901
Theodore Roosevelt leaving the White House. 1897
U.S. battleship Indiana. 1898
U.S. battleship "Oregon." 1898
Wreck of the "Vizcaya." 1898

Birds, Protection of
Aigrette. 1920
Roosevelt, friend of the birds [1] 1924
Roosevelt, friend of the birds [2] 1924
Roosevelt, friend of the birds [3] 1924
Roosevelt, friend of the birds [4]; The Roosevelt Dam [3] 1928
TR [in Louisiana], 1915 [1] 1915
TR [in Louisiana], 1915 [2] 1915
TR [in Louisiana], 1915 [3] 1915
TR [in Louisiana], 1915 [4] 1915
Woman wearing aigrette in her hat. 1920

Black Hills, S.D.
Dedication of Roosevelt Mountain at Deadwood, S.D., 1919. 1919
President Coolidge speaking at Black Hills, S.D., 1927. 1927

Black Skimmer
Roosevelt, friend of the birds [1] 1924
Roosevelt, friend of the birds [2] 1924

Roosevelt, friend of the birds [3] 1924
Roosevelt, friend of the birds [4]; The Roosevelt Dam [3] 1928

Blue Line Sightseeing Tours, inc.
Scenes showing Blue Line Tour route to Roosevelt House in 1925. 1925

Bluets
Scenes of flowers and birds in Washington, D.C. 1920

Boats and boating
TR and expedition party on the [Sepotuba] River [1914] 1914

Bolling, Sallie White
President Wilson arrives in New York to lead fourth Liberty Loan parade [1918] 1918

Borglum, Gutzon
President Coolidge speaking at Black Hills, S.D., 1927. 1927

Borglum, John Gutzon de la Mothe
See Borglum, Gutzon

Boston, Mass.
Calvin Coolidge as Governor of Massachusetts. 1919
Calvin Coolidge as Governor of Massachusetts, 1919. 1919
Calvin Coolidge sworn in for second term as Governor of Massachusetts. 1920
Governors of New England meet in Governor Coolidge's office in Boston to discuss fuel. 1919
[Man speaking at Faneuil Hall, Boston] 1910
Memorializing Roosevelt. 1925
Owen D. Young [1] 1927
Owen D. Young [2] 1927
Roosevelt scenes [1917–1918] 1917
Short scenes of TR [1] 1916
TR attends his son Archie's wedding at Boston, 1917. 1917
TR with naval officers, exterior Navy Club, Boston [1918] 1918

Boston, Mass.—Police strike, 1919
Calvin Coolidge as Governor of Massachusetts. 1919

Boston, Mass. Emmanuel Church
See Emmanuel Church, Boston, Mass.

Boston, Mass. Faneuil Hall
[Man speaking at Faneuil Hall, Boston] 1910

Boston, Mass. Old State House
Calvin Coolidge as Governor of Massachusetts. 1919
Calvin Coolidge as Governor of Massachusetts, 1919. 1919
Calvin Coolidge sworn in for second term as Governor of Massachusetts. 1920
Governors of New England meet in Governor Coolidge's office in Boston to discuss fuel. 1919

Boston, Mass. State House
See Boston, Mass. Old State House

Bowles, Henry L.
Calvin Coolidge sworn in for second term as Governor of Massachusetts. 1920

Boy Scouts
  Scout parade, Cartagena, Colombia, 1920. 1920

Boy Scouts of America
  Brooklyn children attend services, children sew stars on Roosevelt Flag [1919] 1919
  Children sewing stars on flag, placing flag on TR's grave [1919] 1919
  Daniel C. Beard and Ernest T. Seton. 1900
  Daniel C. Beard, TR Jr., and Boy Scouts visit TR's grave, 1920. 1920
  [Flag services for TR at Oyster Bay, October 1919] 1919
  Gen. Pershing speaking to Scouts in New York. 1919
  Memorial services for TR at Van Cortlandt Park, New York, Oct. 1919. 1919
  Memorial services for TR on the steps of the New York Public Library, 1919 [1] 1919
  Memorial services for TR on the steps of the New York Public Library, 1919 [2] 1919
  RMA flag ceremonies, children sew stars on flag, 1919. 1919
  RMA flag service on the steps of New York Public Library, 1919. 1919
  Runners carrying flag to TR's grave [1919] 1919
  Scouts on their way to TR's grave, Daniel C. Beard and TR Jr. attend services, 1920. 1920
  Theodore Roosevelt, great scout [1] 1925
  Theodore Roosevelt, great scout [2] 1925
  Theodore Roosevelt, great scout [3] 1925
  TR memorial services at New York Public Library, 1919. 1919
  Whole nation honors memory of Roosevelt. 1919

Brandenburg Gate, Berlin
  See Berlin. Brandenburger Tor

Braunstein, Cy, source
  TR and Cardinal Gibbons at Balitmore, Md., 1918. 1918
  TR speaking at [Pueblo] Colorado, 1912. 1912
  TR's return to New York, 1910 [1] 1910

Bray (J. R.) Studios
  See Bray Studios, inc.

Bray-Mar Productions
  See Bray Studios, inc.

Bray Pictures Corporation
  See Bray Studios, inc.

Bray Productions
  See Bray Studios, inc.

Bray Screen Products
  See Bray Studios, inc.

Bray Studios, inc.
  Extermination of mosquitoes by spraying swamps. 1910

Bray Studios, inc., source
  Extermination of mosquitoes by spraying swamps. 1910
  Shall we prepare? 1916

Brazil
  Scenes of the River of Doubt photographed by G. M. Dyott, 1926–1927 [1] 1927

Scenes of the River of Doubt photographed by G. M. Dyott, 1926–1927 [2] 1927
  Theodore Roosevelt, great scout [1] 1925
  Theodore Roosevelt, great scout [2] 1925
  Theodore Roosevelt, great scout [3] 1925
  TR and expedition party on the [Sepotuba] River [1914] 1914

Brazil—Description and travel
  The River of Doubt [1] 1928
  The River of Doubt [2] 1928
  The River of Doubt [3] 1928
  The River of Doubt [4] 1928
  The River of Doubt [5] 1928
  The River of Doubt [6] 1928
  The River of Doubt [7] 1928
  Scenes of the River of Doubt photographed by G. M. Dyott, 1926–1927 [1] 1927
  Scenes of the River of Doubt photographed by G. M. Dyott, 1926–1927 [2] 1927

Brazilian Trip
  See Roosevelt-Rondon Scientific Expedition

Breton Island Reservation, La.
  Roosevelt, friend of the birds [1] 1924
  Roosevelt, friend of the birds [2] 1924
  Roosevelt, friend of the birds [3] 1924
  Roosevelt, friend of the birds [4]; The Roosevelt Dam [3] 1928
  TR [in Louisiana], 1915 [1] 1915
  TR [in Louisiana], 1915 [2] 1915
  TR [in Louisiana], 1915 [3] 1915
  TR [in Louisiana], 1915 [4] 1915

Bridges, Suspension
  Scenes of TR on board ship before sailing for West Indies, 1916. 1916

Brooklyn, N.Y.
  Brooklyn children attend services, children sew stars on Roosevelt Flag [1919] 1919
  Memorial services for TR on the steps of the New York Public Library, 1919 [1] 1919
  RMA flag ceremonies, children sew stars on flag, 1919. 1919
  Sarah Bernhardt addresses crowd in Prospect Park, Brooklyn, 1917. 1917

Brooklyn, N.Y.—Parks—Prospect Park
  Sarah Bernhardt addresses crowd in Prospect Park, Brooklyn, 1917. 1917

Brown pelican
  Roosevelt, friend of the birds [1] 1924
  Roosevelt, friend of the birds [2] 1924
  Roosevelt, friend of the birds [3] 1924
  Roosevelt, friend of the birds [4]; The Roosevelt Dam [3] 1928

Brownson, Willard H.
  TR reviews the fleet, 1907. 1907

Bryce, Elizabeth A.
  Lord and Lady Bryce. 1910

185

Bryce, James
Lord and Lady Bryce. 1910

Buchheister, source
Still photographs of TR on motion picture film. 1920

Buckey, Mervyn C.
General Nivelle visits TR's grave [1921] 1921

Buckingham Palace, London
See London. Buckingham Palace

Budapest
Street scenes in Naples, Italy. 1910

Budapest, Országház
Street scenes in Naples, Italy. 1910

Budapest. Parliament (Building)
See Budapest. Országház

Buffalo
McKinley's funeral, 1901. 1901
President McKinley reviewing the troops at the Pan-American Exposition. 1901
President McKinley speaking at Buffalo, 1901. 1901
President McKinley's funeral, 1901 [1] 1901
President McKinley's funeral in Buffalo, Washington, and Canton, Ohio, 1901. 1901
[Scenes of TR, Panama Canal construction, and William McKinley] 1901

Buffalo. City and County Hall
McKinley's funeral, 1901. 1901
President McKinley's funeral, 1901 [1] 1901
President McKinley's funeral in Buffalo, Washington, and Canton, Ohio, 1901. 1901

Buffalo. Pan-American Exposition, 1901
See Pan-American Exposition, 1901

Buffalo. Stadium
President McKinley reviewing the troops at the Pan-American Exposition. 1901

Buffaloes
Scenes of African animals [1911] 1911

Buildings—Models
See Architectural models

Buildings, Public
See Public buildings

Bulloch, Martha
See Roosevelt, Martha Bulloch

Bulloch Hall, Roswell, Ga.
See Roswell, Ga. Bulloch Hall

Bullock, Seth
Dedication of Roosevelt Mountain at Deadwood, S.D., 1919. 1919

Burgess, Frederick
TR at Forest Hills, New York, 1917 [1] 1917
TR at Forest Hills, New York, 1917 [2] 1917

Burnquist, Joseph A. A.
Close-up of TR speaking [1917] 1917
Roosevelt scenes [1917–1918] 1917
TR in St. Paul, Minn. [1917] 1917
TR speaking at [St. Paul, Minnesota, 1917] 1917

Burroughs, John
Scenes of John Burroughs. 1910

Bush, Maud Howard
TR speaking at Newburgh, N.Y. [1918] 1918

Business Men's Club, Cincinnati
TR attends dinner of Cincinnati, Ohio, Business Men's Club, Dec. 14, 1917 [1] 1917
TR attends dinner of Cincinnati, Ohio, Business Men's Club, Dec. 14, 1917 [2] 1917

Business Men's Club, Cincinnati. Reception Committee
TR attends dinner of Cincinnati, Ohio, Business Men's Club, Dec. 14, 1917 [2] 1917

Bussey, Eugene
Commander Dyott sailing from [Hoboken, N.J.] for South America, 1926. 1926

Butler, Joseph G.
President McKinley's memorial dedicated by William Howard Taft at Niles, Ohio. 1917

Butler, Nicholas Murray
TR on Fifth Avenue, New York, near St. Patrick's Cathedral after attending Mayor Mitchel's funeral. 1918

Byrd, Richard Evelyn
Colonel Lindbergh, Admiral Byrd, and Clarence Chamberlin at flying field just before Lindbergh's flight, 1927. 1927

Cactus
The Roosevelt Dam [1] 1928
The Roosevelt Dam [2] 1928

California. Governor, 1911–1917 (Johnson)
[Scenes of TR, 1913–1915] 1913
TR [at Panama-Pacific Exposition, 1915] 1915
TR himself [1] 1926
TR himself [5] 1926
See also Johnson, Hiram W.

California. University
See University of California, Berkeley

Cambridge. University
See Cambridge, Eng. University

Cambridge, Eng.
Still pictures of TR at [Cambridge] 1910. 1910

Cambridge, Eng. University
Still pictures of TR at [Cambridge] 1910. 1910

Cambridge, Mass.
Owen D. Young [1] 1927
Owen D. Young [2] 1927

Camp Albert L. Mills
See Camp Mills

Camp Grant
General Pershing at Camp Grant. 1920
Roosevelt scenes [1917–1918] 1917
Roosevelt scenes from RMA productions. 1912
Short scenes of TR [1] 1916
Theodore Roosevelt in the great war [1] 1930
Theodore Roosevelt in the great war [2] 1930
Theodore Roosevelt in the great war [3] 1930
TR himself [1] 1926
TR himself [2] 1926
TR himself [3] 1926
TR himself [4] 1926
TR himself [5] 1926
TR himself [6] 1926

Camp Mills
Roosevelt scenes [1917–1918] 1917
TR at Camp Mills [1917] 1917

Canal Zone
Dr. William Gorgas. 1900
The Panama Canal. 1927
Panama Canal scenes. 1910
Ships in the Panama Canal [1] 1910
Ships in the Panama Canal [2] 1910
The Story of the Panama Canal [1] 1927
The Story of the Panama Canal [2] 1927

Canal Zone—Views
Dr. William Gorgas. 1900

Canals—Locks
See Locks (Hydraulic engineering)

Canals, Interoceanic
The Panama Canal. 1927
Panama Canal scenes. 1910
Panama Canal; scenes of the finished Canal. 1919
[Scenes of TR, Panama Canal construction, and William McKinley] 1901
Ships in the Panama Canal [1] 1910
Ships in the Panama Canal [2] 1910
The Story of the Panama Canal [1] 1927
The Story of the Panama Canal [2] 1927
William H. Taft in Panama [1910?] 1910

Caney, Battle of, 1898
See El Caney, Battle of. 1898

Caney, Cuba
See El Caney, Cuba

Canoes and canoeing—Brazil
Scenes of the River of Doubt photographed by G. M. Dyott, 1926–1927 [1] 1927

Canonicus (Ship)
International naval review, Hampton Roads, Virginia, 1907. 1907

Canton, Ohio
President McKinley's funeral, 1901 [1] 1901
President McKinley's funeral, Canton, Ohio, 1901 [1] 1901
President McKinley's funeral, Canton, Ohio, 1901 [2] 1901
President McKinley's funeral in Buffalo, Washington, and Canton, Ohio, 1901. 1901
TR attends McKinley's funeral, 1901. 1901
TR attends McKinley's funeral, Canton, Ohio, 1901. 1901

Canton, Ohio. First Methodist Episcopal Church
See First Methodist Episcopal Church, Canton, Ohio

Canton, Ohio. McKinley Club
See McKinley Club

Canton, Ohio. Westlawn Cemetery
See Westlawn Cemetery

Capitol, Washington, D.C.
See Washington, D.C. Capitol

Caribe
Scenes of the River of Doubt photographed by G. M. Dyott, 1926–1927 [1] 1927
Scenes of the River of Doubt photographed by G. M. Dyott, 1926–1927 [2] 1927

Caribe Syndicate L.t.d. Films
Scout parade, Cartagena, Colombia, 1920. 1920

Caricatures and cartoons
Cartoon of Mr. Paul Rainey's African trip [1911] 1911
Cartoon of TR's reception by crowned heads of Europe. 1910
Cartoon: TR's arrival in Africa. 1909
President Roosevelt, 1901–1909. 1930
Roosevelt cartoons. 1910

Carlier, Hector
Roosevelt scenes [1917–1918] 1917
TR receiving Belgian envoys at Sagamore Hill [1917] 1917

Carow, Edith Kermit
See Roosevelt, Edith

Carriages and carts
Admiral Dewey parade, 1899 [1] 1899
Admiral Dewey parade, 1899 [2] 1899

Cartagena, Colombia
Scout parade, Cartagena, Colombia, 1920. 1920

Cartagena, Colombia—Description—Views
Scout parade, Cartagena, Colombia, 1920. 1920

Cartagena, Colombia—Plazas
Scout parade, Catagena, Colombia, 1920. 1920

Cartagena, Colombia—Walls
Scout parade, Cartagena, Colombia, 1920. 1920

Carter, Horace A.
Calvin Coolidge sworn in for second term as Governor of Massachusetts. 1920

Cartier, Emile
President Wilson arrives in New York to lead fourth Liberty Loan parade [1918] 1918

Cartoons
See Caricatures and cartoons

Carver, H. P., source
Americanism wins, Coolidge elected. 1919
Calvin Coolidge sworn in for second term as Governor of Massachusetts. 1920
Col. William Boyce Thompson. 1920
General Pershing at Camp Grant. 1920
Governors of New England meet in Governor Coolidge's office in Boston to discuss fuel. 1919
King Edward's funeral, 1910 [1] 1910
Major General Wm. C. Gorgas. 1910
[Man speaking at Faneuil Hall, Boston] 1910
Senator Hiram Johnson. 1922
Senator Hitchcock. 1910
Senator McCumber of North Dakota. 1920
Senator Penrose. 1910
Senator Pomerene. 1910
Senator Smoot. 1920
Senator Watson. 1921
Senators Curtis, Cummins, Moses, and [Representative] Mondell. 1919
Speaker of the House F. H. Gillett. 1919
[Unidentified man] 1910
Will Hays. 1920

Catedral, Panama (City)
TR speaking from Cathedral steps, Panama. 1906
TR speaking in Panama, November 1906. 1906
TR's arrival in Panama, November 1906 [1] 1906
TR's arrival in Panama, November 1906 [2] 1906
TR's arrival in Panama, November 1906 [3] 1906

Caterpillars
Scenes of the River of Doubt photographed by G. M. Dyott, 1926–1927 [1] 1927
Scenes of the River of Doubt photographed by G. M. Dyott, 1926–1927 [2] 1927

Cathedral of St. Mary, San Francisco
See St. Mary's Cathedral, San Francisco

Catholic Total Abstinence Union of America
TR as Father Curran's guest at Wilkes-Barre, Pa., August 10, 1905. 1905
TR at Wilkes-Barre, Pa., 1905. 1905
TR in Wilkes-Barre, Pa., 1905. 1905

Cemeteries—Belgium—Laeken
The King and Queen of Belgium and premier Poincaré of France [1] 1927
The King and Queen of Belgium and Premier Poincaré of France [2] 1927

Central Park
See New York (City)—Parks—Central Park

Chagres River
Panama Canal; scenes of the finished Canal. 1919

Chamberlin, Clarence D.
Colonel Lindbergh, Admiral Byrd, and Clarence Chamberlin at flying field just before Lindbergh's flight, 1927. 1927

Chambéry, France
Quentin Roosevelt's grave, 1918. 1919
Quentin Roosevelt's grave in France. 1919

Chapman, Frank Michler
Scenes of Dr. Frank Chapman. 1920

Charles, Count of Flanders, 1903 –
The King and Queen of Belgium and Premier Poincaré of France [1] 1927
The King and Queen of Belgium and Premier Poincaré of France [2] 1927

Château-Thierry, France
American Legion lays cornerstone of Roosevelt Bridge at Château-Thierry. 1921

Château-Thierry, France—Bridges—Roosevelt Bridge
American Legion lays cornerstone of Roosevelt Bridge at Château-Thierry. 1921

Cherrie, George K.
The River of Doubt [1] 1928
The River of Doubt [2] 1928
The River of Doubt [3] 1928
The River of Doubt [5] 1928
The River of Doubt [7] 1928
[Scenes of TR on board ship, 1916; Scenes of TR's trip to South America. 1913] 1913

Chessman, A., source
President McKinley speaking, 1901. 1901
Short scenes of TR [2] 1912
TR at Fargo, N.D., during Progressive campaign, 1912 [1] 1912
TR at Fargo, N.D., during Progressive campaign, 1912 [2] 1912
[TR getting into parked car] 1910
TR riding in auto through crowded streets [1912] 1912
TR with Rough Rider friends. 1910

Chicago
Chauncey Depew, Senator Perkins, and Governor Whitman of New York, at GOP Convention, 1916, Chicago, Ill. 1916
General Wood and Calvin Coolidge in Chicago, 1920. 1920
TR reviews and addresses troops [Fort Sheridan, Ill.]; TR riding in auto, Chicago, 1917. 1917

Chicago. Coliseum
Chauncey Depew, Senator Perkins, and Governor Whitman of New York, at GOP Convention, 1916, Chicago, Ill. 1916
General Wood and Calvin Coolidge in Chicago, 1920. 1920

TR speaking at Sagamore Hill [1916–1918] [1] 1916
TR's camp in Africa [1909] 1909

Connaught, Arthur William Patrick Albert, Duke of, 1850-1942
[Scenes of the British royal family] 1918
TR's return from Africa, 1910 [1] 1925
TR's return from Africa, 1910 [2] 1925

Connecticut. Governor, 1915–1921 (Holcomb)
Governors of New England meet in Governor Coolidge's office in Boston to discuss fuel. 1919

Connecticut. Governor's Foot Guards. First Company, Hartford
Governor's Foot Guards, Conn. 1899

Connecticut. Governor's Foot Guards. Second Company, New Haven
Governor's Foot Guards, Conn. 1899

Conservation of natural resources
President Roosevelt, 1901–1909. 1930

Constitution
See United States Constitution

Construction equipment
The Panama Canal. 1927
Panama Canal scenes. 1910
The Story of the Panama Canal [1] 1927
The Story of the Panama Canal [2] 1927

Construction workers
The Panama Canal. 1927
Panama Canal scenes. 1910
The Story of the Panama Canal [1] 1927
The Story of the Panama Canal [2] 1927

Convention of the Loyal Order of Moose, 29th, Pittsburgh, 1917
Short scenes of TR [1] 1916

Conventions, Political
See Political conventions

Convicts
See Prisoners

Cook, Thomas C.
Roosevelt scenes [1917–1918] 1917
TR receiving Belgian envoys at Sagamore Hill [1917] 1917

Coolidge, Calvin, 1908-1924
Americanism wins, Coolidge elected. 1919

Coolidge, Calvin, Pres. U.S., 1872–1933
Americanism wins, Coolidge elected. 1919
Calvin Coolidge as Governor of Massachusetts. 1919
Calvin Coolidge as Governor of Massachusetts, 1919. 1919
Calvin Coolidge sworn in for second term as Governor of Massachusetts. 1920
General Wood and Calvin Coolidge in Chicago, 1920. 1920
Governors of New England meet in Governor Coolidge's office in Boston to discuss fuel. 1919
President Harding and Calvin Coolidge [1] 1920

President Harding and Calvin Coolidge [2] 1920
See also United States. President, 1923–1929 (Coolidge)

Coolidge, Calvin, Pres. U. S., 1872 – 1933—Addresses, essays, lectures
President Coolidge speaking at Black Hills, S. D., 1927. 1927

Coolidge, Calvin, Pres. U. S., 1872 – 1933—Family
Americanism wins, Coolidge elected. 1919

Coolidge, Calvin, Pres. U. S., 1872 – 1933—Homes
Americanism wins, Coolidge elected. 1919

Coolidge, Grace Goodhue
Americanism wins, Coolidge elected. 1919.

Coolidge, John
Americanism wins, Coolidge elected. 1919

Cooper, Jack
TR, Mayor Mitchel and guests at Cooper Sanitarium [1917] 1917

Cooper's Training Camp
Short scenes of TR [1] 1916
TR, Mayor Mitchel and guests at Cooper Sanitarium [1917] 1917

Copenhagen
TR in Norway and Denmark, 1910 [1] 1910
TR in Norway and Denmark, 1910 [2] 1910
TR in Norway and Denmark, 1910 [3] 1910
TR's return from Africa, 1910 [1] 1925

Copenhagen. Amalienborg
TR in Norway and Denmark, 1910 [1] 1910
TR in Norway and Denmark, 1910 [2] 1910
TR in Norway and Denmark, 1910 [3] 1910

Coquille, J. Hippolyte
Roosevelt, friend of the birds [1] 1924
Roosevelt, friend of the birds [2] 1924
Roosevelt, friend of the birds [3] 1924
Roosevelt, friend of the birds [4]; The Roosevelt Dam [3] 1928
TR [in Louisiana], 1915 [1] 1915

Corner stones, Laying of
American Legion lays cornerstone of Roosevelt Bridge at Château-Thierry. 1921
Laying cornerstone of Roosevelt's School, New Rochelle, N. Y. [1920] 1920
Leonard Wood lays cornerstone of Roosevelt House, 1921. 1921
RMA services at [Hearst Greek Theatre, University of California, Berkeley, Calif.]; Laying cornerstone of Roosevelt School at New Rochelle, N. Y. [1920] 1920

Cortelyou, George B.
President McKinley reviewing the troops at the Pan-American Exposition. 1901
President McKinley speaking at Buffalo, 1901. 1901
President McKinley's funeral in Buffalo, Washington, and Canton, Ohio, 1901. 1901

[Scenes of TR, Panama Canal construction, and William McKinley] 1901

Coudert, Frederic R.
Marshal Foch visits Roosevelt House, 1921. 1921
Roosevelt scenes [1917–1918] 1917
TR receiving Belgian envoys at Sagamore Hill [1917] 1917
TR speaking at Oyster Bay, July 4, 1916. 1916

Cove Neck School
See Cove School

Cove School
Brooklyn children attend services, children sew stars on Roosevelt Flag [1919] 1919
Children sewing stars on flag, placing flag on TR's grave [1919] 1919
[Flag services for TR at Oyster Bay, October 1919] 1919
RMA flag ceremonies, children sew stars on flag, 1919. 1919
Roosevelt at home: Sagamore Hill, Oyster Bay, L. I. [2] 1930
Runners carrying flag to TR's grave [1919] 1919

Cowboys
Memorializing Roosevelt. 1925

Cowles, William Sheffield, 1846–1923
President McKinley's funeral, Canton, Ohio, 1901 [1] 1901

Cox, Channing H.
Calvin Coolidge sworn in for second term as Governor of Massachusetts. 1920

Cox, James M.
TR attends dinner of Cincinnati, Ohio, Business Men's Club, Dec. 14, 1917 [1] 1917
Tr attends dinner of Cincinnati, Ohio, Business Men's Club, Dec. 14, 1917 [2] 1917

Crowder, Enoch H.
Dedication of Cuban memorial, 1924 [1] 1924
Dedication of Cuban memorial, 1924 [2] 1924
Roosevelt scenes from RMA productions. 1912

Crowds
Crowd exterior of Buckingham Palace. 1910
King George and Queen Mary of England [1] 1928

Crowley, Mathias
General Pershing at Camp Grant, 1920

Cruisers (Warships)
International naval review, Hampton Roads, Virginia, 1907. 1907
William H. Taft in Panama [1910?] 1910

Crumpacker, Edgar D.
TR's inauguration, 1905 [2] 1905

Cuba
25th Infantry. 1898
Pack mules with ammunition on the Santiago trail, Cuba. 1898
Spanish Mountain Artillery, 1898. 1898
Troops making military road in front of Santiago. 1898

Cuba. Army
See Cuba. Ejército

Cuba, Ejército
Dedication of Cuban memorial, 1924 [1] 1924
Dedication of Cuban memorial, 1924 [2] 1924

Cuba. Presidente, 1921 – 1925 (Zayas y Alfonso)
Dedication of Cuban memorial, 1924 [1] 1924
Dedication of Cuban memorial, 1924 [2] 1924
Roosevelt scenes from RMA productions. 1912

Cuiabá River
The River of Doubt [1] 1928
The River of Doubt [2] 1928
The River of Doubt [3] 1928
The River of Doubt [4] 1928
The River of Doubt [5] 1928
The River of Doubt [7] 1928

Culebra Cut, Canal Zone
See Gaillard Cut, Canal Zone

Cummins, Albert B.
Senators Curtis, Cummins, Moses, and [Representative] Mondell. 1919

Curran, John J.
TR as Father Curran's guest at Wilkes-Barre, Pa., August 10, 1905. 1905

Curry, George
TR in New Mexico, 1916. 1916
TR's reception in Albuquerque, N. M., 1916. 1916

Curtis, Charles
Senators Curtis, Cummins, Moses, and [Representative] Mondell. 1919

Cuyabá River
See Cuiabá River

Daiquiri, Cuba
Dedication of Cuban memorial, 1924 [1] 1924
U. S. Troops landing at Daiquiri, Cuba. 1898

Dalstein, Jean B.
TR in Vincennes, France, 1910. 1910
TR reviews French troops at Vincennes, France, 1910. 1910
TR's return from Africa, 1910 [1] 1925
TR's return from Africa, 1910 [2] 1925

Dalzell, John
TR's inauguration, 1905 [2] 1905

Dams
See Roosevelt Dam

Dams—Arizona
The Roosevelt Dam [2] 1928
Roosevelt, friend of the birds [4]; The Roosevelt Dam [3] 1928
Scenes of Roosevelt Dam. 1911
TR at dedication of Roosevelt Dam, 1911. 1911

TR speaking at the dedication of Roosevelt Dam, 1911. 1911
TR with group of men, 1917; TR speaking at dedication of Roosevelt Dam, 1911. 1911
See also Roosevelt Dam

Dams—Arizona—Design and construction
The Roosevelt Dam [1] 1928
The Roosevelt Dam [2] 1928

Dantz, William T.
Through the Roosevelt country with Roosevelt's friends. 1919

Davidson, Gilbert Aubrey
TR at San Diego Exposition, 1915. 1915

Day, William Rufus, 1849–1923
TR attends McKinley's funeral, 1901. 1901
TR attends McKinley's funeral, Canton, Ohio, 1901. 1901

De Luca, Kennedy
General [Diaz] of Italy visits TR's grave [1921] 1921

Deadwood, S.D.
Dedication of Roosevelt Mountain at Deadwood, S.D., 1919. 1919

Declaration of Independence
See United States. Declaration of Independence

Dedication services
American Legion lays cornerstone of Roosevelt Bridge at Château-Thierry. 1921
Dedication of Roosevelt House, 1923. 1923
Dedication of Roosevelt House, Oct. 27, 1923. 1923
Dedication of Roosevelt Mountain at Deadwood, S.D., 1919. 1919
Laying cornerstone of Roosevelt School, New Rochelle, N.Y. [1920] 1920
Owen D. Young [1] 1927
Owen D. Young [2] 1927
President Coolidge speaking at Black Hills, S.D., 1927. 1927
RMA services at [Hearst Greek Theatre, University of California, Berkeley, Calif.]; Laying cornerstone of Roosevelt School at New Rochelle, N.Y. [1920] 1920
The Roosevelt Dam [1] 1928
The Roosevelt Dam [2] 1928
TR at dedication of Roosevelt Dam, 1911. 1911
TR speaking at the dedication of Roosevelt Dam, 1911. 1911
TR with group of men, 1917; TR speaking at dedication of Roosevelt Dam, 1911. 1911

Demarest, John, source
TR at Forest Hills, New York, 1917 [2] 1917

Demorest, Alice G.
Woman's Roosevelt Memorial Association meeting at Roosevelt House, 1923 [1] 1923
Woman's Roosevelt Memorial Association meeting at Roosevelt House, 1923 [2] 1923

Denby, Edwin
Leonard Wood at Battle Creek, Michigan. 1920

Denmark
TR's return from Africa, 1910 [2] 1925

Depew, Chauncey M.
Chauncey Depew, Senator Perkins, and Governor Whitman of New York, at GOP Convention, 1916, Chicago, Ill. 1916

Derby, Ethel Roosevelt
Still picture of TR and his family. 1907
TR in Norway, 1910. 1910
TR in Norway and Denmark, 1910 [1] 1910
TR in Norway and Denmark, 1910 [2] 1910
TR in Norway and Denmark, 1910 [3] 1910

Desmond, Thomas C.
TR speaking at Newburgh, N.Y. [1918] 1918

Detroit
Leonard Wood at Battle Creek, Michigan. 1920

Detroit. Hotel Statler
Leonard Wood at Battle Creek, Michigan. 1920

Dewey, George
Admiral Dewey on flagship, 1899. 1899
Admiral Dewey on the deck of flagship, 1899 [1] 1899
Admiral Dewey on the deck of flagship, 1899 [2] 1899
Admiral Dewey parade, 1899 [1] 1899

DeWolfe, Florence Kling
See Harding, Florence Kling

Diaz, Armando, duca della Vittoria
General [Diaz] of Italy visits TR's grave [1921] 1921

Diplomatic negotiations in international disputes
Japanese and Russian peace delegates [leaving New York City], 1905. 1905

Diplomats
Elihu Root and Mayor Mitchel of New York, Mr. Root and American delegates return from Russia [1917] 1917
Japanese and Russian peace delegates [leaving New York City], 1905. 1905

Discoveries (in geography)
Scenes of the River of Doubt photographed by G. M. Dyott, 1926–1927 [1] 1927
Scenes of the River of Doubt photographed by G. M. Dyott, 1926–1927 [2] 1927

Discovery Landing, Norfolk, Va.
See Norfolk, Va. Discovery Landing

Dodge Brothers, inc.
Leonard Wood at Battle Creek, Michigan. 1920

Dogs
Roosevelt at home: Sagamore Hill, Oyster Bay, L.I. [1] 1930
Roosevelt at home: Sagamore Hill, Oyster Bay, L.I. [2] 1930

Dogwood
Scenes of flowers and birds in Washington, D.C., 1920
[Scenes of flowers in Washington, D.C.] 1920

D'Olier, Franklin
American Legion lays cornerstone of Roosevelt Bridge at Château-Thierry. 1921

Donnelly (John) & Company
See John Donnelly & Company

Dreadnoughts
See Battleships

Dude ranches
Through the Roosevelt country with Roosevelt's friends. 1919

Duncan, James
Elihu Root and Mayor Mitchel of New York. Mr. Root and American delegates return from Russia [1917] 1917

Dunne, Edward F.
Reviewing Annapolis middies. 1915

Duquesne, Pa.
Charles E. Hughes speaking during campaign, Duquesne, Pa., 1916. 1916

Dynamite
Panama Canal scenes. 1910

Dyott, George M.
Commander Dyott sailing from [Hoboken, N.J.] for South America, 1926. 1926
The River of Doubt [1] 1928
The River of Doubt [2] 1928
The River of Doubt [3] 1928
The River of Doubt [4] 1928
The River of Doubt [6] 1928
The River of Doubt [7] 1928
Scenes of the River of Doubt photographed by G. M. Dyott, 1926–1927 [1] 1927
Scenes of the River of Doubt photographed by G. M. Dyott, 1926–1927 [2] 1927

Dyott, George M., source
Scenes of the River of Doubt photographed by G. M. Dyott, 1926–1927 [1] 1927
Scenes of the River of Doubt photographed by G. M. Dyott, 1926–1927 [2] 1927

Eagles, Fraternal Order of
See Fraternal Order of Eagles

Eastman Kodak Company, source
Roosevelt, friend of the birds [3] 1924
Roosevelt, friend of the birds [4]; The Roosevelt Dam [3] 1928
Theodore Roosevelt, great scout [2] 1925
Theodore Roosevelt, great scout [3] 1925

Eaton, Howard
Through the Roosevelt country with Roosevelt's friends. 1919

Eclair Film Company, source
TR at Baltimore [1918]; TR at Sagamore [Hill, 1918] 1918

Edison (Thomas A.) inc.
Admiral Dewey on flagship, 1899. 1899
Admiral Dewey on the deck of flagship, 1899 [1] 1899
Admiral Dewey on the deck of flagship, 1899 [2] 1899

Pack mules with ammunition on the Santiago trail, Cuba. 1898
President McKinley reviewing the troops at the Pan-American Exposition. 1901
President McKinley speaking at Buffalo, 1901. 1901
Troops making military road in front of Santiago. 1898
U.S. troops landing at Daiquiri, Cuba. 1898

Editorial by the late Theodore Roosevelt [Title]
TR speaking at Sagamore Hill [1916–1918] [1] 1916

Editorial cartoons
Cartoon of Mr. Paul Rainey's African trip [1911] 1911
Cartoon of TR's reception by crowned heads of Europe. 1910
Cartoon: TR's arrival in Africa. 1909
Roosevelt cartoons. 1910

Edward VII, King of Great Britain, 1841–1910
Cartoon of TR's reception by crowned heads of Europe. 1910
King Edward's funeral, 1910 [1] 1910
King Edward's funeral, 1910 [2] 1910
The King of Italy entertains King Edward of England on his yacht. 1907

Edward VII, King of Great Britain, 1841 – 1910—Funeral and memorial services
King Edward's funeral, 1910 [1] 1910
King Edward's funeral, 1910 [2] 1910
TR's return from Africa, 1910 [1] 1925
TR's return from Africa, 1910 [2] 1925

Edward VIII, King of Great Britain, 1894 – 1972
The Prince of Wales visits TR's grave. 1919
TR's return from Africa, 1910 [1] 1925
TR's return from Africa, 1910 [2] 1925

Edward, Duke of Windsor
See Edward VIII, King of Great Britain, 1894–1972

Edward Albert, Prince of Wales
See Edward VIII, King of Great Britain, 1894–1972

Egan, Katharine M.
TR in Denmark, 1910. 1910
TR in Norway and Denmark, 1910 [1] 1910
TR in Norway and Denmark, 1910 [2] 1910
TR in Norway and Denmark, 1910 [3] 1910

Egan, Maurice F.
TR in Denmark, 1910. 1910
TR in Norway and Denmark, 1910 [1] 1910
TR in Norway and Denmark, 1910 [2] 1910
TR in Norway and Denmark, 1910 [3] 1910

Egerton, Edwin H., Sir
The King of Italy entertains King Edward of England on his yacht. 1907

Église Notre-Dame, Laeken, Belgium
The King and Queen of Belgium and Premier Poincaré of France [1] 1927
The King and Queen of Belgium and Premier Poincaré of France [2] 1927

Egrets
See Herons

Ekaterinburg, Russia
See Sverdlovsk, Russia

El Caney, Battle of 1898
Dedication of Cuban memorial, 1924 [1] 1924
Dedication of Cuban memorial, 1924 [2] 1924

El Caney, Cuba
Dedication of Cuban memorial, 1924 [1] 1924
Dedication of Cuban memorial, 1924 [2] 1924

Elections—Massachusetts
Americanism wins, Coolidge elected. 1919

Electric locomotives
Ships in the Panama Canal [1] 1910

Elisabeth, consort of Albert I, King of the Belgians, 1876–1965
The King and Queen of Belgium and Premier Poincaré of
France [1] 1927
The King and Queen of Belgium and Premier Poincaré of
France [2] 1927

Elkhorn Ranch, N.D.
Through the Roosevelt country with Roosevelt's friends. 1919

Elmendorf, Dwight L., source
Admiral Dewey on flagship, 1899. 1899
Admiral Dewey on the deck of flagship, 1899 [1] 1899
Admiral Dewey on the deck of flagship, 1899 [2] 1899
Admiral Dewey parade, 1899 [1] 1899
Admiral Dewey parade, 1899 [2] 1899
Disappearing gun at testing grounds, Sandy Hook, 1898. 1898
Emperor Francis Joseph of Austria greeted by his people.
1910
Spanish Mountain Artillery, 1898. 1898

Elmoran
See Masai

Emery, John G.
American Legion lays cornerstone of Roosevelt Bridge at
Château-Thierry. 1921

Emmanuel Church, Boston, Mass.
TR attends his son Archie's wedding at Boston, 1917. 1917

Emperors
Emperor Francis Joseph of Austria greeted by his people.
1910

Erie County, N.Y. City and County Hall
See Buffalo, N.Y. City and County Hall

Erie County, N.Y. County Hall
See Buffalo, N.Y. City and County Hall

Espinosa, Priscilliano
Dedication of Cuban memorial, 1924 [1] 1924
Dedication of Cuban memorial, 1924 [2] 1924

European War, 1914–1918
Elihu Root and Mayor Mitchel of New York, Mr. Root and
American delegates return from Russia [1917] 1917
Lieutenant-Colonel Theodore Roosevelt arrives in New York
after the World War. 1919
[Quentin Roosevelt]; Clemenceau and Foch, 1917–1919. 1918
Quentin Roosevelt's grave, 1918. 1919
Quentin Roosevelt's grave in France. 1919
Robert Bacon and Army officers. 1918
Roosevelt scenes [1917–1918] 1917
Scene of Clemenceau, Tardieu, Foch, Poincaré and Pershing,
1917–1918. 1918
Scenes of TR and his sons Quentin and Archie, 1917–1918
[1] 1917
Scenes of TR and his sons Quentin and Archie, 1917–1918
[2] 1917
Theodore Roosevelt in the great war [1] 1930
Theodore Roosevelt in the great war [2] 1930
Theodore Roosevelt in the great war [3] 1930
TR receiving Belgian envoys at Sagamore Hill [1917] 1917
TR's sons' regiments during war, 1917–1918 [1] 1918
TR's sons' regiments during war, 1917–1918 [2] 1918

European War, 1914–1918—Aerial operations, American
TR's sons' regiments during war, 1917–1918 [1] 1918

European War, 1914–1918—Finance
Theodore Roosevelt in the great war [1] 1930
Theodore Roosevelt in the great war [2] 1930
Theodore Roosevelt in the great war [3] 1930

European War, 1914–1918—Finance—New York (City)
President Wilson arrives in New York to lead fourth Liberty
Loan parade [1918] 1918

European War, 1914–1918—Finance—Washington, D.C.
President Wilson arrives in New York to lead fourth Liberty
Loan parade [1918] 1918

European War, 1914–1918—Public opinion
Close-up of TR speaking [1917] 1917
Close-up scenes of TR speaking during World War I, 1917–
1918. 1917
Sarah Bernhardt addresses crowd in Prospect Park, Brooklyn,
1917. 1917
TR attends dinner of Cincinnati, Ohio, Business Men's Club,
Dec. 14, 1917 [1] 1917
TR attends dinner of Cincinnati, Ohio, Business Men's Club,
Dec. 14, 1917 [2] 1917
TR, exterior of building, Washington, D.C., 1918. 1918
TR in St. Paul, Minn. [1917] 1917
TR reviews and addresses troops [Fort Sheridan, Ill.]; TR rid-
ing in auto, Chicago, 1917. 1917
TR riding in an auto in Chicago, 1917. 1917
TR speaking at St. Paul, Minn., 1918. 1918
TR speaking at [St. Paul, Minnesota, 1917] 1917
TR speaking during War, 1917–1918. 1917
TR speaking in St. Paul, Minnesota, 1918. 1918

European War, 1914–1918—Religious aspects
[Scenes of the British royal family] 1918

European War, 1914–1918—War work—Y.M.C.A.
Mrs. Theodore Roosevelt Jr. attends Women in War Work
Congress in Paris [1918] 1918.

European War, 1914 – 1918—Women's work
Mrs. Theodore Roosevelt Jr. attends Women in War Work Congress in Paris [1918] 1918

European War, 1914 – 1918—United States
President Wilson arrives in New York to lead fourth Liberty Loan parade [1918] 1918

Evans, Bob, 1846 – 1912
See Evans, Robley D.

Evans, Robley D.
TR reviews the fleet, 1907. 1907

Executive Office Building, Washington, D.C.
See Washington, D.C. State, War and Navy Building

Exhibition buildings
TR [at Panama-Pacific Exposition. 1915] 1915

Exhibitions
President McKinley reviewing the troops at the Pan-American Exposition. 1901
President McKinley speaking at Buffalo, 1901. 1901
Reviewing Annapolis middies. 1915
[Scenes of TR, 1913–1915] 1913
[Scenes of TR, Panama Canal construction, and William McKinley] 1901
TR and Mrs. Roosevelt [at the Panama-California Exposition, 1915] 1915
TR [at Panama-Pacific Exposition, 1915] 1915
TR at Sagamore Hill [1916] 1915
TR at San Diego Exposition, 1915. 1915
TR speaking [at the Panama-Pacific Exposition, 1915] 1915
William H. Taft burns mortgage of Exposition, 1915. 1915
See also flower shows; particular exhibitions, e.g. Pan-American Exposition, 1901; and subdivision Exhibitions under names of cities.

Explorers
Commander Dyott sailing from [Hoboken, N.J.] for South America, 1926. 1926

Expositions
See Exhibitions

Factories
TR speaking in St. Paul, Minnesota, 1918. 1918

Fagan, James J.
William H. Taft burns mortgage of Exposition, 1915. 1915

Fairbanks, Charles W.
TR's inauguration, 1905 [2] 1905

Fairfield, Harry S.
Calvin Coolidge sworn in for second term as Governor of Massachusetts. 1920

Fairs
See Exhibitions

Fall, Albert B.
TR in New Mexico, 1916. 1916

TR with Rough Rider friends. 1910
TR's reception in Albuquerque, N.M., 1916. 1916

Fallières, Armand
See Fallières, Clément Armand, Pres. France, 1841–1931

Fallières, Clément Armand, Pres. France, 1841 – 1931
Cartoon of TR's reception by crowned heads of Europe. 1910

Famous Players-Lasky Corporation, source
Scenes of lions. 1910
Woman wearing aigrette in her hat. 1920

Faneuil Hall, Boston, Mass.
See Boston, Mass. Faneuil Hall

Fargo, N.D.
Crowd listening to TR speak during Progressive campaign, 1912. 1912
Short scenes of TR [2] 1912
TR at Fargo, N.D., during Progressive campaign, 1912 [1] 1912
TR at Fargo, N.D., during Progressive campaign, 1912 [2] 1912
TR scenes purchased from different dealers. 1912
TR speaking from train platform, 1912. 1912

Farm equipment
The Roosevelt Dam [1] 1928
The Roosevelt Dam [2] 1928

Farrar, Geraldine
President Wilson arrives in New York to lead fourth Liberty Loan parade [1918] 1918

Farrow, source
TR wearing army coat standing in auto greeting friends at Oyster Bay, 1910. 1910

Faust, William H.
Leonard Wood at Battle Creek, Michigan. 1920

Feathers
Aigrette. 1920
Woman wearing aigrette in her hat. 1920

Ferdinand I, Czar of Bulgaria, 1861 – 1948
TR's return from Africa, 1910 [1] 1925
TR's return from Aftica, 1910 [2] 1925

Ferris, Joseph A.
Through the Roosevelt country with Roosevelt's friends. 1919

Ferris, Sylvane M.
Through the Roosevelt country with Roosevelt's friends. 1919

Ferris, Sylvanus M.
See Ferris, Sylvane M.

Fiala, Anthony
The River of Doubt [1] 1928
The River of Doubt [2] 1928
The River of Doubt [3] 1928
The River of Doubt [5] 1928

The River of Doubt [7] 1928
[Scenes of TR, 1913–1915] 1913
[Scenes of TR on board ship, 1916; Scenes of TR's trip to South America. 1913] 1913

Fiala, Anthony, photographer
The River of Doubt [1] 1928
The River of Doubt [2] 1928
The River of Doubt [5] 1928
The River of Doubt [6] 1928
The River of Doubt [7] 1928
TR and expedition party on the [Sepotuba] River [1914] 1914

Fiala, Anthony, source
TR and expedition party on the [Sepotuba] River [1914] 1914

Field artillery
See Artillery, Field and mountain

Fighting Irish 69th of New York
See United States. Army. 165th Infantry

Finley, John H.
RMA trustees at Roosevelt House, 1923 [2] 1923

First Company Governor's Guard
See Connecticut. Governor's Foot Guards. First Company, Hartford

First Methodist Episcopal Church, Canton, Ohio
President McKinley's funeral in Buffalo, Washington, and Canton, Ohio, 1901. 1901

Fisher, Joe
President McKinley's memorial dedicated by William Howard Taft at Niles, Ohio. 1917

Fitzpatrick, Elizabeth K.
Memorializing Roosevelt. 1925

Flags
Allied armies in China, 1917–1918. 1918
Brooklyn children attend services, children sew stars on Roosevelt Flag [1919] 1919
Children sewing stars on flag, placing flag on TR's grave [1919] 1919
Flag at half-mast, Oyster Bay, Jan. 1919. 1919
[Flag services for TR at Oyster Bay, October 1919] 1919
Memorial services for TR at Van Cortlandt Park, New York, Oct. 1919. 1919
Memorial services for TR on the steps of the New York Public Library, 1919 [1] 1919
Memorial services for TR on the steps of the New York Public Library, 1919 [2] 1919
President Wilson arrives in New York to lead fourth Liberty Loan parade [1918] 1918
RMA flag ceremonies, children sew stars on flag, 1919. 1919
RMA flag service on the steps of New York Public Library, 1919. 1919
Runners carrying flag to TR's grave [1919] 1919
TR memorial services at New York Public Library, 1919. 1919
Whole nation honors memory of Roosevelt. 1919

Flags—United States
Scenes of the White House. 1920

Flower Show, International
See International Flower Show

Flower shows
Scenes of TR and his sons Quentin and Archie, 1917–1918 [1] 1917
Scenes of TR and his sons Quentin and Archie, 1917–1918 [2] 1917
TR and Leonard Wood at the New York flower show, 1917. 1917

Flowering cherries
[Scenes of flowers in Washington, D.C.] 1920

Flowering trees
Scenes of flowers and birds in Washington, D.C. 1920
[Scenes of flowers in Washington, D.C.] 1920

Foch, Ferdinand
Marshal Foch visits Roosevelt House, 1921. 1921
[Quentin Roosevelt]; Clemenceau and Foch, 1917–1919. 1918
Scene of Clemenceau, Tardieu, Foch, Poincaré and Pershing, 1917–1918. 1918

Folsom, Frances
See Preston, Frances Folsom Cleveland

Forbidden City, Peking
See Peking. Imperial Palace

Ford, Henry, source
TR in auto [1912] 1912

Forest Hills, N.Y.
Roosevelt scenes [1917–1918] 1917
Roosevelt scenes from RMA productions. 1912
Theodore Roosevelt in the great war [1] 1930
Theodore Roosevelt in the great war [2] 1930
Theodore Roosevelt in the great war [3] 1930
TR at Forest Hills, New York, 1917 [1] 1917
TR at Forest Hills, New York, 1917 [2] 1917

Forest Hills Rifle Club
Roosevelt scenes [1917–1918] 1917
Roosevelt scenes from RMA productions. 1912
Theodore Roosevelt, great scout [3] 1925
TR at Forest Hills, New York, 1917 [1] 1917
TR at Forest Hills, New York, 1917 [2] 1917

Fort Sheridan
TR reviews and addresses troops [Fort Sheridan, Ill.]; TR riding in auto, Chicago, 1917. 1917

Foster, source
King and Queen of Spain attend a military review. 1920
Scenes of John Burroughs. 1910
TR reviews and addresses troops [Fort Sheridan, Ill.]; TR riding in auto, Chicago, 1917. 1917
TR speaking at Sagamore Hill [1916–1918] [1] 1916

Fourth of July celebrations
Roosevelt at home: Sagamore Hill, Oyster Bay, L.I. [1] 1930
Roosevelt at home: Sagamore Hill, Oyster Bay, L.I. [2] 1930
TR at Forest Hills, New York, 1917 [1] 1917

TR at Forest Hills, New York, 1917 [2] 1917
TR speaking at Oyster Bay, July 4, 1916. 1916

Fourth of July orations
Sarah Bernhardt addresses crowd in Prospect Park, Brooklyn, 1917. 1917
Short scenes of TR as used in Paramount reel. 1916
TR at Forest Hills, New York, 1917 [1] 1917
TR at Forest Hills, New York, 1917 [2] 1917
TR speaking at Oyster Bay, July 4, 1916. 1916

Fowler, Benjamin A.
The Roosevelt Dam [1] 1928
The Roosevelt Dam [2] 1928
TR at dedication of Roosevelt Dam, 1911. 1911
TR speaking at the dedication of Roosevelt Dam, 1911. 1911
TR with group of men, 1917; TR speaking at dedication of Roosevelt Dam, 1911. 1911

Fox, William, source
Airmen honor TR's memory by dropping American Legion wreath on his grave [1919] 1919
Children visit TR's grave, 1920. 1920
General Goethals. 1923
King Albert of Belgium visits TR's grave, October, 1919. 1919
Mr. Garfield presenting medals to 1929 medalists. 1929
President Harding presenting chair used by TR at the White House to the directors of RMA, October 1921. 1921
TR at Sagamore Hill [1916] 1915
TR at Sagamore Hill [1916–1918] 1916
TR memorial services at New York Public Library, 1919. 1919

Fox Film Corporation
Airmen honor TR's memory by dropping American Legion wreath on his grave [1919] 1919
Children visit TR's grave, 1920. 1920
General Goethals. 1923
King Albert of Belgium visits TR's grave, October, 1919. 1919
TR memorial services at New York Public Library, 1919. 1919

Fox news [Series]
Airmen honor TR's memory by dropping American Legion wreath on his grave [1919] 1919
Children visit TR's grave, 1920. 1920
General Goethals. 1923
King Albert of Belgium visits TR's grave, October, 1919. 1919
TR memorial services at New York Public Library, 1919. 1919

France
TR's sons' regiments during war, 1917–1918 [1] 1918
TR's sons' regiments during war, 1917–1918 [2] 1918

France, Armée
American Legion lays cornerstone of Roosevelt Bridge at Château-Thierry. 1921
[Quentin Roosevelt]; Clemenceau and Foch, 1917–1919. 1918
Quentin Roosevelt's grave, 1918. 1919
Quentin Roosevelt's grave in France. 1919
Scene of Clemenceau, Tardieu, Foch, Poincaré and Pershing, 1917–1918. 1918

France. Armée—Maneuvers
TR in Vincennes, France, 1910. 1910
TR reviews French troops at Vincennes, France, 1910. 1910

France. Armée—Officers
Scene of Clemenceau, Tardieu, Foch, Poincaré and Pershing, 1917–1918. 1918

France. Président, 1913–1920 (Poincaré)
Scene of Clemenceau, Tardieu, Foch, Poincaré and Pershing, 1917–1918. 1918
See also Poincaré, Raymond, Pres. France, 1860–1934

Franchise
See Suffrage

Franz Ferdinand, Archduke of Austria, 1863–1914
TR's return from Africa, 1910 [1] 1925
TR's return from Africa, 1910 [2] 1925

Franz Joseph I, Emperor of Austria, 1830–1916
Cartoon of TR's reception by crowned heads of Europe. 1910
Emperor Francis Joseph of Austria greeted by his people. 1910

Fraser, James Earle
Dedication of Cuban memorial, 1924 [1] 1924
Dedication of Cuban memorial, 1924 [2] 1924

Fraternal Order of Eagles
Gifford Pinchot, 1923. 1923

Frederik VIII, King of Denmark, 1843–1912
TR's return from Africa, 1910 [1] 1925
TR's return from Africa, 1910 [2] 1925

Frederiksborg Castle, Hilleród, Denmark
See Hilleród, Denmark. Frederiksborg slot

Frenchy
Through the Roosevelt country with Roosevelt's friends. 1919

Frist, Cora
See Goodrich, Cora Frist

Fruit trees
Scenes of flowers and birds in Washington, D.C. 1920

Fullam, William F.
Reviewing Annapolis middies. 1915

Fuller, Melville Weston
[TR's inaugural ceremony, 1905] 1905
TR's inauguration, 1905 [1] 1905
TR's inauguration, 1905 [2] 1905

Funeral service
King Edward's funeral, 1910 [1] 1910
King Edward's funeral, 1910 [2] 1910
McKinley's funeral, 1901. 1901
McKinley's funeral, Washington, D.C., 1901. 1901
President McKinley's funeral, 1901 [1] 1901
President McKinley's funeral, 1901 [2] 1901
President McKinley's funeral, Canton, Ohio, 1901 [1] 1901
President McKinley's funeral, Canton, Ohio, 1901 [2] 1901
President Mckinley's funeral in Buffalo, Washington, and Canton, Ohio, 1901. 1901
Still pictures exposed on scene of McKinley's funeral as used

in Paramount reel. 1901
TR attends McKinley's funeral, 1901. 1901
TR attends McKinley's funeral, Canton, Ohio, 1901. 1901
TR on Fifth Avenue, New York, near St. Patrick's Cathedral after attending Mayor Mitchel's funeral. 1918
TR's funeral, 1919. 1919
TR's funeral at Oyster Bay, 1919. 1919
TR's funeral at Oyster Bay, January 1919 [1] 1919
TR's funeral at Oyster Bay, January 1919 [2] 1919
See also Memorial service

Futter, Walter A., source
Count von Bernstorff of Germany. 1910
Czar Nicholas of Russia. 1910
Mayor Mitchel of New York. 1917
TR, Mayor Mitchel, Governor Charles Whitman of New York, and Myron Herrick, 1917. 1917
William H. Taft in Panama [1910?] 1910

Gaeta, Italy
The King of Italy entertains King Edward of England on his yacht. 1907

Gage, Lyman J.
President McKinley's funeral, Canton, Ohio, 1901 [2] 1901
President McKinley's funeral in Buffalo, Washington, and Canton, Ohio, 1901. 1901
TR attends McKinley's funeral, 1901. 1901
TR attends McKinley's funeral, Canton, Ohio, 1901. 1901

Gaillard Cut, Canal Zone
Ships in the Panama Canal [2] 1910

Galt, Edith Bolling
See Wilson, Edith

Ganahal, L., source
Reviewing Annapolis middies. 1915
TR at San Diego Exposition, 1915. 1915

Garden City, N.Y.
Roosevelt scenes [1917–1918] 1917
TR at Camp Mills [1917] 1917

Garfield, James R.
Mr. Garfield presenting medals to 1929 medalists. 1929
Presentation of Roosevelt Medals, May 1925, Washington, D.C. 1925

Gate of Great Harmony, Peking
See Peking. Gate of Great Harmony

Gate of Supreme Harmony, Peking
See Peking. Gate of Great Harmony

Gatun Lake
Panama Canal; scenes of the finished Canal. 1919

Gaumont (Firm), source
Calvin Coolidge as Governor of Massachusetts, 1919. 1919
[Scenes of TR, 1913–1915] 1913
TR with group of men, 1917; TR speaking at dedication of Roosevelt Dam, 1911. 1911

Gaynor, William J.
TR comes back. 1925.
TR on reception yacht in New York Bay, 1910. 1910
TR speaking at Battery Park, New York, June 1910. 1910
TR speaking at the Battery, 1910. 1910
TR's return from Africa, 1910 [1] 1925
TR's return from Africa, 1910 [2] 1925
TR's return to New York, 1910 [1] 1910
TR's return to New York, 1910 [2] 1910

Geiss, A., source
Cartoon: TR's arrival in Africa. 1909
Still pictures of TR at [Cambridge] 1910. 1910

General Film Publicity & Sales Company
TR at Fargo, N.D., during Progressive campaign, 1912 [1] 1912

General Vision Company, source
Crowd listening to TR, Cardinal Gibbons and priests in foreground, 1917. 1917
Quentin Roosevelt's grave, 1918. 1919
Scouts on their way to TR's grave, Daniel C. Beard and TR Jr. attend services, 1920. 1920
TR's funeral, 1919. 1919

Gentry, Caroline
Roosevelt, friend of the birds [4]; The Roosevelt Dam [3] 1928
TR comes back. 1925

Gentry, Caroline, director
President Roosevelt, 1901–1909. 1930
The prize winning design by John Russell Pope for the proposed memorial to Theodore Roosevelt for the city of Washington. 1926
Roosevelt at home: Sagamore Hill, Oyster Bay, L.I. [2] 1930
Roosevelt, friend of the birds [1] 1924
Roosevelt, friend of the birds [2] 1924
Theodore Roosevelt in the great war [1] 1930
Theodore Roosevelt in the great war [2] 1930
Theodore Roosevelt in the great war [3] 1930
TR's return from Africa, 1910 [1] 1925
TR's return from Africa, 1910 [2] 1925

Gentry, Caroline, editor
The Panama Canal. 1927
The River of Doubt [1] 1928
The River of Doubt [2] 1928
The River of Doubt [4] 1928
The River of Doubt [5] 1928
The River of Doubt [7] 1928
The Roosevelt Dam [1] 1928
The Roosevelt Dam [2] 1928
The Story of the Panama Canal [1] 1927
The Story of the Panama Canal [2] 1927
Theodore Roosevelt, great scout [3] 1925

George I, King of the Hellenes, 1845–1913
TR's return from Africa, 1910 [1] 1925
TR's return from Africa, 1910 [2] 1925

George V, King of Great Britain, 1865–1936
King George and Queen Mary of England [1] 1928

King George and Queen Mary of England [2] 1928
[Scenes of the British royal family] 1918
Still photographs of TR on motion picture film. 1920
TR's return from Africa, 1910 [1] 1925
TR's return from Africa, 1910 [2] 1925

George VI, King of Great Britain, 1895–1952
TR's return from Africa, 1910 [1] 1925
TR's return from Africa, 1910 [2] 1925

Georgia Day
Jamestown Exposition, 1907. 1907

Georgia Day at the Jamestown Exposition, June 10, 1907 [Title]
Jamestown Exposition, 1907. 1907

Germany
Kaiser Wilhelm. 1910

Germany. Army
See Germany. Heer

Germany. Heer—Officers
Kaiser Wilhelm. 1910
Kaiser Wilhelm and his admiralty staff attend launching at
Kiel. 1910

Germany. Kreigsmarine
International naval review, Hampton Roads, Virginia, 1907.
1907

Germany. Kriegsmarine—Officers
Kaiser Wilhelm. 1910
Kaiser Wilhelm and his admiralty staff attend launching at
Kiel. 1910

Germany. Navy
See Germany. Kriegsmarine

Gibbons, James
Crowd listening to TR, Cardinal Gibbons and priests in
foreground, 1917. 1917
President Roosevelt, 1901–1909. 1930
Roosevelt scenes from RMA productions. 1912
TR and Cardinal Gibbons at Baltimore, Md., 1918. 1918
TR as Father Curran's guest at Wilkes-Barre, Pa., August 10,
1905. 1905
TR at Baltimore [1918]; TR at Sagamore [Hill, 1918] 1918
TR himself [1] 1926
TR himself [2] 1926
TR himself [3] 1926
TR himself [4] 1926
TR himself [5] 1926
TR himself [6] 1926
TR in Baltimore during Liberty Loan drive, 1918. 1918

Gillain, Cyriaque C.
Scene of Clemenceau, Tardieu, Foch, Poincaré and Pershing,
1917–1918. 1918

Gillett, Frederick Huntington
Speaker of the House F. H. Gillet. 1919

Giraffes
Scenes of African animals [1911] 1911

Gleaves, Albert
TR, Charles E. Hughes, and Mayor Mitchel of New York, on
reviewing stand in front of the New York Public Library
[1917] 1917

Glennon, James H.
Elihu Root and Mayor Mitchel of New York, Mr. Root and
American delegates return from Russia [1917] 1917

Gloria Trumpeters
Dedication of Roosevelt House, 1923. 1923
Dedication of Roosevelt House, Oct. 27, 1923. 1923

Goethals, George W.
The Building of the Panama Canal upon the occasion of a
memorial exhibition held in honor of General George Wash-
ington Goethals. 1928
General Goethals. 1923
The Panama Canal. 1927
The Story of the Panama Canal [1] 1927
The Story of the Panama Canal [2] 1927
William H. Taft in Panama [1910?] 1910

Goethals, George W., source
Ships in the Panama Canal [2] 1910

Goldsborough, Phillips L.
TR and Cardinal Gibbons at Baltimore, Md., 1918. 1918
TR at Baltimore [1918]; TR at Sagamore [Hill, 1918] 1918
TR in Baltimore during Liberty Loan drive, 1918. 1918

Goodhue, Grace
See Coolidge, Grace Goodhue

Goodrich, Cora Frist
Governor Goodrich of Indiana. 1918

Goodrich, James P.
Governor Goodrich of Indiana. 1918

Goodrich, Pierre F.
Governor Goodrich of Indiana. 1918

Gorgas, William C.
The Building of the Panama Canal upon the occasion of a
memorial exhibition held in honor of General George Wash-
ington Goethals. 1928
Dr. Gorgas who had charge of sanitation during building of
the Panama Canal. 1910
Dr. William Gorgas. 1900
Major General Wm. C. Gorgas. 1910
The Panama Canal. 1927
The Story of the Panama Canal [1] 1927
The Story of the Panama Canal [2] 1927

Government buildings
See Public buildings

Government missions, American
Elihu Root and Mayor Mitchel of New York, Mr. Root and
American delegates return from Russia [1917] 1917

Government missions, Belgian
Roosevelt scenes [1917–1918] 1917
TR receiving Belgian envoys at Sagamore Hill [1917] 1917

Governors
Governors are entered under the name of the state or province with subdivision Governors, e.g., Iowa—Governors; *see also* similar headings, e.g., Iowa. Governor, 1917–1920 (Perkins); and individual names of governors, e.g., Pinchot, Gifford.

Governor's Foot Guards, Conn.
See Connecticut. Governor's Foot Guards. First Company, Hartford
Connecticut. Governor's Foot Guards. Second Company, New Haven

Governors Island, N.Y.
15th Infantry leaving Governors Island for China (Boxer Uprising) 1900. 1900

Grand Aerie, Fraternal Order of Eagles
See Fraternal Order of Eagles

Grand Central Palace, New York (City)
See New York (City). Grand Central Palace

Granite sculpture
The prize winning design by John Russell Pope for the proposed memorial to Theodore Roosevelt for the city of Washington. 1926

Granite sculpture—South Dakota
President Coolidge speaking at Black Hills, S.D., 1927. 1927

Grant, Frederick Dent
Jamestown Exposition, 1907. 1907.

Grant, Camp, Ill.
See Camp Grant

Grasshoppers
See Locusts

Great Britain – Peerage
Lord and Lady Bryce. 1910

Great Britain. Army—Colonial forces
[Scenes of the British royal family] 1918

Great Britain. Army—Officers
Robert Bacon and Army officers. 1918

Great Britain. Navy
International naval review, Hampton Roads, Virginia, 1907. 1907

Great Britain. Parliament
[Scenes of the British royal family] 1918

Great Britain. Royal Navy
See Great Britain. Navy

Great Northern Film Company
See Nordisk Films Kompagni, A/s, Copenhagen

Greek revival (Architecture)—Georgia
Bulloch home, Roswell, Georgia, 1923. 1923

Greek Theatre
See Hearst Greek Theatre

Grey, Edward Grey, 1st Viscount, 1862–1933
The Prince of Wales visits TR's grave. 1919

Grimes, Helen
Gifford Pinchot, 1923. 1923

Guanabara Bay
Scenes of the River of Doubt photographed by G. M. Dyott, 1926–1927 [1] 1927
Scenes of the River of Doubt photographed by G. M. Dyott, 1926–1927 [2] 1927

Guanabara Palace, Rio de Janeiro
See Rio de Janeiro. Palácio Guanabara

Guerrero, Manuel Amador
See Amador Guerrero, Manuel, Pres. Panama, 1833–1909

Guggenheim, Solomon R.
[Scenes of TR, 1913–1915] 1913

Guiana (Ship)
[Scenes of TR on board ship, 1916; Scenes of TR's trip to South America, 1913] 1913
Scenes of TR on board ship before sailing for West Indies, 1916. 1916
Short scenes of TR [1] 1916

Gulf of Mexico
Roosevelt, friend of the birds [1] 1924
Roosevelt, friend of the birds [2] 1924
Roosevelt, friend of the birds [3] 1924
Roosevelt, friend of the birds [4]; The Roosevelt Dam [3] 1928
TR [in Louisiana], 1915 [1] 1915
TR [in Louisiana], 1915 [2] 1915
TR [in Louisiana], 1915 [3] 1915
TR [in Louisiana], 1915 [4] 1915

Gun-carriages, Disappearing
Disappearing gun at testing grounds, Sandy Hook, 1898. 1898

Gustaf V, King of Sweden, 1858–1950
King Gustav of Sweden greeted by his people. 1920

Gymnastics
[Scenes of TR, 1913–1915] 1913

Haakon VII, King of Norway, 1872–1957
TR himself [1] 1926
TR himself [2] 1926
TR himself [3] 1926
TR himself [4] 1926
TR himself [5] 1926
TR himself [6] 1926
TR in Norway and Denmark, 1910 [1] 1910
TR in Norway and Denmark, 1910 [2] 1910
TR in Norway and Denmark, 1910 [3] 1910
TR's return from Africa, 1910 [1] 1925
TR's return from Africa, 1910 [2] 1925

Hadley, Herbert S.
Colonel Roosevelt is invited to fly in Arch Hoxsey's plane at St. Louis, Mo., 1910. 1910

Hagedorn, Hermann
Dedication of Roosevelt Mountain at Deadwood, S.D., 1919. 1919
Mr. Hagedorn and Mr. Akeley at Roosevelt House, 1925 [1] 1925
Mr. Hagedorn and Mr. Akeley at Roosevelt House, 1925 [2] 1925
Mr. Hagedorn and Mr. Akeley at Roosevelt House, 1925 [3] 1925
Mr. Hagedorn and Mrs. Wood at Roosevelt House [1924, Long version] 1924
Mr. Hagedorn and Mrs. Wood at Roosevelt House [1924, Short version] 1924
President Harding presenting chair used by TR at the White House to the directors of RMA, October 1921. 1921
RMA pilgrimage to TR's grave, 1930. 1930
RMA trustees at Roosevelt House, 1923 [1] 1923

Hagedorn, Hermann, director
Through the Roosevelt country with Roosevelt's friends. 1919

Haig, Douglas
Scene of Clemenceau, Tardieu, Foch, Poincaré and Pershing, 1917–1918. 1918

Hall of Supreme Harmony, Peking
See Peking. Hall of Supreme Harmony

Hammond, Emily Vanderbilt Sloane
Leonard Wood lays cornerstone of Roosevelt House, 1921. 1921
Marshall Foch visits Roosevelt House, 1921. 1921
Mrs. Roosevelt, Sr., and Mrs. J. H. Hammond photographed on the roof of Roosevelt House, 1927; Mrs. Roosevelt arrives at Roosevelt House. 1927
Woman's Roosevelt Memorial Association meeting at Roosevelt House, 1923 [1] 1923
Woman's Roosevelt Memorial Association meeting at Roosevelt House, 1923 [2] 1923

Hampton Roads
International naval review, Hampton Roads, Virginia, 1907. 1907
TR reviews the fleet, 1907. 1907

Hanna, Marcus A.
President McKinley inauguration, 1901. 1901
President McKinley's inauguration, 1901 [2] 1901

Harbord, James G.
Dedication of Cuban memorial, 1924 [2] 1924

Harding, Florence Kling
General Wood and Calvin Coolidge in Chicago, 1920. 1920
President Harding and Calvin Coolidge [1] 1920
President Harding and Calvin Coolidge [2] 1920

Harding, George T.
President Harding and Calvin Coolidge [1] 1920
President Harding and Calvin Coolidge [2] 1920

Harding, Warren Gamaliel, Pres. U. S., 1865–1923
General Wood and Calvin Coolidge in Chicago, 1920. 1920
President Harding and Calvin Coolidge [1] 1920
President Harding and Calvin Coolidge [2] 1920
President Harding presenting chair used by TR at the White House to the directors of RMA, October 1921. 1921

Harper, Frank
The River of Doubt [1] 1928
The River of Doubt [2] 1928
The River of Doubt [3] 1928
The River of Doubt [5] 1928
The River of Doubt [7] 1928
[Scenes of TR on board ship, 1916; Scenes of TR's trip to South America, 1913] 1913

Harrington, Emerson C.
TR addresses large crowd for the Liberty Loan in Baltimore, 1918. 1918
TR and Cardinal Gibbons at Baltimore, Md., 1918. 1918
TR at Baltimore [1918]; TR at Sagamore [Hill, 1918] 1918
TR himself [1] 1926
TR himself [2] 1926
TR himself [3] 1926
TR himself [4] 1926
TR himself [5] 1926
TR himself [6] 1926
TR in Baltimore during Liberty Loan drive, 1918. 1918
TR scenes purchased from different dealers. 1912.

Harris, James G.
Calvin Coolidge sworn in for second term as Governor of Massachusetts. 1920

Harrisburg, Pa.
Gifford Pinchot, 1923. 1923

Hart, Albert Bushnell, Theodore Roosevelt cyclopedia.
Memorializing Roosevelt. 1925

Hart, Albert Bushnell
RMA pilgrimage to TR's grave, 1930. 1930

Hart, Hastings Hornell
Scenes of Hastings Hart, 1930 medalist. 1930

Harts, William W.
Robert Bacon and Army officers. 1918

Harvard University
Owen D. Young [1] 1927
Owen D. Young [2] 1927

Harvard University. Graduate School of Business Administration
Owen D. Young [1] 1927
Owen D. Young [2] 1927

Harvard University. Library
Memorializing Roosevelt. 1925

Hastings, Thomas
President Wilson arrives in New York to lead fourth Liberty Loan parade [1918] 1918

201

Havana
Dedication of Cuban memorial, 1924 [1] 1924

Havana—Harbor
Dedication of Cuban memorial, 1924 [1] 1924

Havana. Morro Castle
Dedication of Cuban memorial, 1924 [1] 1924

Hays, Will H.
General Wood and Calvin Coolidge in Chicago, 1920. 1920
President Harding and Calvin Coolidge [1] 1920
President Harding and Calvin Coolidge [2] 1920
President Harding presenting chair used by TR at the White House to the directors of RMA, October 1921. 1921
RMA trustees at Roosevelt House, 1923 [2] 1923
TR Jr. and Will Hays. 1920
Will Hays. 1920

Heads of state
King Edward's funeral, 1910 [1] 1910
King Edward's funeral, 1910 [2] 1910
TR's return from Africa, 1910 [1] 1925
TR's return from Africa, 1910 [2] 1925

Health resorts, watering-places, etc.
TR, Mayor Mitchel and guests at Cooper Sanitarium [1917] 1917

Hearst Greek Theatre
RMA ceremonies at [Hearst Greek Theatre, University of California, Berkeley, Calif.] 1919
RMA services at [Hearst Greek Theatre, University of California, Berkeley, Calif.]; Laying cornerstone of Roosevelt School at New Rochelle, N.Y. [1920] 1920

Hearst-Pathe News
President Wilson arrives in New York to lead fourth Liberty Loan parade [1918] 1918
Roosevelt scenes [1917–1918] 1917
TR, exterior of building, Washington, D.C., 1918. 1918
Women suffragettes visit TR at Sagamore [1917] 1917

Hearst-Pathe News [newsreel]
President Wilson arrives in New York to lead fourth Liberty Loan parade [1918] 1918
Roosevelt scenes [1917–1918] 1917
TR, exterior of building, Washington, D.C., 1918. 1918
Women suffragettes visit TR at Sagamore [1917] 1917

Hearst-Selig News Pictorial
TR in a rowboat on Oyster Bay, Archie assists with boat to shore. 1914. 1914

Hearst-Selig News Pictorial [newsreel]
TR in a rowboat on Oyster Bay, Archie assists with boat to shore, 1914. 1914

Hecker, Frank J.
Leonard Wood at Battle Creek, Michigan. 1920

Helm, William P.
Roosevelt at home: Sagamore Hill, Oyster Bay, L. I. [1] 1930
Roosevelt at home: Sagamore Hill, Oyster Bay, L. I. [2] 1930

Scenes of TR at Sagamore Hill, 1912. 1912
TR and Mr. Helm, a newspaper reporter, exterior of Sagamore Hill, 1912. 1912
A visit to Theodore Roosevelt at his home at Sagamore Hill, Oyster Bay, L. I., 1912. 1912

Helsingór, Denmark
TR in Denmark, 1910. 1910
TR in Norway and Denmark, 1910 [1] 1910
TR in Norway and Denmark, 1910 [2] 1910
TR in Norway and Denmark, 1910 [3] 1910

Helsingór, Denmark. Kronborg slot
TR in Norway and Denmark, 1910 [1] 1910
TR in Norway and Denmark, 1910 [2] 1910
TR in Norway and Denmark, 1910 [3] 1910

Hemment, John C., photographer
Scenes of African animals [1911] 1911

Hendricks, Francis
Chauncey Depew, Senator Perkins, and Governor Whitman of New York, at GOP Convention, 1916, Chicago, Ill. 1916

Henry, consort of Wilhelmina, Queen of the Netherlands, 1876–1934
Queen Wilhelmina of Holland, the Prince Consort [and] the Princess. 1920

Hepburn, Emily E.
Woman's Roosevelt Memorial Association meeting at Roosevelt House. 1923 [1] 1923
Woman's Roosevelt Memorial Association meeting at Roosevelt House, 1923 [2] 1923

Herons
Roosevelt, friend of the birds [1] 1924
Roosevelt, friend of the birds [2] 1924
Roosevelt, friend of the birds [3] 1924
Roosevelt, friend of the birds [4]; The Roosevelt Dam [3] 1928

Herrick, Myron T.
TR, Mayor Mitchel, Governor Charles Whitman of New York. and Myron Herrick. 1917. 1917

Herron, Helen
See Taft, Helen Herron

Hickory Hill, Thomson, Ga.
See Thomson, Ga. Hickory Hill

Hicks, Frederick C.
President Harding presenting chair used by TR at the White House to the directors of RMA, October 1921. 1921

High school students—Political activity
Brooklyn children attend services, children sew stars on Roosevelt Flag [1919] 1919
Children sewing stars on flag, placing flag on TR's grave [1919] 1919
[Flag services for TR at Oyster Bay, October [1919] 1919
Memorial services for TR at Van Cortlandt Park, New York, Oct. 1919. 1919

Memorial services for TR on the steps of the New York Public Library, 1919 [1] 1919
RMA flag ceremonies, children sew stars on flag, 1919. 1919
Runners carrying flag to TR's grave [1919] 1919
TR memorial services at New York Public Library, 1919. 1919
Whole nation honors memory of Roosevelt. 1919

Hill, Louis C.
The Roosevelt Dam [1] 1928
The Roosevelt Dam [2] 1928
TR at dedication of Roosevelt Dam, 1911. 1911
TR speaking at the dedication of Roosevelt Dam, 1911. 1911
TR with group of men, 1917; TR speaking at dedication of Roosevelt Dam, 1911. 1911

Hill, Louis W.
TR in St. Paul, Minn. [1917] 1917

Hilleród, Denmark. Frederiksborg slot
TR in Norway and Denmark, 1910 [1] 1910
TR in Norway and Denmark, 1910 [2] 1910
TR in Norway and Denmark, 1910 [3] 1910

Hine, Charles
TR at Camp Mills [1917] 1917

Hippopotamus
African animals, 1909
TR in Africa [1909, 3] 1909

Hispano-American War, 1898
See United States—History—War of 1898

Hitchcock, Ethan Allen, 1835–1909
President McKinley's funeral, Canton, Ohio, 1901 [2] 1901
President McKinley's funeral in Buffalo, Washington, and Canton, Ohio, 1901. 1901
TR attends McKinley's funeral, 1901. 1901
TR attends McKinley's funeral, Canton, Ohio, 1901. 1901

Hitchcock, Gilbert M.
Senator Hitchcock. 1910

Hobbs, William H.
Leonard Wood at Battle Creek, Michigan. 1920

Hoboken, N.J.
Commander Dyott sailing from [Hoboken, N.J.] for South America, 1926. 1926

Holcomb, Marcus H.
Governors of New England meet in Governor Coolidge's office in Boston to discuss fuel. 1919

Hollis, V. P., source
TR in St. Paul, Minn. [1917] 1917
TR speaking at St. Paul, Minn., 1918. 1918
TR speaking in St. Paul, Minnesota, 1918. 1918

Holmes, Burton, source
TR reviews the fleet, 1907. 1907

Hopi Indian Reservation, Ariz.
Hopi Indians dance for TR at [Walpi, Ariz.] 1913. 1913

Hopi Indians – Social life and customs
Hopi Indians dance for TR at [Walpi, Ariz.] 1913. 1913

Horrigan, Edward
Calvin Coolidge sworn in for second term as Governor of Massachusetts. 1920

Horsemen
Rough Riders greet TR during Liberty Loan drive out west [1918] 1918

Horses
Roosevelt at home: Sagamore Hill, Oyster Bay, L. I. [1] 1930
Roosevelt at home: Sagamore Hill, Oyster Bay, L. I. [2] 1930
Scenes of the River of Doubt photographed by G. M. Dyott, 1926–1927 [2] 1927
Spanish Mountain Artillery, 1898. 1898

Horst, source
Roosevelt scenes from RMA productions. 1912

Hotel Alvarado, Albuquerque, N.M.
See Albuquerque, N.M. Alvarado Hotel

Hotel McAlpin, New York (City)
See New York (City). Hotel McAlpin

Hotel Nelson, Rockford, Ill.
See Rockford, Ill. Hotel Nelson

Hotel Statler, Detroit
See Detroit. Hotel Statler

Hovey, Carl
Shall we prepare? 1916
TR scenes purchased from different dealers. 1912

Howe, Lyman, source
Kaiser Wilhelm and his admiralty staff attend launching at Kiel. 1910
King Edward's funeral, 1910 [2] 1910
King Gustav of Sweden greeted by his people. 1920
The King of Italy entertains King Edward of England on his yacht. 1907
TR as Father Curran's guest at Wilkes-Barre, Pa., August 10, 1905. 1905
TR at dedication of Roosevelt Dam, 1911. 1911
TR in San Francisco, 1903. 1903
TR reviews French troops at Vincennes, France, 1910. 1910
TR speaking at the dedication of Roosevelt Dam, 1911. 1911

Hoxsey, Arch
Colonel Roosevelt is invited to fly in Arch Hoxsey's plane at St. Louis, Mo., 1910. 1910

Hoyle, Eli D.
TR, Charles E. Hughes, and Mayor Mitchel of New York, on reviewing stand in front of the New York Public Library [1917] 1917

Hughes, Charles Evans
Charles E. Hughes speaking during campaign, Duquesne, Pa., 1916. 1916
President Harding presenting chair used by TR at the White

House to the directors of RMA, October 1921. 1921
Roosevelt scenes from RMA productions. 1912
Still photographs of TR on motion picture film. 1920
Theodore Roosevelt in the great war [1] 1930
Theodore Roosevelt in the great war [2] 1930
Theodore Roosevelt in the great war [3] 1930
TR, Charles E. Hughes, and Mayor Mitchel of New York, on reviewing stand in front of the New York Public Library [1917] 1917

Hulbert, Murray
Dedication of Roosevelt House, 1923. 1923
Dedication of Roosevelt House, Oct. 27, 1923. 1923

Hunting
Through the Roosevelt country with Roosevelt's friends. 1919
See also Big game hunting

Hunting dogs
Scenes of African animals [1911] 1911

Hurd, Richard M.
TR at Sagamore Hill [1916] 1915

Ibis
Scenes of the River of Doubt photographed by G.M. Dyott, 1926–1927 [1] 1927

Illinois. Governor, 1913–1917 (Edward F. Dunne)
Reviewing Annapolis middies. 1915

Imperial Palace, Peking
See Peking. Imperial Palace

Inauguration Day
President McKinley inauguration, 1901. 1901
President McKinley's inauguration, 1901 [1] 1901
President McKinley's inauguration, 1901 [2] 1901
TR himself [1] 1926
TR himself [2] 1926
TR himself [3] 1926
TR himself [4] 1926
TR himself [5] 1926
TR himself [6] 1926
TR speaking at Sagamore Hill [1916–1918 and scenes of his early career] 1897
[TR's inaugural ceremony, 1905] 1905
TR's inauguration, 1905 [1] 1905
TR's inauguration, 1905 [2] 1905

Indiana. Governor, 1917–1921 (Goodrich)
Governor Goodrich of Indiana. 1918

Indiana (Ship)
U.S. battleship Indiana. 1898

Indianapolis
Governor Goodrich of Indiana. 1918

Indianapolis. St. Vincent's Hospital
See St. Vincent's Hospital, Indianapolis

Indians of North America—Arizona—Employment
The Roosevelt Dam [1] 1928
The Roosevelt Dam [2] 1928

Indians of South America
See Arara Indians; Nambicuara Indians

Indians of South America—Brazil
The River of Doubt [2] 1928
The River of Doubt [3] 1928
The River of Doubt [4] 1928
The River of Doubt [6] 1928
The River of Doubt [7] 1928
Scenes of the River of Doubt photographed by G. M. Dyott, 1926–1927 [1] 1927
Scenes of the River of Doubt photographed by G. M. Dyott, 1926–1927 [2] 1927

Infantry drill and tactics
15th Infantry leaving Governors Island for China (Boxer Uprising) 1900. 1900

Insects—Brazil
The River of Doubt [6] 1928

Insull, Samuel
TR reviews and addresses troops [Fort Sheridan, Ill.]; TR riding in auto, Chicago, 1917. 1917

International Film Service
See International Film Service Company

International Film Service Company
Children sewing stars on flag, placing flag on TR's grave [1919] 1919
Gen. Pershing speaking to Scouts in New York. 1919
The Prince of Wales visits TR's grave. 1919

International Film Service Company, source
Still picture of TR and his family. 1907

International Flower Show, 5th, New York City, 1917
Scenes of TR and his sons Quentin and Archie, 1917–1918 [1] 1917
Scenes of TR and his sons Quentin and Archie, 1917–1918 [2] 1917
Short scenes of TR [1] 1916
TR and Leonard Wood at the New York flower show, 1917. 1917

International News [newsreel]
American Legion lays cornerstone of Roosevelt Bridge at Château-Thierry. 1921

International News Reel Corporation
See International Newsreel Corporation

International news [Series]
General [Diaz] of Italy visits TR's grave [1921] 1921

International Newsreel Co.
See International Newsreel Corporation

International Newsreel Company
See International Newsreel Corporation

International Newsreel Corporation
American Legion lays cornerstone of Roosevelt Bridge at

Château-Thierry. 1921
General [Diaz] of Italy visits TR's grave [1921] 1921

International Newsreel Corporation, source
American Legion lays cornerstone of Roosevelt Bridge at
Château-Thierry. 1921
Children sewing stars on flag, placing flag on TR's grave
[1919] 1919
Daniel C. Beard, TR Jr., and Boy Scouts visit TR's grave,
1920. 1920
Exterior scenes of Sagamore Hill. 1918
General [Diaz] of Italy visits TR's grave [1921] 1921
King Albert of Belgium visits TR's grave, 1919. 1919
Lieutenant-Colonel Theodore Roosevelt arrives in New York
after the World War. 1919
Mrs. Theodore Roosevelt Jr. attends Women in War Work
Congress in Paris [1918] 1918
President Coolidge speaking at Black Hills, S.D., 1927. 1927
The Prince of Wales visits TR's grave. 1919
Scenes of TR on board ship before sailing for West Indies,
1916. 1916
TR addresses large crowd for the Liberty Loan in Baltimore,
1918. 1918
TR and Leonard Wood at the New York flower show, 1917.
1917
TR and several men. 1910
TR calls on neighbors at Christmas, 1917. 1917
TR in a rowboat on Oyster Bay, Archie assists with boat to
shore, 1914. 1914
TR Jr. and Will Hays. 1920
TR seated at his desk in the Outlook office [1914?] 1914
TR speaking during War, 1917–1918. 1917
TR speaking to a group of men from the porch at Sagamore
Hill, 1916. 1916
TR speaking to a group of suffragettes from the porch at
Sagamore Hill, 1917. 1917
TR's funeral at Oyster Bay, 1919. 1919
TR's reception in Albuquerque, N.M., 1916. 1916

International [Series]
Children sewing stars on flag, placing flag on TR's grave
[1919] 1919
The Prince of Wales visits TR's grave. 1919

International [Series] v. 1, no. 37
Gen. Pershing speaking to Scouts in New York. 1919

Iowa—Governors
Senators Curtis, Cummins, Moses, and [Representative]
Mondell. 1919

Ipatiev
Last known home of Czar Nicholas. 1918

Irrigation—Arizona
The Roosevelt Dam [1] 1928

Irrigation farming—Arizona
The Roosevelt Dam [1] 1928
The Roosevelt Dam [2] 1928
Roosevelt, friend of the birds [4]; The Roosevelt Dam [3]
1928

Irvin, Vivian R.
TR in St. Paul, Minn. [1917] 1917

Islands—Louisiana
TR [in Louisiana], 1915 [1] 1915
TR [in Louisiana], 1915 [2] 1915
TR [in Louisiana], 1915 [3] 1915
TR [in Louisiana], 1915 [4] 1915

Italy. Army
See Italy. Esercito—Officers

Italy. Esercito—Officers
General [Diaz] of Italy visits TR's grave [1921] 1921

Izzedin, Yusuf
See Yusuf Izzedin, 1858–1916

Jack Cooper's Health Farm
See Cooper's Training Camp

Jackson, Thomas, source
Colonel Roosevelt is invited to fly in Arch Hoxsey's plane at
St. Louis, Mo., 1910. 1910

Jails
See Prisons

James River
Launch. U.S. battleship "Kentucky." 1898

Jamestown, Va.
Jamestown Exposition, 1907. 1907

Jamestown, Va.—Exhibitions
Jamestown Exposition, 1907. 1907

Jamestown Exposition, 1907
International naval review, Hampton Roads, Virginia, 1907.
1907
Jamestown Exposition, 1907. 1907

Jamestown Ter-Centennial Exposition
See Jamestown Exposition, 1907

Job, Herbert K.
Roosevelt, friend of the birds [1] 1924
Roosevelt, friend of the birds [2] 1924
Roosevelt, friend of the birds [3] 1924
Roosevelt, friend of the birds [4]; The Roosevelt Dam [3]
1928

Job, Herbert K., photographer
Roosevelt, friend of the birds [1] 1924
Roosevelt, friend of the birds [2] 1924
Roosevelt, friend of the birds [3] 1924
TR [in Louisiana], 1915 [1] 1915
TR [in Louisiana], 1915 [2] 1915
TR [in Louisiana], 1915 [3] 1915
TR [in Louisiana], 1915 [4] 1915

Joffre, Joseph J.
Scene of Clemenceau, Tardieu, Foch, Poincaré and Pershing,
1917–1918. 1918

John Donnelly & Company
The prize winning design by John Russell Pope for the pro-
posed memorial to Theodore Roosevelt for the city of
Washington. 1926

Johnson, Hiram W.
[Scenes of TR, 1913–1915] 1913
Senator Hiram Johnson. 1922
TR [at Panama-Pacific Exposition, 1915] 1915
TR himself [1] 1926
TR himself [5] 1926

Juliana, Queen of the Netherlands, 1909–
Queen Wilhelmina of Holland, the Prince Consort [and] the
Princess. 1920

Jusserand, Jean Adrien Antoine Jules
See Jusserand, Jules

Jusserand, Jules
Jules Jusserand, 1924. 1924
TR in Vincennes, France, 1910. 1910
TR reviews French troops at Vincennes, France, 1910. 1910
TR's return from Africa, 1910 [1] 1925
TR's return from Africa, 1910 [2] 1925

Kaiserin Auguste Victoria (Ship)
TR comes back. 1925
TR's return to New York, 1910 [1] 1925
TR's return to New York, 1910 [2] 1925

Kandel, source
Kaiser Wilhelm. 1910
TR attends his son Archie's wedding at Boston, 1917. 1917
TR in Baltimore during Liberty Loan drive, 1918. 1918
TR on porch at Sagamore Hill, 1917. 1917

Kansas. Governor, 1919–1923 (Henry J. Allen)
Memorial services for TR on the steps of the New York Public
Library, 1919 [1] 1919
Memorial services for TR on the steps of the New York Public
Libarry, 1919 [2] 1919
RMA flag service on the steps of New York Public Library,
1919. 1919
TR memorial services at New York Public Library, 1919. 1919
See also Allen, Henry J.

Kearton, Cherry, photographer
African animals. 1909
African natives. 1909
TR in Africa [1909, 1] 1909
TR in Africa [1909, 2] 1909
TR in Africa [1909, 3] 1909
TR in Africa [1909, 4] 1909
[TR planting a tree in Africa] 1909
TR's camp in Africa [1909] 1909

Kearton, Cherry, source
TR in Africa [1909, 1] 1909
TR in Africa [1909, 4] 1909

Kellogg, Frank B.
President Harding presenting chair used by TR at the White
House to the directors of RMA, October 1921. 1921

Kendley, Nitch
Through the Roosevelt country with Roosevelt's friends. 1919

Kentucky. Governor, 1919–1923 (Morrow)
President Harding and Calvin Coolidge [1] 1920
President Harding and Calvin Coolidge [2] 1920

Kentucky (Ship)
Launch, U. S. battleship "Kentucky." 1898

Kenya
African animals. 1909
TR in Africa [1909, 1] 1909
TR in Africa [1909, 2] 1909
TR in Africa [1909, 3] 1909
TR in Africa [1909, 4] 1909
TR's camp in Africa [1909] 1909

Keystone, S. D.
President Coolidge speaking at Black Hills, S. D., 1927. 1927

Kiel
Kaiser Wilhelm and his admiralty staff attend launching at
Kiel. 1910

Kiel, Henry W.
Colonel Roosevelt is invited to fly in Arch Hoxsey's plane at
St. Louis, Mo., 1910. 1910

Kikuyu tribe
African natives. 1909
TR in Africa [1909, 1] 1909
TR in Africa [1909, 2] 1909
TR in Africa [1909, 4] 1909

Kikuyu tribe—Dances
African natives. 1909
TR in Africa [1909, 1] 1909
TR in Africa [1909, 2] 1909
TR in Africa [1909, 4] 1909

Kikuyu tribe—Social life and customs
TR in Africa [1909, 2] 1909

Kineto Company of America
King Edward's funeral, 1910 [1] 1910

King, Evelyn
See Baker, Evelyn King

Kings and rulers
The King of Italy entertains King Edward of England on his
yacht. 1907
TR's return from Africa, 1910 [1] 1925
TR's return from Africa, 1910 [2] 1925

Kinley, Nitch
See Kendley, Nitch

Kinloch, Mo.
Colonel Roosevelt is invited to fly in Arch Hoxsey's plane at
St. Louis, Mo., 1910. 1910

Kinloch, Mo. Lambert Field
Colonel Roosevelt is invited to fly in Arch Hoxsey's plane at

St. Louis, Mo., 1910. 1910

Queen Wilhelmina of Holland, the Prince Consort [and] the Princess. 1920

RMA flag ceremonies, children sew stars on flag, 1919. 1919

RMA flag service on the steps of New York Public Library, 1919. 1919

RMA services at [Hearst Greek Theatre, University of California, Berkeley, Calif.]; Laying cornerstone of Roosevelt School at New Rochelle, N. Y. [1920] 1920

Runners carrying flag to TR's grave [1919] 1919

Senator Smoot. 1920

Senators Curtis, Cummins, Moses, and [Representative] Mondell. 1919

Whole nation honors memory of Roosevelt. 1919

Kinloch Aviation Field, Kinloch, Mo.
See Kinloch, Mo. Lambert Field

Kinloch Field, Kinloch, Mo.
See Kinloch, Mo. Lambert Field

Kinloch Park, Mo. Lambert Field
See Kinloch, Mo. Lambert Field

Kinogram Publishing Company
See Kinogram Publishing Corporation

Kinogram Publishing Corporation
Americanism wins, Coolidge elected. 1919

Calvin Coolidge sworn in for second term as Governor of Massachusetts. 1920

Dedication of Roosevelt Mountain at Deadwood, S. D., 1919. 1919

[Flag services for TR at Oyster Bay, October 1919] 1919

Governors of New England meet in Governor Coolidge's office in Boston to discuss fuel. 1919

The King and Queen at Belgium and Premier Poincaré of France [1] 1927

King George and Queen Mary of England [1] 1928

King George and Queen Mary of England [2] 1928

Laying cornerstone of Roosevelt School, New Rochelle, N. Y. [1920] 1920

Memorial services for TR on the steps of the New York Public Library, 1919 [1] 1919

Owen D. Young [1] 1927

Owen D. Young [2] 1927

Kinogram Publishing Corporation, source
Americanism wins, Coolidge elected. 1919

Crowd exterior of Buckingham Palace. 1910

Herbert Putnam. 1920

Jules Jusserand, 1924. 1924

The King and Queen of Belgium and Premier Poincaré of France [1] 1927

The King and Queen of Belgium and Premier Poincaré of France [2] 1927

King George and Queen Mary of England [1] 1928

King George and Queen Mary of England [2] 1928

Owen D. Young [2] 1927

Owen Wister. 1920

Presentation of Roosevelt Medals, May 1925, Washington, D. C. 1925

Queen Wilhelmina of Holland, the Prince Consort [and] the Princess. 1920

RMA pilgrimage to TR's grave, 1930. 1930

Scenes of Hastings Hart, 1930 medalist. 1930

Street scenes in Naples, Italy. 1910

Kinograms, inc.
See Kinogram Publishing Corporation

Kinograms Publishing Company
See Kinogram Publishing Corporation

Kinograms Publishing Corporation
See Kinogram Publishing Corporation

Kinograms [Series]
Americanism wins, Coolidge elected. 1919

Calvin Coolidge sworn in for second term as Governor of Massachusetts. 1920

Dedication of Roosevelt Mountain at Deadwood, S. D., 1919. 1919.

[Flag services for TR at Oyster Bay, October 1919] 1919

Governors of New England meet in Governor Coolidge's office in Boston to discuss fuel. 1919

The King and Queen of Belgium and Premier Poincaré of France [1] 1927

King George and Queen Mary of England [1] 1928

Laying cornerstone of Roosevelt School, New Rochelle, N. Y. [1920] 1920

Memorial services for TR on the steps of the New York Public Library, 1919 [1] 1919

Owen D. Young [1] 1927

Owen D. Young [2] 1927

Queen Wilhelmina of Holland, the Prince Consort [and] the Princess. 1920

RMA flag ceremonies, children sew stars on flag, 1919. 1919

RMA flag service on the steps of New York Public Library, 1919. 1919

RMA services at [Hearst Greek Theatre, University of California, Berkeley, Calif.]; Laying cornerstone of Roosevelt School at New Rochelle, N. Y. [1920] 1920

Runners carrying flag to TR's grave [1919] 1919

Senator Smoot. 1920

Senators Curtis, Cummins, Moses, and [Representative] Mondell. 1919

Whole nation honors memory of Roosevelt. 1919

Kirby, Gustavus T.
[Scenes of TR, 1913–1915] 1913

Kirkendall, Fred C.
TR as Father Curran's guest at Wilkes-Barre, Pa., August 10, 1905. 1905

Kleine, George, source
International naval review, Hampton Roads, Virginia, 1907. 1907

Japanese and Russian peace delegates [leaving New York City], 1905. 1905

McKinley's funeral, 1901. 1901

McKinley's funeral, Washington, D. C., 1901. 1901

Pack mules with ammunition on the Santiago trail, Cuba, 1898
President McKinley speaking at Buffalo, 1901. 1901
President McKinley's funeral, Canton, Ohio, 1901 [1] 1901
President McKinley's funeral, Canton, Ohio, 1901 [2] 1901
President McKinley's funeral in Buffalo, Washington, and Canton, Ohio, 1901. 1901
President McKinley's inauguration, 1901 [1] 1901
TR attends McKinley's funeral, Canton, Ohio, 1901. 1901
Troops making military road in front of Santiago. 1898
[TR's inaugural ceremony, 1905] 1905
U. S. troops landing at Daiquiri, Cuba. 1898

Kling, Florence
See Harding, Florence Kling

Knox, Frank
See Knox, Franklin

Knox, Franklin
Dedication of Cuban memorial, 1924 [1] 1924

Knox, Philander Chase
President McKinley's funeral, Canton, Ohio, 1901 [2] 1901
President McKinley's funeral in Buffalo, Washington, and Canton, Ohio, 1901. 1901
TR attends McKinley's funeral, 1901. 1901
TR attends McKinley's funeral, Canton, Ohio, 1901. 1901

Koester, Hans Ludwig Raimund Von
Kaiser Wilhelm and his admiralty staff attend launching at Kiel. 1910

Komura, Jutaro
TR himself [1] 1926
TR himself [2] 1926
TR himself [3] 1926
TR himself [4] 1926
TR himself [5] 1926
TR himself [6] 1926

Kronborg Castle, Helsingór, Denmark
See Helsingór, Denmark. Kronborg slot

Labor Day
TR, Charles E. Hughes, and Mayor Mitchel of New York, on reviewing stand in front of the New York Public Library [1917] 1917
TR speaking at Newburgh, N. Y. [1918] 1918

Laeken Belgium
The King and Queen of Belgium and Premier Poincaré of France [1] 1927
The King and Queen of Belgium and Premier Poincaré of France [2] 1927

Laeken, Belgium. Église Notre-Dame
See Église Notre-Dame, Laeken, Belgium

Laidlaw, Harriet B.
Scenes of TR speaking at Sagamore [1916–1918] 1916
Women suffragettes visit TR at Sagamore [1917] 1917

Lambert, Alexander
Presentation of Roosevelt Medals, May 1925, Washington,

D. C. 1925
President Harding presenting chair used by TR at the White House to the directors of RMA, October 1921. 1921
RMA pilgrimage to TR's grave, 1930. 1930
RMA trustees at Roosevelt House. 1923 [1] 1923

Lambert Field, Kinloch, Mo.
See Kinloch, Mo. Lambert Field

Landing operations
U.S. troops landing at Daiquiri, Cuba. 1898

Landscape
Scenes of Oyster Bay. 1924

Lansing, Robert
Original U. S. documents. 1920

Laughing gull
Roosevelt, friend of the birds [1] 1924
Roosevelt, friend of the birds [2] 1924
Roosevelt, friend of the birds [3] 1924
Roosevelt, friend of the birds [4] 1924; The Roosevelt Dam [3] 1928

Launches
TR and expedition party on the [Sepotuba] River [1914] 1914

Laying cornerstone of Roosevelt School at New Rochelle, N. Y. [1920] [Title]
RMA services at [Hearst Greek Theatre, University of California, Berkeley, Calif.]; Laying cornerstone of Roosevelt School at New Rochelle, N. Y. [1920] 1920

Leclercq, Mathieu
Roosevelt scenes [1917–1918] 1917
TR receiving Belgian envoys at Sagamore Hill [1917] 1917

Lee, A., source
Quentin Roosevelt's grave in France. 1919
TR at limousine window, 1917. 1917
TR during Progressive campaign, 1912. 1912
TR speaking at Sagamore Hill [1916–1918 and scenes of his early career] 1897
TR's funeral at Oyster Bay, January [1] 1919

Lee, Georgia Watson
Senator Watson. 1921

Lee Parade Ground, Norfolk, Va.
See Norfolk, Va.—Plazas—Lee Parade Ground

Legislators
[Unidentified man] 1910

Legislators—California
Senator Hiram Johnson. 1922

Legislators—Georgia
Senator Watson. 1921

Legislators—Indiana
Senators Curtis, Cummins, Moses, and [Representative] Mondell. 1919

Legislators—Iowa
Senators Curtis, Cummins, Moses, and [Representative] Mondell. 1919

Legislators—Kansas
Senators Curtis, Cummins, Moses, and [Representative] Mondell. 1919

Legislators—Massachusetts
Speaker of the House F. H. Gillett. 1919

Legislators—Nebraska
Senator Hitchcock. 1910

Legislators—New Hampshire
Senators Curtis, Cummins, Moses, and [Representative] Mondell. 1919

Legislators—New Mexico
Short scenes of TR [1] 1916
TR in New Mexico, 1916. 1916
TR with Rough Rider friends. 1910
TR's reception in Albuquerque, N.M., 1916. 1916

Legislators—New York (State)
Senators Curtis, Cummins, Moses, and [Representative] Mondell. 1919

Legislators—North Dakota
Senator McCumber of North Dakota, 1920

Legislators—Ohio
Senator Pomerene. 1910

Legislators—Pennsylvania
Senator Penrose. 1910

Legislators—South Dakota
Dedication of Roosevelt Mountain at Deadwood, S. D., 1919. 1919

Legislators—Utah
Senator Smoot. 1920

Legislators—Wyoming
Senators Curtis, Cummins, Moses, and [Representative] Mondell. 1919

Leland, Henry M.
Leonard Wood at Battle Creek, Michigan. 1920

Lenihan, Michael J.
Roosevelt scenes [1917–1918] 1917
TR at Camp Mills [1917] 1917

Leonard Wood League of Michigan
Leonard Wood at Battle Creek, Michigan. 1920

Leopold III, King of the Belgians, 1901–
King Albert of Belgium visits TR's grave, 1919. 1919
King Albert of Belgium visits TR's grave, October, 1919. 1919
The King and Queen of Belgium and Premier Poincaré of France [1] 1927

The King and Queen of Belgium and Premier Poincaré of France [2] 1927

Lewis, Samuel, source
Dr. Gorgas who had charge of sanitation during building of the Panama Canal. 1910
Governor Goodrich of Indiana. 1918
Panama Canal; scenes of the finished Canal. 1919

Lewis J. Selznick Enterprises
See Selznick Pictures Corporation

Liberty loan acts
See United States. Laws, statutes, etc. Liberty loan acts

Liberty Loan Committee for Maryland
See Maryland. Liberty Loan Committee

Liberty Loan Committee for New York City
See New York (City). Liberty Loan Committee

Liberty's Altar, New York (City)
See New York (City). Liberty's Altar

Lindbergh, Charles A.
Colonel Lindbergh, Admiral Byrd, and Clarence Chamberlin at flying field just before Lindbergh's flight, 1927. 1927

Lindsley, Henry D.
Memorial services for TR on the steps of the New York Public Library, 1919 [1] 1919
Memorial services for TR on the steps of the New York Public Library, 1919 [2] 1919
RMA flag service on the steps of New York Public Library, 1919. 1919

Linnenkohl, source
TR [in Louisiana], 1915 [2] 1915

Lions
Scenes of African animals [1911] 1911
Scenes of lions. 1910

Little Missouri Badlands, N.D.
Through the Roosevelt country with Roosevelt's friends. 1919

Little Missouri River
Memorializing Roosevelt. 1925
Through the Roosevelt country with Roosevelt's friends. 1919

Livingstone, Colin H.
Theodore Roosevelt, great scout [1] 1925
Theodore Roosevelt, great scout [2] 1925
Theodore Roosevelt, great scout [3] 1925

Lizards—Brazil
Scenes of the River of Doubt photographed by G. M. Dyott, 1926–1927 [1] 1927
Scenes of the River of Doubt photographed by G. M. Dyott, 1926–1927 [2] 1927

Locks (Hydraulic engineering)
The Panama Canal. 1927

Panama Canal scenes. 1910
Panama Canal; scenes of the finished Canal. 1919
Ships in the Panama Canal [1] 1910
The Story of the Panama Canal [1] 1927
The Story of the Panama Canal [2] 1927

Lockwood, Grace S.
TR attends his son Archie's wedding at Boston, 1917. 1917

Locomotives
Scenes of Oyster Bay. 1924

Locusts—Brazil
Scenes of the River of Doubt photographed by G. M. Dyott, 1926–1927 [1] 1927

Lodge, Henry Cabot
General Wood and Calvin Coolidge in Chicago, 1920. 1920
Memorial services for TR on the steps of the New York Public Library, 1919 [1] 1919
Memorial services for TR on the steps of the New York Public Library, 1919 [2] 1919
President Harding and Calvin Coolidge [1] 1920
President Harding and Calvin Coolidge [2] 1920
President Harding presenting chair used by TR at the White House to the directors of RMA, October 1921. 1921
President Roosevelt, 1901–1909. 1930
RMA flag service on the steps of New York Public Library, 1919. 1919
TR memorial services at New York Public Library, 1919. 1919
TR's inauguration, 1905 [2] 1905
TR's return from Africa, 1910 [1] 1925
TR's return from Africa, 1910 [2] 1925

Loeb, William, 1866–1937
Memorial services for TR on the steps of the New York Public Library, 1919 [1] 1919
Memorial services for TR on the steps of the New York Public Library, 1919 [2] 1919
RMA flag service on the steps of New York Public Library, 1919. 1919
RMA pilgrimage to TR's grave, 1930. 1930
RMA trustees at Roosevelt House, 1923 [1] 1923
TR comes back. 1925
TR memorial services at New York Public Library, 1919. 1919
TR's return from Africa, 1910 [1] 1925
TR's return from Africa, 1910 [2] 1925

London
Crowd exterior of Buckingham Palace. 1910
King Edward's funeral, 1910 [1] 1910
King Edward's funeral, 1910 [2] 1910
[Scenes of the British royal family] 1918

London—Monuments
Crowd exterior of Buckingham Palace. 1910

London—Palaces
Crowd exterior of Buckingham Palace. 1910

London—Streets—The Mall
Crowd exterior of Buckingham Palace. 1910

London. Buckingham Palace
Crowd exterior of Buckingham Palace. 1910

London. Queen Victoria Memorial
Crowd exterior of Buckingham Palace. 1910

London. St. Margaret's Church, Westminster
See Westminster, Eng. St. Margaret's Church

Long, Henry F.
Calvin Coolidge sworn in for second term as Governor of Massachusetts. 1920

Long Island, N.Y.
Colonel Lindbergh, Admiral Byrd, and Clarence Chamberlin at flying field just before Lindbergh's flight, 1927. 1927

Los Angeles, Calif.
Short scenes of TR [2] 1912
TR riding in auto through crowded streets [1912] 1912

Louisiana
Roosevelt, friend of the birds [1] 1924
Roosevelt, friend of the birds [2] 1924
Roosevelt, friend of the birds [3] 1924
Roosevelt, friend of the birds [4]; The Roosevelt Dam [3] 1928
TR [in Louisiana], 1915 [1] 1915
TR [in Louisiana], 1915 [2] 1915
TR [in Louisiana], 1915 [3] 1915
TR [in Louisiana], 1915 [4] 1915

Louisiana. Dept. of Conservation
Roosevelt, friend of the birds [1] 1924
Roosevelt, friend of the birds [2] 1924
Roosevelt, friend of the birds [3] 1924
TR [in Louisiana], 1915 [4] 1915

Louisiana Conservation Commission
See Louisiana. Dept. of Conservation

Loyal Order of Moose
Short scenes of TR [1] 1916

Loyal Order of Moose Convention
See Convention of the Loyal Order of Moose

Luncheons
TR attends dinner of Cincinnati, Ohio, Business Men's Club, Dec. 14. 1917 [1] 1917
TR attends dinner of Cincinnati, Ohio, Business Men's Club, Dec. 14, 1917 [2] 1917

Maase, E., photographer
Mr. Hagedorn and Mr. Akeley at Roosevelt House, 1925 [1] 1925
Mr. Hagedorn and Mr. Akeley at Roosevelt House, 1925 [2] 1925
Mr. Hagedorn and Mr. Akeley at Roosevelt House, 1925 [3] 1925
Mr. Hagedorn and Mrs. Wood at Roosevelt House [1924, Long version] 1924
Mr. Hagedorn and Mrs. Wood at Roosevelt House [1924, Short version] 1924

Madeira River
The River of Doubt [2] 1928
The River of Doubt [6] 1928

210

Scenes of the River of Doubt photographed by G. M. Dyott, 1926–1927 [1] 1927

Maine. Governor, 1917–1920 (Milliken)
Governors of New England meet in Governor Coolidge's office in Boston to discuss fuel. 1919
TR attends dinner of Cincinnati, Ohio, Business Men's Club, Dec. 14, 1917 [1] 1917
TR attends dinner of Cincinnati, Ohio, Business Men's Club, Dec. 14, 1917 [2] 1917

Majestic (Ship)
TR's return to New York, 1910 [2] 1910

Maltese Cross Ranch, N.D.
See Chimney Butte Ranch, N.D.

Manhattan (Ship)
TR comes back. 1925
TR on reception yacht in New York Bay, 1910. 1910
TR's return to New York, 1910 [1] 1910
TR's return to New York, 1910 [2] 1910

Manhattan Bridge, New York (City)
See New York (City)—Bridges—Manhattan Bridge

Manning, Mae, editor
President Roosevelt, 1901–1909. 1930
Theodore Roosevelt in the great war [1] 1930
Theodore Roosevelt in the great war [2] 1930
Theodore Roosevelt in the great war [3] 1930
TR's return from Africa, 1910 [1] 1925
TR's return from Africa, 1910 [2] 1925

Manning, William T.
Dedication of Roosevelt House, 1923. 1923
Dedication of Roosevelt House, Oct. 27, 1923. 1923

Manor House
See New York (City). Van Cortlandt House

Manuel II, King of Portugal, 1889–1932
Cartoon of TR's reception by crowned heads of Europe. 1910
TR's return from Africa, 1910 [1] 1925
TR's return from Africa, 1910 [2] 1925

March, Peyton C.
TR's funeral at Oyster Bay, 1919. 1919
TR's funeral at Oyster Bay, January 1919 [2] 1919

Marching
Jamestown Exposition, 1907. 1907
President Wilson arrives in New York to lead fourth Liberty Loan parade [1918] 1918
Reviewing Annapolis middies. 1915
TR at Forest Hills, New York, 1917 [1] 1917
TR at Forest Hills, New York, 1917 [2] 1917
TR reviews and addresses troops [Fort Sheridan, Ill.]; TR riding in auto, Chicago, 1917. 1917

Marching bands
Return of Spanish-American troops, 1898. 1898

Marion, Ohio
General Wood and Calvin Coolidge in Chicago, 1920. 1920

President Harding and Calvin Coolidge [1] 1920
President Harding and Calvin Coolidge [2] 1920

Marne River
American Legion lays cornerstone of Roosevelt Bridge at Château-Thierry. 1921

Marot, Felix
Sarah Bernhardt addresses crowd in Prospect Park, Brooklyn, 1917. 1917

Marshall, Thomas R.
TR's funeral at Oyster Bay, 1919. 1919
TR's funeral at Oyster Bay, January 1919 [2] 1919

Marston, George M.
TR at San Diego Exposition, 1915. 1915

Martens, Jean D.
See Mertens, Jean D.

Martin, Eben W.
Dedication of Roosevelt Mountain at Deadwood, S.D., 1919. 1919

Martin, Paul A.
Leonard Wood at Battle Creek, Michigan. 1920

Mary, consort of George V, King of Great Britain, 1867–1953
King George and Queen Mary of England [1] 1928
King George and Queen Mary of England [2] 1928
[Scenes of the British royal family] 1918

Mary, Princess of Great Britain, 1897–1965
[Scenes of the British royal family] 1918

Maryland—Governors
TR and Cardinal Gibbons at Baltimore, Md., 1918. 1918
TR at Baltimore [1918]; TR at Sagamore [Hill, 1918] 1918
TR in Baltimore during Liberty Loan drive, 1918. 1918

Maryland. Governor, 1916–1920 (Harrington)
TR addresses large crowd for the Liberty Loan in Baltimore, 1918. 1918
TR and Cardinal Gibbons at Baltimore, Md., 1918. 1918
TR at Baltimore [1918]; TR at Sagamore [Hill, 1918] 1918
TR himself [1] 1926
TR himself [2] 1926
TR himself [3] 1926
TR himself [4] 1926
TR himself [5] 1926
TR himself [6] 1926
TR in Baltimore during Liberty Loan drive, 1918. 1918
TR scenes purchased from different dealers. 1912

Maryland. Liberty Loan Committee
TR addresses large crowd for the Liberty Loan in Baltimore, 1918. 1918
TR and Cardinal Gibbons at Baltimore, Md., 1918. 1918
TR at Baltimore [1918]; TR at Sagamore [Hill, 1918] 1918
TR in Baltimore during Liberty Loan drive, 1918. 1918
TR scenes purchased from different dealers. 1912

Masai
African natives. 1909

TR in Africa [1909, 1] 1909
TR in Africa [1909, 2] 1909
TR in Africa [1909, 4] 1909

Masai—Dances
African natives. 1909
TR in Africa [1909, 1] 1909
TR in Africa [1909, 2] 1909
TR in Africa [1909, 4] 1909

Masai—Social life and customs
TR in Africa [1909, 2] 1909

Masonic Temple, Battle Creek, Mich.
See Battle Creek, Mich. Masonic Temple

Massachusetts—Lieutenant-governors
Calvin Coolidge sworn in for second term as Governor of Massachusetts. 1920

Massachusetts—Officials and employees
Calvin Coolidge sworn in for second term as Governor of Massachusetts. 1920

Massachusetts—Politics and government
Calvin Coolidge sworn in for second term as Governor of Massachusetts. 1920

Massachusetts. Council
Calvin Coolidge sworn in for second term as Governor of Massachusetts. 1920

Massachusetts. Executive Council
See Massachusetts. Council

Massachusetts. Executive Department Council
See Massachusetts. Council

Massachusetts. Governor, 1919–1921 (Coolidge)
Americanism wins, Coolidge elected. 1919
Calvin Coolidge as Governor of Massachusetts. 1919
Calvin Coolidge as Governor of Massachusetts, 1919. 1919
Calvin Coolidge sworn in for second term as Governor of Massachusetts. 1920
General Wood and Calvin Coolidge in Chicago, 1920. 1920
Governors of New England meet in Governor Coolidge's office in Boston to discuss fuel. 1919
President Harding and Calvin Coolidge [1] 1920
President Harding and Calvin Coolidge [2] 1920
See also Coolidge, Calvin, Pres. U.S., 1872–1933; United States. President, 1923–1929 (Coolidge)

Mato Grosso, Brazil (State)
The River of Doubt [3] 1928
The River of Doubt [4] 1928
The River of Doubt [5] 1928

Matto Grosso, Brazil (State)
See Mato Grosso, Brazil (State)

Maud, consort of Haakon VII, King of Norway, 1869–1938
TR in Norway, 1910. 1910
TR in Norway and Denmark, 1910 [1] 1910

TR in Norway and Denmark, 1910 [2] 1910
TR in Norway and Denmark, 1910 [3] 1910

Mauretania (Ship)
Lieutenant-Colonel Theodore Roosevelt arrives in New York after the World War. 1919

Mayflower (Yacht)
International naval review, Hampton Roads, Virginia, 1907. 1907
TR reviews the fleet, 1907. 1907

McAdoo, Eleanor
President Wilson arrives in New York to lead fourth Liberty Loan parade [1918] 1918

McAdoo, William Gibbs
Memorial services for TR on the steps of the New York Public Library, 1919 [1] 1919
Memorial services for TR on the steps of the New York Public Library, 1919 [2] 1919
President Wilson arrives in New York to lead fourth Liberty Loan parade [1918] 1918
RMA flag service on the steps of New York Public Library, 1919. 1919
TR memorial services at New York Public Library, 1919. 1919
William Gibbs McAdoo. 1910

McAlpin Hotel, New York (City)
See New York (City). Hotel McAlpin

McAndrews, James W.
[Quentin Roosevelt]; Clemenceau and Foch, 1917–1919. 1918

McCabe, James A.
Brooklyn children attend services, children sew stars on Roosevelt Flag [1919] 1919
Memorial services for TR on the steps of the New York Public Library, 1919 [1] 1919
RMA flag ceremonies, children sew stars on flag, 1919. 1919

McCarter, Margaret Hill
General Wood and Calvin Coolidge in Chicago, 1920. 1920

McCumber, Porter J.
Senator McCumber of North Dakota. 1920

McKenney, James H.
[TR's inaugural ceremony, 1905] 1905
TR's inauguration, 1905 [1] 1905
TR's inauguration, 1905 [2] 1905

McKinley, Helen
President McKinley's memorial dedicated by William Howard Taft at Niles, Ohio. 1917

McKinley, Ida Saxton
President McKinley speaking at Buffalo, 1901. 1901

McKinley, William, Pres. U.S., 1843–1901
President McKinley reviewing the troops at the Pan-American Exposition. 1901
Still pictures exposed on scene of McKinley's funeral as used in Paramount reel. 1901

TR speaking at Sagamore Hill [1916–1918 and scenes of his early career] 1897
See also United States. President, 1897–1901 (McKinley)

McKinley, William, Pres. U.S., 1843–1901—Addresses, essays, lectures
President McKinley inauguration, 1901. 1901
President McKinley speaking, 1901. 1901
President McKinley speaking at Buffalo, 1901. 1901
[Scenes of TR, Panama Canal construction, and William McKinley] 1901

McKinley, William, Pres. U.S., 1843–1901—Funeral and memorial services
McKinley's funeral, 1901. 1901
McKinley's funeral, Washington, D.C., 1901. 1901
President McKinley's funeral, 1901 [1] 1901
President McKinley's funeral, 1901 [2] 1901
President McKinley's funeral, Canton, Ohio, 1901 [1] 1901
President McKinley's funeral, Canton, Ohio, 1901 [2] 1901
President McKinley's funeral in Buffalo, Washington, and Canton, Ohio, 1901. 1901
Still pictures exposed on scene of McKinley's funeral as used in Paramount reel. 1901
TR attends McKinley's funeral, 1901. 1901
TR attends McKinley's funeral, Canton, Ohio, 1901. 1901

McKinley, William, Pres. U.S., 1843–1901—Homes
President McKinley's funeral, 1901 [1] 1901
President McKinley's funeral, Canton, Ohio, 1901 [2] 1901

McKinley, William, Pres. U.S., 1843–1901—Inauguration, 1901
President McKinley inauguration, 1901. 1901
President McKinley's inauguration, 1901 [1] 1901
President McKinley's inauguration, 1901 [2] 1901

McKinley, William, Pres. U.S., 1843–1901—Monuments, etc.
President McKinley's memorial dedicated by William Howard Taft at Niles, Ohio. 1917

McKinley Club
President McKinley's memorial dedicated by William Howard Taft at Niles, Ohio. 1917

McKinley Club, Canton, Ohio
See McKinley Club

McKinley Memorial
See Niles, Ohio. National McKinley Birthplace Memorial

McKnight, Edwin Toil
Calvin Coolidge sworn in for second term as Governor of Massachusetts. 1920

McMaster, William H.
President Coolidge speaking at Black Hills, S.D., 1927. 1927

Mead, William W.
TR himself [1] 1926
TR himself [2] 1926
TR himself [3] 1926
TR himself [4] 1926
TR himself [5] 1926
TR himself [6] 1926

Medalists
Mr. Garfield presenting medals to 1929 medalists. 1929
Professor Henry Fairfield Osborn, RMA medalist, 1923. 1934
Scenes of Dr. Frank Chapman. 1920
Scenes of Hastings Hart, 1930 medalist. 1930

Medora, N.D.
Through the Roosevelt country with Roosevelt's friends. 1919

Medora, N.D.—Description—Views
Through the Roosevelt country with Roosevelt's friends. 1919

Medora, N.D. Rough Rider's Hotel
Through the Roosevelt country with Roosevelt's friends. 1919

Meeker, Arthur, 1866–1946
TR reviews and addresses troops [Fort Sheridan, Ill.]; TR riding in auto, Chicago. 1917. 1917

Memorial rites and ceremonies
Brooklyn children attend services, children sew stars on Roosevelt Flag [1919] 1919
Children sewing stars on flag, placing flag on TR's grave [1919] 1919
Children visit TR's grave, 1920. 1920
[Flag services for TR at Oyster Bay, October 1919] 1919
Friends and admirers visit TR's grave, 1920. 1920
General [Diaz] of Italy visits TR's grave [1921] 1921
General Nivelle visits TR's grave [1921] 1921
King Albert of Belgium visits TR's grave, 1919. 1919
King Albert of Belgium visits TR's grave, October, 1919. 1919
Memorial services for TR on the steps of the New York Public Library, 1919 [1] 1919
Memorial services for TR on the steps of the New York Public Library, 1919 [2] 1919
The Prince of Wales visits TR's grave. 1919
RMA flag ceremonies, children sew stars on flag, 1919. 1919
RMA flag service on the steps of New York Public Library, 1919. 1919
RMA pilgrimage to TR's grave, 1930. 1930
Runners carrying flag to TR's grave [1919] 1919
[Scenes of the British royal family] 1918
Three children visit TR's grave, 1920. 1920
TR memorial services at New York Public Library, 1919. 1919
Whole nation honors memory of Roosevelt. 1919.

Memorial rites and ceremonies—Belgium
The King and Queen of Belgium and Premier Poincaré of France [1] 1927
The King and Queen of Belgium and Premier Poincaré of France [2] 1927

Memorial service
Dedication of Roosevelt Mountain at Deadwood, S.D., 1919. 1919
Laying cornerstone of Roosevelt School, New Rochelle, N.Y. [1920] 1920
RMA services at [Hearst Greek Theatre, University of California, Berkeley, Calif.]; Laying cornerstone of Roosevelt School at New Rochelle, N.Y. [1920] 1920
Scouts on their way to TR's grave, Daniel C. Beard and TR Jr. attend services, 1920. 1920
See also Funeral service

Memorials

President McKinley's memorial dedicated by William Howard Taft at Niles, Ohio. 1917

The prize winning design by John Russell Pope for the proposed memorial to Theodore Roosevelt for the city of Washington. 1926

See also Monuments

Merrifield, A. W.

See Merrifield, Arthur W.

Merrifield, Arthur W.

Through the Roosevelt country with Roosevelt's friends. 1919

Mertens, Jean D.

Roosevelt scenes [1917–1918] 1917

TR receiving Belgian envoys at Sagamore Hill [1917] 1917

Metropolitan magazine

Shall we prepare? 1916

TR scenes purchased from different dealers. 1912

Mexico, Gulf of

See Gulf of Mexico

Michigan. Leonard Wood League

See Leonard Wood League of Michigan

Michigan. University. Michigan Union

Leonard Wood at Battle Creek, Michigan. 1920

Midshipmen

Reviewing Annapolis middies. 1915

[TR's inaugural ceremony, 1905] 1905

TR's inauguration, 1905 [1] 1905

Milburn, John G.

President McKinley reviewing the troops at the Pan-American Exposition. 1901

President McKinley speaking at Buffalo, 1901. 1901

Miles, Basil

Elihu Root and Mayor Mitchel of New York, Mr. Root and American delegates return from Russia [1917] 1917

Miles, H., source

TR at limousine window, 1917. 1917

TR's arrival in Panama, November 1906 [1] 1906

TR's arrival in Panama, November 1906 [2] 1906

TR's arrival in Panama, November 1906 [3] 1906

Military ceremonies, honors, and salutes

General Pershing at Camp Grant. 1920

Jamestown Exposition, 1907. 1907

King and Queen of Spain attend a military review. 1920

President McKinley reviewing the troops at the Pan-American Exposition. 1901

Reviewing Annapolis middies. 1915

TR at Camp Mills [1917] 1917

TR at Forest Hills, New York, 1917 [1] 1917

TR at Forest Hills, New York, 1917 [2] 1917

TR, Charles E. Hughes, and Mayor Mitchel of New York, on reviewing stand in front of the New York Public Library [1917] 1917

Military education—France

TR reviews French troops at Vincennes, France, 1910. 1910

Military maneuvers

TR in Vincennes, France, 1910. 1910

TR reviews French troops at Vincennes, France, 1910. 1910

Military music

President McKinley's funeral, 1901 [1] 1901

President McKinley's funeral, 1901 [2] 1901

Military supplies

Pack mules with ammunition on the Santiago trail, Cuba. 1898

Military training camps—Illinois

General Pershing at Camp Grant. 1920

TR reviews and addresses troops [Fort Sheridan, Ill.]; TR riding in auto, Chicago, 1917. 1917

Military training camps—New York (State)

TR at Camp Mills [1917] 1917

Military transportation

See Transportation, Military

Miller, Leo E.

The River of Doubt [1] 1928

The River of Doubt [2] 1928

The River of Doubt [3] 1928

The River of Doubt [5] 1928

The River of Doubt [7] 1928

[Scenes of TR on board ship, 1916; Scenes of TR's trip to South America, 1913] 1913

Milliken, Carl E.

Governors of New England meet in Governor Coolidge's office in Boston to discuss fuel. 1919

TR attends dinner of Cincinnati, Ohio, Business Men's Club, Dec. 14, 1917 [1] 1917

TR attends dinner of Cincinnati, Ohio, Business Men's Club, Dec. 14, 1917 [2] 1917

Mineola, N.Y.

Roosevelt scenes from RMA productions. 1912

Scenes of TR and his sons Quentin and Archie, 1917–1918 [1] 1917

Scenes of TR and his sons Quentin and Archie, 1917–1918 [2] 1917

Theodore Roosevelt in the great war [1] 1930

Theodore Roosevelt in the great war [2] 1930

Theodore Roosevelt in the great war [3] 1930

TR scenes purchased from different dealers. 1912

Minnesota. Governor, 1915–1921 (Burnquist)

Close-up of TR speaking [1917] 1917

TR in St. Paul, Minn. [1917] 1917

TR speaking at [St. Paul, Minnesota, 1917] 1917

See also Burnquist, Joseph A. A.

Miraflores Lake

Panama Canal; scenes of the finished Canal. 1919

Missions, Government
See Government missions

Missouri. Governor, 1909–1913 (Hadley)
Colonel Roosevelt is invited to fly in Arch Hoxsey's plane at St. Louis, Mo., 1910. 1910

Mitchel, John P.
Elihu Root and Mayor Mitchel of New York, Mr. Root and American delegates return from Russia [1917] 1917
Mayor Mitchel of New York. 1917
Roosevelt scenes from RMA productions. 1912
Still photographs of TR on motion picture film. 1920
Theodore Roosevelt in the great war [1] 1930
Theodore Roosevelt in the great war [2] 1930
Theodore Roosevelt in the great war [3] 1930
TR, Charles E. Hughes, and Mayor Mitchel of New York, on reviewing stand in front of the New York Public Library [1917] 1917
TR, Mayor Mitchel and guests at Cooper Sanitarium [1917] 1917
TR, Mayor Mitchel, Governor Charles Whitman of New York, and Myron Herrick, 1917. 1917
TR on Fifth Avenue, New York, near St. Patrick's Cathedral after attending Mayor Mitchel's funeral. 1918

Mitchell, John, 1870–1919
TR as Father Curran's guest at Wilkes-Barre, Pa., August 10, 1905. 1905

Mitchell, Pell, source
TR [in Louisiana], 1915 [1] 1915
TR [in Louisiana], 1915 [4] 1915

Models, Architectural
See Architectural models

Models (Clay, plaster, etc.)
The prize winning design by John Russell Pope for the proposed memorial to Theodore Roosevelt for the city of Washington. 1926

Moki Indians
See Hopi Indians

Mombasa, Kenya
TR in Africa [1909, 2] 1909
[TR planting a tree in Africa] 1909

Moncheur, Ludovic, Baron
Roosevelt scenes [1917–1918] 1917
TR receiving Belgian envoys at Sagamore Hill [1917] 1917

Mondel, Frank W.
See Mondell, Frank W.

Mondell, Frank W.
Senators Curtis, Cummins, Moses, and [Representative] Mondell. 1919

Monitors (Warships)
See Turret ships

Monkeys
The River of Doubt [6] 1928
Scenes of African animals [1911] 1911
Scenes of the River of Doubt photographed by G. M. Dyott, 1926–1927 [1] 1927
Scenes of the River of Doubt photographed by G. M. Dyott, 1926–1927 [2] 1927

Monroe Palace, Rio de Janeiro
See Rio de Janeiro. Palácio Monroe

Montana
Through the Roosevelt country with Roosevelt's friends. 1919

Montreuil-sur-Mer, France
Robert Bacon and Army officers. 1918

Monuments
The prize winning design by John Russell Pope for the proposed memorial to Theodore Roosevelt for the city of Washington. 1926
See also Memorials; London—Monuments

Monuments—Cuba
Dedication of Cuban memorial, 1924 [1] 1924
Dedication of Cuban memorial, 1924 [2] 1924

Moore, Charles C.
William H. Taft burns mortgage of Exposition, 1915. 1915

Moose, Loyal Order of
See Loyal Order of Moose

Moose Convention
See Convention of the Loyal Order of Moose

Moqui Indians
See Hopi Indians

Morgan, Edwin V.
The River of Doubt [1] 1928
The River of Doubt [2] 1928
The River of Doubt [3] 1928
The River of Doubt [4] 1928
The River of Doubt [5] 1928
The River of Doubt [7] 1928
[Scenes of TR, 1913–1915] 1913
[Scenes of TR on board ship, 1916; Scenes of TR's trip to South America, 1913] 1913

Morin, John M.
Gifford Pinchot, 1923. 1923

Morro Castle, Havana
See Havana. Morro Castle

Morrow, Edwin P.
President Harding and Calvin Coolidge [1] 1920
President Harding and Calvin Coolidge [2] 1920

Mortgage loans
William H. Taft burns mortgage of Exposition, 1915. 1915

Mortgages
William H. Taft burns mortgage of Exposition, 1915. 1915

Moses, George H.
Senators Curtis, Cummins, Moses, and [Representative] Mondell. 1919

Mosquito control
Extermination of mosquitoes by spraying swamps. 1910

Mosquitoes
Extermination of mosquitoes by spraying swamps. 1910

Mosquitoes—Larvae
Extermination of mosquitoes by spraying swamps. 1910

Motion Picture Library
See Roosevelt Memorial Association. Film Library

Mount Roosevelt, S.D.
Dedicaton of Roosevelt Mountain at Deadwood, S.D., 1919. 1919

Mount Rushmore National Memorial
President Coolidge speaking at Black Hills, S.D., 1927. 1927

Mount Theodore Roosevelt, S.D.
See Mount Roosevelt, S.D.

Mounted police
TR's inauguration, 1905 [2] 1905

Mounted police—Chicago
TR riding in auto in Chicago, 1917. 1917

Mounted police—New York (City)
TR's funeral at Oyster Bay, 1919. 1919
TR's funeral at Oyster Bay, January 1919 [2] 1919

Moving-picture journalism
Gifford Pinchot, 1923. 1923

Mrs. Roosevelt arrives at Roosevelt House, 1927 [Title]
Mrs. Roosevelt, Sr., and Mrs. J. H. Hammond photographed on the roof of Roosevelt House, 1927; Mrs. Roosevelt arrives at Roosevelt House. 1927

Mules
Pack mules with ammunition on the Santiago trail, Cuba. 1898
Scenes of the River of Doubt photographed by G. M. Dyott, 1926–1927 [1] 1927
Spanish Mountain Artillery, 1898. 1898

Müller, Lauro S.
The River of Doubt [1] 1928
The River of Doubt [2] 1928
The River of Doubt [3] 1928
The River of Doubt [4] 1928
The River of Doubt [5] 1928
The River of Doubt [7] 1928
[Scenes of TR, 1913–1915] 1913
[Scenes of TR on board ship, 1916; Scenes of TR's trip to South America, 1913] 1913

TR himself [1] 1926
TR himself [2] 1926
TR himself [3] 1926
TR himself [4] 1926
TR himself [5] 1926

Multeers
Pack mules with ammunition on the Santiago trail, Cuba. 1898

Murray, Joe
Memorializing Roosevelt. 1925

Muscle Shoals, Ala.
President Harding and Calvin Coolidge [2] 1920

Museum of Natural History, New York (City)
See American Museum of Natural History, New York

Mutual Film Corporation
Mrs. Theodore Roosevelt Jr. attends Women in War Work Congress in Paris [1918] 1918

Nambicuara Indians
The River of Doubt [1] 1928
The River of Doubt [2] 1928
The River of Doubt [4] 1928
The River of Doubt [7] 1928

Nanbikuara Indians
See Nambicuara Indians

Naples
Street scenes in Naples, Italy. 1910

Naples—Plazas—Piazza del Plebiscito
Street scenes in Naples, Italy. 1910

Naples. Palazzo reale
Street scenes in Naples, Italy. 1910

National Audubon Society
Roosevelt, friend of the birds [1] 1924
Roosevelt, friend of the birds [2] 1924
Roosevelt, friend of the birds [3] 1924
Roosevelt, friend of the birds [4]; The Roosevelt Dam [3] 1928
TR [in Louisiana], 1915 [1] 1915
TR [in Louisiana], 1915 [2] 1915
TR [in Louisiana], 1915 [3] 1915
TR [in Louisiana], 1915 [4] 1915

National McKinley Birthplace Memorial
See Niles, Ohio. National McKinley Birthplace Memorial

National McKinley Birthplace Memorial Association
President McKinley's memorial dedicated by William Howard Taft at Niles, Ohio. 1917

National Theater, Oslo
See Oslo. Nationaltheatret

Naturalists
Scenes of John Burroughs. 1910

Naval ceremonies, honors, and salutes
International naval review, Hampton Roads, Virginia, 1907. 1907

Naval Service Club, Boston, Mass.
Roosevelt scenes [1917–1918] 1917
Short scenes of TR [1] 1916
TR with naval officers, exterior Navy Club, Boston [1918] 1918

Navy Club, Boston, Mass.
See Naval Service Club, Boston, Mass.

Neri
See Nyeri, Kenya

Netherlands
Queen Wilhelmina of Holland, the Prince Consort [and] the Princess. 1920

New, Harry S.
Senators Curtis, Cummins, Moses, and [Representative] Mondell. 1919

New England
Governors of New England meet in Governor Coolidge's office in Boston to discuss fuel. 1919

New Hampshire. Governor, 1919 – 1921 (Bartlett)
Governors of New England meet in Governor Coolidge's office in Boston to discuss fuel. 1919

New Mexico—Governors
TR in New Mexico, 1916. 1916
TR's reception in Albuquerque, N.M., 1916. 1916

New Rochelle, N.Y.
Laying cornerstone of Roosevelt School, New Rochelle, N.Y. [1920] 1920
RMA services at [Hearst Greek Theatre, University of California, Berkeley, Calif.]; Laying cornerstone of Roosevelt School at New Rochelle, N.Y. [1920] 1920

New Rochelle, N.Y. Roosevelt School
See Roosevelt School

New Rochelle, N.Y. Wykagyl
See Wykagyl, N.Y.

New York (City)
Admiral Dewey parade, 1899 [1] 1899
Admiral Dewey parade, 1899 [2] 1899
Dedication of Roosevelt House, 1923. 1923
Dedication of Roosevelt House, Oct. 27, 1923. 1923
Elihu Root and Mayor Mitchel of New York, Mr. Root and American delegates return from Russia [1917] 1917
Gen. Pershing speaking to Scouts in New York. 1919
General Goethals. 1923
Governor's Foot Guards, Conn. 1899
Japanese and Russian peace delegates [leaving New York City], 1905. 1905
Leonard Wood lays cornerstone of Roosevelt House, 1921. 1921
Lieutenant-Colonel Theodore Roosevelt arrives in New York after the World War. 1919

Marshal Foch visits Roosevelt House, 1921. 1921
Mayor Mitchel of New York. 1917
Memorial services for TR at Van Cortlandt Park, New York, Oct. 1919. 1919
Memorial services for TR on the steps of the New York Public Library, 1919 [1] 1919
Memorial services for TR on the steps of the New York Public Library, 1919 [2] 1919
Memorializing Roosevelt. 1925
Moving exhibits into Roosevelt House, 1923. 1923
Mr. Garfield presenting medals to 1929 medalists. 1929
Mr. Hagedorn and Mr. Akeley at Roosevelt House, 1925 [1] 1925
Mr. Hagedorn and Mr. Akeley at Roosevelt House, 1925 [2] 1925
Mr. Hagedorn and Mr. Akeley at Roosevelt House, 1925 [3] 1925
Mr. Hagedorn and Mrs. Wood at Roosevelt House [1924, Long version] 1924
Mr. Hagedorn and Mrs. Wood at Roosevelt House [1924, Short version] 1924
Mrs. Roosevelt, Sr., and Mrs. J. H. Hammond photographed on the roof of Roosevelt House, 1927; Mrs. Roosevelt arrives at Roosevelt House. 1927
President Wilson arrives in New York to lead fourth Liberty Loan parade [1918] 1918
Professor Henry Fairfield Osborn, RMA medalist, 1923. 1934
RMA flag service on the steps of New York Public Library, 1919. 1919
RMA trustees at Roosevelt House, 1923 [1] 1923
RMA trustees at Roosevelt House, 1923 [2] 1923
Roosevelt scenes from RMA productions. 1912
Scenes of Dr. Frank Chapman. 1920
[Scenes of TR, 1913–1915] 1913
Scenes of TR and his sons Quentin and Archie, 1917–1918 [1] 1917
Scenes of TR and his sons Quentin and Archie, 1917–1918 [2] 1917
Scenes of TR on board ship before sailing for West Indies, 1916. 1916
Scenes showing Blue Line Tour route to Roosevelt House in 1925. 1925
Shall we prepare? 1916
Short scenes of TR [1] 1916
Still photographs of TR on motion picture film. 1920
Theodore Roosevelt in the great war [1] 1930
Theodore Roosevelt in the great war [2] 1930
Theodore Roosevelt in the great war [3] 1930
TR and Leonard Wood at the New York flower show, 1917. 1917
TR, Charles E. Hughes, and Mayor Mitchel of New York, on reviewing stand in front of the New York Public Library [1917] 1917
TR, Mayor Mitchel, Governor Charles Whitman of New York, and Myron Herrick, 1917. 1917
TR memorial services at New York Public Library, 1919. 1919
TR on Fifth Avenue, New York, near St. Patrick's Cathedral after attending Mayor Mitchel's funeral. 1918
TR scenes purchased from different dealers. 1912
TR seated at his desk in the Outlook office [1914?] 1914
TR speaking at Battery Park, New York, June 1910. 1910
TR speaking at the Battery, 1910. 1910
TR's return to New York, 1910 [1] 1910
TR's return to New York, 1910 [2] 1910

U.S. battleship "Oregon." 1898

Whole nation honors memory of Roosevelt, 1919

Woman's Roosevelt Memorial Association meeting at Roosevelt House, 1923 [1] 1923

Woman's Roosevelt Memorial Association meeting at Roosevelt House, 1923 [2] 1923

New York (City)—Bridges—Manhattan Bridge

Scenes of TR on board ship before sailing for West Indies, 1916. 1916

New York (City)—Buildings

TR's return to New York, 1910 [2] 1910

New York (City)—Harbor

Scenes of TR on board ship before sailing for West Indies, 1916. 1916

Short scenes of TR [1] 1916

TR comes back. 1925

TR on reception yacht in New York Bay, 1910. 1910

TR's return to New York, 1910 [1] 1910

TR's return to New York, 1910 [2] 1910

New York (City)—Officials and employees

Admiral Dewey parade, 1899 [1] 1899

Admiral Dewey parade, 1899 [2] 1899

New York (City)—Parks—Battery

TR comes back. 1925

TR on reception yacht in New York Bay, 1910. 1910

TR speaking at Battery Park, New York, June 1910. 1910

TR speaking at the Battery, 1910. 1910

TR's return to New York, 1910 [1] 1910

TR's return to New York, 1910 [2] 1910

New York (City)—Parks—Central Park

Gen. Pershing speaking to Scouts in New York. 1919

[Scenes of TR, 1913–1915] 1913

New York (City)—Parks—Van Cortlandt Park

Memorial services for TR at Van Cortlandt Park, New York, Oct. 1919. 1919

Whole nation honors memory of Roosevelt. 1919

New York (City)—Plazas

TR's return to New York, 1910 [1] 1910

New York (City)—Plazas—Madison Square

President Wilson arrives in New York to lead fourth Liberty Loan parade [1918] 1918

Theodore Roosevelt in the great war [1] 1930

Theodore Roosevelt in the great war [2] 1930

Theodore Roosevelt in the great war [3] 1930

New York (City)—Streets

TR comes back. 1925

TR's return to New York, 1910 [1] 1910

TR's return to New York, 1910 [2] 1910

New York (City)—Streets—Fifth Avenue

President Wilson arrives in New York to lead fourth Liberty Loan parade [1918] 1918

TR on Fifth Avenue, New York, near St. Patrick's Cathedral after attending Mayor Mitchel's funeral. 1918

New York (City). American Museum of Natural History

See American Museum of Natural History, New York

New York (City). Church of All Nations

See Church of All Nations, New York (City)

New York (City). City Hall

Elihu Root and Mayor Mitchel of New York, Mr. Root and American delegates return from Russia [1917] 1917

Roosevelt scenes from RMA productions. 1912

New York (City). Grand Central Palace

Scenes of TR and his sons Quentin and Archie, 1917–1918 [1] 1917

Scenes of TR and his sons Quentin and Archie, 1917–1918 [2] 1917

Short scenes of TR [1] 1916

TR and Leonard Wood at the New York flower show, 1917. 1917

New York (City). Hotel McAlpin

Scenes showing Blue Line Tour route to Roosevelt House in 1925. 1925

New York (City). Liberty Loan Committee

Roosevelt scenes [1917–1918] 1917

Scenes of TR speaking at Sagamore [1916–1918] 1916

Short scenes of TR as used in Paramount reel. 1916

TR at Baltimore [1918]; TR at Sagamore [Hill, 1918] 1918

TR at Sagamore Hill [1916–1918] 1916

TR scenes purchased from different dealers. 1912

TR speaking at Sagamore Hill [1916–1918] [1] 1916

TR speaking at Sagamore Hill [1916–1918] [2] 1916

TR speaking at Sagamore Hill [1916–1918 and scenes of his early career] 1897

New York (City). Liberty's Altar

President Wilson arrives in New York to lead fourth Liberty Loan parade [1918] 1918

Theodore Roosevelt in the great war [1] 1930

Theodore Roosevelt in the great war [2] 1930

Theodore Roosevelt in the great war [3] 1930

New York (City). Manhattan Bridge

See New York (City)—Bridges—Manhattan Bridge

New York (City). Pennsylvania Railroad Station

See New York (City), Pennsylvania Station

New York (City). Pennsylvania Station

President Wilson arrives in New York to lead fourth Liberty Loan parade [1918] 1918

New York (City). Public Library

Memorial services for TR on the steps of the New York Public Library, 1919 [1] 1919

Memorial services for TR on the steps of the New York Public Library, 1919 [2] 1919

RMA flag service on the steps of New York Public Library, 1919. 1919

Still photographs of TR on motion picture film. 1920

TR, Charles E. Hughes, and Mayor Mitchel of New York, on reviewing stand in front of the New York Public Library [1917] 1917

TR memorial services at New York Public Library, 1919. 1919

New York (City). Roosevelt House
Dedication of Roosevelt House, 1923. 1923
Dedication of Roosevelt House, Oct. 27, 1923. 1923
Leonard Wood lays cornerstone of Roosevelt House, 1921.
1921
Marshal Foch visits Roosevelt House, 1921. 1921
Memorializing Roosevelt. 1925
Moving exhibits into Roosevelt House, 1923. 1923
Mr. Garfield presenting medals to 1929 medalists. 1929
Mr. Hagedorn and Mr. Akeley at Roosevelt House, 1925 [1]
1925
Mr. Hagedorn and Mr. Akeley at Roosevelt House, 1925 [2]
1925
Mr. Hagedorn and Mr. Akeley at Roosevelt House, 1925 [3]
1925
Mr. Hagedorn and Mrs. Wood at Roosevelt House [1924,
Long version] 1924
Mr. Hagedorn and Mrs. Wood at Roosevelt House [1924,
Short version] 1924
Mrs. Roosevelt, Sr., and Mrs. J. H. Hammond photographed
on the roof of Roosevelt House, 1927; Mrs. Roosevelt arrives
at Roosevelt House. 1927
RMA trustees at Roosevelt House, 1923 [1] 1923
RMA trustees at Roosevelt House, 1923 [2] 1923
Scenes showing Blue Line Tour route to Roosevelt House in
1925. 1925
Theodore Roosevelt, great scout [1] 1925
Theodore Roosevelt, great scout [2] 1925
Theodore Roosevelt, great scout [3] 1925
Woman's Roosevelt Memorial Association meeting at Roose-
velt House, 1923 [1] 1923
Woman's Roosevelt Memorial Association meeting at Roose-
velt House, 1923 [2] 1923

New York (City). Roosevelt Memorial
See New York State Theodore Roosevelt Memorial, New
York

New York (City). Theodore Roosevelt Memorial
See New York State Theodore Roosevelt Memorial, New York

New York (City). Union League Club
TR, Mayor Mitchel, Governor Charles Whitman of New York,
and Myron Herrick, 1917. 1917

New York (City). Van Cortlandt House
Memorial services for TR at Van Cortlandt Park, New York,
Oct. 1919. 1919
Whole nation honors memory of Roosevelt. 1919

New York (State)
Scenes of Hastings Hart, 1930 medalist. 1930

New York (State). Governor, 1915 – 1918 (Charles S. Whitman)
TR, Mayor Mitchel, Governor Charles Whitman of New York,
and Myron Herrick, 1917. 1917
See also Whitman, Charles S.

New York (State). National Guard. 7th Regiment
See New York Infantry. 7th Regiment. 1806–1922 (Militia).
Band

New York (State). National Guard. 65th Regiment
See New York Infantry. 65th Regiment

New York (State). National Guard. 74th Regiment
See New York Infantry. 74th Regiment

New York Aquarium
TR's return to New York, 1910 [2] 1910

New York Bay
Admiral Dewey on flagship, 1899. 1899
Admiral Dewey on the deck of flagship, 1899 [1] 1899
Admiral Dewey on the deck of flagship, 1899 [2] 1899
Scenes of TR on board ship before sailing for West Indies,
1916. 1916
TR comes back. 1925
TR on reception yacht in New York Bay, 1910. 1910
TR's return to New York, 1910 [2] 1910

New York Cavalry. Squadron A
TR's inauguration, 1905 [1] 1905

New York Harbor
[Scenes of TR on board ship, 1916; Scenes of TR's trip to
South America, 1913] 1913

New York Infantry. 7th Regiment, 1806–1922 (Militia). Band
TR speaking to a group of men from the porch at Sagamore
Hill, 1916. 1916

New York Infantry. 65th Regiment
President McKinley reviewing the troops at the Pan-American
Exposition. 1901

New York Infantry. 74th Regiment
President McKinley reviewing the troops at the Pan-American
Exposition. 1901

New York State Theodore Roosevelt Memorial, New York
Professor Henry Fairfield Osborn, RMA medalist, 1923. 1934

New York Yacht Club
Japanese and Russian peace delegates [leaving New York
City], 1905. 1905

New York Zoological Society
Scenes of the River of Doubt photographed by G. M. Dyott,
1926–1927 [1] 1927

Newburgh, N.Y.
Roosevelt scenes [1917–1918] 1917
TR speaking at Newburgh, N.Y. [1918] 1918

Newburgh (Ship)
Roosevelt scenes [1917–1918] 1917
TR speaking at Newburgh, N.Y. [1918] 1918

Newburgh Shipyards Corporation
See Newburgh Shipyards, inc.

Newburgh Shipyards, inc.
TR speaking at Newburgh, N.Y. [1918] 1918

Newell, Frederick H.
The Roosevelt Dam [1] 1928
The Roosevelt Dam [2] 1928

Newport News, Va.
Launch, U.S. battleship "Kentucky." 1898

Newport News Shipbuilding and Dry Dock Company
Launch, U.S. battleship "Kentucky." 1898

Nhambiquaras Indians
See Nambicuara Indians

Nicholas II, Emperor of Russia, 1868–1918
Cartoon of TR's reception by crowned heads of Europe. 1910
Czar Nicholas of Russia. 1910
Last known home of Czar Nicholas. 1918

Niles, Ohio
President McKinley's memorial dedicated by William Howard
Taft at Niles, Ohio. 1917

Niles, Ohio. National McKinley Birthplace Memorial
President McKinley's memorial dedicated by William Howard
Taft at Niles, Ohio. 1917

Nivelle, Robert G.
General Nivelle visits TR's grave [1921] 1921

Nobel prizes
TR himself [1] 1926
TR himself [2] 1926
TR himself [3] 1926
TR himself [4] 1926
TR himself [5] 1926
TR himself [6] 1926
TR in Norway and Denmark, 1910 [1] 1910
TR in Norway and Denmark, 1910 [2] 1910
TR in Norway and Denmark, 1910 [3] 1910

Nolte, Louis
Colonel Roosevelt is invited to fly in Arch Hoxsey's plane at
St. Louis, Mo., 1910. 1910

Norbeck, Peter
Dedication of Roosevelt Mountain at Deadwood, S.D., 1919.
1919

Nordisk Film Company
See Nordisk films kompagni, A/s, Copenhagen

Nordisk films kompagni, A/s Copenhagen, source
TR in Norway and Denmark, 1910 [1] 1910
TR in Norway and Denmark, 1910 [2] 1910
TR in Norway and Denmark, 1910 [3] 1910

Norfolk, Va.
Jamestown Exposition, 1907. 1907

Norfolk, Va.—Plazas—Lee Parade Ground
Jamestown Exposition, 1907. 1907

Norfolk, Va. Discovery Landing
Jamestown Exposition, 1907. 1907

North Dakota
Theodore Roosevelt: fighter for social justice. 1934

Northampton, Mass.
Americanism wins, Coolidge elected. 1919
General Wood and Calvin Coolidge in Chicago, 1920. 1920
President Harding and Calvin Coolidge [1] 1920
President Harding and Calvin Coolidge [2] 1920

Notre-Dame de Laeken (Church)
See Église Notre-Dame, Laeken, Belgium

Nye, Joseph M.
King Albert of Belgium visits TR's grave, 1919. 1919
King Albert of Belgium visits TR's grave, October, 1919. 1919
The Prince of Wales visits TR's grave. 1919

Nyeri, Kenya
African natives. 1909

Nyoac (Steamboat)
The River of Doubt [1] 1928
The River of Doubt [2] 1928
The River of Doubt [3] 1928
The River of Doubt [4] 1928
The River of Doubt [5] 1928
The River of Doubt [7] 1928

Oaths
[TR's inaugural ceremony, 1905] 1905
TR's inauguration, 1905 [1] 1905
TR's inauguration, 1905 [2] 1905

Ocean liners
TR's return to New York, 1910 [2] 1910

Ocean travel
The King of Italy entertains King Edward of England on his
yacht. 1907

O'Connor, Thomas Power
Roosevelt scenes [1917–1918] 1917
TR receiving Belgian envoys at Sagamore Hill [1917] 1917

Ohio. Governor, 1917–1920 (Cox)
TR attends dinner of Cincinnati Ohio, Business Men's Club,
Dec. 14, 1917 [1] 1917
TR attends dinner at Cincinnati, Ohio, Business Men's Club,
Dec. 14, 1917 [2] 1917

Ohio. National Guard. Troop A
President McKinley inauguration, 1901. 1901
President McKinley's inauguration, 1901 [1] 1901
President McKinley's inauguration, 1901 [2] 1901

Ohio Cavalry. Troop A
See Ohio. National Guard. Troop A

Old age pensions—Pennsylvania
Gifford Pinchot, 1923. 1923

Old State House, Boston, Mass.
See Boston, Mass. Old State House

Olympia (Cruiser)
Admiral Dewey on flagship, 1899. 1899

Admiral Dewey on the deck of flagship, 1899 [1] 1899
Admiral Dewey on the deck of flagship, 1899 [2] 1899

Olympic games
Queen Wilhelmina of Holland, the Prince Consort [and] the
Princess. 1920

Opening day, Jamestown Exposition, April 26, 1907 [Title]
Jamestown Exposition, 1907. 1907

Orators
[Man speaking at Faneuil Hall, Boston] 1910

Orchids—Brazil
Scenes of the River of Doubt photographed by G. M. Dyott,
1926–1927 [1] 1927

Ordnance
Disappearing gun at testing grounds, Sandy Hook, 1898. 1898
See also Artillery

Ordnance testing
Disappearing gun at testing grounds, Sandy Hook, 1898. 1898

Oregon (Ship)
The Panama Canal. 1927
The Story of the Panama Canal [1] 1927
The Story of the Panama Canal [2] 1927
U.S. battleship "Oregon." 1898

Oriole Baseball Park, Baltimore
See Baltimore. Oriole Baseball Park

Orioles
Scenes of the River of Doubt photographed by G. M. Dyott,
1926–1927 [1] 1927
Scenes of the River of Doubt photographed by G. M. Dyott,
1926–1927 [2] 1927

Orme, John P.
The Roosevelt Dam [1] 1928
The Roosevelt Dam [2] 1928
TR with group of men, 1917; TR speaking at dedication of
Roosevelt Dam, 1911. 1911

Ormsbee, Elizabeth
See Ormsby, Elizabeth

Ormsby, Elizabeth
Sarah Bernhardt addresses crowd in Prospect Park, Brooklyn,
1917. 1917

Ornithologists
Scenes of Dr. Frank Chapman. 1920

Országház, Budapest
See Budapest. Országház

Osborn, Henry Fairfield
Professor Henry Fairfield Osborn, RMA medalist, 1923. 1934

Oscar Gustaf V Adolf
See Gustaf V. King of Sweden, 1858–1950

Oslo
TR in Norway, 1910. 1910
TR in Norway and Denmark, 1910 [1] 1910
TR in Norway and Denmark, 1910 [2] 1910
TR in Norway and Denmark, 1910 [3] 1910
TR's return from Africa, 1910 [1] 1925
TR's return from Africa, 1910 [2] 1925

Olso. Nationaltheatret
TR In Norway and Denmark, 1910 [1] 1910
TR In Norway and Denmark, 1910 [2] 1910
TR In Norway and Denmark, 1910 [3] 1910

Osterrieth, Leon
Roosevelt scenes [1917–1918] 1917
TR receiving Belgian envoys at Sagamore Hill [1917] 1917

Outlook, The
TR seated at his desk in the Outlook office [1914?] 1914

Oyster Bay, N. Y.
Airmen honor TR's memory by dropping American Legion
wreath on his grave [1919] 1919
American Legion places wreath on TR's grave [1919]; Scenes
of Oyster Bay from the air. 1919
Aviators drop American Legion wreath on TR's grave [1919]
1919
Brooklyn children attend services, children sew stars on Roo-
sevelt Flag [1919] 1919
Children sewing stars on flag, placing flag on TR's grave
[1919] 1919
Children visit TR's grave, 1920. 1920
Close-up of TR's grave, 1920. 1920
Daniel C. Beard, TR Jr., and Boy Scouts visit TR's grave,
1920. 1920
Exterior scenes of Sagamore Hill. 1918
Flag at half-mast, Oyster Bay, Jan. 1919. 1919
[Flag services for TR at Oyster Bay, October 1919] 1919
Friends and admirers visit TR's grave, 1920. 1920
General [Diaz] of Italy visits TR's grave [1921] 1921
General Nivelle visits TR's grave [1921] 1921
King Albert of Belgium visits TR's grave, 1919. 1919
King Albert of Belgium visits TR's grave, October, 1919. 1919
Oyster Bay from the air [1919] 1919
The Prince of Wales visits TR's grave. 1919
The prize winning design by John Russell Pope for the pro-
posed memorial to Theodore Roosevelt for the city of
Washington. 1926
RMA flag ceremonies, children sew stars on flag, 1919. 1919
RMA flag service on the steps of New York Public Library,
1919. 1919
RMA pilgrimage to TR's grave, 1930. 1930
Roosevelt at home: Sagamore Hill, Oyster Bay, L.I. [1] 1930
Roosevelt at home: Sagamore Hill, Oyster Bay, L.I. [2] 1930
Roosevelt scenes [1917–1918] 1917
Roosevelt scenes from RMA productions. 1912
Runners carrying flag to TR's grave [1919] 1919
Scenes of Oyster Bay. 1924
Scenes of Sagamore Hill. 1923
Scenes of TR and his sons Quentin and Archie, 1917–1918
[1] 1917
Scenes of TR and his sons Quentin and Archie, 1917–1918
[2] 1917

Scenes of TR at Sagamore Hill, 1912. 1912
Scenes of TR speaking at Sagamore [1916–1918] 1916.
Scouts on their way to TR's grave, Daniel C. Beard and TR Jr. attend services, 1920. 1920
Shall we prepare? 1916
Short scenes of TR [1] 1916
Short scenes of TR as used in Paramount reel. 1916
Still photographs of TR on motion picture film. 1920
Still picture of TR and his family. 1907
Theodore Roosevelt in the great war [1] 1930
Theodore Roosevelt in the great war [2] 1930
Theodore Roosevelt in the great war [3] 1930
Three children visit TR's grave, 1920. 1920
TR and Mr. Helm, a newspaper reporter, exterior of Sagamore Hill, 1912. 1912
TR at Baltimore [1918]; TR at Sagamore [Hill, 1918] 1918
TR at Sagamore, 1917. 1917
TR at Sagamore Hill [1916] 1915
TR at Sagamore Hill [1916–1918] 1916
TR calls on neighbors at Christmas. 1917. 1917
TR in a rowboat on Oyster Bay, Archie assists with boat to shore, 1914. 1914
TR on porch at Sagamore Hill. 1917. 1917
TR receiving Belgian envoys at Sagamore Hill [1917] 1917
TR reviewing and speaking to 13th Regiment at Sagamore Hill, 1917. 1917
TR scenes purchased from different dealers. 1912
TR speaking at Oyster Bay, July 4, 1916. 1916
TR speaking at Sagamore Hill [1916–1918] [1] 1916
TR speaking at Sagamore Hill [1916–1918] [2] 1916
TR speaking at Sagamore Hill [1916–1918 and scenes of his early career] 1897
TR speaking to a group of men from the porch at Sagamore Hill, 1916. 1916
[TR speaks to group at Sagamore Hill, 1] 1917
[TR speaks to group at Sagamore Hill, 2] 1917
[TR speaks to group at Sagamore Hill, 3] 1917
TR wearing army coat standing in auto greeting friends at Oyster Bay, 1910. 1910
TR's funeral, 1919. 1919
TR's funeral at Oyster Bay, 1919. 1919
TR's funeral at Oyster Bay, January 1919 [1] 1919
TR's funeral at Oyster Bay, January 1919 [2] 1919
A visit to Theodore Roosevelt at his home at Sagamore Hill, Oyster Bay, L. I., 1912. 1912
Women suffragettes visit TR at Sagamore [1917] 1917

Oyster Bay, N. Y.—Description—Aerial
Airmen honor TR's memory by dropping American Legion wreath on his grave [1919] 1919
American Legion places wreath on TR's grave [1919]; Scenes of Oyster Bay from the air. 1919
Aviators drop American Legion wreath on TR's grave [1919] 1919
Oyster Bay from the air [1919]

Oyster Bay, N. Y.—Description—Views
Scenes of Oyster Bay. 1924

Oyster Bay, N. Y.—Harbor
Scenes of Oyster Bay. 1924
TR in a rowboat on Oyster Bay, Archie assists with boat to shore, 1914. 1914
TR scenes purchased from different dealers. 1912

Oyster Bay, N. Y.—Parks—Theodore Roosevelt Memorial Park
Scenes of Oyster Bay. 1924

Oyster Bay, N. Y. Christ Episcopal Church
See Christ Episcopal Church, Oyster Bay, N. Y.

Oyster Bay, N. Y. Sagamore Hill
Exterior scenes of Sagamore Hill. 1918
The prize winning design by John Russell Pope for the proposed memorial to Theodore Roosevelt for the city of Washington. 1926
RMA pilgrimage to TR's grave, 1930. 1930
Roosevelt at home: Sagamore Hill, Oyster Bay, L.I. [1] 1930
Roosevelt at home: Sagamore Hill, Oyster Bay, L.I. [2] 1930
Roosevelt scenes [1917–1918] 1917
Roosevelt scenes from RMA productions. 1912
Scenes of Sagamore Hill. 1923
Scenes of TR and his sons Quentin and Archie, 1917–1918 [1] 1917
Scenes of TR and his sons Quentin and Archie, 1917–1918 [2] 1917
Scenes of TR at Sagamore Hill, 1912. 1912
Scenes of TR speaking at Sagamore [1916–1918] 1916
Shall we prepare? 1916
Short scenes of TR [1] 1916
Short scenes of TR as used in Paramount reel. 1916
Still photographs of TR on motion picture film. 1920
Still picture of TR and his family. 1907
Theodore Roosevelt, great scout [1] 1925
Theodore Roosevelt, great scout [2] 1925
Theodore Roosevelt, great scout [3] 1925
Theodore Roosevelt in the great war [1] 1930
Theodore Roosevelt in the great war [2] 1930
TR and Mr. Helm, a newspaper reporter, exterior of Sagamore Hill, 1912. 1912
TR at Baltimore [1918]; TR at Sagamore [Hill, 1918] 1918
TR at Sagamore, 1917. 1917
TR at Sagamore Hill [1916] 1915
TR at Sagamore Hill [1916–1918] 1916
TR on porch at Sagamore Hill, 1917. 1917
TR receiving Belgian envoys at Sagamore Hill [1917] 1917
TR reviewing and speaking to 13th Regiment at Sagamore Hill, 1917. 1917
TR scenes purchased from different dealers. 1912
TR speaking at Sagamore Hill [1916–1918] [1] 1916
TR speaking at Sagamore Hill [1916–1918] [2] 1916
TR speaking at Sagamore Hill [1916–1918 and scenes of his early career] 1897
TR speaking to a group of men from the porch at Sagamore Hill, 1916. 1916
TR speaking to a group of suffragettes from the porch at Sagamore Hill [1917] 1917
[TR speaks to group at Sagamore Hill, 1] 1917
[TR speaks to group at Sagamore Hill, 2] 1917
[TR speaks to group at Sagamore Hill, 3] 1917
A visit to Theodore Roosevelt at his home at Sagamore Hill, Oyster Bay, L. I., 1912. 1912
Women suffragettes visit TR at Sagamore [1917] 1917

Oyster Bay Park, Oyster Bay, N. Y.
See Oyster Bay, N. Y.—Parks—Theodore Roosevelt Memorial Park

Pack transportation
Pack mules with ammunition on the Santiago trail, Cuba. 1898
Spanish Mountain Artillery, 1898. 1898.

Palácio de Guanabara, Rio de Janeiro
See Rio de Janeiro. Palácio Guanabara

Palácio Guanabara, Rio de Janeiro
See Rio de Janeiro. Palácio Guanabara

Palácio Isabel, Rio de Janeiro
See Rio de Janeiro. Palácio Guanabara

Palazzo reale, Naples
See Naples. Palazzo reale

Paleontologists
Professor Henry Fairfield Osborn, RMA medalist. 1923. 1934

Palmer, Frederick, editor
Shall we prepare? 1916

Palms—Brazil
Scenes of the River of Doubt photographed by G. M. Dyott, 1926–1927 [1] 1927
Scenes of the River of Doubt photographed by G. M. Dyott, 1926–1927 [2] 1927

Pan-American Exposition, 1901
President McKinley reviewing the troops at the Pan-American Exposition, 1901
President McKinley speaking at Buffalo, 1901. 1901
[Scenes of TR, Panama Canal construction, and William McKinley] 1901

Panama
William H. Taft in Panama [1910?] 1910

Panama, Presidente, 1904–1908 (Amador Guerrero)
The Panama Canal, 1927
The Story of the Panama Canal [1] 1927
The Story of the Panama Canal [2] 1927
TR speaking from Cathedral steps, Panama. 1906
TR speaking in Panama, November 1906. 1906
TR's arrival in Panama, November 1906 [1] 1906
TR's arrival in Panama, November 1906 [2] 1906
TR's arrival in Panama, November 1906 [3] 1906

Panama (City)
TR speaking from Cathedral steps. Panama. 1906
TR speaking in Panama, November 1906. 1906
TR's arrival in Panama, November 1906 [1] 1906
TR's arrival in Panama, November 1906 [2] 1906
TR's arrival in Panama, November 1906 [3] 1906

Panama (City). Catedral
See Catedral, Panama (City)

Panama—California Exposition, 1915–1916
Reviewing Annapolis middies. 1915
TR and Mrs. Roosevelt [at the Panama-California Exposition, 1915] 1915
TR at San Diego Exposition, 1915. 1915

Panama-California Exposition, San Diego, Calif., 1915–1916
See Panama-California Exposition, 1915–1916

Panama Canal
The Building of the Panama Canal upon the occasion of a memorial exhibition held in honor of General George Washington Goethals. 1928
Dr. William Gorgas. 1900
Extermination of mosquitoes by spraying swamps. 1910
The Panama Canal. 1927
Panama Canal scenes. 1910
Panama Canal; scenes of the finished Canal. 1919
President Roosevelt, 1901–1909. 1930
[Scenes of TR, Panama Canal construction, and William McKinley] 1901
Ships in the Panama Canal [1] 1910
Ships in the Panama Canal [2] 1910
The Story of the Panama Canal [1] 1927
The Story of the Panama Canal [2] 1927
William H. Taft in Panama [1910?] 1910

Panama Canal—Navigation
Panama Canal; scenes of the finished Canal. 1919

Panama Canal (Government)
See Canal Zone

Panama Canal Company
Dr. William Gorgas. 1900

Panama Canal Zone
See Canal Zone

Panama-Pacific International Exposition, 1915
[Scenes pf TR, 1913–1915] 1913
Theodore Roosevelt in the great war [1] 1930
Theodore Roosevelt in the great war [2] 1930
Theodore Roosevelt in the great war [3] 1930
TR [at Panama-Pacific Exposition, 1915] 1915
TR at Sagamore Hill [1916] 1915
TR speaking [at the Panama-Pacific Exposition, 1915] 1915
William H. Taft burns mortgage of Exposition, 1915. 1915

Panama-Pacific International Exposition, 1915—Buildings
[Scenes of TR, 1913–1915] 1913
TR [at Panama-Pacific Exposition, 1915] 1915

Panama-Pacific International Exposition, San Francisco, 1915
See Panama-Pacific International Exposition, 1915

Panama Railroad Company
See Panama Canal Company

Paper Print Collection
25th Infantry. 1898
The Forbidden City, Pekin. 1903
Governor's Foot Guards, Conn. 1899
Launch, U. S. battleship "Kentucky." 1898
Pack mules with ammunition on the Santiago trail, Cuba. 1898
President McKinley reviewing the troops at the Pan-American Exposition. 1901
Theodore Roosevelt leaving the White House. 1897
Troops making military road in front of Santiago. 1898

U. S. battleship "Oregon." 1898
U. S. troops landing at Daiquiri, Cuba. 1898
Wreck of the "Vizcaya." 1898

Parades
See Processions

Paramount
Queen Wilhelmina of Holland, the Prince Consort [and] the Princess. 1920
Shall we prepare? 1916

Paramount, source
Panama Canal scenes. 1910
President McKinley inauguration, 1901. 1901
President McKinley reviewing the troops at the Pan-American Exposition. 1901
President McKinley's funeral, 1901 [2] 1901
President McKinley's inauguration, 1901 [2] 1901
Return of Spanish-American troops, 1898. 1898
Short scenes of TR as used in Paramount reel. 1916
Still pictures exposed on scene of McKinley's funeral as used in Paramount reel. 1901
Theodore Roosevelt leaving the White House. 1897
TR at Wilkes-Barre, Pa., 1905. 1905
TR attends McKinley's funeral, 1901. 1901
TR speaking from Cathedral steps, Panama. 1906
TR speaking in Panama, November 1906. 1906
TR's inauguration, 1905 [1] 1905
TR's inauguration, 1905 [2] 1905

Paramount pictographs, no. 2
Shall we prepare? 1916

Paramount weekly gazette [Series]
Queen Wilhelmina of Holland, the Prince Consort [and] the Princess. 1920

Paris
Mrs. Theodore Roosevelt Jr. attends Women in War Work Congress in Paris [1918] 1918

Parker, Alton B.
TR, Charles E. Hughes, and Mayor Mitchel of New York, on reviewing stand in front of the New York Public Library [1917] 1917

Parker, John Milliken
Roosevelt, friend of the birds [1] 1924
Roosevelt, friend of the birds [2] 1924
Roosevelt, friend of the birds [3] 1924
Roosevelt, friend of the birds [4]; The Roosevelt Dam [3] 1928

Parks
See subdivision Parks under names of cities, e.g., New York (City)—Parks—Central Park

Parties, Political
See Political parties

Pathe
Chauncey Depew, Senator Perkins, and Governor Whitman of New York, at GOP Convention, 1916, Chicago, Ill. 1916

Commander Dyott sailing from [Hoboken, N.J.] for South America, 1926. 1926
General Nivelle visits TR's grave [1921] 1921
Leonard Wood lays cornerstone of Roosevelt House, 1921. 1921
Marshal Foch visits Roosevelt House, 1921. 1921
Roosevelt at home: Sagamore Hill, Oyster Bay, L.I. [1] 1930
Roosevelt at home: Sagamore Hill, Oyster Bay, L.I. [2] 1930
Scenes of TR at Sagamore Hill, 1912. 1912
TR and Mr. Helm, a newspaper reporter, exterior of Sagamore Hill, 1912. 1912
TR Jr. with group of sailors and soldiers. 1919
TR's funeral at Oyster Bay, January 1919 [2] 1919
A visit to Theodore Roosevelt at his home at Sagamore Hill, Oyster Bay, L.I., 1912. 1912

Pathe, source
Chauncey Depew, Senator Perkins, and Governor Whitman of New York, at GOP Convention, 1916, Chicago, Ill. 1916
Colonel Lindbergh, Admiral Byrd, and Clarence Chamberlin at flying field just before Lindbergh's flight, 1927. 1927
Commander Dyott sailing from [Hoboken, N.J.] for South America, 1926. 1926
Elihu Root and Mayor Mitchel of New York, Mr. Root and American delegates return from Russia [1917] 1917
Flag at half-mast, Oyster Bay, Jan. 1919. 1919
General Nivelle visits TR's grave [1921] 1921
Mrs. Roosevelt, Sr., and Mrs. J. H. Hammond photographed on the roof of Roosevelt House, 1927; Mrs. Roosevelt arrives at Roosevelt House. 1927
President Wilson arrives in New York to lead fourth Liberty Loan parade [1918] 1918
Roosevelt scenes [1917–1918] 1917
Rough Riders greet TR during Liberty Loan drive out west [1918] 1918
Scene of Clemenceau, Tardieu, Foch, Poincaré and Pershing, 1917–1918. 1918
Scenes of Roosevelt Dam. 1911
TR and Mr. Helm, a newspaper reported, exterior of Sagamore Hill, 1912. 1912
TR [at Panama-Pacific Exposition, 1915] 1915
TR, exterior of building, Washington, D.C., 1918. 1918
TR in New Mexico. 1916. 1916
TR Jr. with group of sailors and soldiers, 1919
TR, Mayor Mitchel and guests at Cooper Sanitarium [1917] 1917
TR riding in an auto in Chicago, 1917. 1917
TR with naval officers, exterior Navy Club, Boston [1918] 1918
TR's funeral at Oyster Bay, January 1919 [2] 1919
William Gibbs McAdoo. 1910
William Howard Taft on rear platform of train. 1908
Women suffragettes visit TR at Sagamore [1917] 1917

Pathé Frères
See Pathe

Pathe News, inc.
See Pathe

Pathe News [newsreel]
Chauncey Depew, Senator Perkins, and Governor Whitman of New York, at GOP Convention, 1916, Chicago, Ill. 1916
Commander Dyott sailing from [Hoboken, N.J.] for South

America, 1926. 1926
General Nivelle visits TR's grave [1921] 1921
Leonard Wood lays cornerstone of Roosevelt House, 1921. 1921
Marshal Foch visits Roosevelt House, 1921. 1921
TR Jr. with group of sailors and soldiers. 1919
TR's funeral at Oyster Bay, January 1919 [2] 1919

Peirce, Herbert H. D.
Japanese and Russian peace delegates [leaving New York City], 1905. 1905

Peking
Allied armies in China, 1917–1918. 1918
The Forbidden City, Pekin. 1903

Peking—Description—Views
The Forbidden City, Pekin. 1903

Peking. Forbidden City
See Peking. Imperial Palace

Peking. Gate of Great Harmony
The Forbidden City, Pekin. 1903

Peking. Hall of Supreme Harmony
The Forbidden City, Pekin. 1903

Peking. Imperial Palace
The Forbidden City, Pekin. 1903

Peking. West Flowery Gate
The Forbidden City, Pekin. 1903

Peking. White Pagoda
The Forbidden City, Pekin. 1903

Pelissier, Pete
See Pellessier, Pete

Pellessier, Pete
Through the Roosevelt country with Roosevelt's friends. 1919

Pennsylvania—Governors
Gifford Pinchot, 1923. 1923

Pennsylvania. Governor, 1923–1927 (Pinchot)
Dedication of Roosevelt House, 1923. 1923
Dedication of Roosevelt House, Oct. 27, 1923. 1923
Gifford Pinchot, 1923. 1923
See also Pinchot, Gifford

Pennsylvania Station, New York (City)
See New York (City). Pennsylvania Station

Penrose, Boies
Senator Penrose. 1910

Perkins, Arthur L.
Commander Dyott sailing from [Hoboken, N.J.] for South America, 1926. 1926

Perkins, F. Nathaniel
Roosevelt scenes [1917–1918] 1917
Short scenes of TR [1] 1916

Perkins, George W.
Chauncey Depew, Senator Perkins, and Governor Whitman of New York, at GOP Convention, 1916, Chicago, Ill. 1916
TR himself [1] 1926
TR himself [2] 1926
TR himself [3] 1926
TR himself [4] 1926
TR himself [5] 1926
TR on Fifth Avenue, New York, near St. Patrick's Cathedral after attending Mayor Mitchel's funeral. 1918

Perkins, Nathaniel F.
See Perkins, F. Nathaniel

Pershing, John J.
Gen. Pershing speaking to Scouts in New York. 1919
General Pershing at Camp Grant. 1920
[Quentin Roosevelt]; Clemenceau and Foch, 1917–1919. 1918
Scene of Clemenceau, Tardieu, Foch, Poincaré and Pershing, 1917–1918. 1918

Pétain, Henri Philippe
Scene of Clemenceau, Tardieu, Foch, Poincaré and Pershing, 1917–1918. 1918

Pétain, Philippe
See Pétain. Henri Philippe

Pets
Roosevelt at home: Sagamore Hill, Oyster Bay, L.I. [1] 1930
Roosevelt at home: Sagamore Hill, Oyster Bay, L.I. [2] 1930

Pezet, Federico Alfonso
William H. Taft in Panama [1910?] 1910

Pezet, Frederico Alphonso
See Pezet, Federico Alfonso

Philadelphia
Short scenes of TR [1] 1916
TR scenes purchased from different dealers. 1912

Physicians
Dr. William Gorgas. 1900

Pigs
See Swine

Pilots (Aeronautics)
See Air pilots

Pinchot, Cornelia Bryce
Dedication of Roosevelt House, 1923. 1923
Dedication of Roosevelt House, Oct. 27, 1923. 1923

Pinchot, Gifford
Dedication of Roosevelt House, 1923. 1923
Dedication of Roosevelt House, Oct. 27, 1923. 1923
Gifford Pinchot, 1923. 1923
Memorializing Roosevelt. 1925
Presentation of Roosevelt Medals, May 1925, Washington, D.C. 1925
The Roosevelt Dam [1] 1928
The Roosevelt Dam [2] 1928

Piper, Walter C.
Leonard Wood at Battle Creek, Michigan. 1920

Piranha
See Caribe

Pittsburgh
Charles E. Hughes speaking during campaign, Duquesne, Pa., 1916. 1916
Short scenes of TR [1] 1916

Pittsburgh. Allegheny County Courthouse
See Allegheny Co., Pa. County Courthouse

Plattsburgh, N.Y.
Theodore Roosevelt in the great war [1] 1930
Theodore Roosevelt in the great war [2] 1930
Theodore Roosevelt in the great war [3] 1930

Plattsburgh Barracks
Theodore Roosevelt in the great war [1] 1930
Theodore Roosevelt in the great war [2] 1930
Theodore Roosevelt in the great war [3] 1930

Plazas
Plazas are entered under names of cities, e.g., New York (City)—Plazas; individual plazas located in particular cities are further subdivided by names, e.g., New York (City)—Plazas— Madison Square.

Plymouth, Vt.
President Harding and Calvin Coolidge [1] 1920

Poincaré, Henriette
The King and Queen of Belgium and Premier Poincaré of France [1] 1927

Poincaré, Raymond, Pres. France, 1860–1934
The King and Queen of Belgium and Premier Poincaré of France [1] 1927
The King and Queen of Belgium and Premier Poincaré of France [2] 1927
Scene of Clemenceau, Tardieu, Foch, Poincaré and Pershing, 1917–1918. 1918
See also France. Président, 1913–1920 (Poincaré)

Police—United States
Return of Spanish-American troops, 1898. 1898

Political conventions
Chauncey Depew, Senator Perkins, and Governor Whitman of New York, at GOP Convention, 1916, Chicago, Ill. 1916
General Wood and Calvin Coolidge in Chicago, 1920. 1920

Political parties
Chauncey Depew, Senator Perkins, and Governor Whitman of New York, at GOP Convention, 1916, Chicago, Ill. 1916
General Wood and Calvin Coolidge in Chicago, 1920. 1920
President Harding and Calvin Coolidge [1] 1920
President Harding and Calvin Coolidge [2] 1920
See also names of parties, e.g., Republican Party; and subdivision Politics and government under names of countries, e.g., United States—Politics and government.

Political parties—Colorado
TR speaking at [Pueblo] Colorado, 1912. 1912

Political parties—North Dakota
TR at Fargo, N.D., during Progressive campaign, 1912 [1] 1912
TR at Fargo, N.D., during Progressive campaign, 1912 [2] 1912
TR speaking from train platform, 1912. 1912

Political parties—Washington, D.C.
TR in auto [1912] 1912

Politics and art
Cartoon of TR's reception by crowned heads of Europe. 1910
Roosevelt cartoons. 1910

Polygon, Vincennes, France
See Vincennes, France. Polygon

Pomerene, Atlee
Senator Pomerene. 1910

Pope, John Russell
The prize winning design by John Russell Pope for the proposed memorial to Theodore Roosevelt for the city of Washington. 1926

Portsmouth, Treaty of, 1905
Japanese and Russian peace delegates [leaving New York City], 1905. 1905
TR himself [1] 1926
TR himself [2] 1926
TR himself [3] 1926
TR himself [4] 1926
TR himself [5] 1926
TR himself [6] 1926

Prendergast, William A.
Elihu Root and Mayor Mitchel of New York, Mr. Root and American delegates return from Russia [1917] 1917

Preparedness
Close-up of TR speaking [1917] 1917
Shall we prepare? 1916
Theodore Roosevelt in the great war [1] 1930
Theodore Roosevelt in the great war [2] 1930
Theodore Roosevelt in the great war [3] 1930
TR reviews and addresses troops [Fort Sheridan, Ill.]; TR riding in auto, Chicago, 1917. 1917
TR riding in an auto in Chicago, 1917. 1917
TR speaking at [St. Paul, Minnesota, 1917] 1917

Presidents—United States—Election—1905
President Roosevelt, 1901–1909. 1930

Presidents—United States—Election—1912
Crowd listening to TR speak during Progressive campaign, 1912. 1912
Roosevelt scenes from RMA productions. 1912
Short scenes of TR [2] 1912
Theodore Roosevelt: fighter for social justice. 1934
TR at Fargo, N.D., during Progressive campaign, 1912 [1] 1912

TR at Fargo, N.D., during Progressive campaign, 1912 [2] 1912

TR during Progressive campaign, 1912. 1912

TR in auto [1912] 1912

TR riding in auto through crowded streets [1912] 1912

TR scenes purchased from different dealers. 1912

TR speaking at [Pueblo] Colorado, 1912. 1912

TR speaking from train platform, 1912. 1912

Presidents—United States—Election—1916

Charles E. Hughes speaking during campaign, Duquesne, Pa., 1916. 1916

Chauncey Depew, Senator Perkins, and Governor Whitman of New York, at GOP Convention, 1916, Chicago, Ill. 1916

Scenes of TR speaking at Sagamore [1916-1918] 1916

Short scenes of TR [1] 1916

Short scenes of TR [2] 1912

TR at Sagamore Hill [1916] 1915

TR at Sagamore Hill [1916-1918] 1916

TR in New Mexico, 1916. 1916

TR speaking at Sagamore Hill [1916–1918] [1] 1916

TR speaking at Sagamore Hill [1916–1918] [2] 1916

TR speaking at Sagamore Hill [1916–1918 and scenes of his early career] 1897

TR speaking to a group of men from the porch at Sagamore Hill, 1916. 1916

TR's reception in Albuquerque, N. M., 1916. 1916

Presidents—United States—Election—1920

General Wood and Calvin Coolidge in Chicago, 1920. 1920

Leonard Wood at Battle Creek, Michigan. 1920

President Harding and Calvin Coolidge [1] 1920

President Harding and Calvin Coolidge [2] 1920

Presidents—United States—Inauguration

President McKinley inauguration, 1901. 1901

President McKinley's inauguration, 1901 [1] 1901

President McKinley's inauguration, 1901 [2] 1901

[TR's inaugural ceremony, 1905] 1905

TR's inauguration, 1905 [1] 1905

TR's inauguration, 1905 [2] 1905

Presidents—United States—Nomination

General Wood and Calvin Coolidge in Chicago, 1920. 1920

President Harding and Calvin Coolidge [1] 1920

President Harding and Calvin Coolidge [2] 1920

Roosevelt scenes from RMA productions. 1912

Scenes of TR speaking at Sagamore [1916–1918] 1916

TR at Sagamore Hill [1916] 1915

TR at Sagamore Hill [1916–1918] 1916

TR speaking at Sagamore Hill [1916–1918] [1] 1916

TR speaking at Sagamore Hill [1916–1918] [2] 1916

TR speaking at Sagamore Hill [1916–1918 and scenes of his early career] 1897

TR speaking to a group of men from the porch at Sagamore Hill, 1916. 1916

Presidents—United States—Term of office

President Roosevelt, 1901–1909. 1930

Preston, Frances Folsom Cleveland

TR addresses large crowd for the Liberty Loan in Baltimore, 1918. 1918

TR at Baltimore [1918]; TR at Sagamore [Hill, 1918] 1918

TR himself [1] 1926

TR himself [2] 1926

TR himself [3] 1926

TR himself [4] 1926

TR himself [5] 1926

TR himself [6] 1926

TR in Baltimore during Liberty Loan drive, 1918. 1918

TR scenes purchased from different dealers. 1912

Preston, Thomas J.

TR addresses large crowd for the Liberty Loan in Baltimore, 1918. 1918

TR at Baltimore [1918]; TR at Sagamore [Hill, 1918] 1918

TR himself [1] 1926

TR himself [2] 1926

TR himself [3] 1926

TR himself [4] 1926

TR himself [5] 1926

TR himself [6] 1926

TR in Baltimore during Liberty Loan drive, 1918. 1918

TR scenes purchased from different dealers. 1912

Priests

Crowd listening to TR, Cardinal Gibbons and priests in foreground, 1917. 1917

TR as Father Curran's guest at Wilkes-Barre, Pa., August 10, 1905. 1905

TR at Wilkes-Barre, Pa., 1905. 1905

TR in Wilkes-Barre, Pa., 1905. 1905

Prince Charles Théodore

See Charles, Count of Flanders, 1903–

Prisoners

Scenes of Hastings Hart, 1930 medalist. 1930

Prisoners of war—Sverdlovsk, Russia

Allied armies in China, 1917–1918. 1918

Last known home of Czar Nicholas. 1918

Prisons—New York (State)

Scenes of Hastings Hart, 1930 medalist. 1930

Prisons—Russia—Sverdlovsk

Allied armies in China, 1917–1918. 1918

Last known home of Czar Nicholas. 1918

Prizma Pictures, source

Roosevelt cartoons. 1910

Processions

Admiral Dewey parade, 1899 [1] 1899

Admiral Dewey parade, 1899 [2] 1899

Close-up of TR speaking [1917] 1917

Daniel C. Beard, TR Jr., and Boy Scouts visit TR's grave, 1920. 1920

Emperor Francis Joseph of Austria greeted by his people. 1910

General Pershing at Camp Grant. 1920

Governor's Foot Guards, Conn. 1899

President McKinley inauguration, 1901. 1901

President McKinley's funeral, 1901 [1] 1901

President McKinley's funeral, 1901 [2] 1901

President McKinley's funeral, Canton, Ohio, 1901 [1] 1901

President McKinley's funeral, Canton, Ohio, 1901 [2] 1901

President McKinley's funeral in Buffalo, Washington, and Canton, Ohio, 1901. 1901

President McKinley's inauguration, 1901 [1] 1901

President McKinley's inauguration, 1901 [2] 1901

President McKinley's memorial dedicated by William Howard Taft at Niles, Ohio. 1917

Return of Spanish-American troops, 1898. 1898

Reviewing Annapolis middies. 1915

Roosevelt at home: Sagamore Hill, Oyster Bay, L.I. [1] 1930

Roosevelt at home: Sagamore Hill, Oyster Bay, L.I. [2] 1930

Rough Riders greet TR during Liberty Loan drive out west [1918] 1918

Scene of Clemenceau, Tardieu, Foch, Poincaré and Pershing, 1917–1918. 1918

Scenes of TR and his sons Quentin and Archie, 1917–1918 [1] 1917

Scenes of TR and his sons Quentin and Archie, 1917–1918 [2] 1917

TR as Father Curran's guest at Wilkes-Barre, Pa., August 10, 1905. 1905

TR at Wilkes-Barre, Pa., 1905. 1905

TR comes back. 1925

TR in New Mexico, 1916. 1916

TR in San Francisco, 1903. 1903

TR in St. Paul, Minn. [1917] 1917

TR in Wilkes-Barre, Pa., 1905. 1905

TR reviews and addresses troops [Fort Sheridan, Ill.]; TR riding in auto, Chicago, 1917. 1917

TR riding in an auto in Chicago, 1917. 1917

TR riding in auto through crowded streets [1912] 1912

TR speaking at Sagamore Hill [1916–1918 and scenes of his early career] 1897

TR speaking at [St. Paul, Minnesota, 1917] 1917

TR's arrival in Panama, November 1906 [1] 1906

TR's arrival in Panama, November 1906 [2] 1906

TR's arrival in Panama, November 1906 [3] 1906

[TR's inaugural ceremony, 1905] 1905

TR's inauguration, 1905 [1] 1905

TR's inauguration, 1905 [2] 1905

TR's reception in Albuquerque, N.M., 1916. 1916

TR's return to New York, 1910 [1] 1910

Processions, Ecclesiastical—Cartagena, Colombia
Scout parade, Cartagena, Colombia, 1920. 1920

Progressive Party (Founded 1912)
Crowd listening to TR speak during Progressive campaign, 1912. 1912

Short scenes of TR [2] 1912

Theodore Roosevelt: fighter for social justice. 1934

TR at Fargo, N.D., during Progressive campaign, 1912 [1] 1912

TR at Fargo, N.D., during Progressive campaign, 1912 [2] 1912

TR during Progressive campaign, 1912. 1912

TR himself [1] 1926

TR himself [2] 1926

TR himself [3] 1926

TR himself [4] 1926

TR himself [5] 1926

TR himself [6] 1926

TR in auto [1912] 1912

TR riding in auto through crowded streets [1912] 1912

TR scenes purchased from different dealers. 1912

TR speaking at [Pueblo] Colorado, 1912. 1912

TR speaking from train platform, 1912. 1912

Protection of birds
See Birds, Protection of

Proving grounds
Disappearing gun at testing grounds, Sandy Hook, 1898. 1898

Public buildings
See subdivision Public buildings under names of countries and cities, e.g., United States—Public buildings; and names of particular buildings, e.g., Washington, D.C. Capitol.

Public law no. 192
See United States. Laws, statutes, etc. Liberty loan acts

Public Schools Athletic League, New York
[Scenes of TR, 1913–1915] 1913

Pueblo, Colo.
Theodore Roosevelt: fighter for social justice. 1934

TR speaking at [Pueblo] Colorado, 1912. 1912

Putnam, Herbert
Herbert Putnam. 1920

Mr. Garfield presenting medals to 1929 medalists. 1929

Queen Maud (Ship)
TR in Denmark, 1910. 1910

TR in Norway and Denmark, 1910 [1] 1910

TR in Norway and Denmark, 1910 [2] 1910

TR in Norway and Denmark, 1910 [3] 1910

Queen Victoria Memorial, London
See London. Queen Victoria Memorial

Railroad terminals—New York (City)
TR at Forest Hills, New York, 1917 [1] 1917

TR at Forest Hills, New York, 1917 [2] 1917

Railroads—Passenger cars
Major General Wm. C. Gorgas. 1910

Railroads—Canal Zone
Dr. William Gorgas. 1900

Railroads—New England—Finance
Governors of New England meet in Governor Coolidge's office in Boston to discuss fuel. 1919

Rainey, Paul James
Cartoon of Mr. Paul Rainey's African trip [1911] 1911

Scenes of African animals [1911] 1911

Rainey, Paul James, photographer
Allied armies in China, 1917–1918. 1918

Last known home of Czar Nicholas. 1918

Rainey, Paul James, source
Scenes of African animals [1911] 1911

Ranch life
See Dude ranches

Reclamation of land—Arizona
The Roosevelt Dam [1] 1928
The Roosevelt Dam [2] 1928
Roosevelt, friend of the birds [4]; The Roosevelt Dam [3] 1928
Scenes of Roosevelt Dam. 1911
TR at dedication of Roosevelt Dam, 1911. 1911
TR speaking at the dedication of Roosevelt Dam, 1911. 1911

Reed, Latham R.
TR at Camp Mills [1917] 1917

Reichstagsgebäude, Berlin
See Berlin. Reichstagsgebäude

Reid, Helen Rogers
Scenes of TR speaking at Sagamore [1916–1918] 1916
Women suffragettes visit TR at Sagamore [1917] 1917

Reid, W. W., photographer
Through the Roosevelt country with Roosevelt's friends. 1919

Reiker, M., source
Scenes of flowers and birds in Washington, D.C. 1920

Reporters and reporting
Short scenes of TR as used in Paramount reel. 1916

Republican National Committee
See Republican Party. National Committee

Republican National Convention
See Republican Party. National Convention

Republican Party
Chauncey Depew, Senator Perkins, and Governor Whitman of New York, at GOP Convention, 1916, Chicago, Ill. 1916
General Wood and Calvin Coolidge in Chicago, 1920. 1920
President Harding and Calvin Coolidge [1] 1920
President Harding and Calvin Coolidge [2] 1920

Republican Party. Michigan
Leonard Wood at Battle Creek, Michigan. 1920

Republican Party. National Committee, 1920–1924
General Wood and Calvin Coolidge in Chicago, 1920. 1920

Republican Party. National Convention. 16th, Chicago, 1916
Chauncey Depew, Senator Perkins, and Governor Whitman of New York, at GOP Convention, 1916, Chicago, Ill. 1916

Republican Party. National Convention, 17th, Chicago, 1920
General Wood and Calvin Coolidge in Chicago, 1920. 1920
President Harding and Calvin Coolidge [1] 1920
President Harding and Calvin Coolidge [2] 1920

Republican Party. Notification Committee, 1920
President Harding and Calvin Coolidge [1] 1920
President Harding and Calvin Coolidge [2] 1920

Reservoirs—Arizona
The Roosevelt Dam [1] 1928
The Roosevelt Dam [2] 1928

Reuter, John
Through the Roosevelt country with Roosevelt's friends, 1919

Reuterdahl, Henry, editor
Shall we prepare? 1916

Rew, Robert
General Pershing at Camp Grant. 1920

Rhinoceros
African animals. 1909
Scenes of African animals [1911] 1911

Rhode Island. Governor, 1915 – 1921 (Beeckman)
Governors of New England meet in Governor Coolidge's office in Boston to discuss fuel. 1919

Rickenbacker, Edward V.
[Quentin Roosevelt]; Clemenceau and Foch, 1917–1919. 1918

Rio da Dúvida
See Roosevelt River

Rio de Janeiro
The River of Doubt [1] 1928
The River of Doubt [2] 1928
The River of Doubt [3] 1928
The River of Doubt [4] 1928
The River of Doubt [5] 1928
The River of Doubt [6] 1928
The River of Doubt [7] 1928
Roosevelt scenes from RMA productions. 1912
Scenes of the River of Doubt photographed by G. M. Dyott, 1926–1927 [2] 1927
[Scenes of TR, 1913–1915] 1913
[Scenes of TR on board ship, 1916; Scenes of TR's trip to South America, 1913] 1913
TR himself [1] 1926
TR himself [2] 1926
TR himself [3] 1926
TR himself [4] 1926
TR himself [5] 1926
TR himself [6] 1926

Rio de Janeiro—Harbor
Scenes of the River of Doubt photographed by G. M. Dyott, 1926–1927 [1] 1927
Scenes of the River of Doubt photographed by G. M. Dyott, 1926–1927 [2] 1927
[Scenes of TR, 1913–1915] 1913

Rio de Janeiro. Palácio Guanabara
The River of Doubt [1] 1928
The River of Doubt [2] 1928
The River of Doubt [3] 1928
The River of Doubt [4] 1928
The River of Doubt [5] 1928
The River of Doubt [7] 1928
[Scenes of TR, 1913–1915] 1913
[Scenes of TR on board ship, 1916; Scenes of TR's trip to South America, 1913] 1913

Rio de Janeiro. Palácio Monroe
The River of Doubt [1] 1928

The River of Doubt [2] 1928
The River of Doubt [4] 1928
The River of Doubt [5] 1928
The River of Doubt [7] 1928

Rio Roosevelt
See Roosevelt River

Rio Téodoro
See Roosevelt River

Rio Théodoro
See Roosevelt River

River of Doubt
See Roosevelt River

River of Doubt Expedition
See Roosevelt-Rondon Scientific Expedition

RMA
See Roosevelt Memorial Association

Roads—Cuba—Maintenance and repair
Troops making military road in front of Santiago. 1898

Roberts, Alton F.
Leonard Wood at Battle Creek, Michigan. 1920

Roberts, Margaret
Through the Roosevelt country with Roosevelt's friends. 1919

Robins, Raymond
Presentation of Roosevelt Medals, May 1925, Washington, D.C. 1925

Robinson, Corinne Roosevelt
Leonard Wood lays cornerstone of Roosevelt House, 1921. 1921

Rocco, Saint
See Rochus, Saint, 1295 (ca.)–1327

Roch, Saint
See Rochus, Saint, 1295 (ca.)–1327

Roche, Saint
See Rochus, Saint, 1295 (ca.)–1327

Rochus, Saint, 1295 (ca.)–1327
Scout parade, Cartagena, Colombia, 1920. 1920

Rockford, Ill.
General Pershing at Camp Grant. 1920
Roosevelt scenes [1917–1918] 1917
Short scenes of TR [1] 1916
Theodore Roosevelt in the great war [1] 1930
Theodore Roosevelt in the great war [2] 1930
Theodore Roosevelt in the great war [3] 1930

Rockford, Ill. Hotel Nelson
General Pershing at Camp Grant. 1920

Rondon, Candido Mariano da Silva
The River of Doubt [1] 1928
The River of Doubt [2] 1928
The River of Doubt [3] 1928
The River of Doubt [4] 1928
The River of Doubt [5] 1928
The River of Doubt [6] 1928
The River of Doubt [7] 1928
Scenes of the River of Doubt photographed by G. M. Dyott, 1926–1927 [1] 1927

Roon (Cruiser)
International naval review, Hampton Roads, Virginia, 1907. 1907

Roosevelt, Archibald B.
Scenes of TR and his sons Quentin and Archie, 1917–1918 [1] 1917
Scenes of TR and his sons Quentin and Archie, 1917–1918 [2] 1917
Scenes of TR at Sagamore Hill, 1912. 1912
Still picture of TR and his family. 1907
TR attends his son Archie's wedding at Boston, 1917. 1917
TR himself [4] 1926
TR in a rowboat on Oyster Bay, Archie assists with boat to shore, 1914. 1914
TR scenes purchased from different dealers. 1912
TR's funeral at Oyster Bay, 1919. 1919
TR's funeral at Oyster Bay, January 1919 [2] 1919
TR's sons' regiments during war, 1917–1918 [1] 1918
TR's sons' regiments during war, 1917–1918 [2] 1918
A visit to Theodore Roosevelt at his home at Sagamore Hill, Oyster Bay, L. I., 1912. 1912

Roosevelt, Corinne
See Robinson, Corinne Roosevelt

Roosevelt, Edith
Dedication of Cuban memorial, 1924 [1] 1924
Dedication of Cuban memorial, 1924 [2] 1924
Mrs. Roosevelt, Sr., and Mrs. J. H. Hammond photographed on the roof of Roosevelt House, 1927; Mrs. Roosevelt arrives at Roosevelt House, 1927
The River of Doubt [1] 1928
The River of Doubt [2] 1928
The River of Doubt [4] 1928
The River of Doubt [5] 1928
The River of Doubt [7] 1928
The Roosevelt Dam [1] 1928
The Roosevelt Dam [2] 1928
Roosevelt scenes from RMA productions. 1912
Still picture of TR and his family, 1907
TR and Mrs. Roosevelt [at the Panama-California Exposition, 1915] 1915
TR at San Diego Exposition, 1915. 1915
TR attends his son Archie's wedding at Boston, 1917. 1917
TR in Norway, 1910. 1910
TR in Norway and Denmark, 1910 [1] 1910
TR in Norway and Denmark, 1910 [2] 1910
TR in Norway and Denmark, 1910 [3] 1910
TR reviews the fleet, 1907. 1907
TR speaking from Cathedral steps, Panama. 1906
TR speaking in Panama, November 1906, 1906

TR with group of men, 1917; TR speaking at dedication of Roosevelt Dam, 1911. 1911

TR's arrival in Panama, November 1906 [3] 1906

Roosevelt, Edith Kermit Carow
See Roosevelt, Edith

Roosevelt, Eleanor Butler Alexander
Mrs. Theodore Roosevelt Jr. attends Women in War Work Congress in Paris [1918] 1918

Roosevelt, Ethel Carow
See Derby, Ethel Roosevelt

Roosevelt, George E.
Short scenes of TR [2] 1912

Theodore Roosevelt: fighter for social justice. 1934

TR at Fargo, N.D., during Progressive campaign, 1912 [1] 1912

TR at Fargo, N.D., during Progressive campaign, 1912 [2] 1912

TR during Progressive campaign, 1912. 1912

TR speaking from train platform, 1912. 1912

Roosevelt, Kermit
The River of Doubt [1] 1928

The River of Doubt [2] 1928

The River of Doubt [3] 1928

The River of Doubt [4] 1928

The River of Doubt [5] 1928

The River of Doubt [7] 1928

[Scenes of TR on board ship, 1916; Scenes of TR's trip to South America, 1913] 1913

Still picture of TR and his family. 1907

TR in Norway, 1910. 1910

TR in Norway and Denmark, 1910 [1] 1910

TR in Norway and Denmark, 1910 [2] 1910

TR in Norway and Denmark, 1910 [3] 1910

TR's sons' regiments during war, 1917–1918 [1] 1918

Roosevelt, Martha Bulloch
Bulloch home, Roswell, Georgia, 1923. 1923

Roosevelt, Quentin
[Quentin Roosevelt]; Clemenceau and Foch, 1917–1919. 1918

Quentin Roosevelt's grave, 1918. 1919

Quentin Roosevelt's grave in France. 1919

Scenes of TR and his sons Quentin and Archie, 1917–1918 [1] 1917

Scenes of TR and his sons Quentin and Archie, 1917–1918 [2] 1917

Still picture of TR and his family. 1907

Theodore Roosevelt in the great war [1] 1930

Theodore Roosevelt in the great war [2] 1930

Theodore Roosevelt in the great war [3] 1930

TR's sons' regiments during war, 1917–1918 [1] 1918

Roosevelt, Theodore, 1887–1944
Daniel C. Beard, TR Jr., and Boy Scouts visit TR's grave, 1920. 1920

Friends and admirers visit TR's grave, 1920. 1920

King Albert of Belgium visits TR's grave, 1919. 1919

King Albert of Belgium visits TR's grave, October, 1919. 1919

Laying cornerstone of Roosevelt School, New Rochelle, N.Y. [1920] 1920

Lieutenant-Colonel Theodore Roosevelt arrives in New York after the World War. 1919

The Prince of Wales visits TR's grave. 1919

RMA services at [Hearst Greek Theatre, University of California, Berkeley, Calif.]; Laying cornerstone of Roosevelt School in New Rochelle, N.Y. [1920] 1920

Roosevelt scenes from RMA productions. 1912

Scouts on their way to TR's grave, Daniel C. Beard and TR Jr. attend services, 1920. 1920

Still picture of TR and his family, 1907

Theodore Roosevelt, great scout [1] 1925

Theodore Roosevelt, great scout [2] 1925

TR Jr. and Will Hays. 1920

TR Jr. with group of sailors and soldiers. 1919

TR's sons' regiments during war, 1917–1918 [1] 1918

TR's sons' regiments during war, 1917–1918 [2] 1918

Roosevelt, Theodore, Pres. U.S., 1858–1919
Colonel Roosevelt is invited to fly in Arch Hoxsey's plane at St. Louis, Mo., 1910. 1910

Crowd listening to TR speak during Progressive campaign, 1912. 1912

Hopi Indians dance for TR at [Walpi, Ariz.] 1913. 1913

King Edward's funeral, 1910 [2] 1910

President Harding presenting chair used by TR at the White House to the directors of RMA, October 1921. 1921

President McKinley inauguration, 1901. 1901

President McKinley's funeral, Canton, Ohio. 1901 [1] 1901

President McKinley's funeral, Canton, Ohio. 1901 [2] 1901

President McKinley's funeral in Buffalo, Washington, and Canton, Ohio, 1901. 1901

President Roosevelt, 1901–1909. 1930

Reviewing Annapolis middies. 1915

The River of Doubt [1] 1928

The River of Doubt [2] 1928

The River of Doubt [3] 1928

The River of Doubt [4] 1928

The River of Doubt [5] 1928

The River of Doubt [6] 1928

The River of Doubt [7] 1928

Roosevelt at home: Sagamore Hill, Oyster Bay, L.I. [1] 1930

Roosevelt at home: Sagamore Hill, Oyster Bay, L.I. [2] 1930

The Roosevelt Dam [1] 1928

The Roosevelt Dam [2] 1928

Roosevelt scenes from RMA productions. 1912

Rough Riders greet TR during Liberty Loan drive out west [1918] 1918

[Scenes of TR, 1913–1915] 1913

Scenes of TR and his sons Quentin and Archie, 1917–1918 [1] 1917

Scenes of TR and his sons Quentin and Archie, 1917–1918 [2] 1917

Scenes of TR at Sagamore Hill, 1912. 1912

[Scenes of TR on board ship, 1916; Scenes of TR's trip to South America, 1913] 1913

Scenes of TR speaking at Sagamore [1916–1918] 1916

Short scenes of TR [1] 1916

Short scenes of TR [2] 1912

Still photographs of TR on motion picture film. 1920

Still pictures of TR at [Cambridge] 1910. 1910

Theodore Roosevelt leaving the White House. 1897

Through the Roosevelt country with Roosevelt's friends. 1919

TR and Leonard Wood at the New York flower show, 1917. 1917

TR and Mrs. Roosevelt [at the Panama-California Exposition, 1915] 1915

TR and several men. 1910

TR at Camp Mills [1917] 1917

TR at limousine window, 1917. 1917

TR [at Panama-Pacific Exposition, 1915] 1915

TR at Sagamore Hill [1916] 1915

TR at San Diego Exposition, 1915. 1915

TR at Wilkes-Barre, Pa., 1905. 1905

TR attends dinner of Cincinnati, Ohio, Business Men's Club, Dec. 14, 1917 [1] 1917

TR attends dinner of Cincinnati, Ohio, Business Men's Club, Dec. 14, 1917 [2] 1917

TR attends his son Archie's wedding at Boston, 1917. 1917

TR attends McKinley's funeral, 1901. 1901

TR attends McKinley's funeral, Canton, Ohio, 1901. 1901

TR calls on neighbors at Christmas, 1917. 1917

TR, Charles E. Hughes, and Mayor Mitchel of New York, on reviewing stand in front of the New York Public Library [1917] 1917

TR comes back. 1925

TR, exterior of building, Washington, D.C., 1918. 1918

[TR getting into parked car] 1910

TR in a rowboat on Oyster Bay, Archie assists with boat to shore, 1914. 1914

TR in auto [1912] 1912

TR [in Louisiana], 1915 [1] 1915

TR [in Louisiana], 1915 [2] 1915

TR [in Louisiana], 1915 [3] 1915

TR [in Louisiana], 1915 [4] 1915

TR in San Francisco, 1903. 1903

TR in St. Paul, Minn. [1917] 1917

TR in Vincennes, France, 1910. 1910

TR in Wilkes-Barre, Pa., 1905. 1905

TR, Mayor Mitchel and guests at Cooper Sanitarium [1917] 1917

TR, Mayor Mitchel, Governor Charles Whitman of New York, and Myron Herrick, 1917. 1917

TR on Fifth Avenue, New York, near St. Patrick's Cathedral after attending Mayor Mitchel's funeral. 1918

TR on porch at Sagamore Hill, 1917. 1917

TR on reception yacht in New York Bay, 1910. 1910

TR receiving Belgian envoys at Sagamore Hill [1917] 1917

TR reviewing and speaking to 13th Regiment at Sagamore Hill, 1917. 1917

TR reviews French troops at Vincennes, France, 1910. 1910

TR reviews the fleet, 1907. 1907

TR riding in an auto in Chicago, 1917. 1917

TR riding in auto through crowded streets [1912] 1912

TR scenes purchased from different dealers. 1912

TR seated at his desk in the Outlook office [1914?] 1914

TR speaking at Sagamore Hill [1916–1918 and scenes of his early career] 1897

TR with group of men, 1917; TR speaking at dedication of Roosevelt Dam, 1911. 1911

TR with naval officers, exterior Navy Club, Boston [1918] 1918

TR with Rough Rider Friends. 1910

TR's reception in Albuquerque, N.M., 1916. 1916

TR's return to New York, 1910 [1] 1910

TR's return to New York, 1910 [2] 1910

Women suffragettes visit TR at Sagamore [1917] 1917

See also United States. President, 1901–1909 (Roosevelt)

Roosevelt, Theodore, Pres. U.S., 1858–1919—Addresses, essays, lectures

Close-up of TR speaking [1917] 1917

Close-up scenes of TR speaking during World War I, 1917–18. 1917

Jamestown Exposition, 1907. 1907

The prize winning design by John Russell Pope for the proposed memorial to Theodore Roosevelt for the city of Washington, 1926

The Roosevelt Dam [1] 1928

The Roosevelt Dam [2] 1928

Roosevelt scenes [1917–1918] 1917

Roosevelt scenes from RMA productions. 1912

Scenes of TR and his sons Quentin and Archie, 1917–1918 [1] 1917

Scenes of TR and his sons Quentin and Archie, 1917–1918 [2] 1917

[Scenes of TR, Panama Canal construction, and William McKinley] 1901

Scenes of TR speaking at Sagamore [1916–1918] 1916

Shall we prepare? 1916

Short scenes of TR [1] 1916

Short scenes of TR [2] 1912

Short scenes of TR as used in Paramount reel. 1916

Theodore Roosevelt: fighter for social justice. 1934

Theodore Roosevelt, great scout [1] 1925

Theodore Roosevelt, great scout [2] 1925

Theodore Roosevelt, great scout [3] 1925

Theodore Roosevelt in the great war [1] 1930

Theodore Roosevelt in the great war [2] 1930

Theodore Roosevelt in the great war [3] 1930

TR addresses large crowd for the Liberty Loan in Baltimore, 1918. 1918

TR and Cardinal Gibbons at Baltimore, Md., 1918. 1918

TR and Mr. Helm, a newspaper reporter, exterior of Sagamore Hill, 1912. 1912

TR as Father Curran's guest at Wilkes-Barre, Pa., August 10, 1905. 1905

TR at Baltimore [1918]; TR at Sagamore [Hill, 1918] 1918

TR at Billings, Montana [1918] 1918

TR at dedication of Roosevelt Dam, 1911. 1911

TR at Fargo, N.D., during Progressive campaign, 1912 [1] 1912

TR at Fargo, N.D., during Progressive campaign, 1912 [2] 1912

TR at Forest Hills, New York, 1917 [1] 1917

TR at Forest Hills, New York, 1917 [2] 1917

TR at Sagamore, 1917. 1917

TR at Sagamore Hill [1916] 1915

TR at Sagamore Hill [1916–1918] 1916

TR comes back. 1925

TR during Progressive campaign, 1912. 1912

TR greeting crowds of people, 1917–18. 1917

TR in Baltimore during Liberty Loan drive, 1918. 1918

TR in New Mexico, 1916. 1916

TR reviewing and speaking to 13th Regiment at Sagamore Hill, 1917. 1917

TR reviews and addresses troops [Fort Sheridan, Ill.]; TR riding in auto, Chicago, 1917. 1917

TR scenes purchased from different dealers, 1912

TR speaking at Battery Park, New York, June 1910. 1910
TR speaking at Newburgh, N.Y. [1918] 1918
TR speaking at Oyster Bay, July 4, 1916. 1916
TR speaking at [Pueblo] Colorado, 1912. 1912
TR speaking at Sagamore Hill [1916–1918] [1] 1916
TR speaking at Sagamore Hill [1916–1918] [2] 1916
TR speaking at Sagamore Hill [1916–1918 and scenes of his early career] 1897
TR speaking at St. Paul, Minn., 1918. 1918
TR speaking at [St. Paul, Minnesota, 1917] 1917
TR speaking at the Battery, 1910. 1910
TR speaking at the dedication of Roosevelt Dam, 1911. 1911
TR speaking [at the Panama-Pacific Exposition, 1915] 1915
TR speaking during War, 1917–1918. 1917
TR speaking from Cathedral steps, Panama. 1906
TR speaking from train platform, 1912. 1912
TR speaking in Panama, November 1906. 1906
TR speaking in St. Paul, Minnesota, 1918. 1918
TR speaking to a group of men from the porch at Sagamore Hill, 1916. 1916
TR speaking to a group of suffragettes from the porch at Sagamore Hill [1917] 1917
[TR speaks to group at Sagamore Hill, 1] 1917
[TR speaks to group at Sagamore Hill, 2] 1917
[TR speaks to group at Sagamore Hill, 3] 1917
TR wearing army coat standing in auto greeting friends at Oyster Bay, 1910. 1910
TR with group of men, 1917; TR speaking at dedication of Roosevelt Dam, 1911. 1911
TR's arrival in Panama, November 1906 [2] 1906
TR's arrival in Panama, November 1906 [3] 1906
TR's inauguration, 1905 [2] 1905
TR's reception in Albuquerque, N.M., 1916. 1916
TR's return from Africa, 1910 [2] 1925
TR's return to New York, 1910 [1] 1910
TR's return to New York, 1910 [2] 1910
A visit to Theodore Roosevelt at his home at Sagamore Hill, Oyster Bay, L.I., 1912. 1912

Roosevelt, Theodore, Pres. U.S., 1858–1919—Anecdotes
Memorializing Roosevelt. 1925

Roosevelt, Theodore, Pres. U.S., 1858–1919—Birthplace
Dedication of Roosevelt House, 1923. 1923
Dedication of Roosevelt House, Oct. 27, 1923. 1923
Leonard Wood lays cornerstone of Roosevelt House, 1921. 1921
Marshal Foch visits Roosevelt House, 1921. 1921
Moving exhibits into Roosevelt House, 1923. 1923
Woman's Roosevelt Memorial Association meeting at Roosevelt House, 1923 [1] 1923
Woman's Roosevelt Memorial Association meeting at Roosevelt House, 1923 [2] 1923

Roosevelt, Theodore, Pres. U.S., 1858–1919—Cartoons, satire, etc.
Cartoon of TR's reception by crowned heads of Europe. 1910
Cartoon: TR's arrival in Africa. 1909
Roosevelt cartoons. 1910

Roosevelt, Theodore, Pres. U.S., 1858–1919—Childhood and youth
Theodore Roosevelt, great scout [1] 1925

Theodore Roosevelt, great scout [2] 1925
Theodore Roosevelt, great scout [3] 1925

Roosevelt, Theodore, Pres. U.S., 1858–1919—Family
Roosevelt at home: Sagamore Hill, Oyster Bay, L.I. [1] 1930
Roosevelt at home: Sagamore Hill, Oyster Bay, L.I. [2] 1930
Still photographs of TR on motion picture film. 1920
Still picture of TR and his family. 1907
Theodore Roosevelt in the great war [1] 1930
Theodore Roosevelt in the great war [2] 1930
Theodore Roosevelt in the great war [3] 1930
TR attends his son Archie's wedding at Boston, 1917. 1917
TR himself [1] 1926
TR himself [2] 1926
TR himself [3] 1926
TR himself [4] 1926
TR himself [5] 1926
TR himself [6] 1926
TR's funeral at Oyster Bay, 1919. 1919
TR's funeral at Oyster Bay, January 1919 [2] 1919

Roosevelt, Theodore, Pres. U.S., 1858–1919—Funeral and memorial services
Airmen honor TR's memory by dropping American Legion wreath on his grave [1919] 1919
American Legion places wreath on TR's grave [1919]; Scenes of Oyster Bay from the air. 1919
Aviators drop American Legion wreath on TR's grave [1919] 1919
Brooklyn children attend services, children sew stars on Roosevelt Flag [1919] 1919
Children sewing stars on flag, placing flag on TR's grave [1919] 1919
Daniel C. Beard, TR Jr., and Boy Scouts visit TR's grave, 1920. 1920
Dedication of Roosevelt Mountain at Deadwood, S.D., 1919. 1919
Flag at half-mast, Oyster Bay, Jan. 1919. 1919
[Flag services for TR at Oyster Bay, October 1919] 1919
Friends and admirers visit TR's grave, 1920. 1920
Laying cornerstone of Roosevelt School, New Rochelle, N.Y. [1920] 1920
Memorial services for TR at Van Cortlandt Park, New York, Oct. 1919. 1919
Memorial services for TR on the steps of the New York Public Library, 1919 [1] 1919
Memorial services for TR on the steps of the New York Public Library, 1919 [2] 1919
Oyster Bay from the air [1919] 1919
RMA ceremonies at [Hearst Greek Theatre, University of California, Berkeley, Calif.] 1919
RMA flag ceremonies, children sew stars on flag, 1919. 1919
RMA flag service on the steps of New York Public Library, 1919. 1919
RMA pilgrimage to TR's grave, 1930. 1930
RMA services at [Hearst Greek Theatre, University of California, Berkeley, Calif.]; Laying cornerstone of Roosevelt School at New Rochelle, N.Y. [1920] 1920
Roosevelt scenes from RMA productions. 1912
Runners carrying flag to TR's grave [1919] 1919
Scouts on their way to TR's grave, Daniel C. Beard and TR Jr. attend services, 1920. 1920
Theodore Roosevelt, great scout [1] 1925
Theodore Roosevelt, great scout [2] 1925

Theodore Roosevelt in the great war [1] 1930
Theodore Roosevelt in the great war [2] 1930
Theodore Roosevelt in the great war [3] 1930
TR himself [1] 1926
TR himself [2] 1926
TR himself [3] 1926
TR himself [4] 1926
TR himself [5] 1926
TR himself [6] 1926
TR memorial services at New York Public Library, 1919. 1919
TR's funeral, 1919. 1919
TR's funeral at Oyster Bay, 1919. 1919
TR's funeral at Oyster Bay, January 1919 [1] 1919
TR's funeral at Oyster Bay, January 1919 [2] 1919
Whole nation honors memory of Roosevelt. 1919

Roosevelt, Theodore, Pres. U.S. 1858 – 1919—Homes
Dedication of Roosevelt House, 1923. 1923
Dedication of Roosevelt House, Oct. 27, 1923. 1923
Exterior scenes of Sagamore Hill. 1918
Leonard Wood lays cornerstone of Roosevelt House, 1921. 1921
Marshal Foch visits Roosevelt House, 1921. 1921
Moving exhibits into Roosevelt House, 1923. 1923
Roosevelt at home: Sagamore Hill, Oyster Bay, L.I. [1] 1930
Roosevelt at home: Sagamore Hill, Oyster Bay, L.I. [2] 1930
Scenes of Sagamore Hill. 1923
Scenes of TR at Sagamore Hill, 1912. 1912
TR and Mr. Helm, a newspaper reporter, exterior of Sagamore Hill, 1912. 1912
TR on porch at Sagamore Hill, 1917. 1917
TR reviewing and speaking to 13th Regiment at Sagamore Hill, 1917. 1917
A visit to Theodore Roosevelt at his home at Sagamore Hill, Oyster Bay, L.I., 1912. 1912
See also New York (City). Roosevelt House; Oyster Bay, N.Y. Sagamore Hill

Roosevelt, Theodore, Pres. U.S., 1858 – 1919—Inauguration, 1905
President Roosevelt, 1901-1909. 1930
TR speaking at Sagamore Hill [1916-1918 and scenes of his early career] 1897
[TR's inaugural ceremony, 1905] 1905
TR's inauguration, 1905 [1] 1905
TR's inauguration, 1905 [2] 1905

Roosevelt, Theodore, Pres. U.S., 1858 – 1919—Journey to Africa, 1909 – 1910
African natives. 1909
Cartoon: TR's arrival in Africa. 1909
Theodore Roosevelt, great scout [1] 1925
Theodore Roosevelt, great scout [2] 1925
Theodore Roosevelt, great scout [3] 1925
TR in Africa [1909, 1] 1909
TR in Africa [1909, 2] 1909
TR in Africa [1909, 3] 1909
TR in Africa [1909, 4] 1909
[TR planting a tree in Africa] 1909
TR's camp in Africa [1909] 1909

Roosevelt, Theodore, Pres. U.S., 1858-1919—Journey to Europe, 1910
Cartoon of TR's reception by crowned heads of Europe. 1910

TR in Vincennes, France, 1910. 1910
TR reviews French troops at Vincennes, France, 1910. 1910
TR's return from Africa, 1910 [1] 1925
TR's return from Africa, 1910 [2] 1925

Roosevelt, Theodore, Pres. U.S., 1858 – 1919—Journey to Louisiana, 1915
Roosevelt, friend of the birds [1] 1924
Roosevelt, friend of the birds [2] 1924
Roosevelt, friend of the birds [3] 1924
Roosevelt, friend of the birds [4]; The Roosevelt Dam [3] 1928
TR [in Louisiana], 1915 [1] 1915
TR [in Louisiana], 1915 [2] 1915
TR [in Louisiana], 1915 [3] 1915
TR [in Louisiana], 1915 [4] 1915

Roosevelt, Theodore, Pres. U.S., 1858 – 1919—Journey to Norway and Denmark, 1910
TR in Denmark, 1910. 1910
TR in Norway, 1910. 1910
TR in Norway and Denmark, 1910 [1] 1910
TR in Norway and Denmark, 1910 [2] 1910
TR in Norway and Denmark, 1910 [3] 1910

Roosevelt, Theodore, Pres. U.S., 1858 – 1919—Journey to Panama, 1906
TR speaking from Cathedral steps, Panama. 1906
TR speaking in Panama, November 1906. 1906
TR's arrival in Panama, November 1906 [1] 1906
TR's arrival in Panama, November 1906 [2] 1906
TR's arrival in Panama, November 1906 [3] 1906

Roosevelt, Theodore, Pres. U.S., 1858 – 1919—Journey to South America, 1913 – 1914
The River of Doubt [1] 1928
The River of Doubt [2] 1928
The River of Doubt [3] 1928
The River of Doubt [4] 1928
The River of Doubt [5] 1928
The River of Doubt [6] 1928
The River of Doubt [7] 1928
[Scenes of TR, 1913–1915] 1913
[Scenes of TR on board ship, 1916; Scenes of TR's trip to South America, 1913] 1913
Theodore Roosevelt, great scout [1] 1925
Theodore Roosevelt, great scout [2] 1925
Theodore Roosevelt, great scout [3] 1925
TR and expedition party on the [Sepotuba] River [1914] 1914

Roosevelt, Theodore, Pres. U.S., 1858 – 1919—Journey to the West Indies, 1916
Scenes of TR on board ship before sailing for West Indies, 1916. 1916

Roosevelt, Theodore, Pres. U.S., 1858 – 1919—Medals
Mr. Garfield presenting medals to 1929 medalists. 1929
Presentation of Roosevelt Medals, May 1925, Washington, D.C. 1925
Professor Henry Fairfield Osborn, RMA medalist, 1923. 1934
Scenes of Dr. Frank Chapman. 1920

Roosevelt, Theodore, Pres. U.S., 1858–1919—Memorial services

See Roosevelt, Theodore, Pres. U.S., 1858–1919—Funeral and memorial services

Roosevelt, Theodore, Pres. U.S., 1858–1919—Military leadership

Roosevelt scenes [1917–1918] 1917

Shall we prepare? 1916

TR speaking at Sagamore Hill [1916–1918 and scenes of his early career] 1897

Roosevelt, Theodore, Pres. U.S., 1858–1919—Monuments, etc.

Dedication of Cuban memorial, 1924 [1] 1924

Dedication of Cuban memorial, 1924 [2] 1924

Dedication of Roosevelt Mountain at Deadwood, S.D., 1919. 1919

The prize winning design by John Russell Pope for the proposed memorial to Theodore Roosevelt for the city of Washington. 1926

Roosevelt scenes from RMA productions. 1912

See also New York State Theodore Roosevelt Memorial, New York

Roosevelt, Theodore, Pres. U.S., 1858–1919—Personality

Memorializing Roosevelt. 1925

Roosevelt at home: Sagamore Hill, Oyster Bay, L.I. [1] 1930

Roosevelt at home: Sagamore Hill, Oyster Bay, L.I. [2] 1930

Roosevelt cartoons. 1910

TR himself [1] 1926

TR himself [2] 1926

TR himself [3] 1926

TR himself [4] 1926

TR himself [5] 1926

TR himself [6] 1926

Roosevelt, Theodore, Pres. U.S., 1858–1919—Quotations

Memorializing Roosevelt. 1925

Theodore Roosevelt: fighter for social justice. 1934

Theodore Roosevelt in the great war [1] 1930

Theodore Roosevelt in the great war [2] 1930

Theodore Roosevelt in the great war [3] 1930

Roosevelt, Theodore, Pres. U.S., 1858–1919—Tomb

Airmen honor TR's memory by dropping American Legion wreath on his grave [1919] 1919

Children visit TR's grave, 1920. 1920

Close-up of TR's grave, 1920. 1920

Daniel C. Beard, TR Jr., and Boy Scouts visit TR's grave, 1920. 1920

Friends and admirers visit TR's grave, 1920. 1920

General [Diaz] of Italy visits TR's grave [1921] 1921

General Nivelle visits TR's grave [1921] 1921

King Albert of Belgium visits TR's grave, 1919. 1919

King Albert of Belgium visits TR's grave, October, 1919. 1919

The Prince of Wales visits TR's grave. 1919

Roosevelt scenes from RMA productions. 1912

Scouts on their way to TR's grave, Daniel C. Beard and TR Jr. attend services, 1920. 1920

Three children visit TR's grave, 1920. 1920

Roosevelt Dam

President Roosevelt, 1901–1909. 1930

The Roosevelt Dam [1] 1928

The Roosevelt Dam [2] 1928

Roosevelt, friend of the birds [4]; The Roosevelt Dam [3] 1928

Scenes of Roosevelt Dam. 1911

TR at dedication of Roosevelt Dam, 1911. 1911

TR himself [1] 1926

TR himself [3] 1926

TR himself [4] 1926

TR himself [5] 1926

TR himself [6] 1926

TR speaking at the dedication of Roosevelt Dam, 1911. 1911

TR with group of men, 1917; TR speaking at dedication of Roosevelt Dam, 1911. 1911

Roosevelt Dam [3], The [Title]

Roosevelt, friend of the birds [4]; the Roosevelt Dam [3] 1928

Roosevelt family

Roosevelt at home: Sagamore Hill, Oyster Bay, L.I. [1] 1930

Roosevelt at home: Sagamore Hill, Oyster Bay, L.I. [2] 1930

Roosevelt Film Library

See Roosevelt Memorial Association. Film Library

Roosevelt High School, New York (City)

Memorial services for TR at Van Cortlandt Park, New York, Oct. 1919. 1919

Whole nation honors memory of Roosevelt. 1919

Roosevelt House, New York (City)

See New York (City). Roosevelt House

Roosevelt in Africa [Title]

TR in Africa [1909, 2] 1909

TR in Africa [1909, 3] 1909

Roosevelt in the great war [Title]

Theodore Roosevelt in the great war [1] 1930

Theodore Roosevelt in the great war [2] 1930

Theodore Roosevelt in the great war [3] 1930

Roosevelt Medal for Distinguished Service

Mr. Garfield presenting medals to 1929 medalists. 1929

Presentation of Roosevelt Medals, May 1925, Washington, D.C. 1925

Professor Henry Fairfield Osborn, RMA medalist, 1923. 1934

Scenes of Dr. Frank Chapman. 1920

Scenes of Hastings Hart, 1930 medalist. 1930

Roosevelt Memorial, New York (City)

See New York State Theodore Roosevelt Memorial, New York

Roosevelt Memorial, Washington, D.C.

See Washington, D.C. Theodore Roosevelt Memorial

Roosevelt Memorial Association

Brooklyn children attend services, children sew stars on Roosevelt Flag [1919] 1919

The Building of the Panama Canal upon the oocasion of a memorial exhibition held in honor of General George Washington Goethals. 1928

Bulloch home, Roswell, Georgia, 1923. 1923

Col. William Boyce Thompson. 1920

Commander Dyott sailing from [Hoboken, N.J.] for South

America, 1926. 1926

Dedication of Cuban memorial, 1924 [1] 1924

Dedication of Cuban memorial, 1924 [2] 1924

Dedication of Roosevelt House, 1923. 1923

Dedication of Roosevelt House, Oct. 27, 1923. 1923

Dedication of Roosevelt Mountain at Deadwood, S.D., 1919. 1919

Friends and admirers visit TR's grave, 1920. 1920

Memorial services for TR at Van Cortlandt Park, New York, Oct. 1919. 1919

Memorial services for TR on the steps of the New York Public Library, 1919 [1] 1919

Memorial services for TR on the steps of the New York Public Library, 1919 [2] 1919

Memorializing Roosevelt. 1925

Mr. Garfield presenting medals to 1929 medalists. 1929

Mr. Hagedorn and Mr. Akeley at Roosevelt House, 1925 [1] 1925

Mr. Hagedorn and Mr. Akeley at Roosevelt House, 1925 [2] 1925

Mr. Hagedorn and Mr. Akeley at Roosevelt House, 1925 [3] 1925

Mr. Hagedorn and Mrs. Wood at Roosevelt House [1924, Long version] 1924

Mr. Hagedorn and Mrs. Wood at Roosevelt House [1924, Short version]1924

Presentation of Roosevelt Medals, May 1925, Washington, D.C. 1925

President Harding presenting chair used by TR at the White House to the directors of RMA, October 1921. 1921

President Roosevelt, 1901–1909. 1930

The prize winning design by John Russell Pope for the proposed memorial to Theodore Roosevelt for the city of Washington. 1926

The River of Doubt [1] 1928

The River of Doubt [2] 1928

The River of Doubt [3] 1928

The River of Doubt [4] 1928

The River of Doubt [5] 1928

The River of Doubt [6] 1928

The River of Doubt [7] 1928

RMA ceremonies at [Hearst Greek Theatre, University of California, Berkeley, Calif.] 1919

RMA flag ceremonies, children sew stars on flag, 1919. 1919

RMA flag service on the steps of New York Public Library, 1919. 1919

RMA pilgrimage to TR's grave, 1930. 1930

RMA trustees at Roosevelt House, 1923 [1] 1923

RMA trustees at Roosevelt House, 1923 [2] 1923

Roosevelt at home: Sagamore Hill, Oyster Bay, L.I. [1] 1930

Roosevelt at home: Sagamore Hill, Oyster Bay, L.I. [2] 1930

Scenes of Oyster Bay. 1924

Scenes of Sagamore Hill. 1923

Scenes of the River of Doubt photographed by G. M. Dyott, 1926–1927 [1] 1927

Scenes showing Blue Line Tour route to Roosevelt House in 1925. 1925

Theodore Roosevelt: fighter for social justice. 1934

Theodore Roosevelt in the great war [1] 1930

Theodore Roosevelt in the great war [2] 1930

Theodore Roosevelt in the great war [3] 1930

Through the Roosevelt country with Roosevelt's friends. 1919

TR comes back. 1925

TR himself [6] 1926

TR memorial services at New York Public Library, 1919. 1919

TR's return from Africa, 1910 [1] 1925

TR's return from Africa, 1910 [2] 1925

A visit to Theodore Roosevelt at his home at Sagamore Hill, Oyster Bay, L.I., 1912. 1912

Whole nation honors memory of Roosevelt. 1919

Roosevelt Memorial Association, source

The Building of the Panama Canal upon the occasion of a memorial exhibition held in honor of General George Washington Goethals. 1928

Bulloch home, Roswell, Georgia, 1923. 1923

Cartoon of TR's reception by crowned heads of Europe. 1910

Close-up of TR speaking [1917] 1917

Close-up scenes of TR speaking during World War I, 1917–1918. 1917

Dedication of Cuban memorial, 1924 [1] 1924

Dedication of Cuban memorial, 1924 [2] 1924

Dedication of Roosevelt House, 1923. 1923

Dedication of Roosevelt House, Oct. 27, 1923. 1923

Leonard Wood at Battle Creek, Michigan. 1920

Leonard Wood lays cornerstone of Roosevelt House, 1921. 1921

Marshal Foch visits Roosevelt House, 1921. 1921

Memorializing Roosevelt. 1925

Moving exhibits into Roosevelt House, 1923. 1923

Mr. Hagedorn and Mr. Akeley at Roosevelt House, 1925 [1] 1925

Mr. Hagedorn and Mr. Akeley at Roosevelt House, 1925 [2] 1925

Mr. Hagedorn and Mr. Akeley at Roosevelt House, 1925 [3] 1925

Mr. Hagedorn and Mrs. Wood at Roosevelt House [1924, Long version] 1924

Mr. Hagedorn and Mrs. Wood at Roosevelt House [1924, Short version] 1924

Owen D. Young [1] 1927

The Panama Canal. 1927

President Roosevelt, 1901–1909. 1930

The prize winning design by John Russell Pope for the proposed memorial to Theodore Roosevelt for the city of Washington. 1926

The River of Doubt [1] 1928

The River of Doubt [2] 1928

The River of Doubt [3] 1928

The River of Doubt [4] 1928

The River of Doubt [5] 1928

The River of Doubt [6] 1928

The River of Doubt [7] 1928

RMA trustees at Roosevelt House, 1923 [1] 1923

RMA trustees at Roosevelt House, 1923 [2] 1923

Roosevelt at home: Sagamore Hill, Oyster Bay, L.I. [1] 1930

Roosevelt at home: Sagamore Hill, Oyster Bay, L.I. [2] 1930

The Roosevelt Dam [1] 1928

The Roosevelt Dam [2] 1928

Roosevelt, friend of the birds [1] 1924

Roosevelt, friend of the birds [2] 1924

Sarah Bernhardt addresses crowd in Prospect Park, Brooklyn, 1917. 1917

Scenes of Dr. Frank Chapman. 1920

[Scenes of flowers in Washington, D.C.] 1920

Scenes of Oyster Bay. 1924

Scenes of Sagamore Hill. 1923

Scenes of the Capitol, Washington, D.C. 1920

Scenes of the White House. 1920

Scenes of TR and his sons Quentin and Archie, 1917–1918 [2] 1917

Scenes of TR at Sagamore Hill, 1912. 1912

[Scenes of TR, Panama Canal construction, and William McKinley] 1901

Scenes of TR speaking at Sagamore [1916–1918] 1916

Scenes showing Blue Line Tour route to Roosevelt House in 1925. 1925

Short scenes of TR [1] 1916

The Story of the Panama Canal [1] 1927

The Story of the Panama Canal [2] 1927

Theodore Roosevelt: fighter for social justice. 1934

Theodore Roosevelt, great scout [1] 1925

Theodore Roosevelt in the great war [1] 1930

Theodore Roosevelt in the great war [2] 1930

Theodore Roosevelt in the great war [3] 1930

Through the Roosevelt country with Roosevelt's friends. 1919

TR and Mrs. Roosevelt [at the Panama-California Exposition, 1915] 1915

TR at Billings, Montana [1918] 1918

TR at Camp Mills [1917] 1917

TR at Forest Hills, New York, 1917 [1] 1917

TR at Sagamore, 1917. 1917

TR, Charles E. Hughes, and Mayor Mitchel of New York, on reviewing stand in front of the New York Public Library [1917] 1917

TR comes back. 1925

TR greeting crowds of people, 1917–18. 1917

TR himself [1] 1926

TR himself [2] 1926

TR himself [3] 1926

TR himself [4] 1926

TR himself [5] 1926

TR himself [6] 1926

TR in Denmark, 1910. 1910

TR [in Louisiana], 1915 [3] 1915

TR in Norway, 1910. 1910

TR in Vincennes, France, 1910. 1910

TR receiving Belgian envoys at Sagamore Hill [1917] 1917

TR scenes purchased from different dealers. 1912

TR speaking at Newburgh, N.Y. [1918] 1918

TR speaking at the Battery, 1910. 1910

TR speaking [at the Panama-Pacific Exposition, 1915] 1915

TR speaking from train platform, 1912. 1912

[TR speaks to group at Sagamore Hill, 1] 1917

[TR speaks to group at Sagamore Hill, 2] 1917

[TR speaks to group at Sagamore Hill, 3] 1917

TR's return from Africa, 1910 [1] 1925

TR's return from Africa, 1910 [2] 1925

A visit to Theodore Roosevelt at his home at Sagamore Hill, Oyster Bay, L.I., 1912. 1912

Woman's Roosevelt Memorial Association meeting at Roosevelt House, 1923 [1] 1923

Woman's Roosevelt Memorial Association meeting at Roosevelt House, 1923 [2] 1923

Roosevelt Memorial Association. Board of Trustees

Presentation of Roosevelt Medals, May 1925, Washington, D.C. 1925

RMA trustees at Roosevelt House, 1923 [1] 1923

RMA trustees at Roosevelt House, 1923 [2] 1923

Roosevelt Memorial Association. Film Library

The Panama Canal. 1927

The prize winning design by John Russell Pope for the proposed memorial to Theodore Roosevelt for the city of Washington. 1926

The River of Doubt [1] 1928

The River of Doubt [2] 1928

The River of Doubt [3] 1928

The River of Doubt [4] 1928

The River of Doubt [5] 1928

The River of Doubt [7] 1928

Roosevelt at home: Sagamore Hill, Oyster Bay, L.I. [1] 1930

Roosevelt at home: Sagamore Hill, Oyster Bay, L.I. [2] 1930

The Roosevelt Dam [1] 1928

The Roosevelt Dam [2] 1928

Roosevelt, friend of the birds [1] 1924

Roosevelt, friend of the birds [2] 1924

Roosevelt, friend of the birds [3] 1924

Roosevelt, friend of the birds [4]; The Roosevelt Dam [3] 1928

The Story of the Panama Canal [1] 1927

The Story of the Panama Canal [2] 1927

Theodore Roosevelt, great scout [1] 1925

Theodore Roosevelt, great scout [2] 1925

Theodore Roosevelt, great scout [3] 1925

Theodore Roosevelt in the great war [1] 1930

Theodore Roosevelt in the great war [2] 1930

Theodore Roosevelt in the great war [3] 1930

TR himself [1] 1926

TR himself [2] 1926

TR himself [3] 1926

TR himself [4] 1926

TR himself [5] 1926

TR himself [6] 1926

TR's return from Africa, 1910 [1] 1925

TR's return from Africa, 1910 [2] 1925

Roosevelt Memorial Park, Oyster Bay, N.Y.

See Oyster Bay, N.Y.—Parks—Theodore Roosevelt Memorial Park

Roosevelt Monument, S.D.

Dedication or Roosevelt Mountain at Deadwood, S.D., 1919. 1919

Roosevelt Mountain, S.D.

See Mount Roosevelt, S.D.

Roosevelt Non-Partisan League

Scenes of TR speaking at Sagamore [1916–1918] 1916

TR at Sagamore Hill [1916] 1915

TR at Sagamore Hill [1916–1918] 1916

TR speaking at Sagamore Hill [1916–1918] [1] 1916

TR speaking at Sagamore Hill [1916–1918] [2] 1916

TR speaking to a group of men from the porch at Sagamore Hill, 1916. 1916

Roosevelt River

The River of Doubt [1] 1928

The River of Doubt [2] 1928

The River of Doubt [3] 1928

The River of Doubt [4] 1928

The River of Doubt [6] 1928

The River of Doubt [7] 1928

Scenes of the River of Doubt photographed by G.M. Dyott, 1926–1927 [1] 1927

Scenes of the River of Doubt photographed by G.M. Dyott, 1926–1927 [2] 1927

[Scenes of TR on board ship, 1916; Scenes of TR's trip to South America, 1913] 1913

TR and expedition party on the [Sepotuba] River [1914] 1914

Roosevelt-Rondon Scientific Expedition
The River of Doubt [1] 1928
The River of Doubt [2] 1928
The River of Doubt [3] 1928
The River of Doubt [4] 1928
The River of Doubt [5] 1928
The River of Doubt [6] 1928
The River of Doubt [7] 1928
Roosevelt scenes from RMA productions. 1912
Scenes of the River of Doubt photographed by G.M. Dyott, 1926–1927 [1] 1927
TR and expedition party on the [Sepotuba] River [1914] 1914

The Roosevelt series of history and biography, no. 1
TR himself [5] 1926

Roosevelt [Title]
TR at Fargo, N.D., during Progressive campaign, 1912 [1] 1912

Roosevelt's return from Africa [Title]
TR's return from Africa, 1910 [1] 1925
TR's return from Africa, 1910 [2] 1925

Root, Elihu
Elihu Root and Mayor Mitchel of New York, Mr. Root and American delegates return from Russia [1917] 1917
Memorial services for TR on the steps of the New York Public Library, 1919 [1] 1919
Memorial services for TR on the steps of the New York Public Library, 1919 [2] 1919
President McKinley's funeral in Buffalo, Washington, and Canton, Ohio, 1901. 1901
RMA flag service on the steps of New York Public Library, 1919. 1919
RMA trustees at Roosevelt House, 1923 [2] 1923
TR attends McKinley's funeral, 1901. 1901
TR attends McKinley's funeral, Canton, Ohio, 1901. 1901
TR memorial services at New York Public Library, 1919. 1919

Root's Mission to Russia
See United States. Special Diplomatic Mission to Russia

Roque, Saint
See Rochus, Saint, 1295 (ca.)–1327

Roque, San
See Rochus, Saint, 1295 (ca.)–1327

Rosen, Roman Romanovich, baron, 1847–1921
Japanese and Russian peace delegates [leaving New York City], 1905. 1905
TR himself [1] 1926
TR himself [2] 1926
TR himself [3] 1926
TR himself [4] 1926
TR himself [5] 1926
TR himself [6] 1926

Roswell, Ga.
Bulloch home, Roswell, Georgia, 1923. 1923

Roswell, Ga. Bulloch Hall
Bulloch home, Roswell, Georgia, 1923. 1923

Rotary Club, Santiago, Cuba
See Club Rotario de Santiago de Cuba

Rough Riders
See United States. Army. 1st Cavalry (volunteer)

Rough Riders Association
Dedication of Cuban memorial, 1924 [1] 1924
Dedication of Cuban memorial, 1924 [2] 1924

Rough Rider's Hotel, Medora, N.D.
See Medora, N.D. Rough Rider's Hotel

Rowe, Leo S.
President Wilson arrives in New York to lead fourth Liberty Loan parade [1918] 1918

Royal Tern (Launch)
Roosevelt, friend of the birds [1] 1924
Roosevelt, friend of the birds [2] 1924
Roosevelt, friend of the birds [3] 1924
Roosevelt, friend of the birds [4]; The Roosevelt Dam [3] 1928
TR [in Louisiana], 1915 [3] 1915

Roycroft, source
Gifford Pinchot, 1923. 1923

Ruby, photographer
RMA trustees at Roosevelt House, 1923 [1] 1923
RMA trustees at Roosevelt House, 1923 [2] 1923
Scenes of Oyster Bay. 1924
Scenes of Sagamore Hill. 1923

Runey, source
TR attends dinner of Cincinnati, Ohio, Business Men's Club, Dec. 14, 1917 [1] 1917
TR attends dinner of Cincinnati, Ohio, Business Men's Club, Dec. 14, 1917 [2] 1917

Rushmore, Mount
See Mount Rushmore National Memorial

Russia
Czar Nicholas of Russia. 1910

Russia—Foreign relations—United States
Elihu Root and Mayor Mitchel of New York, Mr. Root and American delegates return from Russia [1917] 1917

Russia—History—Nicholas II, 1894–1917
Czar Nicholas of Russia. 1910

Russia—History—Revolution, 1917–1921
Last known home of Czar Nicholas. 1918

Russia—History—Politics and government—1917
Last known home of Czar Nicholas. 1918

Russia, Armiîa
Czar Nicholas of Russia. 1910
Japanese and Russian peace delegates [leaving New York City], 1905. 1905

Russia. Army
See Russia. Armiîa

Russian Army
See Russia. Armiîa

Russo-Japanese War, 1904–1905
Japanese and Russian peace delegates [leaving New York City], 1905. 1905

Ryan, Charles W.
Leonard Wood at Battle Creek, Michigan. 1920

Ryan, James A.
TR reviews and addresses troops [Fort Sheridan, Ill.]; TR riding in auto, Chicago, 1917. 1917

Sagamore Hill, Oyster Bay, N.Y.
See Oyster Bay, N.Y. Sagamore Hill

Sailors' Club, Boston, Mass.
See Naval Service Club, Boston, Mass.

Saint Paul
See St. Paul, Minn.

Saint Vincent's Hospital, Indianapolis
See St. Vincent's Hospital, Indianapolis

Saints—Cartagena, Colombia—Commemoration
Scout parade, Cartagena, Colombia, 1920. 1920

Salt River, Ariz.
President Roosevelt, 1901–1909. 1930
The Roosevelt Dam [1] 1928
The Roosevelt Dam [2] 1928
Roosevelt, friend of the birds [4]; The Roosevelt Dam [3] 1928
Scenes of Roosevelt Dam. 1911
TR at dedication of Roosevelt Dam, 1911. 1911
TR speaking at the dedication of Roosevelt Dam, 1911. 1911
TR with group of men, 1917; TR speaking at dedication of Roosevelt Dam, 1911. 1911

Salt River Valley, Ariz.
The Roosevelt Dam [1] 1928
The Roosevelt Dam [2] 1928
Roosevelt, friend of the birds [4]; The Roosevelt Dam [3] 1928
Scenes of Roosevelt Dam. 1911
TR at dedication of Roosevelt Dam, 1911. 1911
TR speaking at the dedication of Roosevelt Dam, 1911. 1911
TR with group of men, 1917; TR speaking at dedication of Roosevelt Dam, 1911. 1911

Sampson, William Thomas
Admiral Dewey on flagship, 1899. 1899
Admiral Dewey on the deck of flagship, 1899 [1] 1899
Admiral Dewey on the deck of flagship, 1899 [2] 1899

Admiral Dewey parade, 1899 [1] 1899
Admiral Dewey parade, 1899 [2] 1899

San Diego, Calif.
Reviewing Annapolis middies. 1915
TR and Mrs. Roosevelt [at the Panama-California Exposition, 1915] 1915
TR at San Diego Exposition, 1915. 1915

San Diego, Calif.—Exhibitions
Reviewing Annapolis middies. 1915
TR and Mrs. Roosevelt [at the Panama-California Exposition, 1915] 1915
TR at San Diego Exposition, 1915. 1915

San Diego, Calif.—Plazas—Plaza de Panama
Reviewing Annapolis middies. 1915

San Diego Exposition
See Panama-California Exposition, 1915–1916

San Francisco
President Roosevelt, 1901–1909. 1930
[Scenes of TR, 1913–1915] 1913
Theodore Roosevelt in the great war [1] 1930
Theodore Roosevelt in the great war [2] 1930
Theodore Roosevelt in the great war [3] 1930
TR [at Panama-Pacific Exposition, 1915] 1915
TR at Sagamore Hill [1916] 1915
TR in San Francisco, 1903. 1903
TR speaking [at the Panama-Pacific Exposition, 1915] 1915
William H. Taft burns mortgage of Exposition, 1915. 1915

San Francisco—Exhibitions
[Scenes of TR, 1913–1915] 1913
TR [at Panama-Pacific Exposition, 1915] 1915
TR speaking [at the Panama-Pacific Exposition, 1915] 1915
William H. Taft burns mortgage of Exposition, 1915. 1915

San Francisco—Plazas—Court of the Universe
TR at Sagamore Hill [1916] 1915
TR speaking [at the Panama-Pacific Exposition, 1915] 1915
William H. Taft burns mortgage of Exposition, 1915. 1915

San Francisco—Streets—Van Ness Avenue
TR in San Francisco, 1903. 1903

San Francisco. Cathedral of St. Mary. Van Ness Ave. and O'Farrell Street
See St. Mary's Cathedral, San Francisco

San Francisco. Panama-Pacific International Exposition, 1915
See Panama-Pacific International Exposition, 1915

San Francisco. St. Mary's Cathedral. Van Ness Ave. and O'Farrell Street
See St. Mary's Cathedral, San Francisco

San Juan Hill, Battle of, 1898
Dedication of Cuban memorial, 1924 [1] 1924
Dedication of Cuban memorial, 1924 [2] 1924

Sandy Hook, N.J.
Disappearing gun at testing grounds, Sandy Hook, 1898. 1898

Sandy Hook Proving Ground, N.J.
See United States. Sandy Hook Proving Ground, N.J.

Santiago, Cuba
See Santiago de Cuba

Santiago de Cuba
Dedication of Cuban memorial, 1924 [1] 1924
Dedication of Cuban Memorial, 1924 [2] 1924
Wreck of the "Vizcaya." 1898

Santiago de Cuba—Monuments
Dedication of Cuban memorial, 1924 [1] 1924
Dedication of Cuban memorial, 1924 [2] 1924
Roosevelt scenes from RMA productions. 1912

Santiago de Cuba—Parks
Dedication of Cuban memorial, 1924 [1] 1924
Dedication of Cuban memorial, 1924 [2] 1924

Saxton, Ida
See McKinley, Ida Saxton

Scenes of Oyster Bay from the air [Title]
American Legion places wreath on TR's grave [1919]; Scenes of Oyster Bay from the air. 1919

Scenes of TR's trip to South America, 1913 [Title]
[Scenes of TR on board ship, 1916; Scenes of TR's trip to South America, 1913] 1913

Schools
Laying cornerstone of Roosevelt School, New Rochelle, N.Y. [1920] 1920
RMA services at [Hearst Greek Theatre, University of California, Berkeley, Calif.]; Laying cornerstone of Roosevelt School at New Rochelle, N.Y. [1920] 1920

Scientific expeditions
Commander Dyott sailing from [Hoboken, N.J.] for South America, 1926. 1926
[Scenes of TR on board ship, 1916; Scenes of TR's trip to South America, 1913] 1913
Tr and expedition party on the [Sepotuba] River [1914] 1914

Scissors bill
See Black skimmer

Scott, Hugh L.
Elihu Root and Mayor Mitchel of New York, Mr. Root and American delegates return from Russia [1917] 1917

Scouts and scouting
Theodore Roosevelt, great scout [1] 1925
Theodore Roosevelt, great scout [2] 1925
Theodore Roosevelt, great scout [3] 1925

Screen telegram [Series]
Mrs. Theodore Roosevelt Jr. attends Women in War Work Congress in Paris [1918] 1918

Seamen
Short scenes of TR [2] 1912
TR Jr. with group of sailors and soldiers. 1919

TR with naval officers, exterior Navy Club, Boston [1918] 1918

Seattle post-intelligencer
Americanism wins, Coolidge elected. 1919

Second Company Governor's Foot Guards
See Connecticut. Governor's Foot Guards, Second Company, New Haven

Selznick news [Series]
Senator Hiram Johnson. 1922
Senator Watson. 1921

Selznick Pictures Corporation
Senator Hiram Johnson. 1922
Senator Watson. 1921

Senate Office Building, Washington, D.C.
See Washington, D.C. Capitol. Senate Office Building

Sepotuba River
The River of Doubt [1] 1928
The River of Doubt [2] 1928
The River of Doubt [4] 1928
The River of Doubt [5] 1928
The River of Doubt [7] 1928
TR and expedition party on the [Sepotuba] River [1914] 1914

Sepulchral monuments—Belgium
The King and Queen of Belgium and Premier Poincaré of France [1] 1927
The King and Queen of Belgium and Premier Poincaré of France [2] 1927

Seton, Ernest T.
Daniel C. Beard and Ernest T. Seton. 1900

Seventh Regiment Band, New York (State)
See New York Infantry. 7th Regiment, 1806–1922 (Militia). Band

Seville
King and Queen of Spain attend a military review. 1920

Shaw, Albert
Presentation of Roosevelt Medals, May 1925, Washington, D.C. 1925
President Harding presenting chair used by TR at the White House to the directors of RMA, October 1921. 1921

Sheep Mountain, S.D.
See Mount Roosevelt, S.D.

Sheridan, Fort, Ill.
See Fort Sheridan

Sherrill, Charles Hitchcock
TR, Charles E. Hughes, and Mayor Mitchel of New York, on reviewing stand in front of the New York Public Library [1917] 1917

Shippy, William H.
Leonard Wood at Battle Creek, Michigan. 1920

Ships
  Admiral Dewey on the deck of flagship, 1899 [1] 1899
  Admiral Dewey on the deck of flagship, 1899 [2] 1899
  Commander Dyott sailing from [Hoboken, N.J.] for South America, 1926. 1926
  Japanese and Russian peace delegates [leaving New York City], 1905. 1905
  Panama Canal; scenes of the finished Canal. 1919
  [Scenes of TR, 1913–1915] 1913
  Ships in the Panama Canal [1] 1910
  Ships in the Panama Canal [2] 1910
  TR comes back, 1925
  TR on reception yacht in New York Bay, 1910. 1910
  TR's return to New York, 1910 [1] 1910
  TR's return to New York, 1910 [2] 1910
  William H. Taft in Panama [1910?] 1910
  See also Boats and boating; Steamboats; Warships; Yachts and yachting; Particular names of ships, e.g., Vandyck

Ships—Launching
  Launch, U.S. battleship "Kentucky." 1898
  TR speaking at Newburgh, N.Y. [1918] 1918

Shipyards
  TR speaking at Newburgh, N.Y. [1918] 1918

Siboney, Cuba
  Dedication of Cuban memorial, 1924 [1] 1924

Sidar (Horse)
  Roosevelt at home: Sagamore Hill, Oyster Bay, L.I. [1] 1930
  Roosevelt at home: Sagamore Hill, Oyster Bay, L.I. [2] 1930
  Scenes of TR at Sagamore Hill, 1912. 1912
  TR and Mr. Helm, a newspaper reporter, exterior of Sagamore Hill, 1912. 1912
  A visit to Theodore Roosevelt at his home at Sagamore Hill, Oyster Bay, L.I., 1912. 1912

Sightseeing business
  Scenes showing Blue Line Tour route to Roosevelt House in 1925. 1925

Sloan, Richard E.
  The Roosevelt Dam [1] 1928
  The Roosevelt Dam [2] 1928
  TR at dedication of Roosevelt Dam, 1911. 1911
  TR speaking at the dedication of Roosevelt Dam, 1911. 1911
  TR with group of men, 1917; TR speaking at dedication of Roosevelt Dam, 1911. 1911

Smith, Charles Emory, 1842–1908
  President McKinley's funeral in Buffalo, Washington, and Canton, Ohio, 1901. 1901
  TR attends McKinley's funeral, 1901. 1901
  TR attends McKinley's funeral, Canton, Ohio, 1901. 1901

Smoot, Reed
  Senator Smoot. 1920

Snake-dance
  Hopi Indians dance for TR at [Walpi, Ariz.] 1913. 1913

Society of Black Hills Pioneers
  Dedication of Roosevelt Mountain at Deadwood, S.D., 1919. 1919

Soldiers
  Allied armies in China, 1917–1918. 1918
  American Legion lays cornerstone of Roosevelt Bridge at Château-Thierry. 1921
  Street scenes in Naples, Italy. 1910
  Tr at Camp Mills [1917] 1917
  TR Jr. with group of sailors and soldiers. 1919
  TR reviewing and speaking to 13th Regiment at Sagamore Hill, 1917. 1917
  TR's sons' regiments during war, 1917–1918 [1] 1918
  TR's sons' regiments during war, 1917–1918 [2] 1918

Soldiers—Cuba
  Spanish Mountain Artillery, 1898. 1898

Soldiers' monuments—Belgium
  The King and Queen of Belgium and Premier Poincaré of France [1] 1927
  The King and Queen of Belgium and Premier Poincaré of France [2] 1927

South America
  [Scenes of TR on board ship, 1916; Scenes of TR's trip to South America, 1913] 1913

South American Trip
  See Roosevelt-Rondon Scientific Expedition

South Carolina (Ship)
  TR comes back. 1925
  TR's return to New York, 1910 [2] 1910

South Dakota. Governor, 1917–1921 (Norbeck)
  Dedication of Roosevelt Mountain at Deadwood, S.D., 1919. 1919

Southworth, Charles S.
  Calvin Coolidge sworn in for second term as Governor of Massachusetts. 1920

Spain—History—War of 1898
  See United States—History—War of 1898

Spain. Army
  See Spain. Ejército

Spain. Ejército. Artillería
  Spanish Mountain Artillery, 1898. 1898

Spanish-American War, 1898
  See United States—History—War of 1898

Spider webs
  Scenes of the River of Doubt photographed by G. M. Dyott, 1926–1927 [1] 1927

Spillways
  Panama Canal; scenes of the finished Canal. 1919

Spirit of St. Louis (Airplane)
  Colonel Lindbergh, Admiral Byrd, and Clarence Chamberlin at flying field just before Lindbergh's flight, 1927. 1927

Spooner, John C.
  [TR's inaugural ceremony, 1905] 1905

TR's inauguration, 1905 [1] 1905
TR's inauguration, 1905 [2] 1905

Springfield, Ill.
Roosevelt scenes [1917–1918] 1917
Short scenes of TR [1] 1916
TR himself [1] 1926
TR himself [2] 1926
TR himself [3] 1926
TR himself [4] 1926
TR himself [5] 1926
TR himself [6] 1926

Sprinkle, William
Roosevelt, friend of the birds [1] 1924
Roosevelt, friend of the birds [2] 1924
Roosevelt, friend of the birds [3] 1924
Roosevelt, friend of the birds [4]; The Roosevelt Dam [3] 1928
TR [in Louisiana], 1915 [1] 1915

Squares, Public
See Plazas

St. Louis, Mo. Lambert Field
See Kinloch, Mo. Lambert Field

St. Margaret's Church, London
See Westminster, Eng. St. Margaret's Church

St. Mary's Cathedral, San Francisco
TR in San Francisco, 1903. 1903

St. Paul, Minn.
Close-up of TR speaking [1917] 1917
Roosevelt scenes [1917–1918] 1917
Theodore Roosevelt in the great war [1] 1930
Theodore Roosevelt in the great war [2] 1930
Theodore Roosevelt in the great war [3] 1930
TR in St. Paul, Minn. [1917] 1917
TR speaking at St. Paul, Minn. 1918. 1918
TR speaking at [St. Paul, Minnesota, 1917] 1917
TR speaking in St. Paul, Minnesota, 1918. 1918

St. Vincent's Hospital, Indianapolis
Governor Goodrich of Indiana. 1918

Stadia
President McKinley reviewing the troops at the Pan-American Exposition. 1901

Stadium, Buffalo
See Buffalo. Stadium

Stahlnecker, P. Stephen
Gifford Pinchot, 1923. 1923

Stamford, Conn.
Short scenes of TR [1] 1916
TR, Mayor Mitchel and guests at Cooper Sanitarium [1917] 1917

State, War and Navy Building, Washington, D.C.
See Washington, D.C. State, War and Navy Building

State House, Boston, Mass.
See Boston, Mass. Old State House

State Inaugural Committee
See United States. Congress. Committee on Inaugural Ceremonies

Statesmen—Great Britain
Lord and Lady Bryce. 1910

Statler Hotel, Detroit
See Detroit. Hotel Statler

Statues
See Monuments
See also names of individual statues and subdivision Statues under names of cities.

Steamboats
Scenes of TR on board ship before sailing for West Indies, 1916. 1916

Steel workers
Charles E. Hughes speaking during campaign, Duquesne, Pa., 1916. 1916

Stickney, Victor H.
Through the Roosevelt country with Roosevelt's friends. 1919

Stineman, Ralph P.
Reviewing Annapolis middies. 1915
TR at San Diego Exposition, 1915. 1915

Stingless bees
Scenes of the River of Doubt photographed by G. M. Dyott, 1926–1927 [1] 1927

Storks
Scenes of the River of Doubt photographed by G. M. Dyott, 1926–1927 [1] 1927

Straus, Oscar S.
Elihu Root and Mayor Mitchel of New York, Mr. Root and American delegates return from Russia [1917] 1917
Oscar Straus. 1910
President Harding presenting chair used by TR at the White House to the directors of RMA, October 1921. 1921
TR's funeral at Oyster Bay, 1919. 1919

Straus, Roger, source
Oscar Straus, 1910

Straus, Sara L.
Friends and admirers visit TR's grave, 1920. 1920
Woman's Roosevelt Memorial Association meeting at Roosevelt House, 1923 [1] 1923
Woman's Roosevelt Memorial Association meeting at Roosevelt House, 1923 [2] 1923

Street names
Streets are entered under names of cities, e.g., Washington, D.C.—Streets; individual streets located in particular cities are further subdivided by names, e.g., Washington, D.C.—Streets—Pennsylvania Avenue.

Stripe, F. C., source

Americanism wins, Coolidge elected. 1919

Calvin Coolidge sworn in for second term as Governor of Massachusetts. 1920

Col William Boyce Thompson. 1920

General Pershing at Camp Grant. 1920

Governors of New England meet in Governor Coolidge's office in Boston to discuss fuel. 1919

King Edward's funeral, 1910 [1] 1910

Major General Wm. C. Gorgas. 1910

[Man speaking at Faneuil Hall, Boston] 1910

Senator Hiram Johnson. 1922

Senator Hitchcock. 1910

Senator McCumber of North Dakota. 1920

Senator Penrose. 1910

Senator Pomerene. 1910

Senator Smoot. 1920

Senator Watson. 1921

Senators Curtis, Cummins, Moses, and [Representative] Mondell. 1919

Speaker of the House F. H. Gillett. 1919

[Unidentified man] 1910

Will Hays. 1920

Students

Still pictures of TR at [Cambridge] 1910. 1910

Suffrage

Women suffragettes visit TR at Sagamore [1917] 1917

See also Women—Suffrage

Suffrage—New York (State)

Scenes of TR speaking at Sagamore [1916–1918] 1916

TR scenes purchased from different dealers. 1912

TR speaking at Sagamore Hill [1916–1918] [1] 1916

TR speaking at Sagamore Hill [1916–1918] [2] 1916

TR speaking to a group of suffragettes from the porch at Sagamore Hill [1917] 1917

Women suffragettes visit TR at Sagamore [1917] 1917

Sullivan, Lewis R.

Calvin Coolidge sworn in for second term as Governor of Massachusetts. 1920

Sullivan, Mark

Presentation of Roosevelt Medals, May 1925, Washington, D. C. 1925

President Harding presenting chair used by TR at the White House to the directors of RMA, October 1921. 1921

Suspension bridges

See Bridges, Suspension

Sverdlovsk, Russia

Allied armies in China, 1917–1918. 1918

Last known home of Czar Nicholas. 1918

Sweden—Kings and rulers

King Gustav of Sweden greeted by his people. 1920

Sweden—Queens

King Gustav of Sweden greeted by his people. 1920

Swine—Africa

Scenes of African animals [1911] 1911

T. Roosevelt Memorial Park

See Oyster Bay, N. Y.—Parks—Theodore Roosevelt Memorial Park

Taft, Helen Herron

William H. Taft in Panama [1910?] 1910

Taft, William Howard, Pres. U. S., 1857–1930

The Panama Canal. 1927

Roosevelt scenes from RMA productions. 1912

The Story of the Panama Canal [2] 1927

TR's funeral, 1919. 1919

TR's funeral at Oyster Bay, January 1919 [1] 1919

TR's funeral at Oyster Bay, January 1919 [2] 1919

William H. Taft burns mortgage of Exposition, 1915. 1915

Taft, William Howard, Pres. U. S., 1857–1930—Addresses, essays, lectures

President McKinley's memorial dedicated by William Howard Taft at Niles, Ohio. 1917

William Howard Taft on rear platform of train. 1908

Taft, William Howard, Pres. U. S., 1857–1930—Journey to Panama, 1910

William H. Taft in Panama [1910?] 1910

Takahira, Kogoro

TR himself [1] 1926

TR himself [2] 1926

TR himself [3] 1926

TR himself [4] 1926

TR himself [5] 1926

TR himself [6] 1926

Talmadge, George E.

TR's funeral at Oyster Bay, 1919. 1919

TR's funeral at Oyster Bay, January 1919 [2] 1919

Tana River

African animals. 1909

TR in Africa [1909, 3] 1909

Tardieu, André

[Quentin Roosevelt]; Clemenceau and Foch, 1917–1919. 1918

Teddy bears

Still pictures of TR at [Cambridge] 1910. 1910

Temperance societies

TR as Father Curran's guest at Wilkes-Barre, Pa., August 10, 1905. 1905

TR at Wilkes-Barre, Pa., 1905. 1905

TR at Wilkes-Barre, Pa., 1905. 1905

Tennessee (Ship)

William H. Taft in Panama [1910?] 1910

Terns

Roosevelt, friend of the birds [1] 1924

Roosevelt, friend of the birds [2] 1924

Roosevelt, friend of the birds [3] 1924
Roosevelt, friend of the birds [4]; The Roosevelt Dam [3] 1928
TR [in Louisiana], 1915 [1] 1915

Theodore Roosevelt Association
See Roosevelt Memorial Association; Women's Theodore Roosevelt Memorial Association

Theodore Roosevelt, friend of the birds [Title]
Roosevelt, friend of the birds [1] 1924
Roosevelt, friend of the birds [2] 1924

Theodore Roosevelt High School, New York (City)
See Roosevelt High School, New York (City)

Theodore Roosevelt Memorial, New York (City)
See New York State Theodore Roosevelt Memorial, New York

Theodore Roosevelt Memorial, Washington, D. C.
See Washington, D. C. Theodore Roosevelt Memorial

Theodore Roosevelt Memorial Park
See Oyster Bay, N. Y.—Parks—Theodore Roosevelt Memorial Park

Theodore Roosevelt [Title]
A visit to Theodore Roosevelt at his home at Sagamore Hill, Oyster Bay, L. I.,1912. 1912

Thomas A. Edison, inc.
See Edison (Thomas A.) inc.

Thompson, William Boyce
Col. William Boyce Thompson. 1920
Memorial services for TR on the steps of the New York Public Library, 1919 [1] 1919
Memorial services for TR on the steps of the New York Public Library, 1919 [2] 1919
President Harding presenting chair used by TR at the White House to the directors of RMA, October 1921. 1921
RMA flag service on the steps of New York Public Library, 1919. 1919
TR memorial services at New York Public Library, 1919. 1919

Thomson, Ga.
Senator Watson. 1921

Thomson, Ga. Hickory Hill
Senator Watson. 1921

Tirpitz, Alfred Peter Friedrich Von
Kaiser Wilhelm and his admiralty staff attend launching at Kiel. 1910

Tittoni, Tommaso
The King of Italy entertains King Edward of England on his yacht. 1907

Tombs
Children visit TR's grave, 1920. 1920
Close-up of TR's grave, 1920. 1920
Friends and admirers visit TR's grave, 1920. 1920

Quentin Roosevelt's grave, 1918. 1919
Quentin Roosevelt's grave in France. 1919
Three children visit TR's grave, 1920. 1920

Tombs—Belgium
The King and Queen of Belgium and Premier Poincaré of France [1] 1927
The King and Queen of Belgium and Premier Poincaré of France [2] 1927

Tompkinsville, N. Y.
Admiral Dewey on flagship, 1899. 1899
Admiral Dewey on the deck of flagship, 1899 [1] 1899
Admiral Dewey on the deck of flagship, 1899 [2] 1899

Towing
Ships in the Panama Canal [1] 1910

TR at Sagamore [Hill, 1918] [Title]
TR at Baltimore [1918]; TR at Sagamore [Hill, 1918] 1918

TR riding in auto, Chicago, 1917 [Title]
TR reviews and addresses troops [Fort Sheridan, Ill.]; TR riding in auto, Chicago, 1917. 1917

TR speaking at dedication of Roosevelt Dam, 1911 [Title]
TR with group of men, 1917; TR speaking at dedication of Roosevelt Dam, 1911. 1911

Trade-unions—Miners
TR as Father Curran's guest at Wilkes-Barre, Pa., August 10, 1905. 1905

Trails—Cuba
Pack mules with ammunition on the Santiago trail, Cuba. 1898

Transatlantic flights
Colonel Lindbergh, Admiral Byrd, and Clarence Chamberlin at flying field just before Lindbergh's flight, 1927. 1927

Transportation, Military
Pack mules with ammunition on the Santiago trail, Cuba. 1898
Spanish Mountain Artillery, 1898. 1898
Troops making military road in front of Santiago. 1898

Treat, John J.
TR, Mayor Mitchel and guests at Cooper Sanitarium [1917] 1917

Tree planting—Kenya
TR in Africa [1909, 1] 1909
TR in Africa [1909, 2] 1909
TR in Africa [1909, 4] 1909
[TR planting a tree in Africa] 1909

Trees
Roosevelt at home: Sagamore Hill, Oyster Bay, L. I. [1] 1930
Roosevelt at home: Sagamore Hill, Oyster Bay, L. I. [2] 1930

Trinacria (Ship)
The King of Italy entertains King Edward of England on his yacht. 1907

Trolley buses—Los Angeles, Calif.
TR riding in auto through crowded streets [1912] 1912

Troop A, Ohio National Guard
See Ohio. National Guard. Troop A

Trust companies
President Roosevelt, 1901–1909. 1930

Turret ships
International naval review, Hampton Roads, Virginia, 1907.
1907

Turtles—Brazil
Scenes of the River of Doubt photographed by G. M. Dyott,
1926–1927 [2] 1927

Tusayan Indians
See Hopi Indians

U. S. troops landing at Baiquiri, Cuba [Title]
U. S. troops landing at Daiquiri, Cuba. 1898

Uniforms, Military
Governor's Foot Guards, Conn. 1899

Union League Club, New York (City)
See New York (City). Union League Club

United Mine Workers of America
TR as Father Curran's guest at Wilkes-Barre, Pa., August
10, 1905. 1905

United Spanish War Veterans
Airmen honor TR's memory by dropping American Legion
wreath on his grave [1919] 1919
American Legion places wreath on TR's grave [1919]; Scenes
of Oyster Bay from the air. 1919
Aviators drop American Legion wreath on TR's grave [1919]
1919

United States—Armed Forces
Return of Spanish-American troops, 1898. 1898
See also United States. Army Air Forces; United States. Army;
United States. Marine Corps

United States—Foreign relations—Russia
Elihu Root and Mayor Mitchel of New York, Mr. Root and
American delegates return from Russia [1917] 1917

United States—Government
See United States—History—Politics and government

United States—Government buildings
See United States—Public buildings

United States—History—War of 1898
25th Infantry. 1898
Governor's Foot Guards, Conn. 1899
Return of Spanish-American troops, 1898. 1898
TR at Camp Mills [1917] 1917
Troops making military road in front of Santiago. 1898
U. S. battleship "Oregon." 1898

U. S. troops landing at Daiquiri, Cuba. 1898
Wreck of the "Vizcaya." 1898

United States—History—War of 1898—Afro-American troops
25th Infantry. 1898

United States—History—War of 1898—Campaigns and battles
Dedication of Cuban memorial, 1924 [1] 1924
Dedication of Cuban memorial, 1924 [2] 1924

United States—History—War of 1898—Naval operations
Wreck of the "Vizcaya." 1898

United States—History—War of 1898—Supplies
Pack mules with ammunition on the Santiago trail, Cuba.
1898

United States—History—European War, 1914–1918
See European War, 1914–1918

United States—History, Naval—20th century
TR reviews the fleet, 1907. 1907

United States—Politics and government—1901–1909
President Roosevelt, 1901–1909. 1930

United States—Politics and government—1913–1921
Chauncey Depew, Senator Perkins, and Governor Whitman
of New York, at GOP Convention, 1916, Chicago, Ill. 1916

United States—Politics and government—1919–1933
General Wood and Calvin Coolidge in Chicago, 1920. 1920
President Harding and Calvin Coolidge [1] 1920
President Harding and Calvin Coolidge [2] 1920

Untied States—Public buildings
Herbert Putnam. 1920
Original U.S. documents. 1920
Scenes of the Capitol, Washington, D.C. 1920
Scenes of the White House. 1920
Senator Hitchcock. 1910
Senator McCumber of North Dakota. 1920
Senator Penrose. 1910
See also Washington, D.C. Capitol; Washington, D.C. White
House; United States. Treasury Dept.—Buildings

United States—Public buildings—Balboa, Canal Zone
Panama Canal; scenes of the finished Canal. 1919

United States—Public lands
The Roosevelt Dam [1] 1928
The Roosevelt Dam [2] 1928

United States—Social conditions—1865–1918
President Roosevelt, 1901–1909. 1930

United States. Air Service
See United States. Army Air Forces

United States. American Diplomatic Mission to Russia
See United States. Special Diplomatic Mission to Russia

United States. American Mission to Russia
See United States. Special Diplomatic Mission to Russia

245

United States. Army
American Legion lays cornerstone of Roosevelt Bridge at Château-Thierry. 1921
President McKinley's funeral, 1901 [1] 1901
President McKinley's funeral, 1901 [2] 1901
President McKinley's funeral in Buffalo, Washington, and Canton, Ohio, 1901. 1901
President McKinley's inauguration, 1901 [2] 1901
Quentin Roosevelt's grave, 1918. 1919
Quentin Roosevelt's grave in France. 1919
Return of Spanish-American troops, 1898. 1898
TR, Charles E. Hughes, and Mayor Mitchel of New York, on reviewing stand in front of the New York Public Library [1917] 1917
TR reviewing and speaking to 13th Regiment at Sagamore Hill, 1917. 1917
TR reviews and addresses troops [Fort Sheridan, Ill.]; TR riding in auto, Chicago, 1917. 1917
Troops making military road in front of Santiago. 1898
U.S. troops landing at Daiquiri, Cuba. 1898

United States—Army—Officers
Gen. Pershing speaking to Scouts in New York. 1919
[Quentin Roosevelt]; Clemenceau and Foch, 1917–1919. 1918
Robert Bacon and Army officers. 1918
[Scenes of TR, 1913–1915] 1913
TR [at Panama-Pacific Exposition, 1915] 1915

United States. Army. 1st Cavalry (Volunteer)
Dedication of Cuban memorial, 1924 [1] 1924
Dedication of Cuban memorial, 1924 [2] 1924
Rough Riders greet TR during Liberty Loan drive out west [1918] 1918
TR comes back. 1925
TR speaking at Battery Park, New York, June 1910. 1910
TR with Rough Rider friends. 1910
[TR's inaugural ceremony, 1905] 1905
TR's inauguration, 1905 [1] 1905
TR's reception in Albuquerque, N.M., 1916. 1916
TR's return to New York, 1910 [1] 1910
TR's return to New York, 1910 [2] 1910

United States. Army. 6th Division
General Pershing at Camp Grant. 1920

United States. Army. 7th Field Artillery
TR's sons' regiments during war, 1917–1918 [1] 1918

United States. Army. 9th Cavalry
TR in San Francisco, 1903. 1903
See also Afro-American soldiers

United States. Army. 25th Infantry
25th Infantry. 1898
See also Afro-American soldiers

United States. Army. 26th Infantry
TR's sons' regiments during war, 1917–1918 [1] 1918
TR's son's regiments during war, 1917–1918 [2] 1918

United States. Army. 69th Infantry
See United States. Army. 165th Infantry

United States. Army. 95th Aero Squadron
Theodore Roosevelt in the great war [1] 1930
Theodore Roosevelt in the great war [2] 1930
Theodore Roosevelt in the great war [3] 1930
TR's sons' regiments during war, 1917–1918 [1] 1918

United States. Army. 165th Infantry
TR at Camp Mills [1917] 1917

United States. Army. A.E.F., 1917–1920
Theodore Roosevelt in the great war [1] 1930
Theodore Roosevelt in the great war [2] 1930
Theodore Roosevelt in the great war [3] 1930

United States. Army. Air Forces
See United States. Army Air Forces

United States. Army. Air Service
See United States. Army Air Forces

United States. Army. Cavalry
TR's inauguration, 1905 [1] 1905

United States. Army. Cavalry—History
TR in San Francisco, 1903. 1903

United States. Army. Infantry—Drill and tactics
15th Infantry leaving Governors Island for China (Boxer Uprising) 1900. 1900

United States. Army. Signal Corps
Robert Bacon and Army officers. 1918

United States. Army. Signal Corps, source
Lord and Lady Bryce. 1910
[Quentin Roosevelt]; Clemenceau and Foch, 1917–1919. 1918
Robert Bacon and Army officers. 1918
[Scenes of the British royal family] 1918
TR's sons' regiments during war, 1917–1918 [1] 1918
TR's sons' regiments during war, 1917–1918 [2] 1918

United States. Army. Signal Corps. Army Pictorial Service, source
Scenes of TR and his sons Quentin and Archie, 1917–1918 [1] 1917

United States. Army Air Forces
Airmen honor TR's memory by dropping American Legion wreath on his grave [1919] 1919
American Legion places wreath on TR's grave [1919]; Scenes of Oyster Bay from the air. 1919
Aviators drop American Legion wreath on TR's grave [1919] 1919
Oyster Bay from the air [1919] 1919

United States. Army Air Forces, source
TR speaking at [St. Paul, Minnesota, 1917] 1917

United States. Bureau of Reclamation
The Roosevelt Dam [1] 1928
The Roosevelt Dam [2] 1928

United States. Bureau of Reclamation, source
Hopi Indians dance for TR at [Walip, Ariz.] 1913. 1913
TR speaking at Sagamore Hill [1916–1918] [2] 1916

United States. Coast Artillery
President McKinley reviewing the troops at the Pan-American Exposition. 1901

United States. Congress. Committee on Inaugural Ceremonies
[TR's inaugural ceremony, 1905] 1905
TR's inauguration, 1905 [1] 1905
TR's inauguration, 1905 [2] 1905

United States. Congress. House
Speaker of the House F. H. Gillett. 1919

United States. Congress. Joint Committee on Inaugural Ceremonies
See United States. Congress. Committee on Inaugural Ceremonies

United States. Congress. Senate. Office Building
See Washington, D.C. Capitol. Senate Office Building

United States. Constitution
Original U.S. documents. 1920

United States. Constitution—Signers
Original U.S. documents. 1920

United States. Corps of Marines
See United States. Marine Corps

United States. Declaration of independence
Original U.S. documents. 1920

United States. Dept. of Agriculture, source
Ships in the Panama Canal [1] 1910

United States. Dept. of State
Original U.S. documents, 1920

United States. Laws, statutes, etc. Liberty loan acts
President Wilson arrives in New York to lead fourth Liberty Loan parade [1918] 1918
Roosevelt scenes [1917–1918] 1917
Roosevelt scenes from RMA productions, 1912
Rough Riders greet TR during Liberty Loan drive out west [1918] 1918
Scenes of TR speaking at Sagamore [1916–1918] 1916
Short scenes of TR as used in Paramount reel. 1916
Theodore Roosevelt in the great war [1] 1930
Theodore Roosevelt in the great war [2] 1930
Theodore Roosevelt in the great war [3] 1930
TR addresses large crowd for the Liberty Loan in Baltimore, 1918. 1918
TR and Cardinal Gibbons at Baltimore, Md., 1918. 1918
TR at Baltimore [1918]; TR at Sagamore [Hill, 1918] 1918
TR at Billings, Montana [1918] 1918
TR at Sagamore Hill [1916–1918] 1916
TR in Baltimore during Liberty Loan drive, 1918. 1918
TR scenes purchased from different dealers. 1912
TR speaking at Sagamore Hill [1916–1918] [1] 1916
TR speaking at Sagamore Hill [1916–1918] [2] 1916

TR speaking at Sagamore Hill [1916–1918 and scenes of his early career] 1897

United States. Library of Congress
Herbert Putnam. 1920
Memorializing Roosevelt. 1925

United States. Marine Corps
President McKinley reviewing the troops at the Pan-American Exposition. 1901
President McKinley's funeral, 1901 [1] 1901
President McKinley's funeral, 1901 [2] 1901
President McKinley's funeral in Buffalo, Washington, and Canton, Ohio, 1901. 1901
Return of Spanish-American troops, 1898. 1898

United States. Military Academy, West Point
President McKinley's inauguration, 1901 [1] 1901
[TR's inaugural ceremony, 1905] 1905
TR's inauguration, 1905 [1] 1905
TR's inauguration, 1905 [2] 1905

United States. Naval Academy, Annapolis
Reviewing Annapolis middies. 1915
[TR's inaugural ceremony, 1905] 1905
TR's inauguration, 1905 [1] 1905

United States. Naval Reserve
Memorial services for TR on the steps of the New York Public Library, 1919 [1] 1919
Memorial services for TR on the steps of the New York Public Library, 1919 [2] 1919
RMA flag service on the steps of New York Public Library, 1919. 1919
TR memorial services at New York Public Library, 1919. 1919

United States. Navy
Japanese and Russian peace delegates [leaving New York City], 1905. 1905
President McKinley's funeral, 1901 [1] 1901
President McKinley's funeral, 1901 [2] 1901
President McKinley's funeral in Buffalo, Washington, and Canton, Ohio, 1901. 1901
Return of Spanish-American troops, 1898. 1898
TR reviews and addresses troops [Fort Sheridan, Ill.]; TR riding in auto, Chicago, 1917. 1917
TR with naval officers, exterior Navy Club, Boston [1918] 1918
Wreck of the "Vizcaya." 1898

United States. Navy—History
TR reviews the fleet, 1907. 1907

United States. Navy—History—War of 1898
Admiral Dewey on flagship, 1899. 1899
Admiral Dewey on the deck of flagship, 1899 [1] 1899
Admiral Dewey on the deck of flagship, 1899 [2] 1899
Admiral Dewey parade, 1899 [1] 1899
Admiral Dewey parade, 1899 [2] 1899

United States. Navy—Officers
Admiral Dewey on flagship, 1899, 1899
Admiral Dewey on the deck of flagship, 1899 [1] 1899
Admiral Dewey on the deck of flagship, 1899 [2] 1899

Admiral Dewey parade, 1899 [1] 1899
Admiral Dewey parade, 1899 [2] 1899
[Scenes of TR, 1913–1915] 1913
Short scenes of TR [1] 1916
TR [at Panama-Pacific Exposition, 1915] 1915
TR reviews the fleet, 1907. 1907
TR with naval officers, exterior Navy Club, Boston [1918] 1918

United States. Navy—Service clubs
Short scenes of TR [1] 1916
TR with naval officers, exterior Navy Club, Boston [1918] 1918

United States. Navy. Asiatic Fleet
Admiral Dewey parade, 1899 [1] 1899

United States. Navy. Atlantic Fleet
International naval review, Hampton Roads, Virginia, 1907. 1907

United States. Ordnance Dept.
Disappearing gun at testing grounds, Sandy Hook, 1898. 1898

United States. President, 1897–1901 (McKinley)
McKinley's funeral, 1901. 1901
McKinley's funeral, Washington, D.C., 1901. 1901
The Panama Canal. 1927
President McKinley inauguration, 1901. 1901
President McKinley reviewing the troops at the Pan-American Exposition. 1901
President McKinley speaking, 1901. 1901
President McKinley speaking at Buffalo, 1901. 1901
President McKinley's funeral, 1901 [1] 1901
President McKinley's funeral, 1901 [2] 1901
President McKinley's funeral, Canton, Ohio, 1901 [1] 1901
President McKinley's funeral, Canton, Ohio, 1901 [2] 1901
President McKinley's funeral in Buffalo, Washington, and Canton, Ohio, 1901. 1901
President McKinley's inauguration, 1901 [1] 1901
President McKinley's inauguration, 1901 [2] 1901
[Scenes of TR, Panama Canal construction, and William McKinley] 1901
Still pictures exposed on scene of McKinley's funeral as used in Paramount reel. 1901
The Story of the Panama Canal [1] 1927
The Story of the Panama Canal [2] 1927
TR attends McKinley's funeral, 1901. 1901
TR attends McKinley's funeral, Canton, Ohio, 1901. 1901
See also McKinley, William, Pres. U.S., 1843–1901

United States. President, 1901–1909 (Roosevelt)
International naval review, Hampton Roads, Virginia, 1907. 1907
Jamestown Exposition, 1907. 1907
The Panama Canal. 1927
President McKinley's funeral, Canton, Ohio, 1901 [1] 1901
President McKinley's funeral, Canton, Ohio, 1901 [2] 1901
President McKinley's funeral in Buffalo, Washington, and Canton, Ohio, 1901. 1901
Still picture of TR and his family. 1907
The Story of the Panama Canal [1] 1927
The Story of the Panama Canal [2] 1927

TR as Father Curran's guest at Wilkes-Barre, Pa., August 10, 1905. 1905
TR at Wilkes-Barre, Pa., 1905. 1905
TR attends McKinley's funeral, 1901. 1901
TR attends McKinley's funeral, Canton, Ohio, 1901. 1901
TR in San Francisco, 1903. 1903
TR in Wilkes-Barre, Pa., 1905. 1905
TR reviews the fleet, 1907. 1907
TR speaking from Cathedral steps, Panama. 1906
TR speaking in Panama, November 1906. 1906
TR's arrival in Panama, November 1906 [1] 1906
TR's arrival in Panama, November 1906 [2] 1906
TR's arrival in Panama, November 1906 [3] 1906
[TR's inaugural ceremony, 1905] 1905
TR's inauguration, 1905 [1] 1905
TR's inauguration, 1905 [2] 1905
See also Roosevelt, Theodore, Pres. U.S., 1858–1919

United States. President, 1909–1913 (Taft)
William H. Taft in Panama [1910?] 1910
See also Taft, William Howard, Pres. U.S., 1857–1930

United States. President, 1913–1921 (Wilson)
President Wilson arrives in New York to lead fourth Liberty Loan parade [1918] 1918
Theodore Roosevelt in the great war [1] 1930
Theodore Roosevelt in the great war [2] 1930
Theodore Roosevelt in the great war [3] 1930

United States. President, 1921–1923 (Harding)
President Harding presenting chair used by TR at the White House to the directors of RMA, October 1921. 1921
See also Harding, Warren Gamaliel, Pres. U.S., 1865–1923

United States. President, 1923–1929 (Coolidge)
The Panama Canal. 1927
President Coolidge speaking at Black Hills, S.D., 1927. 1927
The Story of the Panama Canal [1] 1927
The Story of the Panama Canal [2] 1927
See also Coolidge, Calvin, Pres. U.S., 1872–1933; Massachusetts. Governor, 1919–1921 (Coolidge)

United States. Reclamation Service
See United States. Bureau of Reclamation

United States. Sandy Hook Proving Ground, N.J.
Disappearing gun at testing grounds, Sandy Hook, 1898. 1898

United States. Secret Service
TR's inauguration, 1905 [1] 1905

United States. Special Diplomatic Mission to Russia
Elihu Root and Mayor Mitchel of New York, Mr. Root and American delegates return from Russia [1917] 1917

United States. State Dept.
See United States. Dept. of State

United States. Treasury Dept.—Buildings
President Wilson arrives in New York to lead fourth Liberty Loan parade [1918] 1918

Universal animated weekly
TR reviews and addresses troops [Fort Sheridan, Ill.]; TR riding in auto, Chicago, 1917. 1917

Universal animated weekly, v. 4, issue no. 40
Charles E. Hughes speaking during campaign, Duquesne, Pa., 1916. 1916

Universal animated weekly, v. 5, issue no. 93
President McKinley's memorial dedicated by William Howard Taft at Niles, Ohio. 1917

Universal current events [Series]
TR's funeral at Oyster Bay, 1919. 1919

Universal Film Manufacturing Company
Charles E. Hughes speaking during campaign, Duquesne, Pa., 1916. 1916
President McKinley's memorial dedicated by William Howard Taft at Niles, Ohio. 1917
Scenes of TR and his sons Quentin and Archie, 1917–1918 [1] 1917
TR reviews and addresses troops [Fort Sheridan, Ill.]; TR riding in auto, Chicago, 1917. 1917
TR's funeral at Oyster Bay, 1919. 1919

University of California, Berkeley
RMA ceremonies at [Hearst Greek Theatre, University of California, Berkely, Calif.] 1919
RMA services at [Hearst Greek Theatre, University of California, Berkeley, Calif.]; Laying cornerstone of Roosevelt School at New Rochelle, N.Y. [1920] 1920

University of California, Berkeley. Hearst Greek Theatre
See Hearst Greek Theatre

University of Michigan Union
See Michigan. University. Michigan Union

Urban, Charles, source
American Legion places wreath on TR's grave [1919]; Scenes of Oyster Bay from the air. 1919
Aviators drop American Legion wreath on TR's grave [1919] 1919
Brooklyn children attend services, children sew stars on Roosevelt Flag [1919] 1919
Close-up of TR's grave, 1920. 1920
Dedication of Roosevelt Mountain at Deadwood, S.D., 1919. 1919
[Flag service for TR at Oyster Bay, October 1919] 1919
Friends and admirers visit TR's grave, 1920. 1920
Laying cornerstone of Roosevelt School, New Rochelle, N.Y. [1920] 1920
Memorial services for TR at Van Cortlandt Park, New York, Oct. 1919. 1919
Memorial services for TR on the steps of the New York Public Library, 1919 [1] 1919
Memorial services for TR on the steps of the New York Public Library, 1919 [2] 1919
Oyster Bay from the air [1919] 1919
RMA ceremonies at [Hearst Greek Theatre, University of California, Berkeley, Calif.] 1919
RMA flag ceremonies, children sew stars on flag, 1919. 1919

RMA flag service on the steps of New York Public Library, 1919. 1919
RMA services at [Hearst Greek Theatre, University of California, Berkeley, Calif.]; Laying cornerstone of Roosevelt School at New Rochelle, N.Y. [1920] 1920
Runners carrying flag to TR's grave [1919] 1919
Three children visit TR's grave, 1920. 1920
Whole nation honors memory of Roosevelt. 1919

Urban popular classics [Series]
King Edward's funeral, 1910 [1] 1910

Ursel, Louis, comte d'
Roosevelt scenes [1917–1918] 1917
TR receiving Belgian envoys at Sagamore Hill [1917] 1917

Usher, Nathaniel Reilly
TR, Charles E. Hughes, and Mayor Mitchel of New York, on reviewing stand in front of the New York Public Library [1917] 1917

Utiariti, Brazil
The River of Doubt [1] 1928
The River of Doubt [3] 1928
Scenes of the River of Doubt photographed by G.M. Dyott, 1926–1927 [1] 1927
Scenes of the River of Doubt photographed by G.M. Dyott, 1926–1927 [2] 1927

Utiarity, Brazil
See Utiariti, Brazil

Vail, Robert W.G.
Theodore Roosevelt, great scout [1] 1925
Theodore Roosevelt, great scout [2] 1925
Theodore Roosevelt, great scout [3] 1925

Valkenburg, Edwin A. Van
See Van Valkenburg, Edwin A.

Van Cortlandt House Museum
See New York (City). Van Cortlandt House

Van Cortlandt Mansion, New York (City)
See New York (City). Van Cortlandt House

Van Cortlandt Park
See New York (City)—Parks—Van Cortlandt Park
Van Dyck (Ship)
See Vandyck (Ship)

Van Dyke (Ship)
See Vandyck (Ship)

Van Valkenburg, Edwin A.
Presentation of Roosevelt Medals, May 1925, Washington, D.C. 1925
President Harding presenting chair used by TR at the White House to the directors of RMA, October 1921. 1921
RMA trustees at Roosevelt House, 1923 [2] 1923
Short scenes of TR [1] 1916
TR and several men. 1910
TR scenes purchased from different dealers. 1912

Van Wyck, Robert A.
Admiral Dewey parade, 1899 [1] 1899

Vanderbilt, Cornelius, 1873–1942
TR speaking at the Battery, 1910. 1910
TR's return from Africa, 1910 [1] 1925
TR's return from Africa, 1910 [2] 1925
TR's return to New York, 1910 [1] 1910
TR's return to New York, 1910 [2] 1910

Vandyck (Ship)
Commander Dyott sailing from [Hoboken, N.J.] for South
America, 1926. 1926
The River of Doubt [1] 1928
The River of Doubt [2] 1928
The River of Doubt [3] 1928
The River of Doubt [5] 1928
The River of Doubt [6] 1928
The River of Doubt [7] 1928
[Scenes of TR on board ship, 1916; Scenes of TR's trip to
South America, 1913] 1913

Vandyke (Ship)
See Vandyck (Ship)

Vare, William S.
Gifford Pinchot, 1923. 1923

Vermont. Governor, 1919–1921 (Clement)
Governors of New England meet in Governor Coolidge's
office in Boston to discuss fuel. 1919

Vessels (Ships)
See Ships

Veterans
American Legion lays cornerstone of Roosevelt Bridge at
Château-Thierry. 1921
Memorial services for TR on the steps of the New York Public
Library, 1919 [1] 1919

Victor Emmanuel III, King of Italy
See Vittorio Emanuele III, King of Italy, 1869–1947

Victoria, consort of Gustavus V, King of Sweden, 1862–1930
King Gustav of Sweden greeted by his people. 1920

Victoria, Princess of Great Britain, 1868–1935
The King of Italy entertains King Edward of England on his
yacht. 1907
[Scenes of the British royal family] 1918

Victoria Alexandra Alice Mary
See Mary, Princess of Great Britain, 1897–1965

**Victoria Eugenia, consort of Alfonso XIII, King of Spain,
1887–1969**
King and Queen of Spain attend a military review. 1920

Victoria Memorial, London
See London. Queen Victoria Memorial

Vienna
Emperor Francis Joseph of Austria greeted by his people.
1910

Viktoria, consort of Gustavus V, King of Sweden, 1862–1930
See Victoria, consort of Gustavus V, King of Sweden,
1862–1930

Vincennes, France
TR in Vincennes, France, 1910. 1910
TR reviews French troops at Vincennes, France, 1910. 1910

Vincennes, France. Polygon
TR in Vincennes, France, 1910. 1910
TR reviews French troops at Vincennes, France, 1910. 1910

Vincennes, Château de
TR in Vincennes, France, 1910. 1910
TR reviews French troops at Vincennes, France, 1910. 1910

Violets
Scenes of flowers and birds in Washington, D.C. 1920
[Scenes of flowers in Washington, D.C.] 1920

Visit to the illustrious colonel, A [Title]
A visit to Theodore Roosevelt at his home at Sagamore Hill,
Oyster Bay, L.I., 1912. 1912

Vittoria, Armando Diaz, duca della
See Diaz, Armando, duca della Vittoria

Vittorio Emanuele III, King of Italy, 1869–1947
Cartoon of TR's reception by crowned heads of Europe. 1910
The King of Italy entertains King Edward of England on his
yacht. 1907

Vizcaya (Ship)
Wreck of the "Vizcaya." 1898

Von Tirpitz, Alfred Peter Friedrich
See Tirpitz, Alfred Peter Friedrich Von

Voting
Americanism wins, Coolidge elected. 1919

Voyages and travels
The King of Italy entertains King Edward of England on his
yacht. 1907
[Scenes of TR on board ship, 1916; Scenes of TR's trip to
South America, 1913] 1913
TR in Denmark, 1910. 1910
TR in Norway and Denmark, 1910 [1] 1910
TR in Norway and Denmark, 1910 [2] 1910
TR in Norway and Denmark, 1910 [3] 1910
See also Brazil—Description and travel; Discoveries (in geo-
graphy);Yachts and yachting

Voyages around the world
TR reviews the fleet, 1907. 1907

Wadsworth, James W., 1877–1952
Senators Curtis, Cummins, Moses, and [Representative] Mondell. 1919

Wagstaff, Cyril M.
Robert Bacon and Army officers. 1918

Wallace, Henry C.
President Harding presenting chair used by TR at the White House to the directors of RMA, October 1921. 1921

Walpi, Ariz.
Hopi Indians dance for TR at [Walpi, Ariz.] 1913. 1913

Wanamaker, Rodman
Gen. Pershing speaking to Scouts in New York. 1919
The Prince of Wales visits TR's grave. 1919

Wannigan, Dutch
See Reuter, John

War games
TR in Vincennes, France, 1910. 1910
TR reviews French troops at Vincennes, France, 1910. 1910

War memorials—Belgium
The King and Queen of Belgium and Premier Poincaré of France [1] 1927
The King and Queen of Belgium and Premier Poincaré of France [2] 1927

War of 1914
See European War, 1914–1918

Warner Brothers, source
Crowd listening to TR speak during Progressive campaign, 1912. 1912
TR on reception yacht in New York Bay, 1910. 1910
TR reviewing and speaking to 13th Regiment at Sagamore Hill, 1917. 1917
TR speaking at Battery Park, New York, June 1910. 1910
TR speaking at Oyster Bay, July 4, 1916. 1916
TR's return to New York, 1910 [2] 1910

Warships
TR's return to New York, 1910 [2] 1910

Warships—Visits to foreign ports
International naval review, Hampton Roads, Virginia, 1907. 1907

Washington, D.C.
General Wood and Calvin Coolidge in Chicago, 1920. 1920
Herbert Putnam. 1920
McKinley's funeral, Washington, D.C., 1901. 1901
Memorializing Roosevelt. 1925
Origanal U.S. documents. 1920
Presentation of Roosevelt Medals, May 1925, Washington, D.C. 1925
President Harding and Calvin Coolidge [2] 1920
President Harding presenting chair used by TR at the White House to the directors of RMA, October 1921. 1921
President McKinley inauguration, 1901. 1901
President McKinley's funeral, 1901 [1] 1901
President McKinley's funeral, 1901 [2] 1901
President McKinley's funeral in Buffalo, Washington, and Canton, Ohio, 1901. 1901
President McKinley's inauguration, 1901 [1] 1901

President McKinley's inauguration, 1901 [2] 1901
President Wilson arrives in New York to lead fourth Liberty Loan parade [1918] 1918
The prize winning design by John Russell Pope for the proposed memorial to Theodore Roosevelt for the city of Washington. 1926
Scenes of flowers and birds in Washington, D.C. 1920
[Scenes of flowers in Washington, D.C.] 1920
Scenes of the Capitol, Washington, D.C. 1920
Scenes of the White House. 1920
Scenes of TR and his sons Quentin and Archie, 1917–1918 [1] 1917
Scenes of TR and his sons Quentin and Archie, 1917–1918 [2] 1917
Senator Hitchcock. 1910
Senator McCumber of North Dakota. 1920
Senator Penrose. 1910
Senator Pomerene. 1910
Speaker of the House F. H. Gillett. 1919
Still pictures exposed on scene of McKinley's funeral as used in Paramount reel. 1901
Theodore Roosevelt in the great war [1] 1930
Theodore Roosevelt in the great war [2] 1930
Theodore Roosevelt in the great war [3] 1930
Theodore Roosevelt leaving the White House. 1897
TR, exterior of building, Washington, D.C., 1918. 1918
TR in auto [1912] 1912
TR speaking at Sagamore Hill [1916–1918 and scenes of his early career] 1897
[TR's inaugural ceremony, 1905] 1905
TR's inaugural ceremony, 1905 [1] 1905
TR's inaugural ceremony, 1905 [2] 1905
[Unidentified man] 1910

Washington, D.C.—Description—Aerial
President Harding and Calvin Coolidge [2] 1920

Washington, D.C.—Public buildings
Theodore Roosevelt leaving the White House. 1897
TR speaking at Sagamore Hill [1916–1918 and scenes of his early career] 1897

Washington, D.C.—Statues
Scenes of the Capitol, Washington, D.C. 1920

Washington, D.C.—Streets—Fifteenth Street, N.W.
President McKinley's inauguration, 1901 [1] 1901
[TR's inaugural ceremony, 1905] 1905
TR's inauguration, 1905 [1] 1905
TR's inauguration, 1905 [2] 1905

Washington, D.C.—Streets—Pennsylvania Avenue, N.W.
President McKinley inauguration, 1901. 1901
President McKinley's inauguration, 1901 [1] 1901
President McKinley's inauguration, 1901 [2] 1901
TR's inauguration, 1905 [1] 1905
TR's inauguration, 1905 [2] 1905

Washington, D.C. Capitol
Herbert Putnam. 1920
McKinley's funeral, Washington, D.C., 1901. 1901
President McKinley's funeral, 1901 [1] 1901
President McKinley's funeral, 1901 [2] 1901
President McKinley's funeral in Buffalo, Washington, and

Canton, Ohio, 1901. 1901
Scenes of the Capitol, Washington, D.C. 1920
Senator Hitchcock. 1910
Senator McCumber of North Dakota. 1920
Senator Penrose. 1910
Senator Pomerene. 1910
Speaker of the House F. H. Gillett. 1919
Still pictures exposed on scene of McKinley's funeral as used
  in Paramount reel. [1901]
[TR's inaugural ceremony, 1905] 1905
TR's inauguration, 1905 [1] 1905
TR's inauguration, 1905 [2] 1905
[Unidentified man] 1910

Washington, D.C. Capitol. Senate Office Building
General Wood and Calvin Coolidge in Chicago, 1920. 1920
President Harding and Calvin Coolidge [1] 1920

Washington, D.C. Executive Office Building
See Washington, D.C. State, War and Navy Building

Washington, D.C. Roosevelt Memorial
See Washington, D.C. Theodore Roosevelt Memorial

Washington, D.C. Senate Office Building
See Washington, D.C. Capitol. Senate Office Building

Washington, D.C. State, War and Navy Building
Theodore Roosevelt leaving the White House. 1897
TR speaking àt Sagamore Hill [1916–1918 and scenes of his
  early career] 1897

Washington, D.C. Theodore Roosevelt Memorial
The prize winning design by John Russell Pope for the pro-
  posed memorial to Theodore Roosevelt for the city of
  Washington. 1926

Washington, D.C. Washington Monument
Senator McCumber of North Dakota. 1920

Washington, D.C. White House
President Harding presenting chair used by TR at the White
  House to the directors of RMA, October 1921. 1921
Scenes of flowers and birds in Washington, D.C. 1920
[Scenes of flowers in Washington, D.C.] 1920
Scenes of the White House. 1920
Theodore Roosevelt in the great war [1] 1930
Theodore Roosevelt in the great war [2] 1930
Theodore Roosevelt in the great war [3] 1930
Theodore Roosevelt leaving the White House. 1897
TR speaking at Sagamore Hill [1916–1918 and scenes of his
  early career] 1897

Washington, D.C. Willard Hotel
See Willard Hotel, Washington, D.C.

Washington Monument, Washington, D.C.
See Washington, D.C. Washington Monument

Wason, George B.
Calvin Coolidge sworn in for second term as Governor of Massachusetts. 1920

Water-birds
Roosevelt, friend of the birds [1] 1924
Roosevelt, friend of the birds [2] 1924
Roosevelt, friend of the birds [3] 1924
Roosevelt, friend of the birds [4]; The Roosevelt Dam [3]
  1928
TR [in Louisiana], 1915 [1] 1915
TR [in Louisiana], 1915 [2] 1915
TR [in Louisiana], 1915 [3] 1915
TR [in Louisiana], 1915 [4] 1915

Water-power electric plants—Arizona
The Roosevelt Dam [1] 1928
The Roosevelt Dam [2] 1928

Water-storage—Arizona—Salt River
TR with group of men, 1917; TR speaking at dedication of
  Roosevelt Dam, 1911. 1911

Waterfalls—Brazil
Scenes of the River of doubt photographed by G. M. Dyott,
  1926–1927 [1] 1927
Scenes of the River of Doubt photographed by G. M. Dyott,
  1926–1927 [2] 1927

Watson, Georgia Doremus
Senator Watson. 1921

Watson, Thomas E.
Senator Watson. 1921

Weddings
TR attends his son Archie's wedding at Boston, 1917. 1917

Weiss Brothers, source
[Scenes of TR on board ship, 1916; Scenes of TR's trip to South
  America, 1913] 1913

The West
Theodore Roosevelt, great scout [3] 1925

West Flowery Gate, Peking
See Peking. West Flowery Gate

West Point, N.Y. Military Academy
See United States. Military Academy, West Point

West Point Military Academy
See United States, Military Academy, West Point

Westlawn Cemetery
President McKinley's funeral, 1901 [1] 1901
President McKinley's funeral in Buffalo, Washington, and
  Canton, Ohio, 1901. 1901

Westminster, Eng. St. Margaret's Church
[Scenes of the British royal family] 1918

Weygand, Maxime
[Quentin Roosevelt]; Clemenceau and Foch, 1917–1919. 1918
Scene of Clemenceau, Tardieu, Foch, Poincaré and Pershing,
  1917–1918. 1918

Whigham, Henry J.
President Harding presenting chair used by TR at the White House to the directors of RMA, October 1921. 1921

White Dagoda, Peking
See Peking. White Pagoda

White House, Washington, D.C.
See Washington, D.C. White House

White Pagoda, Peking
See Peking. White Pagoda

Whitehouse, Vira B.
Scenes of TR speaking at Sagamore [1916-1918] 1916
Women suffragettes visit TR at Sagamore [1917] 1917

Whitlock, Brand
King Albert of Belgium visits TR's grave, October, 1919. 1919

Whitman, Charles S.
Chauncey Depew, Senator Perkins, and Governor Whitman of New York, at GOP Convention, 1916, Chicago, Ill. 1916
TR, Mayor Mitchel, Governor Charles Whitman of New York, and Myron Herrick, 1917. 1917

Whitman, Olive H.
Chauncey Depew, Senator Perkins, and Governor Whitman of New York, at GOP Convention, 1916, Chicago, Ill. 1916

Whittall, Matthew J.
Calvin Coolidge sworn in for second term as Governor of Massachusetts. 1920

Wild flowers
Scenes of flowers and birds in Washington, D.C. 1920
[Scenes of flowers in Washington, D.C.] 1920

Wildlife conservation
Aigrette. 1920
Woman wearing aigrette in her hat. 1920
See also Birds, Protection of

Wildlife refuges
See Breton Island Reservation, La.

Wildlife refuges—Louisiana
Roosevelt, friend of the birds [1] 1924
Roosevelt, friend of the birds [2] 1924
Roosevelt, friend of the birds [3] 1924
Roosevelt, friend of the birds [4]; The Roosevelt Dam [3] 1928
TR [in Louisiana], 1915 [1] 1915
TR [in Louisiana], 1915 [2] 1915
TR [in Louisiana], 1915 [3] 1915
TR [in Louisiana], 1915 [4] 1915

Wilhelm II, German Emperor, 1859-1941
Cartoon of TR's reception by crowned heads of Europe. 1910
Kaiser Wilhelm. 1910
Kaiser Wilhelm and his admiralty staff attend launching at Kiel. 1910
TR's return from Africa, 1910 [1] 1925
TR's return from Africa, 1910 [2] 1925

Wilhelmina, Queen of the Netherlands, 1880-1962
Queen Wilhelmina of Holland, the Prince Consort [and] the Princess. 1920

Wilkes-Barre, Pa.
President Roosevelt, 1901-1909. 1930
TR as Father Curran's guest at Wilkes-Barre, Pa., August 10, 1905. 1905
TR at Wilkes-Barre, Pa., 1905. 1905
TR in Wilkes-Barre, Pa., 1905. 1905

Willard Hotel, Washington, D.C.
President McKinley inauguration, 1901. 1901

William II, Kaiser
See Wilhelm II, German Emperor, 1859-1941

Williams, Harry H.
Calvin Coolidge sworn in for second term as Governor of Massachusetts. 1920

Williams, John Sharp
TR's inauguration, 1905 [2] 1905

Wilson, Edith
President Wilson arrives in New York to lead fourth Liberty Loan parade [1918] 1918

Wilson, Eleanor Randolph
See McAdoo, Eleanor

Wilson, George T.
Elihu Root and Mayor Mitchel of New York, Mr. Root and American delegates return from Russia [1917] 1917
Roosevelt scenes [1917-1918] 1917
TR receiving Belgian envoys at Sagamore Hill [1917] 1917

Wilson, James, 1835-1920
President McKinley speaking at Buffalo, 1901. 1901
President McKinley's funeral in Buffalo, Washington, and Canton, Ohio, 1901. 1901
[Scenes of TR, Panama Canal construction, and William McKinley] 1901
TR attends McKinley's funeral, 1901. 1901
TR attends McKinley's funeral, Canton, Ohio, 1901. 1901

Wilson, Margaret Woodrow
President Wilson arrives in New York to lead fourth Liberty Loan parade [1918] 1918

Wilson, Woodrow, Pres. U.S., 1856-1924
President Wilson arrives in New York to lead fourth Liberty Loan parade [1918] 1918
Theodore Roosevelt in the great war [1] 1930
Theodore Roosevelt in the great war [2] 1930
Theodore Roosevelt in the great war [3] 1930

Wilson Dam
President Harding and Calvin Coolidge [2] 1920

Windsor, Edward, Duke of
See Edward VIII, King of Great Britain, 1894-1972

Wingate, George W.
[Scenes of TR, 1913–1915] 1913

Winslow, Cameron M.
TR's funeral at Oyster Bay, 1919. 1919

Wister, Owen
Mr. Garfield presenting medals to 1929 medalists. 1929
Owen Wister. 1920

Witte, Sergeĭ I͡Ul'evich, graf, 1849–1915
Japanese and Russian peace delegates [leaving New York City],
1905. 1905
TR himself [1] 1926
TR himself [2] 1926
TR himself [3] 1926
TR himself [4] 1926
TR himself [5] 1926
TR himself [6] 1926

Woman's Roosevelt Memorial Association
See Women's Theodore Roosevelt Memorial Association

Women—Legal status, laws, etc.
TR speaking to a group of suffragettes from the porch at
Sagamore Hill [1917] 1917

Women—Suffrage—New York (State)
The prize winning design by John Russell Pope for the pro-
posed memorial to Theodore Roosevelt for the city of Wash-
ington. 1926
Roosevelt scenes from RMA productions. 1912
Scenes of TR speaking at Sagamore [1916–1918] 1916
TR scenes purchased from different dealers. 1912
TR speaking at Sagamore Hill [1916–1918 [1] 1916
TR speaking at Sagamore Hill [1916–1918 [2] 1916
TR speaking to a group of suffragettes from the porch at
Sagamore Hill [1917] 1917
Women suffragettes visit TR at Sagamore [1917] 1917

Women's rights—New York (State)
Scenes of TR speaking at Sagamore [1916–1918] 1916
TR scenes purchased from different dealers. 1912
TR speaking at Sagamore Hill [1916–1918 [1] 1916
TR speaking at Sagamore Hill [1916–1918 [2] 1916
TR speaking to a group of suffragettes from the porch at
Sagamore Hill [1917] 1917
Women suffragates visit TR at Sagamore [1917] 1917

Women's Roosevelt Memorial Association
See Women's Theodore Roosevelt Memorial Association

Women's Theodore Roosevelt Memorial Association
Dedication of Roosevelt House, 1923. 1923
Dedication of Roosevelt House, Oct. 27, 1923. 1923
Leonard Wood lays cornerstone of Roosevelt House, 1921.
1921
Marshal Foch visits Roosevelt House, 1921. 1921
Memorializing Roosevelt. 1925
Moving exhibits into Roosevelt House, 1923. 1923
Mr. Hagedorn and Mrs. Wood at Roosevelt House [1924,
Long version] 1924
Mr. Hagedorn and Mrs. Wood at Roosevelt House [1924,
Short version] 1924

Mrs. Roosevelt, Sr., and Mrs. J. H. Hammon photographed
on the roof of Roosevelt House, 1927; Mrs. Roosevelt arrives at Roosevelt House, 1927
Woman's Roosevelt Memorial Association meeting at Roosevelt House, 1923 [1] 1923
Woman's Roosevelt Memorial Association meeting at Roosevelt House, 1923 [2] 1923
See also Roosevelt Memorial Association

Wood, Elizabeth Ogden Brower
Marshal Foch visits Roosevelt House, 1921. 1921
Mr. Hagedorn and Mrs. Wood at Roosevelt House [1924,
Long version] 1924
Mr. Hagedorn and Mrs. Wood at Roosevelt House [1924,
Short version] 1924

Wood, Leonard
Dedication of Roosevelt Mountain at Deadwood, S.D., 1919.
1919
General Wood and Calvin Coolidge in Chicago, 1920. 1920
Leonard Wood at Battle Creek, Michigan. 1920
Leonard Wood lays cornerstone of Roosevelt House, 1921.
1921
Short scenes of TR [1] 1916
Theodore Roosevelt in the great war [1] 1930
Theodore Roosevelt in the great war [2] 1930
Theodore Roosevelt in the great war [3] 1930
TR and Leonard Wood at the New York flower show, 1917.
1917
TR's funeral at Oyster Bay, 1919. 1919

Wood (Leonard) League of Michigan
See Leonard Wood League of Michigan

Wood, Louisa Smith
Leonard Wood at Battle Creek, Michigan. 1920

Wood League of Michigan
See Leonard Wood League of Michigan

Woods, Thomas Francis
Admiral Dewey parade, 1899 [1] 1899
Admiral Dewey parade, 1899 [2] 1899

World War, 1914–1918
See European War, 1914–1918

Wurster, Earnest A.
See Wurster, Ernst E.

Wurster, Ernst E.
Leonard Wood at Battle Creek, Michigan. 1920

Wykagyl, N.Y.
Laying cornerstone of Roosevelt School, New Rochelle, N.Y.
[1920] 1920
RMA services at [Hearst Greek Theatre, University of Cal-
ifornia, Berkeley, Calif.]; Laying cornerstone of Roosevelt
School at New Rochelle, N.Y. [1920] 1920

Wyoming
Through the Roosevelt country with Roosevelt's friends. 1919

Yachts and yachting
International naval review, Hampton Roads, Virginia, 1907. 1907
TR reviews the fleet, 1907. 1907

Yachts and yachting—Italy
The King of Italy entertains King Edward of England on his yacht. 1907

Yellow fever—Panama Canal—Prevention
The Panama Canal. 1927
The Story of the Panama Canal [1] 1927
The Story of the Panama Canal [2] 1927

Yellowstone National Park
President Harding and Calvin Coolidge [2] 1920

YMCA
See Young Men's Christian Associations

Young, Owen D.
Mr. Garfield presenting medals to 1929 medalists. 1929
Owen D. Young [1] 1927
Owen D. Young [2] 1927

Young, Robert
Commander Dyott sailing from [Hoboken, N.J.] for South America, 1926. 1926

Young Men's Christian Associations
Dr. William Gorgas. 1900
Mrs. Theodore Roosevelt Jr. attends Women in War Work Congress in Paris [1918] 1918

Young Men's Christian Associations, source
TR speaking [at the Panama-Pacific Exposition, 1915] 1915

Young's Memorial Cemetery
See Youngs Memorial Cemetery

Youngs Memorial Cemetery
Airmen honor TR's memory by dropping American Legion wreath on his grave [1919] 1919
Children sewing stars on flag, placing flag on TR's grave [1919] 1919
Children visit TR's grave, 1920. 1920
Close-up of TR's grave, 1920. 1920
Daniel C. Beard, TR Jr., and Boy Scouts visit TR's grave, 1920. 1920
[Flag services for TR at Oyster Bay, October 1919] 1919
Friends and admirers visit TR's grave, 1920. 1920

General [Diaz] of Italy visits TR's grave [1921] 1921
General Nivelle visits TR's grave [1921] 1921
King Albert of Belgium visits TR's grave, 1919. 1919
King Albert of Belgium visits TR's grave, October, 1919. 1919
The Prince of Wales visits TR's grave. 1919
RMA flag service on the steps of New York Public Library, 1919. 1919
RMA pilgrimage to TR's grave, 1930. 1930
Runners carrying flag to TR's grave [1919] 1919
Scouts on their way to TR's grave, Daniel C. Beard and TR Jr. attend services, 1920. 1920
Three children visit TR's grave, 1920. 1920
TR himself [1] 1926
TR himself [2] 1926
TR himself [3] 1926
TR himself [4] 1926
TR himself [5] 1926
TR himself [6] 1926
TR's funeral, 1919. 1919
TR's funeral at Oyster Bay, 1919. 1919
TR's funeral at Oyster Bay, January 1919 [1] 1919
TR's funeral at Oyster Bay, January 1919 [2] 1919

Young's Memorial Cemetery, Oyster Bay, N.Y.
See Youngs Memorial Cemetery

Yusuf Izzedin, 1858–1916
TR's return from Africa, 1910 [1] 1925
TR's return from Africa, 1910 [2] 1925

Zahm, John A.
The River of Doubt [1] 1928
The River of Doubt [2] 1928
The River of Doubt [3] 1928
The River of Doubt [4] 1928
The River of Doubt [5] 1928
The River of Doubt [7] 1928
[Scenes of TR, 1913–1915] 1913
[Scenes of TR on board ship, 1916; Scenes of TR's trip to South America, 1913] 1913

Zayas, Alfredo
See Zayas y Alfonso, Alfredo, Pres. Cuba, 1861–1934

Zayas y Alfonso, Alfredo, Pres. Cuba, 1861–1934
Dedication of Cuban memorial, 1924 [1] 1924
Dedication of Cuban memorial, 1924 [2] 1924
Roosevelt scenes from RMA productions. 1912

Zebras
Scenes of African animals [1911] 1911

Bibliography

This bibliography includes all sources used in the research for the cataloging of the Theodore Roosevelt Association Collection. Sources consulted for general background information, as well as those used only for one or two films, are listed. Research was completed in June 1978, so works published after that date do not appear. The bibliography is visually oriented and its purpose is to provide pictorial, as well as textual, documentation.

Full bibliographic information has been provided for each source rather than the short citations used in the reference sources note in the individual title catalog entries. Because different pages, sections, volumes, and dates of the same source were often used for different films, specific information is not cited in the bibliography. The researcher must refer to the reference sources noted in the individual title entries for specific citations. With the exception of trips to Sagamore Hill, the National Archives, and Harvard University, all research was done at the Library of Congress. The order and form of the entries are those used in the public catalog and in the catalogs and finding aids of the special collections of the Library of Congress at the time the research was done. One inconsistency is the citation for the Prints and Photographs Division at the Library. In individual entries the division is listed as P&P; in the comprehensive bibliography its official form is used: U.S. Library of Congress. Prints and Photographs Division.

Abbot, Willis J. *Panama and the Canal: The Story of Its Achievement, Its Problems and Its Prospects.* New York: Dodd, Mead and Company, 1914.

Abbott, Lawrence F. *Impressions of Theodore Roosevelt.* Garden City, N.Y.: Doubleday, Page & Company, 1919.

Abell, Carl. *The Campus, University of California: A Collection of Views and Art Photographs.* [Oakland, Calif.: Press of Bray & Mulgrew] c1919.

Aften Posten, Oslo.

Album of American History. James Truslow Adams, editor in chief [and others] New York: Scribner, 1944–[61]

Albuquerque Journal.

Alfonso, Oscar M. *Theodore Roosevelt and the Philippines, 1897–1909.* Quezon City: University of the Philippines Press, 1970.

All about the Pan-American City and Vicinity . . . Buffalo, N.Y.: Baldwin Pub. Co., 1901.

Along the Apache Trail of Arizona: A Story without Words. [Washington: Press of Gibson Bros., 191–?]

American Museum of Natural History, New York. *Annual Report.* New York: The Museum [1870–]

The Anaconda Standard.

Angle, Paul. *Crossroads: 1913.* Chicago: Rand McNally [1963]

Arizona: Its People and Resources. Rev. 2d ed. by members of the faculty of the University of Arizona. Tucson: University of Arizona Press [1972]

Arizona Republican, Phoenix.

Arnold, C. D. [Pan-American Exposition, Buffalo, N.Y., 1901] lot 4654. P&P

The Atlanta Journal.

Audubon Magazine.

Avery, Ralph E. *America's Triumph at Panama: Panorama and Story of the Construction and Operation of the World's Giant Waterway from Ocean to Ocean.* Edited by William C. Haskins. Chicago: Regan Printing House [c1913]

Azan, Paul J. L. *Souvenirs de Casablanca.* Paris: Hatchette et Cie., 1911.

Azoy, Anastasio C. M. *Three Centuries under Three Flags: The Story of Governors Island from 1637.* Governors Island, N.Y.: Headquarters First Army, 1951.

Bain, George Grantham. [News Photos of Return of U.S. Navy Fleet from Cruise around the World.] lot 11282. P&P.

———. [News Photos of U.S. Navy Atlantic Fleet in New York Harbor, ca. 1910–1915.] lot 11276. P&P.

———. [News Photos of Woman Suffrage in the United States, Mostly New York City, 1905–1917.] lot 11502. P&P.

Bakenhus, Reuben E.; Knapp, Harry S.; and Johnson, Emory R. *The Panama Canal: Comprising Its History and Construction, and Its Relation to the Navy, International Law and Commerce.* New York: J. Wiley & Sons, 1915.

Baltimore American.

Barck, Oscar T. [and] Blake, Nelson M. *Since 1900: A History of the United States in Our Times.* New York: Macmillan, 1947.

Barrett, John. *Panama Canal, What It Is, What It Means* . . . Washington, D.C.: Pan American Union, 1913.

Barry, Richard H. *An Historic Memento of the Nation's Loss: The True Story of the Assassination of President McKinley at Buffalo, with Many Scenes and Pictures Connected with the Tragedy, Including the Last Tributes of Respect at Washington and Canton.* Buffalo, N.Y.: R. A. Reid, 1901.

Beale, Howard K. *Theodore Roosevelt and the Rise of America to World Power.* Baltimore: Johns Hopkins Press, 1956.

Beard, Daniel C. *Hardly a Man Is Now Alive: The Autobiography of Dan Beard.* New York: Doubleday, Doran & Company, 1939.

Blum, John M. *The Republican Roosevelt.* Cambridge: Harvard University Press, 1954.

Boruff, Blanche F., comp. *Women of Indiana: A Work for Newspaper and Library Reference.* Contributing editors, Kathryn E. Pickett, Mary E. Ramier [and others] . . . Indianapolis: Indiana Women's Biography Association; M. Farson, Publisher [c1941]

The Boston Daily Globe.

The Boston Herald.

Boston Post.

The Boston Sunday Globe.

Boys' Life.

Bragdon, Henry W. *Woodrow Wilson: The Academic Years*. Cambridge: Belknap Press of Harvard University, 1967.

Brewton, William W. *The Life of Thomas E. Watson*. Atlanta: The author, 1926.

Brook-Shepherd, Gordon. *Uncle of Europe: The Social and Diplomatic Life of Edward VII*. New York: Harcourt Brace Jovanovich, 1976.

The Brooklyn Daily Eagle.

Buckley, Harold. *Squadron 95*. Paris: Obelisk Press, 1933.

Buffalo Courier.

Buffalo Morning Express.

Bullock, Albert E., ed. *Westminster Abbey and St. Margaret's Church*. London: J. Tiranti, 1920.

Byrd, Richard E. *Skyward: Man's Mastery of the Air as Shown by the Brilliant Flights of America's Leading Air Explorer, His Life, His Thrilling Adventures, His North Pole and Trans-Atlantic Flights, together with His Plans for Conquering the Antarctic by Air*. New York and London: Putnam, 1928.

Cadenhead, Ivie E. *Theodore Roosevelt: The Paradox of Progressivism*. Woodbury, N.Y.: Barron's Educational Series [1974]

Canal Zone. *August 15, 1914: The Panama Canal, Twenty-fifth Anniversary, August 15, 1939*. [Mount Hope, C.Z.: Panama Canal Press, 1939]

The Canton Repository. *Pictorial Life of William McKinley, Twenty-fifth President of the United States, in Commemoration of the One Hundredth Anniversary of His Birth*. Canton, O., 1943.

Carruth, Gorton, ed. *The Encyclopedia of American Facts and Dates*. New York: Crowell [c1970]

Cartagena, Colombia. Camara de Comerico. *Souvenir History of Cartagena de Indias*. [Cartagena?] Imprenta Departmental, 1925.

Castelot, Andre. *Ensorcelante Sarah Bernhardt*. [Nouv. ed.] Paris: Perrin [1973]

Century Association, New York. *Theodore Roosevelt: Memorial Addresses Delivered Before the Century Association, February 9, 1919, Resolutions Adopted February 9, 1919*. New York, 1919.

Cherrie, George K. *Dark Trails: Adventures of a Naturalist*. New York and London: Putnam, 1930.

The Chicago Daily News.

Chicago Daily Tribune.

Chidsay, Donald B. *The Spanish-American War: A Behind-the-Scenes Account of the War in Cuba*. New York: Crown [1971]

Chrislock, Carl H. *The Progressive Era in Minnesota, 1899–1918*. St. Paul: Minnesota Historical Society, 1971.

The Christian Science Monitor.

The Cincinnati Enquirer.

Coan, Charles F. *A History of New Mexico*. Chicago and New York: American Historical Society, 1925.

Collier's.

The Columbia Lippincott Gazetteer of the World. Edited by Leon E. Seltzer with the geographical research staff of Columbia University Press and with the cooperation of the American Geographical Society. Morningside Heights, N.Y.: Columbia University Press [1962]

Connecticut. Governor's Foot Guard. Second Company, New Haven. *Second Company Governor's Foot Guards: Souvenir History 150th Anniversary, 1775–1925*. [New Haven, Conn.: Tuttle, Morehouse & Taylor Company, 1925]

The Daily Argus-Leader, Sioux Falls, S.D.

The Daily Telegraph, London.

D'Ami, Rinaldo D., ed. *World Uniforms in Colour*. London: Patrick Stephens, 1968.

Damon, Charles R., comp. *The American Dictionary of Dates, 458–1920* . . . Boston: Richard G. Badger [c1921]

[Daniels, Josephus] . . . *USS Missouri, USS Ohio, and USS Wisconsin in Various Parts of the Panama Canal on July 15–16, 1915*. lot 5415. P&P.

[Davis, Oscar K. and Mumford, John K.] *The Life of William McKinley, Including a Genealogical Record of the McKinley Family and Copious Extracts from the Late President's Public Speeches, Messages to Congress, Proclamations, and Other State Papers*. New York: P. F. Collier & Son, 1901.

The Detroit Free Press.

Detroit Photographic Co., 1899. *The Dewey Land Parade*. lot 6325. P&P.

_____. [Cuba. 1898–1914] lot 9320. P&P.

_____. [Havana, Cuba. 1898–1914] lot 9319. P&P.

_____. [Panama and the Panama Canal. 1914–15] lot 9681. P&P.

Dicionario Geografico Brasileiro. 2 ed. Porto Alegre: Editora Globa [1972]

Dorn, Frank. *The Forbidden City: The Biography of a Palace*. New York: Scribner [1970]

Dunphy, Edward P. *Newburgh in the World War: A Review of the Part Played by Residents of the City of Newburgh and the Towns of Newburgh, New Windsor and Vicinity in the Great Conflict*. [Newburgh, N.Y.]: Newburgh World War Publishing Co., 1924.

Ellis, Frank H. and Ellis, Elsie M. *Atlantic Air Conquest: The Complete Story of All North Atlantic Flights and Attempts During the Pioneer Years from 1910–1940*. London: W. Kimber [1963]

Empire State Notables, 1914. New York: H. Stafford [c1914]

Enaud, François. *Le Château de Vincennes*. [Paris] Caisse Nationale des Monuments Historiques, 1964.

Enjalric, Marcel. *Château de Vincennes*. Paris: Nouvelles Editions Latines [1975?]

Eskew, Garnett L. *Willard's of Washington: The Epic of a Capital Caravansary*. New York: Coward-McCann [1954]

The Evening Star, Washington, D.C.

The Evening Sun, Baltimore.

The Fargo Forum.

Federal Writers' Project. Massachusetts. *Massachusetts: A Guide to Its Places and People*. Boston: Houghton Mifflin [c1937]; reprint ed., St. Clair Shores, Mich.; Somerset Publishers, 1973.

Federal Writers' Project. New York (City). *New York City Guide*. [Rev. ed.] New York: Random House [c1939]; reprint ed., St. Clair Shores, Mich.: Somerset Publishers, 1972.

Federal Writers' Project. South Dakota. *A South Dakota Guide*. [Pierre, S.D.: State Publishing Company] 1938.

Fernández Almagro, Melchor. *Historia del reinado de don Alfonso XIII*. Ed. ilustrada. Barcelona: Montaner y Simon, 1933.

Fielding, Raymond. *The American Newsreel, 1911–1967*. Norman: University of Oklahoma Press [1972]

Le Figaro, Paris.

The Film Daily Year Book of Motion Pictures.

Fite, Gilbert C. *Mount Rushmore*. Norman: University of Oklahoma Press [1952]

_____. *Peter Norbeck: Prairie Statesman*. Columbia: Univ. of Missouri, 1948.

Fitzpatrick, George and Caplin, Harvey. *Albuquerque: 100 Years in Pictures, 1875–1975*. Albuquerque, N.M.: Bank Securities, 1975.

Fort Sheridan Association. *The History and Achievements of the Fort Sheridan Officers' Training Camps.* [Chicago?] Fort Sheridan Association [c1920]

Fowles, Lloyd W. *An Honor to the State: The Bicentennial History of the First Company, Governor's Foot Guard, Hartford, Connecticut, 1771-1971.* [Hartford, Conn.: Bond Press, 1971]

Freidel, Frank B. *The Splendid Little War.* Boston: Little, Brown [1958]

[Fullerton, Charles B.] ed. *The Twenty-sixth Infantry in France.* [Montabaur-Frankfurt-M., Ger.: Printing Office M. Flock & Co.] 1919.

Funcken, Liliane and Funcken, Fred. *The First World War.* London: Ward Lock, 1974.

Fyfe, Henry Hamilton. *T. P. O'Connor.* London: G. Allen & Unwin [1934]

Gabrielson, Ira N. *Wildlife Refuges.* New York: Macmillan, 1943.

Gardner, Joseph L. *Departing Glory: Theodore Roosevelt as ex-President.* New York: Scribner [1973]

Garraty, John A. *Henry Cabot Lodge, a Biography.* New York: Knopf, 1953.

_____. *Theodore Roosevelt: The Strenuous Life.* New York: American Heritage Pub. Co.; distribution by Harper & Row [1967]

Gatewood, Willard B. *Theodore Roosevelt and the Art of Controversy: Episodes of the White House Years.* Baton Rouge: Louisiana State University Press [1970]

Gernsheim, Helmut and Gernsheim, Alison. *Edward VII and Queen Alexandra: A Biography in Word and Picture.* London: F. Muller [1962]

Gildea, James. *King Edward VII: The Peacemaker.* London: Eyre & Spottiswoode, 1914.

Gorgas, Marie D. and Hendrick, Burton J. *William Crawford Gorgas, His Life and Work.* Garden City, N.Y.: Doubleday, Page and Company, 1924.

Goudy, Frederic W., comp. *Why We Have Chosen Forest Hills Gardens for Our Home.* Forest Hills Gardens, N.Y.: Village Press, 1915.

The Graphic, London. *Funeral of King Edward.* [London: G. R. Parker] 1910.

Gros, Raymond. ed. *T. R. in Cartoon.* Akron, O., New York [etc.] Saalfield Publishing Co. [c1910]

Hagedorn, Hermann. *A Guide to Sagamore Hill: The Place, the People, the Life, the Meaning.* New York: Theodore Roosevelt Association [1953]

_____. *The Magnate: William Boyce Thompson and His Time 1869-1930.* New York: Reynal & Hitchcock [c1935]

_____. *The Roosevelt Family of Sagamore Hill.* New York: Macmillan, 1954.

_____. *Roosevelt in the Bad Lands.* Boston and New York: Houghton Mifflin, 1921.

Hamlin, Talbot F. . . . *The American Spirit in Architecture.* New Haven: Yale University Press, 1926.

Handlin, Oscar. *Harvard Guide to American History.* Cambridge: Belknap Press of Harvard University Press, 1954.

Harbaugh, William H. *The Life and Times of Theodore Roosevelt.* Rev. ed. New York: Collier Books [1963]

Harper's Magazine.

Harvard Business Reports. Chicago & New York: A. W. Shaw Company, 1925-

Harvard University. Library. *Theodore Roosevelt Collection: Dictionary Catalogue and Shelflist.* Cambridge: Distributed by the Harvard University Press, 1970.

The Havana Post.

Hays, Will H. *Memoirs.* Garden City, N.Y.: Doubleday, 1955.

Heald, Jean S. *Picturesque Panama, the Panama Railroad, the Panama Canal.* [Chicago: Printed by Teich & Company, c1928]

The Helena Independent.

Hendricks, Gordon. *Beginnings of the Biograph: The Story of the Invention of the Mutoscope and the Biograph and Their Supplying Camera.* New York: Beginnings of the American Film, 1964.

[Hening, Horace B.] comp. *Albuquerque, New Mexico: Chief City of a New Empire in the Great Southwest.* [Albuquerque, c1908]

Heraldry & Regalia of War. Edited by Bernard Fitzsimons. London: Phoebus, 1973.

Herringshaw's American Blue Book of Biography: Prominent Americans of 1914 . . . Edited and compiled under the supervision of Thomas William Herringshaw . . . Chicago: American Publishers' Association, 1914.

Herringshaw's Blue Book of Biography: New Yorker's [sic] of 1917, Ten Thousand Biographies. Edited by Mae Felts Herringshaw. Chicago: Clark J. Herringshaw, 1917.

Historical Records Survey, New York (City). *Presidential Executive Orders, Numbered 1-8030, 1862-1938.* Clifford L. Lord, editor, Joseph E. Vaughan, Charles E. Baker, associate editors . . . New York: Archives Publishing Company, a division of Hastings House [1944]

History of Woman Suffrage. (. . . Ida H. Harper . . .) New York: Arno Press, 1969.

Hitchings, Sinclair H. and Farlow, Catherine H. *A New Guide to the Massachusetts State House.* Boston: John Hancock Mutual Life Insurance Co. [1964]

Hughes, Charles Evans. *The Autobiographical Notes of Charles Evans Hughes.* Edited by David J. Danelski and Joseph S. Tulchin. Cambridge: Harvard University Press, 1973.

The Illustrated London News. The Funeral Procession of King Edward VII. 1910.

The Illustrated War News.

L'Independance Belge, Brussels.

The Indianapolis News.

The Indianapolis Star.

Internationaler Atlas. The International Atlas. El Atlas Internacional. L'Atlas International. Braunschweig: G. Westermann [c1974]

James, Theodore. *Fifth Avenue.* With photos by Elizabeth Baker. New York: Walker [1971]

Jamestown Exposition. 1907. *Official Catalogue with Maps, Illustrations of Grounds and Exhibits.* [Norfolk, Va.: Jamestown Official Publication Co., 1907]

_____. . . . *Official Guide of the Jamestown Ter-centennial Exposition, Held at Sewell's Point on Hampton Roads, near Norfolk, Va., April 26 to November 30, Nineteen Hundred Seven.* Comp. and ed. by W. H. Bright, Norfolk, Va.: A. Hess, c1907.

Jamestown Exposition, Norfolk, Va. April, 1907. Stereographs of Military Parades at the Exposition. lot 2836. P&P.

_____. Stereographs of the Exposition Commemorating the 300th Anniversary of the First Permanent English Settlement in America. lot 2832. P&P.

Jamestown Magazine.

Jamestown Official Photograph Corporation. *The Jamestown Exposition Illustrated: Photographs Made with Goerz Lenses by Jamestown Official Photograph Corporation . . .* Published by Jamestown Official Photograph Corporation . . . the trade supplied by American News Company . . . New York: Press of I. H. Blanchard Company, 1907.

_____. *Scenes at the Jamestown Exposition, with Historic Sites in Old Virginia . . .* Published by Jamestown Official Photograph Corporation . . . the trade supplied by American News Company . . . New York: Press of I. H. Blanchard Company [1907]

Jane's Fighting Ships. [1st] 1898– [London: S. Low, Marston & Co.]; New York: Arco [1969–

Jessup, Philip C. *Elihu Root.* New York: Dodd, Mead & Company, 1938.

Johnson, Edward A. *History of Negro Soldiers in the Spanish-American War, and Other Items of Interest.* Raleigh: Capital Printing Co., 1899.

Johnston, Frances B. [Pan-American Exposition, Buffalo, N.Y. 1901] lot 2967. P&P.

Johnston, William Davison. *T. R., Champion of the Strenuous Life: A Photographic Biography of Theodore Roosevelt.* New York: Farrar, Straus and Cudahy [1958]

Kearton, Cherry. *Adventures with Animals and Men.* London, New York [etc.] Longmans, Green and Co. [1935]
_____. *Photographing Wild Life across the World.* London: J. W. Arrowsmith [1923]
_____. *Wild Life across the World.* London, New York [etc.] Hodder and Stoughton [1914]

Keller, Allan. *The Spanish-American War: A Compact History.* New York: Hawthorn Books [1969]

Keller, Morton, comp. *Theodore Roosevelt: A Profile.* New York: Hill and Wang [1967]

King, Moses, comp. *The Dewey Reception and Committee of New York City: An Album of One Thousand Portraits, Scenes, Views, etc.* [New York: Moses King, c1899]
_____. *King's Handbook of New York City: An Outline History and Description of the American Metropolis, with over One Thousand Illustrations from Photographs Made Expressly for This Work.* Boston: Moses King [1893]
_____. *King's Views of New York.* [New York: Moses King, c1915]

Kinross, John P. D. B. *The Windsor Years: The Life of Edward, as Prince of Wales, King, and Duke of Windsor.* New York: Viking Press [1967]

Klein, Philip S. and Hoogenboom, Ari. *A History of Pennsylvania.* New York: McGraw-Hill [1973]

La Fargue, Thomas E. *China and the World War.* New York: H. Fertig, 1973.

Lang, Lincoln Alexander. *Ranching with Roosevelt.* Philadelphia and London: J. B. Lippincott Company, 1926.

Leaders of the Twentieth Century, New York City, 1918. New York: Unico News Service [c1918]

League of Women Voters in the United States. . . . Women Active in the Women's Suffrage Movement and as Members of the National League of Women Voters. lot 5544. P&P.

Leary, John J. *Talks with T. R., from the Diaries of John J. Leary, Jr.* Boston and New York: Houghton Mifflin, 1920.

La Libre Belgique, Brussels.

Lindbergh, Charles A. *The Spirit of St. Louis.* New York: Scribner, 1953.

Londres L 'Independance Belge, London.

Lorant, Stefan. *The Life and Times of Theodore Roosevelt.* Garden City, N.Y.: Doubleday [1959]

Lord, Walter. *The Good Years: From 1900 to the First World War.* New York: Harper [1960]

Los Angeles. Municipal Art Dept. *Mayors of Los Angeles.* [Los Angeles, 1965]

Los Angeles Times.

Louisiana History.

Lukas, Jan. *Naples: A Book of Photographs.* London: Spring Books [c1965]

MacFarquhar, Roderick. *The Forbidden City.* New York: Newsweek [1972]

Mackey, Frank J. and Jernegan, Marcus Wilson. *Forward—March!* Chicago: The Disabled Veterans of the World War, Dept. of Rehabilitation [1935]

Manucy, Albert C. *Artillery Through the Ages: A Short Illustrated History of Cannon, Emphasizing Types Used in America.* Washington, D.C.: U.S. Govt. Print. Off., 1949.

Martin, Clarece. *A Glimpse of the Past: The History of Bulloch Hall and Roswell, Georgia.* Roswell, Ga.: Historic Roswell [1973]

Martin, John S., ed. *A Picture History of Russia.* New York: Crown Publishers [1945]

Le Matin, Paris.

McCoy, Donald R. *Calvin Coolidge: The Quiet President.* New York: Macmillan [1967]

McHale, Francis. *President and Chief Justice: The Life and Public Services of William Howard Taft.* Philadelphia: Dorrance & Company [c1931]

McNaughton, Arnold. *The Book of Kings.* New York: Quadrangle/New York Times Book Co., 1973.

Metropolitan Magazine.

Miller, Leo E. *In the Wilds of South America: Six Years of Exploration in Colombia, Venezuela, British Guiana, Peru, Bolivia, Argentina, Paraguay, and Brazil.* New York: Scribner, 1918.

Moore, William Emmet and Russell, James C. *U.S. Official Pictures of the World War, Showing America's Participation: Selected from the Official Files of the War Department, with Unofficial Introductory Photographs.* Washington, D.C.: Pictorial Bureau, 1928.

Moran, Philip R., comp. *Calvin Coolidge, 1872–1933: Chronology, Documents, Bibliographical Aids.* Dobbs Ferry, N.Y.: Oceana Publications, 1970.

The Morning Post, London.

Morris, Richard Brandon, ed. *Encyclopedia of American History.* Rev. and enl. ed. New York: Harper [1961]

Mothner, Ira. *Man of Action: The Life of Teddy Roosevelt.* New York: Platt & Munk [1966]

Motion Picture News

The Moving Picture World.

Mowry, George E. *The Era of Theodore Roosevelt, 1900–1912.* New York: Harper [1958]

Murlin, Edgar L., comp. . . . *The United States Red Book, Containing the Portraits and Biographies of the President and His Cabinet, Senators and Members of the House of Representatives, with a Description . . . of the Chief Buildings in Washington and Statistical Tables . . . Showing the Financial Condition . . . of the United States for . . . 1895.* Albany: J. B. Lyon, 1896.

Murray, William D. *The History of the Boy Scouts of America.* New York: Boy Scouts of America, c1937.

Nankivell, John H. *History of the Twenty-fifth Regiment, United States Infantry, 1896–1926.* [Denver: Smith-Brooks Printing Company, c1927]

The National Cyclopedia of American Biography. v. 1–2 [New York] J. T. White, 1893– [v. 1. 1898]

National McKinley Birthplace Memorial Association. *The National McKinley Birthplace Memorial, Erected by the National McKinley Birthplace Memorial Association, Corner Stone Laid November Twentieth, Nineteen Fifteen, Dedicated October Fifth, Nineteen Seventeen.* [Cleveland, O.: Penton Press, c1918]

[Neale, Walter] *Autobiographies and Portraits of the President, Cabinet, Supreme Court, and Fifty-fifth Congress . . .* Washington, D.C.: Neale Company, 1899.

New Haven Journal-Courier.

New York (City). *Mayor's Committee on Celebration of Twenty-fifth*

Anniversary of the Greater City of New York: Official Book of the Silver Jubilee of Greater New York, May Twenty-sixth to June Twenty-third, Nineteen Hundred and Twenty-three. [New York: The Committee, 1923]

New York (City). Roosevelt House. Photographic file.

New York (State). Board of Trustees of the Roosevelt Memorial. *Annual Report 1st–9th, 1925–1933.* Albany, 1927–34.

_____. *The New York State Theodore Roosevelt Memorial, Dedicated January Nineteen, Nineteen Thirty-six.* Prepared under the direction of the Board of Trustees by George N. Pindar, secretary. [Albany: J. B. Lyon Company, Printers, 1936]

New York (State). Roosevelt Memorial Commission. . . . *Report of the Roosevelt Memorial Commission [1920–1925]* Albany: J. B. Lyon Company, Printers, 1921–26.

New York American.

New York, Greetings from the Great Metropolis Beautiful. [New York: Home Life Publishing Company, 19—?]

The New York Herald.

The New York Herald Tribune.

New York Herald Tribune, Paris.

The New York Times.

The New York Times Mid-week Pictorial.

New York Times Mid-week Pictorial. *Portfolio of the World War: Rotogravure Etchings.* [New York: New York Times, c1917]

The New York Times Obituaries Index, 1858–1968. New York: New York Times, 1970.

New York Tribune.

Newton, Wilfrid Douglas. *Westward with the Prince of Wales.* New York and London: D. Appleton and Company, 1920.

Niver, Kemp R. *Motion Pictures from the Library of Congress Paper Print Collection, 1894–1912.* Berkeley: University of California Press, 1967.

Official Programme of Exercises and Illustrated Inaugural History Commemorating the Inauguration of Theodore Roosevelt as President of the United States, Charles W. Fairbanks as Vice-President of the United States. Washington, D.C.: O. A. Sontag, 1905.

Ohio State Journal, Columbus.

Olin, Spencer C. *California's Prodigal Sons: Hiram Johnson and the Progressives, 1911–1917.* Berkeley: University of California Press, 1968.

Our Patriotic President: His Life in Pictures, Famous Words & Maxims, Anecdotes, Biography. New York: Columbia Press [1904]

Our State Capitol Illustrated. Boston: A. M. Bridgman & Company [1894]

The Outlook.

The Patriot, Harrisburg, Pa.

Paulsen, Valdemar E. *U.S. Army Facts and Insignia: How to Recognize Rank and Service in the Army of the United States.* Edited by Major Lucius A. Hine. Chicago and New York: Rand, McNally & Co. [c1918]

Peattie, Roderick, ed. *The Black Hills.* The contributors: Leland D. Case [and others] New York: Vanguard Press [1952]

Pershing, John J. *My Experiences in the World War.* New York: Frederick A. Stokes Company, 1931.

_____. Papers, 1882–1949. In Library of Congress, Manuscript Division.

_____. [Views and Activities of Military Import, 1902–1921.] lot 7729. P&P.

The Philadelphia Inquirer.

Photographic History of the Spanish-American War: A Pictorial and Descriptive Record of Events on Land and Sea with Portraits and Biographies of Leaders on Both Sides. New York: Pearson Pub. Co. [1898]

The Pittsburgh Dispatch.

The Pittsburgh Post.

Politiken, Copenhagen.

Portrait and Biographical Record of Arizona. Chicago: Chapman Publishing Co., 1901.

The Post-Intelligencer, Seattle.

Pourade, Richard F. *Gold in the Sun.* [San Diego]: Union-Tribune Pub. Co. [1965]

Power, Lionel J. B. *The Royal Ladies of the Netherlands, Queen Wilhelmina and Princess Juliana.* London: S. Paul & Co. [1939]

Practical Politics.

Pringle, Henry F. *The Life and Times of William Howard Taft: A Biography.* New York and Toronto: Farrar & Rinehart [c1939]

_____. *Theodore Roosevelt: A Biography.* New York: Harcourt, Brace and Company [c1931]

Public Ledger, Philadelphia.

Ramsaye, Terry. *A Million and One Nights: A History of the Motion Picture.* New York: Simon and Schuster [1964, c1926]

Rankin, Robert H. *Uniforms of the Army.* New York: Putnam [1968]

Reiss, Toby A. *Denmark in Pictures.* Rev. ed. London and Melbourne: Oak Tree P., 1966.

Republican Party. National Convention, 16th, Chicago, 1916. *Official Report of the Proceedings of the Sixteenth Republican National Convention, Held in Chicago, Illinois, June 7, 8, 9 and 10, 1916, Resulting in the Nomination of Charles Evans Hughs, of New York, for President and the Nomination of Charles Warren Fairbanks, of Indiana, for Vice-President.* New York: Tenny Press [1916]

Republican Party. National Convention, 17th, Chicago, 1920. *Official Report of the Proceedings of the Seventeenth Republican National Convention, Held in Chicago, Illinois, June 8, 9, 10, 11 and 12, 1920, Resulting in the Nomination of Warren Gamaliel Harding, of Ohio, for President, and the Nomination of Calvin Coolidge, of Massachusetts, for Vice-President.* New York: Tenny Press [c1920]

Rhodes, James F. *The McKinley and Roosevelt Administrations, 1897–1909.* Port Washington, N.Y.: Kennikat Press [1965, c1922]

Rickett, Harold W. *Wild Flowers of the United States.* General editor, William C. Steere. Collaborators: Rogers McVaugh [and others] New York: McGraw-Hill [1966–73]

Rocky Mountain News, Denver.

Roosevelt, Edith; Roosevelt, Belle W.; Derby, Richard H.; and Roosevelt, Kermit. *Cleared for Strange Ports.* New York and London: Scribner, 1927.

Roosevelt, Eleanor Butler Alexander. *Day Before Yesterday: The Reminiscences of Mrs. Theodore Roosevelt, Jr.* Garden City, N.Y.: Doubleday [1959]

Roosevelt, Kermit. *The Happy Hunting-grounds.* New York: Scribner, 1920.

_____. *A Sentimental Safari.* New York: Knopf, 1963.

Roosevelt, Nicholas. *Theodore Roosevelt: The Man as I Knew Him.* New York: Dodd, Mead & Co. [1967]

Roosevelt, Theodore, Pres. U.S., 1858–1919. *Addresses and Presidential Messages of Theodore Roosevelt, 1902–1904.* New York and London: Putnam, 1904.

_____. *African and European Addresses by Theodore Roosevelt.* New York and London: J. P. Putnam's Sons, 1910.

_____. *The Hunting and Exploring Adventures of Theodore Roosevelt.* Told in his own words and edited by Donald Day. New

York: Dial Press, 1955.

_____. *Letters*. Selected and edited by Elting E. Morison; John M. Blum, associate editor, John J. Buckley, copy editor. Cambridge: Harvard University Press, 1951–1954.

_____. *Letters from Theodore Roosevelt to Anna Roosevelt Cowles, 1870–1918*. New York and London: Scribner, 1924.

_____. *Papers, 1759–1920*. In the Library of Congress, Manuscript Division.

_____. *Papers, 1878–1940*. In the Library of Congress, Manuscript Division.

_____. *Presidential Addresses and State Papers of Theodore Roosevelt*. New York: P. F. Collier & Son [1905?]

_____. *Roosevelt in the Kansas City Star: War-time Editorials by Theodore Roosevelt*. Boston and New York: Houghton Mifflin, 1921.

_____. *Theodore Roosevelt, an Autobiography . . .* New York: Scribner, 1920.

_____. *Theodore Roosevelt Cyclopedia*. Edited by Albert Bushnell Hart . . . and Howard Ronald Ferleger . . . New York: Roosevelt Memorial Association [c1941]

_____. *Through the Brazilian Wilderness*. 1914. Reprint. New York: Greenwood Press [1969]

_____. *The Works of Theodore Roosevelt*. New York: Scribner, 1926.

Roosevelt, Theodore, 1887–1944. *Average Americans*. New York and London: Putnam, 1919.

Roosevelt House Bulletin.

Roosevelt Memorial Association. *Analostan Island, the Site for the National Memorial to Theodore Roosevelt in Washington*. New York: Roosevelt Memorial Association, 1931.

Roosevelt Memorial Association. *Report . . . 1919/21–1932*. New York: Roosevelt Memorial Association, 1921–[32]

_____. *The Panama Canal* (script)

_____. *Plan and Design for the Roosevelt Memorial in the City of Washington, John Russell Pope Architect*. [New York: The Pynson Printers, 1925]

_____. *Program of a Competition to Select the Artist or Group of Artists Who Will Be Commissioned to Design and Direct the Construction of a Monumental Memorial to Theodore Roosevelt in the City of Washington*. [New York: Roosevelt Memorial Association, c1925]

_____. *President Roosevelt* (script)

_____. *The River of Doubt* (script)

_____. *Roosevelt at Home* (script)

_____. *The Roosevelt Dam* (script)

_____. *Roosevelt, Friends of the Birds* (script)

_____. *T. R. Himself* (script)

_____. *Theodore Roosevelt, Fighter for Social Justice* (script)

_____. *Theodore Roosevelt, Great Scout* (script)

_____. *Theodore Roosevelt in the Great War* (script)

_____. *Theodore Roosevelt, the Great Scout* (script)

_____. *Theodore Roosevelt's Return from Africa* (script)

The Roosevelt Quarterly.

Russell, Francis. *A City in Terror: 1919, the Boston Police Strike*. New York: Viking Press, 1975.

San Francisco Chronicle.

San Francisco Chronicle. *The City San Francisco in Pictures*. [San Francisco, San Francisco Chronicle] 1961.

San Francisco Examiner.

Schlesinger, Arthur M. *History of American Presidential Elections, 1789–1968*. New York: Chelsea House [1971]

Scott, James B. *Robert Bacon: Life and Letters*. Garden City, N.Y.: Doubleday, Page, c1923; reprint ed., New York: Arno Press, 1975.

Scribner's Magazine.

Shaw, Albert. *A Cartoon History of Roosevelt's Career*. New York: Review of Reviews Company [c1910]

Shumway, Harry I. *Albert, the Soldier-king: Being the Life Story of Belgium's Beloved Ruler*. Boston: L. C. Page & Company [1934]

Sloan, Richard E., ed. *History of Arizona*. Phoenix: Record Publishing Co., 1930.

Smith, Cleveland H. & Taylor, Gertrude R . . . . *United States Service Symbols*. New York: Duell, Sloan and Pearce, c1942.

Smith, Edmund B. *Governors Island, Its Military History under Three Flags, 1637–1922*. New York: Valentin's Manual, 1923.

Smith, Gene. *When the Cheering Stopped: The Last Years of Woodrow Wilson*. New York: Morrow, 1964.

Snap Shots of Scenes at the Panama-Pacific Exposition, San Francisco, 1915: 115 Late Views of the Panama-Pacific Exposition. San Francisco: Amos Publishing Co., c1915.

Social Register, New York, 1905. New York: Social Register Association, 1904.

Society of Black Hills Pioneers. *Constitution and By-laws together with a Roll of Members*. [Deadwood, S.D.: Times Job Print. House, 1891]

Souvenir of the Visit of Colonel Mr. Theodore Roosevelt, ex-President of the United States of America, to Chile. Santiago de Chile: Sociedad imprenta y litografia "Universo," 1914.

Spears, Edward L. *Prelude to Victory*. London: J. Cape [1930]

St. Louis Globe-Democrat.

St. Louis Republic.

St. Paul Pioneer Press.

Steward, Julian H., ed. *Handbook of South American Indians*. Washington: U.S. Govt. Print. Off. 1946–59.

Tarbell, Ida M. *Owen D. Young, a New Type of Industrial Leader*. New York: Macmillan, 1932.

Terraine, John. *The Great War, 1914–1918: A Pictorial History*. New York: Macmillan [1965]

Tharp, Louise H. *Saint-Gaudens and the Gilded Era*. Boston: Little, Brown [1969]

Thomas, Addison C. *Roosevelt Among the People: Being an Account of the Fourteen Thousand Mile Journey from Ocean to Ocean of Theodore Roosevelt, Twenty-sixth President of the United States*. Chicago: L. W. Walter Company [c1910]

Thompson, Charles Willis. *Party Leaders of the Time: Character Studies of Public Men at Washington, Senate Portraits, House Etchings, Snapshots at Executive Officers and Diplomats, and Flashlights in the Country at Large*. New York: G. W. Dillingham Company [1906]

The Times-Picayune, New Orleans.

The Times, London.

Todd, Frank M. *The Story of the Exposition: Being the Official History of the International Celebration Held at San Francisco in 1915 to Commemorate the Discovery of the Pacific Ocean and the Construction of the Panama Canal*. New York and London: Pub. for the Panama-Pacific International Exposition Company by Putnam, 1921.

Trevelyan, George M. *Grey of Fallodon: The Life and Letters of Sir Edward Grey, afterwards Viscount Grey of Fallodon*. Boston: Houghton, Mifflin, 1937.

Tuchman, Barbara W. *The Guns of August*. New York: Macmillan, 1962.

Twitchell, Ralph E. *The Leading Facts of New Mexican History*. Albuquerque: Horn & Wallace, 1963.

Unger, Frederick W. . . . *Roosevelt's African Trip: The Story of His Life, the Voyage from New York to Mombasa, and the Route through the Heart of Africa, including the Big Game and Other Ferocious*

Animals, Strange Peoples and Countries Found in the Course of his Travels. [Philadelphia, c1909]

U.S. Congress. *Biographical Directory of the American Congress, 1774–1971, the Continental Congress, September 5, 1774, to October 21, 1788, and the Congress of the United States, from the First through the Ninety-first Congress, March 4, 1789, to January 3, 1971, Inclusive.* [Washington, D.C.] U.S. Govt. Print. Off., 1971.

U.S. Congress. House. Committee on the Library. . . . *Change Name of Roosevelt Island to Theodore Roosevelt Island . . . . Report to Accompany H. R. 14228. . .* [Washington, D.C.: U.S. Govt. Print. Off., 1933]

U.S. Congress. Senate. Committee on Interior and Insular Affairs. *Designating Pelican Island Wilderness Area: Report to Accompany S.126.* [Washington, D.C.: U.S. Govt. Print. Off.] 1969.

_____. *Establishment of the Theodore Roosevelt Birthplace and Sagamore Hill National Historic Sites, N.Y.: Report to Accompany H. R. 8484.* [Washington, D.C.: U.S. Govt. Print. Off., 1962]

U.S. Jamestown Ter-Centennial Commission . . . . *Final Report of the Jamestown Ter-Centennial Commission.* Washington, D.C.: U.S. Govt. Print. Off., 1909.

U.S. Library of Congress. *Herbert Putnam, 1861–1955: A Memorial Tribute.* Washington, D.C.: Library of Congress, 1956.

U.S. Library of Congress. African Section.

U.S. Library of Congress. Manuscript Division. *Index to the Theodore Roosevelt Papers.* Washington, D.C.: [for sale by the Supt. of Docs., U.S. Govt. Print. Off.] 1969 [i.e. 1971]

U.S. Library of Congress. Prints and Photographs Division. Geographic file.

_____. Portrait file.

_____. Presidential file.

_____. Stereo file.

U.S. Library of Congress. Science and Technology Division.

U.S. National Archives and Records Service. Audiovisual Archives Division.

U.S. Ordnance Dept. *Report of the Chief of Ordnance, to the Secretary of War.* Washington, D.C.: U.S. Govt. Print. Off., [1826–1918]

U.S. President, 1901–1909 (Roosevelt) . . . *Special Message of the President . . . Concerning the Panama Canal, Communicated to the Two Houses of Congress on December 17, 1906.* Washington, D.C.: U.S. Govt. Print. Off., 1906.

U.S. War Dept. General Staff. *Catalogue of Official A. E. F. Photographs Taken by the Signal Corps, U.S.A.* Washington, D.C.: U.S. Govt. Print. Off., 1919.

Vorpahl, Ben M. *My Dear Wister: The Frederic Remington-Owen Wister Letters.* Palo Alto, Calif.: American West Pub. Co. [1972]

Washington, D.C. Inaugural Committee, 1901. *Official Souvenir Program, Inaugural Ceremonies, March 4, 1901.* [1901]

Washington, D.C. Inaugural Committee, 1905. *Inauguration of Theodore Roosevelt as President of the United States, March 4, 1905: Membership and Duties of Committees in Charge of Inaugural Ceremonies.* Washington, D.C.: Headquarters of the Inaugural Committee, c1905.

Washington Post.

Werstein, Irving. *1898: The Spanish-American War, Told with Pictures.* New York: Cooper Square Publishers; distributed by Pocket Books. 1966.

_____. *Shattered Decade, 1919–1929.* New York: Scribner [1970]

Whitney, David C. *The Graphic Story of the American Presidents.* Edited by Thomas C. Jones. Chicago: J. G. Ferguson Pub. Co.; [New York] Distributed to the book trade by Doubleday [1975]

Who Was Who in America: A Companion Biographical Reference Work to Who's Who in America. vol. 1, 1897–1942. Chicago: A. N. Marquis Company, c1942.

Who's Who in State Politics, 1914. Boston: Practical Politics, 1914.

Wile, Frederic W. *Men around the Kaiser.* 1913.

Williams, Dion. *Army and Navy Uniforms and Insignia: How to Know Rank, Corps and Service in the Military and Naval Forces of the United States and Foreign Countries.* New York: Frederick A. Stokes Company [c1918]

Wilshin, Francis F. *Sagamore Hill and the Roosevelt Family, Sagamore Hill National Historic Site*, N.Y. [Denver] Denver Service Center, National Park Service, 1972.

Wilson, Robert L. *Theodore Roosevelt: Outdoorsman.* Political background by G. C. Wilson. [New York] Winchester Press [1971]

Wister, Owen. *Owen Wister out West: His Journals and Letters.* Edited by Fanny Kemble Wister. [Chicago] University of Chicago Press [1958]

Wittemann, Herman L. [Panama-California Exposition, San Diego, Calif., 1915.] lot 6930. P&P.

Writers' Program. California. *San Francisco, the Bay and Its Cities.* New York: Hastings House, 1940.

Writers' Program. Georgia. *Atlanta, a City of the Modern South.* New York: Smith & Durrell [1942]

Zahm, John A. . . . *Through South America's Southland, with an Account of the Roosevelt Scientific Expedition to South America.* New York and London: D. Appleton and Company, 1916.